South Dakota War Stories

The Great Plains to Southwest Asia

Protecting America's Freedom

Lieutenant Colonel
George A. Larson
USAF (Ret.)

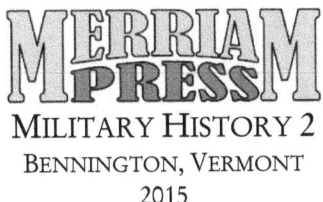

MILITARY HISTORY 2
BENNINGTON, VERMONT
2015

First published in 2015 by the Merriam Press

First Edition

Copyright © 2015 by George A. Larson
Book design by Ray Merriam
Additional material copyright of named contributors.

All rights reserved.
No part of this book may be used or reproduced in any manner whatsoever without written permission, except in the case of brief quotations embodied in critical articles or reviews.

WARNING
The unauthorized reproduction or distribution of this copyrighted work is illegal. Criminal copyright infringement, including infringement without monetary gain, is investigated by the FBI and is punishable by up to five years in federal prison and a fine of $250,000.

The views expressed are solely those of the author.

ISBN 9781576383988
Library of Congress Control Number: 2015953243
Merriam Press #MH2-P

This work was designed, produced, and published in
the United States of America by the

Merriam Press
133 Elm Street Suite 3R
Bennington VT 05201

E-mail: ray@merriam-press.com
Web site: merriam-press.com

The Merriam Press publishes new manuscripts on historical subjects, especially military history and with an emphasis on World War II, as well as reprinting previously published works, including reports, documents, manuals, articles and other materials on historical topics.

Dedication

CITIZENS and veterans of South Dakota have served with distinction in the U.S. military since early 1800. There are many interesting stories which I am calling "South Dakota War Stories." I began writing stories about South Dakota in 1994 after moving to Rapid City. Now as a member of the South Dakota Veterans Writing Group, it became evident that a history of these events was nonexistent. I dedicate these stories to all South Dakotans and the role they played in settling the Great Plains, service in the U.S. Armed Forces and stories of the Native American tribes of South Dakota, which are a part of this history. It is impossible in one book to tell all stories. These stories are a simply a snapshot of years of history in South Dakota with emphasis on service to the protection of the United States.

Lt. Col. George A. Larson, USAF (Ret.)

Contents

Lewis and Clark Corps of Discovery in South Dakota 11
The Conclusion of the Indian Wars in South Dakota 21
The Dakota Territory Cavalry Companies for service in the U.S. Civil War 1861 to 1865 37
South Dakota National Guard, Birth of the South Dakota National Guard 41
Early Railroad Development in the Black Hills 43
Fort Meade Historic Army Post in the western Dakotas 45
South Dakota National Guard, 1889-Statehood 49
South Dakota National Guard, 1893-the Guard is Renumbered 49
South Dakota National Guard, 1898-The Spanish-American War 49
South Dakota State Soldier's (1886 to 2012) Veteran's Home, Hot Springs, South Dakota 51
Spanish American War (1898 to 1902), South Dakota Volunteers, 1st South Dakota Volunteer Infantry Regiment and 3rd United States Volunteer Cavalry Regiment 61
Camp Rapid, South Dakota National Guard 65
Battle Mountain Sanitarium, Department of Veterans Medical Center, Hot Springs, South Dakota 69
Armored Cruiser USS South Dakota 75
Renold Schat, "World War I U.S. Army experience in France on the Western Front" 79
South Dakota National Guard Service on the U.S.-Mexico Border in 1916 ... 89
The U.S. Army's 1916 Punitive Expedition, "The hunt for Poncho Villa," Fourth South Dakota Infantry 91
South Dakota National Guard, World War I 95
Stratobowl Balloon Launches, The United States Race into Space with the Soviet Union 97
Mely Rahn, "A girl remembers the Nazi occupation of France during World War II" 103
Sonja Cody, "A girl remembers the London Blitz" 109
Claire Peterson, "A Civilian Conservation Corps recruit looks back on a Black Hills experience" 117
South Dakota National Guard, World War II Pacific Theater of Operations 125
South Dakota National Guard, World War II European Theater of Operations 125
Black Hills Ordnance Depot, Edgemont, South Dakota 127
John Burnfin, Fire Chief, U.S. Naval Air Station, Ford Island, Pearl Harbor, Hawaii, 7 December 1941 139
Stan Lieberman Remembers the Japanese Attack on Pearl Harbor, 7 De-

cember 1941 147
Victor Weidensee, 3rd Air Commando Group 153
Tom McDill, "Survivor of Bataan during World War II" 161
World War II Rationing in South Dakota 171
Luverne 'Vern' A. Kramer, "Civil Air Patrol hunting German U-boats off the U.S. East Coast" 179
Rextroat Ola, "Women Air Force Service Pilots in World War II" 185
History of Ellsworth Air Force Base 189
North Bombing Range World War II, Support for training operations at Rapid City Army Air Base 195
Clarence Carsner, 34th Infantry Division, 109th Engineer Regiment, "Combat duty in North Africa and Italy, World War II" 199
Marion J. Larkin, "Boeing B-17s in North Africa" 203
Clair Patterson, DD USS McGowan, "Pacific Combat" 213
Joe Foss, United States Marine Corps, Fighter Ace over Guadalcanal 223
Lt. Col. Don Wicker, USAF (Ret.), "World War II to the Cold War" 227
Edwin Petranke, Four-Time Purple Heart Recipient, 36th Infantry Division, World War II 229
Gordon Lease, United States Coast Guard, "1943 Salerno amphibious operation" 233
Joseph Munro, World War II LT. J.G., "USS Shelton (DE-407) and USS Ray K. Edwards (APD-96)" 235
Arthur T. Jansen, United States Marine Corps, "World War II Pacific Combat" 245
Jerry Teachout, United States Army Air Corps 253
Harry Nollsch, U.S. Army 3rd Infantry Division-North Africa, Sicily, Italy, Southern France and Germany 259
Charles Gerlach, "Capture of U-515 in the North Atlantic" 263
George W. Larson, "A Seabee's Story, Tinian and Okinawa, 1944-1945" 267
Had Taylor, German Prisoner of War, Stalag 17, Krems, Austria 275
Lt. Commander, John C. Waldron, USS Hornet, the Battle of Midway, May 1942 277
Thomas K. Oliver, "B-24 down over Yugoslavia, May 1944" 285
"Operation Frantic," Eighth Air Force shuttle bombing missions of Germany from England to Russia and back 293
Peter Dahlberg, U.S. Army World War II, "The Bridge at Remagen" 303
Dean Shaffhausen, "Amphibious Group Nine, Leyte Gulf" 309
Gordon Lease, World War II Coast Guardsman 313
Harold Jansen, U.S. Navy, World War II 315
World War II Consolidated B-24E Liberator Training Crash, Meadow, South Dakota 317
Japanese balloon firebombing attacks against the United States, and South Dakota during World War II 322
Personal look at the "Battle of the Bulge," Three South Dakota veterans recall the historic battle 331

Paul Priest, Bridging the Rhine at Remagen 341
Gale Holbrook, 96th United States Naval Construction Battalion, Philippines and China 351
Carl Anderson, "A personal View of the United States Occupation of Japan after World War II" 359
114th Fighter Wing, South Dakota Air National Guard, Joe Foss Field, Sioux Falls, South Dakota 367
Weaver Air Force Base B-29s deploy to Europe in support of the Berlin Airlift, SAC forward deploys its atomic capable bombers 371
South Dakota National Guard, 1950 to 1953, Korean War 383
Colonel Dale Friend, USA (Ret.), Korea, Vietnam, Germany, "Disputing myths about the U.S. military in the Vietnam War" 385
Gerald (Jerry) Teachout, "Focus on Korea, 1951" 391
R.A. Jacobsen, "Prisoner of War (POW) Riots by North Korean and Communist Chinese Prisoners during the Korean War" 401
Raleigh H. Watson, Jr., Convair B-36, 77th Bomb Squadron, 28th Bomb Wing, Ellsworth Air Force Base Electronic Countermeasures Mechanic 409
How Ellsworth Air Force Base got its Name 411
Ralph Whitaker, B-36 crewman, Ellsworth Air Force Base 415
Matador Cruise Missile, South Dakota Missileers in America's First Nuclear Ground-to-Ground Guided Missile 417
Titan I Intercontinental Ballistic Missiles at Ellsworth Air Force Base 423
MSgt Robert O'Daniel, U.S. Navy and U.S. Air Force, 54th Fighter-Interceptor Squadron, Air Defense Command-Clear, Alaska and "Operation New Life," Wake Island 429
First Lieutenant Charlie Piper, USAF (Ret.), F-86D Pilot, 54th Fighter Interceptor Squadron, Ellsworth Air Force Base, South Dakota 443
Minuteman I and II Intercontinental Ballistic Missiles at Ellsworth Air Force 445
South Dakota National Guard, The Berlin Blockade and resulting international crisis 455
MSgt. Robert O'Daniel, Ballistic Missile Early Warning Station (BMEWS), Clear, Alaska 457
Gerald Teachout, USAF, Air Force Pilot in Vietnam, 1964 461
USS Proteus, Cold War Nuclear Submarine Ballistic Missile Tender, Apra Harbor, Guam 467
Alan B. Walker, May 28, 1968 "Foxtrot Ridge" South Vietnam 477
Mark St. Pierre, December 1968, "Operation Fayette Canyon" 483
Dean Muehlberg, U.S. Army, REMF "War Stories": 17th CAG-Nha Trang, Vietnam-1969 489
William L. Walker, "U.S. Army, Sketch of my daily life in Vietnam" 509
Donald R. Smith, World War II, Korea War and Vietnam War, Airmen's Career covers 32 years 511
South Dakota National Guard, Rapid City Flood-June 1972 515

Linebacker II, The end of the Vietnam War 517
South Dakota National Guard, Service during the Vietnam War 529
The Capture of South Vietnam by North Vietnamese Forces, The end of
    America's 10,000-day war in Southeast Asia 531
Review of Operation New Life on Wake Island, Report prepared for
    Commander Naval Forces Guam 539
Airmen Bring New Life to South Vietnamese Refugees on Wake Island 541
Pacific Backwater comes to Life again, Wake Island, "Operation New
    Life" 543
Refugee Business Rewards with Memories, Wake Island, "Operation New
    Life" 545
Lucky Rains, Hard Work, Mark Early Success, Wake Island, "Operation
    New Life" 547
Wake Island Reviewed, "Operation New Life" 549
Second Honor Roll Listed, "Operation New Life," for 15th Air Force
    Personnel 551
B-52Ds in the Defense of the Republic of South Korea 553
B-52 Stratofortress Reconnaissance Missions during the Iran-Iraq War,
    "Operation Busy Observer" 557
South Dakota National Guard, "Operation Desert Storm" 561
A Unique View of the "Cold War" between the United States and Soviet
    Union, After the tearing down of the Berlin Wall and fall of the "Evil
    Empire" 563
South Dakota National Guard, Spencer Tornado of May 30, 1998 569
South Dakota National Guard, Oglala Tornado of 1999 571
South Dakota Veterans War Memorial at Pierre, South Dakota 573
South Dakota National Guard-Jasper, Flagpole and Maitland Fires (2000)... 577
South Dakota National Guard, "Operation Enduring Freedom Afghani-
    stan" 579
South Dakota National Guard, "Operation Iraqi Freedom" 581
South Dakota National Guard, "Operation Noble Eagle" 583
South Dakota National Guard, "Operation Enduring Freedom Afghani-
    stan," To War in Southwest Asia 585
South Dakota National Guard Goes to War to Protect America, March
    19, 2003 587
Major Bob Liebman, B-1B Weapons Officer, "Combat Southwest Asia,
    28th Bomb Wing" 589
Senior Airmen James Pyeatt, 28th Munitions Squadron, "B-1Bs in
    Southwest Asia" 593
SSgt. Ryan Walker, 34th Maintenance Squadron, 28th Bomb Wing, "B-
    1Bs in Southwest Asia" 595
Major Brian (Sea Bass) Witkowsky, 34th Bomb Squadron, 28th Bomb
    Wing, "B-1Bs in Southwest Asia" 597
Lieutenant Colonel Lucien Case, Chief of Plans, 28th Bomb Wing, Oper-
    ations Group 601

Major Eric Upton, 37th Expeditionary Controller Squadron, 28th Bomb Wing 603
South Dakota Army National Guard in Afghanistan, Lt. Col. John P. Weber, Commander, South Dakota Embedded Training Team 605
South Dakota Air and Space Museum, Berlin Airlift Memorial Dedicated (October 3, 2008) 609
Battleship USS Arizona Memorial, Preservation Project, A South Dakota School of Mines engineering contribution 611
South Dakota National Guard, January 2010 Blizzard Relief 619
South Dakota National Guard, James River Flood Support 621
Operation Odyssey Dawn, 28th Bomb Wing, "B-1Bs over Libya" 623
South Dakota National Guard, Missouri River Flood, May 2011 625
South Dakota National Guard, The End of the War in Iraq 627
175 Years of Serving the United States, Celebration of the U.S. Army National Guard, Birthday Celebration of the South Dakota National Guard, 1862 to 2012 629
Visit to Camp Rapid to Celebrate 150 years of National Guard History 633
South Dakota National Guard, 2012: Countdown to Withdrawal from Afghanistan 635
SSN 790 South Dakota: The third U.S. Navy warship named for South Dakota 637

Lewis and Clark

Corps of Discovery in South Dakota

THE Voyage of Discovery by Lewis and Clark opened the Great Plains, including the Dakotas, to the westward migration and settlement of eastern Americans into the area. This fulfilled the existing slogan of Manifest Destiny with the United States eventually expanding all the way to the Pacific Ocean. The sudden meeting of the Americans and the Native American Indians set off a clash of cultures and wars into the 1880s on the Great Plains.

When Thomas Jefferson took the oath of office as the third President of the United States on March 4, 1801, the country had a population of 5,308,483 (based on a census of the time, which excluded slaves and Native American Indians). The United States stretched west from the Atlantic Ocean to the Mississippi River, south from the Great Lakes to the Gulf of Mexico, covering one million square miles. Only a relative small area was occupied (by Euro-Americans, excluding the Native American Indian tribes), with two-thirds of the population living within 50 miles of the Atlantic Ocean.

By 1803, only four roads crossed the Appalachian Mountains, providing access to the interior of the country, limiting settlement of the west. The Mississippi River formed the western boundary of the United States. If added to the United States, the unexplored area in the west, the country could become a powerful nation state. President Jefferson was eager to learn as much as possible about this area. On January 18, 1803, President Jefferson sent a confidential communication to Congress..."The River Missouri and the Native American Indians inhabiting it, are not as well-known as is rendered desirable by their connection with the Mississippi River, and consequently with us. An intelligent officer with ten or twelve chosen men might explore the whole line, even to the western ocean."

However, the area on the Missouri River, west of the Mandan Indian settlement (in what is now southern North Dakota) was an unknown. It would require someone to travel the route, exploring the area, taking measurements to draw maps. An expedition would record the local flora, fauna, rivers, mountains, and native population. President Jefferson requested Congress to authorize a military expedition to explore west of the Mississippi River, up the Missouri, into an area claimed by England, France and Spain. Meanwhile, President Jefferson sought permission from the government of France, which administered the upper Missouri River basin (Spain had given its administration to France to prevent it from coming under the control of England), to pass through the Louisiana Territory (as President Jefferson referred to the area). Despite the Spanish government's objection, President Jefferson decided to conduct a clandestine exploration of the Louisiana Territory. Congress approved expenditure of $2,500 to fund exploration of the Louisiana Territory. The final bill for the exploration of the Louisiana Territory totaled $38,722.

Meanwhile, President Jefferson requested, through diplomatic channels to the French government an offer to buy the Port of New Orleans, at the mouth of the Mississippi River. This would allow the United States to gain control of the river, guaranteeing the flow of commerce from the interior of the United States to the Gulf of Mexico and beyond. With France fighting a war with England, Emperor Napoleon Bonaparte needed money. He offered, not only to sell the port of New Orleans, but the entire Louisiana Territory for $15,000,000, an area of 820,000 square miles. President Jefferson agreed and sent the purchase to Congress, which approved it on April 30, 1803 (announced on July 4, 1803).

The purchase of the Louisiana Territory doubled the size of the United States and allowed the expedition to proceed openly up the Missouri River, into the unexplored west. President Jefferson appointed his personal White House Secretary, Captain Meriwether Lewis to lead the "Corps of Discovery," the exploration of the "Louisiana Purchase." To assist in leading the expedition, Captain Lewis selected Lieutenant William Clark (President Jefferson promised Captain Lewis that he would submit the necessary paperwork to Congress to get Lieutenant Clark promoted to the rank of Captain. However, the promotion did not reach the Corps of Discovery base at the mouth of the Missouri River prior to the expedition beginning. However, Captain Lewis considered Clark as a Captain during the expedition).

Once Captain Lewis was appointed to lead the Corps of Discovery, he conducted detailed planning sessions with President Jefferson for the trip west of the Mandan Indian village. In order to prepare, Captain Lewis traveled to Philadelphia for instructions from scientists on natural sciences (astronomy, botany, navigation, medicine, biology, and other scientific disciplines). Captain Lewis spent $2,500 on two tons of supplies (mathematical instruments, camp supplies, presents for the Native American Indians, clothing, arms and ammunition, medicine and medical supplies, and a small traveling library), including the construction of a keel boat and three large canoe boats.

President Jefferson gave Captain Lewis specific instructions on what information to collect during the Corps of Discovery: what were the Native American Plains Indians like; what were their languages, customs, and medical habits; describe details of plant and animal life, minerals, topography; and possibilities for trade with the Native American Plains Indians. Because Captain Lewis exhausted appropriated funds from Congress for the Corps of Discovery, President Jefferson gave him a one-page letter..."pledging the faith of the United States to reimburse anyone for any goods or services needed."

Captain Lewis traveled from Washington to Pittsburgh to oversee the construction of a 55-foot long keelboat and three smaller boats during the summer and fall of 1803. At this time, Captain Lewis began recruiting members for the Corps of Discovery's permanent party, those individuals who would explore the area west of the Mandan Indian village and support personnel who would travel to the Mandan Indian village and return south to St. Louis with the keelboat. Captains Lewis and Clark recruited 45 men for the Corps of Discovery: woodsmen, enlisted Army personnel, and local boatman who would return to St. Louis after the permanent party of 33 pushed into the unexplored area west of the Mandan Indian village (their planned 1804 to 1805 winter camp).

The Corps of Discovery reached its staging base at the junction of the Mississippi and Missouri Rivers near St. Louis in December 1803. The expedition made winter camp at the mouth of the Wood River on the Illinois side of the Mississippi River, opposite the mouth of the Missouri River. The Corps of Discovery's journey to the Pacific Ocean began on the morning of May 14, 1804, to transit 3,700 miles through the present states of Missouri, Kansas, Iowa, Nebraska, South Dakota, North Dakota, Montana, Idaho, Oregon and Washington. Throughout the summer, the Corps of Discovery rowed or pulled the keelboat up the Missouri River, traversing sunken tree snags, sand bars, collapsing riverbanks, high winds and thunderstorms. The route through South Dakota was an important part of the eventually subjugation of the Plains Indians as Americans moved from the east to the west. This was not a peaceful westward expansion, with many fierce conflicts between the Native American Indian tribes in the area of the Dakotas (North and South Dakota). On August 20, 1804, at what is now Sioux City, Iowa, the Corps of Discovery suffered its first and only casualty, when Sergeant Charles Floyd died from complications of a burst appendix. He was the first U.S. Army soldier to die west of the Mississippi River.

Relations with the Native American Indians on the lower Missouri River, who had previous contact with English, French, and Spanish fur traders, were friendly. These tribes were accustomed to white men and expected to receive bribes from those traveling up the Missouri River. The Corps of Discovery had prepared for these demands with presents labeled for each of the Native American Indian tribes on the lower Missouri River (Missouri and Oto). The Corps of Discovery traveled up the Missouri River in a large keelboat, bigger than anything the Native American Indians had ever seen. It had a swivel cannon mounted on the bow. Most Native American Indians, living along or near the Missouri River, were astonished when the Corps of Discovery crew fired the cannon, impressed by the power of these white men. In addition, the number of white men to arrive at one time was unusual.

Over the course of the expedition, Captains Lewis and Clark developed a ritual used when meeting Native American Indian tribes. Captain Lewis would begin speaking to the tribal chiefs…"You've got a new father, we're going to be trading with you, we're going to bring you all the benefits that British and Spanish have been bringing you, only we're gonna sell you better goods at cheaper prices, and you should join up in this great American trading empire that we're gonna be building." Captain Lewis added…"You are now part of the United States. You gotta stop fighting one another. You know, it doesn't help us for trade, it doesn't help us, you know, as a nation, and you're fighting one another." Captains Lewis and Clark did not understand why fighting for Native American Plains Indians was a way of life. Various tribes had different objectives on the plains: protection of their hunting grounds, conducting raids as part of a warrior's development, and maintenance of their culture.

Captains Lewis and Clark's Native American Indian diplomacy described as the "Great Traveling Medicine Show." First, European style technology was shown off in a parade. The Corps of Discovery wanted to display Euro-American trade goods, so the "great country store" was pulled out of the keelboat. They wanted to show Native American Indians the trade items available from St. Louis. After this demonstration, Captains Lewis and Clark conducted treaty talk, council making, and showing the United States flag. The chief of the tribe was presented a peace medal. The presentation signified the Native American Indian tribe's recognition of American sovereignty over them. To these Native American Indians all this was strange. For many years, European fur traders had rowed up river, but these white men were different.

These white men with the Corps of Discovery were a large group, well-armed, traveling in big boat, who did not want to trade, but instead insisted on talking, making maps, gather plants and animals, use instruments to determine location, always on the move, make treaties, and stop warfare on the great plains. The Corps of Discovery voyage was a meeting of two different cultures. The Corps of Discovery did not encounter many dangerous confrontations with the Native American Indians. This was because they were the first large group of Euro-Americans to travel through the area and did not threaten the Native American Indians way of life. However, this would change as more white men and settlers moved into the area. In addition, the Corps of Discovery could not survive without support from Native American Indians tribes along their route of travel. President Jefferson instructed Captain Lewis..."to have good and peaceful relations with native people."

The Corps of Discovery left present day Sioux City, Iowa on the morning of August 21, 1804, entering present day South Dakota. On 22 August, the Corps of Discovery camped at present day Elk Point. On 24 August, they reached present day Vermilion and Yankton on 29 August. It was here the expedition encountered the Yankton Sioux Indians. The Yankton Sioux Indians were ready to trade with the United States. They had previously traded with British and French traders. Somehow, they sensed those individuals were to be swept away by these white men. Most of all, they wanted firearms. The first council took place on 30 August, when 70 Yankton Sioux Indians were welcomed into the Corps of Discovery's camp. Their chief, Weuche, explained how poor the Yankton Sioux were and desperately needed trade. They did not get any firearms from the Corps of Discovery. Captain Lewis described the Yankton Sioux..."as a stout, bold looking people and well made. The greater part of them makes use of bows and arrows. Some few rifles I observe among them, not withstanding, they live by bow and arrow. They do not shoot so well as the northern Indians. The warriors are very much decorated with paint, porcupine quills and feathers, large leggings and moccasins, all with buffalo robes of different colors. The squaws wore petticoats and a white buffalo robe with their black hair turned back over their necks and shoulders.

The Corps of Discovery left the Yankton Sioux Indian main village on the morning of September 7, 1804. By 17 September, they reached present day Oacoma, close to Chamberlain. Captain Lewis in a journal entry..."Found the country in every direction for about three miles intersected with deep ravines and steep irregular hills of 100 to 200 feet high. At the tops of these hills, the country breaks off as usual into a fine level plain extending as far as the eye can reach. From this plain I had an extensive view of the river below, and irregular hills which border the opposite sides of the river...to the west a high range of hills, stretch across the country from north to south and appeared distant about 20 miles. They are not very extensive as I could plainly observe their rise and termination. No rock appeared on them."

On 23 September, the Corps of Discovery camped near East Medicine Knoll Creek (present day Pierre) where they met the Teton Sioux (the Lakota) for the first time. The Lakota occupied two villages, one village on the Missouri River and the second, along the Bad River. The Lakota were known among Native American Plains Indians as aggressive, controlling passage up or down the river, demanding gifts from passing traders, resorting to violent tactics if not paid. Given this characteristic, the Lakota's relations with the Arikara Indians living to the north is interesting. The Lakota Indians were more powerful than the Arikara Indians. The Arikara Indians were superior farmers, growing corn and trading it to the Lakota Indians, which used the meal ground from corn as a staple of their diet. Consequently, the Arikara Indians survived, because they were needed for survival by those living around them.

Upon meeting the Lakota Indians, Captains Lewis and Clark went through their ritual, parading in uniform and demonstrating their armaments. However, this display did little to impress the Lakota. They viewed these white men as competitors for control of the Missouri River. As a result, tension increased between the Corps of Discovery and Lakota, nearly resulting in hostilities. Fortunately, Lakota Chief Black Buffalo restrained his warriors. After Chief Black Buffalo calmed his warriors, he welcomed the Corps of Discovery into the Lakota camp. As a precaution, Captain Lewis moored the Corps of Discovery keelboat one mile from the Lakota camp, under guard.

Captain Lewis described the Lakota..."These people show great anxiety. They appear sprightly, generally ill looking and not well made; their legs and arms small; high cheekbones, prominent eyes. They grease and paint themselves with coal when they dress. The distinguished men make use of hawk feathers. This consists of Calumet feathers with Porcupine quills fastened to the top of the head and falls backward about their heads. The men wear a robe, and each a polecat's skin. Fond of dress and show. They are badly armed with rifles...The squaws are cheerful, fine-looking women, not handsome; high cheeks; dressed in skin; a petticoat and robe, which folds back over their shoulder, do all the laborious work, and I may say, perfect slaves to the men, as all squaws of nations, or where the women are more numerous than men." None of the men in the Corps of Discovery spoke Lakota and it was this inability to communicate which lead to misunderstandings. After one such misunderstanding over the Lakota's demand for more good than the expedition had for moving up the Missouri River, the Corps of Discovery departed on the morning of 28 September.

On October 1, 1804, the Corps of Discovery reached the mouth of the Cheyenne River. By 8 October, they reached the Grand River, at present day Mobridge, and the Arikara Indians. In the 1780s, the Arikara Indians were ravaged by small pox. The disease hard hit their population of 30,000 that by 8 October, when the Corps of Discovery arrived, only few Arikara Indians remained. The Corps of Discovery passed one abandoned Arikara Indian village after before reaching the three remaining settlements at the mouth of the Grand River. These Arikara Indian villages contained approximately 2,000, who lived in round, earth-covered lodges, and the first of this type encountered by the Corps of Discovery. The Arikara Indians were farmers, growing corn, beans, squash, tobacco, watermelons, and pumpkins. When crops were scarce, they hunted buffalo and other game. The women did the farming. The crops not only provided them food to get through the winter, but as trade with other Native American Indians, such as the Lakota Indians to the south. In return, they received trade goods levied from traders moving up or down the Missouri River.

The Corps of Discovery stayed with the Arikara Indians for five days, maintaining friendly and warm relations. Most of Captains Lewis and Clark's negotiations centered on trade with the United States. The Arikara Indians, like the Missouri and Oto Indians, agreed to send a delegation down river to St. Louis and onto Washington to meet with President Jefferson. They also agreed to make peace with their enemy to the north, the Mandan Indians. Captain Lewis described the Arikara Indians..."Their men tall and proportioned, women small and industrious, raise great quantities of corn, beans, squash, and tobacco. They collect all the wood and do the drudgery, as is common among savages. These people are dirty, kind, poor, and extravagant, possessing national pride, not beggarly, receive what is given with great pleasure, live in warm houses, large and built in an octagon pattern, forming a cone on top which is left open for smoke to pass. Those houses are generally 30 or 40 feet in diameter, covered with earth on poles with willows and grass to prevent earth passing through. These people express an inclination to be at peace with all nations. The Lakota, who trade the goods they get from British traders for their corn, have great influence over the Arikiara Indians, poison their minds and keep them in perpetual dread. Dress of the men of this nation is simply a pair of moccasins, leggings, flap in front, and a buffalo robe, with their hair, arms, and ears decorated. The women wore moccasins, leggings fringed, and a shirt of goatskins, some with sleeves. This garment is long and generally white and fringed, tied at the waist, with a robe."

More than anything else, it was the personal slave of Captain Lewis, a Negro called York, which occupied the attention of the Arikara Indians. They had never seen a black man. York played with the Arikara Indian children, telling them he was a wild creature who had been captured and trained by Captain Lewis. The Arikara Indian adults were so astonished by York's presence with the Corps of Discovery that they believed he had special spiritual power, nicknaming him "Big Medicine." York was big, dark, strong, agile, and a natural athlete. He was about Captain Clark's age, possibly younger. He had been Clark's life-long companion, with ownership passing down from Clark's father, whose companion had been York's father.

On the morning of 14 October, the Corps of Discovery took to their boats, moving up the Missouri River. The next day they entered present day North Dakota, heading toward the Corps of Discovery Winter camp with the Mandan and Hidatsa Indians near present day Bismarck, reaching their villages on 24 October. The Corps of Discovery made a secure position across the river from the Mandan camp, setting out the winter and preparing for the continued spring re-movement up the Missouri.

The peaceful interaction of the Corps of Discovery with Native American Indians living in present day South Dakota would not be repeated by those who followed, setting off an unstoppable Euro-American conquest of the west, ending in 1891, with forceful subjugation of the Native American Plains Indians. These occupiers of the west were forced onto reservations and their traditional way of life, customs, culture, and language assaulted by the white men who sought to change them into Euro-Americans. The Corps of Discovery maintained a strong military posture and it worked most of the time. Some of the encounters with the Lakotas were tense, because they were heavily armed, but Captains Lewis and Clark managed to end up with friendly exchanges. This is of historical significance, given the seeds of hostility and conflict, which subsequent U.S. Army expeditions did not attempt to copy.

The area of the west which the Corps of Discovery transited through along the Missouri River in present day South Dakota contained many Native American Plains Indian tribes. However, from a Euro-American perspective, the Corps of Discovery charted uninhabited lands, ready for the settlement by those living in the east, expanding the western border of the United States to the Pacific Ocean, claiming everything between. The Corps of Discovery was the first to conduct an extensive exploration of the area west of the Mandan Indian villages. Their detailed maps provided direction for those who followed, but at great cost to the Native American Indians. During the Corps of Discovery return trip down the Missouri, on 30 August, Captain Lewis wrote in his journal a most accurate prophecy about the future of the Native American Plains Indians, when meeting Lakota warriors (The Corps of Discovery did not row to shore but continued downstream)..."I told those Indians that they had been deaf to our counsels, and ill-treated us as we ascended the river two years past; that they had abused all white who had visited them since."

Captain Lewis wrote what would come to pass when the U.S. Army and Euro-Americans reached this area of the United States..."We viewed them as bad people and no more traders would come to them, and whenever the white people wished to visit the Lakotas, they would come sufficiently strong to whip any villainous party who dared oppose them, and other words to the same."

In 1813, Thomas Jefferson wrote about the ideals of the Corps of Discovery, which Captain Lewis maintained while completing a most difficult mission of exploration, which unfortunately for the Native American Indians living in the Louisiana Purchase was not continued with by following Presidents of the United States. Jefferson..."Of courage undaunted, possessing a firmness and perseverance of purpose which nothing but impossibilities could divert from its direction, careful as a father of those committed to his charge. Yet steady in the maintenance of order and discipline, intimate with the Indian character, customs and principles, habituated to the hunting life." Today, South Dakota is a mix of Native American and European-American History.[1]

---

[1] The author, in 1996, prepared a presentation and historical paper on the voyage up the Missouri River into present day South Dakota by Lewis and Clark for the annual Keystone History Conference. The South Dakota
continued...

...continued
State Historical Society in Pierre South, Dakota provided information for this presentation.

The Conclusion of the Indian Wars in South Dakota

TO Euro-Americans immigrants, who settled along the eastern seaboard of North America, few influences exerted themselves more powerfully upon the frontier, as it moved west across the Appalachian Mountains, than the Native American Indians who resisted the westward advance of the white man. At first, the Native American Indians were friendly but as the white man increased in numbers, the pressure on their hunting lands and traditional living areas increased, they became more hostile. Therefore, it was inevitable that Native American Indians came into conflict with the westward advancing white man, forever changing their way of life.

The initial movement of Native American Indians into the western plains began sometime in the 1600s, pushing into what is now South Dakota from the east and south, moving across the plains. There probably were previous groups in this region but their numbers and existence is hard to verify, other than widely scattered bands. These migrating groups consisted of the Hidatsa, Crow, Mandan, Arikara, Cheyenne, Ojibwa, and Sioux Indians.

Native American Plains Indians followed a way of life, directed by the "Spirits" who told them through visions and signs as to the various places of ritual. Daily life was not easy for them, but it gave each what needed for their bodies, minds, and hearts, without taking too much from the land, unlike what the white man did upon reaching the west.

For the Native American Plains Indians, the buffalo was the giver of life and an integral part of their culture. It provided them nearly every material want and a major part of their religious beliefs and practices. After the buffalo herds were hunted to near extinction (by white men), it was a catastrophe to them, something they never recovered from.

On March 30, 1743, French traders, Louis Joseph and Francois La Verendrye reached present day Pierre, South Dakota, along the Missouri River, beginning the white man's intrusion into the west and onto the Dakota plains. Many others followed these first white men onto the western plains. At first, Native American Plains Indians only had limited contacts with white traders, limited primarily to trading buffalo hides and other furs for hard goods such as knives, beads, blankets, and firearms. The mating of the gun to the horse allowed the Native American Plains Indians to be hunters that were more aggressive and increased their ability to support larger families and growing settlements.

In 1803, the United States completed negotiations for Louisiana Territory (Louisiana Purchase), gaining rights to the Dakotas, introducing the concept of Euro-American land ownership to the western plains, which was foreign to the Native American Plains Indians. President Thomas Jefferson sent an expedition, led by Captain William Clark and Lieutenant Meriwether Lewis to explore the Missouri river from its mouth at the Mississippi river to its source, as well as attempting to find a water route to the Pacific. In 1804, the expedition traveled up river through South Dakota and in 1806, passed south, going down stream. From this time on, the white man's pressure on the North American Plains Indians way of life increased, forcing their culture to move away from traditional values to that of the encroaching white man, resulting in cultural confusion and erosion.

Pressure on the Native American Plains Indian culture and Black Hills increased during the 1850s, with the Oregon Trail cutting through the Dakota Territory. It was the main route west to the gold fields of Colorado, Montana, and California. At this time, gold remained a secret in the Black Hills, although its existence was speculated. Many of this humanity moving west, settled at various points along the route, crowding the Sioux's territory by hunting and building homes. Many Sioux fought to protect their hunting grounds and violation of the sacred Black Hills.

The Sioux did not divide, buy, or sell land. But, from 1855 to 1866, as cheap eastern U.S. land (primarily east of the Mississippi River, then quickly advancing west to the Missouri River, between Iowa and Nebraska) became scarce, eastern farmers saw a chance to get a new start in the Dakotas. To increase settlement into the western plains, Congress established boundaries for the western Dakotas (still not considered as a territory because of the lack of a sizable white population, discounting the Native American Plains Indians). Surveyors and mapmakers provided layout for townships, sections, quarter sections to make them easier to sell and/or homestead titles (settled), at the expense of the Native American Plains Indians already in the area.

In 1851, nine Dakota Native American Plains Indian tribes signed the Fort Laramie Treaty, agreeing to stay away from the Oregon Trail, allowing the passage of whites to the gold fields and areas west of the Black Hills. Native American Plains Indians gave up much of their self-sufficiency and nomadic way of life. The U.S. government promised to provide them food and goods for 15 years. The treaty of April 19, 1858, forced the Native American Plains Indians to give up approximately 14,000,000 acres of land between the Missouri and Big Sioux Rivers.

Congress, in 1861, created the Dakota Territory, the area north of Nebraska, west of Minnesota, and east of the Rocky Mountains. The Fort Laramie Treaty of 1868, created the Great Sioux Reservation, comprising 43,000 acres, including all western South Dakota, blocking the area for white settlement. Even before the ink on the treaty was dry, prominent eastern investors and bankers began to scheme to find a way to change the treaty to allow settlement and economic exploitation of the area.

Article II of the Fort Laramie Treaty of 1868 stated..."The United States agrees that the following district of country, commencing on the east bank of the Missouri river where the 46th Parallel North Latitude crosses the same, thence along the low-water mark down said east bank to a point opposite where the northern line of the state of Nebraska strikes the river, thence west across said river, and along the northern line of Nebraska to the 104th Degree of Longitude West from Greenwich, thence north on said meridian to a point where the 46th Parallel of North Latitude intercepts the same, thence due east along said parallel to the place beginning; and in addition thereto, all existing reservations of the east bank of said river, shall be and the same is, set apart for the absolute and undisturbed use and occupation of the Indians herein named, and for such other friendly tribes or individual Indians as from time to time they may be willing, with the consent of the United States, to admit amongst them; and the United States now solemnly agrees that no persons, except herein designated and authorized so to do, and except such officers, agents, and employees of the government as may be authorized to enter upon Indian reservations in discharge of duties enjoined by law, shall ever be permitted to pass over, settle upon, or reside in the territory described in this article, or in such territory as may be added to this reservation for the use of said Indians, and henceforth they will and do hereby relinquish all claims or right in and to any portion of the United States or territories, except such as is embraced within the limits a foresaid, and except as here in after provided."

Under provisions of the Fort Laramie Treaty of 1868 (beginning on July 2, 1874, and for the next 60 days, covering approximately 1,200 miles), Lt. Col. George Armstrong Custer led a U.S. Army expedition into the area. The expedition consisted of 1,000 troops, 1,900 horses and mules, 300 cattle, and 110 wagons, to survey the northern sector of the Dakota Territory referred to as the Black Hills.

In 1871, Congress approved the Indian Appropriations Act, which ended the practice of treating Native North American Plains Indian tribes as sovereign nations by directing that all Native American Plains Indian tribes be treated as individuals, legally designated as "wards" of the Federal government. The act was justified as a way to avoid further misunderstanding in treaty negotiations, where Euro-Americans have often wrongly assumed that a Tribal Chief is also that Tribes Chief-of-State. It was an overt attempt to continue the dismantlement of the tribal structure of the Native American Plains Indians.

Lt. Col. Custer wrote about the expedition into the Black Hills on August 15, 1874..."We have discovered a rich and beautiful country and I have the proud satisfaction of knowing that our explorations have exceeded the most sanguine expectations." He announced that two geologists were on the expedition discovered gold in the Black Hills. Consequently, the rush of fortune seekers that followed set the eventual course for war on the northern plains, a war in which the Black Hills eventually passed into the hands of the white man, at the expense of the Native American Plains Indians.

The U.S. Army did not have enough troops to enforce the Fort Laramie Treaty of 1868, satisfying neither the Native American Plains Indians or the white settlers and miners (who wanted to get into the Black Hills to look for gold). Army troops had to patrol approximately two and half million square miles of territory between the Missouri river and the eastern slope of the Sierra Mountains. There were never more than 15,000 soldiers, scattered among 100 forts and outposts. They had the almost impossible task of defending settlers, ranchers, miners, and railroad crews, as well as keeping thousands of Native American Plains Indians confined to their reservations while keeping tens of thousands of white men off reservation lands. Even though Army pay was low ($13.00 a month), at this time, steady jobs were scarce during the economic slump that followed the U.S. Civil War. Army ranks filled with immigrants, some of whom could speak almost no English, while others joined to escape bad marriages or the law. Because of the need for men, no questions were asked, and many former Confederate Army soldiers enlisted in the U.S. Army of the West, including many officers.

In 1875, a U.S. Senate Commission, meeting with Chief Red Cloud and other Lakota chiefs to negotiate legal access for miners rushing into the Black Hills, attempted to purchase the region for six million dollars. The Lakota chiefs refused to alter the terms of the Fort Laramie Treaty of 1868, and declared..."We will protect their lands from intruders (the white men) if the government would not."

To keep the Army, settlers and Native American Plains Indians supplied with food and other goods, steamboats transported items up the Missouri River, delivering supplies for overland shipment. Prior to the railroad bridges being built across the Missouri River, off-loaded steamboat supplies were moved west by wagons pulled by horses or mules. It was a slow delivery process, no guarantee the goods would arrive to those ordering and paying for them. The wagons were easy targets for thieves, weather, breakage or spoilage of the cargo, and periodic Native American Plains Indians raids to get supplies.

By early 1876, the Overland Stage was maintaining at best, a supplement to wagon transport. Although it primarily carried passengers and mail, it hauled limited amounts of high priority freight. The Overland Stage helped the U.S. Army maintain better communications in the Dakotas, pending the installation of the telegraph and building of the railroads. Both increased pressure to open the North American Plains Indians' lands to settlement. However, the Fort Laramie Treaty of 1868, and its large reservations blocked the westward expansion in the Dakotas.

One of the largest Native American Plains Indian Agencies was the Red Cloud Indian Agency. The Red Cloud Indian Agency established in 1873, for Chief Red Cloud and his Oglala band, as well as for other Native American Plains Indians, totaling nearly 13,000. This and other Native American Plains Indian agencies served as issuing points for supplies to the Sioux, Cheyenne, and Arapaho. However, everything was not as it should have been at the agencies. Many Indian agents requested and usually provided U.S. Army protection.

At the Red Cloud Agency, shortly after its set up, a growing faction of North American Plains Indians living on the reservation surrounding the agency, harassed the employees, threatening area ranchers, and often rode through the unfinished agency stockade shooting out windows and scaring everyone inside.

In March 1874, the U.S. government authorized the establishment of a military camp at the Red Cloud Agency on the White River. The Red Cloud Agency quickly earned the reputation as one of the most troublesome spots on the plains because of the reports filed by its agents and personnel, often presenting a one-side, non-Native American Plains Indian point of view. Camp Robinson, later Fort Robinson, played an important role in the Indian Wars of 1876 to 1890.

Federal authorities ordered the Lakota chiefs to return to their reservations and when they did not, an opportunity to alter the provisions of the Fort Laramie Treaty of 1868 developed. The Army moved 2,500 troops into the field to force the Native American Plains Indians back onto the reservations. General George Crook took troops from Fort Fetter on the North Platte River; General Alfred H. Terry (with Lt. Col. George Custer attached) moved west from Fort Abraham Lincoln at Bismarck, North Dakota; and Colonel John Gibbon marched east from Fort Ellis, Montana.

The original Army plan for defeating and subjugating the Lakota called for three troop forces under the field command of General Crook, Col. Gibbon, and Lt. Col. Custer to trap the bulk of the Lakota and Cheyenne between the three columns, dealing the Native American Plains Indians a crushing defeat. Lt. Col. Custer however, advanced much more quickly than ordered. He neared what he thought was a large Lakota and Cheyenne village on the morning of June 25, 1876. Lt. Col. Custer's rapid advance put him far ahead of Col. Gibbon's slow moving infantry brigades, and unbeknownst to him, General Crook's column had been blocked and forced to temporarily withdraw from its advance by Chief Crazy Horse and his followers at the battle of Rosebud Creek, a victory for the Lakota warriors.

On the verge of what seemed to Lt. Col. Custer a certain and glorious victory for both the U.S. Seventh Cavalry and himself, he moved to attack the village in front of him. Contemptuous of Native American Plains Indians military prowess, Lt. Col. Custer split his force into three parts, to make certain fewer hostiles escaped (Lt. Col. Custer's reference for the Native American Plains Indians).

Lt. Col. Custer's attack was one of the greatest fiascoes for the U.S. Army and on the opposite side, a tremendous victory for the thousands of Lakota, Cheyenne, and Arapaho warriors. These warriors forced Lt. Col. Custer's troops back from their village, onto a long dusty ridge running parallel to the Little Big Horn River, surrounded, and killed all 266.

This was an important battle and victory for the Sioux and their allies under Chief Gall and the Lakota medicine man, Sitting Bull. However, after their victory over Lt. Col. Custer and supporting units, the warriors broke into smaller bands, never again fighting as a single large force (a large unified military force was not the traditional way Native American Plains Indians fought). Chief Gall and Sitting Bull, along with their followers, crossed the northern U.S. border into

Canada, seeking safety from the "Great White Mother across the sea" (Queen Victoria of England) and permission to live on her land.

On August 15, 1876, U.S. Congress passed the Indian Appropriation Bill. It included a threat that if the Black Hills, as well as the lands outside reservations, not given up by the Sioux, no more food or provisions would be shipped to the Tetons to feed those still on the reservations, most who had taken no part in any military action against the U.S. Army. It was the white man's backlash to Lt. Col. Custer's defeat (Native American Plains Indian victory over the white man) at the hands of savage hostiles.

Consequently, the Manypenny Treaty Commission forced the Native American Plains Indians to sign the agreement, or face starvation without rations and supplies, and forever give up their sacred Black Hills. Meanwhile, the remaining bands of roaming Native American Plains Indians suffered greatly, constantly pursued by units of the U.S. Army, and facing starvation, had no other option but to surrender. Other small bands and groups of starving Native American Plains Indians began drifting into the Red Cloud Agency to surrender, by March 1877. Chief Dull Knife surrendered at the Red Cloud Agency in April.

In May 1877, Chief Crazy Horse and his starving band surrendered at the Red Cloud Agency. However, even in apparent defeat, Chief Crazy Horse remained an independent spirit. In September 1877, when he left the reservation without authorization (a white man's restriction which was foreign, given their nomadic culture and former way of life), to take his sick wife to her parents (she had suffered greatly while hiding from pursing U.S. Army units, in the cold of the winter); he was considered to be a threat. General Crook ordered Chief Crazy Horse arrested, fearing that he was plotting to gather disgruntled Native American Plains Indians around him and return to battle the U.S. Army in the west.

Chief Crazy Horse did not resist arrest by Army troops, believing he was going home under Army guard to the reservation and warned not to leave without first obtaining approval from the Red Cloud Indian Agent. However, he was sent to Fort Robinson to be placed in into custody in fort's guardhouse. On September 5, 1877, Chief Crazy Horse was marched under guard by U.S. Army Sioux Troopers to the guardhouse and not home, and he began to resist. In the fulfillment of one of his visions, he foretold of death at the hands of one of his own people, while his arms were pinned to his side by a soldier, a Sioux trooper ran him through with a bayonet.

In late 1880, Chief Gall and his followers entered the United States from Canada, surrendering to the U.S. Army on January 31, 1881. He was moved to the Standing Rock Reservation in the Dakota Territory. Once on the reservation, Chief Gall developed a close relationship with the Indian Agent, James McLaughlin, who became Sitting Bull's most determined and vocal antagonist.

On July 19, 1881, Sitting Bull, and his starving followers, crossed the U.S. border with Canada, surrendering to the U.S. Army. He asked for the right to be able to cross back into Canada whenever he wished, for a home near the Black Hills, and the right to hunt where and whenever he pleased. Instead and not surprisingly, the U.S. Army took him east, to the Standing Rock Reservation. The transfer resulted from a politically motivated goal by Indian Agent McLuaghlin. Once at the reservation, Sitting Bull found his daughter and many who had fought with him at the battle of the Little Big Horn. Those on the reservation, reduced to surviving on government rations were forbidden to speak their own language, and denied their religious customs.

Between 1876 and 1890, the Sioux lived on various reservations, under a constantly changing system of government aid and rules, which totally ignored their beliefs, traditions, previous nomadic life style, and confusing interpretation of the white man's way of life. At the Red Cloud Indian Agency storehouse and issue point, those living on the reservation were issued sugar, coffee, salt pork, beans, and wheat flour. The Sioux preferred traditional corn meal flour, however, the Red Cloud Indian Agent considered its purchase too expensive. Often, Indian Agents skimmed funds off the top of yearly authorizations, transferring funds into their bank accounts. More than one completed their time as an Indian Agent with Large bank accounts, at the expense of those who were supposed to receive these funds on the reservations.

The U.S. Army provided beef cattle on the hoof to replace the Native American Plains Indians reliance on hunting the buffalo. For example, beef arrived at the Red Cloud Agency to meet the treaty obligations of the Fort Laramie Treaty of 1868. However, beef delivery was frequently delayed, reduced, and only reluctantly completed after Lt. Col. Custer's defeat in 1876. Again, Indian agents often reported all required beef arrived, when many head were sold to private individuals or even for stock for Indian agent's ranch herds. It was a system ripe for abuse and fraud, with the Native American Plains Indians suffering because of short rations.

In a further attempt to get the Native American Plains Indians off the reservations and reduce support to the various agencies, the U.S. Congress passed the Dawes Allotment Act of 1887. It granted to the head of each Native American Plains Indian household, 160 acres of land. It was an overt attempt to destroy their tribal system.

As Native American Plains Indian lands became available through forfeiture of previously set aside reservation land, starting in 1873, and continuing until 1896, the white population of the Black Hills increased, dramatically changing the Euro-American cultural make-up of the Black Hills as increasing numbers of immigrants arrived (from the east and west coast ports).

Additional pressure on the Native American Plains Indians way of life resulted as previous empty plains grasslands and traditional hunting grounds became cattle ranching areas, replacing the buffalo. Later, most of the open rangeland disappeared as cattle ranchers acquired the land and fenced it, to move from open range grazing to cattle ranching, trying to eliminate the effects of harsh winter weather.

The open prairie grasslands, not fenced by cattle ranchers, were offered for homesteading land (often not very high quality) advertised in the east. Between 1878 and 1998, thousands of homesteaders moved onto the plains, cutting up the thick prairie sod, planting crops, helped by years of adequate rain, survived in a hostile environment (broiling summer sun and terrible winter cold). In 1870, the population of the southern Dakotas was 10,000 whites (the Native American Plains Indians not counted, or considered as residents of the region), 80,000 by 1880 and 333,000 by 1890.

At the same time, surface gold mining and timber cutting for homes and mine use in the Black Hills reduced the area of traditional Lakota tribal lands. As the Euro-American population increased in the Black Hills, stone quarries appeared to provide stone for permanent buildings, including many church sponsored Native American Plains Indian schools established on the reservations, as well as railroad and road bridges, and many substantial buildings in the Black Hills.

The surrender of the Sioux and Cheyenne did not end trouble at the Red Cloud Agency and for the U.S. Army troops stationed at Fort Robinson. In May 1877, 1,000 Northern Cheyenne, including Chiefs Little Wolf and Dull Knife, were removed from the Red Cloud Agency, shipped by railroad cars to a bleak reservation in Oklahoma, far to the south of their homeland. Once there, they found life on this reservation unbearable and sought a way to return to their traditional home in the Black Hills. In September 1878, 300 of these uprooted Cheyenne left the Oklahoma reservation, heading toward the Nebraska Sand

Hills area. Upon reaching this area, they split into two groups.

Chief Little Wolf took one of the groups to winter in the shelter of Cherry Valley. Meanwhile, Chief Dull Knife took the second group, primarily women and children, to surrender at the Red Cloud Agency. Chief Little Wolf and his band were captured by the U.S. Army in October 1877 and escorted under guard to Fort Robinson for detention.

After one of Dull Knife's warriors escaped from Fort Robinson into the surrounding hills, Chief Dull Knife and his followers were confined in one of the fort's unused barracks, which had been turned into a warehouse. The Red Cloud Indian Agent and U.S. Army officers tried to persuade them to return to the Oklahoma reservation. Chief Dull Knife refused, saying they preferred to die instead of going back to Oklahoma. Consequently, in an attempt to starve them into submission, food and water cut off. After five days, they burst out of the warehouse, and using weapons hidden before lock up, began firing at U.S. Army guards. Many fled across the White River Bridge at the fort's saw mill. Over the next 12 days, in bitter sub-zero cold, periodic fighting occurred. Finally, on January 22, 1879, 78 Cheyenne were captured and 64 killed.

Following the breakout of the Cheyenne from Fort Robinson and their capture, some were taken to Kansas, tried for murder. A few settlers reportedly died at the hands of the Cheyenne during the trip to the Nebraska Sand Hills. However, all were released due to a lack of evidence, transported to the Tongue River Reservation in Montana.

Railroad expansion, such as the Fremont, Elkhorn & Missouri Valley Railroad ran through the Fort Robinson Military Reservation by January 1885 (Later acquired by the Chicago & Northwestern Railroad). Railroads helped the settlement of the western plains and Dakotas. It was a rapid process. In 1870s, no railroads existed in western Dakotas. By 1880, 750 miles existed and by 1890, there were 2,500 miles. However, as population moved and mineral deposits played out or discovered in different areas and railroad lines stopped operations. There are hundreds of such miles of abandoned railroad right of way in the Black Hills.

On November 2, 1889, President Grover Cleveland signed the Omnibus Bill, creating North Dakota (39th state) and South Dakota (40th state), with Pierre becoming the capital of South Dakota (not permanently finalized as the state's capital until the election of 1909). At the same time, the Omnibus Bill gave permanence to the Dakota reservations: Sisseton, Standing Rock, Cheyenne River, Crow Creek, Lower Brule, Pine Ridge, Rosebud, and Yankton.

On February 10, 1890, the General George Crook Commission forced the Sioux to give up the Great Sioux Reservation. This breakup, started by the Omnibus Bill, formalized by the Sioux signing the agreement (of which, they had no other choice), opened vast areas of western South Dakota to one more rush of white settlement, which the Sioux could do nothing about.

This rush to settlements in the Black Hills was best characterized by the bustling Deadwood mining camp. By 1877 the Euro-American conquest of the west was nearly complete. For every Native American Plains Indian in the West, there were 40 whites, and as the Indian Wars ended, the last obstacle to Euro-American domination dropped away, and the country readied itself to assert control over the entire region. Between 1877 and 1887, four and half million Euro-Americans came west. Almost half settled on the western plains. Some came seeking freedom, land of their own (at the expense of the Native American Plains Indians freedom and loss of their sacred areas, such as the Black Hills), and opportunities they could not find in the east or in their own country.

Others found in the west, as surface mining was replaced by more permanent underground hard rock exploitation, a place to change their lives and start over. But, as more Euro-Americans arrived in the west, there was less and less room for the Native American Plains Indians (according to the settlers who distrusted the Native American Plains Indians). Native American Indians' lives changed overnight, with pressure from the United States to forget their old ways and make themselves over in the image of their conquerors.

By 1890, no Native American Plains Indians anywhere in the west lived freely on their former traditional lands. They were controlled by Indian agents (such as those at the Red Cloud Indian Agency), with reservations, on which they struggled to survive on, broken up, the best of their lands going to white settlement under the provisions of the Dawes Act. Because of Congressional cuts to Indian appropriations, rations were drastically reduced (also effected by graft and greed of the various Indian agents), as well as effects of the white man's epidemics of measles, influenza, and whooping cough.

1890 is considered by most Euro-American historians as the period referred to "as the passing of the American frontier," at the July 12, 1893, meeting of the American Historical Association in Chicago, Illinois by the historian Frederick S. Turner. By 1890, many Sioux no longer accepted the white man's way of life. This denial of acceptance resulted because:

Broken treaty promises.
1. Native American Indians could not adapt themselves to agricultural.
2. Poor crop conditions.
3. Reduced government issued rations.
4. Epidemics of pneumonia, measles, and whooping cough which resulted in hundreds to thousands of deaths.
5. Dismantlement of the Great Sioux Reservation by forced agreement in 1889, opposed by influential Sioux.
6. Rise of the "Messiah Craze," (Ghost Dance) added fanaticism to the Native American Plains Indians discontent.

On the Standing Rock Reservation, straddling North and South Dakota, Sitting Bull was living quietly in his cabin, still regarded with respect by many Lakotas who remembered the amazing accuracy of his visions during the time when they fought Lt. Col. Custer. However, the Lakota, divided, struggled to come to term with the white man's world. In the fall of 1890, Sitting Bull was visited by a Miniconjou Lakota name Kicking Bear, just back from a train trip to the far west, bearing remarkable news. A ceremony called the "Ghost Dance" was sweeping through many tribes of the west.

It was part of a message of hope for all Native American Plains Indians preached by a Paiute medicine man or prophet named Wovka. Wovka's gospel of salvation was a mix of Christian and Native American Indian elements. Men and women were first to purify themselves and forswear alcohol and violence. Then they would dance in a large circle, chanting and appealing to the spirits of their ancestors. When they did, Wovoka promised them the whites would vanish and the buffalo would cover the earth again.

Like most Native American Plains Indians, Sitting Bull remained skeptical of the ceremony's promised powers. However, he agreed to let the Ghost Dance be taught to those at the Standing Rock Reservation who wanted to learn it. In the Lakota version of the ceremony, the dancers wore special shirts, said to be stronger than the white man's bullets.

Native American Plains Indians, wearing the sacred Ghost Dance shirt and feathers, formed a ring, joining hands. Everyone was respectful and quiet, expecting something wonderful to happen. The leaders beat time and sang as the people danced, going round to the left in a sidewise step. Occasionally, someone fell unconscious into the center of the dance circle. As each one came to, he or she slowly sat up and looked about, bewildered, and then began wailing inconsolably.

On November 12, 1890, the Pine Ridge Indian Agent telegraphed U.S. Army officials..."We need protection and we need it now, Indians dancing in the snow, wild and crazy. The leaders should be arrested and confined at some military post until the matter is quieted, and this should be at once." Responding to the pleas of the frightened Pine Ridge Indian Agent, federal government officials ordered General Nelson A. Miles and 5,000 troops, including a reconstituted Seventh Cavalry, to put down the reported Native American Plains Indians unrest reported by the Pine Ridge Indian Agent. At the Pine Ridge and Rosebud Indian reservations, the Ghost Dancers feared the approaching U.S. Army troops were coming to attack them, and fled to a remote plateau surrounded by cliffs. Nervous area whites soon began referring to this area as "The Stronghold."

Meanwhile, at the Standing Rock Reservation, Native American Plains Indian Police, charged with keeping peace among their own people, heard a rumor that Sitting Bull was about to join the Ghost Dancers (told to them by the Indian Agent, James McLaughlin). Forty-three Lakota Police were dispatched by McLaughlin to bring in Sitting Bull under arrest. As backup, two troops of U.S. Army cavalry followed at a visible distance.

Before dawn on December 15, 1890, the Lakota Police burst into Sitting Bull's cabin, ordered him to his feet, and pushed him to his feet. Once outside, Sitting Bull's followers began to gather, taunting the Lakota Police, vowing to keep them from taking their leader. Sitting Bull hesitated, unsure of what to do. At about the same time, one of his followers raised a rife, shot one of the Lakota police. Both sides began firing. A Lakota police trooper fired a bullet through Sitting Bull's head.

Sitting Bull's grieving and scared followers fled toward the Cheyenne River Reservation, where they joined a Miniconju band lead by Chief Big Foot. He had once been an enthusiastic Ghost Dancer. However, now he was no longer certain to undergo transformation. Chief Big Foot decided to take his band to the Pine Ridge Reservation and see if there was not some way to reconcile the situation.

Unfortunately, General Miles misunderstood what Chief Big Foot was doing and ordered the Seventh Cavalry, commanded by Colonel John Forsyth, to intercept him. A unit of the Seventh Cavalry caught up with Chief Big Foot's band on December 28, 1890. Chief Big Foot, riding in a wagon, too ill with pneumonia to sit-up, flew a white flag from the wagon to indicate his peaceful intentions. Troopers transferred Chief Big Foot to a U.S. Army field ambulance, and escorted his followers to Little Wounded Knee Creek for the night.

There were 120 men, 230 women and children settled in for the night. The troopers distributed rations to Chief Big Foot's followers. A U.S. Army field surgeon did what he could for sick Chief Big Foot. Troopers positioned four cannon and two Hotchkiss guns (early version of the Gatling gun) on the top of a rise overlooking the camp below. On the morning of 29 December, troopers began moving from tipi to tipi, confiscating anything, capable of implemented as a weapon, sometimes seizing a rifle. A medicine man began to dance and shout: "Do not fear, but let your hearts be strong. Many U.S. soldiers are about us and have many bullets, but I am assuring you the bullets cannot penetrate us." Suddenly, scooping up a handful of dirt, he tossed it up into the air, and with eyes turned toward the sky implored…"Great Spirit, scatter the surrounding soldiers."

Almost simultaneously with the medicine man throwing dirt into the air, troopers were attempting to disarm a Lakota who appeared to be deaf. He hung onto his rife, and a struggle resulted, and it accidentally went off. A few seconds later, troopers on the rise above the camp opened fire with rifles, revolvers, cannon, and Hotchkiss guns. Cannon shells exploded on and throughout the tipis, flatting them, causing great damage and injury. The Lakotas attempted to fight back. When the shooting and cannon fire stopped, 300 Lakota men, women, and children were dead, with others fled into the surrounding countryside.

The Seventh Cavalry suffered 31 killed, almost entirely to friendly fire, because few of the Lakotas had guns. Secret U.S. Army reports reported the soldiers killed by the Hotchkiss guns, which produced very nasty wounds. For several days, the dead Lakotas laid where fallen, while Seventh Cavalry troops contended with sporadic fighting on the reservation.

After a heavy snowfall and bitter cold temperatures, a burial party arrived at the massacre site. Many of the troopers picked the pockets and pulled off items from the dead for souvenirs. They dug a large rectangular trench in the frozen ground, and disregarding Lakota burial ceremony, dumped the bodies into the common grave, covering them up.

During the next 12 days, skirmishes continued between the fleeing Lakotas, settlers, and troopers. One of the U.S. Army's all-black cavalry units, from Fort Robinson, relieved a unit of the Seventh Cavalry, which had become surrounded. On January 15, 1891, Chief Kicking

Bear and 4,000 of his followers surrendered to General Miles at the Pine Ridge Indian Agency.

The tragedy at Wounded Knee was much more than a brief, one-sided engagement between a band of Lakota and U.S. Army troops, taken in total as just one of the battles in the Sioux Ghost Dance War of 1890 to 1891 (white man's reference). The significance for the Euro-Americans of Wounded Knee was that it ended a 400 year struggle between them and the Native American Indians for mastery of the continent. Wounded Knee was the last of the U.S. Army's campaigns of subjugation against the Native American Plains Indians.

The Native American Plains Indians were back on the various reservations, virtual wards and in some minds, prisoners of the federal government. With their confinement to the reservations, the fabric of the Native American Plains Indians culture, religious, and Centuries old society torn apart. After Wounded Knee, the assault on the Native American Indians way of life intensified, but this time from different Euro-American religious dominations operated on and off the reservations. They proposed to the Indian agents that Native American Indian children to be physically taken from their families, and re-educated at special Indian schools, disregarding their tribal, language, and cultural heritage.

By 1900, these various Euro-American religious dominations and other private groups had created 24 off reservation Indian boarding schools, with another 81 boarding and 147 day schools operating on the reservations. These schools attempted to eradicate their students' tribal identities and educate them, "Not as Native American Indians, but as Euro-Americans."

For the Native American Plains Indians after 1890, there was no viable alternative but to submit and try to adapt to a new and foreign way of life. For Native American Indians in South Dakota, it was "The end of a way of life," never to be recreated. For those who want more information, the South Dakota State Historical Society museum at Pierre, South Dakota has a wealth of information and displays. Also, please visit the Journey's gift shop and Crazy Horse Museum gift shop for books on this subject.[2]

---

[2] The author, in 1996, prepared an accompanying paper and presentation to the Keystone History Conference which showed the effects of Lewis and Clark's exploration of the Louisiana Purchase, up the Missouri River to its headwaters and then onto the Pacific Ocean. The author wants to acknowledge the assistance provided for the paper and presentation from
continued...

...continued
    the Crazy Horse Memorial Association. This story is not effectively told when one looks at the settlement of the Great Plains by the United States. It is included in this book to provide a history from the perspective of the Native American Indian populations in South Dakota.

The Dakota Territory Cavalry Companies for Service in the U.S. Civil War 1861-1865

IN the fall of 1861, the U.S. War Department in Washington, DC authorized the governor of the Dakota Territory to raise two volunteer companies of cavalry for the "War of the Rebellion" (the U.S. Civil War between northern military forces and the southern Confederacy). These cavalry companies were to be organized, trained and deployed in the Dakota Territory to conduct military patrols and garrison duties. Governor Jayne, The Dakota Territory Governor set up three recruiting locations by signed proclamation on December 7, 1861. The recruiting stations were at Yankton, Vermillion and Bob Homme. The three towns were the largest in the area. Governor Jayne appointed the brother-in-law of the Dakota Territory Secretary Hutchinson as the recruiting officer at Yankton, Nelson Miner at Vermillion and James M. Allen at Bon Homme. The three appointed recruiting officers began their duties immediately. Company A raised its full complement of volunteers by the winter of 1862, mustered into active federal service at Yankton in April 1862. Company A's officers were: (Vermillion) Captain Nelson Miner, (Yankton) 1st Lt. J.K. Fowler and (Bon Homme) 2nd Lt. Frederick Ploghoff. Company A joined up at Yankton, pending formal mustering in to active service of the Union Army. The citizens of Yankton claimed Company A to be a local unit, even though only one-third of its volunteers had been residents of the future South Dakota country prior to enlistment, the balance of the volunteers from Clay, Cole, Bon Homme and one from Nebraska. Company A's personnel included several Regular Army troops. Mustering in for Company A at Yankton was held on April 29, 1862, with Lt. M.R. Luce, 41st Regiment, Iowa Volunteers as the swearing in officer. Company A was to serve for three years during the Civil War in the Dakota Territory.

During the years after the Civil War, members of the 6th and 7th Iowa Cavalry, along with Bracket's Minnesota Cavalry patrolled out of isolated Army posts in the Colorado, Dakota and Nebraska Territories. Given emphasis during the Civil War, the number of U.S. Army posts in these territories increased from five in 1860 to 30 by 1868. These were primarily small garrisons, containing one to two cavalry companies, built along water sources (lake or river), by the cavalry troops, usually unskilled enlisted personnel. These troops collected and used available local building materials (wood, stone and earth turned into plaster for chinking the log buildings). These garrisons were widely separated, isolated from settlements and in the midst of hostile Indian areas. These garrisons were not forts but more in appearance of a rural village. The Army considered a coordinated Indian attack unlikely. Consequently, the garrisons usually lacked wood stockades or heavy defenses. Garrison troops had to guard against raiding Sioux Indians attempting to steal horses, or conducting hit and run raids against the few settlers on the open range, which the Indians considered to be their tribal home. The buildings were usually enclosed by a wood rail fence to coral the horses, making it easier them easier to guard, take care of and mount for patrols.

The Federal (Union) government, at the start of the Civil War, feared the Native American tribes would unite and attack settlers in the Colorado, Dakota and Nebraska Territories. All remained quiet until August 1862, when the Santee Sioux in Minnesota started attacking area settlers. The Indian conflict spread into the Dakota Territory. The fear of being killed by attacking Sioux Indians (with the Confederacy supplying guns, knives and ammunition) caused undue panic in the small towns in the Dakota Territories. Sioux Falls City residents fled their homes built in 1856 out of fear of Indian attack. The Sioux Indians burned the town to the ground after it was found abandoned. The Santee Sioux Indian and Indian tribes of the Western Sioux united in their hatred of the white men invading their land in the Dakotas, not protected as promised by the Great White Father (President of the United States). From 1863 to 1864, volunteer cavalry units tried to stop the Sioux Indian attacks, usually ending in extermination attacks by both parties. By 1865, the Sioux and Cheyenne Indians united to drive the white men out of the Dakotas in fierce attacks on isolated settlements, ranches, farms and wagon supply trains.

With the end of the Civil War, the Federal government had troops to send west. After the killing and destruction of the Civil War, thousands of former Union and Confederate soldiers and their families moved west for a new start. The U.S. Army moved into the burned out town of Sioux Falls City on May 5, 1865, manned by the 7th Iowa Cavalry. A second garrison was set up along Firesteel Creek, nicknamed Fort Brookings, manned by the 6th Iowa Volunteer Cavalry.

The 6th was relieved by men of Company "M" of the 7th Volunteer Cavalry in the fall of 1865. They were re-enforced by a company of Brackett's Minnesota Cavalry Battalion. This was a temporary assignment with Brackett's Minnesota Cavalry mustered out of active federal service in the spring of 1866. The 7th soldiered on until relieved by Company D (82 men) assigned to the 13th U.S. Infantry on June 8, 1866. The company was transported by the river steamer Rubicon to Sioux City, Iowa. The company traveled overland to Fort Randall, then onto Fort Brookings. What they found was discouraging: two enlisted men barracks, stone commissary and stable. The post was renamed Fort Dakota. The company built fourteen more buildings. The fort was commanded by Colonel Kilburn Knox. After the Civil War, the wartime volunteer and state units were slowly pulled out of the Dakota Territories, replaced by regular Army units.

At Fort Dakota, troopers were assigned "fatigue duty," or manual labor to improve the fort, conduct general maintenance and daily support activities. These troopers spent more time as laborers and not training as professional soldiers. They became permanent garrison troops, not actively patrolling against the perceived Indian threat in the Dakota Territories. This was because the threat from attacking Indian tribes had been reduced to nothing. By 1867, Congress received a petition from the Territorial governor to close Fort Dakota. The area was drawing settlers and real estate speculators wanted the land to sell to these settlers, removing Federal title to the land, which centered on and around the fort. This was a time of westward expansion with settlers setting up unauthorized homesteads on Indian lands, refusing to leave, requiring reluctant troops to remove them, replaced by other settlers as soon as they disappeared over the nearest hill. It was a losing situation, viewed by the Sioux Indians as encroachment on their tribal lands. Eventually a bill was passed in the U.S. House of Representatives on December 13, 1869 to vacate Fort Dakota.[3]

---

[3] "The Dakota Territory during the Civil War, 1861-1865," Territory, Volume I., George W. Kingsbury, 1915, Pierre, South Dakota: South Dakota Historical Society.

South Dakota National Guard

Birth of the South Dakota National Guard

THE state of South Dakota was originally part of the Dakota Territory organized in 1861. It became a state in 1889. Territorial Governor Jayne in 1862 ordered the formation of six companies of militia composed of cavalry and infantry. By September 1862, Companies A and B, First Dakota Cavalry were federalized and served until November 1865. These units were attached to General Sully, Commander, Upper Missouri and covered an area from Sioux City, Iowa up the Missouri River into present day Montana. The first Dakota Cavalry protected the area's settlers from Native American Indian attack during the U.S. Civil War. It was involved in the "Battle of Killdeer Mountain" and the "Battle of the Badlands," both of which are in present day North Dakota.[4]

---

[4] Lt. Col. George A. Larson, USAF (Ret.), "South Dakota National Guard, Birth of the South Dakota National Guard." Visit to Camp Rapid, The South Dakota National Guard's open house to celebrate the National Guard's 150 years of service, display set up in the Headquarters Lobby, "2012: Countdown to Withdrawal," June 9, 2012.

Early Railroad Development in the Black Hills

THE settlement of the west was part of a series of armed conflicts conducted by the United States Army against the Native American Indian tribes on the Great Plains, including the Sioux Indians of the Black Hills. Even though an undeclared war, it was a war nevertheless between the United States and the Native American Indian tribes, who were supposedly keeping the settlement of the Great Plains from becoming a reality by eastern United States citizens. In the history of South Dakota, the building and operation of railroads played a significant and important role in the settlement and development of the Dakota Territory. The first miles of railroad ties and rails were laid down in the eastern part of the Dakota Territory in 1872. The tracks came out of western Minnesota and Iowa in eastern Dakota Territory was of limited mileage. However, the discovery of gold in the Black Hills by U.S. Army Lt. Col. George Armstrong Custer's exploration of the area changed the momentum of laying track into the territory and sealed the fate of the Native American Indians in the Great Plains to the Black Hills. It was not until the forceful subjugation of the Sioux Indians, whose belief in the sacred Black Hills and personal attachment to the area. The signing of a treaty in 1877 between the Sioux Indians and U.S. government, forced an end to the warfare in the area. The rush was on to develop the western Dakota Territory, especially the area of the Black Hills. Earlier, settlement had been spurred on by the Homestead Act of 1862, which placed emphasis on the movement of people into the empty Great Plains, Black Hills, which at the time was contested by Native American Indian tribes who did not want to give up their lands or way of life.[5]

---

[5] Lt. Col. George A. Larson, USAF (Ret.), "Railroad development in South Dakota," paper and presentation, Keystone Historical Conference, Rapid City, South Dakota, 2001.

Fort Meade

Historic Army Post in the Western Dakotas

FORT George Gordon Meade was created in 1978 as a U.S. Army cavalry fort to protect new settlements throughout the northern Black Hills, especially near gold mining operations around Deadwood. Several stage and freight lines passed through Fort Meade on the trails to Deadwood to the southwest. This was rugged country between Fort Meade and Deadwood. The fort provided a stopover rest area. The U.S. Army's inability to keep settlers and miners out of the Black Hills precipitated the U.S. Army's Indian Campaign of 1876. Native American Indian tribes in the Black Hills fought settler's takeover and good seekers destruction of their lands, withdrawing to their traditional hunting grounds on their designated reservations, by the U.S. Army imposed deadline of January 31, 1876. The U.S. Army referred to these Native American Indians as hostiles, requiring a military campaign to subdue and return them to their designated reservations. The U.S. Army 7th Cavalry confronted the Sioux Indians and their Cheyenne allies on the Little Big Horn River in Montana on June 25, 1876. The combined Indian tribes defeated units of the 7th Cavalry in what is commonly referred to as "Custer's last stand." After their impressive victory, the Native American Indian tribes scattered, no longer fighting as a unified force, making them vulnerable to isolation and capture by constantly pressuring U.S. cavalry units, killing many and forcing the majority of Native American Indians of the Great Plains onto Indian reservations.

Because of the long period of the Indian Wars, a term the U.S. Army used to describe its actions on the Great Plains, U.S. Army Brigadier General Alfred H. Terry, Commanding Officer, U.S. Army Department of Dakota, recommended the Army construct a strong Army post in the northern Black Hills. The post would be near Bear Butte, with an estimated construction cost of $50,000, considered a great expenditure in the late 1870s. On July 1, 1878, Companies C, F, I and K, assigned to the First Infantry and Companies D and G, assigned to the Eleventh Infantry set up a camp and supply depot at Spring Creek, two miles west of Bear Butte. The location of the fort was determined by strategic implications to control and protect the area of the Black Hills. It straddled three ground routes to Bear Butte as well as travel routes for Native American Indians from the Sioux Indian Agencies to their hunting grounds in the Powder River Country. Under U.S. Army General Order Number One, dated August 28, 1878, the fort's construction started, referred to as Camp Ruhlen. On December 31, 1878, U.S. Secretary of War changed the name to Fort Meade in honor of George C. Meade, Civil War commander at the battle of Gettysburg and Commander of the Army of the Potomac. As with many Army construction projects in isolated areas of the west, actual costs exceeded estimates. An additional $23,000 had to be authorized under a supplemental War Department appropriation to complete the construction.

Fort Meade's band was the first to play the Star Spangled Banner as part of its formal retreat ceremony every evening, starting in 1892. U.S. Army Colonel Caleb H. Carlton, Commander Eighth Cavalry started the U.S. military retreat ceremony/tradition, 41 years before the Star Spangled Banner became the U.S. National Anthem. In 1896, Fort Meade went through an expansion construction program with 25 sets of officers' quarters built south of the parade ground, Quartermaster storehouse, commissary, band quarters, Post Exchange, ten stables, granary, hospital, and non-commissioned officers quarters along the bank of Bear Butte Creek. As of 1906, Fort Meade's primary mission was that of an Army post for operations against remaining, freely roaming Native American Indians. The fort had a footnote in the history of American-Native American Indian relations and their final subjugation. In 1906, the Sixth Cavalry was ordered to proceed to Montana to locate and apprehend a small group of 432 Ute Indians, led by Chief Red Cap, attempting to escape the United States into Canada, away from their treatment on the reservation. This group of Native American Indians was taken into custody, northwest of the Black Hills peacefully, taken to Fort Meade for temporary internment for the winter, transported to the Cheyenne Indian Reservation in the spring. This became the final Indian campaign conducted by the U.S. Army and from Fort Meade.

Another expansion on Fort Meade was conducted from 1900 to 1910, consisting of seven single and two double barracks, seven sets of officers' quarters, eight cavalry stables, and upgrade to the administration building, quartermaster storehouse, post exchange, guardhouse and bakery. Interestingly, at the conclusion of the construction program, the fort was inactivated with only a small caretaker unit maintaining the fort's facilities. In 1917, the 109th Engineers of the South Dakota Army National Guard arrived for training prior to shipment overseas to combat on the Western Front in France, after the United

States declared war on Germany because of unrestricted submarine warfare in the North Atlantic. The Fourth U.S. Cavalry took over the post on May 1, 1922. It was assigned as a special U.S. Presidential Guard unit for President Calvin Coolidge's summer 1927 vacation in the Black Hills.

During the U.S. Great Depression, 1933 to 1935, Fort Meade served as headquarters for administering the Civilian Conservation Corps (CCC) camps located in South Dakota. The Fourth Cavalry provided troops to assist and maintain security, as well as ground support for U.S. Army and National Geographic Society balloon flights in the stratosphere from the Strato Bowl basin in 1935 to 1936, south of Rapid City. During World War II, Fort Meade was occupied by the 620th Engineer General Service Company. The 620th was manned under a unique situation, officered by cleared personnel, with general manning consisting of German, Japanese and Italian origin American citizens, whose loyalty as Americans was brought into question, although never proved. The 620th was assigned non-combat duties. In early 1943, the company was transferred to Camp Hale, California. As the war continued, Fort Meade became more important. In February 1943, the U.S. Army assigned glider infantry troops from the 88th Infantry, North Carolina to the fort. They trained at the fort until November 1943, preparing for combat operations in England and specifically, cross channel airborne operations during D-Day, June 6, 1944 (Normandy, France). In a shift of operations, in the fall of 1944, Fort Meade converted operations to a POW camp for 600 German troops captured by Allied forces in North Africa. German POWs were housed in former CCC buildings on the west side of the post. The German POWs worked manual, non-military labor, in the local agricultural sector until 1946, when they were finally shipped home to Germany, after the fall 1945 harvest. The war in Europe was over in May 1945, but German POWs were retained until sufficient U.S. servicemen were demobilized, shipped home to pick up the slack in agricultural production. Great quantities of food were needed to feed the populations of liberated areas in Europe, Pacific and China.

On September 1, 1944, Fort Meade's administrative control was transferred to the Veterans Administration (VA). It became an important VA neuro-psychiatric hospital for badly wounded World War II servicemen from Nebraska, South Dakota, Montana and Wyoming at the end of the war. To care for these wounded veterans, an upgraded medical and surgical unit was added. In 1948, the Black Hills National Cemetery was created, enclosing the onsite existing 200 graves on the fort, and then closed for further burials. The VA hospital expanded again in 1967, with the construction of a modern hospital complex north of the previous fort buildings. The Army decided to demolish older buildings remaining on the fort. Fortunately, in 1971 destruction of these buildings stopped because they were placed on the Registry of Historic Place by efforts of Sturgis residents to preserve the buildings as a reminder of South Dakota's military history. This resulted in the creation of the Fort Meade Historic District, which preserved eight of the old buildings from destruction. This was important because during its 66 years of operations, Fort Meade served as the longest active U.S. Army installation in the U.S. Northern Plains.

Fort Meade is a historic military installation. Beginning in 1878, many different U.S. Army Cavalry units were stationed on the fort: 7th Cavalry after its defeat by the Sioux and Cheyenne Indians at the battle of the Little Big Horn, Buffalo-Afro-American soldiers of the U.S. Army's 10th Cavalry during its upgrade from horses to mechanized equipment. Today, Fort Meade is a training installation for the South Dakota National Guard, Army National Guard Officer Candidate School and VA medical facility.[6]

---

[6] Lt. Col. George A. Larson, USAF (Ret.), "Fort Meade, Historic Army Post of the West," presentation and paper for the Keystone History Conference, Rapid City, South Dakota, 2002.

South Dakota National Guard

1889 TO STATEHOOD

BY 1889, statehood was coming for North and South Dakota territories and it required the division of existing militia units between the two newly created states. North Dakota formed the 1st Regiment and South Dakota the 2nd Regiment. The Dakota Territory split into two states by the Enabling Act of Congress. With an estimated population of 400,000 and 27 years as a territory, South Dakota was in the forefront of the statehood drive and generally considered the most deserving[7]

1893, THE GUARD IS RENUMBERED

The South Dakota Regiment was renumbered and became the 1st South Dakota Infantry on September 9, 1893. This change made sense since it was confusing to have a 2nd Regiment with a 1st Regiment. The Guard was then organized as a brigade consisting of the infantry regiment and Battery A. The total strength of the South Dakota National Guard was 100 officers and 800 enlisted.[8]

1898, THE SPANISH-AMERICAN WAR

In April 1898, the First Infantry Regiment was federalized and left South Dakota for service in the Philippine Islands in May 1898. It returned to South Dakota in October 1899, where they were welcomed home by President William McKinley at Aberdeen, South Dakota.

---

[7] Lt. Col. George A. Larson, USAF (Ret.), "South Dakota National Guard, 1889-Statehood." Visit to Camp Rapid, The South Dakota National Guard's open house to celebrate the National Guard's 150 years of service, display set up in the Headquarters Lobby, "2012: Countdown to Withdrawal," June 9, 2012.

[8] Lt. Col. George A. Larson, USAF (Ret.), "South Dakota National Guard. 1893-the Guard is Remembered. Visit to Camp Rapid, The South Dakota National Guard's open house to celebrate the National Guard's 150 years of service," display set up in the Headquarters Lobby, "2012: Countdown to Withdrawal," June 9, 2012.

They served 129 days in combat in the Philippines under General MacArthur, the division commander. South Dakota also furnished five troops of cavalry in 1898, which were assigned to the 3rd U.S. Volunteer Cavalry Regiment, known as "Grigsbys Cowboys." They went to Camp Chick-Maunga, Georgia and served out their term there and discharged in December 1898.[9]

---

[9] Lt. Col. George A. Larson, USAF (Ret.), "South Dakota National Guard, 1898-The Spanish-American War." "Visit to Camp Rapid, The South Dakota National Guard's open house to celebrate the National Guard's 150 years of service," display set up in the Headquarters Lobby, "2012: Countdown to Withdrawal," June 9, 2012.

South Dakota State Soldier's Home 1886 to 2015

Veteran's Home, Hot Springs, South Dakota

THE early history of the home is tied to the Dakota's Department (at that time, the current states of South and North Dakota were part of the Dakota Territories) of The Grand Army of the Republic, through their efforts and Hot Spring backers that the Soldier's Home came into creation. The Grand Army of the Republic was created at Decatur, Illinois in 1866, as a patriotic organization for persons served in the U.S. Army, Navy, Marine Corps or State Militia Regiments in active service under U.S. general officers during the U.S. Civil War, 1861 to 1865. The auxiliary units were the Women's Relief Corps and Sons of the Veterans. The Grand Army of the Republic's membership reached its maximum of 409,489 in 1890. During the Civil War, South Dakota was not a state and did not furnish many troops to the fighting during the war. After the war, veterans moved west into the Dakota Territory to homestead, timber and mining, and set up businesses in new towns, especially as the railroads extended tracks into the territory. This was part of the great west migration after the Civil War into the area of the Great Plains. There had been limited informal discussions on possibility of a Solder's Home for the Dakota Territories in The Grand Army of the Republic, with more serious deliberations at the Third Encampment at Watertown, SD in 1886. This resulted in a resolution introduced and adopted to send onto the Territorial Legislature on establishing the home.

 The area of Hot Springs had support of The Grand Army of the Republic because of its reported medicinal properties of the natural springs in the city, a healthful climate and desire by Hot Spring residences to have a soldier's home in their city. There were many political obstacles to setting up a soldier's home. The Territorial Governor, Church, on February 21, 1889 vetoed Territorial Legislator Bill 39, authorizing $45,000 for construction on donated land. The governor said the funds authorized were "insufficient for the purpose contemplated." However, the Territorial Legislator passed the bill over Church's veto on February 27, 1889. The path to creating a soldier's home was set. At the sixth Annual Encampment of The Grand Army of the Republic in Aberdeen, South Dakota in March 1889, indicated the pleasure of the organization on the passage of the bill. "The crowning act of the last Territorial Legislature was the establishment of a Soldier's Home." The Dakota Territories was first to fund and set up a home for veterans.

Plans for the building of the Soldiers' Home was submitted by W.H. Porry of Mitchell, South Dakota were adopted by the Soldier's Home Board at the July 5, 1889 meeting of the Builder's Notice for Soldiers' of Dakota. The home's buildings were to be built of stone, quarried around Hot Springs, known as the Dakota Sandstone of Upper Cretaceous Age. Construction bids were open by the Soldiers' Home Board on August 7, 1889, with the $34,224 bid from Jacob Wright and C. Oleson as the lowest. Fred T. Evans and John L. Burke were sureties for $30,000. Providing water to the home had to be pumped from the Jennings Springs. Work on the building has progressed rapidly because most of the materials were purchased locally. Sandstone came from a quarry near Hot Springs, lumber from a local sawmill and lime for cement also procured locally. Iron and glass had to be purchased from out of state manufacturers.

The primary building was to be 132 feet long, 85 feet wide, full basement, three stories, with a capacity of 200. Four towers were designed to give it a distinctive architecture feature. Initially the basement was for a kitchen, dining room and Quartermaster, with the other levels as a dormitory. The cornerstone was laid on November 11, 1889. It contains copies of the Hot Spring's local newspaper, Hot Springs Star, Minnekahta Herald and Deadwood Times and Pioneer, cards of the Knights Templers in attendance at the cornerstone ceremony and a Masonic memento. Even during its construction, funding continued to be a concern. South Dakota's first governor, Mellette on January 7, 1890 reminded the first South Dakota Legislator in session that funds were needed for maintenance of the Soldier's Home. The legislators appropriated $10,500, with more funding in following years.

As construction neared completion and occupancy the Soldier's Home Board on June 3, 1890 set rules, although somewhat amended later so final rules were as follows:

First: Admit veterans who are desirous of availing himself of the benefits of the Soldiers' Home. All such have a preference.
Second: Admit those who desire to the inmates temporarily.
Third: Admit those who are financially able to pay the actual

cost of the entertainment. All shall pay to the State the sum named hereafter by the Board.

Fourth: All persons making application for admission to the Home shall exhibit an honorable discharge or Pension certificate or certificate from the War Department of honorable discharge.

The buildings for the State Soldiers' Home were accepted from the contractor in late November 1890. The Soldiers' Home Board moved quickly to admit ten qualified veterans as the hone's first residents. The first veterans moved in on November 15, 1890. There was no furniture, no stove, and no medicines. The first room of furniture was given to the home by the Woman's Relief Corps of Watertown, South Dakota in late November. The Yankton Woman's Relief Corps of Yankton, South Dakota sent a large U.S. flag (ten by twenty feet) to fly from the home's flagpole. The men cooked for the first time on the fire in the firebox of the boiler. They ate off a board set across two barrels. One year later in 1891, an epidemic of pneumonia broke out in the Black Hills, including the State Soldier's Home. The outbreak of pneumonia highlighted the lack of hospital facilities at the home. Personnel at the home set up a temporary hospital ward for eleven veterans with pneumonia. The ward did not have correct staffing: registered nurse, hospital steward, on hand stocks of medicine or a resident surgeon. The Grand Army of the Republic collected $3,000 for a hospital cottage. This was only a stopgap measure, permanent medical facilities required. In October 1894, the Soldiers' Home Board biannual report indicated..."There is an urgent need for more room, a resident surgeon, competent nurses, an allowance for instruments and appliances that should be owned by the hospital, and a more generous allowance for medicines, dressings and other supplies for the sick."

At this time, the Soldiers' Home Board made admission and operation changes:

Any veteran of the army or navy who has an honorable discharge and who has lived in South Dakota for one full year.

Any veteran who has a family dependent upon him and who is unable to work, and who has not to exceed $400 per year, income from all sources, including pension, rent of houses or farms, interest, etc.

Any veteran without dependent family whose income does not exceed $250 per year.

If a veteran's income exceeds these amounts, it may be possible for the Board of Admission to admit him for treatment, during which time he shall have the rights and benefits of the Home but cannot claim a suit of clothes. The Board of Admission to be the sole judges of the privileges, and duration of, his membership and clothing allowance.

Causes for dishonorable discharge set up by the Soldiers' Home Board, as listed at the end of 1894.

For bringing whiskey into the Home, second offense.
For being repeatedly drunk and disorderly.
For language or conduct unbecoming a gentleman.
For repeated disobedience of orders and a refusal to do such work as the member is liable to do when detailed.
For filthiness.

In 1894, a Memorial Association was formed to raise money to erect a stature of General John A. Logan, "The Black Eagle of Illinois," who instituted the tradition of Memorial Day in the United States. Logan was born on February 9, 1826, died December 26, 1886. He took over temporary command of the Army of Tennessee when McPherson was killed. He fought in the battles of Belmont, Donnellson, Shiloh, Vicksburg, Lookout Mountain, Missionary Ridge, the march to Bentonville and Raleigh. Memorial Association President Mrs. Charles M. Cleveland gave an address on July 23, 1989, to approximately 600 people, and then pulled the ropes holding the canvas covering over the statue. The statue cost $19,142, carved by K.H. McVay.

In 1913, an article in the *Hot Springs Star* described a visit by one of its reporters to the state home. We first visited the new detention hospital, which has just been completed and will be occupied this week. This is one of the neatest, best-arranged institutions we have ever seen. One wing is for the accommodation of tubercular patients and will accommodate nine beds. The center building is arranged into a kitchen, dining room and storeroom with a large basement for supplies. On the left of this extending to the other wing is five neatly arranged rooms for bedridden patients and from this part of the institution many valuable pointers might be gained by other hospitals. The extreme left wing is for the accommodation of lady patients and for the nurses' quarters. As the United States inspector remarked on a recent visit… "This hospital is the finest of its kind in the United States."

In July 1920, the State of South Dakota Legislator, among the appropriations made for state institutions and departments during the special session of the legislature is one in which Hot Springs people are particularly interested. According to an article in the *Hot Springs Star*..."the Legislature provided for needed improvements at the State Soldiers Home in the way of increased safety and permanence of its buildings. The following amounts were asked for and voted on and approved on a joint bill: Moving and enlarging the ice house, $1,500; rebuilding boilers, $4,200; rebuilding coal sheds, $4,300; purchasing fire hose, $405; rebuilding milk and cold storage rooms, $1,200; rebuilding laundry and machine shop, $2,800; additional funds for maintenance, $8,000; additional funds for salaries, $1,500. Two quarries belonging to the state home, which are situated west of the buildings will be opened and the stone needed for building taken out. It is expected that the work will be begun at an early date."

By 1924, South Dakota's provisions for the aged and incapacitated ex-soldiers of the state are far from adequate. The 1923 South Dakota State Legislature refused an appropriation for a new building for the State Home, a building that is urgently needed for the occupancy of the veterans whose wives are at the Home with them, and of widows who are not admitted to membership in the Home. Eventually, funds were made available in 1925, for $215,000, for a Women's building. On April 27, 1950, on the State Home's grounds, a ceremony was performed, the turning of the first shovel of dirt for a new $377,500 men's dormitory, with construction following. In 1963, a 228,000 renovation and remodeling of the infirmary. In 1964, $120,000 for a commissary and laundry building, as well as rewiring the Administration building, new windows, elevator and fire escape for the Women's building.

A June 1988 article in the *Hot Springs Star* provided an excellent description of the State Home's facilities. "It sits atop a hill, 193 acres of woods, pasture, green lawns and stately buildings." It is often confused with the other veteran's facility on Hot Springs, the Veterans Administration Medical Center. It once was described by a four year old visitor "as the place where the old warriors live." However, residents who live here agree, "Once you've seen it, you'll never forget the South Dakota State Veteran's Home." Mild, dry weather and the neighborliness of a small community make Hot Springs the perfect setting for retirement. The services offered by the State Veteran's Home make it an attractive retirement choice. Members pay a maintenance fee based on a percentage of income. It entitles the member to receive a room, furnishings except a telephone, bedding, laundry of bedding and personal clothing, meals, medical services, pharmaceutical services, activities and social services. A member is able to retain a minimum monthly income.

All buildings are protected by a central fire-smoke alarm system. Every building had other life safety features such as modern fire exits, sprinkler systems and stairway enclosures. Wheelchair ramps, hallway handrails and talking clocks are among the many assistive devices found throughout the State Veterans' Home. Every residential floor has a lounge, variously furnished with cards, games, puzzles, books, magazines, TVs, easy chairs, aquariums, plants, pianos, and other homey accents. The billiards room, card room, canteen and auditorium are centrally located and well equipped. There are sewing, laundry, cooking and hobby shop areas for personal projects and activities. Rooms for weaving, macramé, painting, photography, electronics and other arts and crafts are also available. Outdoors there are picnic tables, pleasantly situated benches and walking paths through a shaded lawn area. Individuals may use the horseshoe pits or grow flowers and vegetables in three gardens.

A local physician comes to the State Veterans' Home regularly and is on call for other medical services. Prescribed medications are available to members without extra charge at the State Veterans Home Pharmacy operated by a Registered Pharmacist. A licensed physical therapist provides restorative therapy on an individual basis. Members may choose to utilize exercise equipment located in easy access areas of each building. The Chaplain conducts church services, hymn services, Bible study, funerals and other religious activities. Catholic and Protestant services are held weekly with additional services on special holidays.

The State Veterans' Home has a library with many large print novels, current magazines and hometown newspapers. Mail is distributed twice a day at the State Veterans' Home Post Office where members are assigned their own boxes. Van transportation for members is scheduled daily to downtown Hot Springs and to the Hot Springs Veterans Administration Medical Center. In addition to individual activities, members may choose to participate in group activities. Many enjoy outings such as picnics, tours of Black Hills attractions, fishing trips, shopping trips, parades, horse shows, rodeos, nature walks and community events. Volunteers from veteran's organizations provide evening bingo once a week.

On November 11, 1989, the South Dakota Veterans' Home celebrated 100 years of service to the state's veterans. A time capsule, only eight-inches by 16-inches, was opened at the celebration for a century of continuous operations. The time capsule held a two-piece Grand Army of the Republic Veteran's Medal, dated 1866 and a GAR history book. Included was an old coin, papers pertaining to the GAR and various local business cards. The papers, particularly newspaper of the day, were unyellowed by time and easy read. The contents were displayed the next day for visitors to the Home, then wrapped in plastic, placed back in the time capsule and returned to its resting placing in the cornerstone, sealed and to remain for another 100 years.

On September 22, 1998, South Dakota Governor Bill Janklow announced that the South Dakota Veterans' Home to be renamed in honor of Michael J. Fitzmaurice, who was awarded the Congressional Medal of Honor. He earned America's most coveted award at Khe Sanh, Republic of South Vietnam in March 1971, while under attack by North Vietnamese troops. He was seriously injured in the fierce fighting by an explosive device, and is credited with saving the lives of several of his fellow soldiers. He was cited for extraordinary heroism and gallantry above and beyond the call of duty. The official name changing ceremony was held at the South Dakota Veterans Home on October 3, 1998.

On February 24, 2008, another time capsule was opened from the hospital built in 1907, eight-inches, by three-inches, by three-inches. The items inside were carefully removed and placed on temporary display for visitors. Items inside included: a 1907 Liberty nickel, newspapers, text of a speech delivered by the then State Veterans' Home chief doctor Hamilton H. Wilcox. The small box only allowed placing a few new items into the time capsule: a South Dakota quarter, copies of the *Hot Springs Star* and the home's *Fitz Bitz* publication. It was resealed and replaced in the cornerstone of the building, there to remain until 2107.

On June 18, 2010, a famous resident of the state's veteran home, Clarence Wolf Guts died at the age of 86. He was the last surviving Oglala Lakota World War II Code Talker member. The code was never broken by German or Japanese intelligence personnel, helping Allied forces to win the terrible world war. Most Americans only are slightly aware of the 450 Navajo code talkers who have been portrayed in movies about the American fighting against the Japanese, especially during the battle for Saipan in the Mariana Islands in 1944. In reality, there were 15 other Native American Indian tribes who sent their sons to fight in World War II, using their native language and developed codes to openly send radio messages on the battlefield. Clarence was the last surviving South Dakota World War II Oglala Lakota veteran who fought for his country using his native language to confuse a determined enemy.

In December 2011, veterans at the Michael J. Fitzmaurice State Veterans Home became concerned that the grid-lock in Congress would affect a proposed 34.6 million dollar upgrade to the facility. Larry Wilcox, Superintendent..."Worry is widespread among the 131 residents now at the home. They are also watching with concern as the U.S. Department of Veterans Affairs outlines its proposal to close the main Hot Springs Veterans Administration Medical Center in their community as part of a restructuring plan in the Black Hills." The current census of 131 veterans at the home: 52 nursing-home care, with 79 in assisted living and independent living area of the facility. Even though the Veterans Administration has not decided (as of February 2012) on how it will restructure medical care in the Black Hills, on 10 February, the state home received good news. The Washington, District of Columbia office of U.S. Senator Tim Johnson announced... "The state of South Dakota will receive 21.4 million dollars to help build a new 35 million dollar state veterans home in Hot Springs after the project ranked 10th in the nation on a priority list for building state facilities for veterans." The Veterans Administration with pay 65 percent of the project's cost with the state of South Dakota issuing bonds to pay the remaining 12 million dollars. Current governor of South Dakota, Dennis Dauguard released a press statement after hearing about the federal funding. "The federal funding will be not being available until the end of the current federal budget year, and the state has to complete some final steps in the grant process by June to receive the federal money by 30 September 2012."

On October 1, 2013, South Dakota Governor Dennis Dauguard led ground breaking ceremonies for the new veterans' home modernization and expansion. Participating in the ceremony was Michael Fitzmaurice, age 91, the state's last living Congressional Medal of Honor recipient. Lt. Governor Matt Michels..."This home and much of our state was built by Civil War veterans." The ceremony took place in building No. 4, previously used as an infirmary, which will be demolished when the new building is completed.

The newly designed veterans' home is a 130,000 square foot stacked two-story building with a lower walkout main entrance. The 100-bed facility will be used to serve South Dakota veterans and will contain 52 skilled nursing beds on the main level and 48 non-skilled or residential beds on the upper level. The living spaces will be broken into eight neighborhoods in eight wings. Each neighborhood will include a living room, dining room and kitchen area that will provide a home-like environment to the 12 to 13 occupants housed in each neighborhood. The design incorporates residential type furnishings and finishes, and warm, welcoming colors to reduce the institutional look and give the spaces a more comfortable feel.[10]

---

[10] The development of the State Soldier's Home, located in Hot Springs, South Dakota since 1889. Information courtesy of the South Dakota State Soldier's Home to author.

Spanish American War
1898 to 1902

South Dakota Volunteers

1st South Dakota Volunteer Infantry Regiment

3rd United States Volunteer Cavalry Regiment

AMERICA declared war on Spain after the U.S. Navy battleship Maine was sunk by an explosion while anchored in Havana Harbor, Cuba on February 15, 1898. At the time, the War Department claimed the Cuban military placed a mine or explosives under the battleship. In the 1990s, a technical review of the explosion indicated that the explosion resulted from accumulation of explosive coal dust inside the battleship's coalbunkers. But in the heat of war demanding headlines, on 25 April, the U.S. Congress declared ..."that as of 21 April, a state of war had existed between the United States and Spain." However, mobilizing, training and equipping troops for the U.S. Army were a difficult task for the U.S. War Department. Volunteers from South Dakota filled two units during the Spanish American War. Andrew E. Less was governor of South Dakota during the war.

South Dakota set up Camp George Dewey, a temporary military encampment along the Sioux River at Sioux Falls, South Dakota in April 1898. The encampment was set up (basically a tent city, with ten troopers assigned to each tent) to process South Dakota volunteers to fight in the war against Spain. Two troops of the 3rd U.S. Volunteer Cavalry were formed up at the encampment, departing on May 29, 1898.

The 1st South Dakota Volunteer Infantry was created from the South Dakota National Guard organization, mobilized into federal service on April 30. 1898, commanded by Colonel Alfred S. Frost. The volunteers mustered into active federal service from 12 May to May 19, 1898, reaching strength of 46 officers and 983 enlisted. At this time, as during the U.S. Civil War (1861 to 1865), diseases ran wild through tent encampments, especially measles, killing some of the volunteers at Camp Dewey. The volunteers were not issued uniforms, because the

War Department struggled to acquire clothing manufacturers to produce U.S. Army uniforms in large quantities for the influx of state volunteers. If it had not been for the citizens of Sioux Falls, providing meals most would have gone hungry. The Army also struggled to provide field kitchens, cooks and food for the mobilizing encampments around the United States. The Army pulled rifles from armories used by troopers on the Great Plains in the 1870's, the 1987 Springfield .45-70 "Trapdoor Rifle." The South Dakota volunteers were not issued modern weapons, using smokeless powder, which would have not comprised the position of U.S. troops to Spanish troops. In contrast, Spanish troops were equipped with German smokeless rifles, pistols and machine guns supplied by German armaments companies.

The 1st departed Camp Dewey for Camp Merritt, California near the Presidio on 28 May by passenger train. The War Department, as during the Civil War, issued substandard manufactured Army uniforms to the troops in California. However, the blue dye of the heavy wool uniforms faded, changing more to a brown color, forcing the Army to take back the defective uniforms and issue new ones. The uniforms were not suitable for tropical weather and the blue color highlighted them against surrounding green foliage to Spanish soldiers.

The 1st departed Camp Merritt for the long sea voyage to the Philippines on July 23, 1898, along with volunteer troops from Colorado and Minnesota. The troops boarded the U.S. Navy transports Saint Paul and Rio de Janeiro, arriving nine days later in Honolulu, Hawaii. The 1st was barracked in the Queen Liliuokalani's Palace. On 10 August, they boarded the transports for the longer voyage to the Philippines, landing at Cavite in Manila Bay on 31 August. Interestingly, during World War II, South Dakota troops still took 21 days to reach their combat locations in the Philippines. An escorted convoy could only sail at the speed of its slowest ship. The 1st was barracked in the Cathedral of Cavite. The 1st did not take part in any fighting against Spanish troops, which ended on 13 August, with the signing of the armistice between Spain and the United States, referred to as the Treaty of Paris. Spain gave up control of Cuba (became an independent country, but revolutionaries remained, not settled until Fidel Castro's Communist revolutionaries won control of the island 1959), ceded Puerto Rico and Guam to the United States, with the United States purchasing the Philippine Islands for 20 million dollars.

In September the 1st moved to Manila, with the First and Third Battalions barracked in the former residence of a Spanish Officer, with the 2nd Battalion assigned quarters in the Malacanan Place. The three battalions performed guard duty at the San Lazarus Leper Hospital, Bilibib Prison, the Bridge of Spain and the military headquarters set up at the Malacanan Palace occupied by the area commander, Major General Elwell S, Otis and General Douglas MacArthur and Ellis. The 1st only participated in limited fighting against Spanish troops, but not the one originally envisioned. On February 4, 1899, the Philippine American War started in the Philippines between U.S. Army troops and Filipino insurgents led by Filipino General Emilio Aguinaldo. Aguinaldo wanted immediate freedom for the Philippines, not trading control of the Spanish government for that of the United States, creating the Filipino Republic. Fighting raged for two years. Against an estimated force of 40,000 troops, the U.S. Army had to build up forces available in the Philippines, which led to over 100,000 troops transferred to the Philippines. It should be pointed out, the state Army Guard volunteers had to be sent home at the end of their enlistments, approximately some 9,000 troops. Fighting in the Philippines did not end until July 4, 1902, after General MacArthur replaced General Otis in May 1900 (General Otis, at that time, believed the fighting was over).

The First South Dakota Volunteer Infantry engaged Filipino insurgents around Manila in limited fighting. Over the time of its overseas deployment, the 1st suffered the following casualties. One officer killed (official report indicated he died of drowning when crossing a fast moving jungle stream), three officers suffered combat wounds, 34 enlisted died from effects of disease (primarily Malaria), one enlisted died in an accident, 90 enlisted received wounds during the fighting, four enlisted deserted, and 59 enlisted were released from active federal service due to disabilities. On August 11, 1899, the South Dakota troops boarded the U.S. Navy transports Indiana and Morgan City in Manila Bay, sailing first to Tokyo Bay, Japan and onto San Francisco, California. They were mustered out of active Federal service in October 5, 1899 at that location, shipped home by rail passenger car transport to Sioux Falls, South Dakota. From there, they returned to their home of record.

The wartime service of the 3rd U.S. Volunteer Cavalry was a history of non-combat duty. The cavalry unit comprised volunteers from North and South Dakota, Montana and Nebraska, mustered into active federal service at Camp Dewy, Sioux Falls, South Dakota from May 12-23, 1898, commanded by the then Attorney General of South Dakota, Melvin Grigsby. The cavalry unit soon earned the nickname of "Grigsby's Rough Riders," emulating a cavalry unit in Cuba, "Roosevelt's Rough Riders." The cavalry unit consisted of 45 officers and

961 enlisted. The South Dakota volunteers were formed into Troops A, B, C, D and E. The 3rd was transferred to Camp Thomas, set up on a former U.S. Civil War battlefield, Chickamauga, Georgia. The encampment was set up as an Army training facility, getting troops prepared for a long overseas war with Spain. The encampment expanded to 10,000 troops by early August 1898. With the signing of the armistice between the United States and Spain on 13 August, the need for these troops ended. The 3rd U.S. Volunteer Cavalry was mustered out at the training camp on 8 September, Although not involved in any overseas fighting, the 3rd still suffered loss of personnel: nine enlisted died due to the effects of disease, 22 enlisted discharged because of disability, two enlisted court-martialed, and four enlisted deserted. [11]

---

[11] The author, while assigned to the Defense Intelligence Agency (DIA), Alternate National Military Command Center (ANMCC), 1981 to 1985, researched information at the nearby U.S. War College for an article submission to Military History, "Centennial of the Spanish American War," to be published in 1998. The researched material was not used for the magazine.

Camp Rapid

South Dakota National Guard

THE National Guard, the oldest of the U.S. Armed Forces and one of the nation's longest enduring institutions, celebrated its 375th birthday in 2011. The National Guard traces its history back to the earliest English colonies in North America. Responsible for their own defense, the colonists drew on English-military tradition and organized their able-bodied male citizens into militias. The colonial militias protected their fellow citizens from Indian attack, foreign invaders, and later helped win the Revolutionary War against the British. Following independence, the authors of the U.S. Constitution empowered Congress "to provide for organizing, arming, and discipline the militia." However, recognizing the militia's state role, the founding fathers reserved the appointments of officers and training of the militia to the individual states.

Today's National Guard remains a dual state-federal force. Throughout the 19th Century, the size of the Regular Army was small, and the militia provided the bulk of the troops during the Mexican War, the early months of the Civil War and the Spanish-American War. In 1903, important national defense legislation increased the role of the National Guard (as the militia was now called) as a Reserve Force for the U.S. Army. When the U.S. entered World War II in 1917, the National Guard made up 40 percent of the U.S. combat divisions in France. In World War II, National Guard units were among the first to deploy overseas and fight.

Following World War II, National Guard aviation units, some of them dating back to World War I, became the Air National Guard, the nation's newest reserve component. Today's National Guard continues its historic dual mission, providing to the states units trained and equipped to protect life and property, while providing to the nation units trained, equipped and ready to defend the United States and its interests all over the globe.

With its proud 152 year (as of 2015) heritage of serving as the state's militia, the South Dakota National Guard finds its origins dating back to 1862, as part of the Dakota Territory. Since that time, South Dakota's National Guard units have served in nearly every major war conflict since the Civil War. The SDNG has seen combat during the Spanish America War, World War I, World War II, "Operation JUST CAUSE," and "Operation DESERT STORM." The SDNG was also called during the Mexican Border Conflict, Korean War, Berlin Crisis and peacekeeping missions in Bosnia and Kosovo.

Since the September 11, 2001 terrorist attacks on the United States, each of South Dakota's 28 National Guard communities has experienced a unit mobilization in support of "Operation NOBLE EAGLE," "Operation ENDURING FREEDOM," "Operation IRAQI FREEDOM," and "Operation NEW DAWN." More than 4,600 soldiers and 1,500 airmen have been deployed in support of these operations and continued to deploy time and time again.

The National Guard is the only military component that holds a dual-mission, consisting of both federal and state roles. The federal mission is to maintain trained and equipped units available for prompt mobilization for war or a national emergency. At the state level, the governor reserves the ability, under the U.S. Constitution, to call up members of the National Guard in times of domestic emergencies.

Through the years, national disasters have called forth the guard's spirit of teamwork and sacrifice to battle floods, fires, blizzards and tornado destruction. From the Rapid City flood of 1972, to the 1997 Spencer Tornado to Hurricane Katrina and Rita in 2005, and most recently, the 2011 Missouri River flood, the SDNG has helped its fellow South Dakotans and Americans in times of need.

Today's SDNG remains strong with nearly 4,400 soldiers and airmen available to execute its dual-mission on the State and Federal level. The guard is now in 28 communities throughout South Dakota and is comprised of 64 separate Army Guard units and detachments, and 16 Air Guard units. These units perform a variety of missions: everything from command and control, administration, engineering, field artillery, transportation, logistics, communications, maintenance, aviation, public affairs, military police, fire fighting and medical.

The guard is no longer a strategic reserve to the active component, but an operational force directly integrated into active-duty deployments and missions. The force directly integrated into active-duty deployments and missions. The force structure of the SDNG is designed to meet the needs of the future force, giving the guard an enhanced capability to respond in times of emergencies and natural disasters and to support the global war on terrorism.

The SDNG had a significant impact on South Dakota's economy with more than 180 million dollars in expenditures and wages in 2011. The SDNG is also one of the largest employers in the state with more than 960 full time employees, along with nearly 3,400 traditional guard members who train on a part-time basis while pursuing a career or civilian education. These full-time employees, along with state employees and civilian contractors, work to assist the traditional guardsman by providing administrative and logistical support. This support collectively goes into helping units meet mobilization and readiness requirements. The SDNG remains strong with nearly 3,400 soldiers available for state and federal missions. The nerve center for the SDNG resides at the state headquarters at Camp Rapid in Rapid City, South Dakota; a 84 acre training site first developed in 1924.

Camp Rapid is a SDNG installation located on the west side of Rapid City, inside the northeastern edge of the Black Hills. Although the state's capital is in the center of the state, Pierre, the State Adjutant General's office and headquarters is at Camp Rapid. Camp Rapid developed as a summer encampment site of the SDNG in the early 20th Century, using land borrowed from the Bureau of Indian Affairs "Sioux Sanatorium" and Rapid City Indian School (present site of Indian Health Service or HIS) Sioux San Hospital, located west of Camp Rapid. It became a permanent installation during and immediately after World War I, when it was used for mobilization of National Guard units for fighting in France, on the Western Front against Germany. Its use continued during the 1920s and 1930s, and it was taken over as a federal installation during World War II.

During the Cold War, Camp Rapid continued to host and support National Guard activities, including a series of annual exercises involving National Guard troops from many states conducting operations in the Black Hills. In the early 1990s, a new group of building projects replaced concrete tent pads, brick and metal tents with permanent structures for use as armories, barracks and support buildings. Security of Camp Rapid was upgraded significantly in the early 2000 as part of nation-wide security improvements. Construction provided new barracks, dining hall, administrative officers and parking areas.[12]

---

[12] http://sdguard.ngb.army.mil/pages/history.aspx. [Publisher's Note: This link is no longer valid.]

Battle Mountain Sanitarium

Department of Veterans Medical Center
Hot Springs, South Dakota

SENATOR R.F. Pettigrew (U.S. Senator, South Dakota) introduced a bill in the U.S. Congress, No. 2791, for the erection and maintenance of the Northern Branch of National Home for disabled Volunteer Soldiers at Hot Springs, South Dakota. In September 1898, The National Encampment of the Grand Army of the Republic held in Cincinnati, Ohio, passed a resolution requesting the U.S. Congress to establish a national sanitarium in Hot Springs, South Dakota. On May 29, 1902, President Teddy Roosevelt signs the bill authorizing the Battle Mountain Sanitarium. The bathhouses and sanitariums of Hot Springs already attracted visitors from every state in the United States, from the 1880s to 1920s, taking the baths as cure-resorts for many ailments. Only a few of the hot baths remain in operation in Hot Springs.

The report of the Board of Managers for the National Home for Disabled Volunteer states that between 1902 and 1904, $575,000 appropriated by the U.S. Congress for the construction of the Battle Mountain Sanitarium, at Hot Springs. The report, dated December 1, 1905, also stated..."the construction of the sanitarium has not progressed as was anticipated when the last annual report of the Board of Managers was submitted. The weather at Hot Springs, SD during the winter of 1904 to 1905 was unprecedented in severity, and work was at a standstill for several months. In the spring, disastrous floods again interrupted operations. It appears now improvable that the sanitarium can be open for the reception of patients before July 1906." Ground was broken for this great sanitarium on August 17, 1903, and the main group of buildings completed on April 1, 1907, with outbuildings completed later that same year. The main group comprises the administration building, service building, bath house, chapel, library, laundry building and six ward buildings whose ends joined by a circular arcade. This arcade surrounds a circular fountain court, 180 feet in diameter, and provides an enclosed and heated walk during cold weather and cool lunging space during the summer months, having removable widow panels. Outside the Sanitarium group of buildings were other necessary buildings: a fine stable and carriage barn, a conservatory for raising flowers and propagating plants, a large commodious residence for the governor and surgeon (one officer held both positions), suitable residences for the treasurer, quartermaster, chief engineer and gardener.

The medical care offered in the first national homes was largely at the infirmary level. Initially, care was limited to Union veterans who suffered from disabilities incurred in the Civil War. Men over 75 years of age were not admitted unless "well-preserved and unless beneficial results were presumed," and all patients were required to bathe on admission and at least once each week thereafter. All patients thoroughly examined at time of admission and those that required it, vaccinated. It was not in several publications that the construction plan centered the Executive Force in the Administration building and provided for the performance of its duties from that center. One of the impressive features was the breathtaking rotunda allowing access to the several floors from circular walkways with an amazing internal view. The sanitarium was designed by Thomas Rogers Kimball. The operation room was located in the administration area and was "north and top lighted to eliminate shadows and provide the very best light"... "absolutely sanitary, including its dependencies, waiting, anesthetizing and sterilizing rooms." Initially, 475 beds were available in the sanitarium and this number could be increased to 525 whenever necessary. The new sanitarium boasted an intercommunications system of twenty-five telephones running to all parts of the buildings. A power station furnished steam and hot air for heating and pumped water for use in the facility from a hot spring near the juncture of Hot and Cold Brooks. The *Hot Springs Star* reported the completion in May 1907. "Battle Mountain Sanitarium for Disabled Soldiers of the United States at Hot Springs, SD, at a cost of nearly a million dollars." It is assumed that the costs above the $575,000 initial appropriation were due to furniture, machinery, equipment, etc.

Battle Mountain Sanitarium National Cemetery was also completed in 1907. The cemetery was established for interment of veterans who died while residing at the Battle Mountain Sanitarium. An obelisk located on the southeast corner of the cemetery, at its highest elevation of approximately 32 feet high and 42 feet around the base. "National Home, Disable Volunteer Soldiers, Battle Mountain Sanitarium 1914" and "In memory of the men who offered their lives in the defense of their country." There are 1,484 graves (two civilians who died in accidents during construction) in the cemetery (veterans from the U.S.

Civil War 1861 to 1865, Spanish-American War 1898 to1902, World War I 1917 to 1918 and World War II 1941 to1945). The only Medal of Honor recipient burred at the cemetery is Lt. Charles L. Russell (Civil War, Company H, 93rd New York Infantry). The last veteran burial in the cemetery was May 1963 and in 1964, it was closed to burials. Two more burials did occur, both wives of veterans buried in the cemetery.

The Tubercular barracks was constructed in 1908 "a hospital for consumptives." The barracks contained 40 beds and the primary treatment was rest, fresh air and sunshine" and "tubercular pavilion had 50 beds." In 1915, the spacious auditorium and library were added between two of the ward buildings. An ornamental circular stairway of pink sandstone and concrete leading from the current head of River Street by the current Evans Apartments was constructed during 1915, costing $5,000. It replaced a deteriorating single wooden stairway. The grand staircase is a beautiful and substantial structure with one hundred and forty steps, ten platforms, and rest stops on either side, with seats. There are areas for plants, which have been tended over the years by veteran patients, employees and volunteers. In 1925, with the burden of providing a hospital in the Tenth District for tuberculosis veterans and for additional medical/surgical patients, the Veterans Bureau Committee chose Battle Mountain Sanitarium as the location for this hospital. The main hospital building, with north and south wings, constructed on the former site of the Tubercular Barrack, was completed in October 1926.

The American Legion Auxiliary adopted the traditional red poppy as its memorial flower at the organization's first convention in Kansas City, Missouri in 1921. Major John McCrae, a Canadian Officer was at Flanders Field, Belgium during World War I, wrote the famous poem that begins…"In Flanders fields the poppies blow between the crosses, row on row." Wild poppies, blooming in the battle cemeteries of France and Belgium in 1918, constituted "nature's tribute" to the war dead and thus began…"wear a poppy to remember." The poppy making program was initiated in 1926, by the South Dakota Department of American Legion as therapy and additional spending money for veteran participants. The VFW and DAV also have poppy making programs for veterans. In 1930, an Executive Order, provided for the newly formed Veterans Administration to assume the functions of three agencies: The Veterans Bureau, the Pension Bureau and the National Homes for Disable Volunteer Soldiers. With a few years after the main hospital was constructed, the need for additional bed capacity and enlarged surgical facilities developed. Consequently, the construction of an addition to the hospital was undertaken in 1937, and completed in 1938.

Many updates were completed 1932-to-1957. The major medical upgrades consisted of a WPA built laundry in 1943, dietetic building 1950, nurses quarters 1956, dental clinic 1957, X-ray facility 1957, medical library and medical conference room in the 1950s. In the 1950s, drug therapy eliminated the requirement for tubercular care, creating the new mission for the sanitarium to that of general medical care. From 1957 to 1982, a few milestones were reached: VA domiciliary almost reached maximum capacity of 548 and the first VA Contract Nursing Home Program in the country was established in the 1960's between the VA and Southern Hills General Hospital in Hot Springs.

The Freedom Shrine was donated to the VA Medical Center in 1995, by the Rapid City Exchange Club. Located in the rotunda of the primary building, the shrine is a collection of 28 original historic American documents photographically reproduced and attractively displayed in thousands of locations throughout the United States. The purpose of the shrine is to remind all Americans that freedoms, which they enjoy today, are, in essence, a gift from the past, the product of idealism, determination and sacrifice of vast numbers of courageous men and women. The shrine also serves to remind all of us that so precious a gift as freedom must be continually guarded and protected. In 1996, the VA Black Hills Health Care System was established with the consolidation of the VA Medical Centers at Fort Mead and Hot Springs, enhancing the quality and access to health care for veterans in the Black Hills.

There has been a tremendous increase in service to the homeless population. In addition to 50 residential beds, for the homeless in the domiciliary at Hot Springs, there are 134 grant and per diem beds for the homeless population. These beds are paid for by VA but run by non-VA entities, such as the Cornerstone Rescue Mission in Rapid City. These grant and per diem beds are available on Pine Ridge, Cheyenne River and Standing Rock Native American Reservations in addition to what is available in Rapid City. One of the most important changes for the seriously mentally ill population is the recovery module, which focuses on assisting people to live as full a life as possible instead of traditional warehousing or living a life of dependence and futility. They are assisted in finding appropriate jobs and taking control of their lives and treatment.

Compensated work therapy (CWT) was initiated in the 1980s to provide veterans an opportunity to work while in recovery. CWT now has become a prominent component in the best practices in the recovery process. Funding has been provided for the program and it is mandatory that all VA Medical Centers have a CWT program, which contracts with employers in the community as well as with the VA Medical Center to provide employment for veterans. The Black Hills Health Care System operates CWT at Hot Springs, Pine Ridge, Fort Meade, McLaughlin and Eagle Butte in South Dakota. Typically, over 120 are involved in CWT at any given time. In 2006, over 150 veterans worked in the Hot Springs and Pine Ridge CWT programs and earned over $400.000. The VA Medical Center at Hot Springs opened a CWT Transitional Residence in July 2005. A duplex was converted into an eleven-bed residence with funds received from the Veterans Integrated Service Network 23. This assists veterans in returning to the community while working CWT. To be eligible, they must have completed one month of CWT in the domiciliary and are required to pay rent and provide their own food. Any length of stay in the transitional residence is limited to six months. In 1984, the Veterans Administration assumed the mandate to provide priority treatment to former POWs and developed an outreach program to meet the needs in the areas of disability compensation, health care and rehabilitation.

The primary mission of the domiciliary today is rehabilitation of veterans to improve quality of life and become a productive member of society and their community. The VA Domiciliary at Hot Springs is one of two of its kind in the upper Midwest. Significant cost containment at Hot Springs VA Medical Center was begun in 1986, by admitting veteran patients requiring a higher level of care directly from the domiciliary into community nursing homes and bypassing the costly interim transfer to the VA hospital. In 1996, with the consolidation of the Hot Springs and Fort Mead VA Medical Center, Hot Springs gradually become an ambulatory surgery center. Surgical patients requiring overnight stays are transferred to Fort Meade for care. The Ambulatory Surgery Center operates during daytime hours, Monday through Friday, supported by part time or contract surgeons, and a full time anesthetist.

Diagnostic services are the result of the merger of nuclear medicine and radiology in 1998, and the addition of a laboratory in 1999. The eye clinic consists of three refracting lanes, a dispensary, a laser room, a visual field room and a digital imaging room. State of the art testing and treatment equipment include digital retinal imaging and fluorescein angiograms, ocular coherence, tomography, multifocal laser, YAG laser and automated visual perimeter. Contract ophthalmology services are provided several times a month, which include cataract surgery and laser treatment of retinal disease and glaucoma. Students in their fourth (final) year of optometry school train in the clinic and rotate through every three months. Affiliations are established with Pacific University College of Optometry and the Illinois College of Optometry.

Dialysis began at the VA Medical Center in December 1973. They began with one patient who dialyzed three days a week. By 1981, the unit had grown to 1,000 dialysis treatments a year. Today, the dialysis unit has grown to 22 patients, provides over 3,000 dialysis treatments a year, and is open six days a week. Of utmost significance is the fact that Hot Springs has the only VA dialysis unit the country to be Medicare certified to provide care to non-veteran (local) patients through a sharing agreement. The pharmacy service has strived to provide veterans with optimal pharmaceutical care making patient safety a priority.

Veterans are still served in the original dining room but smaller tables are in place and a cafeteria line is used instead of family style dinning. Hospitalized veterans receive a tray at their bedside. Dietitians spend more of their time planning therapeutic diets and providing education for a healthier lifestyle including diet. The color and style of uniforms has changed and, currently, blue shirts and navy or white pants are worn by both men and women along with hairnets for women and caps for men.

Early in 1997, the new ambulatory care area was dedicated. This included the new main entrance for ambulatory care, ambulance entrance, emergency room, outpatient desk area, total renovation of ground east, providing many new exam rooms, new patient waiting areas, and the new file room. VA Medical Center, Hot Springs mission for veterans is "To be your partner in achieving health and well-being." Its vision is that "We will be the health care system of choice, providing compassionate quality care, efficient service, and enhanced access. We will be a responsible community member, an employer of choice and a leader in education." [13]

---

[13] Department of Veterans Affairs Medical Center, "Battle Mountain Sanitarium, 1907-1997" and "Celebrating a century of caring for America's heroes, 1907-2007," Hot Springs, South Dakota.

Armored Cruiser USS South Dakota ACR-9

The First South Dakota Warship

THE state of South Dakota has a long military history, from the settlement of the western great plains through the men and women serving in the U.S. military forces. To honor that tradition, USS South Dakota (ACR-9), an armored cruiser of the Pennsylvania-Class, was built by (launched on July 21, 1904) the Union Works of San Francisco, California.

The South Dakota was assigned to the Armored Cruiser Squadron, Pacific Fleet. The cruiser left San Francisco on September 15, 1908, later cruising off the Pacific Ocean approach to Central and South America, returning to Mare Island, California on June 22, 1909. The cruiser returned south, operating off the western approach to the Panama Canal, sailing to Bremerton Navy Yard in August as part of the U.S. Navy's participation in the Alaska-Yukon-Pacific Exposition held in Seattle, Washington.

On 5 September, the Armored Cruiser Squadron, consisting of California, Colorado, Maryland, Pennsylvania, South Dakota and West Virginia departed San Francisco on September 5, 1909, reaching Honolulu, Hawaii on the 11 September. The cruiser sailed to the Admiralty Islands, Pago Pago on Tutuila Island in American Samoa, Philippines, Japan and China, returning to Honolulu on January 21, 1910. In February, the South Dakota and cruiser Tennessee cruised off the pacific coast of South America before the South Dakota entered dry dock at San Francisco in October to allow yard workers to scrape the hull's bottom and repaint the hull below the waterline. After dry dock and painting, the cruiser resumed operations in the Pacific in 1911, rejoining the Armored Cruiser Squadron, sailing to the Hawaiian Islands, Guam and the Philippines. Outside Manila Bay, the cruiser damaged its starboard propeller requiring repairs in the Dewey Dry Dock. While it was in dry dock, Philippine workers scraped and painted the cruiser's lower hull, repairing the anchor engine. The cruiser joined the squadron in time to sail into Yokohama, Japan. After leaving Japan, the cruiser broke its main shaft on the trip back to Honolulu. The shaft was damaged when the propeller bent and the resulting misalignment unnoticed while in dry dock.

The cruisers California, Colorado, South Dakota and West Virginia came together at Santa Monica, California on October 7, 1911. The South Dakota resumed participation in squadron level exercises after August 1912. The cruiser entered reserve status on December 30, 1913 at Puget Sound Navy Yard. On April 17, 1914, the cruiser came out of reserve status for possible combat operations against Mexico. On 18 April, four companies of the 4th Marine Regiment boarded the cruiser, sailing to Marie Island. It joined the collier USS Jupiter, loading the balance of the 4th Marine Regiment. On 19 April, the two ships sailed south to a holding position off the Pacific coast of Mexico. They rendezvoused with the cruiser West Virginia, in preparation to land Marines if necessary but these troops were not needed. On 6 July, the South Dakota returned to California.

In August 1914, the cruiser sailed to Honolulu, returning to Bremerton, going into reserve on 28 September. It was designated as Flag Ship, Reserve Force, Pacific Fleet from January 21, 1915 to February 1916. The cruiser was removed from reserve, sailing south to and through the Panama Canal on May 20, 1917, joining the Atlantic Fleet to support naval operations against Germany during World War I. It was assigned patrol duties along the coast of Brazil. In 1918, the cruiser performed troop convoy escort duty from the U.S. east coast to mid-Atlantic, relieved by British Royal Navy warships for the remaining portion of the convoy transit to French ports on the English Channel. On one escort mission, the cruiser broke a propeller shaft in the heavy North Atlantic sea swells, requiring dry dock for repair in a U.S. east coast repair facility. After the armistice ending World War I, the cruiser participated in two trips from Brest, France to New York harbor transporting U.S. troops from the fighting on the western front. During a voyage to New York on January 7, 1919, the cruiser was badly damaged during a violent North Atlantic storm, requiring extensive repairs, not completed until May. With the drawn down of Atlantic Fleet activities after the Armistice, repair space became limited on the east coast. The cruiser was released from the Atlantic Fleet, transiting through the Panama Canal, back to the Pacific, assigned Flagship U.S. Asiatic Fleet of 26 ships. The Imperial Japanese Navy closely monitored the forward deployments of the U.S. Asiatic Fleet, determining and planning counter-measures as necessary.

During the winter of 1920, the South Dakota and USS Albany were ordered to Vladivostok, Russia to assist American troops ashore (U.S. military intervention in the Russian Civil War after the end of World War I). The cruiser departed Vladivostok in March 1920, sailing to Japan, then returning to Vladivostok in April. The cruiser departed Russian waters, sailing to Chefoo, China for short-range battle and director practice in May. The cruiser's name was changed to the Huron on June 7, 1920 designating it as a heavy cruiser, freeing its name for a new battleship then under construction. After the devastating Japanese earthquake of September 1, 1923, the U.S. Asiatic Fleet undertook humanitarian assistance to the people of Japan. The Huron was replaced by the Pittsburgh as Flagship, U.S. Asiatic Fleet on December 23, 1926 at Chefoo, China. The Huron reached Puget Sound Navy Yard on March 3, 1927, decommissioned on June 17th removed from the active Navy list on November 15, 1929. The cruiser was sold on November 11, 1930 for scrap in order to meet U.S. commitments to the signed London Treaty for the Limitation and Reduction of Naval Armaments. This set up major warship allocations between the Imperial Japanese Navy, the British Royal Navy and the U.S. Navy. The Huron was stripped of usable engineering equipment and armaments, with the superstructure cut down to the waterline, sold to the Powel River Company Limited of British Columbia, Canada. The Huron was used as a floating breakwater for a log pond and paper mill operations. The hulk was ballasted and anchored, with pumps periodically removing water to keep the hulk floating. The ship slowly rusted but remained as a functional floating breakwater until a violent Northwest Pacific storm on February 18, 1961 sent waves over the ship, swamping it, sinking it to the log pond's bottom in 80 feet of water where it rests today.[14]

---

[14] Lt. Col. George A. Larson, USAF (Ret.), "War ships in transition: Armored cruiser South Dakota, America's first all-steel warships were a transition from the wood-and-iron mixed construction introduced in the Civil War era, Sea Classics, February 2011.

Renold Schat

World War I U.S. Army Experience in France on the Western Front

WORLD War I grew out of the assignation of Archduke Franz Ferdinand, heir to the Austro-Hungarian throne, in Sarajevo on June 28, 1914, by a member of the Blackhand, a Nationalist Sect Society in the Austro-Hungarian Empire. Three weeks later, Austria-Hungary sent an ultimatum to Serbia, demanding the arrest of the assassin and brought to justice. Serbia had an alliance with Russia at this time. In response, Austria-Hungary set in motion a series of events, which rapidly got of hand, leading to the First World War and death of millions of civilians and military. Austria-Hungary, unsatisfied with Serbia's response to the assignation, declared war on Serbia on July 28, 1918, believing it would be a short and localized (regional) conflict. However, Russia began six weeks of war mobilization to deploy its military forces in striking areas so it could support its ally, Serbia. This started a chain of event, which did not end until turning into a world war. In response to the Russia Army military threat, Germany honored its military treaty with Austria-Hungary, declaring was on Serbia. Russia declared war on Germany and Austria-Hungary on 3 August. England supported France, declaring war on Germany on 4 August, with the objective of defending Belgium from invasion by German troops attempting to swing north through the country into France, with the ultimate objective of capturing Paris, ending the war quickly. Then troops from the British Colonial Empire entered the war to support England: Australia, Canada, India, New Zealand and the Union of South Africa. In addition, Japan honored its military agreement with England, declaring war on Germany on 23 August and on Austria-Hungary on 25 August. This allowed Japan to seize Germany's Pacific Colonial Empire, something it wanted to do after defeating Russia in the Far East during the Russo-Japanese War. Italy did not honor its military treaties with Germany or Austria-Hungarian Empire, only later joining the spreading European-Mediterranean War on the side of the Allies on May 1915. Consequently, the supposedly regional Balkans War rapidly escalating into a total world war which cost millions of lives in senseless trench warfare of frontal assaults against each other's trenches into the muzzles of massed machine guns, mortars, artillery and rifle fire.

Entangling alliances resulted in:

Austria-Hungarian Empire declared war on Serbia.
German Empire declared war on France, England and Russian Empire.
Russian Empire declared war on German Empire and Austria-Hungarian Empire.
British and French Colonial Empires declared war on German Empire.
Japan declared war on the German Empire and Austria-Hungarian Empire.

On April 6, 1917, U.S. Congress approved a joint resolution declaring that a state of war existed between the Imperial German Government, the Government and the people of the United States and making provisions to prosecute the same.

After the U.S. entered World War II on April 7, 1917, Renold Schat, Clear Lake, South Dakota, felt he should help serve his country in its battle for freedom. He enlisted in the U.S. Army even though he was 29 years old, with a business. He enlisted in the U.S. Army at Sioux Falls, South Dakota on May 12, 1917, ordered to Jefferson Barracks, St. Louis, Missouri for military induction and initial basic training. By the end of May, he transferred to Fort Bliss at El Paso, Texas, where Renold joined the 5th Artillery as a Private, starting artillery training. In the rapidly wartime expanding U.S. Army, the process took new enlistees, draftees and added a small number of experienced men from existing unites, forming new battalions. On June 21, 1917, a number of regular Army personnel from the 5th Artillery became nucleus of a new unit, Battery "C," 13th Field Artillery.

New enlistees and draftees brought the artillery regiment to strength, trained on 4.7-inch cannons in Texas through the summer and fall of 1917. With so many new recruits, promotions advanced easy with Renold promoted to Corporal on July 21, 1917, Sergeant on 28 July. It was not all work for the recruits, after a tough day of training, there was time for leisure with baseball the main attraction. Renold hung out near the baseball practice field after completing a day's work and finally got on the team. He was a fair pitcher, good hitter, could fill in as catcher and fit into other positions.

For Renold, after a period of reorganization and strenuous training with the regiment, the regiment departed Texas to join the Fourth Division at Camp Greene, North Carolina on December 10, 1917. On May 12, 1918, they departed North Caroline, boarded a two-day troop train trip to Camp Merritt, New Jersey. The division embarked from New York harbor on May 22, 1918 on the USS Great Northern. They crossed the rough, rolling seas of the Atlantic, landing at Brest, France. They stayed for eight days at Camp Pontenezen Barracks, France, under mandatory quarantine. On June 7, 1918, they were loaded (crammed) into what historians refer to as World War I's infamous 40 by 8 wood railroad boxcars (The same type and size of railroad boxcars used during World War II by Nazi SS troops to transport Jews, political prisoners and undesirables to concentration camps for Hitler's "Final Solution," death camps. There was standing room only, with many transported dying of exhaustion, lack of food and water or succumbing to disease and beatings), for the three-day rail trip to Camp de. Songe at Bordeaux, France.

Even though Renold's artillery regiment trained on 4.7-inch cannons in the United States prior to overseas deployment, they were forced to transition and learn French 155mm cannons, necessary because of standardized, high-number production and distribution of artillery shells to front line units on the Western Front (Allied artillery battalions which used thousands of shells daily). This required retraining on the French artillery and the horrible conditions they would encounter of the Western Front. Renold was selected by the company commander to attend Advanced Cannoneer School on French 155 mm cannons. Renold had always been good at math and understood the principle of sectors, trajectories, aiming by compass and positioning the cannons. When they moved to a new site, he helped set the cannons and sight them. Renold was also the sergeant of the signal platoon with 23 men under him. They had various jobs, including scouts, telephone operators, instrument and linemen. They took wire off reels, stringing it from the cannons at the firing site, to the front lines and often out into "No Man's Land," amid the destruction and perils from German artillery, machine gun and mortar fire. Forward positioning allowed Renold's personnel to observe and report where the rounds fell, advising the cannon crews on required adjustments to hit the specified targets. While in France, Renold took a Signal Corps training course on motorcycles and drove the Indian motorcycle, fitted with a sidecar to carry maps, instruments and high-priority gear needed for his job as a sergeant of a forward observation team.

French artillery moved their 155mm cannons by teams of horses during most of the war, placing them into position at night to hide the newly set up batteries from German aerial reconnaissance. Conditions were horrible in the winter for men and horses moving the heavy artillery through mud, without lights and as quietly as possible giving the constant noise from the horses and movement of the artillery. There were few hard-surface roads; it was cold, wet and muddy, with the heavy equipment difficult to move at night. Near the end of the war, selected artillery units were equipped with trucks and tractor-crawlers to move cannons into position. The war was going against Germany and the noise from the mechanized equipment did not compromise firing positions. Even during World War II, the German Army used large numbers of horses to tow artillery. Their industrial output could not match the United States in production of trucks, jeeps, and heavy movers for a mechanized war.

For Renold, all too soon, they moved out of their training camp, moved to the front for combat. At this time in fighting on the Western Front, the Germans were threatening a break-through toward Paris for what they hoped to be a knockout blow to end the war before the full weight of arriving American troops, equipment and supplies, which would change the balance of forces fighting on the Western Front in favor of the Allies. German Army divisions advanced against French Army divisions in the Chateau-Thierry area. The U.S. 3rd Division and 2nd Marines joined French troops to stop the German advance. The U.S. 13th Field Artillery moved forward to provide artillery support to U.S. infantry trying to slow and then stop the German advance in their sector.

Renold remembered that food was simple but nourishing. Hot meals were rare on the front lines in the trenches, easier to provide at semi-fixed artillery positions behind the trench lines. As the war dragged on, the Germans had great difficulty in feeding their troops, with the civilian population on near starvation rations. U.S. Army hot kitchens were more common in reserve position areas, set up when the battalion pulled out of the front lines, given a rest period from trench warfare.

After two months, the battery's artillery moved back to the front and the 13th Field Artillery departed Camp de Songe on 29 July by train. The railroad cars arrived at Chateau-Thierry on 30 July. That evening, they began movement to the front lines, crossing the Marie River, with the men receiving their first introduction to German aircraft dropping bombs on the roads leading into the city. Before dawn on 1 August, the battery slowly moved into Belleau Wood, remaining under cover during the day to hide from German aerial reconnaissance. The next night they moved into a reserve position near Fere en Tardenois. After dark on 5 August, the battery moved forward and took up position to the left of Chery, moving in under scattered German Artillery shelling. Their first shot fired from this position was at noon on 6 August, with effective fire concentrated against German positions near the villages of Perles, Bazoches, Long u Val and Valixere in the Vesle Sector. While at this position, the battery tasted real combat on the evening of 13 August. While the gun crews were in action, a German artillery shell registered a direct hit between the battery's second and third guns. Another shell hit between the battery's billets and kitchen facility. It killed five and wounded twenty-seven. Despite the hit from German artillery, no men from the battery wavered. Coolly and without fear, the men of the battery went about the tasks of caring for the wounded and repairing the shell damage while under heavy German artillery attack. The decision was made to shift positions to hide the guns from the Germans and within two hours, the battery began firing at German positions with two undamaged guns. Battery personnel worked to repair the remaining two guns. Battery personnel were cited in a citation for bravery under fire.

Leaving Chery during the night of 17 August, the battery moved to Laterte Gaucher, where it was back into 40 by 8 French railroad boxcars for the trip to Marieulles, arriving on 21 August. They enjoyed a rest period behind the front lines and replaced personnel to bring the battery back to full operational strength. Major Burr, advanced from captain, moved up to command level in the regiment, replaced by Captain Charles McCleary within the battery. Between 6 to 8 September, the battery moved into a second line reserve position in the Toulon Sector near Yeps. Another night move forward on 8 September shifted the battery to a position bear Rupt on the St. Mihiel front to support the U.S. Army 26th Division.

The battery's guns moved to a new position on 11 September. At 1 a.m., the battery commenced firing at the start of the St. Mihiel offensive. The battery bombarded the German trench lines and rear reserve areas before the Allied infantry climbed out of their trenches, going over the top in the accepted military tactic of frontal assault, which had killed millions of Allied and German soldiers. They had maps marked in artillery reference coordinates so they could shell German trench positions. During regular bombardment support, the battery might begin firing at 6 a.m., or midnight, or 2 or 3 p.m., starting three to four minutes prior to zero hour. They would lay down a barrage of smoke shell in front of the trenches for two to three minutes to screen U.S. infantry troops climbing out of the trenches into exposed positions to cross "No Man's Land" into German artillery, machine gun, mortar and massed rifle fire range. The cannons were reset to lay down a second barrage of smoke shells at 200 to 300 yards into "No Man's Land" ahead of the advancing infantry. Advancing infantry moved forward taking covering positions wherever possible in shell craters, then advancing as the smoke shell barrage moved closer to German trench positions. As the advance approached the German trenches, the smoke shells continued to provide cover until the last moment of breaching German positions. At this point, artillery fire stopped or shifted farther ahead of the troops to support the advance through the first German or front line trenches into the following secondary of reserve trench (fall back) defenses. This sounds easy on paper, but was dangerous, hard to complete, and when done so, usually at high cost to the attacking infantry. This is why casualties on the Western Front were so high, with military commanders unwilling or unable to shift tactics in face of modern technological advanced killing weapons.

Renold had one noteworthy experience when a few of his men suffered after the effects of a German shelling. Linemen had to go out into "No Man's Land" when German shells frequently cut the battery's telephone lines to the forward observer's position. Some suffered concussions from the incoming German shells if caught in the open moving from one shell hole to another. One man came back with effects of shell concussions, not knowing anything or his immediate surroundings, evacuated to the U.S. Army Field Hospital in the rear area for rest and treatment. When he returned to the battery at St. Mihiel, he suffered another incident of heavy German shellings, suffered a replace, again sent to the rear for medical care, but did not return to the battery, deemed unfit for duty.

Renold, after suffering for a week or ten days with a sore throat, which continued to worsen, his tonsils, swelled. He was afraid he would not be able to swallow or possibly breathe. While they were behind the front lines in reserve position, he went to the U.S. Army aid station to ask for medical treatment. After a long wait, a doctor checked him over. The doctor said... "This is a wound and we don't have room for you, but I will look at your tonsils." After backing Renold against a tree near the medical tent, he lanced the tonsils. Renold spit out about a cup of pus and blood, but started to breathe better. He was sent back to his unit where he had to sleep sitting up. The next day his throat felt better. Renold was lucky that the bad infection did not result from the primitive medical care without proper antiseptic or clean operating conditions, which was deadly during World War I, causing the almost as many deaths as on the battlefield, infections killing millions during the war.

The regiment's battery spent seven days at St. Miehiel and 41 days at Meuse-Argonne, which turned out to be their longest time at one operational location. After a heavy battle, the area between the trenches was a horrible sight: dead men, broken and discarded equipment abandoned everywhere with tress blown apart, leaving on jagged stumps. Burial details performed terrible work. Battery personnel frequently worked on burial details, laying men in long open trenches dug deep into the ground, identified with disks or dog tags hanging from crude wood crosses. This was a terrible job and not for the faint of heart and made, many men despaired their duty. After several gun position moves, the battery pulled out of the rear area on the night of 14 September, going to Bois de Souilly. Moving at night to hide from German aerial reconnaissance, they took a forward position near Egnes on 25 September. The battery commenced firing early the next day. Another night on 27 September and the battery commenced its first heavy artillery shelling over "No Man's Land," moving forward to Cuisy, taking positions near Bois de Septasrages under heavy German artillery shelling. A German artillery shell landed near the battery's position on 6 October, killing one and wounding six. From 14 to 23 October, the battery remained near Nantillois, moving into the rear area by truck transport to the second reserve line near Moncyville.

On the night of 29 October, the battery was ordered to move forward into a position near Montfaucon. They remained under cover throughout the day and resumed movement at night, reaching a position near Cunel. Starting at midnight on 31 October, the battery took part in conducting a concentrated artillery barrage to clear the Germans from the left flank, opening up the way for a sustained offensive to push back the Germans. On 6 November, the battery moved under the cover of darkness to a new position near Doulcon, under German shelling. After one day of artillery fire, the battery moved across the Meuse River to a position near Murveaux. The battery remained at this location until 11 November, when combatants (Allied forces and German forces and its allies) signed the Armistice at 5 a.m., November 11, 1918, effective 11 a.m. Even though the armistice ended World War I, it planted the seeds for the Second World War. Many historians, including the author, believed there was no break in the World War from its beginning with the politically motivated assassination in Sarajevo on June 28, 1914, continuing until the signing of unconditional surrender by representatives of the Japanese military and civilian government cabinet members with Allied representatives on September 2, 1945, on the Iowa class battleship USS Missouri in Tokyo Bay. Formal interpretive historians mark the end of World War I as November 11, 1919.

The U.S. Army War College summary of the U.S. involvement in World War I summarized that 24,234,021 men registered for the military draft with 3,099,000 serving in the U.S. Armed Forces, only three percent of the population. When compared to other Allied, German combatants and its Central Powers, U.S. commitment was small but provided the turning point in winning the war.

The Allied powers forced Germany to withdraw from Luxembourg under observation by the U.S. Army, followed by formal liberation. On November 18, 1918, U.S. Army General John Pershing issued a proclamation to the people of Luxembourg, indicating troops of the U.S. Third Army would transit through their country to take up positions to occupy the area of the German Rhineland, as Allies and not as invaders..."After four years of violation of its territory, the Grand Duchy of Luxembourg is to be fortunately liberated. American troops will enter the Grand Duchy of Luxembourg as friends and will abide rigorously by the rules and conduct of international law. Their presence will not be extended longer than is necessary; will not be a burden upon you. The operation of the government and institutions will not be impeded. Your lives and livelihoods will not be disturbed. Your person and your property will be respected."

Renold and his fellow troops, leaving the now silent battlefield front on the afternoon of 11 November, made a five-day trek to a rest camp at Commercy. U.S. Army Quartermaster Corps personnel issued new clothes and equipment to the men. They prepared to march into Germany with the U.S. Army, part of the Allied Army of Occupation. German troops had already left for their homeland within a day of the signing of the armistice. Most were tired, hungry and psychologically beaten, with orders to be out of Allied controlled territory within two weeks. On 21 November, khaki-clad U.S. troops began the long journey into the Rhineland as part of the Allied Army of Occupation. They marched for almost a month, through dusty, devastated battle torn up areas, through Luxembourg, along the Moselle River, arriving at the town of Gevenich, Germany near Coblenz. On 18 December, they took up quarters in Gevenich, above the Valley of the Moselle.

Enlisted men were barracked in school buildings or public (government) buildings, not in civilian homes. However, officers and NCOs were assigned rooms in private homes. Under the terms of the armistice, the German civilian populations were ordered to cooperate with the Allies, but fortunately, the relationship between U.S. occupying forces and the German people was cordial and business like. The bridgehead across the Rhine River at Coblenz was a major transportation point and a prime concern in the Allied Occupation Army's security of vital supply and communications lines. There was time for U.S. troops to enjoy the local community and make friends, especially with the children who suffered greatly from the years of war, living in Germany.

In the spring, the Coblenz bridgehead control was transferred to French occupation forces (which greatly upset the German civilian population, setting up the rise of Nazism in Germany). The 13th Field Artillery moved to Arhweiler near Dusseldorf along the Rhine River. The troops enjoyed this location and one of Renold's favorite memories was about trips to many local castles, which were located on many hills overlooking the Rhine River. He seemed to be partial to the Katz castle and enjoyed the story about the "Rock of the Lorelie," where sweet songs of beautiful maidens lured sailors to their doom. They had a little more time for recreation and enjoyed the countryside along the Rhine River. They remained at this location until departing for the United States in July 1919. They packed all their equipment for shipment back to the United States as well as all personal items for sea transportation home.

After they cleaned equipment and clothes for the trip home, the French government and military planned a large and elaborate victory parade in Paris, through the Arc de Triomphe, on Bastille Day 1919. A select portion of the U.S. Army sent to France during World War I was scheduled to march in the parade, so a color guard was chosen for each battalion participating in the parade. The men chosen were tall, rugged in physical appearance and excellent examples of American troops. Renold was included in one of these color guard detachments, so he would not be going home with the bulk of the 13th Field Artillery. Renold's packed duffle bag was shipped home with friends in the artillery battery. The trip to Paris was fun, going to new places, meeting new and cheering crowds. Crowds were large and celebrations overwhelming, but the experience of marching through the Arc De Triomphe on July 14, 1919 was a once in a lifetime experience for Renold.

Captain McCleary addressed Renold and the men of the battery before they departed France..."For over two years we have been together. Friendships have been formed which will never be forgotten. Friendships with that solid foundation which arises only from such comradeship as was ours through this, the greatest struggle in world history. Side by side, we have gone through that struggle. The burdens of hardships, sorrows and pain of one, like the burden, hardship, sorrow and pain of all. Facing together the onslaught of battle with spirit so characteristic of the American Army, a spirit that could not be other than victorious. Now comes the time of parting. Amid the joyous hurry and confusion in anticipation of soon being again with loved ones at home, we may perhaps forget for the moment that which will mean much in other years."

From the parade in Paris, Renold and other members of the color guard traveled to London, England to participate (march) in a military parade for British King George and Queen Mary. It was an outstanding parade held in front of hundreds of thousands of cheering British citizens. Renold and the color guard shipped home to the United States on a troop transport, with other U.S. troops returning home. Interestingly, due to a clerical entry or administrative misunderstanding, their return trip's quarters were in the troop transport steerage section, far below deck. This happened because their unit (color guard) designation was listed as "colored." At that time, in the segregated U.S. Army, colored troops were assigned separated and third class quarters on U.S. transports. Regardless, the trip across the North Atlantic was rough and uncomfortable due to bad weather and high seas. Most of those on the transport became seasick. When Renold arrived in New York, he found out his duffle bag had been stolen. He lost his diary, clothes and souvenirs. After landing, Renold was shipped to Camp Dodge, north of Des Moines, Iowa for military procession and separation from the Army on August 14, 1919.[15]

---

[15] Material provided by Ralph Schat, Rapid City, South Dakota, "Renold Schat in World War I," interview, Lt. Col. George A. Larson, USAF (Ret.), June 2009.

South Dakota National Guard

Service on the U.S.-Mexico Border in 1916

ON July 15, 1916, the South Dakota Fourth Infantry Regiment mustered into service for duty along the U.S.-Mexico border. They departed Camp Hagman near Redfield, South Dakota on July 31, 1916 for San Benito, Texas. Along with the First Oklahoma Infantry. They served until March 3, 1917. The First Louisiana Infantry and the 26th U.S. Infantry were assigned to the First Separate Brigade, commanded by Colonel Robert Bullard, U.S. Army. The South Dakota troops spent seven months on the border training and watching. They were mustered out of active Federal duty at Fort Crook, Nebraska on March 3, 1917.[16]

---

[16] Lt. Col. George A. Larson, USAF (Ret.), "South Dakota National Guard, Service on the U.S.-Mexico Border in 1916." Visit to Camp Rapid, The South Dakota National Guard's open house to celebrate the National Guard's 150 years of service," display set up in the Headquarters Lobby, "2012: Countdown to Withdrawal," June 9, 2012.

The U.S. Army's 1916 Punitive Expedition

The Hunt for Poncho Villa
Fourth South Dakota Infantry

BEGINNING in 1911, Mexico's international political instability overflowed toward the southern border of the United States. During the summer of 1911, President William Howard Taft authorized the U.S. Army to transfer additional troops to the southwest, garrisoned at San Antonio, Texas. Political and military unrest continued to grow inside Mexico.

Following the mobilization of 1911, the Army patrolled the frontier with small units, but when the insurrectionists overthrew the Mexican government in 1913, President Howard Taft decided on a show of force similar to the earlier concentration of troops. On 21 February, President Taft ordered Major General William H. Carter, Central Department, to assemble the most fully manned of the U.S. Army's divisions, the 2nd Division, on the Gulf Coast of Texas. Unlike its mobilization of the Maneuver Division in 1911, the War Department transmitted a five line telegram to deploy the 2nd Division. General Carter, who arrived with his staff in Texas within three days, established the division headquarters and its 4th and 6th Brigades at Texas City and the 5th Brigade at Galveston. The 2nd Division lacked, however, some field artillery, medical, signal, and engineer elements and all its trains.

Tensions remained high between the United States and Mexico in 1914, and in response, President Woodrow Wilson adjusted the deployment of military units to protect American interests. U.S. naval forces occupied Vera Cruz, Mexico with U.S. Army troops relieving the sailors ashore. On 30 April, the 5th Brigade, 2nd Division, augmented with cavalry, field artillery, engineer signal, bakery and aviation units, and almost the entire divisional staff, took up positions in the city. To placate uneasy U.S. citizens along the U.S.-Mexico border, the 2nd Division and 8th Brigade, elements of the 1st and 3rd Divisions, and some smaller united, moved to the southern frontier of the United States with Mexico. In November, the crisis at Vera Cruz ended and the 5th Brigade returned to Galveston, but activity resumed the following months when the 6th Brigade, 2nd Division, deployed to Waco, Arizona. For the next few months, no major changes took place in the disposition of U.S. forces. In August 1915, a hurricane struck Texas City and Galveston, killing 13 U.S. Army enlisted men, causing considerable damage to the 2nd Division's equipment and supplies. The War Department decided the 2nd Division was no longer needed along the border with Mexico and transferred to other military posts in the Southern Department. The divisional headquarters was demobilized on October 18, 1915.

On March 9, 1916, violence crossed the U.S. southern border when Mexican bandits raided Columbus, New Mexico, killing and wounding several U.S. soldiers and town civilians. The following day, the Southern Department commander, Major General Frederick Funston, ordered Brigadier General John J. Pershing, Commander, 8th Brigade, to apprehend the perpetrators. For his mission, General Pershing organized a provisional division and designated it as "The Punitive Expedition, U.S. Army." Violence intensified along the border during the spring of 1916, creating a general mobilization. After a raid in May (against Glen Springs, Texas), President Wilson called up (mobilized) the National Guard of Arizona, New Mexico and Texas into active federal service. After another raid by Mexican bandits across the U.S.-Mexico border on 16 June, President Wilson federalized all U.S. Guard units assigned to tactical divisions in the Stimson Plan (reorganization of the Army to be better prepared for war mobilization).

As a result, the South Dakota Fourth Infantry Regiment was mustered into active federal service on July 15, 1916, to support operations and security along the U.S.-Mexico border. The Fourth Infantry Regiment formed up at Camp Hagman, Redfield, South Dakota, departing by passenger trains to Benito, Texas on 31 July, east of Brownsville, Texas on the Gulf Coast. The Fourth Infantry Regiment was assigned to protect the U.S.-Mexico border from possible cross-border raids/incursions by Poncho Villa's Army, part of the political and military revolutionary activities in Mexico. The regiment was operational assigned as the First Separate Brigade with the 22nd U.S. Infantry, 1st Louisiana and 1st Oklahoma. These federalized troops became garrison troops, taking no part in military operations inside Mexico. These federal troops participated in large scale Army maneuvers in preparation for involvement in the European War, especially since German U-boats continued attacks on merchant vessels in the North Atlantic. The South Dakota Fourth Infantry Regiment was shipped home in March 1917, demobilized (released) from active federal service. On April 2, 1917, President Wilson went before a joint session of Congress, requesting a declaration of war against Germany, with Congress declaring war on 6 April. On 15 July, the South Dakota Fourth Infantry Regiment and First Cavalry Regiment were mobilized into active federal service for combat in France, on the Western Front.[17]

---

[17] Lt. Col. George A. Larson, USAF (Ret.), "Hunting Poncho, The 1st Aero Squadron's air operations in support of the Army's 1916 Punitive Expedition," Air Classics, July & August 2004.

South Dakota National Guard

World War I

THE Fourth South Dakota had barely returned from its service on the Mexican border in 1916 and 1917, when the United States entered World War I. The 3rd Battalion was called back into Federal service in the middle of 1917, performing guard duty on vital installations through South Dakota. By October 1917, the entire regiment was called up to active Federal service. Upon arriving at Camp Greene, North Carolina, the regiment discovered that it was being split up to form the 147th Field Artillery Regiment, the 116th Supply Train, also the 146th and 148th Machine Gun Battalions. The SDNG rendered good service with the 147th becoming one of the premier American artillery units in France. A second South Dakota regiment, the South Dakota Cavalry was sworn into active Federal service, but suffered a similar fate, as did the 4th Infantry. The 1st Cavalry had been reorganized in early 1917, as the 5th Infantry, but the War Department ordered it turned back to a cavalry unit in May 1917. Lessons of the deadly trench warfare with massed artillery and machine gun defenses made the traditional cavalry charge obsolete and suicidal.[18]

---

[18] Lt. Col George A. Larson, USAF (Ret.), "South Dakota National Guard in World War I." Visit to Camp Rapid, The South Dakota National Guard's open house to celebrate the National Guard's 150 years of service," display set up in the Headquarters Lobby, "2012: Countdown to Withdrawal," June 9, 2012.

Stratobowl Balloon Launches

The United States Race into Space with the Soviet Union

THE 1960s, often viewed or referred to as an intense period in the superpowers confrontation when the Cold War between the United States and the Soviet Union nearly turned into a hot, thermonuclear exchange over the placement of Russian medium range ballistic missiles (MRBM) and intermediate range ballistic missiles (IRBM) on the island of Cuba, 90 miles south of Miami, Florida. The "Cuban Missile Crisis," sometimes referred to as the "Missiles of October," was avoided, but the space race between the two superpowers (term coined after World War II as the two main combatant allies, which defeated Nazi Germany, Italy and Japan) continued. Earlier, in the 1930s, the United States had been in competition with the Soviet Union to carry men to the edge of the earth's atmosphere and return them safely. A site in western South Dakota was selected for this first near space exploitation and scientific research attempt. In 1933, the United States Army Air Corps (USAAC) Captain Albert W. Stevens, who had a long standing interest in aerial photography and high altitude scientific observation submitted a proposal to USAAC Headquarters for a high altitude, scientific balloon flight. The flight would gather data on the composition of air wind direction and velocity, temperature, pressure, cosmic rays. Solar spectrum and effects of altitude on radio transmission. USAAC General Benjamin D. Foulois approved the proposal with the stipulation that someone besides the USAAC fund the project, which covered the purchase of the balloon, gondola, instruments, hydrogen or helium to inflate and lift the balloon to the desired altitude.

Captain Stevens convinced the National Geographic Society to cooperate in a joint, high altitude balloon project, with the Society paying the project's expenses and USAAC providing the flight and ground support personnel. Meanwhile, the U.S. Navy conducted a high altitude balloon launch and flight on its own to investigate the upper stratosphere. On November 20, 1933, U.S. Navy Lt. Commander G.W. Settle and U.S. Marine Corps Major Chester Fordney took off in a hydrogen balloon (a 600,000 cubic foot balloon designed and built by the Goodyear Company) and set an unofficial high altitude balloon record flight of 61,237 feet. Half way around the world, the Soviet Union launched its own stratospheric balloon on January 29, 1934, establishing a new high altitude record of 72,000 feet. Unfortunately, the three-man crew died when the gondola struck the ground at high speed after the parachute retarding system failed.

The Goodyear Company designed and fabricated a 3,000,000 cubic foot balloon for the next stratospheric flight, which would use helium rather than hydrogen, therefore the larger size. Helium gas was more stable and less volatile, thus the larger volume needed to compensate for reduced lifting capacity per volume of hydrogen gas. The balloon was named "Explorer I." The Dow Chemical Company designed and produced the gondola. The gondola was pressurized, air tight, hollow spherical shaped, constructed of Dow metal, a light magnesium alloy, 100-inches in diameter. The gondola's shell was only 1/5th-inch thick. The sphere's interior shell and floor was constructed of similar lightweight material, resulting in an inside diameter of 60-inches.

Most of the gondola's instruments were designed and fabricated by Captain Stevens, with remaining instruments commercially produced and bought from various electronic companies. Instruments were mounted inside and outside the gondola (on top or hanging below on ropes), designed to measure and record conditions in the upper stratosphere. To lighten the gondola's weight as it neared the ground, most of the instruments and equipment were jettisoned from or thrown out of the gondola, dropped to the ground by parachute for subsequent retrieval by Army chase personnel.

Captain Stevens was designated Flight Scientific Observer; Major E. Kepner, Flight Commander; and Captain Orvil A. Anderson in charge of ground operations and alternate pilot. They scouted for and selected a launch site 12 miles southwest of Rapid City, SD in the Black Hills, nicknamed as "Stratosphere" or "Strato Bowl." The natural basis was deep enough to protect the balloon from prevailing wind gusts during inflation process and wide enough to allow ground support personnel to move the balloon from one side of the natural basin to the other to allow a launched balloon to take off from the up wind side, thereby clearing the basin's rugged rim above.

On July 28, 1938, Explorer I was ready for its flight. After launch, the flight predicted (expected) parameters until reaching 60,000 feet, at which time, the three-man crew noticed a tear in the gas envelope's fabric. Immediately, they began an emergency vent of helium for stop the climb, bringing the gondola to the ground. At 18,000 feet, the crew opened the gondola's hatch to inspect damage to the balloon. Major Kepner determined the damage would not prevent a safe landing, saving the gondola, instruments and the crew onboard. However, during the descent below 18,000 feet, bottom panels of the balloon's fabric completely came loose, drifting away from the balloon. The remaining fabric panels resembled a large parachute, threatening to deflate, resulting in a high-speed fall toward the ground and fatal crash. The crew agreed to be positioned to jump out of the gondola, parachuting to the ground. Suddenly, the balloon's fabric seams burst, with the three crew immediately jumping out of the gondola, opening their parachutes, safely descending to the ground. The gondola smashed into the ground up wind from the three-crew members.

Ground inspection of the damaged balloon fabric panels resulted in a design change on the next balloon, Explorer II. Goodyear Company used the same fabric on the lower panels, strengthening the upper panels, increasing total capacity to 3,700,000 cubic feet. On the top, six panels down, two-ply fabrics panels were inserted around the balloon, thereby strengthening the fabric for the helium gas expansion and provide a higher degree of safely margin during climb to altitude. The balloon's rip (manual deflation panel) designed was altered to the one used on U.S. Navy non-rigid airships. This was more reliable and safer way to quickly release helium from the balloon but strong enough to prevent accidental tearing of the balloon's fabric at high altitude because of the pressure from the expanding helium. Explorer II's gondola was redesigned to reduce weight, lessening strain on the balloon's fabric. This was one of the reasons Explorer I's balloon fabric could not support the July 18, 1935 mission flight's helium capacity and gondola weight. Mission planners reduced the crew from three to two. The redesign and mission weight management reduced Explorer II's weight by 14,000 pounds (18,000 pounds lighter than Explorer I). Engineers reduced lead dust ballast weight to 1,000 pounds. The release of lead ballast dust during climb to altitude maintained the programmed ground to altitude flight profile. Today, the Environmental Protection Agency would not allow the release of lead dust into the atmosphere and its subsequent contamination of ground water, farm and ranch fields, agricultural products, animals and humans.

Explorer II required 220,000 to 230,000 cubic feet of helium to inflate the large balloon envelope. The balloon was fitted with an auxiliary inflation sleeve to permit adding more helium to compensate for water weight accumulating on the balloon's exterior from frost or rain. This balanced the launch load so the balloon could reach the desired altitude.

On July 11, 1935, Explorer II was inflated for launch. However, during initial inflation, one of the fabric panel seams tore loose, even after redesign, dropping the gondola to the ground, trapping the two-man crew in the gondola. This was fortunate it happened during inflation and not after launch. Ground support personnel rescued the two Army officers in the gondola, carefully removing the crumpled fabric from on top and around the gondola. The crew was uninjured, except for scratches during exiting through the gondola's hatch. The failed fabric panel ripped seams had not been double stitched, pulling loose, deflating the balloon. The damaged panels were repaired. However, the launch was held, waiting for favorable weather. For the next launch. Volunteer ground observers spread out 30 miles apart in a fan shaped area on November 10, 1935 to monitor the flight of Explorer II. These observers were positioned east of Oakland Lakes, northeast of Brookings, South Dakota and to Quinn, Nebraska. The balloon's flight was constantly monitored by radio communications between the onboard crew and launch site. Once the observers received launch confirmation, they recorded the location and measured the angle of the passing balloon, providing verification of its altitude to compare with onboard instrument recordings.

The operations plan for Explorer II started with its uncrating from an airtight crate at 1 p.m., one day prior to launch. Inflation began at 4 or 5 p.m., to be completed prior to midnight, for a dawn launch. The inflation order triggered the Strato Bowl's staff to request military support from Fort Meade. Three hundred officers and enlisted men assisted in handling the 3,700,000 cubic foot fabric balloon and patrol the rugged cliff areas overlooking the launch site.

On 10 November, at 6:30 p.m., the ground crew started balloon inflation. This began later than programmed because the troops were careful to properly attached the balloon to the gondola, spread the fabric on the ground properly to prevent wrinkling which could cause the thin fabric to stress and tear. Fort Meade troops transported 1,600 helium gas cylinders to the launch site's temporary storage area.

Military police from Fort Meade patrolled the rim above the launch area at the bottom of the basin to control the expected 21,000 spectators gathered for the balloon lift off. They patrolled the Strato Bowl's rim, guarding open campfires to keep the collected people from freezing in the sub-zero temperature, directing arriving cars and trucks to designated parking areas. Military police reunited separated family members, directed spectators to viewing points on the rim, preventing open fires from getting out of control and spreading to the surrounding forest.

Inflation proceeded normally until 10:45 p.m., when the ground crew noticed a 20 foot tear in the fabric above them. It took the ground crew an hour to patch and reinforce the torn fabric. The near tragic ending of Explorer I's flight in July 1934 was on the minds of those repairing the tear in the supposedly redesigned and improved Explorer II balloon. The repair was so close to original construction, Goodyear engineers could not locate the repair area until pointed out by those who did the repair. Inflation resumed until 135,000 cubic feet of helium was pumped (vented) into the balloon at 2:50 a.m. The helium rose to the top of the balloon approximately 350 feet in height.

The inflated balloon set several records prior to its launch. The balloon's 3,700,000 cubic foot capacity, consisting of 115,845 square feet of fabric made it the largest fabricated balloon built. The gondola, nine feet in diameter, with a volume of 382 cubic feet, was the largest spherical gondola constructed for stratospheric exploration. The instruments inside and mounted outside the gondola, the most varied to date to collect and measure high altitude data.

The scientific instruments carried into the upper stratosphere operated automatically, with readings recorded every 90 seconds by machine driven cameras. The setting of a high altitude ascent record was secondary to the measurement of temperature and barometric pressure changes from the ground to the flight's ceiling. The collected air samples were analyzed at the National Geographic Society laboratories in Washington, District of Columbia. The flight studied cosmic rays to learn more of their nature, behavior and origin. Some instruments studied sunlight and skylight to learn more about the earth's protective ozone layer, as well as observing sky, sun and earth brightness at high altitude.

As dawn approached, the ground crew moved the inflated balloon, with the suspended gondola below, to the west edge of the basin because of a strong westerly wind. The crew for this mission: Captain Orvil A. Anderson (pilot) and Captain Albert W. Stevens (commander). At 7 a.m., the lines holding the balloon to the ground were released.

The balloon's gondola cleared the Strato Bowl's rim by 50 feet. The balloon was 8,000 pounds lighter than originally estimated. The balloon's launch was earlier than expected because of a shift in wind from northwest to west, requiring the launch as soon as possible to clear the basin's rim above. At 50 feet above the rim, an unexpected down draft struck the rising balloon, with only quick action by the crew, releasing 750 pounds of lead dust ballast to keep the gondola from backing down onto the rim amongst the thousands of spectators.

At 7:15 a.m., the balloon reached 11,700 feet. At 7:37 a.m., USAAC Captain H. K. Baisley, observing the climbing balloon from a trailing airborne aircraft, radioed that the balloon reached 17,200 feet, over the Cheyenne River, southeast of Rapid City. He watched the crew rig instruments outside and underneath the gondola, then disappearing inside, securing the hatch. Instruments automatically started operating, along with the gondola's air purification system. The balloon climbed at 400 feet a minute. At 10:28 a.m., Captain Anderson radioed to the ground..."We are at 60,000 feet. We're not going to stop until we hit the ceiling and we'll stay there about an hour and a half. The atmosphere in the gondola is fairly dry, but the windows were frosting. The inside temperature in six degrees below." Captain Stevens then came on the radio..."The instruments were O.K., indicating the earth's radiance at 200 candles." As the balloon reached maximum altitude, Captain Anderson reduced rate of climb to 200 feet a minute. The balloon reached 73,000 feet approximately four hours after takeoff. At 11:22 a.m., the balloon reached 79,000 feet. Captain Anderson adjusted trim to maintain this altitude for 100 minutes. The balloon was at a position over the Niobrara River in Nebraska.

Captain Anderson attempted to locate and identify stars but was unable to do so. The sky was dark blue, tinged to a purple color. Approximately 14 miles below, the earth lost most of its detail, with the horizon an indistinctive blur. Railroad tracks and highways were scarcely visible, with only rivers, towns and small checkerboard patterns of farms distinguishable.

At 12:30 p.m., Captain Anderson opened the release valve, venting helium for a controlled descent. At 1:47 p.m., the balloon reached 40,000 feet, 75 miles southeast of Valentine, Nebraska. At 2:13 p.m., the balloon was down to 31,000 feet, 50 miles west of Yankton, South Dakota. The balloon landed safely, November 11, 1935 near White Lake, South Dakota. The camera film was flown to Washington, DC for analysis. The gondola was shipped to Washington, DC and on display at the Smithsonian Air and Space Museum. The record breaking high altitude flight helped launch the United States into the space race with the Soviet Union during the early years of the Cold War.[19]

---

[19] Lt. Col. George A. Larson, USAF (Ret.), "Flight into the Stratosphere over South Dakota," Friends Journal, spring 2000.

Mely Rahn

A Girl Remembers the Nazi Occupation of France During World War II

ON May 10, 1940, the German Army and Air Force attacked France, ending what British and French leaders referred to as the "Phony War," resulting in the evacuation of British Expeditionary Forces and limited numbers of French troops from Dunkirk by June 4, 1940 (with France surrendering on 22 June). Mely Rahn of Rapid City, South Dakota was a young child in France when the Germans occupied the country. Rahn..."My father, Albert de Nuefville, was a native German; however, his mother was of Jewish ancestry. This Jewish heritage caused problems after Adolf Hitler came to power in Germany. Hitler and Nazi Party leaders used the Nuremberg Laws of 1935 to divide Jews into four categories." The Nuremberg Laws stripped German Jews of their: rights and German citizenship, prohibited Jews from serving in the German military, could not hold German Civil Service jobs, Jews prohibited from the teacher profession, and Jews were not allowed to marry members of the Aryan race. Rahn..."Under these new restrictions, my father was determined to be a Mischling First Degree, anyone with two Jewish grandparents and two non-Jewish grandparents, who was either baptized and brought up a Christian or practice no religion. His was a stifling stigma. When he applied to marry my mother Hilda, German State officials denied his request. My father and Hilda left Germany, settling in southern France. Vignaux, after German troops occupied northern France, came under the control of the Nazi puppet regime referred to as Vichy.

"My mother died after I was born. My father hired a nurse (from Strasbourg, France) to take care of me. The area of Alsace-Lorraine, annexed by Germany in 1871, followed by France's defeat during the France-German War 1875 to 1878, returning to French control after the Germany forced to sign the Treaty of Versailles (1919) after its defeat by the Allies in World War I. It was not pleasant for my nurse to return to the area of Alsace-Lorraine. The French government interned my father, who spoke French and German, twice as an enemy combatant, because of his German ancestry, at Le Vernt. We were fortunate, our landlord knew the internment camp commandant and convinced him to release my father in 1939. My father was again interned after Germany invaded France on May 12. 1940. He was released from the second internment camp in June 1940, as German forces completed their invasion and defeat of the French and British forces. A French protestant agency found a house for my father in Vignaux. My nurse, Lina Gaunher and I joined him in Vignaux a year later (1941). The village we lived in was only two hours from the boundary line between Vichy controlled and German occupied France. My father, nurse and I were refugees during the war. The residents of the tiny southern French village of Vignaux hid us for three years. They probably saved our lives. I will be forever grateful to the people in that tiny village."

After the end of the war in Europe (V-E Day), the Nuremberg Trials were held at Nuremberg, Germany, between November 1945 and October 1946, before an International Military Tribunal, bringing to trial twenty-two "German War Criminals," which included Hermann William Goring (Commander of the Luftwaffe), Rudolf Hess (Nazi Party Deputy) and Albert Speer (German Armaments Minister). Prosecution was assisted by Allied capture of detail German records. Captured records included a written order (part of minutes from a January 20, 1942 during a meeting of representatives of various German War Ministries and Agencies of the SS (Schutzstaffel) and SD (Sicherheitsdienst) at Wannsee, a Berlin suburb) from Adolf Hitler, transmitted by Goering to Reinhardt Heydrich (at the time, Reich's Protector in Prague, Czechoslovakia). The order was entitled "Final Solution of the Jewish Problem." This affected Mely Rahn and her father hiding in Vignaux, France. At this time in the war, it should be pointed out, it appeared Germany was on the verge of winning the war against Russia on the Eastern Front, against British forces in North Africa and German U-boats appeared to be closing the sea lanes around England in the "Battle of the North Atlantic." In 1942, there were approximately 750,000 Jews in France. The minutes of this meeting recorded Heydrich's comments on the Final Solution..."The Jews should now in the course of the Final Solution be brought to the East...for use as labor. In big labor gangs, with separation of sexes, the Jews capable of work are brought to these areas and employed in road building, in which the task undoubtedly a great part will fall through natural diminution. The remnant that finally is able to survive all this, since this is undoubtedly the part with the strongest resistance, must be treated accordingly, since these people, representing a natural selection, are to be regarded as the germ cell of a new Jewish development." In other words, the Jews of Europe were first to be transported to the conquered east, then worked to death, and the few tough ones who survived, put to death.

At the Nuremberg Trials Albert Speer stated..."France was the most important of Nazis controlled industrial countries. After he became Armaments Minister he stopped the shipment of French forced labor workers from the country to increase production at existing French war factories." This did not stop SS forces from rounding up and shipping rounded up Jews to concentrations camps to the east, as part of the "Final Solution."

Rahn..."My father was trained as a mechanical engineer. In Vignaux he farmed to grow our own food. During the war, there was a lot of hunger, because the Germans requisitioned most our food, cows, hogs and horses. By the end of the war, there were no horses anywhere. The German Army used hundreds of thousands of horses, especially on the Eastern Front to move artillery and supply wagons. I never saw any Germans in the village. We were fortunate that the village did not contain any German collabators who probably would have told the German Gestapo my father and I were of Jewish ancestry, due to my mother being Jewish. People in the village protected us. I remember people were starving all over the area. I remember one day seeing a man on a bicycle rapidly peddling away from our neighbor's house, with a wicker basket full of honking geese. Our neighbors lost the geese to someone else who would like the geese for meat. It got so bad that our allowance of meat rationing was only two ounces per person, per week. Although, children did receive a somewhat larger ration. I remember seeing contrails of Allied aircraft above the Village and waving to them. I was warned not to do this because if seen by a German, I would be arrested. We did not suffer any Allied bombing because our village was not a strategic target.

"There was a school in the village, divided into a class for boys and girls. I did not go to the school, although I sometimes looked through the school's window. I read in my father's diary from June 6, 1944..."D-Day, Allies landed." Most of my father's diaries were lost after we came to the United States. In August 1944, my father received a Red Cross message from his brother. He helped us get out of the village in December 1944. One of my uncles, from the United States, was in U.S. Army Intelligence assigned to interrogate captured Germans. He did not serve in active combat, but as an intelligence specialist behind the lines. He located some of our relatives who survived the war in Germany. However, one of my cousins was in the German Army, in a tank (Panzer) battalion, killed on April 27, 1945 (V.E. Day was on May 8, 1945, which stopped the fighting in Europe) by Russian troops while trying to reach American lines and surrender. German troops wanted to surrender to either American or British troops, not to Russian troops, which for them was a death sentence.

"We lived in Vignaux until my father's uncle; a soldier in the American Army brought us to Paris in December 1945. My nurse and I went to Charters, south of Paris, while my father remained in Paris. However, my nurse left that same month, returning home. My father sent me to Switzerland, staying with a foster family there during the winter of 1945 to 1946. Before my sixth birthday, in 1946 we immigrated to the United States. My father remarried and had a second daughter. In the United States, I never forgot the faces I left behind. Over the years, I was always curious about the village, but my father didn't talk much about his wartime experiences. Curiosity compelled me to return while visiting Europe in 1980. That first attempt at reunion never panned out as planned. I brought my two boys with me (11 year old Michael and nine year old Jeffrey) so they might meet some if the people I knew as a child in the small French village. We hiked from the train station to the village, finding it deserted with shuttered buildings. I found my old house, but not knowing where anyone lived, I was too timid to ask questions. I did not have the courage to knock on doors, so we hiked back to the train station. In 2010, I made a second trip to Vignaux, determined to track down familiar faces this time. I printed several of dad's old photos to take with me. I thought the photographs would aid me in the search. Unfortunately, I forgot to pack and take the photographs with me. Again, I did not meet anyone from the village.

"I couldn't bear the thought of never reconnecting with the families who took me in, so in the fall of 2011, I planned a third trip to France. I decided that I was going to go there and knock on doors until someone let me in. I made sure to pack my photos for this trip. The day before my 8 October departure, I searched online for any information on Vignaux. I found the name and address of the village's mayor. I wrote Mayor Claude Zaccariotto a note in French and mailed it off that same day. It was on a whim. I never expected the letter to reach its intended recipient before I arrived. It was just luck that the mail went through. Mayor Zaccariotto responded to my inquiry by organizing a welcome party of villagers who remembered me. I used the opportunity to pass around my father's photos. Well-wishers recognized the pint-sized versions of themselves in the prints. I had pictures of nearly everyone. It was just a really neat experience to go back and remember with this group of people that I hadn't seen in 67 years.

"The village of Vignaux is the stuff of my earliest childhood memories. I still can remember the house I lived in, the garden and fruit trees adjacent to our home, the well that served as a backdrop for several of the old photographs and the 'lavior,' the open-air washhouse for laundry. I had my photograph taken at the same well as when I had a photograph taken as a young child. There was a sign on the gated well, indicating the water is not safe to drink. However, we used the well during our three year stay at the house. At the close of my happy reunion, my newfound friends and I toasted our walk down memory lane with champagne and apple tart.

"I remain in contact with the villagers in Vignaux. We continue to swap stories and photos. I feel deeply indebted to these villagers who took my father in when they could have turned him over to Vichy officials and to the SS for shipment to a concentration camp. The Germans had not yet overrun that part of France when we arrived. German occupation eventually came and life the primitive village changed." On November 11, 1942, the German Army extended its control into southern France, no longer under control by the Vichy government. Rahn..."The French people were starving. They weren't supposed to harbor men like my father (a Jew). The people of Vignaux temporarily lost their undisturbed way of life to the occupying Germans, but they didn't lose their decency. They chose to show kindness to a stranger and I am forever grateful. What impressed me so much it that they took my father in and nobody ever denounced him. They were just wonderful."[20]

---

[20] Mely Rahn, Rapid City, South Dakota, interview, Lt. Col. George A. Larson, USAF (Ret.), February 21, 2012.

Sonja Cody

A Girl Remembers the London Blitz

SONJA Cody, during World War II was a young girl living in England during the "Battle of Britain," marrying a U.S. Army enlisted man, moving to Rapid City, South Dakota after the war. The "Battle of Britain," referred by the Germans as "Luftsch/Acht um England," was a gigantic series of flowing air to air engagements over the English Channel and England between the Royal Air Force (RAF) and German Air Force (GAF or Luftwaffe) in the summer and fall 1940. The aerial combat consisted of four distinctive phases or segments.

> Phase One: 10 July to August 1940. The English Channel battles (in German called "Kamalkampf).
> Phase Two: August 12-23, 1940. The German air assault, called "Eagle Attack" (in German called Adlerangriff) as the GAF attacked RAF airfields along the coastal areas of England.
> Phase Three: 24 August September 1940. The GAF attacked RAF airfields within its aircraft's fuel limits to obtain air superiority to allow a seaborne invasion of England by the German Army, supported by the German Navy across the English Channel.
> Phase Four: September 7, 1940 to May 11, 1941. The GAF bombed English cities, relieving pressure on RAF airbases, aircraft, personnel and pilots.

Sonia Cody... "Before World War II, I went to India with my family. My father though it was important for me to go to a local school, not to a segregated British school, learning on a classroom with Indian children. I learned to speak Hindi and read it as well. Today, I must admit to having forgotten most of that language. After my father received a transfer back to England, I had to learn how to speak and talk correct English. The sea voyage from India took something like six to eight weeks in a convoy because we were at war with Germany after that nation's attack on Poland on September 1, 1939. I was a young girl in England and my experiences during the bombing are very difficult to talk about, especially when remembering the terrible death and destruction all around me. My father transferred to the fighting in North

Africa with the British Army. While my father was in North Africa, our home destroyed by a German bomb. My mother, brother and I fled London to Cambridge, where my mother's brother lived. Unfortunately, for those who had rooms to rent, children were not welcomed and this was active discrimination, no rooms to rent to those with children. My mother finally located a place for us to live, in an antique shop. She did not believe in taking protection inside an air raid shelter when the Germans bombed. When we entered the antique shop, the man asked us kinds 'Are you hungry?' He took us through the shop into the back, into the kitchen, where his wife gave my brother and me a meal we never forgot. He then told us 'Each of you children will have a bedroom of your own.' We stayed with them for two years."

The appearance of German bombers in the skies over London during the daylight hours of September 7, 1940 marked a change in Adolf Hitler's efforts to bring England to its knees. During the previous two months, the GAF attacked RAF airfields and radar stations to destroy them to clear the way for the invasion of England. When the GAF could not defeat the RAF, Hitler had to cancel the invasion. Hitler switched strategic emphasis to that of destroying London and England's major cities to demoralize the civilian population. The pre-war concept of strategic terror bombing was set in motion by the GAF. At 4 p.m., September 7, 1940, 348 German bombers escorted by 617 fighters bombed London until 6 p.m. Two hours later, guided by fires, a second group of bombers attacked until 4:30 a.m. the next morning. The attack was on the radio and in the London papers. It was the start of the "Blitz," which lasted until May 1941, with 57 days of intense and terrifying bombing of England by the GAF. On May 11, 1941, Hitler halted the intense bombing campaign against England, moving GAF units to the east, in preparation for the attack on the Soviet Union.

Cody..."My grandmother lived in London throughout the Blitz and the war. My mother, brother and I took a blackout train from Cambridge to London. Grandmother's flat had holes in the walls from GAF aircraft strafing and bombings. When the strafing started, grandmother laid down on the floor to survive while shells whistled overhead. A family we knew lived down the street from my grandmother. Their four-story home was destroyed by a German bomb, killing the entire family, except for the son who was walking home from school.

"My uncle worked at PWE Radio as the CEO. He spoke fluent German. When the war broke out, he stopped all contacts with Germany and the German people. I always comment to people about my Blitz experiences that other children also suffered throughout Europe, growing up in the middle of the disaster of war. I get very emotional when I talk about this. From my uncle, we found out our home had been bombed right after we left London. My mother stored our furniture in a warehouse. All we had was one suitcase. The warehouse was bombed and destroyed by fire. We thought everything was destroyed in the fire. After the war, my mother received a letter from the government indicating the warehouse owner was profiteering from the misery of others. He sold people's furniture out the back door of the warehouse as items were signed in for storage through the front door. The government apologized for his behavior but that was all. My mother did not get anything.

"My mother had to work to earn enough to provide for us. She worked in a Greek restaurant. We were always cold at night due to the lack of heat caused by coal rationing. She walked home at night and she was cold when she got into bed with me. As a six year old, I was scared and shivering in bed. Mom was an air raid warden. I got to the point where I could listen to the sounds of aircraft flying at night, telling mom if they were German, British or American. After the war, when I was 12 years old, I joined the Junior Red Cross as a volunteer. During the war, we kept moving from one place to the next.

"When living with others, we pooled our ration coupons to stretch our food as far as possible. We received small sacks of food at schools (three eggs, three potatoes, cheese and bacon) to last for a week. It is hard for me now to believe food was so short during the war, even with food supplies arriving from the United States.

"During air raids, we did not go to an air raid shelter. My mother always held me when we were in the home during an air raid attack. When I was outside, looking up, I could see barrage balloons tethered over Cambridge. The balloons were tethered to the ground to keep German aircraft from flying low over the city. At night, when the searchlights probed the sky I thought it was pretty. When I was a school during the day, our playground had an underground air raid shelter, covered with dirt and grass to conceal it from German bombers. If I was in class and the air raid siren went off, we were directed to the air raid shelter. My teacher gave each if us a small piece of Body Rock Hard Candy to suck on to stop children from crying. We still had to do our schoolwork, air raid or not. When the all clear siren sounded, it made me sick from the high pitch sound down to the end stop sound. All the parks had air raid shelters to allow civilians to duck into one when an air raid commenced. For fun, we scrounged rectangular tin pans, climbing to the top of a shelter, sliding down one side as if sliding down a snow-covered hill in winter in South Dakota. I also climbed trees, as all children tend to do, even during the war.

"When the Americans arrived in England, they were young, well dressed and groomed. One afternoon, after school I was outside with my brother, who was bouncing a ball off a brick wall along the sidewalk. An American soldier came up to him and asked, 'Do you have a sister?' My brother turned and pointed toward me. The American looked at me, smiled and said, 'Well, you are too young!' At that time, neither of us thought much about it, since we were too young and not aware of many things adults did.

"On my seventh birthday, my mother saved her ration coupons to make six small jam tarts, one for me and five of my friends. What a treat this was for all of us. Americans, on their bases, positioned a large wood packing crate, with its top open, near the entrance to the base. One their way out of the base, American soldiers dropped in candy, gum and other sweets. When it was full, a U.S. Army truck took it to a town market, handing out the sweets. They averaged a stop in our town square every two months. On Christmas Day, the Americans opened the base and had a great party for the local children with lots of food, entertainment and gifts from Santa Claus.

"One afternoon I was playing with a group of boys when an American soldier walked by and sat down with a British woman on a nearby park bench. They were eating something white with a wood spoon out of a cardboard container. The boys urged me to walk up and ask them what they were eating. The American handed me the container and the wood spoon and told me 'Take this ice cream and play mother to the boys so you all can have a spoon of ice cream.' It tasted very good and there was enough so each of us had one spoon. We just felt safer when the Americans were around. The U.S. Army set up a donut wagon in the town's square to serve coffee and donuts to American servicemen. I walked past the wagon coming home from school and the smell as great. The sergeant in charge soon recognized me every day. One day he came out to the wagon and said, 'I have something for you. Take these donuts home and share with you family. I made them especially for you.' I was not allowed to take anything like this from strangers, but I took the sack, went home, and gave it to my mother. She took me right back to the donut wagon, verifying that I had not asked for them. The sergeant would not take them back. When we were back home they were so good and what a treat. The

Americans always seemed to show unbelievable kindness toward British children and expected nothing in return. This was a story many Americans do not know about.

"My father was an officer assigned to the Black Watch and badly injured in North Africa. The right side of his face was nearly gone. British Army doctors allowed him to come home for three days but he was not very good. When he left the house to go to the hospital, he disappeared, not showing up at the medical facility. The British Army thought he deserted and cut off my mother's limited payments for six months until he wandered into a military base. My mother had to ask for money from relatives, two who were RAF Spitfire pilots. The British Army started my mother's check again when they found him, but we got no back pay. His memory was affected by the head wounds and he did not know where he was. The British Army put him into a hospital in Scotland and he never got better or able to come home. We took a train to see him but he did not recognize us. He passed away after the war from his wounds. He was a brave man and a good person, another war victim, not killed on the battlefield but paid the price for defeating the Nazi military.

"My two uncles flew Spitfires with the RAF. They survived the Battle of Britain. I felt sadness of these two men flying fighters to kill German fighter pilots, each not knowing the other. I wanted to be a pilot when grown up. My uncles took a large cardboard box and turned it into a make believe aircraft cockpit, complete with dials and instruments drawn on the forward inside of the cardboard box, with a cockpit window to lookout. With the war news and deaths of so many pilots, I realized how dangerous flying an aircraft could be.

"We had an aunt living in Liverpool. We stayed with her. The house was near the beach and we could walk along the designated roped off areas. A man was walking his dog when it got off the beach and headed out into the sand near the water, stepping on a land mine, blowing up. The sound was deafening, even where we were staying away from the beach. On another occasion, I was sitting on the porch in a rocking chair when a violent explosion shook the house. A couple walking on the beach did not pay attention to where they were going, strayed off the marked path, stepped on a mine, killing both. Another time, my mother and I were walking on the beach when I spotted a body in the surf, washed up onto the beach, probably from a ship bombed in the English Channel by a German aircraft. My mother quickly covered my eyes, took me off the beach and notified the local air raid warden about the dead body on the beach. They would have to bring in a British Army unit that had a map of the mines on the beach to retrieve the body without setting off the mines. This very dangerous work was necessary to retrieve the body.

"The British government conducted an evacuation to move vulnerable citizens out of urban areas and those near prime military targets for German bombers. It was decided to move as many children as possible into rural areas, away from the death and destruction in the cities. The evacuation was code named 'Operation PIED PIPER.' The British government started the evacuation before the Germans invaded Poland on September 1, 1939 and during the period when British troops were in France, before the disaster at Dunkirk. Trains moved the children if their parents wanted to get them out of the urban areas. During evacuations, actual numbers were hard to define, with estimates of approximately 3,500,000 moved out of the urban areas into the countryside. Interestingly, estimates included 2,000,000 whose parents or they could afford to buy passage out of England to Canada, Australia, South Africa, United States and to the Caribbean Islands. Government officials halted evacuations in September 1944, with London remaining a prohibited return area until June 1945.

"The Battle of Britain actually lasted for five years until VE-Day in Europe when the Germans surrendered. The Germans attacked us to affect our morale and call a stop to the war in the same manner. British night bombing campaign, followed by the American bombing during daylight to stop German production and affect the morale of the German people. If the German bombers could not locate their assigned targets, they would drop their remaining bombs on cities, rather than carry the bombs back to base. The V-1 or Flying Bomb Blitz or Buzz Bomb or Doodlebug as I heard them called was terrifying. After the war, British newspapers printed a recap of the aerial bombs: 2,450 hit London, killing 6,180 and injuring 18,000. It was a terrifying weapon for those of us on the ground. The Doodlebugs fell on London and other cities when their engine stopped. The Germans were trying to hit and knock out PWE Radio outside Cambridge. One afternoon I went to a movie theater to watch cartoons. All of a sudden, the air raid siren went off. They turned off the movie and herded us out of the movie theater. When outside, I started to head for home when the air raid warden yelled, 'Get down!' I looked up to see a Doodlebug barely clear the roof of our house by 10 to 12 feet, slamming into an open area on the other side, exploding with a great roar. The debris was thrown everywhere. Inside our home, there was a steel kitchen shelter table six foot long, three to four feet wide, with steel mesh on either end of the table, and on one side. The steel table and mess were designed to protect those inside the house if they would be unable to get into an air raid shelter.

"The incendiary or fire bombing attacks burned down many homes, businesses, schools, churches and public buildings, with people losing their lives. Even with the war raging around us, we tried to live a normal life. After the war, when I turned 18, my mother was diagnosed with cancer. She had no life of her own during the five years of war and it was hard for parents to take care of children with destruction all around.

"For the British, the local pub was a vital part of daily life, not just a place to go and drink. One night we were in the pub getting something to east when an American soldier walked in, went to the bar, saying 'Drinks for everyone!' My mother commented, 'Some would think the American was throwing his money around and showing off.' In reality, we heard him say to the woman behind the bar, 'I want to share with those in the pub.' I found most Americans were aware of our hardship and did as much as possible to help, although others did not. Most had nowhere to go, away from home for the first time and wanted to be with someone. We became acquainted with an American pilot who also came into the pub, sharing with us whenever possible. We tried to make him feel as at home as possible. The American in his uniform looked neat and he was well groomed. He took off on a combat mission, got his aircraft shot down, crashing as he cross the English Channel. The aircraft burst into flames. The rescue crews could only locate the pilot's wings and not the body. An American enlisted man brought the pilot's wings to my mother, saying, "I want to give these wings to you because you were so good to him!" My mother kept these with her for as long as I remembered.

"My grandfather was a minister who immigrated to the United States and moved to California. During the Battle of Britain, he sent a telegram asking us to come to the United States and live with him in California. The British government set up a program to move women and children by ship to the United States, away from the destruction in England. My mother went to the government agency handling the evacuation of children out of England. We were posted to the list. My brother had been infected with Malaria when in India and just after we qualified to leave England, he had a relapse of Malaria. My brother's relapse made him, and of course, the rest of the family ineligible for the evacuation from England and then the train trip to California. We were very lucky! The transport we were to sail on the, SS City of Benares, leased by the British Children's Overseas Reception Board (CORB) to relocate British children and their mothers away from England. The transport sailed out of Liverpool harbor on September 13, 1940, scheduled to dock at Quebec and Montreal, Canada. The transport assigned to Convoy QB-213, torpedoed on 17 September by a German U-boat. The sinking stopped the evacuation of children out of England. My mother told me my brother saved our lives. Seventy-seven of the 90 children on the transport killed.

"I remember more about the pub in Cambridge. It was near our home, on a corner, with a row of houses on one side and nestled against an electric power sub-station. Those in the pub commented that the sub-station was an ideal target. One night, a huge explosion occurred inside the sub-station, with those inside the pub running out to get away from the German bombing. Firemen responded quickly, putting out the flames. The pub's brick wall kept the fire from spreading inside, destroying the pub. The firemen went into the pub to celebrate their putting out the fire, caused by an electrical short, not a German bomb.

"It was a hard time for everyone. Evacuation of children was by parent's choice only. When we left London, we had to go somewhere. Many people were trying to get out of the urban areas or even leave England. Once into the countryside, the children were sometimes treated badly. Those who took the children in thought no one would find out. Most took good care of them, while others exploited the children. Government officials did not have the manpower or time to check on everyone. For our family, we were more concerned about our neighbors who were suffering alongside us from others who we knew nothing about.

"After the war, I married an American Army enlisted man who was a military driver. We moved to Rapid City, South Dakota. He served in South Vietnam during the fighting there and exposed to Agent Orange. He became very sick and died of cancer. I taught school at the Douglas School System (outside the School Gate, Ellsworth Air Force Base, east of Rapid City) for twenty-six years. I want to tell everyone of the generosity of Americans knows no bounds."[21]

---

[21] Sonja Cody, "A girl remembers the London Blitz," material provided to Lt. Col. George A. Larson, USAF (Ret.) for article submission to the Armourer Militaria Magazine, United Kingdom, June 2010.

Claire Peterson

A Civilian Conservation Corps Recruit Looks Back on a Black Hills Experience

THE Great Depression that gripped the United States for a decade following the stock market crash on October 29, 1929 was years in the making. After the fighting of World War I ended and wartime price controls removed, the U.S. economy ran at full steam. Beginning in the 1920s, inflation and over-production began reducing farm income on states like South Dakota, while the national economy burst ever higher. Much of the prosperity based on speculation, however, and as 1929 neared its end, the stock market crash dropped the U.S. into a long period of economic depression that spread to other nations around the world. Suddenly, millions of Americans became unemployed as the effects of the depression rippled throughout the country. Voters responded to the crisis by ousting Republican Party office holders, electing Franklin D. Roosevelt as President in November 1932. President Roosevelt presented the American people with his "New Deal," a wide array of innovative (at that time) programs designed to tackle the lingering economic depression and revitalize the country. It would take another global confrontation, World War II, for the country to emerge from the hard times that beset the nation in the 1930s.

Among the most popular and successful New Deal programs were those that put unemployed to work on public improvement projects around the country. The Emergency Conservation Act, which passed the U.S. Congress and President Roosevelt, signed on March 31, 1933, led to the creation of the Civilian Conservation Corps (CCC), which gave thousands of unemployed men temporary jobs on projects relating to forest and soil conservation. President Roosevelt called for 250,000 men from families who were on relief to sign up for CCC work on state and federal lands by July 1933.

To help solve the logistical problems of moving thousands of recruits, many who lived in the eastern U.S. were assigned to work in the western United States the Army came in to provide mobilization assistance. The U.S. railroad system and trucks were used to move CCC enlistees to their respective work camp locations. The U.S. Department of Agriculture and Department of Interior were responsible for determining and overseeing work projects, ranging from tree thinning and planting to land terracing and dam building. Through its local and state relief offices, the U.S. Department of Labor recruited and enrolled men for the CCC. Director Robert Fechner, who President Roosevelt appointed on April 5, 1933, headed this unprecedented administrative arrangement. By the end of 1935 there were 2,650 CCC work camps were operating in the United States, housing 505,782 recruits. Counting Army personnel, work-detail supervisors, educators and administrators, the total exceeded 600,000.

The CCC not only provided men with jobs on worthwhile projects but also benefited their families and local economies of those enrolled in the program. Each CCC recruit earned $30.00 per month, with $25.00 sent home. This pumped 72 million dollars into local economies short of cash. Each CCC camp pumped an average of $5,000 per month into the economies of the local communities around the camp by purchasing food and supplies. Local men with experience in manual labor were hired to instruct recruits, many of whom came from cities and never worked outside.

Enrollees in the CCC were required to be between eighteen and twenty-five years old, although later the enlistment age reduced to seventeen. They were unmarried and come from a family on relief. Veterans of any age and marital status who were on relief were allowed to enlist and the age requirement did not apply to local men who served as instructors. In addition to paid work and three meals a day, the CCC provided recruits educational opportunities. An estimated 40,000 men were taught to read and write on their free time, including vocational training, which gave recruits a better chance of obtaining employment after CCC enlistment. The CCC also enrolled 80,000 Native American Indians, 20,000 older men and 250,000 veterans.

At its peak of operations in South Dakota, the CCC maintained 33 camps, with the average of 19 operating. By the time the program ended in 1942, a total of 32,471 personnel had been employed at the camps. Besides the day to day work done on resource conservation projects, the largest CCC project completed in the state was the Lake of Pines Dam, creating Sheridan Lake in the Black Hills, southwest of Rapid City. The CCC had a great economic impact on South Dakota, returning an estimated 6.2 million dollars to workers' families.

Among the hundreds to thousands of recruits joining the CCC, one was Claire Patterson. Patterson..."I was born in Custer County, South Dakota, in a small town called Folsom on March 6, 1923. When

I was very young, my parents moved from Folsom to the southeastern part of South Dakota to a small town called Mission Hill. When I turned seventeen in 1940, I talked to my parents onto letting me join the CCC for three months, although I stayed in the organization longer. My folks had to sign the CCC enrollment papers. I went by train to Sioux Falls and from there I took another train to Rapid City. At Rapid City, I boarded a narrow-gauge railroad line running east and west. The narrow gauge no longer exists, as with many others previously operational in the Black Hills. This railroad was called the Crouch Line. It weaved around hills and obstacles. It went through an area now called Johnson Siding. I eventually ended up in a small town called Mystic. CCC trucks were waiting for one hundred recruits and me. Most of us were from eastern South Dakota. We all enlisted about the same time. We were driven to a CCC side camp called Black Fox, supported by a larger Camp Roubaix.

"At Camp Black Fox, we lived in tents with wood floors. The tents were canvas stretched over a wood framework. They were quite comfortable, especially with the raised wood floors, able to hold eight men. These tents were home for us in the side camp into the middle of October 1940. We arrived in the side camp in March 1940, near the end of the month. It was supported and run by the U.S. Army from Fort Meade, where our officers and camp doctors came from. For the first few days in camp, it was as if we were in Army basic training. We were given Army physicals, shots, clothes and other supplies.

"On the first workday in camp, I chopped wood. Within one week, we were taught how to fight forest fires, especially which tools to use on various type and sizes of fires that might break out in the Black Hills. This amounted to seven to ten days of training, during which we built a fire line around our camp, three to four feet wide. This line was more of a trail than what today is called or referred to as a firebreak. Later, we were driven in trucks into the Black Hills to cut firewood, using two-man cross cut saws and double-edge axes for trimming off the branches of down trees. We received considerable instruction on how to safely swing a double-edged axe, which weighed from three to four pounds. When we carried this axe to and from our work sites, the edges were covered with a rubber protector.

"The people who were training us were recruited from the local area of the Black Hills and some served as our camp foreman. There were usually six foreman assigned to each camp. Each foreman took out his own work detail into the surrounding area. In a CCC camp of two hundred men, work groups consisted of twenty to thirty men.

With a work group of twenty men, only one truck was needed to haul men to the work site and back to camp. On one such detail I was on we had six to eight men assigned to build water troughs for cattle feeding in the forest area during spring, summer and into the early fall.

"We would locate a large dead and dry tree, approximately 30-inches in diameter, cut it down and then cut it into a workable length of six to eight feet. Two of us began working, standing back to back, using a flat bladed axe to flatten one side of the log for stability so it could be positioned on the ground when completed and not roll or move when filled with water. Once this was finished, we rolled the log onto the flat side, allowing us to begin to hollow the top side of the log. Again, we worked back to back, moving from the center to the end of the log, hollowing it out to form a water trough. This process usually took us from two to three days. We constructed these troughs to a natural spring. We would run a metal pipe downhill from the water source to the trough. This would fill up the wooden trough, allowing cattle to drink when grazing on government land. Early in November, we would return to these natural springs, disconnect the metal water feed pipe, and roll the trough over one a small support logs to keep it off the ground and prevent water from freezing inside during the winter, which would crack the wood. For me, this was one of the most interesting projects I worked on while in the CCC.

"One of the other primary projects we worked on was large-scale tree planting in areas that had been burned by fire or damaged due to erosion. In the fall of 1940, I was one of 60 to 70 men assigned to one area, moving in one line, planting young trees. We planted Douglas fir trees, which were not natural to the Black Hills, but were planted as an experiment in reforestation. We used the 'skip' method to plant trees. We each carried a canvas water bag with the top cut off to hold the plantings. The trees came in bundles of one hundred, six to eight-inches tall. The 'skip' method required us to use a three-inch wide axe spade, which we drove into the ground, pulling the handle back to create a space to drop in one of the Douglas fir trees. Withdrawing the axe and using the heel of our boot, we stomped the tree into a vertical position. We then moved onto the next tree spot and repeated the process. We planted Douglas fir trees for approximately two months. With 60 to70 of us planting an average of 500 trees a day, we estimated a total of 35,000 each day.

"On another project, during the winter, we thinned trees to promote strong healthy growth and reduce fire during hot and dry weather. We were taught how to go into a thick stand of trees and use proper techniques to thin them to the correct number of healthy trees per 125 square feet in order to maximize straight growth. We each took an area and moved three steps forward and three steps forward and three steps forward and three steps to either side, with the goal of clearing an area of approximately 125 square feet. No matter what size the tree, if had a crotch, the tree was cut down. If it had a dead spike top, it was cut down. The remaining trees selected not to be cut had to be perfectly healthy. The trees we had to cut down were further cut to manageable lengths, hauled to a centralized location, and stacked in a teepee arrangement, ready to be burned once sufficient snow had fallen in winter to keep the fires from spreading to standing trees. I spent many days in the winter burning these slash fires.

"We stayed at the side camp until October 15, 1940, moving into the main Camp Roubaix for winter operations. At this camp, we lived in permanent wood barracks, with electricity and stoves for heat. Each building was heated by two square metal stoves, with a slide-opening top for wood, one at each end of the barracks. On a rotating basis, two men in each barracks were assigned to keep the fires going at night or when we were in camp during cold weather. There was no running water in the barracks, so if the temperature did fall below freezing, there was no damage. The shower and lavatory were in a separate building and constantly heated by wood stoves. Everything in the camp was fueled by wood.

"We were issued clothes while assigned to the CCC. One set of clothes was similar to the Army's tan uniforms. For the winter and cold weather, we had heavy jackets, shirts and wool caps with pull-down earflaps for protection against high wind chills when working outside. We wore blue denims on work details and when back in camp, we took a shower and changed into tan uniforms. We wore black scarves for ties and stood inspection, followed by the day's retreat ceremony. We then marched into the mess hall; the tan uniform with black scarf was our admission ticket. We had good food while in the CCC.

"Some of those in the camp who either selected or volunteered to be cooks, served for two or three months as assistants under the primary cooks. While we were on cooking detail, we worked three days with two days off, worked two days and three days off, with every other weekend, getting three days off. I eventually ended up as a cook first class in the CCC, referred to as a 45, meaning I received forty five dollars per month. Initially, I was a 36, receiving thirty-six dollars per month. Because we had to send twenty five dollars home each month, money was always in short supply and had to be stretched as far as possible. The CCC did provide for all our basic needs and it was not too difficult for me to stay within the limited funds each month. The raise while I was on cooking detail helped. Almost everyone in the camp was into smoking during their free time, including me. However, we could not afford packaged cigarettes. We would go to the camp store and buy a carton of Bull Durham, containing twenty-four tobacco pouches for one dollar. We then rolled our own cigarettes.

"When I was working as a cook, we served a lot of hamburger, which we ground from hindquarters of beef. The meat was stored in a large walk-in cooler along with other fresh food items requiring refrigeration due to the bulk nature of the food supplies needed to feed all this in the camp three meals a day. The meat was delivered in quarter sections, which we cut to meet that day's requirements. For two meals, lunch and supper, we served mashed potatoes. As one might estimate, we went through large quantities of potatoes every week, which had to be peeled, cleaned, boiled and mashed. Meals served for lunch and supper would include a salad and some type of desert, usually canned fruit or ice cream. We did not have a cafeteria style set up but one that can best be described as family style eating. For family style, all the food would be set on each table. Our mess helpers would set up the table first, with each plate positioned upside down, coffee cup on top of the plate and silverware on either side. The cooks would dish up large bowls of beef, potatoes, gravy, salad and fruit if ice cream was not going to be served from one gallon tin cans, which the mess helpers placed on each table. Every table had to be set up completely before the camp members were allowed to march inside and be fed.

"After all the tables were set with food, the camp's CCC personnel marched into the mess hall with groups of eight assigned to a specific table, taking position behind the long bench on that side of the table. The Mess Sergeant blew his whistle and everyone sat down, turning over their plates and filling them from the food in the bowls. When one of the serving bowls was empty, someone at the table would hold up the empty bowl so one of the mess helpers could retrieve it to the kitchen to be filled and brought back to the table. After a long workday, those in the mess hall had a large appetite. If we served ice cream, no fruit was served; we waited until the tables were cleared by the mess helpers, leaving a spoon for each man on the table. A mess helper pushed a wheeled cart with piles of bowls, passing out bowls to as required to each table, followed by others with ice cream in paper containers, from which two scoops of ice cream were dished into each bowl.

"For breakfast, we had individual boxes of cereal, one set of at each plate, with a bowl on top of the plate and a one pint glass bottle of milk with a cardboard pull-opening cap. Quite often, instead of cold cereal, we served hot oatmeal from large serving bowls on the table, along with a pint glass bottle of milk. Later in mess hall operations, we set up a cafeteria-style serving operation, with aluminum trays and silverware picked up by each person going through the serving line. Mess helpers dished out individual servings of food onto the tray, receiving various food items as the person moved through the serving line. We began this serving style in October 1941. Someone always wanted an extra serving, used to the previous family-style dining we used.

"In 1940, we were tasked to build a forest-fire lookout tower at the top of Flag Mountain. This construction was going to be a difficult project because the closest we could haul building materials up the mountain because of the steep grade was two hundred to three hundred feet. The tower's lower base was built out of local stone, cut on location. The top part of the tower was built of wood. Our CCC engineers designed, and we built a simple but efficient delivery system to move materials the remaining distance up to the top of the mountain. The two to three hundred feet up the steepest part of the grade. Rock cutters prepared the stones to the required size below the final tower site, as determined by the engineers for a specific section of the tower's base. The cut stone was loaded into a metal bucket, two to two and one half feet in diameter. The metal bucket was attached to a steel cable from the work preparation area to the tower's construction location. The bucket could hold up to one hundred pounds. A pulley was attached to a tree at the lower part of the slope and to the framework of the tower above. Two of us were assigned to put on leather harnesses, which each one had a small steel cable leading to a larger cable. At the top of the grade, after placing tension of the harness lines, we walked downhill, pulling the loaded bucket to the top. When there was a stone in the bucket, it would be taken out and the flagman would signal us to walk back up the hill, allowing the empty bucket to go back down the slope to be reloaded. This process was repeated over and over to move the cut stone to the tower construction site, as well as sand and mortar mix to cement the stones. Cement was mixed at the top of the grade. This method was the only efficient way to move the cut stone, sand and mortar to the top of the mountain where the lookout tower was located near what became Deer Field Lake. At that time, the lake was part of the master construction plans for the Black

Hills, with construction of a dam planned later. The lookout tower no longer remains, but it was a project I vividly remember.

"In late October 1941, we moved out of Camp Roubaix to Camp Galena, whose real name under CCC control was Park Creek. Once in camp, our purpose was to dismantle it for closure. By December 1941, employment opportunities in the United States were more plentiful as the country created jobs for war in industries supporting Lend Lease, as well as increased orders for armament of America's military. It was only considered a matter of time before the United States entered the war in Europe against Germany and Italy on the side of England.

"In some areas, such as South Dakota, jobs were still scarce because it took time for the trickle-down effect to get into the state. It was picking up although according to letters from my parents, but slowly. I was assigned to dispose of excess kitchen equipment in the camp and telephoned Fort Meade to determine if they were interested. They agreed to receive the equipment. I still had to maintain meals at the camp, so equipment had to be shipped out in our CCC trucks in phases. I was cooking on Sunday morning December 7, 1941, when the Japanese attacked Pearl Harbor. We had a small portable radio and were listening to music when a flash bulletin came on announcing that the Japanese had attacked. I did not know where Pearl Harbor was located. Someone finally told me it was in Hawaii, in the Pacific, far west of the California coast, and that it was a large United States Navy installation.

"It did not take long for a military detachment from Fort Meade to come into camp to start giving us close order military drill and other instructions. We found out the Army was getting ready to transfer CCC members in the camp into the Army. I grabbed my hat and told them I was done, which was my right under the enlistment terms since I had completed my initial enlistment. I was able to get a ride in one of the remaining CCC trucks to Rapid City. Once there, I was given an honorable discharge for the CCC and a one way train ticket home. I got off the train at Yankton and then various people gave me rides into Mission Hill. This ended my experience with the CCC in South Dakota, a part of my life I remember very well." [22]

---

[22] Beyond Mount Rushmore, "Clair Peterson, a CCC recruit looks back on a Black Hills experience," Lt. Col. George A. Larson, USAF (Ret.), South Dakota Historical Society, Pierre, South Dakota, 2010.

South Dakota National Guard

World War II Pacific Theater of Operations

ON November 25, 1940, units of the South Dakota Army National Guard were called up for a one year training period. The 147th Field Artillery Regiment was the first to go on active duty at Camp Ord, California. After training at Camp Ord, they embarked on November 22, 1941 for duty in the Philippine Islands. They departed Pearl Harbor, Hawaii on November 30, 1941 and were west of Pearl Harbor on December 7, 1941 when the Japanese attacked Pearl Harbor, diverted to Brisbane, Australia. They were in Australia until 1943 and after some reorganizations, they began the long battle of retaking various islands in the Pacific and were part of the U.S. occupation forces entering Japan at the end of the war. The unit was inactivated in January 1946. [23]

World War II European Theater of Operations

On February 10, 1941, the 109th Engineer Regiment, 109th Quartermaster Regiment and the 34th Signal Company were called to active Federal Service and assembled with the 34th Division, which contained the South Dakota units, set sail for Ireland on January 14, 1942. The 1st Battalion, 109th Quartermaster and Company A, 109th Engineers were part of this movement. They participated in the North Africa campaign, the Italian campaign and the occupation of northern Italy after May 1945. The South Dakota troops were discharged in 1945 and 1946 as individuals, not units. [24]

---

[23] Lt. Col George A. Larson, USAF (Ret.), "South Dakota National Guard, World War II Pacific Theater of Operations." Visit to Camp Rapid, The South Dakota National Guard's open house to celebrate the National Guard's 150 years of service," display set up in the Headquarters Lobby, "2012: Countdown to Withdrawal," June 9, 2012.

[24] Lt. Col George A. Larson, USAF (Ret.), "South Dakota National Guard, World War II European Theater of Operations." Visit to Camp Rapid, The South Dakota National Guard's open house to celebrate the National Guard's 150 years of service," display set up in the Headquarters Lobby, "2012: Countdown to Withdrawal," June 9, 2012.

Black Hills Ordnance Depot

Edgemont, South Dakota

BY 1939, Adolf Hitler and a revitalized (illegal according to the terms of the signed Armistice ending World War I), armaments industry started equipping a modern Army, Navy and Air Force while the United States neglected its Armed Forces preparedness and modernization (although small improvements were made in aircraft carrier and aircraft modernization). After the German military conquest of Poland (September 1939) and France (May 1940), the U.S. Congress relented, increased the existing $436,000,000 munitions and rearmament program to $1,442,000,000 in September 1940, $913,000,000 in March 1941 to support Lead Lease commitments to England, $1,339,000 in June 1941 to replace depleted U.S. munitions stock and $3,000,000 in August 1941. The increases came prior to U.S. official entry into World War II. Later, armaments expenditures skyrocketed, making it even more difficult for the U.S. Army Ordnance Department to manage weapons and munitions procurement.

The U.S. Army Ordnance Department was responsible for the design, procurement, distribution and maintenance of ordnance. Its mission was to meet weapons' specifications of the USN; U.S. Army infantry, armored units and Air Force; manufacture or purchase of items produced to meet the services' design specifications; storage, inspection and issue of this material; and maintenance of replacement parts and salvage. However, in the United States prior to 1939, there was practically no civilian armaments industry, with no explosive, shell trading or bag-loading ammunition production facilities. Even with Congressional authorization for funds to expand ordnance/armaments productions, the U.S. Army's six arsenals could only meet five percent of the ordered ordnance production increases. The existing arsenals were Springfield Armory (small arms), Wateruliet Arsenal (cannons), Watertown (gun carriages and forgings), Rock Island (artillery recoil mechanisms, gun carriages and combat vehicles), Frankford (small arms ammunition, explosives and propellants). By 1940, the U.S. Army Ordnance Department managed the operations of 26 storage facilities which increased to 42 after the building of 16 new depots, increasing storage capacity ten times original capacity by 1943.

The U.S. Army Ordnance Department had to build, equip and

bring into production chemical and explosive plants necessary to provide an adequate ammunition industry build a tank arsenal and other facilities for which there were no civilian counterparts and to convert private industry to war production. The process of selecting sites for new ammunition plants was complicated. The U.S. Army Ordnance Department was directed to spread out plants as widely as possible to meet wartime security concerns, which increased freight distances between plants and seaports for loading and shipment to overseas combat theaters of operations. The U.S. Ordnance Department was restricted from building new plants within 200 miles of the nation's borders. It was believed to be necessary to locate new munitions plants away from coasts. The U.S. military wanted to prevent enemy attacks (sea launched commando raids, shelling from enemy surfaced submarines at night, from disguised enemy surface raiders at night which sneaked close to shore for quick shelling prior to withdrawal back into the night's dark ocean, and outside the aircraft launch range of Imperial Japanese aircraft carriers along the U.S. Pacific coast). These threats never were real and did not materialize.

In 1941, the expansion program was in full swing as construction on 25 munitions plants began, with an average time of nine months to complete each plant. The U.S. Army Ordnance Department had to direct construction of new production facilities while dealing with emergency the situation of supplying large stocks of arms and ammunition to England after its military (British Expeditionary Force or BEF) evacuation from Dunkirk, France, under terms the Lend Lease. The transfer of large quantities of weapons and munitions to England reduced the Ordnance Department's stocks by 25 to 30 percent, further reduced by the country's increasing military training and mobilization demands.

Nebraska was one of the states, which met the U.S. Army Ordnance Department's requirements of geographic isolation and security. The Nebraska Ordnance Plant was located one half mile south of Mead, Nebraska and west of Omaha, Nebraska. Construction began in March 1941 as part of initial U.S. armaments industry buildup, completed one year later. The plant was built on 17,000 acres of flat farmland to accommodate four ammunition load lines, an ammonium nitrate plant, warehouses, administration buildings and maintenance shops. During its World War II operations, the Nebraska Ordnance Plant produced three million bombs and sixteen million booster powder artillery and naval shell propellant charges. Additional ordnance plants in the state were built at Grand Island and Sidney, Nebraska.

Nebraska's ordnance plants and others throughout the United States helped the U.S. Army Ordnance Department meet its war munitions production goals. From Pearl Harbor to V-J Day, the U.S. Army Ordnance Department provided the U.S. military and 43 foreign nations military with 47 billion rounds of ammunition, eleven million tons of artillery ammunition, twelve million rifles and carbines, 750,000 artillery pieces and 3,500,000 military vehicles. Lend Lease, beginning in 1941 through October 1945, provided America's allies with more than 46 billion dollars of goods and services, nine billion dollars of which consisted of ordnance and ordnance equipment. Under Lead Lease, 99 percent of this aid was shipped to England, Russia, China and Free French forces. The principal war benefit the U.S. received from Lead Lease aid was the damage inflicted on Germany, Italy and Japan by recipient countries. Lead Lease was an effective method of waging war, saving American lives and shortening the war, saving American lives.

The U.S. Army Ordnance Department managed munitions production, facilities construction and distribution while undergoing a dramatic personnel expansion program. The U.S. Army Ordnance School at Aberdeen, Maryland increased in capacity throughout 1942, reaching 1,500 students. By 1943, the school's capacity leveled off at 5,000 officers, 1,800 officer candidates and 15,000 enlisted trainees. The school's facilities covered over 275 acres, over 300 buildings, teaching 70 different ordnance technical courses. Although U.S. Army Ordnance troops were not officially classified as combat soldiers, all efforts were made to physically and mentally prepare them to work and fight alongside combat troops. By the end of World War II, the U.S. Army Ordnance Department trained more 300,000 military and civilian personnel in all forms of ordnance handling procedures and operations.

The expansion of the U.S. Army Ordnance Department run depots was important to the U.S. and Allied war effort. The first new depots were located in the four corners of the United States to support to U.S. Army troops, which might have to resist an enemy invasion. These depots were Fort Wingate, New Mexico; Umatilla, Oregon; Ravenna, Ohio and Anniston, Alabama. Ammunition was being shipped into all four depots by November 1941. As munitions productions expanded as new ammunition and munitions plants came on line, there was an urgent demand for additional storage space to prevent disruption of supplies to rearm the U.S. military and support expanding demands of Allied forces under Lead Lease. Part of the expansion resulted in the construction of two plateau depot sites, selected because of low moisture storage environment, which minimizes munitions determination. The large South Dakota Black Hills Ordnance Depot was isolated sufficiently to store poisonous gas munitions as well as meeting the plateau criteria.

The U.S. Army conducted the first possibility survey and inspection for an ordnance depot in southwest South Dakota in October 1941 (before the Japanese attack on Pearl Harbor and the United States entry into World War II). The U.S. Army wanted a depot site to store surplus gas ammunition. The U.S. military did not use nerve gas during World War II but was prepared to do so if Germany or Japan did use such agents. The fear was that Germany, if backed into a corner would use nerve gas on advancing Allied troops or worse, in bombs dropped on London. Hitler was unstable and the early intelligence, kept from the American public, that Germany had created slave labor or concentration camps to eliminate populations from subjugated areas. It was not until later that intelligence collected indicating the Germans were using concentration camps as "death camps." Since Germany used mustard gas during World War I trench warfare, there was the possibility that they would use even more deadly nerve agents in World War II. Fortunately and somehow, the German General Staff convinced Hitler not to use these weapons.

To store these nasty weapons, it was necessary for a special type of storage facility to be located, built and operated in a sparsely populated area. The U.S. Army's requirements were fully met in southwest South Dakota, because the closest rail line (passenger/freight station at Provo) was two miles from the proposed depot site, with a population of only twelve. The city of Edgemont was located eight miles from the proposed depot, although its population was approximately 1,000. There also were no other populated settlements within 35 miles, which counter-acted Edgemont's population. The Black Hills Ordnance Depot became a major World War II engineering and construction project of the U.S. Army ordnance Department's munitions storage and distribution expansion to support the U.S. military and its Allies in fighting a global war. The Black Hills Ordnance Depot name ignored Edgemont residents' suggestion it be called the Edgemont Ordnance Depot. After the depot was completed and operations started, those working at the sprawling complex nicknamed the area as "Igloo," because of the hundreds of concrete, igloo constructed, earth covered munitions storage bunkers. The igloo bunkers had been built by the U.S. Army since 1926, storing all types of munitions.

J.A. Terteling and Sons Construction Company, an Idaho based company, which built other U.S. army ammunition depots and airfields after the U.S. entered World War II, won the contract for building the depot. The contract was large enough that J.A. Terteling and Sons Construction Company subcontracted the electrical distribution system, heating plant, administration buildings, railroad distribution and shipping network along with other components to additional construction companies to meet the U.S. Army completion deadline (timetable). Construction work was delayed because of heavy April and May rains in 1942, which turned everything in the construction area into a sea of deep mud. Construction contracts immediately affected local communities around the depot as construction companies advertised and hired every able bodied worker to build the depot, also bringing in contract workers from outside the area, including Native American Indians from nearby reservations. Instantly, a housing shortage developed, with a housing boom starting in Provo and Edgemont, suddenly pumping money in the area's depressed economy. This part of South Dakota had suffered greatly from the U.S. "Great Depression" of the 1930s. What the New Deal programs had been unable to do, the run up to World War II and rearming of the U.S. military pulled America out of the lasting effects of the depression, the 1940's version of a Federal stimulus package.

Prior to start of construction on the depot, administrative control was under the U.S. Army Ordnance Department. The depot was to serve as a reserve storage and distribution facility for Ogden, Utah; Rock Island, Illinois; Rossford and Stockton, California depots in the receiving, storing and issuing of all categories of ammunition and general ordnance supplies. By September 1943, J.A. Terteling and Sons Construction Company laid off several thousand construction workings as building activity declined. At the same time, announcements were posted for permanent workers, including women, for permanent staff positions at the depot. The depot's payroll had a significant economic impact of the area's economy until it closed in 1967. By December 1943, the majority of the depot's buildings were complete. Construction workers built 802 ordnance igloos, laid out in nine blocks of 88 to 90, adjacent to the depot's in house rail line. Each block was serviced by a platform type unloading and loading platform, similar to railroad depots throughout the U.S. western small towns. The igloos were built at or on ground level, with a concrete slab floor, end wall and arched roof, 30 feet wide and 60 to 100 feet long. The igloo was covered with dirt except at the front entrance where a concrete slab 30 feet wide by 15 feet high was fitted with a heavy door and a small entry concrete slab to reduce mud and dirt from being tracked into the igloo. The above ground storage area was equipped with personal protective shelters, referred to as "foxholes," a heavy concrete rectangular shaped building, designed with an open door an enclosed interior to protect workers from accidental exploding munitions if one or more igloos detonated. The storage area contained a packing, shipping and receiving buildings. Twelve munitions and one black powder magazine were built with concrete slab floors, brick walls and wood windows, doors and roofs. The wood roofs were designed that in case of an accident, any explosion blew upward. The depot's warehouses were large buildings with concrete floors, rows of heavy wood vertical roof support posts and trusses, 400 to 500 feet wide, 800 to 1,000 feet long. The warehouses stored everything the Army used except food, explosive or ammunition.

The depot's administration area consisted of many buildings, guardhouse and dispensary. The utilities area consisted of railway locomotive and machine shops, and a central heating plant complex. The bundle ammunition packing and shipping area consisted of a field office and four ammunition-packing buildings. At the depot site, the ammunition crating process sealed 75mm and 105mm artillery shells into fiber cases, three to a wood case, which was called a "clover leaf," because of the case's end pattern. The depot's labor force in the crating center was predominately women. There was one accident when phosphorous shells caught fire and resulted in flares going up all day into the evening. The lumber storage area had a fully equipped carpenter's shop, at which workers custom made most the of the depot's furniture, munitions crates and repaired all types of items made of wood. The housing area contained 105 single, five double and two-bachelor officer quarters, 18 enlisted quarters, six barracks and three apartments. Due to its isolation, civilian housing provided eleven single dormitories and 17 apartments, eighty five single, forty duplex, nineteen four plex and 50 six plex married housing units. Coming off the effects of the "Great Depression," these modern housing units were considered a luxury for those who claimed jobs at the depot, as well as the wartime paychecks that went along with the jobs. For this part of southwest South Dakota, the depot provided great economic security and valuable wartime support for the U.S. military and Allied forces fighting around the world.

The depot was serviced by 158 miles of hard surfaced roads, 38 miles of railroad track age and all the necessary utilities to support the sprawling complex and housing area. It was not until the middle of

1943 that the hospital and housing areas were completed. Most of the depot's buildings were considered temporary structures, designed to last five to seven years, primary because of the estimated length of the war. However, it was restrictions placed by the Army on the type of building materials, costs, construction techniques and types of construction, which limited the building's lifespan. Most of the sixteen U.S. Army Ordnance Department depots built during World War II did not normally include on site housing. However, the extreme isolated location of the Black Hills Ordnance Depot made housing, schoolrooms, medical, commissary and post exchange an absolute necessity. Thousands of people worked, lived, children attended school and shopped on the depot. During World War II, it was a large, self-sustaining community that operated around the clock, seven days a week, support America's war effort. Without their sacrifices, the U.S. military and its Allies would have been hard pressed to maintain an ever-increasing demand for munitions.

The first ammunition shipment arrived at the depot on November 4, 1942. The depot's receiving, processing and shipping activity peaked in January-to-March 1943, when 3,194 rail freight cars (loaded with ordnance) were handled. The workload was heavy and the wartime shipping timetables were tight, with 12 hour, seven day weeks standard. Consequently, work shifts severely disrupted workers' family life, especially since by this time, 46 percent of the depot's work force was women. It was the war and Americans work hard, greatly sacrificing their lives to bring an end to the was as soon as possible. These workers and families read the daily newspaper's headlines and stores of rising U.S. casualties. This was especially true in the Pacific, with each amphibious invasion the climbing deaths and wounded, increasing the closer U.S. forces came to the Japanese home islands. Even with a large female work force at the depot, war workers were also in short supply. The U.S. Army attempted to ease the labor shortage by using Italian POWs at the depot, beginning in December 1943. Under the rules of the Geneva Convention and U.S. Army guidelines on the use of POW labor, Italian POWs, as well as cleared German POWs (non-hardcore Nazis POWs). German POWs could volunteer to work in non-direct, war-related civilian and government labor. They worked in civilian supply, clerk assistance, depot cleaning (gloried name for garbage collection, lawn mowing, weed cutting, tree trimming and picking up wood shipping crates for reuse) and vehicle maintenance in the motor pool. Italian POW status changed after Italy surrendered to the Allies after the southern half of the country was under Allied control (south of Rome). The Italian government switched to the side of the Allies against Germany in the summer of 1944. German forces controlled the northern one-half of Italy and fought tenaciously for every yard of ground. At this time, Italian POWs living in secure barracks received similar status to that of U.S. Army Service troops, becoming part of the newly formed and created Italian Service Units. These Italian personnel could now work in the majority of the depot's munitions operations, especially heavy work of unloading and loading rail freight cars.

After V-J Day, the depot's operational levels and intensity declined. The depot's primary function switched to receiving and storing surplus ammunition then currently in the production and distribution pipeline. The depot also began disposal of excess war material, equipment and supplies; along with storing, renovating and maintaining retained military equipment. From 1945 to 1950, the depot's civilian labor force reduced to 700, affecting the economies of surrounding communities, reducing government purchases, spending in stores, bars and restaurants with reduced incomes from rental housing. This result in a double impact to the areas because in the southwest part of the state, finding jobs for those released from the depot and returning servicemen was nearly impossible. Many depot women workers lost their wartime well-paying jobs, especially with the general attitude they should go back to being mothers and housewives, not in the full time work force of a post-war economy. The end of the war in the Pacific required an immense readjustment from all-out war economy to a peacetime consumer economy. The downward spiral of depot employment and economic influence was temporarily stopped after the Communist North Korea Army invaded South Korea on June 25, 1950. The level of activity increased again after the Communist Chinese Army sent troops into North Korea to stop the total subjugation of North Korea. This resulted in a new war as Chinese troops drove South Korean, U.S. and United Nations troops south of the 38th Parallel, capturing Seoul for the second time in the war. The depot's work force increased to 1,300, returning to 700 after the armistice was signed in July 1953, ending the fighting but not ending the war between North and South Korea, maintaining the 38th Parallel as the dividing line between the two Koreas. The depot's function returned to receiving and storing surplus munitions.

Regardless of the depot's fluctuating employment levels, the ordnance facility remained an important boost to economies of Edgemont and Provo, pumping in needed dollars. After the Korean War armistice, area city officials began hearing repeated U.S. Army proposals that the depot would close. The U.S. Army conducted utilization studies on the depot's military support functions in the early 1960s, in light of "Cold War" realities with the Soviet Union. Edgemont and Provo business leaders, community groups and city officials did everything possible to convince the Army of the importance of the depot's continued operations to the area economy and support to future U.S. military operations. On April 24, 1964, the Secretary of Defense announced the depot would go through a phased drawn down over a three year period, closing on June 30, 1967.

During its operations from 1943 to 1967, the Army stored two types of dangerous nerve agents at the depot, which created many problems for area residents once the depot closed. The first nerve gas agent stored was the 1930 to 1940 manufactured "G" nerve gas agent, which was extremely violate, turning from a liquid to gas at a temperature of 72 degrees. The second nerve gas agent was the "V" nerve gas manufactured during the 1950s, based on intelligence information that the Soviet Army had produced and stockpiled a similar gas agent, with the assistance of captured German scientists. This nerve agent was an oily liquid, which made it even more dangerous. Further complicating the storage of these two dangerous nervous gas agents was the onsite destruction of tens of thousands of leaking mustard gas bombs and shells at the depot. The following sounds incredible today under tight EPA rules, regulations and guidelines. Depot personnel dug open slit trenches, unlined to prevent chemical seepage into ground water, open to the air and windblown chemical vapors, which produced airborne contamination, to burn the leaking mustard gas bombs and shells. Leaking weapons were laid in the bottom of the trenches, carefully stacked, diesel fuel poured into the trench until covering the bombs and shells, with a flare gun firing an flare into the trench to set the diesel fuel a blaze. The Army determined this was an acceptable procedure at the time and necessary due to the large numbers of leaking mustard gas weapons in storage and limited availability of on site, high-temperature, enclosed kilns to destroy the mustard gas weapons. High-temperature kilns not only destroyed the mustard gas agents, the casings but also the toxic vapors so only harmless gas released at the top of the kiln's smoke stack. This is the acceptable destruction procedure for these toxic gas agents. There were exposed ground areas near the open burning pits, on top of a hill overlooking the igloos where no vegetation grew. A U.S. Army report stated "The depot's chemical and conventional ammunition was removed or destroyed prior to the Federal government's selling most of the depot's land and facilities to the

City of Edgemont, with the remaining area transferred to the U.S. Forest Service. Edgemont, in turn, sold the land to private individuals and companies. Cattle and hog feeding operations were conducted on open grass areas, along with light manufacturing. With the identification of contamination, these activities were stopped.

A 1976 U.S. Army report indicated "An initial decontamination was conducted in 1966, before the depot closed, with ground areas and structures inspected, tested, washed and rinsed. Possible contaminated areas within the bomb disposal and burning grounds were surfaced cleaned and all areas decontaminated to the most reasonable possible extent." Edgemont city officials believed in 1973 that the Army's efforts were not sufficient and wanted additional testing concerning possible ground water contamination. With upgraded EPA guidelines of that time, additional cleanup was necessary. Consequently, because of concerns and urgings of area resident, the U.S. Army Corps of Engineers, beginning in June 1995, tested surface water and soil areas to determine if any contaminates remained. The author and his son went through all the areas of the depot in March 1994, taking photographs, recording conditions of the depot for this story, and viewed the contaminated areas, burning pits, storage igloos, remaining World War II buildings. This was one of the last open access allowed to the former munitions storage facility. In 1995, if any contaminates were identified and seeping off the depot into surrounding land areas, the areas had to be cleaned. Although the Federal government responsible Pentagon officials reported that no nuclear weapons were handled, processed or stored at the depot, radiation testing was added to the depot's cleanup checklist. U.S. Navy personnel conducted a test of one igloo, setting off a large conventional demolition explosive inside to determine if it could withstand a low-level (partial) nuclear detonation. Post-test detonation inspections determined the former depot's igloos could safely store conventional but not nuclear munitions. Concern over possible radiation contamination surfaced after a local resident found a radioactive chemical near one igloo in the munitions handling area. U.S. Army report stated... "Charcoal was one of the materials used for packing around conventional munitions shipped out of the depot and it was natural, low-level occurring radiation, not from any nuclear munitions."

During testing, crews used special equipment to avoid drilling into undetected buried ordnance to prevent explosions and release of contaminates into the ground. Additional cleanup at the depot was conducted in two phases. Phase one consisted of conventional ordnance and explosive waste materials. Phase two consisted of hazardous and toxic wastes. Explosive waste materials consisted of mustard gas residue. Depot cleanup moved to the track range and burning grounds where defective ordnance had been destroyed. Destruction of various types of ordnance was conducted at a time when there were not adequate safeguards for protecting the surrounding environment. After World War II, destruction of unused ordnance in the Pacific Theater of Operations was similar, with equipment and munitions frequently dumped into the Pacific Ocean. The author talked to Seabees who were on Tinian after the end of World War II, used bulldozers to push unrepairable B-29s, munitions, 55 gallon fuel drums and metal Quonset huts into the waters around the island.

U.S. Army Corps of Engineers continued cleanup of remaining bombs and ammunition identified and recovered in 1996, with removal of identified chemical weapons or waste materials in 1997. Given the large area of the depot, removal of identified contaminates was a long-term and expensive process.

The Black Hills Ordnance Depot was an importance and significant part of South Dakota's war and national defense efforts from May 1942 through June 1967. With the shift in munitions types used and modernization of the U.S. Armed Forces, the U.S. Army Ordnance Department indicated the depot's lifespan had been reached. Since 1967, the depot became a western ghost town. However, rows of concrete igloos remain, easily visible miles from Edgemont, south of Highway 18. The depot served America's war needs, but with lasting environmental impacts, although not an isolated EPA identified "Super Fund" cleanup site.[25]

---

[25] Lt. Col. George A. Larson, USAF (Ret.), "South Dakota munitions and support during World War II." 2003 award winner as best paper and presentation, 11th annual West River History Conference, October 9-11, 2003, Rapid City, South Dakota.

John Burnfin

Fire Chief, U.S. Naval Air Station, Ford Island, Pearl Harbor, Hawaii, December 7, 1941

ON Sunday, December 7, 1941, referred to as the "Day of Infamy" in U.S. history, is more than the results and effects of the attack by Japanese against the U.S. Navy Pearl Harbor Naval Base and supporting Army facilities. At this time, John Burnfin was Fire Chief, U.S. Naval Air Station, Ford Island, Pearl Harbor, Hawaii. His wife Dakota, nicknamed Coty, was the manager of a beauty shop on Ford Island. She offers a personal perspective on the Japanese attack. Even at 92 years of age (at the time of her interview in 2005), her memory was still sharp. She resides in Belle Fourche, South Dakota (northwest of Rapid City and north of I-90). During her story of the Japanese attack, she refers to her husband as Bernie.

Coty... "On December 5, 1941, we saw the whole Pacific Fleet come into Pearl Harbor. The battleships tied up around our part of the island." The Japanese were hoping to catch the U.S. Navy's Pacific Fleet aircraft carriers as well as the battleships along with their supporting auxiliaries anchored in Pearl Harbor. The Japanese assigned attack waves one and two to attacks and sink these targets. Fortunately, for the U.S. Pacific Fleet, the aircraft carriers and escorts were not in the harbor. Task Force 8 (TF8) had delivered USMC Scout Bomber Squadron 231 to Midway Island and was still out to sea, on its return to Pearl Harbor. The task force consisted of aircraft carrier Lexington; heavy cruisers Astoria, Chicago and Portland; destroyers Dayton, Flasser, Lamson, Mahan and Porter. Task Force 12 (TF12) had delivered USMC Dive-Bomber Squadron 221 to Midway island and they were still out to sea, returning to Pearl Harbor by a separate route than TF8 so as not to provide the Japanese concentrated targets because of increase possibility of imminent hostilities with the Empire of Japan. TF12 consisted of the aircraft carrier Enterprise; heavy cruisers Indianapolis, Northhampton and Salt Lake; destroyers Balach, Benham, Craven, Ellet, Fanning, Gurdley, MacCall and Maury, supported by five converted destroyer/minesweepers. On the return to Pearl Harbor the heavy cruiser Indianapolis broke off from TF12, accompanied by the five destroyer/minesweepers to conduct amphibious bombardment training off Johnston Island. The Third Pacific Fleet aircraft carrier, Saratoga, was at the U.S. Naval Base at San Diego, California.

Other Pacific Fleet warships were outside Pearl Harbor. The heavy cruiser Minneapolis and four destroyer/minesweepers patrolled south of Oahu. The heavy cruiser Pensacola was escorting the tender Niagara, U.S. Navy transport Charmont and Phoenix, two Army transports and three-freighters to Manila, Philippines. After receiving a radio message on the Japanese attack on Pearl Harbor the convoy diverted to anchorage at Suva, Fiji. The heavy cruiser Louisville was escorting transports Hugh L. Scott and President Coolidge outbound from Manila, Philippines. Additional Pacific Fleet warships were away from Hawaiian waters. The battleship Colorado was a Bremerton Navy Yard, Puget Sound for overhaul. Six destroyers and five submarines were at Mare Island Navy Yard. One light cruiser, three World War I era four-stack destroyers and four submarines were at San Diego, California. The submarine Gar was patrolling off Mexico's Pacific coast. The light cruiser Trenton was patrolling of the Panama Canal's Pacific coast entrance. The light cruiser Richmond was patrolling off Peru's Pacific coast. Numerous fleet submarines were absent from Pearl Harbor, either training or on active patrol. Tambor and Triton were patrolling off Wake Island. Trout patrolled the area around Midway Island. Thresher was training, conducting simulated torpedo attack runs against the destroyer Litchfield, south of Oahu. Plunger, Pollaoka and Pompano were conducting training northeast of Oahu.

This left 104 ships in Pearl Harbor the morning of December 7, 1941, when Japanese carrier aircraft attacked the harbor and surrounding Army installations: eight battleships, nine cruisers, 31 destroyers, five submarines, 24 mine ships and 27 various auxiliaries. Coty..."Bernie said it was a rare occurrence, as the whole Pacific Fleet hardly ever came in at the same time. The weekend before, we had an alert. We had gone on a drive around the island of Oahu and we mentioned that they had really put security on everything. Even bridges around the island had guards on them."

On November 27, 1941, a war warning was sent to U.S. Army Major General Walter Short, Commander U.S. Army Hawaiian Department and U.S. Navy Admiral Husband E. Kimmel, Commander U.S. Naval Forces Pearl Harbor. It stated..."to undertake such reconnaissance and other measures you deem necessary...execute an appropriate defense deployment preparatory to carrying out the tasks assigned in WPL-46." U.S. Joint Navy Basic War Plan 46, drafted on May 26, 1941, referred to as "Rainbow 5," defined U.S. and British military operations if a general war broke out and America entered the conflict, with primary emphasis on defeating Germany and Italy. In the Pacific, WPL-46 stated the U.S. Navy was tasked to support Allied operations for the defense of the Malay Barrier by diverting Japanese naval forces to respond to attacks on the Marshall Islands. (The U.S. Navy attacked the Marshall Islands on February 1, 1942) The U.S. Navy was tasked to conduct raids on sea communications and positions of Japanese forces, support British Navy forces south of the Equator and west to Longitude 155 degrees east and prepare to capture the Marshall and Caroline Islands.

Coty..."Bernie's friend, Heine, was assigned to the Utah and on the weekend of December 7, 1941, he was staying with us. We all were sleeping on Sunday morning when the Japanese began the attack against Pearl Harbor."

Prior to this attack, the Japanese attack force was approaching 230 miles from the north and east of Pearl Harbor. The attack force consisted of aircraft carriers Akagu, Kaga, Hiryu, Skokaku, Soryu and Ziukaku; battleships Hiei and Kirishama; cruisers Chikuma and tone; destroyers Akigumo, Arare, Hamakaze, Isokaze, Kagero, Kasumi, Shiranuhi, Tanikaze and Urakaze. The six Japanese carriers launched 43 Mitsubishi AGM Zero-Sens (common name, "Zero" or Zeke), 51 Aichi D3A dive-bombers and 89 Nakajima B5N Kate dive-bombers (40 armed with torpedoes). This provided an air attack force of 183 aircraft in the first wave against Pearl Harbor. The initial Japanese air attack was against Kaneohe Air Station at 7:48 a.m. Ford Island and Hickam airfield were attacked at 7:55 a.m.

Coty..."I just put on a house coast over my pajamas. Bernie jumped into his uniform and took off for the fire station. I watched him go. The Japanese planes were diving and strafing him, with some of the bullets going between his legs into the truck's right seat. The planes were so low I could see the pilot and Rising Sun red insignia painted on the underside of the wings. By this time Heine was up and insisting we go to the playground of the school that was just in front of our quarters. All of the other families were gathered there. We just walked around. Heine had a hold of my arm and afterwards my arm was black and blue from his heavy clutch. Believe me, it wasn't easy to just keep moving in that small space, with bombs, bullets and explosions going on around us! We weren't their targets, but all the ships around Ford Island were the Japanese targets. The battleship Arizona was moored behind us, with the battleships Oklahoma and West Virginia beside our location on Ford Island. Debris was flying everywhere. The noise was horrendous. I don't know how long it lasted, but Heinie had a hard time keeping me in the open. One's instinct is to get under cover. I really wanted to get somewhere else, but Heinie knew the meaning of survival during the attack, get away from the buildings were flying debris was worse. When the first wave ended, we were taken to the Admiral's quarters, which had a basement."

The second Japanese attack wave consisted of 36 Zeros, 81 Vals and 54 Kates. These 171 aircraft continued the air attack on Pearl Harbor, beginning at 8:40 a.m., completed by 9:55 a.m. Coty..."Heine went back to his ship, the Utah, to find it sunk." At this time in its Navy duty with the Pacific Fleet, the Utah was classified as a target ship, without defensive armament. The Utah was hit by two torpedoes, listed and rolled over, a total loss by 8:12 a.m. The Utah was never salvaged, remains where it sank, a permanent underwater memorial in Pearl Harbor. Coty..."During the Japanese second attack on Pearl Harbor, we sat on the floor of the basement in the Admiral's house, all around the exterior walls. The racket was terrible and the walls shuddered and shook. The dead and wounded were brought lying face down on stretchers. I kept looking for Bernie's feet. I still had slippers on. We were kept on the Admiral's basement until the second wave of bombing was through. All of the families spent the night in bachelors officer quarters and were given breakfast the next morning. I don't remember just when I got back to our quarters, or when Bernie got there, but everything looked so drab and eerie. The smoke and soot were so thick. Our yard was covered with white hats and various parts of uniforms hanging from the trees, with debris everywhere."

The Japanese attack against Pearl Harbor destroyed 188 aircraft with 18 ships sunk or damaged. The USS Arizona (BB-39) took one torpedo hit forward, one bomb penetrating the forward magazine. The resulting explosion caused extensive damage around it as well as the release of oil from the ruptured fuel bunkers, setting the surrounding water on fire. The battleship was not salvaged, written off as a complete loss, with only the superstructure removed. After the war, it was dedicated as a permanent memorial to honor those who dies on the ship and remained entombed below the water line or killed during the attack. The USS California (BB-44) took two torpedo and two bomb hits. It was refloated on March 24, 1942, repaired sufficiently to sail under its own power to Bremerton Navy Yard for a complete overhaul, modernization and refitting, eventually returning to combat duty with the Pacific Fleet. The USS Maryland (BB-46) was protected by the Oklahoma, but was hit by one fragmentation and one 16-inch armor-piercing bomb. It was repaired to sea worthy condition, sailing to Bremerton Navy Yard of repairs, modernization, returning to the Pacific Fleet. It was the first Pearl Harbor damaged battleship to return to Pacific combat duty. The USS Nevada (BB-36) was moored astern of the Arizona. It took one torpedo hit forward and three bomb hits. The crew was able to get the ship underway, but as it headed toward the harbor's entrance, it came under heavy air attack, with two bombs hitting the ship, forcing beaching at Waipo Point, south of Ford Island. The USS Oklahoma (BB-37) took five torpedo hits, causing it to roll over, bottom up. The battleship was righted in March 1943 to clear the berthing area but not repaired. After the war, the useless hulk was sold for scrap and towed to the United States and cutting torches. The USS Pennsylvania (BB-38) was in dry dock with two other ships. The battleship took one bomb hit, repaired, departed dry dock on 12 December, sailing to Bremerton Navy Yard for final repairs, modernization, returning to the Pacific Fleet. The USS Tennessee (BB-43) was moored inboard of West Virginia, taking two bomb hits. By 20 December, the battleship was repaired sufficiently to sail to Bremerton Navy Yard for extensive repairs, modernization, returning to the Pacific Fleet. The USS Utah took two torpedo hits, capsizing. It remains where sunk. The USS West Virginia (BB-48) was struck by seven torpedoes on the portside and two bomb hits. It sank upright to the bottom of the harbor. On May 19, 1942, it was refloated, repaired, sailed to Bremerton Nay yard for further repairs, modernization, returning to the Pacific Fleet. The cruisers Helena, Honolulu and Raleigh were repaired, returning to duty with the Pacific Fleet. The destroyers Cassin and Dune were written off as unrepairable, the Shaw repaired, returning to combat duty with the Pacific Fleet.

 The Japanese lost 29 aircraft and five two-man midget submarines. One major tactical error was that the Admiral Nagumo cancelled the planned third attack wave, leaving the dry docks, submarines and facilities, and oil/fuel storage farms intact. This allowed ships to be repaired at Pearl Harbor without returning to the U.S. West Coast, able to refuel and operate from Pearl Harbor. The Pacific Fleet submarines were able to sortie, starting unrestricted attacks against Japanese merchantmen, especially oil tankers, and warships. Interestingly, it was unrestricted German U-boat sinkings in the Atlantic, which nearly brought the U.S. into a declared war against Germany and its ally Italy. At the start of the war U.S. submarine commanders were frustrated from torpedo failures for one year, until improved detonators corrected the detonation malfunctions. Warships entering Pearl Harbor were refueled and sortied against the Japanese fleet, but without tanker support. The timing of the third attack wave might have caught the returning U.S. carriers entering Pearl Harbor, extending the Imperial Japanese Naval supremacy in the Pacific, but not changing the eventual outcome once America's industrial base built up to produce the warships necessary to fight back across the expanse of the Pacific to the Japanese home islands.

Coty..."Bernie had been fighting fires during the two attacks. The water main to Ford Island was cut when the forward magazine of the Arizona detonated. Bernie improvised and pumped water out of the harbor. I'll never know how he got through it. He fought fires during the bombing and the rest of the day. Bernie said the only wound he got from the Japanese attack was a blister on his heel from wearing house slippers. Bernie took me to view a dead Japanese carrier pilot in our back yard. He had no shoes on, just gray socks. His plane was scattered across the airstrip." Fay Carbone, Coty's sister, added to her sister's story about the Japanese attack on Pearl Harbor. At the time of the attack she had no idea of the fate of her sister. Fay..."I was 14 years old and it seems mom, dad and I were driving back from a visit to a friend at their ranch, when we heard of the Japanese attack on Pearl Harbor. The next day we huddled around our radio to listen to President Franklin D. Roosevelt as he spoke before a joint session of Congress." President Roosevelt... "Yesterday, December 7, 1941, a date which will live in infamy, the naval and air forces of the Empire of Japan...?" Fay..."Mom and dad worried constantly and slept very little, wondering if Coty and Bernie would inquire about them. What a great day it was when that post card came with Coty's signature and the box checked... 'We are OK.' That news went around town fast."

Coty..."I had washed clothes and hung them on the line on Saturday after I came home from work. The sailors who had been lucky enough to swim away from their ships, through oil, somehow reached our yard. I used the clothes to wipe the oil from their bodies. Our quarters were still standing, but pretty much a mess inside from shrapnel and fire. Bomb concussions had dumped everything out of the cupboards and off the shelves. We expected another attack at any time. Bernie, of course, had to stay at the fire station and I stayed alone in our quarters. It was really frightening. Bernie was able to come to our quarters for a few minutes each day. He helped me put up blackout curtains over the windows. There was a complete blackout throughout the islands and we were without water and electricity. The nights alone were scary. There was a lot of activity in the harbor. Those on shore would shout out 'ship alone, identify yourself and your destination!' These cries went on throughout the night. I slept in my clothes for the first week after the bombing. Several times a day, sailors would come to my door and tell me to stay inside, as they had the unfortunate duty of retrieving bodies, which washed ashore from the ships.

"The battleship Arizona was right behind our quarters. The battleships Oklahoma and West Virginia were right along the bank, next to our backyard. I got so I knew when they came to my door what they were going to do. They wore masks and carried litters. The stench of death was almost unbearable. If I dared to look out the window, I would see one or two bodies floating along or lodged against the shoreline near our quarters, always bloated, with their uniforms bursting at the seams. Things finally settled down and by Christmas, we had electricity restored but still were under strict back out conditions. I could finally let my family on the mainland know we were OK. A printed post card was made available where we could mark OK or wounded and sign it. My folks got it two weeks after the Pearl Harbor attack. On Christmas day, Bernie, Heine and several of Bernie's fire crew came to our quarters. I served canned ham and someone brought a gallon of whiskey, so we got around a circle, ate ham, drank whiskey and sang Christmas carols. That, I will never forget.

"Then the evacuation of dependents started. Pregnant women and women with children were sent back to the U.S. West Coast ports by passenger ship. On December 30, 1941, Bernie took me to my ship, the USS Garfield for passage to San Francisco. However, we remained in port for three days. The passenger capacity of the Garfield was 90, but it was increased to 180. Every little nook and cranny had a cot in it. I was assigned a cot in the ship lounge along with many others. Six destroyers escorted us out of Pearl Harbor with one leading the transport, two on either side, and one trailing the convoy. We sailed under strict wartime conditions, zigzagging all the way, with the destroyer escorts regularly changing positions. We had many 'General Alarm' during which everyone rushed to their lifeboat station. We didn't know if it was for real or practice but believe me, we were all there! We wore life jackets at all times, except when sleeping. Even then, it was within quick reach. The normal five-day crossing took 10 days. After arriving in San Francisco, I took a train to Bowman, North Dakota."

Fay..."Coming back from Bowman, North Dakota, where we picked up Coty from the train station, she was so apologetic for crying and being so emotional. Dad reminded her she had held it in so long that it was time to let it go. She was a nervous wreck. If a door slammed or something dropped, any sudden noise would terrify her and she would burst into tears. It got easier as time went by, but she never spent a moment without concern for Bernie's safety."

Coty..."Bernie was recommended for the Navy Cross, but he refused it. He didn't do any more than the men under him. He did accept a Presidential Unit Citation." [26]

---

[26] Lt. Col. George A. Larson, USAF (Ret.), "Pearl Harbor, A wife remembers the Japanese attack," Military, December 2006.

Stan Lieberman Remembers the Japanese Attack on Pearl Harbor December 7, 1941

STAN Lieberman, Rapid City, South Dakota..."I was born at Worcester, Massachusetts on July 15, 1917. I attended high school there, graduated in 1935, and joined the military in 1940. I have an interesting story of how I joined the Army. I went down to the U.S. Post Office in Worcester with Fred Levine, a friend of mine, to enlist in the Navy. He and I were high school friends and wanted to join the military together. We knew a war was coming and we figured we might as well enlist, and thought there should be some advantage in enlisting so we walked into the Naval Recruiting Office. The recruiter went over the enlistment and what he could offer us, which sounded pretty- good. I asked him how long we would be enlisting for and he said 'six years.' I looked at Levin and said it was time to go outside and talk over this six year term. While we were in the hall of the Post Office, we saw the Army recruiting poster on the wall. We both thought the Army pilot program sounded interesting. We enlisted in the Army for three years with an offer of three different assignments outside the United States: Philippines, Panama Canal Zone or Hawaii. We took Hawaii and later, when the war broke out with the Empire of Japan, we considered ourselves lucky, especially concerning the 'Death March on Bataan,' in the Philippines after the Japanese starved out U.S. Army and Filipino troops.

"After completing the enlistment paperwork, each of us was issued a train ticket to Fort Solkum, New York. My first job in the Army was as a dockhand on the ferry running between Fort Solkum to the mainland. After four months, we left New York on a Navy transport, the USS Washington, a former German luxury passenger liner. We went through the Panama Canal on our way to the Hawaiian Islands. The officers on the transport had staterooms, while we were assigned sleeping quarters in the hold, with rows of three high wood bunks. It was hot in the cargo hold, there was no air conditioning at that time, so we slept on the deck where there was a breeze, and it made the trip livable.

"My friend, Frank Levin, was on the transport with me, but when he walked down the gangplank in Honolulu, he stumbled and fell hard on the dock, severely injuring himself. He was taken to Fort Shaftner's hospital and the Army sent him back to the States and gave Levin an honorable discharge, with disability. That ended Levin's six months of Army service.

"The 86th Observation Squadron was attached to a fighter squadron stationed at Wheeler Field, but we moved to Bellows Field on the other side of the island from Pearl Harbor. I was assigned to the 86th Photo Section, as I was the only person who flew. At Bellows, we had a small photo lab in a trailer and I flew photo missions over the entire island. I was at aerial reconnaissance school when the Japanese attacked.

"I want to start somewhat earlier, prior to the Japanese attack to provide a look at what was going on in Hawaii. The entire island had been on alert for one week. Planes had been moved out of Wheeler Field and dispersed to alternate emergency airfields around the island. We had six of our squadron's aircraft dispersed to Haleiwa Field and all planes flew back into Wheeler Field on Saturday morning, 6 December, after the alert was cancelled. They were parked in rows to prevent sabotage and not at the edges of the airfield.

"I had Saturday and Sunday off, as was usual for the weekend. We were still at peace. I was going to visit my friends at Bellows Field, then hitch a ride across the island into Honolulu for Saturday night. I intended to go with my squadron commander, Jim Stuart. He was one of the finest men I knew and became a General by the end of the war. He flew from Bellows Field to Wheeler Field and back on weekends or when he had duty because his family loved in Wheeler Field's officer quarters. I was going to fly with him from Wheeler Field to Bellows Field. While I was waiting for him, I saw two fuel trucks slowly going down the line of parked P-40s, refueling each one."

In a warning message sent to U.S. Army Major General Walter Short, Commander U.S. Army Hawaiian Department from the War Department on November 27, 1941..."Undertake such reconnaissance and other measures you deem necessary." The alert was cancelled with troops and aircraft returned to their bases.

Lieberman... "I said to the fuel truck drivers, wouldn't these parked aircraft make a Hell of a target if the Japanese attacked? There had been all kinds of rumors. That morning, U.S. Army trucks were headed back to Schofield Barracks, bumper to bumper, returning from defensive positions around the island after being taken off alert. On Saturday, everything was returning to pre-alert status and we were on holiday. When the squadron commander did not fly in from Bellows Field, I hitched a ride to downtown Honolulu. I had lunch and that night I went to a USO dance.

"On Sunday morning, the U.S. Navy Harbor Report indicated there were 94 ships at Pearl Harbor: eight battleships, target battleship Utah, nine cruisers, 31 destroyers, five submarines, 24 mine ships and 27 auxiliaries. The aircraft carriers were away from Pearl Harbor, delivering aircraft to Midway and Wake Islands. On Sunday morning, I was bombed out of my bed. I was on the top bunk on the third floor when I heard and felt a tremendous explosion. Later, we found out the bomb impacted across the street in a housing area, but in an open area. The Japanese pilot released the bomb to hit the barracks but it barely cleared the top floor before striking the ground and detonating.

"The first bomb dropped scored a direct hit on Wheeler's Mess Hall, killing 300 soldiers on Sunday morning. Most of us slept in rather than going to breakfast, which was served at 0700. It was not a mandatory formation on the weekends, so that is why I was still in bed when the explosions woke me up. The first thing we did was run down to the ground floor, a mere 50 to 60 yards from the fully fueled P-40s parked on the concrete aircraft apron. We ran into the armament's shack and told the sergeant to hand out the guns. He would not open the locked gate without a signature from an officer so we went ahead tore down the wire and grabbed the guns. There was a .50 caliber machine gun inside. I had never fired a gun the entire time I had been in the Army. Some of the aircraft armorers knew nothing about machine guns. Some of these guys ran down to the flight line armaments shack to retrieve the .50 caliber machine gun ammunition and bring the belts to the barracks. We set up the machine gun on its tripod and my job was to feed the ammunition belt into the gun.

"The Japanese were flying below the tops of the buildings, strafing and bombing. This went on for about an hour, with a 30 minute pause before the second wave of Japanese aircraft attacked. I could see the Japanese aircrews with their leather helmets, goggles and scarves. The rear gunners on the dive and horizontal bombers fired their .30 caliber machine guns at us on the ground. When we started firing the .50 caliber machine gun, it froze after 15 to 20 rounds. We did not know it was necessary to pump water into the machine gun's cooling jacket to keep it from overheating. The guys with me were more familiar with the operation of air-cooled .50 caliber machine guns on the P-40s. We learned a quick lesson on the operation of a .50 caliber machine gun.

"We lay down in the open area next to the barracks on a concrete pad. Someone handed me a 1905 Springfield rifle and showed me how to load it with a single bullets, because there weren't any .30 caliber clips available for the rifles. They went down and got some .30 caliber ammunition from the flight line armaments shack. I added bullets into the rifle and got ready to fire at the attacking Japanese aircraft. As Japanese aircraft flew low at a distance of 60 yards, with flaps down to slow its speed, I fired directly at the pilot and squeezed the trigger. My bullet passed to the rear of the aircraft. I knew nothing about leading a moving target since this was the first time I fired a gun in the Army.

"We went down to the flight line after the end of the first Japanese bombing attack wave to one of the hangars packed with .30 and .50 caliber ammunition boxes. The hangar was burning and flames spread to the wood ammunition boxes. I noticed a bombshell fragment on the hangar floor and stuck it in my pocket while I began to drag out non-burning ammunition boxes. The Japanese second wave was bombing and strafing while we were dragging out the undamaged ammunition crates.

"I am not a big guy and the ammunition boxes were heavy. There was an aircraft tug close by, used to pull aircraft around the aircraft parking apron, fitted with a thick curved steel bumper. Japanese .30 caliber machine gun shells were piercing the steel bumper and this was not a pleasant sight.

"On the previous morning, on the bulletin board, there was a picture of a wounded Chinese civilian with burns on his arms from a reported Japanese mustard gas attack. I was scared to death of a similar attack and I had a practice gas mask in my locker on the third floor of the barracks. It was not very practical but it might provide a limited amount of protection. I got up and started to run up to the third floor to retrieve my gas mask, but every time I put my foot on the first step, a bomb exploded. Finally, I got the courage to run up the stairs to get my gas mask. If I had been half-smart, I would have gone down into the basement of the concrete barracks for protection.

"That night, after the first few shots on the .50 caliber machine gun removed from the armory, I was considered a machine gun expert. We were assigned to go into the housing area with the .50 caliber machine gun and set up a defensive position there. We were expecting a Japanese attack sometime during the night and I was put in charge of the machine gun crew, even though I was a Private, I had five or six guys working with me. We built a machine gun nest using cement bags because we didn't have sand bags available. When it was all set up I was in charge of the gun's position. About midnight, the loudest racket you ever heard broke out. One of my guys was firing the machine gun into the air marked by tracers and he was not the only one firing into the black night sky. I asked him what he was shooting at and he said he didn't know, but everyone else was shooting into the night sky. I told the kid to stop firing and after that, we heard a random shot now and then. Anything that moved, a cat or dog, was shot at. The entire island was trigger-happy.

"I had not taken any pictures during the Japanese attack and on Monday morning, I thought I had better get back to work at the photo lab. I showed up and started to help others get things organized. I was told to grab my photographic equipment and my parachute, and head to the flight line. I was going up in a B-18 Bolo to take photographs of the destruction in Pearl Harbor and surrounding military installations on the island. Master Sergeant Gorges was in charge of the photo lab and he was going along on this aerial photographic mission as my navigator. We flew at an altitude of 200 to 300 feet over Pearl Harbor for a couple of hours, taking pictures to create a mosaic of the damage. We had to guess on the flight path on each run because we did not have any reference points. Below us were hundreds of small boats in the oil-blackened water. There were fires and smoke everywhere, increasing the difficulty of flying a precise route. The USS Oklahoma had capsized, with its bottom up and covered with hundreds of men using air hammers and cutting torches trying to reach the men trapped inside. We flew low enough to see the faces of the men working on the battleship. I had a close up view of the destruction and damage below. The boats in the water were looking for and pulled dead bodies out of the water. We landed and I went back to the lab to develop the black and white film into 10 by 14-inch photographs, creating a mosaic of the harbor.

"Shortly after this, I had the opportunity to apply for pilot training as I intended to do in 1940 when enlisting in the Army. As long as I was going to continue flying, I might as well be the one doing the flying. The flight surgeon checked me out and told me he could pass me, but that my eyes would not pass on the pre-flight physical in the States. I asked him to sign it and he did, I was given orders for returning to the States. Prior to boarding a military transport out of Pearl, an Officer asked if I had anything of a military nature in my footlocker. Without thinking, I opened it and handed him my copies of the 10 by

14-inch photos of Pearl Harbor. That was the last time I saw them."[27]

The Japanese attack on Pearl Harbor pushed the United States into World War II, ending America's neutrality. The war did not officially end until 2 September, with the signing of the Allied terms of unconditional surrender onboard the U.S. Navy battleship New Jersey, anchored inside Tokyo Bay, Japan.

---

[27] Stan Lieberman, World War II, Pearl Harbor, Hawaii, 7 December 1941, Rapid City, South Dakota, interview author, June 2009.

Victor Weidensee

3rd Air Commando Group

VICTOR Weideness... "It was a usual day of relaxing for a group of young college students at South Dakota State College (SDSC) on December 7, 1941. We were having our noon meal together in the boarding house where we stayed when suddenly one of the students who were listening to a radio announcement of the Japanese attack on Pearl Harbor, which was the moment that forever changed our lives. After some discussions of the event we all know that we were going to be called to military duty because we were enrolled in the Reserve Officers Training Corps (ROTC) and we had been told by our ROTC instructors of the possibility of war with Japan. How they knew about a war with Japan was coming I do not know. I was a 18 year old freshman in college at this time. I was not interested in a career in the military. My father had been in the U.S. Army in World War I and told me that was futile, not a glorious business and hope fully neither my younger brother nor I would ever get involved in one.

"The next week we were informed that because we were ROTC students, we would be mustered into the military once and received my Military Identification (ID) card, number 17085439, which would be my ID number through the time I was in the service. I can't remember other numbers but I still remember this number even though I no longer have my name tags, which had that number on them. My date of enlistment was December 4, 1942 and entered active duty on April 12, 1943. We were allowed to stay in school until we were called up and reported to Fort Snelling, Minnesota where we were finally 'branded into the real Army.' From there we were sent by troop train to and first basic training at Camp Wolters near Mineral Wells, Texas. Before leaving Fort Snelling we were told we would have our choice of service and many of us wanted to join the Army Air Corps.

"When we got to Camp Walters and met our regular Army Master Sergeant Pointdexter we found out that we were not in the Air Corps, but in the 'foot slogging' infantry. I had taken and passed the Air Corps tests, and had been accepted for the Air Corps Pilot Training Program. I was shocked to find out that the Army did not keep its word. So much for volunteering. MSgt. Pointdexter said to us our first day in camp...'I hate college students...Don't worry about calling your mother for the next 13 weeks, I am your mother.' I spent 13 Hellish weeks in basic training during the hot days of summer in Texas and learned how to be a soldier according to MSgt. Pointdexter.

"In the meantime, I finally found out that my request to join the Air Corps had been accepted and when I finished basic training with several others we had requested transfer were sent to Dickinson College in Carlyle, Pennsylvania to begin our training. I just had turned 19 years of age. My class was made up of mostly airmen who had been gunners on B-17s, Eighth Air Force, England against Nazi targets in Europe, who wanted to be pilots. This was a tough bunch of chaps who knew what the score was. I flew in Cub aircraft, a dream to fly, neared solo time hours.

"While at Dickenson College, I was able to play in the band with some of the finest musicians I have ever known. I was a trumpet player. We did not do much drilling, playing for those who did. I also learned to play the clarinet and Saxophone, taking lessons for two months from professionals including one who had played in a band with Spike Jones. He told me I was not a very good trumpet player. I was just a green kid who played music with professionals in some major dance bands before the war. I had great time during this experience.

"After a month or so, we were told the Air Corps was closing the Cadet Pilot Training Programs and we were sent by train to a replacement camp in Miami, Florida where we were to receive orders. We were put on permanent KP duty for one month. I never want to see another KP kitchen at 4:30 a.m., washing pots and pans. While on KP we received Air Corps basic training, not as hard as Army Infantry Basic Training. This was in the hot steamy summer and needless to say there were many unhappy campers. The only thing that made it bearable was that we were housed in luxurious Miami Beach hotels, which at that time were not air conditioned. In 2006, I went back to Miami Beach, located the same hotel, now upgraded and modernized which also included air conditioning. When not on duty or KP, with many going on sick call to get out of KP, we were able to swim on the sea and play on the beach.

"After six weeks, we were asked if we would like to transfer to either Gunnery School, Mechanics School, or Radio School. About this time, we were asked if we would like to volunteer for a new group that was being formed. We who put up our hands met Colonel Arvid Olson, who had been a member of the American Volunteer Group (AVG), under the command of Chinese General designated officer,

General Claire Chennault in China before Pearl Harbor, intercepting Japanese fighters and bombers attacking National Chinese cities and industrial targets. Colonel Olson was the General's number two man in the AVG. The Colonel informed us he was forming the 3rd Air Commando Group. He then told us the group would be similar to the 1st Air Commando Group, which operated into the China-Burma-India (CBI), and we would be trained to operate behind enemy (Japanese) lines. The group would consist of fighter squadrons of P-51 Mustangs, liaison squadron of Stinson L-5, troop carrier squadrons of C-47s and WACO CG-4A gliders.

"To me this sounded like an adventure and anything was better than KP. We were organized and sent to Drew Field, Florida, to begin our training. The group was activated on May 1, 1944. No one liked to be in gliders and released from the towing C-47, you had one way in and no way out, unless towed back out by a C-47, ground take-off or airborne snatch. The gliders were shipped on a cargo transports to the Pacific. They were lost, never delivered to our destination and our group.

"We were issued a .45 automatic pistol, which had a pearl handle, and either a carbine or a machine gun as our weapons. The training included work in guerrilla fighting, how to operate behind enemy lines, lots of physical training, as well as how to live off the land. We also learned how to use gliders and communications equipment. We spent a lot of time flying in the C-47 transports and the L-5s on maneuvers, simulating behind the lines combat. This was along with plenty of physical training to assure we were fit for whatever might come along, completed our training. Our mission was to establish and maintain an airstrip behind enemy lines, to provide for our own supply and air defense, to attack targets in the enemy's rear areas and to furnish air support for ground troops.

"After training period was complete, we were sent to San Francisco, California and departed for the Pacific passing under the Golden Gate Bridge, in early November 1944. The fighter squadron personnel and the C-47 transports flew to New Guinea where they picked up new P-51 aircraft. The other members of the 3rd Commando Group departed on a troopship in early November. One of the worst experiences of my life was on the troop ship. It was crowded with several thousand troops and we were soon out to sea after passing under the Golden Gate Bridge, the rough seas made most everyone sea sick. I never left my bunk for several days. I was far enough down into the ship and when I hit the steel side, I knew I was below the waterline. I lived on boiled eggs, which a friend, who did not get sea sick, brought me. When I recovered, the rest of the trip was OK, even though we enlisted men were unaware of our destination.

"After a rather boring trip on the transport, we arrived at Leyte in the Philippine Islands on December 1, 1944, which was shortly after the invasion by American forces. When we finally got organized, the fighter squadrons were active bombing and strafing the enemy air bases on Mindanao, taking off from a base on Tacloban. The troop carrier planes dropped supplies to the ground forces and also transported wounded. It was while at this base we were attacked by Japanese airborne troops on December 6-7, 1944, who destroyed many of our L-5s that were parked on the air base. Our P-51s and C-47s were not on the field. We saw, what we thought were two C-47s approaching to make a landing. Then we realized they were Japanese with airborne troops jumping out of the two aircraft. Once on the ground the Japanese lobbed grenades into the revetments containing our L-5s. The two transports were destroyed by antiaircraft artillery. Thank goodness for the infantry who blunted the attack and in a short time restored order. There were dead Japanese bodies everywhere on the airfield.

"With the invasion of Luzon, the group moved from Leyte to Magaldan airfield on Luzon in late December 1944. The ground personnel went from Leyte to the Lingayen Gulf on an LST and while on this trip we went through a typhoon. The weather was so bad and the sea so rough that at times we thought we would capsize. However, on this sea trip I did not get sick even though I spent much time sitting on the seat of a 6 by 6 truck, chained to the open deck. The Navy crew did not want Army troops in the enclosed cargo deck area because it was full of 50 gallon barrels of gasoline and a single spark could have set it off with a bang. Needless to say, this was not a cruise ship and I wondered how the Navy sailors could stand the service very long. Again, we lived for several days on boiled eggs, as this was all the cooks could prepare.

"When we got out of the storm, the trip was fine and it was on this trip that I saw a Kamikaze attack on the ships in the invasion fleet. It was not very intense, but was the first and only time that I observed this type of warfare.

"When the group set up at Magaldan airfield, the fighters provided ground support to the troops and patrolled the air for enemy aircraft. The troop carrier C-47s evacuated wounded soldiers and carried supplies where needed, including beer flights to Australia. L-5s of the liaison squadron worked in evacuation, combat spotting for artillery, communication and transport of officers in the field. One of our L-5 pilots, TSgt. Head flew while smoking a cigar. He took off, only reaching 100 feet when the L-5 crash landed in the top of a huge tree. We ran up and thought we would find him dead. He was alive, leaning out of the aircraft yelling, 'How in the Hell do I get out?' We yelled at him, 'Climb down.' He reached the ground, unhurt, but the L-5 was a total loss. L-5s were also often used by high-ranking officers, generals to get a 'bird's eye' view of what was happening on the ground. General Joe Stillwell came to the air base and wanted to go up in an L-5. He wore his World War I cavalry hat. One of the sergeants took him up. The general stuck his head out of the right side L-5 window and his hat blew off, floated into the water below. When the general landed, he wanted the Navy to search for his hat. The hat was gone.

"The local friendly guerrillas around the base liked to fish to supplement their food. We gave them an idea on how to catch fish. We threw a grenade into the water. When it detonated, the shock wave brought up dead and stunned fish to the water's surface where they were picked up.

"In April the group moved to Laoay on the northern tip of Luzon, 150 miles behind enemy lines. The group operated the airfield and was supplied by the troop carrier squadron. The P-51s provided ground support for the Army and Philippine guerrilla forces as well as staffing missions to Formosa. In June 1945, the air base became the staging field for combat operations against Formosa. The base also served as an emergency-landing place for aircraft that had been damaged in combat or had mechanical problems and needed a safe place to land.

"To me, this was an exciting time and I made many friends of the personnel in the guerrilla army. These folks provided great protection for us Yanks from the Japanese. We also were giving the opportunity to get to know these folks and I can recall many positive social contacts. With the guerrillas we had danced and parties with them, drinking Tobac liquor, a great time. The Philippines was a Catholic nation. We danced with the local girls, after dancing first with their mother. War was not all Hell! It was an exciting time for me.

"In August 1945, the group moved to Le Shima in the Ryukus. I remember the first attempt to fly to this island in a fully loaded C-47. The weather was bad and we were forced to return back to Laoay air base, but no one had told is and when we arrived back on the aborted flight, we were surprised because we though the new base was so similar to what we had left. So much for communications from the C-47's crew to us passengers. What I remember of this flight was that I shared the plane with a jeep and piles of other equipment, which was not really tied down. My seat, if I remember, was sitting in a jeep, without a seat belt.

"It was while we moved to Laoay that we received a new group commander (CO). He was Lt. Col. Walker Mahurin, who had transferred from the Eighth Air Force to the Fifth after a successful tour of duty as a fighter pilot in Europe. He was the first American Ace to shoot down/destroy 20.75 enemy aircraft. He had received every medal that the Army gave except the Congressional Medal of Honor, the Purple Heart and the Soldier's Medal. He was an energetic driven person and I believe when we met him he was about 29 years old. He was a fellow who led by example and everyone liked him once he got established. I became a friend of his as he paid little attention to rank. I was an Air Operations Staff Sergeant who, along with Master Sergeant McNally, pretty much ran the air base. He was an aggressive pilot and led the fighters on many missions to Formosa. On one mission, he lost three aircraft to enemy fire and was forced to bail out into the ocean. He survived in a rubber life raft until rescued by the Air Sea Rescue people. He tried to get the base medical doctor to say he was wounded because he had sores on his butt from sitting in salt water in the life raft, but was unable to do this and did not get his Purple Heart. He was later actually wounded and earned his Purple Heart.

"The group was at Le Shima Air Base when the Japanese surrendered. We were elated with the news and looked to our next assignment. In October 1945, the group moved to Chitose Air Base on the northern island of Hokkaido in Japan. When we went over to the barracks, we found they were infested with fleas. We were all sprayed with DDT and spent the first weeks cleaning up our quarters. While at Chitose Air Base we were all counting our points to see when we could go home to the United States.

"I believe most of the men enjoyed being part of the occupation forces and while we were always on our guard, we found no difficulty with the Japanese in the area.

"Lt. Col. Mahurin had access to a two-seat P-40. I flew sight-seeing missions over Hiroshima where I saw the destruction of the city from the atomic bomb. To view this type of destruction made me hate war. Lt. Col. Mahurin also flew a C-47 back to Manila to pick up supplies. He simply walked up to an empty jeep, got in, started it up, and we drove into town. Once into Manila, we stopped at the San Miguel Brewery. We saw U.S. infantrymen with 250 gallon water tanks in jeep trailers, loading (pouring) beer into the tanks with hoses.

"While waiting to see if I would go home, I was thrilled when I found that I had 85 points, enough to return home to the United States, and leave the military. When I told the Co and Master Sergeant McNally of my desire to leave, they tried to get me to change my mind and remain in the service. However, I decided I wanted to continue my education and really wanted to go home. Furthermore, the group was to be deactivated in February 1946, and all personnel re-assigned to other units.

"I left the group and went to Tokyo. I saw the destruction caused by incendiary bombs dropped from B-29s during night bombing raids. I did not want to get into another war. I was assigned to go home in a converted 'Jeep' or escort aircraft carrier. The crew welded three high steel bunks in neat rows from one end of the hangar deck to the other, that when the elevator doors were open the sea breeze made it cool and a comfortable trip home. We docked at San Francisco. At that time, I found out someone on the ship had opened my trunk and stole all my Japanese souvenirs, pearl handled .45, jungle knife, and my 'burp' machine gun. It had to be one of the sailors on the ship. I took a train to Fort Leavenworth, Kansas where I was discharged from the Navy on 19 December 1945.

"At that time, the group was awarded several commendations and I received the Soldier's Medal for action in the Philippines for which I saved a man from drowning in waters off Luzon. I was awarded the following for my service in New Guinea, the Philippines, the South Pacific and the Army: The Distinguished Unit Badge, Philippines Liberation Ribbon with Bronze Star, the Good Conduct Medal and the Soldier's Medal. After receiving an honorable discharge from the Army Air Corps, I took a train to Gettysburg, South Dakota, where I was united with my parents and friends and I was ready for a new chapter in my life." [28]

---

[28] Victor Wedensee, Rapid City, South Dakota. Retired music Professor, Black Hills State University. During World War II, served in the Philippines with the 3rd Air Commando Group. Black Hills Veterans Writing Group, Western Dakota Technical Institute, Rapid City, South Dakota, May 12, 2012.

Tom McDill

Survivor of Bataan During World War II

THE Japanese attack on the Philippine Islands on December 8, 1941, after the surprise attack against Pearl Harbor, grabbed newspaper headlines in the United States and around the world. Even though the Japanese had been on the same World War I alliance with the United States, war in the closing days of 1941 appeared to be not if, but when and where. The U.S. created various war plans, designated by color, as did Germany. One of Germany's war plans was for the invasion of Poland, implemented on September 1, 1939, beginning World War II in Europe. For the United States, War Plan Orange-3 (WPO-3) was prepared to defend the western Pacific, including the Philippines. Prior to the outbreak of war in the Pacific, the U.S. War Department recognized that against a full scale Japanese amphibious landing, air and naval attack against the Philippines, the only area that realistically could be defended was Manila Bay and the Bataan Peninsula. However, U.S. and Filipino troops were not expected to hold out for more than six months. During this time period, it was hoped the U.S. Navy could force a relief convoy from Pearl Harbor to relieve the Philippines. Unfortunately, the lack of preparations by General MacArthur to set up supply depots (food, ammunition and medical supplies), prepare defensive lines on Bataan and disperse his vulnerable air force speeded Japanese subjugation of the Philippines. More significantly, the Japanese attack on Pearl Harbor and other Empire Japanese Navy successful operations in the western Pacific made WPO-3's timeline impossible.

The American-British-Chinese (ABC-1) staff agreement, signed on March 27, 1941, in Washington, DC, set the future war effort to defeat Germany first (once the U.S. entered the war), but the Pacific area of operations was not overlooked. ABC-1 stated:

1. The United States Fleet will:
    A. Support Allied operations for the defense of the Malay Barrier by diverting enemy strength through attacks on the Marshall Island and raids sea communications and positions.
    B. Support British naval forces south of the equator and

west 155 degrees longitude east.
C. Protect Allied territory and sea communications in the Pacific.
D. Prepare to capture the Marshall and Caroline Islands.

2. The United States Army, in conjunction with the Pacific Fleet and Army Air Forces will:
A. Hold Oahu.
B. Defend the Panama Canal and the Pacific Coast of the United States and Canada, including Alaska.
C. Support the republics of the west coast of South America

The Orange War Plans were replaced by Rainbow War Plans (such as Rainbow V), which mandated the defense of the Western Hemisphere, the American continent above 10 degrees north, with the dispatch of American forces to Europe to first defeat Germany and Italy. If a two-ocean war broke out, the U.S. would have to adopt a defensive position strategy against the Empire of Japanese, based on the defense of the Aleutian-Hawaii-Panama triangle area.

Steps were implemented to improve Philippine defenses. General MacArthur was appointed commander of all U.S. Army forces in the Far East and initiated a mobilization and training of the Philippine Army. It took time to move troops, equipment and supplies to the Philippines, especially under growing demands to provide England was materials to fight Germany and Italy. The transfer of equipment was made easier with the passage of Lend Lease by Congress, providing money for war material, shipped on British flag carriers to England and other U.S. allies, especially China. Supplies were in the pipeline from the United States, which by July 1942, would have increased Philippine defenses against a possible Japanese attack.

One U.S. Army enlisted man assigned to the Philippines was Tom McDill (2006, lived north of Custer South, Dakota, dying in 2015, 95 years old). McDill..."I was born in Lincoln, Nebraska on October 14, 1921, and in the summer of 1940, I was on the 'bum' with a close friend from Chadron, Nebraska, riding a freight train into Yakima, Washington. Along the way, we saw U.S. Army requiring posters. My friends said, 'We ought to join the U.S. Army.' So, we went to the local Army Recruitment Center in Yakima. The recruiter had two openings in the Philippines, U.S. Army Air Corps (USAAC). This later became the U.S. Army Air Forces (USAAF) on June 20, 1941. We were sent to nearby Fort Lawton, three miles northwest of downtown

Seattle. I was only 18 years at the time, so I had to obtain signatures from my parents. They preferred to let me enter the U.S. Army rather than riding boxcars, doing nothing. We went by train to San Francisco, California, then to Fort McDowell on Angel Island. This was the U.S. Military Embarkation Center for personnel transiting to Pacific duty locations. I boarded the U.S. troops transport USS Cottle (APA 147) for the 21 day sea voyage to Manila, arriving September 1940. I was assigned to Nichols Field, located on the outskirts of Manila. I received little recruit (basic military instruction) training, so I was assigned to guard duty at the field's ammunition dump. The guard detail consisted of three men: me, another private and one Private First Class (PFC) (commander of the detail). The PFC took the day shift and the remaining two of us broke up the evening's duty into two equal time shifts, 1800 to 2400 and 2400 to 0600. I was on guard duty for almost one year. I managed to get off it by volunteering for the 409th Signal Company Aviation and got training to be a signal lineman.

"The 409th Signal Company Aviation Company was a service detachment, activated three months before the Japanese attack on the Philippines. This was good duty. We had Filipino bunk boys who made our beds, pulled mosquito netting over the beds and did other cleaning. We also had boys to do KP so we did not have to pull that duty either. We really didn't have any concerns about Japan attacking the Philippines, although a lot of military prevention activities were apparent, especially with the arrival of B-17 Flying Fortresses."

On December 8, 1941, Clark Field was placed on alert to the possibility of a large-scale Japanese air attack from Formosa. Aircraft took off at 0830. The airborne force landed to refuel. At 1245, Japanese fighters and bombers attacked Clark Field and other U.S. airfields, including Nichols Field. The Japanese attack destroyed one third of U.S. fighters and one-half of the bombers, stripping MacArthur's command of air defense against following Japanese air attacks and amphibious landings. Japanese troops landed on Luzon on 10 December. MacArthur's over-optimistic defensive operations plan was to holdout against the Japanese attacks for a maximum of six months.

McDill..."I was at Nichols Field when the Japanese air attack occurred, hiding behind a truck. A bomb landed on the opposite of the truck, sending a piece of shrapnel through the vehicle, hitting me in the leg, slightly wounding me. We picked up our personal equipment and were trucked to Manila, where we boarded a motor launch to Mariveles and into the Bataan Peninsula. We went by truck up the west side of Bataan on the China Sea side, north of Ciabobo Point.

Our primary task was to string communications wire to front line positions, connecting artillery and field commanders together. We also patched broken sections when Japanese artillery or bombs cut the wires, which were usually strung along the edges of roads or trails. For those of us in the signal company, it was like we were out on maneuvers. When we were fixing breaks in the wire, we got very close to the fighting and our main camp was close to a field artillery position. Shells fired from these guns sounded like boxcars rumbling overhead."

As the situation on Bataan worsened, President Roosevelt ordered General MacArthur to leave Philippines to prevent his being captured by the Japanese. On March 11, 1943, General MacArthur, his family and 15 staff members escaped from Corregidor by motor torpedo boats. They reached Macajalar Bay on the north coast of Mindanao. They went to a nearby airfield, boarded two B-17 Flying Fortresses for the flight to northern Australia. On 9 April, Major General Edward P. King surrendered all troops on Bataan to Japanese Colonel Nakayama, 14th Japanese Army Senior Operations Officer.

McDill..."At the time of surrender, I was on the west side of Bataan, 20 miles north of Mariveles. Japanese troops searched us, taking weapons, personal items of value and equipment. Most of the U.S. troops were not prepared for the harsh treatment handed out by the Japanese troops. Japanese soldiers were taught not to surrender and it was considered a dishonor to do so. The Japanese planned to use trucks to transport POWs out of Bataan to Camp O'Donnell, twelve miles northwest of Clark Field, but there were not enough trucks.

"Camp O'Donnell was a military training base for the Philippine Army and it would prove inadequate as a POW camp, holding too many U.S. and Filipino soldiers. The Japanese gathered U.S. and Filipino troops, marching us north through a series of small towns. Most of the captured troops were weak from the effects of reduced rations and constant jungle fighting. Known as the Bataan Death March, Japanese troops clubbed, bayoneted and shot POWs along the hot march route north to San Fernando. The Japanese captured 12,000 U.S. and 64,000 Filipino troops. During the 55 mile forced march, 2,330 U.S. and 7,000 Filipino troops perished. Thousands more died during the harsh period of captivity. We were forced to march along the sides of the road while Japanese trucks drove down the center, toward the tip of Bataan. Corregidor surrendered on May 7, 1943, ending organized resistance against the Japanese, although a guerrilla movement started, increasing throughout the war as time passed.

"San Fernando was our first food stop on the long march. It was a railhead stop to load POWs into boxcars for the trip to Camp O'Donnell. Everyone was hungry and thirsty. I was fortunate that I still had iodine tablets, which Japanese troops searching me had not confiscated and my canteen. Without getting shot, I was able to fill my canteen with water along the road and drop in the iodine tablets, drink and not become sick. The guards were a rough lot, constantly keeping us moving. I saw one guard shoot and bayonet fellow POWs without reason. My signal company had been broken up on Bataan, so I lost track of nearly all of them.

"At San Fernando, in groups of 100, we were loaded into metal boxcars for the eight hour train trip to Capras. The heat inside the boxcar soared to over 100 degrees, and 10 to 15 men per car didn't survive. Once at Capras, the survivors were unloaded and marched to Camp O'Donnell. Once at the camp, I was assigned to a barracks. Because crowding in the camp was severe and deaths averaged 40 to 60 a day, I decided to volunteer for work details outside the camp. It was worse at the Filipino camp across the road, where deaths averaged 200 to 300 a day. A friend and I got out of camp to work down at the river in the pump house, which supplied water to the camp's kitchen. We were able to contact guerrillas operating in the surrounding area and smuggle in food, cigarettes and occasionally, candy. The Japanese, because of Camp O'Donnell's over-crowding, decided to set up additional POW camps, established at Cabanatuan, 25 miles northeast of Capras. Camp Number One was located four miles away from Cabanatuan. Camp Number Two was located four miles east of Camp Number One. Camp Number Three was located six miles east of Camp Number Two. These three camps had been set up as Philippine Army camps before the Japanese invasion.

"I was sent to Camp Number One and assigned to a 50 to 60 man barracks. We raised our own vegetables for food, which also fed the Japanese guards, who at this camp were primarily from Formosa. In this camp, we had doctors and medics, but almost no medicine. Again, we were placed on short rations, usually rice and a watery soup. The Japanese used POWs for various work details, especially on the construction of airfields, transporting us back and forth by truck.

"At Camp Number One, we did not have contact with guerillas as at Camp O'Donnell. There were no escapes from the camp because the Japanese assigned 10 men to what became known as a 'death squad.' If one POW escaped, the remaining nine POWs in the assigned squad would be immediately executed. Slowly, the Japanese began shipping American POWs out of the Philippines in what became known as

'Hell Ships,' a good description of their fate during the sea voyage. I tried to avoid this as long as possible, but I did not prevail."

The Japanese began moving POWs to Japan, retaining them as slave labor, on what became known as "Hell Ships." This brief description of what happened to the POWs on these Hell Ships is not intended to be a complete listing but a sampling of what the Japanese did and how they moved the POWs to Japan. The Asaku Maru, on 6 July 1942, carried 60 male and 19 female POWs from Rabaul, New Britain to Yokohama, Japan. On October 3, 1942, the Tamahoko Maru transported 269 POWs from Camp Cassisang, Mindanao to Manila. On another trip, on June 13, 1944, the transport was carrying 772 POWs, sailing from Manila to Takao, Formosa. On its final sea leg to Japan, the transport was stalked, torpedoed and sunk by the U.S. submarine Tang on June 24, 1944. The sinking and subsequent actions by the Japanese cost the lives of 560 out of the 772 POWs onboard. At this time in the war, the U.S. had no intelligence the Japanese were moving POWs in unmarked transports, not properly designated with Red Cross or POW markings. In desperation, as the U.S. submarine onslaught against Japanese transports increased, the Japanese Navy falsely marked transports with the Red Cross symbol in order to move high-priority cargoes to their destinations. Both Japanese actions violated Geneva Convention rules, which the Japanese repeated violated during the war.

The Noto Maru on August 27, 1944, departed Manila with 1,035 POWs. McDill..."I was shipped to Japan on the Noto Maru. We were loaded into the forward hold of the Japanese transport, which carried no markings that it was a POW transport. We were fortunate in that our ship was not torpedoed by a U.S. submarine. The cargo hold we were in was nine feet high, 90 feet long and 50 feet wide, divided into two wooden tiers, creating three spaces, three feet high. The hold was hot and the steel sides so hot you could not touch them. We were fed only two small handfuls of rice each day and if we got water, it was one small cup. There were no lights inside the hold and the conditions were terrible. Sanitary facilities consisted of four or five wooden buckets and many POWs suffered from dysentery and sickness. Japanese guards were at the small, wooden hatch entrance at the top of the hold to prevent any POWs from attempting to escape. I found out after the war that two of my friends on the Arisan Maru were killed when torpedoed by a U.S. submarine."

On September 5, 1944, the Shinyo Maru sailed from Davo, carrying 750 POWs. The transport was torpedoed by the U.S. submarine

Paddle (SS 263) on 7 September, killing 667 POWs. POW deaths occurred from the torpedo hit, Japanese guard machine gun fire, drowning and death from wounds incurred during the sinking. Only 38 POWs survived. The Japanese completed movement of the majority of Allied POWs to Japan before U.S. submarines and wide-ranging aircraft carrier air attacks cleared the waters around the Japanese home islands of merchant shipping. The remaining Japanese merchant ships were further endangered by sea mines dropped in the main shipping lanes as part of the USAAF's "Operation STARVATION." B-29s dropped 1,000 and 2,000 pound sea mines by parachute into Japan's inland shipping lanes. Once a mine splashed into the water, the parachute automatically jettisoned, allowing the mine to sink to the bottom. B-29s conducted aerial mining in the Shimonoseki Strait and major Inland Sea harbors entrances. Naval sea mines sank more Japanese shipping than all other Allied offensive actions.

McDill..."Moji, Japan was our point of entry on the Noto Maru. We were loaded onto a well-guarded ferry for the sea trip to Shimonoseki on 6 September and then loaded into a sealed passenger railroad car, with the window shades pulled down for the three day trip north to Hanawa. Once off the train, we were marched into a small POW camp, designated as Camp 6B, a copper mining operation. The mine was located two miles up a mountain, northwest from the POW camp, and this is where we worked from 5 a.m. to 5 p.m., Monday through Saturday. The work was dangerous because the mine was very old and I often worked in cold standing water. We used steel sledgehammers to break lose the copper bearing ore, pulling back the loosened ore with a diamond shaped hoe, then shoveling the ore into an ore hopper car. A track led to an open hole in the mine where we dumped the copper ore, which went down to a smelter plant at the base of the mountain. The Japanese civilian "Honchos" in the mine were brutal, constantly pushing us. Copper was a scare mineral, critical to Japan's limited high-tech war production.

"After we were back in the hands of U.S. military personnel, I found out that the Japanese were living on less than 2,000 calories per day. Since we were POWs, we were at the bottom of the available food chain. We constantly had to scavenge for food, eating what can best be described as garbage. We were fed millet, not rice, which was hard to digest and we all suffered. Sometimes, we were given soup, more colored water than an actual soybean soup.

"There was a lot of snow at this camp during the winter. We shoveled narrow walkways bordered by snow up to the tops of the 30 foot high wood barracks. For heat, we had one small stove, but little or no wood to burn. Workers in the copper mine, myself included, smuggled any wood we could find back to the camp. We somehow managed to smuggle the wood past the guards into camp and then burn the wood in the stove. We also had a great problem with fleas and just could not get rid of them.

"The Japanese guards never told us anything about the war, especially how badly it was going against Japan. I never saw any Boeing B-29 Superfortresses flying over the camp until after Japan surrendered. On August 19, 1945, finally, the Japanese guards told us that Japan had surrendered and the war was over. We were allowed to mark the camp with large letters, 'PW' visible from the air. The next day, a USN torpedo bomber flew low over the camp, dropping K-rations, which we eagerly picked up. This food was welcomed by all and quickly consumed."

The dropping of the atomic bombs on Hiroshima and Nagasaki saved the lives of over 300,000 Allied POWs held by the Japanese. The Japanese Kempeitai Military Police received orders on August 14, 1945, to begin the execution of Allied POWs to be completed prior to the Allied invasion of Japan. The surrender of the Japanese saved these POWs from death. On August 17, 1945, the 20th Air Force was tasked to deliver emergency supplies by air to POW camps, set up by the Japanese prior to entry by Allied troops or movement out by the POWs to collection points. The B-29 was ideal for this operation because of its long range and large bomb bay, which could haul the supplies to be parachuted into POW camps. The first airdrops consisted of essential supplies: clothing, medicines (along with detailed instructions for their use) and three days of food: soups, fruit, juices, extracts and vitamins. The second airdrops consisted of seven days of rations. Follow-on airdrops were scheduled as required until the POW camps were liberated or the prisoners moved to transfer points. The supplies were packed inside 55-gallon drums for protection, dropped by parachute. However, when the parachute failed to deploy and open, the drum smashed hard into the ground, spilling its contents over the ground, still rapidly picked up by POWs. Between 29 August and September 20, 1945, there were 1,066 POW supply flights, with 900 dropping their supplies into POW camps. B-29s delivered 4,470 tons of supplies to 63,500 POWs.

McDill..."We were in Hanawa for three weeks after Japan surrendered. As to be expected, the Japanese camp guards became very friendly, telling us that two large bombs had been dropped by B-29s, one on Hiroshima and the second on Nagasaki. I saw a B-29 for the first time when one dropped food and supplies into the camp. It was finally arranged for us to be taken into nearby Hanawa, moved by passenger train south to Shiogama Harbor. We were transferred to a USN LST, No. 252, with its ramp lowered so we could walk inside and then moved out beyond the harbor to a large hospital ship, the USS Rescue. The hospital ship sailed to Yokohama, arriving on 15 September. Some of those onboard were taken off the ship, while others were brought on. Some, like myself, remained onboard. The hospital ship sailed across the Pacific, stopping at Pearl Harbor before sailing to San Francisco, from which I had sailed so many months previously in September 1940. I was bused to Letterman Army Medical Center for a stateside medical evaluation and treatment, and then by passenger train to Fitzsimmons Army Medical Center in Denver, Colorado. I remained at Fitzsimmons for one month, enjoying the mountain air, food and a chance to slowly transition from a POW to a human being. At this time, I made the decision to remain in the Army, while others elected to get out as quickly as possible. While at Fitzsimmons, I collected my back pay and then transferred to Fort Riley, Kansas. I was given 90 days leave and an additional 90 days temporary duty leave, which was six months of my own time with no work, but still being paid as a U.S. soldier. This ended my World War II POW experience and began my transition from an enlisted soldier to that of an officer.

"After the extended leave, I reported to Offutt Field, Nebraska and was given the rank of Staff Sergeant. While there, the change was made to the Air Force, transferring me from the USAAF to the USAF. I saw Pentagon Circular Number 101, which indicated that if you were an NCO during World War II, you could apply to be commissioned as a Second Lieutenant, USAF Reserve. I filled out the necessary forms and promptly forgot about them. A Staff Sergeant friend of mine also completed the forms and sent in the application. He was called to duty as a Second Lieutenant at the beginning of the Korean War, assigned to F.E. Warren Air Force Base at Cheyenne, Wyoming. By that time, I had been promoted to Technical Sergeant and assigned to Fort Benjamin Harrison at Indianapolis, Indiana. This was a location, which I did not like. I arranged for a transfer to Hill Air Force Base at Salt Lake City, Utah. I was only there for five months before being transferred to Seattle, Washington where I became Chief Clerk of the orderly room. I then went to F.E. Warren as an instructor at the Air Force Administrative School and promoted to Master Sergeant.

"The Korean War was in full swing and there was a constant need for Company Grade officers. The Air Force found my Reserve Officer application, which I had sent but forgot about, and I became a Second Lieutenant, USAFR. I remained at F.E. Warren, moving up the officer ranks to that of a Captain. I spent three years in Spain and then back to F.E. Warren, retiring in June 1961, with 11 years as enlisted and 10 years as an officer." [29]

---

[29] Lt. Col. George A. Larson, USAF (Ret.), "Survivor of Bataan, A look back on being a Japanese Prisoner," Military, April 2006.

World War II Rationing in South Dakota

Home Front Contribution to Winning the War

THE United States actively entered World War II against the Japanese Empire on December 8, 1941; one day after the Imperial Japanese Navy launched an air attack from six of its Fleet carrier, northwest of the Hawaiian Islands against Pearl Harbor and its associated military installations. Adolf Hitler in German, wanting to support Japan against Britain and the United States, believing the Japan would also declare war against Russia in the east and invade Soviet territory, declared war against the United States on December 11, 1941. On that day, the U.S. Congress declared war against Germany and Italy, finalizing sides during the Second World War, a global combat with far reaching significance once the fighting ended in August 1945. To Hitler's disappointment, Japan honored its non-aggression pact with Russia and did not declare war and create a second front against Stalin's military. This allowed Russia to withdraw Army divisions and equipment from the Far East, moving these forces on the Trans-Siberian Railway to the Eastern Front, launching a winter offensive against German forces in front of Moscow, driving them away from the capital.

The United States had to fight a global war in which it had to train, equip its current and planned military forces, feeding the U.S. civilian population and troops, Allied troops and most of their civilian populations. It took time to switch from a consumer-based economy to one of full wartime production, complicated by continuing effects in 1941 from the 1929 economic depression. Prior to Pearl Harbor, the U.S. had anticipated its eventual involvement in a global war. In February 1941, prices started to increase because the British began quantity purchases of military equipment, ammunition, food and supplies, paying in hard currency, transporting these items in their own ships across the North Atlantic to English ports. British merchantmen had to run a gauntlet of German U-boats patrolling west of the British Isles to sink as many British merchantmen and tankers as possible to disrupt the supply line from the United States. To control this rise in prices, on April 11, 1941, the U.S. Office of Price Administration and Civilian

Supply (OPACS) began operation. For the British, food was vitally important because they could not grow enough food to feed their civilian population and deployment military. The British finally reached the point where they could no longer pay in hard currency for food and war material from the United States. The U.S. Congress passed the Lend Lease Act of March 11, 1941, which authorized President Roosevelt to give the British what they needed with the stated qualification these items would be returned after the war. Food was a significant part of Lend Lease shipments to England.

Rationing was already part of war life in Europe. After invading Poland on September 1, 1939, Germany initiated food rationing. However, Germany only planned to fight a short war, expecting to knockout France and British forces in the west with British forces retreating to England, initiating a lighting strike against Russia to force the Soviet military into complete defeat, surrendering all of eastern Russia and its Caucus oil fields to Germany. This would place the entire western and eastern European Continent under Nazi control, screened from attack by the seizure of North Africa, the Suez Canal and Middle East coast of the Mediterranean, isolating the British Isles, forcing England to sign a peace treaty with Germany. Germany did not begin World War II with a full war mobilization needed to fight and win a protracted multi-front war. It would only be after Albert Speer, Hitler's Armaments Minister, took control of the Germany economy that there was full wartime mobilization. By this time in the war, it was too late to change or alter the outcome of the fighting only prolonging the overwhelming defeat of the German military and destruction of the economy.

England began meat rationing in December 1939, followed in January 1949 by the rationing of bacon, butter and sugar. By June 1941, clothing was added to rationed items. German U-boats sank huge tonnages of Lend Lease supplies headed for England. It was not until the middle of 1943 that U.S. Liberty ship construction added more shipping tonnage capacity than lost to German military submarine and long-range air attacks. The British civil population suffered a 22 percent reduction in their standard of living during the war. German U-boats nearly won the "Battle of the Atlantic," cutting off supplies from the United States. Not enough submarines were on patrol at any given time to cut off the flow of supplies and once production increased, Allied defenses took a heavy toll. It was the introduction of large numbers of escorts for convoys, long-range air patrols, introduction of escort carriers to provide constant air coverage over the convoys, which dealt German U-boats a fatal blow.

There was recognition in the United States that it needed to prepare for a long war, which prompted the creation of the Office of Price Administration (OPA) in August 1941. Its mandate was to prevent spiraling prices, rising costs, profiteering and inflation. OPA established 8,000 local rationing boards, staffed by 60,000 salaried civil servants, assisted by 200,000 volunteers to administer the rationing program. Rationing started with foodstuffs, first sugar and meat. Clothing was added to the list, especially silk and nylon. Foreign sources of silk was nearly stopped by the Japanese military control of the Chinese coastline and control of the Burma Road, the only ground route into China. Initial rationing in the United States was not heavily controlled, but quickly shifted into a system, which touched the daily lives of all Americans. After the attack on Pearl Harbor, the Japanese military seized Malaya and the Dutch East Indies, cutting of U.S. access to sources of raw rubber. Many different ideas were tried to save rubber: collection of used tires, rubber raincoats, tennis shoes, boots and anything else made out of rubber. This never met demand. Fortunately, U.S. chemists developed a formula and production process for synthetic rubber from agricultural and forest products, referred to as butyl rubber. This allowed the rubber wheeling of the U.S. military and its allies, especially Lend Lease trucks sent to Russia for use on the Eastern Front.

Gasoline rationing was initiated in 17 eastern U.S. states in May 1942. U.S. civilian consumption of gasoline was reduced for civilians to five gallons per week. By December 1942, over one half of the automobiles in the United States carried an 'A' sticker on the windshield, reducing the purchase allotment to four gallons a week. The majority of the remaining vehicles were issued a 'B' sticker given to authorized war related workers, with fuel usage and purchase based on driving to and from work for one week. Car pools were the norm and not an exception, further reducing weekly consumption. The 'C' sticker was issued to people requiring unlimited gasoline purchases such as doctors, police and those living in rural areas and western states where distances between towns, farms and ranches were long. Truck drivers were issued the 'T' sticker, allowing the purchase of unlimited gasoline necessary to haul the goods to fuel America's economy geared for maximum war production. As with all rationing, a black market developed in stolen and counterfeit fuel stickers.

War Ration Book One was issued in May 1942. It was not a complicated printing, done on letter size paper, with regulations governing its use, information in the book filled out by the owner identifying its owner and 28 White War Ration stamps. Each stamp, when declared valid, could be redeemed to purchase coffee, sugar, shoes, etc., depending on the designation of the stamp. Every member of a family was eligible to receive a War Ration Book. The War Ration book prescribed how much and what type of food could be purchased in one week. It did not take too long for local ration boards to be overwhelmed with complaints that recently issued ration books had been lost, stolen or accidentally destroyed. Lost ration books were worth more than money. You needed ration book stamps to purchase food. Stores were told not to make any exception for those who did not have a valid War Ration Book.

Sometimes store clerks had to remind customers that a purchase required money as well as a ration stamp. It was truly an education process for War Ration Book One users. Stores also had to indicate the number of War Ration Book stamps, along with the price of each item on the store's shelves, in a refrigerator or meat cooler. This constantly changed and usually a blackboard at the store's entrance indicated any changed prices, required War Ration Stamps for each purchase and costs of merchandise. This triggered a constant displeasure with the rationing system. Adding to the pressure on rationing were the constant drives to collect scrap metal, newspaper, tin cans and everything else needed for war production. City residents became frustrated on leaning farmers cattle, chickens (poultry was not rationed and farmers sold these to city residents), pigs, eggs and vegetables were being used to barter for manufactured items, outside the rationing process and restrictions. In August 1942, meat was rationed, further reducing what could be purchased. With the approach of winter, heating fuel rationing began in October. Coal was the primary source of heat for homes in the United States. Many Americans in cities did not have access to alternate fuel sources such as wood (corn cobs on farms in rural areas), making it difficult to heat their home during the bitter cold months. There was no other option but to seal off as many rooms as possible, heat provided by a coal fired fireplace or cast iron kitchen stove. Many farmers in South Dakota used corn cobs to heat their homes during the winter, guarding their property from city and town dwellers sneaking onto their land to cut standing trees for firewood.

Hoarding was another problem, with people collecting as many rationed goods as possible, sometimes buying up existing stocks of store items that were scheduled to go onto the rationing program. Those with money were accused of profiteering at the determinant of the working poor. It is the same tune protesters state during their protests against Wall Street. They protest the widening gap of 99 percent of Americans to the one percent who control the majority of wealth in the United States in 2015. The same feelings arose during World War II. It seemed that those with money could always get around rationing restrictions. The author's mother frequently saw storeowners sell rationed goods at higher prices to those with cash without the use of War Ration book coupons. There were other ways to get around rationing restrictions. Many of the items purchased in such manner were used to barter for other scarce items. Sometimes efforts to profiteer backfired when items announced to go a ration list, did not. Sometimes this process was used to discourage profiteering and affect those who used excess cash to buy up items.

Most Americans might have thought the rationing of sugar would be the most troublesome, because baking and sweetening food required sugar, but it was coffee rationing, which began on November 29, 1942, that caused the most vocal complaints. Coffee consumption was set at one pound per adult for five weeks. Coffee ration stamps were removed from children's War Ration books for those under the age of fifteen, which set off a wave of complaints from parents and coffee drinking family members. The author's grandmother, used a double glass ball coffee maker, keeping old coffee grounds and using them many times, adding new coffee grounds as little as possible. It was black, thick, strong and better than no coffee at all. In addition, when stateside service members were shipped overseas, their War Ration books had to be turned into their Local Ration Board and could not be used by their family members. Non-coffee drinkers bartered their coffee ration stamps for clothes, shoes and scarce items, especially from local farmers and ranchers. Coffee rationing ended in July 1943. Gasoline rationing in the United States became universal in December 1942 for all 48 states.

As with all World War II U.S. programs, war rationing responses went from complete acceptance to black marketers and profiteers who abused the system to make money from the hardship of others. This was especially true for dairy shortage. A severe butter shortage developed in February 1943. After the war, declassified reports indicated that many local rationing boards followed and practiced favoritism. Most Americans considered rationing as an inconvenience. American cities were not bombed nor were foreign troops occupying the nation. Americans were more worried about their sons, fathers, brothers and family members, and as the war continued, even women served in the military.

Responding to food shortages and war propaganda posters, Americans planted "Victory Gardens" anywhere possible to supplement their rationed goods. Canning had always been popular and increased during World War II. Canned vegetables and meat added to the variety of food available on family dinner tables, easing rationing effects, allowing large families the quantities and varieties to feed everyone. Many Americans felt cheated when they were penalized for doing what the government wanted, plant a "Victory Garden" and grow food. Their rationing items were reduced.

One of the most important U.S. contributions to the war effort was pre-packed field rations, designated as Type C, D and K. The series was created by the U.S. Army in late 1939. By the end of the war, the U.S. produced over one billion field rations, feeding millions of troops and civilians in liberated areas when no other food was available. Russian Army troops were fed "K" rations, delivered under Lend Lease by sea transport to Murmansk, and then trucked to the Eastern Front in their fight against the German Army.

Type C field ration was created to feed troops when no setup or field kitchens were available. The food was packed in six small cans: three of meat and three of bread. Type "D" field rations were to be used to feed troops for short periods, one or two days, when other food was not available, providing 1,770 calories a day. It was a simple four ounce food bar consisting of chocolate, sugar, dry milk, coco fat, oat flour and flavoring. It was also included in the mass produced Type "K" Field rations.

The Type "K" field ration provided three different meals of 3,000 calories: breakfast, dinner and supper. "K" rations were designed to feed troops for two to three days. However, in combat, this was often extended to two or three weeks. Each ration was sealed in a wax covered cardboard container, making it weigh less and able to be carried by a soldier for three days of food. Soldiers who ate these rations were constantly hungry and anxious to get to a location where a field hospital; was set up, breakout their mess kits for a hot meal serving. During heavy snows in the west, including South Dakota, "K" rations were airdropped to isolated Indian reservations, small towns and cut off farms and ranches.

War Ration book One was just the start. It was followed in sequence by War Ration Book Two to increase control over consumption in the United States. Americans planted Victory Gardens and canned excess food. Unfortunately, during the application process for

War Ration Book Two, households had to provide a complete listing of all their food in the home (purchased or canned). This had to be signed to determine food availability. This penalized those who grew some of their food, curbed excesses and lived by wartime rules. The book contained colored stamps, red and blue, lettered A to Z, with point numbers printed in denominations of 1, 2, 5 and 8. Red stamps allowed the holder to purchase margarine, butter, meat, canned fish, cheese, fats (such as lard and vegetable oil) and canned milk. To increase the number of War Ration Book red stamps, for every pound of meat droppings or fat brought into a collection point, the consumer earned two War Ration book stamps. Blue stamps, sometime colored brown or green, allowed the holder to purchase canned vegetables, canned and dried fruit, canned juices and baby food.

Even with all the planning on issuing and using ration stamps, no change could be made or returned on purchases if not using the entire dominations of stamps surrendered to the store clerk. If an item cost four ration points, and the consumer only had a five point stamp, unfortunately, a one-point ration stamp was not given to the consumer in change.

During World War II, only one-third of food items in the United States were rationed. War Ration book Three was issued at the same time as War Ration Book Two. This book contained ration stamps printed with airplane, aircraft carrier, tank and artillery stamps. Shoes could be purchased with airplane stamps and other stamps were designated for specific items.

The War Production Board (WPB) also changed clothing styles to reduce the amount of material needed for civilian clothes. The WPB banned the following clothing trim: double-breasted suits, vests, trouser cuffs, patch pockets, pleaded skirts, hemlines shortened to save fabric. Even with increasing rationing controls, civilian consumption of goods and services in the United States increased by 13 percent. The war did not stop the building of new stores, with an increasing variety of goods available to the American consumer, a great change from the previous economic effects of the depression. As the United States expanded its wartime economy to fight a global war, mobilization literally spent the country out of the effects of the depression. In May 1944, meat rationing was cancelled, except for steaks and choice cuts of meat. By December 1944, meat went back on the ration list, although butter rationing ended.

War Ration Book Four corrected the deficiency of previous ration books in that change could now be given on purchases, saving precious stamps. Change was in the form of red or blue round tokens, about the size of a dime, made from cardboard, with a non-expiring date. The author found a quart size glass canning jar half full of these cardboard tokens saved by his mother. She saved these for holiday baking, birthdays and special purchases. By December 1945, with full production capacity reached by synthetic rubber plants, tire rationing ended. Even during rationing, food consumption in the United States increased nine percent. The number of available calories increased, partly to feed war workers and others involved in the war effort. A study made during the war, indicated draftees and volunteers who entered the U.S. military were under weight, often suffering from malnutrition and in need of a well-balanced diet during military training to be able to be ready for overseas combat.

By 1945, the American agricultural system was feeding the country's civilian population, its military, Allied populations and troops, along with civilian populations in the liberated countries around the world. In Europe, during the war occupation of conquered countries, Germany shipped all available agricultural, diary and meat products from the occupied countries back to Germany, with little regard for that country's civilian population. There was a huge demand for food after the war from the United States to feed liberated populations in Europe, western Pacific, Asia and China. American agricultural production increased and met the demand. During World War II, America was constantly short of farm workers. After Allied victories in North Africa, hundreds of thousands of German POWs, along with Italian troops were transported to the United States in empty transports, moved by secured passenger trains to POW camps throughout America. As many of these POWs as possible were politically cleared for work outside the camps which helped harvest crops. These POWs assisted in food production so adequate food stocks could be shipped throughout the world. Rationing helped the United States win the battle of war production, which could not be matched by Germany, Italy or Japan. OPA ended rationing on gasoline, fuel oil and processed food on August 6, 1945, followed in June 1946 by the end of sugar rationing. The United States committed itself to winning the war, allowing it to dictate the terms of unconditional surrender to its wartime enemies. [30]

---

[30] Lt. Col. George A. Larson, USAF (Ret.), "War Rationing in the United States during World War II," Armourer, March-April 2005. In 2003, the author interviewed Rapid City residents about rationing during World War II.

Luverne "Vern" A. Kramer

Civil Air Patrol Hunting German U-boats Off the U.S. East Coast

ONE of the lesser reported on stories and organizations operating during World War II were the Civilian Air Patrol (CAP) and the role it played in diminishing the German submarine or U-boat threat along the U.S. Atlantic Sea Frontier, Caribbean and Gulf of Mexico. The CAP today is an auxiliary of the United States Air Force but had its origins in the late 1930s. At this time, American aviation activist Gill Wilson began lobbying the U.S. War Department to strengthen and augment existing air assets for the USAAC, in preparation for a projected future entry into a war against Germany and Italy in Europe and North Africa. On December 7, 1941, Fiorello H. LaGuardia, Mayor of New York and Director, Office of Civil Defense (OCP), signed an order creating the CAP. Gill Wilson was assigned its first Executive Officer, with USAAC Major General John Curry its first commander.

After the Imperial Japanese Navy attack on Pearl Harbor on December 7, 1941, the U.S. declared war on the Empire of Japan on December 8, 1941. Adolf Hitler, honoring Germany's commitment under the Tripartite Pact with Japan (although not required to do so under the pact's protocols), declared war in the United States (dragging Italy into the war against the United States) on December 8, 1941. The U.S. Congress quickly responded, declaring war on Germany and Italy the same day. Fortunately, for the untrained and unprepared U.S. military forces along the seacoasts, it took time for U-boats to be deployed from the large German submarine base at Lorient, France. The first group of U-boats sailed out of Lorient on 23 December, transiting across the Atlantic to assume patrol stations along the U.S. east coast. The first U-boat sinking occurred on January 11, 1943, 300 miles east of Cape Code, Massachusetts by U-123, the first of many U-boat sinkings in American coastal waters.

The newly created USAAF and USN scrapped together available aircraft to create close in and in-shore anti-submarine patrols to search and locate U-boats. On December 8, 1941, the AAF directed 1st Air Support and 1st Bomber Command to begin air patrols along the U.S.

Eastern Sea Frontier. With limited air assets, 1st Air Support Command's observation and fighter aircraft patrolled to an off shore distance of forty miles from Portland, Maine and south to Wilmington, North Carolina. However, at this time in the war against Germany, one day's allocation of patrol aircraft was less than ten. The 1st Bomber Command's available aircraft included the twin-engine Douglas B-18 Bolo and North American B-25 Mitchell, allowing patrols to be extended out to 300 miles. The AAF only had a few four-engine Boeing B-17 Flying Fortresses on the east coast, able to conduct patrols out to 600 miles. Until March 1942, 1st Bomber Command could only maintain a daily sortie rate of six aircraft (three from Mitchell Field, New York and three from West Field, Massachusetts). There were not enough military aircraft available to cover all possible U-boat operating areas during daylight and none were equipped for night anti-submarine patrols.

The AAF brought in aircraft from the recently organized CAP to augment 1st Bomber Command's hunt for U-boats. The CAP consisted of civilian pilots volunteering to fly their own small aircraft over water, conducting air defense patrols against U-boats, assisting in locating and guiding warships to the location of torpedoed or those sunk by gunfire from surfaced submarines to allow survivors to be rescued. CAP pilots were initially only authorized to receive limited government support. The first group of CAP pilots began flying out of Atlantic City, New Jersey on March 8, 1942.

German U-boat captains quickly shocked U.S. military on the ease and great success in sinking freighters and tankers sailing along the Atlantic Eastern Sea Frontier. Early in the effort to counter German U-boats, U.S. air assets were stretched thin. The movement of refined gasoline and petroleum products was hampered by German U-boat sinkings of tankers, greatly reduced the flow of fuel and vital war supplies scheduled to be shipped to England. German U-boats operated in relative safety from surface or air attack, often within sight of civilians on beaches. Tankers and freighters were sunk in large numbers. For support to military air assets, but before U.S. military defenses increased to perform anti-submarine warfare, the War Department required an initial 90 day operations trail early in 1942, in order to prove civilian pilots could conduct U-boat patrols. Twenty-one airfields were selected to station CAP aircraft for anti-submarine patrols.

Because of their civilian status, CAP personnel setting up these bases, without military priorities or authorizations, equipment and spare parts, often without personnel replacements, had many problems. Initially CAP pilots purchases their own aviation fuel, and in most states paid fuel tax. The CAP begged, borrowed and took any excess or surplus equipment available to set up operating airfields. The CAP also received gifts from local towns around airfields being established, along with county governments, chamber of commerce, state governments, individuals and corporations. By the middle of 1943, CAP pilots had spent over one million dollars of their own funds to keep aircraft flying, looking for German U-boats. Beginning in January 1942, German U-boats had extracted a heavy toll on tankers sailing unescorted along the U.S. East Coast. German U-boats were hidden in the black water while tankers were visible, outlined from the lights on shore not shut off, only later disappearing as blackout restrictions were imposed and enforced. It did not take too long before oil companies; beginning with Sunoco, took collections at their gasoline stations, and by placing service charges on the stations helping to pay CAP operating expenses. U.S. oil companies needed tankers to move oil and refined petroleum products from Texas oil fields and terminals to fuel storage locations along the U.S. east coast. A system of land petroleum distribution pipelines was incomplete, although construction continued with great emphasis and urgency. Fuel supplies were scarce as rationing reduced consumption to meet growing and urgent demands of a two-ocean war. Oil companies created sink-a-sub clubs to collect money for CAP units. This money was essential because the War Department had only cut loose minimal reimbursements of $8.00 per day for CAP pilots. However, for CAP pilots their reimbursements took months to receive due to the wartime bureaucracy to process payments in a timely manner.

In March 1942, the CAP support 1st Bomber Command completed over 8,000 patrol hours. This equaled the previous two months flying hours (January and February). Unarmed CAP aircraft and pilots quickly made aerial encounters with U-boats, giving German submarine commanders and crews an uncomfortable sight of an enemy aircraft above. Even though CAP were initially unarmed, U-boat captains had to dive their boats, change course underwater, head for deeper water, running away from the sighting position to avoid vectored AAF and USN aircraft, and surface warships. To give CAP aircraft sting, bomb racks were fabricated. This allowed lightweight bomb(s) or depth charge(s) to be carried. The pilot was assisted by a simple and inexpensive bombsight in the cockpit.

CAP's primary value during the time of heavy U-boat attacks and sinkings along the U.S. coastal shipping lanes was to locate disabled ships or survivors in lifeboats/life rafts. CAP's aircraft's low-flying speeds enabled pilots to locate many survivors on the water not noticed by higher and faster flying military aircraft. By June 1942, the USN along with AAF/CAP aircraft forced German U-boats to disengage from attacks in the close-in U.S. east coastal shipping lanes, moving out into more fertile hunting grounds in the Caribbean and Gulf of Mexico (off the entrance to the Panama Canal and in the Texas tanker shipping lanes around the Florida Keys. This switch should have been expected by U.S. military defenses, which again were unprepared for the U-boat onslaught and subsequent high-level of merchant ship and tanker sinkings.

One of the CAP pilots flying along the U.S. east coast was Luverne "Vern" A Kramer, currently living in Deadwood, South Dakota. On December 7, 1941, he was working in the Homestake Gold Mine's sawmill. In March 1942, he drove to Wichita, Kansas to begin working in the Boeing Aircraft Company's B-29 Superfortress engine assembly plant. He was a member of the CAP in Wichita and accepted a position in Atlantic City, New Jersey, arriving in April 1943. It took him three days to drive from Wichita to Atlantic City. By the time Vern arrived, the routine for flight activities was well established. On April 29, 1943, the CAP was operationally transferred from control of OCD to the War Department, and in May 1943, an Auxiliary of the AAF. CAP strength at Atlantic City consisted of forty aircraft of various types and sizes. The only standard shared was the CAP emblem painted on the side of the aircraft's fuselage and wings. The emblem was an adaption of the U.S. Civil Defense emblem, with a three-blade propeller in a white triangle. The U.S. was added to conform to military markings. CAP aircraft were multi-colored because they were privately owned, no constant color scheme. The Atlantic City CAP base launched its daily flight operations at dawn, with two aircraft flying out to Cape May to locate and pickup ships sailing down from Rehobeth Beach, Delaware. Planes flew out to a distance of 25 miles to 50 miles off shore, flying at 500 feet, using a compass for navigation. There were no radio navigation aids for CAP pilots. Interestingly, the wreckage accumulated in the shipping lanes from previous U-boat sinkings, hulls and superstructures above the sunken wrecks, created known visible navigation markers. Because of the intensity of the war and threat from U-boats, no attempts had been made to salvage the wrecked ships. Once CAP pilots identified ships to be escorted, they slowly circled the ships under way, keeping a watch for German U-boats in the area. These CAP aircraft flying out of Bar Harbor, Maine;

Portland, Maine and Falmouth, Massachusetts conducted air escort missions for the Boston to Halifax bound convoys. None of the CAP pilots flying convoy escort mission had been trained on military close escort procedures.

Vern Kramer..."If CAP pilots spotted anything, especially survivors in the water, they would drop a marker so a U.S. Coast Guard cutter or other ship could locate and pick up survivors or recover bodies. After a four hour, patrol mission another CAP aircraft would take over and the previously patrolling aircraft would return to base. These patrols required improvising to keep flying, even after the military officially recognized the CAP as a valuable resource to keep U-boats below the surface. Original personal safety equipment for the CAP aircrews was limited, consisting of inflated inner tubes, which the pilots threw into the aircraft's baggage compartment. They also had lift rings and eventually issued a "Zoot Suit" (a rubber suit worn while flying over cold water). These "Zoot Suits" were designed to protect its wearer who had to ditch into or parachute into the cold (freezing) Atlantic Ocean. Unfortunately, they were hot and awkward to wear inside a small aircraft. Usually, the observer in the aircraft would take his arm out of the rubber suit while flying because he could not write comments on the mission log. This led to problems if the aircraft went down into the cold Atlantic Ocean because the Zoot Suit would rapidly fill with the water, making the unfortunate wearer weighing several hundred additional pounds that the U.S. Coast Guard rescuer would have to lift out of the water. Finally, they were issued inflatable Mae West life preservers. I never went down into the cold water. However, those who did were made members of the CAP Dick Club."

One of the outstanding qualities of the CAP during World War II was its flexibility and freedom from the need (requirement) to go through military channels. For example, if the USN needed something of high priority moved my air, such as time expiring blood plasma to a bomb sight, or message delivered to a ship off shore, the CAP delivered it quickly. Often, if bad weather grounded military aircraft, CAP frequently continued to fly.

Kramer..."After a long mission, I often found my aircraft maintenance skills needed. There were always aircraft, which needed work before their next mission. I learned aircraft maintenance at Spearfish Airport before the war."

Because of a combination of increasing military aircraft, USN warship convoy escorts, blackout restrictions along the U.S. east coast, along with low-level CAP flights, German Navy Commander, Admiral Karl Donitz on August 31, 1943, ordered the withdrawal of his U-boats from the U.S. Atlantic coastal shipping lanes. In an ultimate compliment, a German U-boat commander wrote in his log (captured by U.S. Navy intelligence officers after the surrender of German military forces, on file in the U.S. Naval War College library) wrote that German submarines were withdrawn..."because of those dammed little red and yellow airplanes of the Civil Air Patrol." As CAP aircraft were withdrawn, these volunteers took on new assignments such as guarding airfields, towing aerial gunnery targets (for airborne and anti-aircraft gunnery training), flying courier and liaison sorties, along with continued search and rescue flights.

Kramer..."After the Atlantic City base closed, I transferred to Hadley Field, New Jersey and onto Rehobeth Field, Delaware. I also went to Hyde Field, near Clinton, Maryland. I transferred to Baltimore, Maryland to work in the maintenance facility for CAP aircraft before returning them back to the civilian owners. I also performed two target missions consisting of a CAP aircraft, which reeled out of the rear or bottom of the aircraft for shore gunnery units to conduct live gunnery practice. Each gunnery unit coated its ammunition with a different color of paint so when the target sleeve was recovered, the gunnery unit could see how accurate their fire was on the target. CAP aircraft would release their target sleeve or banner over the gun emplacement so it could be recovered and reviewed on the spot. CAP pilots often decorated tow banners before a mission. Night missions were especially challenging because their aircraft was not equipped with night instruments and interior lights sometimes were not available, or of lighted, so bright as to reduce outside visibility which placed the pilots in jeopardy. Often, these missions were flown during cold weather, making it difficult for the pilots to do their mission in an unheated cockpit. The pilots wore fur lined clothes and heavy flying boots. Usually, the CAP aircraft's fuselage had a hole cut on the bottom, through which a banner sleeve could be lowered. Consequently, there was a constant flow of cold air blowing into the aircraft." [31]

---

[31] Lt. Col. George A. Larson, USAF (Ret.), "Civil Air Patrol searches for German U-boats during World War II," article submission to South Dakota Historical Society, Pierre, South Dakota, October 2004.

Rextroat Ola

Women Air Force Service Pilots in World War II

D URING the run-up for the United States to transition from neutrality to active participation against Germany, Italy and Japan, the male dominated military pilot image slowly cracked from pressure by American women pilots. The Women Flying Training Detachment (WFTD) and the Women Auxiliary Ferry Squadron (WAFS) used women pilots in military support functions. The Women Air Force Service Pilots (WASP) replaced the WFTD and WAFS to provide non-combat support for U.S. military aviation, on August 5, 1943.

After the narrow victory by the RAF over the German Air Force, two American women aviation pioneers in the summer of 1941 (Jacqueline Cochran and Nancy Harkness Love) separately submitted proposals to allow women pilots to perform non-combat flight support for the USAAF. Women would free men for combat duty by ferrying military aircraft from U.S. aviation factories to military state side bases and overseas shipment points, while assisting military training by performing repetitive duties (towing drones and aerial target sleeves). General Henry H. Arnold, Commanding General USAAF, decided not to implement the two proposals.

However, Air Transport Command (ATC) was over-committed in 1942. To meet demands of a two-ocean war, the USAAF decided to adopt Nancy love's proposal to allow women pilots to assist ATC in moving aircraft across the country to meet U.S. war demands. Twenty-five pilots completed recruitment into the program, with each averaging 1,000 hours flight time. Jacqueline Cochran convinced General Arnold to authorize and begin training women pilots to serve in non-combat support for military aviation duties in the United States.

The USAAF created the 319th WFTD at Houston, Texas Municipal Airport, with Cochran as its commander. The Second Ferrying Group, WAFS at New Castle Army Air Base, Delaware started operations. In July 1943, General Arnold combined the WAFS and WFTD into the WASP. Women pilot training began in November 1942, under a civilian contract for a military pilot training school at Howard Hughes Airport, Houston, Texas. Pilot training increased, expanded numbers required a larger facility with more room for ground school and flight training aerial operations. Training moved to Avenger Field, Sweetwater, Texas. WASP training program consisted of:

1. 135 hours flight training.
2. 180 hours ground school instruction.

Program training modifications consisted of:

1. Declining flight experience of candidates required changes to flying instruction.
2. Candidates complained the instruction program was not meeting their needs.
3. Declining proficiency of graduates forced assigned of women pilots to non-ferry flight operations.
4. No air to air gunnery training.
5. Limited formation flying training.
6. No aerobatic training.
7. Candidates received standard flight procedures: stalls, loops, spins, lazy eights, snap rolls, etc.
8. Washout rates for women candidates same or slightly less than male pilot training candidates.

Ola Rextroat, member of the Oglala Lakota Native American Indian tribe, joined the WASP after graduating from High School. After completing pilot training, she was assigned to tow aerial target sleeves for gunnery trainees to shot at. Each trainee had their ammunition painted a certain color to allowing scoring once the sleeve was released from the tow aircraft, floating to the ground for recovery by personnel in a jeep, then taken to a scoring area to determine the proficiency of the gunner. USAAF records indicate Rextroat as the only Native American Indian woman qualifying for, completing training and serving in the WASP.

WASP was given choice of duties after completing training.

1. The type of aircraft to fly.
2. Selection of primary operating or home air base.
3. Preference to pilots to be assigned with.

Assignments were based on the trainee's records.

1. Flight time.

2. Ground school performance.
3. Link trainer performance.
4. Physical training performance and evaluation.
5. Performance as a student officer.
6. Evaluation by staff advisors.

Those graduating WASP with the best overall ratings were usually granted the type of plane they wanted to fly. Most WASP flew light aircraft but others flew multi-engine aircraft including B-17s, B-24s and B-29s. WASP served at 120 air bases throughout the United States. They accumulated over 60,000,000 air miles of ferry operations consisting of:

1. Flights from aircraft factories to ports of overseas embarkation.
2. Delivery of combat aircraft to training bases.
3. Towed airborne target sleeves for aerial interception, aerial gunnery, anti-aircraft live fire, simulated air-to-ground strafing attacks against ground troops to assist in their training for combat.
4. Transporting cargo throughout the United States.
5. Delivery of 78 different types of aircraft, a total of 12,650 (50 percent of WASP ferry flights).

During WASP operations

1. Eleven killed during training.
2. Twenty-seven killed during operational flights. [32]

---

[32] "Rextroat Ola. Congressional Gold Medal ceremony in honor of Women Air Force Service Pilots," March 11, 2010. Information courtesy Eric Bursch, Legislative Assistance, Office of Congresswoman Stephanie Herseth-Sandlin, South Dakota to Lieutenant Colonel George A. Larson, USAF (Ret.)

Brief History of Ellsworth Air Force Base

Rapid City, South Dakota

ON January 2, 1942, the U.S. War Department established Rapid City Army Air Base as a training location for B-17 Flying Fortress crews. From September 1942, when its military runways first opened, until mission needs changed in July 1945, the field's instructors taught thousands of pilots, navigators and gunners from nine heavy bombardment groups and numerous smaller units. All training focused on the Allied drive to overthrow Axis powers in Europe.

After World War II, the base briefly trained weather reconnaissance and combat squadrons flying the P-61 Black Widow, P-38 Lightning, P-51 Mustang and B-25 Mitchell aircraft. When these missions ended, Rapid City Army Air Field temporarily shut down from September 1946 to March 1947. After operations resumed in 1947, the base became an Air Force asset. The primary unit assigned to Rapid City AFB was the 28th Bombardment Wing (BMW) flying the B-29 Superfortress.

The installation changed names a few more times during its early years. In January 1948, Air Force Chief of Staff, General Carl A. Spaatz renamed it Weaver AFB, in honor of Brigadier General Walter R. Weaver, one of the pioneers in the development of the Air Force as an independent military service. In June of that year, in response to overwhelming public appeals, Secretary of the Air Force Stuart Symington returned the base to its previous name. The base was declared a "permanent installation" in early 1948.

Shortly after additional improvements in July 1949, the 28th BMW started conversion from B-29s to B-36s. In April 1950, the Air Staff reassigned the base from 15th to 8th Air Force administrative control. The base experienced one of its worst peacetime tragedies in March 1953, when a RB-36H crashed, killing the entire crew of 23 in Newfoundland while returning from a routing training exercise in Europe. On June 13, 1953, President Dwight D. Eisenhower made a personal visit to dedicate the base in memory of Brigadier General Richard E. Ellsworth, Commandeer 28th Strategic Reconnaissance Wing (SRW), who lost his life in the crash.

Military organizations periodically upgraded manpower and equipment periodically to meet new national security requirements. Ellsworth AFB's organizations were no exception. Headquarters SAC reassigned the 28th BMW from 8th to 15th Air Force in October 1955. Approximately one year later, SAC set plans in motion to replace the 28th's B-36s with the B-52 Stratofortress. The last B-36 departed Ellsworth on May 29, 1957 and the first B-52 arrived sixteen days later. In 1958, all base units came under the command of the 821st Strategic Aerospace Division, headquartered at Ellsworth AFB.

In October 1960, Ellsworth entered the "space age" with the activation of the 850th Strategic Missile Squadron (SMS), initially assigned to the 28th BMW. For more than a year, this squadron prepared for the emplacement of Titan I ICBMs, which arrived in 1962, shortly after the activation of the 44th SMW in January. At that time, Headquarters SAC named the 44th SMW as host wing at Ellsworth AFB. The Titan I's life span was short in western South Dakota. In July 1962, SAC effectively rendered it obsolete with the activation of the 66th SMS, the first of such units slated to operate 150 Minuteman I ICBMS with the 44th SMW. The 67th SMS joined the 44th in August, followed by the 68th in September 1962.

On June 1, 1971, SAC inactivated the 821st Strategic Aerospace Division. By October, an upgraded Minuteman II ICBM replaced the Minuteman I ICBM. Ellsworth soon became known as "the showplace of SAC" as it continued to fight the Cold War by maintaining two legs of America's strategic triad: strategic bombers and ICBMs. It carried out these important missions for more than 15 years with relatively little change. The 1980s brought new challenges. In 1986, the base and 28th BW made extensive preparations to phase out the aging B-52 fleet and became the new home for the advanced B-1B Lancer. Contractors completed new unaccompanied enlisted dormitories in March; a new security police group headquarters in October, and gave Ellsworth's 13,497 foot runway a much needed upgrade. In addition, they completed new aircraft maintenance facilities for the base's new aircraft. The last 28th BMW B-52H departed Ellsworth in early 1986. In January 1987, the wing received the first of its 35 B-1B Lancer bombers.

The 12th Air Division moved to Ellsworth AFB in July 15, 1988. This organization was responsible for training B-1B, B-52 and KC-135 Stratotanker aircrews. Headquarters SAC activated a third wing, the 99th Strategic Weapons Wing at Ellsworth on August 10, 1989. This wing assumed primary responsibility for B-1B and B-52 advanced aircrew training.

Internationally, the destruction of the Berlin Wall in October 1989 symbolized the imminent demise of the Soviet Union over the next several months. It should be pointed out, beginning in 2000, the Russian Federation flush with oil money is rebuilding its nuclear strike force and modernizing its military to the point where in rattles potential movement of weapons if the United States builds a missile shield defense in former Eastern Bloc countries as protection against future Iranian missile attacks, possibly armed with nuclear warheads. During this transition, the Air Force shuffled its organizations and resources to meet a diminishing, although shifting worldwide threats. Changes came quickly. On January 3, 1990, SAC redesignated the 812th Combat Support Group as the 812th Strategic Support Wing (SSW), which, for a short time became Ellsworth's fourth wing. The 812th SSW consolidated all combat support activities into one organization. On July 31, 1990, SAC replaced the 12th Air Division with the Strategic Warfare Center (SWC), which provided operational command and administrative control over Ellsworth's subordinate units. Later, as part of SAC's intermediate headquarters and base level organization plan, on September 1, 1991, SAC redesignated the 28th BMW to 28th Wing, the 44th SMW, the 44th Wing, 99th SWW and the 99th Tactics and Training Wing. Ten days later, SAC inactivated the SWC and 812th SSW. The 28th became Ellsworth's host organization and it absorbed all previous 812th SSW functions. It was also during this time that in acknowledgement of the elimination of the Warsaw Pact (the military presence of the Soviet Union in Eastern Europe), the Secretary of Defense ordered nuclear alert to stand-down. The decades of instant nuclear retaliation Cold War ended.

On June 1, 1992, as part of the first major reorganization since the creation of an independent Air Force, SAC was inactivated SAC, assigning Ellsworth's organizations (including a renamed 28th BW) to the newly activated Air Combat Command (ACC). After, less than a year under ACC, the 28th's mission changed from strategic bombardment to worldwide conventional munitions delivery. The mission of the 99th Tactics and Training Wing (later redesignated as the 99th Wing) continued modified training operations to match the new force concept. The 44th MW completed its assigned deterrence mission. On December 3, 1991, the missile wing began pulling the first Minuteman II ICBM from its silo. On April 6, 1992, the first Launch Control Center (LCC) was deactivated. The entire missile complex was deactivated by April 1994. In keeping with its America's patriotic tradition of the American

Revolutionary War tradition, the 44th MW inactivated on July 4, 1994.

In March 1994, Ellsworth welcomed the 34th BS, a geographically separated unit awaiting airfield upgrades before it could return to its parent organization, the 366th BW at Mountain Home AFB, Ohio. The 34th's B-1BS (at that time) were part of the Air Force's composite wings, equipped with F-15s, F-16s and KC-135s. Also during 1994, the Air Force selected Ellsworth as the exclusive location from which to conduct a congressionally mandated operational readiness assessment of the B-1B, referred to as "Dakota Challenge." After six months of hard work, under peacetime and simulated wartime conditions, the 28th BW and Ellsworth AFB passed the test with flying colors and proved the B-1B to be a reliable and capable weapons system, the mainstay of America's heavy bomber fleet for years to come. Interestingly, at that time, it was believed the B-52 would not be the modern bomber it has become today after modifications, which increased electronic bombing accuracy, command, control and communications, reduced aircraft and updated cockpit flat screen technology. The B-52 and the B-2 were ACC's nuclear capable bombers with the B-1B currently a conventional munitions delivery platform.

In 1995, the 99th Wing departed for a new assignment at Nellis AFB, Nevada, although a small contingent formerly attached to that wing, remained behind to continue tactics training and radar munitions scoring from a handful of dispersed detachments. 1995 also saw the activation of one of Ellsworth's oldest units, the 77th BS. While the unit (as an administrative entity) departed to save Air Force funds for the development of a follow-on to B-1B munitions, the organization's aircraft remained at Ellsworth (in a flying reserve status) under the care of its sister unit, the 37th BS.

A reversal of fortune occurred early in 1996, when on 26 March; the Air Force announced the 77th BS would return to Ellsworth AFB. On 1 April, the squadron was activated at Ellsworth as the geographically separated 34th BS completed its transfer back to the 366th Wing at Mountain Home AFB, Idaho. By June 1998, the 77th had six of its B-1Bs pulled out of the reconstitution reserve, balancing those lost by the 34th BS.

In March 1999, the Air Force announced a reorganization plan that made Ellsworth AFB and 28th BW partners in the new Expeditionary Air Force (EAF) concept. The 28th BW was named a lead wing in the EAF. Under this plan, the 77th BS gained six B-1Bs and Ellsworth gained 100 military personnel. The expeditionary forces were designed to help the Air Force quickly respond to any worldwide crisis while making life more predictable for military members and their families. Although, during the fighting in Iraq and Afghanistan, deployments were continuous and hard on military personnel and their families, not to mention aircraft and equipment.

It was not too long before Ellsworth and the 28th BW took the lead in the EAF concept. Five B-1Bs from the wing joined NATO assets in "Operation ALLIED FORCE," and began attacks on military targets in Kosovo on April 1, 1999. By the end of the conflict in June, Ellsworth B-1Bs had flown 100 combat sorties, dropping 1,260 tons of MK-82 general-purpose bombs. The B-1B and Team Ellsworth proved itself invaluable to the security of America's national interests overseas.

After September 1, 2001, Team Ellsworth answered the call by deploying a number of B-1Bs in support of "Operation ENDURING FREEDOM." Aircraft from the 37th BS joined additional B-1Bs from the 34th BS at Mountain AFB and formed the 34th Expeditionary BS. This squadron, along with other elements from Ellsworth, deployed to Diego Garcia and joined the 28th Air Expeditionary Wing (AEW) where they recorded an impressive record against terrorist factions with their stated mission to attack and inflict harm and death on the United States. B-1B's combat effectiveness was exceeded 95 percent by only flying five percent of the total strike aircraft missions. They dropped 39 percent of the total tonnage of bombs, which was more than any other NATO strike aircraft. The amount of ordnance dropped was tremendous. During their deployment, the 28th BS dropped 2,974 JDAMS, 1,471 MK-82s, 135 MK-84S and 70 CBU-87s. The 28th BW and personnel continue to participate in deployments in support of operations around the world.

On September 19, 2001, the 34th BS joined the Ellsworth Team, arriving from Mountain Home AFB. Due to a drawdown in the number of B-1Bs, the 77th BS was inactivated and the "Thunderbirds" of the 34th BS moved to Ellsworth AFB to take its place as an operational squadron.

On April 20, 2015, the 28th BW switched from AAC to Air Force Global Strike Command (AFGSC), with headquarters at Barksdale Air Force Base, Louisiana. AFGSC now manages the nation's entire bomber fleet: B-1B, B-2 and B-52H. With this change, Ellsworth AFB will be the only pure conventional bomber base in AFGSC. The B-1B fleet at Ellsworth and Dyess AFB, Texas remains the cornerstone of the Air Force's air defense and global conventional strike force. With the newly expanded Power River Training Complex, authorized by the Federal Aviation Agency, the nation's B-1Bs from Ellsworth and B-

52Hs from Minot Air Force Base have a large area to perform tactical training. This change places Ellsworth at the top of probable bases to base the programmed Air Force's Long Range Strike Bomber (LRS-B) scheduled to replace the B-1B and B-52H.[33]

---

[33] "History of Ellsworth Air Force Base," Ellsworth Air Force Base, 28th Bomb Wing, Historian Office, July 2003.

North Bombing Range During World War II

Support for Training Operations at Rapid City Army Air Base

During World War II, 1941-1945, there was an area northeast of Newell, South Dakota, on Old Route 212, commonly referred to as the "Bombing Range." It was used by the Army Air Corps flying out of Rapid City Army Air Base, Rapid City, South Dakota. The site was located in a summer sheep pasture owned by Alexander and Preston "Buster" and Mabell Hill. Later, the Hill's family purchased it outright. It had been cordoned off; targets set so fake "dummy" bombs could be dropped by B-25s to fly over for target practice. For night exercisers, the targets were illuminated by power from a generator and guided with a voice from the radio tower. By 1942, the site was equipped with personnel barracks, a mess hall, a radio tower and a water tower. The men would drive to Rapid City for supplies, which would take an entire day, traveling at a top speed of 40mph to make the round trip. The wartime rationing system was in place, however, the airmen received special treatment and would get all the food and gasoline they needed. The men were rotated after their training, so none were in the area more than a few months at a time. The airmen generally drove into Newell on Saturday nights to attend dances, attended movies, played pool or watched baseball games. It is said, the local young men of Newell did not particularly appreciate these airmen coming into town, dating their young women. However, the young women rather enjoyed it because the airmen always seemed to have money to speed, unlike their counterparts to spend on food, movies and dances. Many of the airmen became friends with the Newell citizens, business owners, farmers or ranchers. The bombing range ceased use after the war was declared over and the equipment was left to rust and rot into the earth. The Hill family children enjoyed playing and exploring the site and did retrieve several empty bomb casings. In order to utilize his entire grazing range, Preston Hill pushed the rubble into a pile and with that, the North Bombing Range disappeared.[34]

LeRoy Faigan during World War II was assigned to the North Bombing Range. LeRoy..."The Old Route 212 appears to be the road we took from Newell to the Bombing range and I believe it was all gravel at the time. Also, the road leading into the range may have been gravel. I do remember when it rained we had trouble with a rear wheel drive dump truck constantly sliding off the road into the ditch. We called the surface 'gumbo,' it was mud and did not get very deep but was as slippery as ice. I used to drive a 6 by 6 Army truck once a week to Rapid City, for three months, and if memory serves me correctly, it took the better part of a day to get there, loading up supplies at Rapid City Army Air Base and get back."[35]

Faigan..."The bombing range water tower started leaking badly and someone got the brilliant idea to tar the inside. Well, you can imagine what the water tasted like after that, even showering with that water was unpleasant. The practice bombs used were filled with a small amount of explosive and something to create smoke. As I recall, they weighed about 100 pounds each and were about four feet long. Before I stopped flying because of injuries sustained in an airplane crash on June 14, 1941, then assigned to the bombing range, part of my job was to take pictures of the bomb strikes from the plane. When I was stationed at the range, there were actually times when we were right on the target repairing it when bombs were dropped. We used to kid around and say it was the safest place to be. But we did get off and away very quickly. The only reason we were there was because we had been told there would be no bombing at that time."[36]

Faigan..."I used to drive to the base for supplies and got to know the Supply Sergeant at Rapid City Army Air Base pretty well so we had lots of fresh meat and all the butter we wanted. So we decided one

---

[34] Linda Velder, Newell Museum, "North Bombing Range," Newell Centennial Book, Newell, South Dakota: Centennial Committee, 2010, to author, May 24, 2012.

[35] LeRoy Faigan during World War II was assigned to the North Bombing Range. He put together his remembrances of the bombing range in an e-mail to Linda Velder, Newell Museum on October 12, 2001, to author on May 24, 2012.

[36] LeRoy Faigan during World War II was assigned to the North Bombing Range. He put together his remembrances of the bombing range in an e-mail to Linda Velder, Newell Museum on November 13, 2001, to author on May 24, 2012.

night to make French fried potatoes cooked in butter and not oil. Well of course, they were horrible to eat and we did not do that again."[37]

Faigan..."There was another target somewhere quite a distance from the one I was stationed at. It had just a generator, which had to be tended by one of our fellows who would go there twice a day, morning and evening to service the generator and turn the target lights on and off. In traveling back and forth, I met a family who lived some miles from nowhere, lots of kids, two or three trucks, and what they did I do not know. Well, I became quite 'friendly' with one of the daughters and occasionally would spend the night there. He asked me to go along for the ride one time and stopped by there at about lunch time. They were very hospitable and asked us to stay for lunch. I diplomatically declined, no screens, windows and doors wide open in August. Chickens were running through the house and jumping on the table. It was strictly like something out of a Steinbeck novel."[38]

---

[37] LeRoy Faigan during World War II was assigned to the North Bombing Range. He put together his remembrances of the bombing range in an e-mail to Linda Velder, Newell Museum on November 15, 2001, to author on May 24, 2012.

[38] LeRoy Faigan during World War II was assigned to the North Bombing Range. He put together his remembrances of the bombing range in an e-mail to Linda Velder, Newell Museum on December 13, 2001, to author on May 24, 2012.

Clarence Carsner

34th Infantry Division, 109th Engineer Regiment

Combat Duty in North Africa and Italy, World War II

CLARENCE Carsner enlisted in the U.S. Army, South Dakota National Guard on June 19, 1940, some 18 months prior to the Imperial Japanese Navy carrier launched attack on U.S. military installation in and around Pearl Harbor, Hawaii on December 7, 1941. He was assigned to the 109th Engineer Regiment Headquarters and Service Camp. The 109th was a Black Hills National Guard Regiment with operational units in Rapid City, Sturgis and Hot Springs. President Franklin D. Roosevelt, as part of the U.S. military buildup prior to Pearl Harbor, under Presidential Order Number 8635, dated February 10, 1941, changed the status of the South Dakota National Guard unit to an active U.S. Army regiment assigned to the 34th U.S. Infantry Division, nicknamed the "Red Bull Division."

The 109th was shipped to Camp Claiborne, Louisiana, arriving at the Army training camp on February 26, 1941. Training was developed to prepare troops for an undefined combat threat, which at this time meant a possible involvement in the war against Germany and Italy. The training evolved in August 1941 into a War Department, Army designated "Louisiana Maneuvers," a large peacetime war game, which consisted of multiple divisions, enemy versus friendly forces. War training ramped up after Pearl Harbor. The 109th did not leave Camp Claiborne until January 2, 1942, traveling by train to Fort Dix, New Jersey for advanced training. The 109th Engineer Regiment was reorganized as the 109th Engineer Battalion, with parts of the original group assigned to the 34th Infantry Division, others assigned to other Army units to fill out their personnel quotas needed to be fully manned for combat duty.

Carsner was assigned to the 109th Engineer Battalion, sailing on February 19, 1942, on the transport USAT American Legion for combat in Europe. The transport, two days out of port suffered major mechanical problems, forcing it to drop out of the convoy, return to port without an escort. The transport reached Halifax, Nova Scotia but the ship required more extensive repairs than available in the convoy assembly port. It sailed south to the Boston Ship Repair Yard. After the transport docked, the 109th departed the ship, trucked to a temporary quarters at Camp Edward, Massachusetts, where the battalion resumed combat training. On 29 April, the 109th boarded its replacement transport, the Mexico, joining another convoy for the trip across the North Atlantic, reaching Belfast, Ireland on 12 May. The battalion was assigned to Camp Killadas, Ireland.

The 109th commenced additional combat training for a future landing in North Africa, supporting "Operation TORCH." Company C, 109th Engineers landed at Algeria on November 8, 1942. On January 4, 1943, the 34th Division and remaining 109th personnel landed at Oran, Algeria to prepare and take part in offensive actions against German forces in Tunisia. German Field Marshall Erwin Rommel did not wait for the General Eisenhower to attack, he moved first, attacking the 34th Division, including elements of the 109th Infantry Battalion. Rommel had combat hardened troops, better artillery (88mm dual-purpose: anti-aircraft and anti-armor), and superior armor (tanks with heavier frontal armor and larger caliber guns with tremendous armor penetrating power and longer range). The first U.S. contact against Rommel's troops was a disaster, forever referred to as the "Kasserine Pass" on February 20, 1943, hitting the U.S. II Corps. The U.S. lost 1,000 combat troops, large numbers of destroyed armor, artillery, jeeps, trucks, with hundreds of troops captured. General Eisenhower relieved General Fredendall as commander of II Corps, with General George Patton on March 3, 1943.

The 34th Division attacked "Hill 609" in April, securing the objective on 1 May, continuing on to Chouigui Pass, reaching Tebourba and Ferryville. The 34th Division landed at Salerno, Italy on 25 September. The 109th assisted in the crossing of the Calore River on 28 September, supporting the 34th Division's attack north to Benevento. The 109th assisted the division in crossing the winding Volturno River three times in October and November. The 34th Division was part of a larger force attacking Mont Patano and only able to occupy one of the four hilltops on the mountain prior to being pulled out of the line on 9 December for Rest & Relaxation (R & R).

Beginning in January 1944, the 34th Division took part in the attack on the German defensive position, called "The Gustav Line." This was a fall back defensive line across the Italian peninsula to stop the northward advance of Allied troops out of southern Italy, built quickly by German engineers as a fall back defensive line. The defensive line ran east from the Tyrrhenian Sea to the east end of the existing Bernhardt Line, which stopped at Minturno. The new line jogged north to Costle Forte, east to the Garigliano and Rapido Rivers into the bastion of Monte Casino, east to Sbiago, reconnecting to the remaining portion of the Bernhardt Line ay Alfredina. It took advantage of the mountainous terrain and rapid flowing rivers to create a formidable defense against which Allied forces would have to constantly attack uphill. The 34th Division was pulled out of the line on 13 February for R & R.

The division went from the meat grinder of the fight for Monte Casino to the fire to take part in the flank amphibious landing behind German lines at Anzio on 25 March. Unfortunately, Major General John Lucas had landed on 22 January; he stopped below the hills surround Anzio, deciding to build up forces, equipment and supplies before attacking east toward Rome. This timidity allowed German Field Marshall Kesselring to seal off the Anzio beachhead with scraped together troops, armor and artillery. After the Germans annihilated an armed reconnaissance force, General Lucas was relieved of command, replaced by General Truscott on 22 February. It took until 23 May for Truscott to breakout of Anzio, which allowed General Mark Clark to capture Rome on June 5, 1944, one day after the Allied invasion of Normandy on D-Day. The 34th Division was pulled out of the line for R & R, then attacked and captured Mount Belmonte in October 1944. Winter weather effectively stopped Allied offensive operations, with the 34th Division taking up defensive positions south of Bologna. On April 15, 1945, the advance continued north with the 34th Division, capturing Bologna on 21 April. Allied offensive operations stopped on May 2, 1945, after German forces ceased combat operations. On 8 May (VE-Day), German commanders surrendered to General Eisenhower's forces, stopping the war in Europe.

Carsner and the 109th Battalion participated in 600 days of military service in North Africa and Italy. The U.S. Army War College World War II records indicate this was a longest of any U.S. combat unit during the war. After returning to the United, he was discharged from the 109th in July 1945, even though fighting continued in the Pacific against remaining Japanese military forces. Fierce fighting did not end until the Japanese civil government and military agreed to accept the Allied terms of unconditional surrender with the provision that they could retain their Emperor, stopping the fighting on 15 August, with the signing of the surrender documents onboard the battleship Missouri in Tokyo Bat on September 2, 1945. Carsner rejoined the South Dakota

National Guard in March 1947, retiring with the rank of Colonel in 1978.[39]

---

[39] Clarence Carsner, U.S. Army World War II, "Combat duty in the Mediterranean Theater of Operations in World War II," Veterans of Foreign Wars, Post 1273, Rapid City, South Dakota.

Marion J. Larkin

Boeing B-17s in North Africa

MEMBERS of the United States Armed Forces who served in past wars can vouch that sometimes an earned military decoration can take a while to work its way through the bureaucratic paper mill to be verified and presented. Not many veterans have to wait 52 years after the World War II combat mission that earned him a Distinguished Flying Cross to be presented and receive the medal. But, this is what happened to Marion J. Larkin of Rapid City, South Dakota. During World War II, Larkin was a U.S. Army Air Forces (USAAF) Boeing B-17F Flying Fortress copilot and later, pilot, assigned to the 99th Bomb Group (BG). Larkin was a college senior at Kansas State University when the Japanese attacked the U.S. military installations at Pearl Harbor, Hawaii on the morning of December 7, 1941. He drove a bunch of his college friends to the U.S. Army recruiting office in Lawrence, Kansas so they could enlist. While his friends were signing up, the Army recruiter asked him also to enlist. However, Larking wanted to graduate first. The Army recruiter explained to him that if he signed up now, he could be paid for the drive to Lawrence would wait until graduation before being called up to active military duty. He signed up and in one week he was called up into the USAAF.

Larkin received primary cadet flying training at Oxnard, California starting on June 13, 1942, learning to fly the Boeing/Stearman PT-17 trainer. He then went to the next level of training at Gurdner Field at Taft, California, flying the Vultee BT-13 Valiant trainer. Next, he flew the North American AT-6 Texan, then onto the twin-engine Cessna AT-17. This aircraft was used to qualify pilots for advanced training in heavier, multi-engine aircraft: Boeing B-17 Flying Fortress and Consolidated B-24 Liberator. The B-17 was a long-range, four-engine strategic bomber. Lt. Larkin trained on the B-17 and assigned to the 99th BG, part of a Flying Fortress crew. The 99th BG was constituted on January 29, 1942, activated on June 1, 1942 at Orlando AAFB, Florida. On September 30, 1942, Lt. Larkin joined a newly formed B-17 crew assigned to Walla Walla, Washington for basic four-engine familiarization training, gunnery practice, bombing practice and crew combat coordination training. The B-17 crew went to Sioux City

AAFB at Sioux City, Iowa for advanced bomber formation flying training using the B-17E. Sioux City AAFB was as a training base prior to bomber crews transitioning to a separate base where the crew picked up the aircraft to fly to England or North Africa for theater combat operations. The crew boarded a train to the Boeing Aircraft Company's production plant at Salinas, Kansas, picking up a factory fresh B-17F.

1st. Lt. Charles Bliss named the B-17F after his three-year old daughter, Coreen Ann, painting the name "Queen Ann" on the aircraft's number 42-29512, a Boeing B-17F-55-BO, on the nose of the bomber. Larkin was the bomber's copilot. The crew flew the new B-17F to Derrider, Louisiana for over the water, long-range navigation and flight crew familiarization training to prepare them for combat operations. The training was primarily designed to give B-17 aircrews simulated combat experience, preparing them to navigate over the English Channel and the North Sea to targets in Nazi controlled Europe. When B-17s began flying from air bases in North Africa and later Italy, over water navigation was critical. The long-distance over water navigation had a practical purpose to aircrews to fly from the United States, over the Atlantic to bases in England and North Africa.

The Queen Ann and other 99th BG B-17s landed at Navarin, Algeria, North Africa on February 23, 1943. Rather than fly onto heavy bomber bases in England and combat with the Eighth Air Force, the 99th BG remained in North Africa, assigned to the Twelfth Air Force. The 99th BG was needed because German Field Marshall Erwin Rommel was pressing vigorously with ground attacks against the non-combat tested U.S. Army troops, seriously disrupting General Dwight D. Eisenhower's planned Allied ground offensive east, out of Morocco and Algeria into Tunisia. Unfortunately, the 99th BG's ground echelon, mess facilities and cooks, and administrative personnel moved directly to England by sea transport. Army troops on the base hastily scrapped together enough personnel to create a make shift ground support team, providing aircrews with pup tents to sleep at night in the cold desert night temperatures. Many aircrew members decided to sleep inside their bomber to be somewhat protected from the desert night's winds. The aircrews had to find as much shelter as possible because the cold temperatures in North Africa created a dramatic contrast from the day's searing temperatures.

Aircrews also had to guard their bombers to keep out roaming Arab tribesmen from sneaking along the flight line's edge at night, entering the bombers, stealing anything not welded to the body of the aircraft, and any personal items. During daylight hours, aircrews loaded bombs, fueled the aircraft, inserted guns and ammunition, and anything else needed to conduct their assigned combat sortie. This bare bones existence was hard on the 99th's aircrews, especially without mess facilities and no regular hot food servings. The aircrews, whenever possible, ate in surrounding Army infantry and artillery units, support troops and British Army units. They all opened their mess facilities for the 99th, serving hot meals before and after a combat mission. There was a problem for each aircrew's four officers, including those on the Queen Ann. Under strict interpretation of U.S. Army regulations, officers could not eat with enlisted personnel, and hot food was only available at the enlisted mess facilities close to the base. The Queen Ann's enlisted crewmembers told their officers "take off all rank and act like one of us." The enlisted crewmembers took good care of their officers, creating an elite combat aircrew. The surrounding mess facilities prepared box lunches for the aircrews to take on combat missions.

The 99th entered combat in March 1943, starting bombing missions against German and Italian airfields, harbor facilities, railroad transfer points, viaducts, bridges and other strategic targets in Tunisia, Sardinia, Sicily and Italy. On July 5, 1943, the 99th attacked Gerbini airfield, Sicily. Bombers fought their way through intense Bf-109 fighter attacks and flak to destroy hangars, fuel tanks and ammunition dumps on and around the airfield. At the end of the bombing raid, 99th gunners credited with shooting down or destroying on the ground, one hundred enemy fighters. These bombing raids, prior to the Allied invasion of Sicily, rendered Gerbini airfield and its seven satellite airfields unserviceable. U.S. Army Air Force Intelligence officers, after the invasion of Sicily made a thorough ground inspection of these airfields, counting over 1,000 enemy aircraft either damaged or destroyed. The German Air Force withdrew remaining operation aircraft to airfields in northern Italy prior to the withdrawal from Sicily.

On these missions, the Queen Ann's crew feared anti-aircraft artillery aerial bursts the most, followed closely by Bf-109 fighter attacks. Fw-190 fighters also attacked, assigned to the Herman Goring "Yellow Nose" Group, considered to be one of the German Air Force elite fighter groups. The Queen Ann's crew was amazed at the tenacity, which German fighter pilots took when attacking Flying Fortress groups, plowing straight ahead through concentrated .50 caliber machine gun fire, pressing home attacks. After completing fifteen combat missions on Queen Ann, Lt. Bliss received orders and transferred to a position in the group, as check out pilot. Lt. Larkin became Queen Ann's pilot. The rest of the crew remained the same, with copilots, flying with other crews but never permanently assigned to Larkin's crew. Larkin completed 19 combat missions as pilot/aircraft commander of the Queen Ann.

On July 16, 1943, the 99th BG, including 1st Lt. Larkin's crew, attacked the railroad yards at San Giovanni, Italy. This was Larkin's 35th combat mission. The Queen Ann was flying on the left wing in a three ship B-17 formation. The 99th BG flew straight and level after turning onto the target run from the Initial Point (IP), so all 26 B-17s would be properly lined up for the final bombing run on the railroad yards, releasing all bombs along its long axis to allow for maximum number of bombs striking the target. The Germans used Giovanni Railroad Yard to ship large quantities of equipment, supplies and ammunition south to support German Army units manning defensive positions across the Italian peninsula, blocking Allied troops attempt to reach Rome from the south. The 99th BG dropped its bombs on their assigned target.

After the Queen Ann's bombardier released bombs, Larkin pushed the aircraft's nose over, descending from bombing altitude of 29,000 feet to get away from heavy caliber flak. However, one flak burst exploded in front of the aircraft, followed group flak bursts straddling the left side of the B-17F, causing considerable damage. Black smoke filled the aircraft's cockpit, while at the same time the aircraft began to roll toward another bomber because control lines to the tail were severed. Larkin engaged the autopilot, which brought the damaged bomber to level flight control. The bomber lost engine number two, propeller on engine three running wild, creating an out of control aircraft. Larkin could not feather engine three. Number three engine's propeller fell off. The aircraft was shuddering and shaking, with the autopilot functioning but providing only a limited degree of flight control. The autopilot's controls were located on the wings where flat bursts did not cut the control wires. The autopilot kept the bomber from rolling completely over onto its top, continuing into an uncontrollable spin and crash. Even with the autopilot functioning, Larkin had difficulty controlling the damaged bomber. It was like driving a car downhill without a steering wheel or brakes. Engines two and three were gone. In a four-engine aircraft, engines are numbered one through four, beginning with engine one, left outboard; engine two, left inboard; engine three, right inboard and engine four, right outboard. On the damaged B-17F, two engines remained functioning. One on each side of the fuselage, evenly spaced, engines one and four. Larkin was having problems with engine number four, which could only operate at a reduced power setting of 50 percent. To keep the bomber flying level, power was reduced on number one engine.

Even though the radio in the damaged aircraft was not functioning, the intercom remained operational. Through this system, Larkin knew two of his gunners were badly wounded requiring emergency medical attention. The navigator, Lt, Banasiack, carrying a portable oxygen tanks hooked in his facemask's oxygen hose, crawled to the rear of the aircraft to check on the condition of the two wounded gunners. These two had wounds in the legs and abdomen. A third gunner suffered a wound behind his ear from a small piece of shrapnel.

The flight engineer, SSgt. Delano, began slowly crawling along the shredded left side of the fuselage, attempting to splice severed control cable lines together. He was able to complete repairs, allowing Larkin to regain a limited degree of lateral flight control, giving him slow and gradual flight directional changes. With only two engines operating, and those two at 50 percent power, the bomber had to drop out of formation because it could not keep up. More of an immediate concern for the crew was the loss of altitude. Slowly dropping to a lower altitude, a lone aircraft or straggler became a "sitting duck" for any German fighter attacking the bomber. The crew had a tough decision, to parachute, ditch or execute a controlled crash landing in Allied controlled territory. These were serious choices. If the crew parachuted or ditched, the wounded crewmembers might not survive. To keep the damaged aircraft flying, the crew lightened it as quickly as possible, throwing anything out of the bomber not bolted down, except machine guns and ammunition. The guns provided some level of protection against attacking German fighters. The damaged B-17F was still over German occupied/controlled territory with the crew deciding to try to reach Allied control territory, then throw out the remaining guns and ammunition. Up to this time, the crew was fortunate, the bomber had not been attacked by German fighters.

All of a sudden one of the crew yelled "German fighters." In the air, a German Bf-109 and RAF Spitfire looked similar. B-17 and B-24 gunners often mistakenly opened fire on RAF Spitfires before correctly identifying the type of aircraft approaching the aircraft. A gunner only had a few seconds to fire or not fire, with any mistake resulting on an enemy fighter firing at close range, severely damaging the bomber or knocking it down. Consequently, RAF Spitfire pilots developed the tactic of executing what they referred to as a "flesh up" maneuver. This was a high-speed roll away from the bombers, clearly showing the

British markings on the underside of the fighter. This was a dangerous maneuver, but one, which saved many RAF pilots from being, shot down by B-17 and B-24 gunners. The three fighters approaching the "Queen Ann" executed this maneuver and were identified as RAF fighters. They joined on the B-17 flying close to the visibly wounded bombers, providing close-in fighter escort. Now the gunners could throw out their .50 caliber machine guns and ammunition, flak vests, helmets and expended .50 caliber machine gun shell casings from the bomber's floor. The B-17 continued to vibrate and lose precious altitude.

The preferred emergency airfield was on the British controlled island of Malta. Malta's airfield assisted U.S. bombers flying out of North African airfields, bombing targets in Sicily and Italy, prior to the Allied invasion of those two enemy occupied territories. Headquarters Desert Air Force provided fighter escort for the bombers whenever they could be made available. Also, Malta based RAF fighters were often launched to provide escort of American heavy bombers exiting German target areas after bomb release. Frequently, wounded bomber crewmembers were able to receive medical treatment quicker at Malta than making the long flight back to a North African base. Badly damaged bombers also used Malta as an emergency landing field, rather than risk the longer over the water flight to their North American air bases.

By now, the B-17 was below 10,000 feet, so oxygen was no longer required. The crew continued to throw out any unnecessary equipment from the aircraft. Now even the oxygen tanks, masks and oxygen hoses could be thrown out. Lt. Larkin decided the aircraft could not make it to Malta, which was over 100 miles away with the aircraft losing altitude. So rather than be forced to ditch in the sea on the way to Malta, Larkin headed the aircraft south, flying along the east coast of Sicily, hoping to bring the aircraft to some type of controlled landing when it lost remaining altitude or he found a suitable emergency landing area.

British General Montgomery and U.S. General George Patton commanded troops, which invaded Sicily on July 9, 1943. Because of this successfully Allied landing, Larkin hoped to make an emergency landing in Allied controlled territory there. The B-17 was badly damaged, so low that Larkin was unable to change direction to any great degree, There was another dangerous situation developing, the bomber was now flying over British Royal Navy battleships, slowly steaming off shore, firing on German positions on Sicily, inland from the amphibious landing beaches. The large shells were going in shore and at the same time, German artillery shells were going out to sea toward the battleships. Larkin was running out of options. The B-17 continued to lose altitude, actually flying through out-going British Navy shells and incoming German long-range defensive artillery shells. The "Queen Ann's" crew could see splashes from the German shells around the British battleships.

As the "Queen Ann" flew past Port Syracuse, near Cape Passero, Larkin identified a fairly level stretch of hard sand beach over which might be a possible emergency crashing landing area. As best as possible, given the aircraft's limited controllability remaining, Larkin lined up the damaged B-17 for wheels up crash landing. By now, the bomber was so low there was no alternative but to land. The spliced control wires broke, at this moment, but Larkin engaged the autopilot while jockeying the power setting on the two operating engines to keep the landing area directly ahead of the rapidly descending aircraft. This turned out to be a very interesting emergency.

As Lt. Larkin prepared to make an emergency landing on what initially appeared from a distance and closer, to be a sandy flat beach area, he suddenly realized he was actually landing in a swamp containing heavy brown mud. He had no choice, with altitude and speed almost gone, but to land. The copilot lowered the aircraft's flaps, but only the left side of the landing gear came down. Larkin ordered flaps to be raised, correcting the descending bomber's lateral direction by again using the throttles to decrease power to the left engine. The B-17 was nearly to the ground, approaching with wheels up, flaps up, nearing the aircraft's stall speed, but at a high landing speed. Interestingly, the three RAF fighters remained close by the bomber, even flying through the off shore shell fire. One of the RAF fighter pilots radioed British Army Headquarters on Sicily that a badly damaged American bomber was going to crash land behind British Army front lines.

As the B-17 crossed the edge of the brown sandy appearing area, the bomber stalled, falling out of the air, dropping into what was actually mud. It plowed through thick mud with dirty water filling the bomber's interior. A thin layer of mud created a crush over the five foot deep swamp water, which gave the area the appearance of a sandy beach from the air.

Even though badly damaged, the B-17 did not break upon impact or burst into flames. As the crew scrambled to get out of the aircraft, they found shrapnel from German flak had shredded the lift raft stowed inside the bomber's fuselage right side. The crew pulled out the remaining life raft, inflated it as they threw it out the aircraft. Part of the crew climbed into the lift raft out of the right side of the aircraft. Other crew members jumped into the muddy water, which was up to their necks, making it a struggle for them to reach firm ground. After struggling in this muddy water for 30 minutes, they saw British Army medics wading toward them, yelling, "good show Yanks!"

Once onto firm ground, the British Army medics took the "Queen Ann's" crew to their Army field hospital, at which time British Army doctors treated the two badly and one slightly wounded gunners, keeping the two waist gunners at their hospital. Most of the crew was treated for various minor wounds suffered during the crash landing.

Lt. Larkin never found out what happened to the two badly wounded waist gunners treated in the British Army field hospital. He and his copilot were driven in a British Army Lorry to an airstrip on Sicily, where a U.S. C-47 flew them back to their base at Oudna, Tunisia. The other crew members were flown in a RAF C-47 to Malta, from there picked up by a 99th BG training crew flying a B-17 for the return flight to Oudna, Tunisia. Lt. Larkin and remaining "Queen Ann" crewmembers and replacements were assigned another B-17F, which the crew named "Bugs," aircraft number 42-9526 after the cartoon character Bugs Bunny. The composite crew flew another 15 combat missions. They were reassigned to Fifteenth Air Force in November 1943, moving to Tortorella Airfield, Italy on December 11, 1943. Later, they transferred to Marcianise, Italy on December 18, 1943. After reaching 50 combat missions, now Captain Larkin was ordered to return to the United States on December 1, 1944. He was assigned as a B-17 Flying Fortress instructor at Rapid City Army Air Base, Rapid City, South Dakota.

Larkin was then transferred to Davis Monthan Air Base at Tucson, Arizona to help transition B-17 and B-24 pilots coming from Europe to fly the B-29 for Pacific combat operations. After months of training B-29 crews, Larkin began to train and fly with one crew, which probably meant they were about to be transferred to the Pacific Theater of Operations (Guam, Tinian or Saipan), assigned to the Twentieth Air Force. By this time in World War II, Germany and Italy had surrendered. The Allies planned to concentrate military forces to attack the Japanese home islands. At this point in the war, the USAAF began reviewing Airman records to determine who should be retained on active duty, even though the war against Japan was ongoing. If an airman accumulated a certain number of points, he could request release from active service. Captain Larkin qualified and discharged on July

25. 1945. His World War II service included over 1,600 flying hours, earning the following military decorations: Air Medal with nine Oak Leaf Clusters, American Campaign Medal, European-Africa-Middle East Campaign Medal, World War II Medal and Distinguished Flying Cross. [40]

---

[40] Lt. Col. George A. Larson, USAF (Ret.), "B-17 warrior: The strategic bombing campaign from North Africa, Friends Journal, Volume 31, Number 1, Spring 2008.

Clair Patterson

DD USS McGowan, Pacific Combat

CLAIR Patterson..."I was born in a small town of Folsom, Custer County, South Dakota on March 6, 1923. When I was very young, my parents moved from Folsom to the southern part of South Dakota to a small town called Mission Hills. When I turned 17 in 1940, I convinced my parents to let me enroll in the Civil Conservation Corps (CCC), in which I served from the middle of October 1940 to the middle of December 1941, receiving an honorable discharge and returning home from working in the Black Hills of South Dakota, to Mission Hills. Outside Mission Hills, my father worked in a cattle ranch, feeding cattle for the farm's owner who increased the number of cattle in anticipation of large orders from the Federal government due to the war against Germany, Italy and Japan. The $25.00 I sent home each month while in the CCC helped my parents because rural South Dakota suffered because of the depression in the United States. It was a lot of money for people who did not see that much money at the same time. This was one of the purposes of the CCC, giving unemployed men work and sending money home to ease the effects of the depression.

"My father was feeding over one hundred fifty head of cattle for the owner and he was glad to see me come home from the CCC. I stayed with my parents on the cattle ranch, helping take care of the herd. However, being patriotic after Pearl Harbor and the United States entering World War II, I drive into Yankton to enlist in the USN. From my experience in the CCC, I decided not to enlist in the U.S. Army. At that time, there were openings so I could enlist in the USN. The recruiter told me I would have to wait until a draft notice was sent and then come back to enlist in the USN. I went back to work on the farm in anticipation of receiving a draft notice, but one never came, which I thought was unusual given the huge mobilization going on the months after Pearl Harbor in the United States and South Dakota. I waited for three months and still no draft notice. I drove to Yankton to talk the situation over with the local draft board. I found out that the owner of the cattle ranch had requested a deferment for me (granted, due to my working in agriculture and considered necessary to support the war). However, I really wanted to enlist in the

USN. I was blocked from doing so until the deferment was cancelled.

"I went to the ranch owner and asked him to request my deferment be cancelled. He refused because the price for cattle was rising and he wanted to add more cattle to the feeding operation and needed me to stay on the ranch and help my father. Because I could not convince him to submit a request to cancel the deferment, I told him my desire not to work for him and I would no longer work for him. Later, I found out he was on the Yankton Draft Board and he pulled my deferment. A few days after quitting the farm, I received my 1A Draft Notice, which I wanted all along. I drove into Yankton and enlisted in the USN. One week later, I was on my way west out of South Dakota to begin Navy Boot Camp training. I took a passenger rail train from Yankton to Sioux Falls, then west to the brand new USN Boot Camp Training and Advanced Training Facility at Farragut, Idaho."

The author is familiar with the World War II history of the USN Training Station, Farragut, Idaho because his father George W. Larson attended Boot Camp training and Advanced Gunnery School training at this military training base. After the USN entered World War II, the USN had an urgent and immediate, long-term requirement to train thousands of recruits. The USN built three new, large Boot Camp and training facilities to meet the urgent wartime expansion to fight a two-ocean war. The training facility at Farragut, Idaho was located at the southern end of Lake Pend Oreille. The other two large USN training bases were Bainbridge, Maryland and Sampson, New York. At Farragut, Idaho, the base consisted of 4,050 acres. The USN was concerned after Pearl Harbor that a large training center in the western part of the United States, located far enough inland from the U.S. Pacific coast to be secure from Imperial Japanese Navy aircraft carriers. In reality, this was never in the plans of the Japanese Navy but caused many initial security concerns for the U.S. military. Base construction started in April 1942, with the training facility commissioned on August 2, 1942. The training facility was large, consisting of six separate boot camps, allowing a new training class to be assigned each week, with a boot camp group graduating every 6 to 8 weeks. At its peak capacity, the training facility consisted of 538 family housing units and barracks for station training personnel. The nearby town of Farragut grew to 65,000, becoming the largest city in Idaho (at that time). The training facility became the second largest military training station in the United States. It also contained advanced training schools for hospital corpsman, cooks, bakers, electricians, gunner's mates, Class C instructors and boat handlers.

Patterson..."Once at Farragut, Idaho, a USN trainer asked me about my civilian qualifications and training in the CCC. I did not tell him of learning to cook, fearing I would be assigned to that skill. I kept quiet on this learned skill because I wanted to be in combat and not as a support person. I was on boot camp basic training for two months. Many in my class wanted to go onto gunner's mate training. I also signed up for this advanced training. The Chief called me into his office and told me I was to be sent to Treasure Island, California for advanced gunnery training. For one month after boot camp, I received basic gunner's mate instruction at Farragut."

The author's father also trained at Treasure Island as a gunner's mate. Treasure Island facility was created in 1937. By building this artificial island, nearby shallow shoals were eliminated and a dumping location provided for dredging operations in San Francisco Bay. The man-made island was the site of the 1939-1940 Golden Gate International Exposition. Temporarily, Treasure Island served as San Francisco's airport, provided a land runway and seaplane launch/recovery ramp. Treasure Island is connected to the natural island of Yerba Buena by a causeway to the mainland and then onto San Francisco by the Golden Gate Bridge. With the war in Europe, starting on 1 September 1939, but before Pearl Harbor, the USN acquired Treasure Island, renaming it U.S. Naval Station, Treasure Island. The USN converted the island into a large military reception, training and embarkation center, along with Headquarters 12th Naval District. During peak activity during World War II, the island's facilities processed up to 12,000 military personnel daily for shipment to various Pacific Combat Zones and after the war discharged returning military personnel for re-entry into civilian life.

Patterson..."I worked hard while at Treasure Island's advanced gunnery school earned good grades. I lived in the barracks, originally built for the Golden Gate International Exposition. In the barracks, I could look out the barrack's window and see the large island in the harbor, Alcatraz, used as a maximum Federal prison. The Chief at the training location on Treasure Island said I could select my next assignment. I responded immediately asking for destroyer duty along the U.S. east coast. Two or three days passed before I was told my next posting was to the USN base at Kearny, New Jersey. I was given a passenger train ticket from California to New Jersey in December 1942. I was going to serve on board a brand new Fletcher Class destroyer, DD-678, USS McGowan. It was still in the process of final putting out. I first had to go to the USN base at Norfolk, Virginia while the destroyer was finishing final fitting out, joining other members of the crew.

"After the destroyer was ready, we took a train to the Flushing Avenue barracks in New York City, New York. The barracks was a building ten stories tall. It was a big deal for me to be in the barracks and in New York City. We marched over to the Brooklyn Navy Yard and onto the McGowan. We went out to sea for our first sea trials. We came back to make the necessary repairs. The follow on sea trials were held off Bermuda, a real good shakedown cruise for the new destroyer. Unfortunately, we burned out a turbine, requiring replacement, which had to be completed at the Brooklyn Navy Yard. A large section of the steel deck, eight feet wide and twenty feet long had to be cut out by shipyard workers, to allow the turbine to be hoisted out of the ship and a new turbine installed. This was a complicated engineering process, taking a considerable amount of time and skill by the shipyard workers. Once the new turbine was installed, the deck had to be lifted back onto place, welded seams ground smooth as before the repair started and repainted.

"We were going to be granted leave while the destroyer was undergoing repairs in the Brooklyn Navy Yard. This set up an interesting opportunity for me. The ship's starboard watch side of the destroyer could go on leave for a period of four to five days. Then the ship's portside watch could go on leave for the same amount of time. However, I could not take a passenger train from New York City to Keystone, South Dakota, where my family had moved in that amount of time. A friend of mine on the ship could not make it home for the same reason because his parents lived in Florida. I said how about $50.00 for his leave, if I could add those days to mine. First, I had to talk to the Chief Gunner's Mate. He had to discuss this option with the Executive Officer, who indicated this was all right with him. He had to discuss this with the Captain. Very quickly, I heard my name announced over the ship's speaker system. I had my ten days of leave. I was told to go to Grand Central Station in New York City to purchase a passenger train ticket home. I boarded a fast passenger train to the west coast with one of its stops at Cheyenne, Wyoming. I took a bus to Rapid City and onto Keystone. I was lucky, this only took me three days, giving me four days at home. I went back to Cheyenne to catch a fast passenger train to New York City. I got back to the ship twelve hours prior to my leave running out. It was a great trip to get home and see my parents before going on extended combat duty on the destroyer.

"After our leaves were over, we were to go out on another shakedown cruise. We sailed out into the North Atlantic. All ship's systems performed perfectly. We were then assigned to convoy escort duty, sailing from the U.S. east coast to Iceland and back again for six months. The Chief Gunner's Mate told us we were going to transit the Panama Canal and go into the Pacific Theater of Operations. We stopped at the large USN base at San Diego, California. We took on food, fuel, and restocked the ship's stores, then sailed for Pearl Harbor, Hawaii. I was finally going to see Pearl Harbor, which I first heard about the morning of December 7, 1941, when working as a cook in the CCC camp at Galena, South Dakota. It was very exciting for me. We lined the rail of the destroyer when entering Pearl Harbor, past the sunken battleship Arizona. It was a very emotional time for all of us on the destroyer.

"We sailed out of Pearl Harbor to Eniwetok, prior to going to the Marianas, which would be our first combat action, participating in the invasion of Saipan. Of course, the fighting was all over when we dropped anchor in Eniwetok Atoll, which had been turned over into a major USN base and anchorage. Our first combat engagement was off Saipan."

The McGowan's log. For naval fire support during the invasion of Saipan, the McGowan was assigned to Fire Sector four, the northwest one-half of the island. The fire support ships consisted of battleships Colorado and Maryland, cruiser Louisville with destroyers McDermott, McGowan, Melvin McNair. During Saipan combat operations these and other USN ships fired star shells at night to illuminate the battlefield to break up Japanese attacks. During Saipan operations, USN ships fired 5,882 star shells.

Patterson..."While operating off Saipan, we nearly ran out of food, reducing our meal choices to beans and tomato sauce. Our destroyer squadron was relieved and went back to Eniwetok for re-provisioning and rearming. We were resupplied with mutton as our primary meat from New Zealand. I thought it tasted good but this was not the comments from many of my crewmates who did not like this meat. We went back to the Marianas to support the invasion of Tinian, located two and one-half miles south of Saipan. Tinian was generally flat (ideal for the construction of long and wide B-29 Superfortress runways). We worked with the battleships off Tinian."

McGowan's log...The McGowan was assigned to Fire Sector two, located midway along Tinian's west coast from Gurguan Point to Faibus San Hilo Point. The fire support force consisted of the cruiser

Birmingham, along with destroyers McDermott, McGowan and Renshaw. These ships, prior to the amphibious invasion of Tinian fired a combined 1,960 rounds of various caliber ammunition. The destroyers fired their 5-inch main armament and the cruiser its 6-inch main and 5-inch secondary guns.

Patterson…"During our fire support against Tinian, the 5-inch shell casings piled up on the deck near the 5-inch mounts. During lulls in fire support, we pitched these shell casings into the water to clear the ship's deck resuming combat operations. Off Tinian, my 5-inch gun suffered a miss fire. A miss fire inside a 5-inch gun mount is a very dangerous situation that must be taken care of immediately to clear the gun's barrel. I learned in gunnery school how to handle a miss fire and correct procedures to clear the gun. A 5-inch shell is three feet long. After the miss fire, I ordered everyone out of the gun mount. I opened the breech mechanism, and then slowly pulled out the 5-inch shell. I carefully carried it out of the gun mount, heaving the shell over the side of the ship into the water. It only took a few seconds. I previously prepared for a possible miss fire. I took the heads off two shells, pouring the powder into plastic buckets. I took the shells and cut them to one foot long. I replaced that much powder and placed an inert warhead on the shell. I inserted one of these blanks into the gun barrel, shut the breech mechanism and fired it to finish cleaning the gun. If a full round was inserted, there was a possibility the breech mechanism might not completely close and seal due to pressure buildup. With the short shell removed, the gun was ready for firing. Most Americans do not realize the importance destroyers played in knocking out enemy positions. During Japanese counter attacks, for support at night, we fired star shells over our troop positions on the islands. We were eventually relieved from operations off the Marianas and sailed to Eniwetok for re-provisioning. We restocked the ship, checked all guns, engines and equipment.

"Our next combat assignment was to support the U.S. Marine Corps invasion of the island of Iwo Jima. We wanted to capture Iwo Jima for many reasons. The Japanese were using the island's airfields to refuel single-engine fighters and twin-engine bombers for one-way attack bombing missions against B-29 airfields on Saipan and Tinian, which they viewed as a strategic threat to the Japanese home islands. The Japanese used Iwo Jima as an early warning radar site to warn Japan of approaching B-29 raids. The U.S. military wanted to build B-29 emergency runways on Iwo Jima to save badly damaged bombers, which could not make the long over the water return flight to the

Marianas or short on fuel and had to land to refuel to make the return flight. Iwo Jima was an ideal location to station long-range North American P-51 Mustang fighters to escort B-29s over Japan. When we operated off Honshu Island, in the Japanese home islands. I saw a low-flying B-29s heading for Iwo Jima, often with one or more engines feathered. Our destroyer never pulled B-29 lifeline patrols between Iwo Jima and the Marianas Islands. Although, we did pull many USN pilots out of the water when they either ditched their aircraft near the destroyer or ones we spotted in parachutes floating down to the water. I remember three USN pilots we picked up in July 1945, and took them back to their aircraft carrier. They were transferred to the carrier by boson's chair, and in return, we received ice cream for our crew. This was a real treat.

"We were relieved of Pacific combat and headed toward Adak Island in the Aleutians, for the Great Northern Circle Route home, a shorter sailing distance then going via Pearl Harbor. Our replacement destroyer was hit by a Japanese Kamikaze and sank. We were ordered to turn around and resume combat operations. Another replacement destroyer relieved us. Again, we set sail for Adak Island and back to San Francisco, California. Again, we did not make it. Two B-29s from North Field, assigned to the 509th Composite Group, dropped two atomic bombs on Japan (Hiroshima on August 6, 1945 and Nagasaki on August 9, 1945), forcing the subsequent surrender of Japan and our return to Japan. We were told the destroyer was headed to Hokkaido to assist in clearing sea mines. Our job was to trail, at a safe distance, wooden hull minesweepers, which were cutting loose moored sea mines. Some of these mines were Japanese, with the majority dropped from B-29s to close Japanese ports to sea traffic and limit food and strategic imports. When the mines were cut loose and floated to the surface, we used our 20mm and 40mm guns to explode the mine. We continued this until the battleship USS Missouri's sailing into Tokyo Bay prior to the final Japanese surrender on that combat ship. We had the privilege of entering Tokyo Bay, using our Captain's gig to pick up the Japanese dignitaries to be taken onboard the USS Missouri on September 2, 1945, to sign the terms of unconditional surrender. We did not pick these dignitaries up after the signing ceremony.

"We were relieved again from duty in the Pacific after the Japanese signed the formal terms of unconditional surrender on the USS Missouri and we headed for home, by the way of Pearl Harbor to San Francisco. I was on duty at night when I spotted the lighthouse outside the entrance to San Francisco Bay. We were standing four hour watch-es. I could feel the speed of the ship through the vibrations of the turning shaft while at the helm. We were scheduled to berth at San Francisco Navy Yard. The war was over and we arrived at midnight, so we had to circle outside the entrance to San Francisco Bay, waiting for daylight and a harbor pilot. With the war over, there was no urgency to get warships into San Francisco Bay. We put on extra lookouts on the destroyer to watch for approaching ships, now running with full lights on because the war was over and peacetime regulations were in effect. We slowed down, cruising in wide easy circles. The harbor pilot came out to the destroyer at first light. He took us into San Francisco Bay. World War II defense mines were still in place, requiring a specific entrance route into the harbor. We eventually docked at the naval yard.

"We were granted leave once the ship was secured to the dock and engineering machinery secured and shut down, with a security detail remaining the ship. After getting off the destroyer, I took a bus to Oakland, across the bay, to catch a passenger train home. There was no direct train service departing San Francisco. I beat the entire crew to the Oakland train station. The ticket agent said the train was due to come into station and then depart for the east coast was completely booked. The ticket agent indicated I would have to wait for another eastbound train. I told him to sell me a ticket to Cheyenne, Wyoming, with a return, and I would find somewhere to get onto the train. After shipping him a bribe, I got a ticket. I went to the train platform. The train came into the station and I was able to get onto the train, I found an empty seat and sat down because I had a valid ticket. I got off the train at Cheyenne and took a bus to Rapid City. At this time, after the end of World War II, an old building in Rapid City, of which I cannot remember its location, was used as a one night hotel, for the cost of one dollar. That was enough for me and I was able to get a good night's sleep. The next morning I got up, threw my sea bag over my shoulder and started walking down one of the streets in Rapid City, hoping to catch a ride to Keystone. I barely started walking when someone stopped and picked me up, driving me all the way into Keystone. Once leave was completed, I took the train back to Oakland and a bus to the destroyer. I helped put the ship into mothballs prior to the destroyer being towed into the storage area in the bay. We took all the guns out of operation and sprayed the ship's exterior surfaces with a protective sealant. This was designed to keep out salt water from the interior of the ship, as well as primary and secondary armaments. This took two months to secure the ship from combat status and prepare it for long-term storage. Once done, I took a train to Minneapolis, Minnesota, where I mustered out of the USN and then home to Keystone, South Dakota. This ended my World War II service."[41]

---

[41] Clair Patterson, Keystone, South Dakota, interview Lt. Col. George A. Larson, USAF (Ret.), November 20, 2004.

Joe Foss

United States Marine Corps, Fighter Ace over Guadalcanal

Governor of the State of South Dakota

JOE Foss was born on April 17, 1915, near Sioux Falls, South Dakota. After graduating from high school, he attended Augustana College, Sioux Falls College, eventually graduating from the University of South Dakota with a Business degree in 1940. Prior to the Japanese attack on Pearl Harbor, Foss enlisted in the United States Marine Corps (USMC) in June 1940, in August 1940 discharged to become an aviation cadet in the USMC Reserve, active duty into the USMC the same month, assigned to Pensacola, Florida for primary flight training. After completion of initial flight training, Foss earned his pilot wings, commissioned in the USMC as a Second Lieutenant in March 1941. He was promoted to 1st Lt. and then Captain. His primary aircraft was the Grumman F4F Wildcat, assigned as Executive Officer, Squadron VMF-121. The squadron loaded onto the escort aircraft carrier Copahee, destination Guadalcanal in the Solomon Islands, providing air cover for USMC troops on Guadalcanal against fierce Japanese air attacks in an attempt to wrestle the island back from the USMC troops. Events in the Solomon Islands forced the United States military into its first large-scale amphibious operations against the Japanese in World War II. The Japanese, after the naval defeat at the Battle of the Coral Sea and Midway Island, followed Admiral Yamamoto's plan to capture the small British port of Tulagi on Florida Island to build a naval seaplane base prior to occupying the larger Guadalcanal 20 miles to the south. By stationing Japanese Zero floatplanes for defense and long-range four-engine seaplanes for aerial reconnaissance, Allied naval movements could be observed and attacked. On May 13, 1942, the Japanese occupied Tulagi, using two large transports to land troops, supplies and equipment needed to build a seaplane base. During unloading operations, an Australian PBY reconnaissance aircraft identified the Japanese invasion force, reporting the landing to Allied Headquarters in Australia. The Japanese plan was to severe U.S. shipping lanes from the United States to New Zealand and Australia.

On May 28, 1942, the Japanese landed on Guadalcanal, surveying and laying out an airfield on 19 June. The runway was 3,778 feet long, 160 feet wide, confirmed by a U.S. B-17 photoreconnaissance flight on July 5, 1942. Japanese engineers and laborers only had 197 feet in the center of the runway to complete before it was operationally ready for bombers and fighters. USMC troops landed on Guadalcanal and Tulagi on 7 August. Fierce fighting followed after Japanese troops on the island withdrew into the jungle and hills surrounding the runway under construction. Seabees landed, using Japanese equipment and supplies, added to their own equipment and material to surface a 75 foot by 2,500 foot section of the runway (now called Henderson Field) with metal Marston Mat sections, the minimum length for a fighter to take-off and land. The arrival of fighters provided the ability to hold onto the airstrip, attacking Japanese bombers and fighters, transports and warships approaching south from Rabaul down the "slot" to Guadalcanal. After Seabees completed laying down Marston Mats on a 150 foot and 2,500 foot section, fighters could operate from two parallel runways. If one section was damaged from Japanese bombs or naval warship shells, it could be roped off, while flight operations continued on the undamaged section. After the entire 150 foot by 5,600 foot runway was covered with Marston Mat sections, there were in effect, four separate fighter strips, with bombers able to operate from the wider and longer area of the runway. The Seabees provided Henderson Field fighters with four separate fighter strips. This proved important when intense Japanese warship shelling or heavy bomb damage tore up sections of the steel Marston Mat runway sections.

On October 9, 1942, VMF-121 took-off from the aircraft carrier Copahee, landing on Henderson Field on Guadalcanal. Captain Foss would be in aerial command of four F4Fs. His airborne comrades quickly earned the nicknamed as "Foss Flying Circus." His exploits were highlighted in the black and white movie; starring James Cagnie called "Gallant Hours" about the U.S. fight against the Japanese on and around Guadalcanal. While stationed with the Defense Intelligence Agency (DIA) and Joint Chiefs of Staff (JCS), the author was able to request and access USMC historical files on the aerial combat at Henderson Field, Guadalcanal.

On October 13, 1942, pilots of VMF-121 scored their first (two) Japanese aircraft kills. Captain Foss lead (12) F4Fs after these two kills from Henderson Field to intercept a large force of 32 Japanese Zero fighters and Betty bombers. He shot down one Zero, although his F4F was badly damaged by other Zeros. He was able to land back on Henderson Field. On 14 October, Captain Foss shot down a Zero fighter. On 18 October, Captain Foss and his flight intercepted a large flight of Zero fighters, with a loss of one F4F to the Japanese fighters. Foss was able to climb above the Zero fighters, diving down and shooting one down, hit a second, attacking another. He located a group of Betty bombers, diving through the bomber formation, pulling up and attacking from below, shooting down one of the bombers. This gave Captain Foss five aerial kills, earning him the title of fighter ace. On 20 October, Foss shot down two Zero fighters.

On 23 October, Captain Foss shot down one Zero, engaging a second, also shooting it down at the top of a loop maneuver. He fired at a second Zero that was executing a slow roll. As with any airborne hunter, in the heat of combat, he became separated from the other F4Fs in the flight, jumped and shot up by two Zero fighters. Foss managed to get the damaged fighter back to Henderson, landing, with the F4F declared a total loss, cannibalized for parts to keep other F4Fs flying. USMC and Army pilots flying from Henderson Field, if shot up by Japanese Zero fighters, could attempt to land back at Henderson Field or ditch in the waters around Guadalcanal, picked up by Navy warships. If Japanese aircraft were shot down, the fighter pilots and bomber crews knew that Admiral Yamamoto would not commit Navy warships to pick them up or send in amphibious aircraft to attempt an open ocean rescue and return them to combat. Captain Foss was credited with shooting down eleven Japanese aircraft, making him a double ace. On 25 October, he shot down two more Japanese aircraft on a morning flight and a third in the afternoon.

On 7 November, Captain Foss and seven F4Fs were tasked to attack a group of Japanese destroyers and a cruiser in the 'slot' approaching Guadalcanal. Foss shot down a cruiser float biplane, but he got too close to the rear gunner who fired and hit the F4F's engine, which seized and quit, forcing an ocean ditching because Foss was too low to parachute out of the mortally wounded fighter near Malaita Island. He was lucky that a group of local missionaries picked him up in an open boat, taking Foss to shore, where they used a radio of contact Henderson Field. He was picked up by an Army PBY on 8 November. When he reached Henderson Field, Captain Foss was awarded the Distinguished Flying Cross, personally pinned on this uniform by the area Commander, Admiral William Halsey. Captain Foss was back in a F4F on 12 November, shooting down one Betty bomber and one Zero. In the afternoon, he shot down another Betty bomber.

Physical stress from intense aerial combat and disease (malaria) finally did what the Japanese could not, knock him out of combat for six weeks. He was flown from Henderson Field on a C-47 to New Caledonia and onto Australia for medical treatment and rest. By this time, Captain Foss had been credited with shooting down 23 Japanese aircraft. He returned to Henderson Field on January 1, 1943. On 15 January, he shot down three more Japanese aircraft, raising his total to twenty-six. The USMC pulled him out of aerial combat, flying Captain Foss back to the United States. In May 1943, at the White House, President Franklin Roosevelt awarded him the Congressional Medal of Honor.

Captain Foss was assigned as a training advisor at the Santa Barbara USMC Air Station. Later he was assigned Commander, USMC VMF-115, Pacific Theater. Under Foss's photograph in the state capital of South Dakota, at Pierre lists his post-war accomplishments and service to the state of South Dakota. After World War II, Foss was commissioned in the South Dakota Air National Guard, organizing the guard. He was elected to the South Dakota House of Representatives. During the Korean War, returning to active duty as a Colonel. He was appointed Chief of Staff, South Dakota National Guard with the rank of Brigadier General. In 1954, he was elected Governor of South Dakota, re-elected in 1958. He passed away on January 1, 2003, at Scottsbluff, Arizona, buried at Arlington National Cemetery.[42]

---

[42] The author, while researching information of Seabees (United States Naval Construction Battalions–USNCBs) on Guadalcanal Island and the "Cactus Air Force," came from the Admiral Nimitz Museum archives at Fredericksburg, Texas (renamed as The National Museum of the Pacific War). Part of the article is included on Henderson Field to assist in telling the story of USMC ace, Joe Foss, later Governor of South Dakota. The balance of the information was researched at the South Dakota State Historical Society in Pierre, South Dakota.

Lt. Col. Don Wicker, USAF (Ret.)

World War II to the Cold War

DON Wicker..."I traveled in December 1942 to Minneapolis, Minnesota where I was inducted into the U.S. Army at Fort Snelling. Army basic training was at Jefferson Barracks, Missouri, boot camp, lasting 30 days. Then, back to Minnesota at College training detachment, St. Cloud for cadet classification. Headed to Santa Ana, California where I did not qualify as a pilot, reassigned as a navigator. Went to Ellington, Field, Texas for pre-flight training. Onto aerial gunnery school at Harlingen, Texas. On October 1, 1943, to navigator school at Hondo, Texas (Class 44-3). Onto bombardier school at Roswell, New Mexico. My B-25 crew training was at Columbia, South Carolina. Our port of embarkation was Miami Beach, Florida. In December 1944, reach Feni, India, east of Calcutta, flying B-25G and H models, a total of 50 missions. We flew sorties into China and southern Burma. On one mission, ran out of fuel. Due to bad weather, our primary and alternate airfields were closed. We found Cox's Bazzar, an RAF airfield. The pilot had three green lights showing the tricycle landing gear down and locked. On touchdown, the nose wheel collapsed. We came to a complete stop, walked away from the destroyed aircraft with no injuries. We were assigned to the 12th Bomb Group, 83rd Bomb Squadron. We moved onto Pandaveswar.

"July to October 1945, flew the Douglas B-26. We completed transition training and on this base received news of Japan's surrender on August 14, 1945 with the signing of unconditional surrender on the battleship USS Missouri, Tokyo Bay. From November 1945 to May 1946, we ferried B-26s from India to Munich, Germany. I ended at a Replacement Depot near Paris, France. I was there for two months. The Red Cross consisted of great people, with who I could eat donuts, drink coffee, while waiting for reassignment.

"Stayed with B-26s, moving to a former World War II German Air Force field, Schliescham Air Base, near Dachau Concentration Camp. Destruction all around the base, but our quarters were OK. I wanted to remain in the military as an officer, but even though I was a senior 1st Lt., the CO said that was not going to happen because I did not have a college degree. In May 1946, returned to the U.S. by Victory Ship, landing at New York, sailing across the North Atlantic from

LaHarve, France.

"I was in the reserves for five years. I attended South Dakota State University for four years, earning a degree in education and sociology under the G.I. Bill. Attended West Colorado for one year, working on a Master's degree. Did not finish, recalled to active duty in the Air Force, rank of Captain in the summer of 1952. Attended navigator school at Ellington, Field. Flew the B-26 in Virginia before going to Pusan Air Base, Republic of South Korea (January 1953 to June 1953). I flew 56 night intruder missions with the same crew. My pilot was a Second Lieutenant. We had a crash landing at Pusan. The nose wheel collapsed with my Norden bomb sight flying over my head. The pilot kept the aircraft on the pierced steel planking mat runway. He did not brake which prevented the aircraft from flipping over onto its back. No injuries.

"I went back to the states, transferred to C-54 transports at Great Falls, Montana. We flew from Great Falls to Kodiak, Alaska to Fairbanks to Anchorage to Adak and back to Great Falls. I transferred to Travis Air Force Base flying C-47s for two years. We flew to Hickam Air Force Base, Hawaii, to Wake Island, to Hameda Air Base near Tokyo, Japan to Midway Island, to Hickam and back to Travis. This took us nine days.

"I was Commandant of Cadets, Air Force Reserve Officer Training Corps, Air University for three years at the University of North Dakota. While at Grand Forks, promoted to Major. Moved to Mather Air Force Base, near Sacramento, California.

"I attended radar-navigator school for B-52s at Castle Air Force Base, California in 1960. First B-52 active duty base SAC assignment was at Travis Air Force Base, California flying B-52Gs. I moved up in the squadron becoming the Domestic Target Study Officer, then Chief of Bomb Nav. Went to March Air Force Base on the Alternate Command Post. I spent four years as operations planner. Went to Elmendorf Air Force Base, Anchorage, Alaska in a Joint Command, Chief of ALMCC. In 1972 transferred to Ellsworth Air Force Base, assigned to 4 ACCS. I retired in October 1975 as a Lieutenant Colonel." [43]

---

[43] Don Wicker, Lt. Col. USAF (Ret.), Rapid City, South Dakota, "World War II to the Cold War," interview, Lt. Col. George A. Larson, USAF (Ret.), May 18, 2012.

Edwin Petranke

Four Time Purple Heart Recipient

36th Infantry Division, World War II

EDWIN Petranke..."I was born September 9, 1916 at White River, South Dakota. In 1943, I enlisted in the U.S. Army at Vermillion, South Dakota. I went to basic army training then onto Fort Benning, Georgia. In September 1943, departed the United States on a troop transport, arriving North Africa on October 14, 1943, assigned either to Company A or B (various times), 143rd Regiment, 1st Battalion, 36th Infantry Division as a replacement officer. The division had landed in North Africa on April 13, 1944. I trained personnel at Arzew and Rabat, assigned to VI Corps, but attached to Services of Supply, North African Theater of Operations U.S. Army (NATOUSA) for supply functions and support to combat troops. The 36th Division was fighting in Italy when I was assigned to the division. We went into the front lines on 15 November south of Venafro in the Liri Valley. I had been promoted to First Lieutenant, platoon leader as well as Company Executive Officer. We made our first attempt to force a crossing over the Volturno River but the Germans repulsed our attack and we stayed there for 30 days. After the battle there was a temporary truce to allow the Germans to retrieve their dead and wounded from our lines and the Germans did the same for us in their lines. We dug into the slopes of Mount Cairo, behind Cassin Ridge and Castellone Ridge on the near boundary. I remember British Dragoons assigned to our part of the line. They carried very sharp knives. They used the knives in direct, close-in combat, at night. We were told to wear our dog tags outside of our uniforms at night when in foxholes. These British troops silently passed through our lines into the German lines without making a sound. Like the Germans, we were usually four to a foxhole. As the British troops came upon a foxhole, if they felt a dog tag, they moved on. If no dog tag, they slit the throats of three of the four men in the foxhole, leaving one to wake up to the blood and terror of the death of three comrades. In the mornings, we often heard the screams of German soldiers when they found the dead with them in the foxhole, often running to the rear. Sometimes we could get a shot at these running Germans. On our second attempt to cross the Volturno River I was wounded in my front left shoulder from a mortar shell shrapnel fragment. The fragment tore through my shoulder, carrying with it a piece of my coat fabric. This became infected and two months later, doctors cut open the back to the same shoulder, removing the fabric piece and cleaning out the wound.

"On 15 August we landed in southern France. The next day we liberated our first French Village. My second Purple Heart was earned at Montelimar, 250 miles north of our amphibious landing area on the Mediterranean Sea, fighting the German 19th Army. An Army Corpsman patched me up and sent me right back into the line. My third Purple Heart was prior to entering the Vosges foothills, near Belfort. I received a shrapnel would from a German 88mm gun. Again, I was patched up and sent back into the line. My fourth and final Purple Heart was won in the Colmar Pocket, along the southwest border of Germany with France. This was a serious wound. I was hit by a German machine gun with shrapnel fragments penetrating my leg. I was carried to an aid station on a stretcher. I was given a shot, passed out, taken to Paris. Again the doctors knocked me out and I don't remember much. I was told I was flown to a military hospital in England. I had four surgeries, pinning my left leg and knee to repair my shattered femur. The bullet is still embedded in the bone. I was in the English hospital for three months,

"In order to ship me home, they placed me in a total body cast, except my head and arms. I was carried to an ambulance, driven to the dock area (not sure which one), carried up a gangplank onto a Swedish liner the SS Olaf. We landed at New York City Port. An Army doctor asked me where I wanted to be sent to. I said Des Moines, Iowa, the closest point I could be to home by train. However, for some reason, I was shipped all the way across the United States to Oregon. I was taken to a military hospital, and after three weeks, they cut off the top of the body cast, leaving the bottom section intact for two weeks. At that time, I was able to sit up and get out of the cast on my own. They asked me if I wanted to be mustered out at this time. I said no. I wanted to wait until all my medical records caught up with me due to my multiple wounds. I was sent to Camp Roberts, California, assigned limited duty, again as a Company Executive Officer. I was transferred to Ford Ord, California for re-evaluation and medical review. Then onto to Camp Beale, in north California. At this time, my medical records and personnel files caught up with me. I had enough points to be discharged. I was sent home to Vermillion, South Dakota."

Petranke handed the author a short overview of the history of the 36th Infantry Division. After 400 days of combat, five campaigns in Italy, France, Germany and Australia, two major amphibious operations, the men of the division capture 175,806 enemy troops, won 12 Congressional Medals of Honor, received six Presidential Citations, 12 Distinguished Service plaques, a host of other commendations, medals and awards. The division's casualty lost was the third highest in the European Theater of Operations was 3,974 killed, 19,052 wounded and 4,317 missing in action.[44]

---

[44] Edwin Petranke, World War II, 36th Infantry Division (Long-care facility, Veterans Medical facility, Fort Mead, South Dakota), interview, author, 21 July 2012

Gordon Lease

United States Coast Guard, 1943
Salerno Amphibious Operation

TROOPS of the U.S. Fifth Army landed at Salerno, a vital port located south of Naples, Italy during the Allied invasion of Italy after victory in Sicily. On September 9, 1943, German forces moved into southern Italy to block Allied forces. U.S. forces were reenforced by the U.S. Army's 82nd Airborne Division. Naval gunfire knocked out the bulk of German forces around Salerno. This allowed the U.S. Fifth Army to join up with the British Eighth Army inland on 15 September.

Gordon Lease remembers a strange incident during the Salerno operation. Lease..."I noticed an RAF Spitfire on the beach with U.S. Air Corps markings. No one knew where it came from or why it had U.S. markings. It took until 1989 for me to find about this aircraft. At our Coast Guard crew reunion in St. Louis, meeting at the same hotel, an Air Corps squadron was also having a reunion. I found out that the squadron did not have any aircraft when formed so the RAF gave them Spitfires to fly during the Sicily operations and then for the invasion of southern Italy at Salerno. The Spitfire was shot down by German Anti-aircraft batteries at Salerno." [45]

---

[45] Gordon Lease, Rapid City, South Dakota, "U.S. Coast Guard, 1943 Salerno amphibious operation," interview, Lt. Col. George A, Larson, USAF (Ret.), Black Hills Veterans Writing Group, Western Dakota Technical Institute, Rapid City, South Dakota, May 12, 2012.

Joseph Munro

World War II Lt. J.G.

USS Shelton (DE-407) and USS Ray K. Edwards (APD-96)

THE USS Shelton (DE-407) was a John C. Butler-class destroyer escort (DE) built for the United States Navy during World War II. It was named for Ensign James A. Shelton, a naval aviator who was reported missing during the Battle of Midway. This was the first of two U.S. Naval vessels to bear the name. The Shelton was laid down on November 1, 1943, by Brown Shipbuilding Company of Houston, Texas. The destroyer was launched on December 18, 1943, sponsored by Mrs. John Shelton, commissioned on April 4, 1944, with Lieutenant Lewis B. Salomon, U.S. Naval Reserve (USNR), in command. Much of the crew was assembled at that time from the U.S. Navy Sub Chaser Training School. After the destroyer was commissioned, it moved down the Houston Ship Channel under its own power, accompanied by the destroyer Edmonds, to Galveston, where it took on supplies. After a few days of that, it sailed onto Bermuda for a shakedown cruise. During shake down activities, it took almost daily cruises to get experienced in running the ship and to find out if anything required correction. The shake down activities took at least a couple of weeks. At their conclusion, each ship had to pass an operations test to determine that it and the crew was capable of going to meet the enemy. Everyone and the ship passed. On the way to Boston, the ship passed through the Cape Cod Canal, which eliminated the necessity of going around Cape Cod. The overhaul or correction time in Boston took two weeks.

While in Boston, the ship's crew attended a two day fire-fighting school. The school used a concrete building that was 30 feet square, without a roof. The bottom was filled with fuel oil and steel grating above the floor to create the deck grating of a ship. There was also a steel stairway in its obstacles. Instructors ignited the oil and after it was burning very well, the crew would go into the building with a water fog nozzle to extinguish the fire, carefully making certain the fire did not get behind them. Another training exercise was with a large

Christmas tree like structure that had nozzles all over it. Gasoline was sprayed out of all the nozzles and when the instructors set it off, it created a large fire. The crew put that fire out with water nozzle that had a very fine spray.

After the Shelton departed Boston, it transited through the Panama Canal, sailing onto San Diego, arriving on July 6, 1944. The destroyer's crew loaded supplies and ammunition. After a couple of days, the destroyer sailed to Pearl Harbor, Hawaii. The destroyer's cruising speed was 15 knots. The destroyer had maximum speed of 20 knots, with a combat or flank speed of 24 knots. The destroyer spent several weeks in Pearl Harbor, doing various activities. The crew spent several days at target practice, consisting of aerial target shooting. A tow plane would fly in our area with a target sleeve in tow. The 5-inch ammunition came as a separate shell and then a canvas encased propellant charge. The 5-inch shells were then fixed with proximity fuses. The shell didn't have to hit the target to explode, close was good enough to penetrate the aerial enemy with deadly shrapnel. The propellant charge was in a casing 6-inches in diameter and approximately 30-inches long.

While at Pearl Harbor, the destroyer and its crews would go out and perform as plane guard for an aircraft carrier. The destroyer's job was to trail the aircraft carrier on one side and pick up any aircraft personnel who for any reason might miss or run off the carrier's flight deck. Fortunately, this didn't happen too often. The biggest challenge was keeping up with the carrier. One day while acting as plane guard, General Quarters sounded on the destroyer. What happened was that a plane was sitting in launch position on the carrier with its engine idling. The catapult was accidently tripped and the plane was rammed forward, but with the engine on idle, it didn't go much more than fall off the front of the flight deck and into water. Unfortunately, the carrier plowing ahead brushed the torpedo bomber with three aircrew on board. The destroyer speeded to the aircraft, which was by then partly submerged. After slowing and stopping, the destroyer lowered its lifeboat, powered by a small engine, which served as the Captain's gig. The boat crew rescued the uninjured pilot, injured radioman. The rear gunner's compartment was submerged and the pilot indicated that his area took the full brunt of the carrier's impact. The pilot believed the gunner was dead. The two aircrew members were transferred back to the carrier. The pilot by a canvas seat on a cable and the injured radioman on a stretcher on the same cable.

The Shelton departed Pearl Harbor on 26 July and sailed southwest across a good part of the Pacific in a small task group to Manus

Island. Manus is the largest island in the Admiralty Group which is located north of New Guinea and three degrees below the equator. Manus is about 50 miles long and 20 miles wide, it had a big harbor that was almost entirely closed by land. There were quite a few ships there, one of which was a battleship. On September 11-12, 1944, the destroyer departed Manus with a small invasion task force, included with quite a few escort ships were three aircraft carriers and some troop transports. These were not regular fleet carriers, but were rather oil tankers that had been converted to aircraft carriers. While they could carry only a limited number of aircraft, there was a method of providing greater total strike capability. The destroyer's destination was Morotai Island, which is the northernmost island of the Halmahera Group, which is about 300 miles south of the Philippines. Information available was that the island was needed to establish a PT base to help with the invasion of the Philippines.

The invasion of Morotai was scheduled for 15 September, assigned to Task Force 77 (Morotai Attack Force). The destroyer's responsibility during the invasion was to act with other escorts to form a screen for the carriers that would detect and attack any Japanese submarines that might be in the area. Since the Shelton was operating with the carriers, it was seldom within sight of land. The invasion schedule predicted that the carriers would depart the area about 18 September. However, plans never go awry as much as they do in war. On 3 October, the Shelton was still off Morotai in screen for escort carriers Fanshaw Bay and Midway, patrolling back and forth. The day dawned in the usual routine format, but at 0810 hours, General Quarters sounded. The bridge rung up flank speed and suddenly, disaster struck. Imperial Japanese Navy submarine RO-41 attacked the two carriers, with a torpedo wake sighted at 1,500 yards from the escort. At flank speed, the Shelton evaded the first torpedo but hit on the starboard screw by a second torpedo. It was as if the bulkhead at the rear of the engine room had been hit with a giant hammer. There was no boom, just a tremendous hammer striking noise. The after engine room was the area nearest to the explosion in which no one was killed or injured. Immediately after the torpedo impact, the propeller drive shafts and the turbine reduction gears started making grinding noises and came to a quick stop. Boiler safety valves started to blow because the flow of steam to the main propulsion turbine had stopped. The destroyer went dead in the water. The ship continued to have electric power because the boilers and the steam turbine electric generators were not damaged.

The destroyer was heavily damaged. The main deck at the rear of the 5-inch gun mount was vertical. The rear part of the ship was missing. The men in the steering station and laundry areas were gone. Three officers in the rear aft officers' quarters were also gone. Some enlisted men in the rear personnel or bunk area were killed and injured. A total of 15 men were lost. Some of the crew on the deck at the time of the attack and said they saw one body fly up over the ship and land in the water ahead of the ship. Some small pieces of flesh were brushed off the back of the Captain's shirt, which was on the Flying or Outside Bridge when the explosion happened. The two carriers were barely visible of the horizon, disappearing rapidly. Two sister destroyer escorts were scurrying around the ocean looking for the Japanese submarine with their underwater gear. Within 20 minutes, the fuel pumps supplying oil to the boilers lost suction due to the tilt of the destroyer, which was down in the water at the stern and high at the bow. Steam pressure was lost in the boilers and with that, electric power was also lost. While the rear of the ship was missing, the ship was in danger of quickly sinking. The closing of watertight doors prevented any additional flooding that may have continued. To lighten the ship, the three torpedoes were fired off on a course to nowhere. Heavy tools and moveable equipment was thrown overboard.

After a few hours, the DE Richard M. Rowell came along side and took off Shelton's crew. Three wounded enlisted personnel were taken aboard the Rowell on stretchers. During the interval between the torpedo hit and being picked up the Rowell, the Shelton drifted a couple of miles. After the Shelton was abandoned, still a drift, the Rowell retraced the Shelton's drift path. It was easy to follow because of the oil slick made by leaking oil tanks as well as a small amount of debris in the water. When the Rowell got to the approximate area of the attack, contact was made with a Japanese submarine using sonar equipment. The logical assumption was that it was the attacking Japanese submarine. To be certain a code consisting of three letters of the alphabet was sent out underwater by the sonar gear. These letters changed for every day of the year. The sequence of recognition was that after the surface ship sent out the inquiry signal, the submarine would respond with its three letter code, which also changed each day. The suspect submarine responded with what was received as "AAA," which in Navy language was "Able, Able, Able." It was the wrong response. The Rowell's captain responded, "I'll Able, Able, Able you, you SOB." The ship's loudspeaker announced that a hedgehog attack was being made on the Japanese submarine. After getting the Rowell into position, the hedgehog was fired. The hedgehogs made the sound 'pop, pop, pop, pop, pop' as the projectiles fired off. They went up approximately 150 feet in the air, spread out and then arched over toward the sea to form the oval pattern when they hit the water. Then they penetrated into the water. After a short time period, there was a bump that could be felt, then another, and a hit. Suddenly, a large amount of air burped out of the water. This was followed by small sections of wood strips that formed the walking surface on submarines.

Immediately, there were shouts of jubilation, joy and celebration. This submarine had severely damaged the Shelton, but in turn, the Rowell got the submarine. The Rowell was the only ship in the area, so it headed back to Manus. After the Shelton's crew walked off the Rowell at Manus, Tokyo Rose broadcast the report of the Shelton's sinking. The Shelton's crew asked the question, "How could that happen if the Japanese submarine had been destroyed by the Rowell?" The Japanese submarine would have no opportunity to radio in a report of the attack on an American destroyer. Worse than that, was that the USS Sea Wolf, a U.S. Navy Fleet submarine was last reported in that area and had not been heard from since the night of 2 October. Worse still, it had become apparent that the attack on the submarine had been made in an area that had been designated as a U.S. submarine sanctuary, an area in which no attack should be made on any submarines. The submarine the Rowell attacked and sunk was the USS Sea Wolf. Its crew number about sixty.

"What happened to the Shelton?" After the Rowell departed the area, another destroyer received orders to take the adrift Shelton in tow to a repair port in Australia. The Shelton was towed for two days, when it rolled over on its side and sank. The Shelton never fired a shot at the Japanese in combat. At Manus, the Shelton's crew noticed the harbor was packed with ships of every type. They knew something big was about to happen. One morning the Shelton's crew got up and looked outside their on shore quarters and the harbor was empty. They had all gone to take part in the invasion of the Philippines.

On 12 October, the remaining nine Shelton's officers (including Lt. J.G. Munro) that survived the Japanese torpedo attack, received orders to proceed to the United States and upon arriving report to the Commandant of the nearest Naval District. Four of the officers flew across the Pacific on a Navy four-engine flying boat. It wasn't designed for carrying passengers, so there were very few built-in seats. The Shelton's officers sat and slept on mailbags or whatever was available in the aircraft. The flying boat landed in Johnson harbor to refuel. The flying boat's final landing destination was the Oakland Naval Air Station.

The Shelton's crew reported to the Commandant, San Francisco Naval District. The battered officers received allowance for new uniforms and one store stayed opened in the evening to allow them to purchase and fit their new uniforms. On 25 October, the four officers received orders to report to the Naval Training Center at Miami, Florida. However, these officers had a delay in reporting for one month. The reporting date, with travel time was set for 11 December. The one month delay was awarded for those naval personnel whose ship was sunk by enemy action.

They took the train from Chicago to Miami, for the Sub Chaser Training Center. They got a room with cooking privileges in a home in Miami. The school ended in February. The former Shelton officers received orders on 19 March to proceed to the Charleston Navy Yard near Charleston, South Carolina for duty on the USS RAY K. Edwards (APD 96). The crew seeing the Edwards for the first time was a big surprise. They had expected a finished product and it was deep in the process of undergoing refit and modification. A good bit of heavy construction remained to be done on it. APDs were designated as a high-speed troop transport. They were actually remodeled destroyer escorts on which the rear 5-inch gun turret was removed and that area converted to a cargo hold with a boom and winches on the deck. The torpedo tubes were removed and four landing craft mounted on the ship's superstructure with davits for handling them into and out of the water. What had been open deck along the sides of the destroyer escorts was enclosed with folding bunks to make it possible to carry 200 troops.

The Charleston Shipyard was a large installation. Some of the ships in the yard were getting repairs from war damage and some of those ships were really beat up. While the former officers of the Shelton were in Charleston, the war in Europe ended. The Ray K. Edwards was laid down as the Rudderow-class destroyer escort USS Ray K. Edwards (DE-237) on December 1, 1943 by the Charleston Navy Yard and was launched on February 19, 1944, sponsored by Mrs. Lena M. Edwards. The ship was reclassified as a Crosley-class high-speed transport and redesignated APD-96 on July 17, 1944. After conversion to its new role, the APD-96 was commissioned on June 11, 1945.

During the latter part of June 1944, the ship departed on its shakedown cruise to Guantanamo Bay, Cuba. The ship returned to the Norfolk, Virginia Navy Yard for shakedown repairs and modifications. Just a day or two before leaving Norfolk, there was a report in the newspaper about a giant bomb that had been exploded in Japan. The

Edwards left Norfolk, sailing south. However, just an hour or two after getting out to the ocean and up to cruising speed. At that time, one of the propeller drive shaft bearings was over-heating. It just kept getting hotter and hotter. The only way to stop the shaft was to shut down both propeller shafts. Engineering crewmembers opened the bearing and they found that somehow grinding compound had been added to the oil. After cleaning the bearing and oil slump, they closed it up and the ship resumed its cruising speed.

After transiting the Panama Canal, the Edwards turned northward to the U.S. West Coast. One or two days after leaving the western entrance to the Panama Canal, a radio report came to the ship that the war was over in the Pacific. After a short stay in Long Beach, California to load supplies, the Edwards sailed west to become a minor cog in the occupation force of Japan. The ship stopped at Pearl Harbor, after which it stopped at Eniwetok Atoll in the Marshall Islands. Eniwetok was later the site of atomic and hydrogen bomb explosions as part of America's atomic and thermonuclear testing programs. The ship sailed into Buckner Bay, Okinawa. As the ship neared Okinawa, radio reports were received of a typhoon heading into the area. The destroyer increased speed from 15 to 20 knots, which used fuel at a high rate. The fuel tanks were low as ship neared Buckner Bay. As the ship entered the harbor, the ships in the harbor were hurrying to get out to the open sea. A harbor is the worst place to be in a typhoon. The first thing the Edwards captain accomplished was finding a tanker to refuel. After refueling, the Edwards sailed out of Buckner Bay to the open sea to clear from the path of the typhoon.

In heavy weather like this, the sea could be quite rough. The bow of the ship would go up and down. A real big wave would strike the bow and it would really send a shudder through the length of the ship, after which it would come back to the bow, but with less intensity. In rough weather, the wardroom was equipped with fiddle boards that came in sections that fastened together and fit over the wardroom table. The boards had holes that fit the sizes of plates and glasses to prevent them from sliding. The wardroom table went lengthwise across the width of the ship. The Captain's place was at the end of the table. Several times after a decision was made not to fit the fiddle boards on the wardroom table, all of the meal and dishes the officers couldn't grab, would end up in the Captain's lap. At times, the destroyer would have to refuel from a tanker, while underway, that was exciting. The destroyer would come alongside at about 10 knots. The tanker would extend hoses over to the destroyer on a boom. The crew would grab the hoses and attach them to fill pipes, tie them down, and they'd start receiving the oil from the tanker. During the refueling process, the destroyer might get close to the tanker, sometimes within two feet. The Captains of the tanker and destroyer talked over the radio and moved apart. Both Captains had to be careful not to get too far apart, watching the ropes and hoses become taut and strained. Those near the hoses would be ordered to clear the area because in rough weather there was a danger that the hoses would rip out of their fill pipes. However, that never happened. One time, for some reason the destroyer had to refuel from a fleet aircraft carrier. If the destroyer got too close, the overhand of the flight deck could tear off the rigging for the mast and do great damage to the radar antenna. After a couple days of sailing around, the Edwards returned to Buckner Bay. The crew witnesses the power of a typhoon. Every ship that couldn't get out of the harbor to the ocean was up on dry land. They could never be refloated.

From Okinawa, the Edwards sailed up into the Inland Sea of Japan. The destroyer anchored off Kure at the southwestern end of the sea. The crew had an opportunity to go ashore and witness the effects of the B-29 bombings, which decimated the area. The destroyer also anchored in another area that was more remote. There were small villages on the hillside and the 29,900 ton Japanese battleship Ise, which was armed with 14-inch guns. It had been attacked and sunk but its crew managed to beach the warship before it sunk in deeper water. The crew boarded the damaged battleship, climbed all over it. They had their pictures taken on while sitting on the forward 14-inch twin turret, with Lt. J.G. Munro straddling one barrel, just behind the open muzzle. The crew went further ashore, cut down a pine tree to serve as ship's Christmas tree. No one appeared to admonish the crew that this couldn't be down. The destroyer also sailed to Wakavama, at the northeastern end of the Inland Sea. The small city had been hit by a B-29 fire raid.

The only thing remaining in the town's business area was a safe for each store or office. Some of the crew walking around that area and out into the country a little way, an older man motioned for them to come with him. He took them into his personal Shinto shrine. They crew took off their shoes and went in. He chanted from a scroll while tapping a stick to a hollow piece of wood. One of these places at which some of the crew stopped had been a port area with piers and warehouses, but it had been severely damaged by an earthquake sometime during the war. The pier surfaces were broken and undulated. The warehouses on the piers were twisted. The area had been rendered unusable. Lieutenant Solomon became somewhat friendly with some boys in the area and it was from them that he traded 10 pounds of sugar for a Japanese Samurai sword. These boys taught some of the crew how to count up to ten in Japanese. The crew also traded cigarettes for beer with the boys and then gave the beer back to them to drink while they counted to ten in Japanese.

During the time the Edwards was in the Inland Sea, it functioned as a single ship operation. For a few days, the destroyer trailed an old cargo ship around one entrance to the Inland Sea. The cargo ship was acting as a minesweeper as it went over an area suspected to be mined and they were supposed to explode. If the cargo ship, the Edwards was to pick up the crew. It didn't happen. Lieutenant Solomon was careful to keep the destroyer in the wake of the cargo ship.

The Edwards sailed for home, without some of its officers and enlisted who had already received orders and sent home by other means of transportation. Returning home to the United States, the Edwards transited the Panama Canal on April 24, 1946 and, after visits to Boston, Massachusetts; Jacksonville, Florida and Charleston, South Carolina she was towed to Mayport, Florida, arriving on August 13, 1946. The destroyer was decommissioned on 30 August, berthed at the Green Cove Springs, Florida, as part of the Atlantic Reserve Fleet. The destroyer was stricken from the Navy List on June 1, 1960, and sold on June 15, 1961 to Diamond Manufacturing Company of Georgia for scrapping. Lieutenant J.G. Munro returned home. [46]

---

[46] Joseph Munro during World War II was a U.S. Navy Lt. J.G. The following information was provided by Joseph Munro, to author, based on a World War II personal history of Lt. Commander Lewis G. Salmon of the USS Shelton (DE-207) and USS Ray K. Edwards (APD-96), written by his son, William R. Salmon, entitled "What dad did during the war." It provides a look at the U.S. Navy workhorses of World War II, sometimes referred to as the "Greyhounds of the fleet," the destroyers.

Arthur T. Jansen

United States Marine Corps
World War II Pacific Combat

ARTHUR T. Jansen..."I entered the United States Marines Corps on December 21, 1943 at the Marine Recruiting Station in Portland, Oregon. I was sent to the Marine Corps Center in San Diego, California for eight weeks of Boot Camp. During that time, we trained with many different weapons and different types of combat. We were subjected to rigorous physical training and marksmanship skills. The Marine Corps base at San Diego was mainly sand reclaimed from the Pacific Ocean, so, moving around in our heavy combat boots and the loose sand was great exercise for your legs and lungs, especially since you never walked. We were always expected to double-time in formation wherever we went. That meant double time to chow, double time to the obstacle course, double time to hand to hand combat training, double time to the head and double time to get your shots. The whole point was you never walk anywhere. For mental gymnastics, we were required to memorize our dog tag number and our rifle serial number. During the time I spent in the Corps, I had so many different weapons I cannot remember any of the serial numbers, but I will never forget my dog tag number, 934309. If my information is correct, I was the 934,309 enlisted Marine to serve in the Marine Corps since it became a military force in 1775.

"One of the great experiences during boot camp was inspections. The drill instructors inspected your sea bag to make sure you only had G.I. issue items in it and everything was in a proper order. They inspected your rifle to determine how dirty it was, because they never considered how clean it was. They checked your cot to make sure the corners were correctly folded and the blanket was stretched tight enough to play Yankee Doodle Dandy on it with a half dollar.

"I remember one interesting training event when we were introduced to the hand grenade. Everyone in the platoon was instructed on the proper procedure for handling and throwing hand grenades. After we had a chance to throw a couple of grenades from a bunker, the instructor explained that it took approximately 10 seconds for the grenade to go off after it was released. He emphasized that if a grenade was accidentally dropped in a crowd after the pin had been removed, the best way to handle it would be to pick it up, unscrew the top, and remove the primer. He explained this would prevent it from going off. A short time later during the lesson (you guessed it), he accidentally dropped a grenade after he pulled the pin and of course, everyone scrambled for cover. No one approached the grenade, it was a dud.

"During the eight weeks in San Diego, we spent two weeks at Camp Mathews Rifle Range honing our skills with the M-1 rifle and perfecting our close order drill. We continued to double-time in formations everywhere we went. We also learned that you clean a rifle with soap and water and then dry it thoroughly and put a light coat of oil on it. I had always thought water and metal were mortal enemies. However, the Marine Corps taught me I was wrong. My time at Camp Mathews also provided me with a raise in pay. If you fired 'expert' on the range you received $5.00 a month more.

"Following Camp Mathews, we all felt salty coming back to the Marine Corps base in San Diego. Everyone there when we returned there were new recruits with shaved heads and bewildered looks. We had one week, as I recall, and then we graduated or if we had not measured up, we were sent back to a remedial platoon. We lost a couple of platoon members. One, if I remember, who couldn't swim and one who could not read. Other than that, the rest of us were pronounced fit for combat. After boot camp, we all got a leave to go home and see our folks. I had been gone since August, when Tex Malone I went to Vancouver, Washington to work in the shipyards. We worked for Kaiser on building baby (escort) aircraft carriers. Little did I know that one day I would be aboard one, possibly one I had worked on. What I remember most about my leave, which was in February, was how cold it was in Hot Springs and Rapid City, South Dakota. While I was in Rapid City, we went to Deadwood to see my step grandparents. Apparently, Deadwood wasn't very popular with the local military brass because they had stationed Army Air Forces Military Police at all the entrances to the city and they permitted military personnel to enter only if you could convince them you had a reason they approved of for entering. They also kept your orders until you returned and you had to give them a time when you would return. I think they believed me when I told them I was going to visit my grandparents. I spent some time in Deadwood when I was in High School and Deadwood was a pretty wild place even then and I am sure it got wilder with all the GI's from the Rapid City Army Air Base coming into town.

"Following boot camp, I spent a couple of months working out with the base track team at the Marine Corps base in San Diego. I was a pole-vaulter. While I was stationed at the Marine Corps base, I got a 48 hour leave one weekend and went to Los Angles and met some of the guys from Hot Springs who were stationed in California. The one who put the reunion together was Don Getty, U.S. Army who was also a former classmate of mine in High School. He was stationed at Fort Ord, California and through letters, he was able to round up some of the other guys we both knew. Jack Hopper was an Army Air Corps cadet, Jerry Krutsch joined the U.S. Army, and I can't seem to remember who the others were, but they were not classmates. Following that get together, I began to feel guilty that I wasn't contributing to the war effort and asked for a transfer to a unit going overseas. The First Sergeant was a little testy about my asking for a transfer just before a track meet. In addition, being on the track team, I had to perfect a skill that could be used anywhere in the Marine Corps. In addition to feeling guilty, I also hated learning to play the bugle. When asked what I would prefer, I inquired about the tank corps and the next thing I remember I was in the infantry company training at Camp Elliot near San Diego.

"At Camp Elliot we went through all the possible combat situations, crawling on our bellies under barbwire with machine guns firing overhead, sometimes in a down pour of rain, crouching in foxhole (reinforced with railroad ties) while a tank drove over the top of us. However, of course, I didn't see too many enemy tanks either. One of my fond memories of Camp Elliott was that we were too young to buy beer off base but we could purchase 'Miller High Life-The Champagne of Bottled Beer' for 10 cents a bottle at the 'Slop Shop' (Marine name for the base post exchange), which we took advantage of every chance we got.

"After completing infantry training with the 64th Replacement Regiment at Camp Elliot, the Marine Corps turned the camp over to the Navy. We were shipped to a new camp called Pendleton, near Oceanside, California. After a week there, we shipped out to Hawaii where we also spent about a week. During that time, President Roosevelt visited the island and we stood in formation while he rode by in an open limousine. Before we left Pearl Harbor, we were assigned to a unit. I was assigned to the Third Marines of the Third Marine Division. The Third Division was made up of the 3rd, 9th and 21st Regiments. During the trip to Guam from Hawaii, we were sailing on a ship called the SS Degross, a French freighter refitted to carry troops. It was old and had trouble keeping up with the other ships. One night, we were sailing with the without lights because we were passing Wake Island and didn't want to be detected. During the night, our ship lost its rudder and was going wild in the convoy. Suddenly we heard foghorns sounding all around us, and the ship stopped. They put a diver over the side and he was able to repair the rudder. In the meantime, the rest of the convoy kept moving. They left one destroyer behind to escort our ship and the next day we did finally catch up. When I arrived on Guam on August 15, 1944, I was assigned to "L" Company, 3rd Battalion, 3rd Regiment, 3rd Marine Division. 'L' Company had suffered nearly a 50 percent casualty rate during the invasion of Guam. I was assigned to a 60mm mortar squad and remained with the squad through the end of the war.

"The retaking of Guam was one of the toughest battles the Third Division had been involved in to that time. Guam had been a territory of the United States since 1898. Prior to the attack on Pearl Harbor on December 7, 1941, the military had decided not to increase the amount of equipment or manpower it would require to defend the island. To try to fortify it would probably give the enemy added equipment and fortifications when they did take it. There was no doubt that the island, with its small detachment of Marines and very little defensive equipment, would not be able to repel an invasion by a large Japanese force. They did take the island on December 8, 1941. The Japanese had fortified Guam as much as they could during the time they occupied the island. The initial attack by the 3rd Division of U.S. Marines occurred on July 21, 1944. By the time of the final sweep of the island was completed during the first three days of November 1944, the Marines had suffered 677 killed in action, 3,200 wounded and 9 missing in action. By January 1, 1945, the enemy had lost 9,811 killed and 469 captured. The mop up of the island continued until the end of the war in August 1945.

"During the time, I was on Guam, 'L' Company sent out patrols on a daily basis searching for Japanese soldiers that had hidden out in the hills and jungles. They were very elusive and the patrols mainly kept them from any kind of guerrilla organization. During one sweep of the island, the entire division moved across the island. However, in spite of this effort, daily patrols and area sweeps, there were still ambushes taking place into 1946.

"One of my memories of Guam was a fishing trip we took in the Agana Bay using a Duck (a military amphibious vehicle) for a fishing boat. They provided the poles and reels but for bait, they provided canned tuna. There was no way you could keep that flaky canned tuna on a hook, so most of the afternoon was just riding around in the bay in the duck. Another experience that didn't live up to its billing was a trip to the beach to go swimming. We had a picnic and played some football in the sand and really had a good time, but when we went swimming, I got a real shock. I had never swum in salt water before and I had learned to swim in fresh water, so I always swam with my eyes open. Big mistake in salt water.

"September of 1944, our company was bivouacked in a jungle clearing. We slept in shelter-halves, cooking in our helmets. I remember on 1 September, I woke up in the morning and crawled out of the shelter half. The next thing I remember I woke up on a stretcher two days later in a field hospital. I had contracted Dengue Fever, I believe it is a type of Malaria. I had blood poison in my right arm from a mosquito bite on my right wrist. These was a red streak running up to my armpit and I felt terrible. About a week later and 10 pounds lighter, I returned to the company. We continued patrols through 1944 and into 1945. During a company sweep of a suspected area, my mortar squad was moving up on the right flank of one of the rifle squads when we encountered a bunker. It didn't appear there had been any activity in the area, but the rifle squad decided not to take any chances and fired a bazooka into the bunker. A large fragment from the explosion hit me just above the ankle. After a few days in the hospital, I returned to the company and spent the next three to four weeks on crutches (referred to as limited duty).

"The Third Marine Division established a base on Guam and trained during 1944 and 1945 for the battle of Iwo Jima. The division boarded ships in February 1945, and of course none of the enlisted and probably most officers had no idea of where we were going. By 25 February, we were approaching Iwo Jima which was about five miles long and maybe two and one-half miles wide at the widest point. D-Day was 27 February and nearly 30,000 Marines of the 3rd, 4th and 5th Divisions, and some units attached to these divisions were committed to the invasion. My battalion was held in reserve, as we were told, because we had so many new replacements. The battalion had been decimated during the invasion of Guam.

"We could see almost everything happening on Iwo as it took place during the daylight. At night, we could see the mortars and artillery explosions and the tracer bullets from the rifles. On the morning of the 28th or 29th, I saw a Navy reconnaissance plane hit by ground fire. The tail separated from the rest of the plane just behind the cockpit and two crewmembers bailed out of the airplane, parachuting into the ocean. They were picked up by the Navy. I suppose that as I look back on this, I was lucky not to have been sent ashore. However, at the time, nearly every one of us on that ship wanted in the worst way to be involved. We discussed ways we might get off the ship and go ashore. Apparently, the unit commander heard about our clandestine plans and an announcement came over the PA system telling us that anyone who left the ship without authorization would be court marshaled. We would probably still have done it if we could, we didn't feel we had come this far just to be spectators.

"The battle for Iwo Jima was the bloodiest battle of World War II. There was only one battle in the history of our country that had more American causalities than Iwo Jima, and that was the battle of Gettysburg during the U.S. Civil War. There were 22,000 highly trained Japanese defenders dug in on the island. They had miles of tunnels, some were three levels deep and big enough for the Japanese to stand up straight and run in. They had underground electrical systems so the tunnels could be lighted and underground lines for their communications. The command post on the island was 60 feet underground and reinforced with concrete. Their defenses in addition to the 22,000 men, included hundreds of pillboxes, bunkers, block houses and caves with heavy artillery, mortars, machine guns and small arms. The Japanese had the island completely covered with concealed firing points. It was said that if Marines stayed in one place too long they would suffer a barrage of mortar or artillery fire.

"During the battle, Marines suffered 26,000 causalities. This was the only battle where we had more causalities than the enemy. The Third Marines had 5,569 causalities, of which, 1,131 were killed in action. Out of the 22,000 enemy troops on the island, only about 1,000 survived.

"The importance of Iwo Jima was twofold. First, the airfields provided the Japanese with control of the Pacific south of Japan. With their airfields, they locate and bomb or strafe our Navy ships and they could intercept our bombers from Guam, Tinian and Saipan on their runs to Japan. Second, we needed the airfields for emergency landings for our aircraft coming or going to, or coming back from Japan. One aircraft made an emergency landing on Iwo Jima before the island was secure. During the remainder of the war, 2,400 aircraft (the majority Boeing B-29 Superfortresses) made emergency landings on Iwo Jima, saving the lives of some 27,000 pilots and crewmembers.

"Following Iwo Jima, we returned to Guan and began training for the next engagement. Of course, after they dropped the atomic bombs, the Japanese surrendered and the war was over. We discovered the next engagement we were preparing for, according to the maps posted on the Company bulletin board, would have been the island of Japan. If there is anything, a Democratic President ever did that I am grateful for, it was Harry Truman and his decision to drop the bombs. It could very well have saved my life and the lives of hundreds of thousands of other Marines, Army and Navy personnel, and probably millions of Japanese.

"After we returned to Guam from Iwo Jima, I had the good fortune to run across two guys I had gone to school with them in Hot Springs, South Dakota. First was Jack Trow who was a couple of years behind me in high school and was in the Third Division, Ninth Division. We were able to get together a couple of times and talk about good times back home. Jack received the Bronze Star for his action on Iwo Jima. The second was Maurice (Ozzie) Asemissen, we had graduated from Hot Springs, South Dakota. Ozzie was in the Navy and assigned to submarines. There was a submarine base on Guam and I don't remember who found out we were both there. I enjoyed going to the sub base to see Ozzie, because they always had great food and we always had a great time getting caught up on news from other classmates in the service and on the home front.

"I was sent back to the States in February 1946. We left Guam and almost immediately ran into a typhoon. I can remember standing on the bow of the ship and looking at the waves. They appeared to be thirty or forty feet above the bow of the ship and suddenly I would be looking down at a hole in the water that was below the bow of the ship. I was fortunate not to be affected by seasickness, but some of the men onboard actually turned green. It was a real challenge to get in the chow line and walk by where someone had gotten sick and couldn't make it to the rails, or even worse if it happened in a gangway where they had no place else to go. We landed at Treasure Island in the Bay of San Francisco. After being fitted with new uniforms and checked by doctors, we boarded a small Kaiser built Jeep aircraft carrier for the short sea trip down the coast of California to San Diego. One great mistake was that the unit commander decided to hold a little close order drill and inspection of the flight deck. Being so close to shore the aircraft carrier was rocking from side to side so badly we couldn't help but lunge forward and back as the ship rolled, it was so bad the detachment was soon dismissed. This could have been on one of the 'Jeep' aircraft carriers I worked on at the Vancouver, Washington shipyard three years before.

"At this point, the Third Marine Division had been retired and all of us who were in for the duration were being discharged. I was asked where I would like to be discharged. I had heard there was a Marine Corps detachment in Hastings, Nebraska and I opted to go there. However, true to form, I was sent to Naval Station at Bainbridge, Maryland. I really thought this was great. I could have never been able to do all that traveling on my own and it was great seeing so much of the country. All the travel was by rail passenger car. Following my discharge at Bainbridge, I was able to see Washington, DC and take a trip to New York City with a fellow Marine I had met at Bainbridge. He had relation living in New York City so we got a quick tour of the city. I remember seeing the Empire State Building at night, but the clouds were so low, you could only see up about 50 stories."[47]

---

[47] Arthur T Jansen, USMC, 1943-1946, attended high school in Hot Springs, South Dakota and provided the highlights of his Marine Corps service during World War II in a letter to author, June 2006.

Jerry Teachout

United States Army Air Corps

JERRY Teachout..."The decision to try to become an Air Corps pilot came early in my humble beginnings. I was to probably stay on the farm, like other neighbor boys and be satisfied with the fate, even though there were other options available. The one I took changed my whole life. During my high school years, there had been the opportunity of taking short trips to Omaha and Kansas City for livestock shows and other things. Now, for a farm kid in the day and age, Omaha and Kansas City were in another world, even if they were only miles from home. I was born to parents that never traveled unless there was a relative involved, and that was darned seldom. Fremont County, Iowa was the place of my birth (October 12, 1924). I started first grade at the tender age of four, meaning that I would graduate from high school before I was seventeen. On one of those trips to Omaha, it was suggested that the municipal airport was a good side trip, just to watch the big airplanes take-off and land. With our noses poked through the wire fence that kept people from going out on the concrete aircraft parking area, we witnessed an Army Air Corps pair of pilots approach a very close by airship, parachutes slung over a shoulder then into the cockpit. One of the airmen walked around the plane checking the control surfaces, engine, tail and many other things unbeknownst to us. It was not too long before he settled in the front cockpit, strapped himself in, placed a pair of headsets over his 50 mission cap and proceeded to start the engine. It whined, belched, shot a lot of smoke out of the exhaust and finally ran on its own. Being that close to a real airplane, a real crew, a real experience it was. Was that the instant that started putting dreams in my young head? Wish I knew because I've never forgotten that incident to this day. Little did I know about the world situation in 1938 that would lead to World War II.

"About a year later, I was helping my dad by driving the tractor hooked to a hayrack piled high with alfalfa, headed for the barn. I had turned onto a dirt road with nary a thought in my mind except to finish the assigned task. The noise of the tractor probably drowned out the sound of an approaching airplane following the road at a very low altitude, coming from the rear. All of a sudden, it was over me, past me and was disappearing in the distance, and if left with me a resolve. That if he could do that, I could too! Only later was I to know that it probably was a Martin B-26 Marauder being test flown by a couple of hot rod Air Corps pilots from the Omaha-Martin B-26 factory at Fort Crook, Bellevue, Nebraska! That was the turning point that really started me on an aviation career that has never ended.

"Three days before Pearl Harbor I left to go to Wichita, Kansas, to an aviation school with the dream in mind that I could learn about building an airplane but without the confidence that I could fly one of them. After all, it took a smart educated cookie to reach the rank of pilot and I was certain that I would never be of that class. About a week before finishing school, I was called in to the school's President office, to be informed that I had to be 18 before I could work in any factory that built airplanes, such as Boeing, Cessna or Beechcraft, local manufacturers that had government contracts. I was offered a bus ticket back to Iowa, or I could stay and work for the school! The farm in Iowa didn't call near as loud as the opportunity to work for a school that had to do with airplanes. I wouldn't be 18 for about a year and that seemed like a forever term in my mind and in time. I could and did learn everything the school had to offer, engines, propellers, instruments, hydraulics, electric circuits, control systems, and many things this farm boy had never heard of. My first job was in the tool crib issuing tools to be used by students to the things that I had already learned. I think that lasted about two weeks when the head of the blueprint/math department stopped by the tool crib and asked if I'd be interested in helping somewhere in his department, he'd already cleared it up with higher ups. To make a long story short, I of course took the job, advanced until I was the only teacher on many occasions and when the school moved to Detroit, Michigan in June of 1942, I had both departments because the retired university professor, my mentor, could not move because his wife was dying of cancer in Wichita.

"I wouldn't be 18 until October and this was only June. Again, this was forever! In the meantime, the possibility of becoming an aviation cadet loomed bigger all the time. After all, education standards had come down, the war was under way, the U.S. Army needed pilots very bad, and hope was rising that, there might be a possibility. I took the entrance exams, both mental and physical for aviation cadets, passed both with flying colors, worked hard at my job in inspection in a real factory, building my ego and hopes with prayers that I might make the grade. I got the call from the Air Corps to report for infantry style basic training, reporting date was June 18, 1943. I was on my way!

"No one ever worked harder for a goal than this kid. I was strictly on my own, what I did and accomplished was mine and only mine, if I goofed up, there was no one else to blame but me. Basic Soldier Training taught me discipline and respect for authority, a furtherance of what I had learned from my folks. Use of a Springfield rifle was just plain fun because I grew up with a gun in my hand. I learned very fast that an educated, inquiring mind got the gravy ahead of others. Listening to smarter heads was a virtue, selecting the best of available options became a habit! I even got to go to college while still in training, more learning, hoping, praying, and all the whole of our forces in the theaters of operations were taking it on the chin. There was not a doubt that if I made it through flying training, I would go to other parts of the world to help turn the tide. Thoughts of getting scared entered the picture even though classmates paid the total price.

"The tragedy of losing my mother in March of 1944 became a comma in the sentence of my life. I was delayed before I ever got into an airplane by her death. As I look back now, I think the 'old man' upstairs delayed me for a reason, one to be explained years later when I found out that many of my flying classmates had been shot down on raids over Tokyo and in the Pacific. Why had I been delayed?

"Flying school was probably one of the hardest lessons to be learned yet. There was never any time to slack off because if you did, someone else could take your spot. In all phases of flying training there was always the fear that someone was better than you, and 'wash out' was ever present. It was always a test of good judgment, skill and luck. The war was not yet won by a long shot, but had started to wind down, with the smell of victory all around. Primary flying took place at Cimarron Field near Yukon, Oklahoma, followed by basic flying near Garden City, Kansas. I could hardly dream of the 'silver wings' that lay ahead if I kept my head screwed on straight! Advanced flying training at Eagle Paris, Texas taught me a whole lot about fighter tactics, because that was what I wanted to fly, in the worst way. An additional month of flying training was added to advance flying at Moore Field, Mission, Texas, but I got into a real fighter, P-40 of Flying Tigers fame. By the time graduation day rolled around, December 23, 1944, I thought there wasn't anything I couldn't do, look what I just did. I was a Second Lieutenant, I had a pair of silver wings on my chest, and I was on top of the world! Woe be unto the Axis! That uniform was the pinnacle of success and I had done the impossible and somewhere along the line, I realized that the airplane seen at the Omaha Airport so long ago was the same airplane I had learned to fly in advance training, the AT-6 Texan, made by North American, flown by thousands of cadets and it certainly included me.

"After a very short graduation leave, I found out that officers got leave and airmen got furloughs. I had orders to a pilot pool at Waco Airfield Number 1, Waco, Texas. From there, we were to get further assignment supposedly in accordance with our previous training. Rumor had it that our next job was to fly gliders. That did not set too well with me because an airplane with an engine gave you a lot more choices as to where you wanted to go. One day shortly after the glider rumor mill had started, my buddy and I were walking past the orderly room, an airman was posting something for everyone to read on the outside daily bulletin board, quickly read by at least two of us. It basically said the B-24 aircraft commanders were needed and if you were interested, report to such and such in the orderly room. I don't think the door had shut before both of us were there, willing to fly anything, but not gliders. A couple of days later found the two of us on a bus to Courtland, Alabama, arriving there on Saturday evening. All was well and good, we thought, until we heard an obvious four engine aircraft flying in at not too far distant traffic pattern. Boom! No more four engines were heard, only later, upon arriving at the air base by bus, did we learn that war weary and unmodified B-24s had a nasty habit of blowing up as the gear was lowered. It didn't take an aeronautical engineer to learn just what went wrong.

"The B-24 took a lot of muscle to fly, especially with two engines out on one side. That notice on the bulletin board said 5 foot 7-inches was the minimum height and 140 pounds the minimum weight. I weighed 141 and was 5 foot 7-1/4 inches, just above minimums, and it didn't take long to follow the reasoning behind all this. There just wasn't enough trim tab and muscle to keep that airplane level even during practice sessions, and we weren't even in combat yet. The idea of herding four engines, not one, nine other crewmembers, not as fighter training had taught was another facet of training. The Aircraft Commander had to look out for all the rest, make all the decisions, in other words, had to be the boss. Only another crewmember would understand this, and the better boss you were, the better crew integrity resulted. I often wonder if the average person realizes that crew camaraderie after the show is over means so much. Lives were at stake, a wrong analysis of a tight situation by any crewmember could put the whole crew in jeopardy. Is it any wonder that trust became the order of the day, a weak link in the chain showed up very quickly. Training?

"You bet, fast and furious, either learn it or get out of the way! B-24 school went fast, and a few of us were picked to go on to the B-29 at Maxwell Field, Alabama.

"The time was July of 1945. While in B-24 training, VE-Day had been declared, all fighting in Europe ceased, but the workload of training never stopped. Did this help win World War II? I was too busy learning about the biggest, longest, highest flying aircraft in the world. I was now training to be a copilot on B-29s. It wasn't hard to see why crew training in B-24 school was so important in flying the B-29. More of the same, but additional crewmembers were thrown into the pot, and they seemed to have had more experience. For instance, there was added to the crew a CFC or Central Fire Control member, almost always a Master Sergeant. He fired the tail guns by radar, a brand new device at the time. My aircraft commander was a senior Major who had graduated from flying school in 1938. In my opinion, he couldn't land the B-29 worth a hoot, the instructor pilots seemed to know this, the result was that I got a lot of stick time not usually afforded to a copilot trainee. Our missions were eight hours long, and we learned about the unusual characteristics of the B-29, finally finishing the course with orders to report to the Replacement Depot in Lincoln, Nebraska. The aircraft commander and myself, in three days, were to pick the rest of the crew and head for Guam. Something happened on the way to Lincoln that I'll never forget, V.J. Day was declared. The flight engineers, also a rated pilot and myself were traveling together, by express train from Birmingham to Chicago. Very early in the morning the trains stopped, out in the middle of nowhere. The conductor didn't even know where we were. Hours passed, we disembarked from the train until the conductor got a wave from somewhere that we had better get back onboard. Slowly, the train rolled thru Kankakee, Illinois, giving us some idea of where we were. We stopped again, this time a newspaper boy came onboard selling the most important paper ever printed, V.J. Day!

"We arrived in Lincoln, instead of a three day stay, it lasted for three months. I was assigned to the flight line as an instructor in the AT-6 to give other pilots their four hours per month for them to draw their flight pay. What goes around comes around, the same type of airplane shows up again! My hometown was just eighty miles down the section line east of Lincoln, and it got a going over quite often. To this day, any of the old timers that are left stop me on infrequent visits and have something to say about the tricks I used to do with the AT-6.

So much for World War II.

Flying and aircraft were solidly implanted in my blood. The farm kid was ready for anything but the future of military aviation looked mighty dim. After I was released from active duty, eventually I stayed in the Reserve Air Corps, assigned to Offutt Air Base near Omaha and flew any military plane that was available. In the meantime, Civilian Flight Instructor School was in the mix and I got to fly some 12 different airplanes as a result. My single and four-engine training paid off because it wasn't too long until the Active Reserve got its ducks in a row and started a Reserve Troop Carrier Wing. More training resulted to get checked out in a C-46, and I soon became an instructor pilot. Once again, training paid off, when South Korea was invaded and President Truman called us to active duty. It was guys like me that were ready for anything we were assigned to do. History calls it the 'Forgotten War,' but those that participated in it won't and don't forget!

"I stayed in military service for a little more than 28 years. I can honestly say that every flight was a training flight, with always something new to learn. I always cautioned a new student pilot, 'The day that you think you know more than the airplane, is the day you should quit flying it, because the next day it will kill you."[48]

---

[48] Jerry Teachout, Rapid City, South Dakota to author, August 28, 2003.

Harry Nollsch

U.S. Army 3rd Infantry Division

North Africa, Sicily, Italy, Southern France and Germany

HARRY Nollsch, born in 1919, spent three years of his young life in the service of his country, traveling a good part of three continents in the war that throttled the hegemonic daydreams of Japan and Germany. He was transferred from infantry machine gun crew to aircraft maintenance school. Prior to entering the U.S. Armed Forces, in 1936 Nollsch joined the Civil Conservation Corps (CCC), a social program set up by the Roosevelt administration that allowed young men, impacted by the U.S. "Great Depression," to enlist in a para-military organization in an area that put them to work on public projects. These men earned $30.00 per month, of which, $25.00 was sent home to assist those there, with $5.00 left for the worker's needs. Outside this small stipend, the men got room and boards, not a bad thing in those difficult times.

In 1941, Nollsch got a chance to go away to the National Youth Administration for training in aircraft maintenance, the move that later saved him from the fate of the machine gun crew. He was drafted in June 1942. He traveled from Sturgis to Fort Crook, Nebraska onto Fort Leavenworth, Kansas then to Camp Pickett, Virginia. It was whole training as a basic infantryman in a machine gun crew that he was called out and told he was going to Fort Sill, Oklahoma for Field Artillery Observation School. He trained there in L-2, L-3 and L-4 aircraft. The L-4, Piper Cub, was America's most used observation/liaison aircraft used during World War II, and the one he became the most acquainted with as a crew chief, responsible for its maintenance and readiness for scoping our enemy artillery.

On completion of the course, Nollsch was assigned to the 2nd Armored Division, Fort Bragg, North Carolina. He took a very cold rail car trip in the fall of 1942, accompanying self-propelled 105mm artillery pieces on open flatbed railroad cars to Fort Dix, New Jersey. He had to wear everything item of clothes he brought with him as well as any borrowed clothes to keep warm. It was not a pleasant railroad trip north to Fort Dix.

By November 1943, the 2nd Armored Division had landed in Morocco, North Africa where Nollsch began his trek across the northern tier of the continent, the Allied forces driving back the Germans and Italians, their eyes on Sicily. He continued onto Anzio, with intermediate trips through Sicily and southern Italy. Somewhere along the line he was assigned to the 9th Field Artillery Battalion, an element of the U.S. 3rd Infantry Division. He was part of the landing in the south of France in August 1944. He saw Winston Churchill passing the landing craft and ships of the landing force, waving to the men on the various boats and ships.

Nollsch remembered men in Sicily hiding in grain sacks next to the airstrip as protection from strafing German aircraft, as if that would do them any good. People in Sicily asked him to stay for lunch and in Palermo, the population holding out bottles of wine to passing troops. He remembered seeing an Italian fall off a two wheel cart, the horse continuing on and the driver running after the animal and cursing. He remembered the three-inch deep foxholes that a man used to try to escape from a German fighter strafing attack, with two men piling on top of the first in a vain attempt to gain safety from the impacting shells. Heavy caliber machine gun rounds will do that to men. He recalled observing the devastation caused by Allied aircraft, which strafed a several mile long column of German troops, equipment and horses. It was a view into holocaust that stayed in his mind.

In Sicily, Nollsch had an unexpected customer show up in a jeep at his unit, wanting to go up in Harry's L-4 to observe the progress of the battle was General George Patton. The general got what he wanted, and the respect of Nollsch for wanting to go into the immediate area of the conflict.

In France, he was picked to drive a jeep for some officers that were on a trip to Grenoble for a break. His uniform and that of the officers were basically the same so he was treated like an officer for those couple of days. He didn't do much except to enjoy the break from the hostilities. He didn't want to learn the ski because he didn't want to take the chance of being injured and separated from his buddies.

Somewhere in the Vosges Mountains in France, Nollsch and his friends were invited by a French family to dinner. While sitting down to a table to eat, a neighbor to the family came by and upbraided the head of the family which Harry took to be an attack for treating the American soldiers with respect. The family patriarch proceeded to take the intruder outside and cuff him quite well.

In October 1944, Nollsch was wounded in France while waiting in line in a tent to get his haircut. A German artillery shell landed just outside the temporary barbershop. He was hit in the arm with shrapnel and the man getting his haircut was hit in the side of the head. Later, in April 1945, at Salzburg, Austria, he received a Purple Heart for the wound. He was awarded the medal on the same stage that the famous 3rd Infantryman, Lieutenant Audie Murphy received one of his many medals.

While bivouacked in Salzburg, Austria in the immediate days after the end of the war in Europe, a G.I. came down the road pushing a handcart loaded with a huge silver bowl filled with linen taken from Adolf Hitler's mountain retreat, the Eagle's Nest. He asked Harry if he wanted a souvenir and gave him a towel with the initials AH embroidered on it. Unfortunately, the towel has been misplaced somewhere in the many moves his family made over the years.[49]

---

[49] Courtesy, Dean Muehlberg, Black Hills Veterans Writing Group, "Reluctant heroes plus one, Harry Nollsch and the Third Infantry Division," to author, June 2010.

Charles Gerlach

Capture of U-515 in the North Atlantic

CHARLES Gerlach..."I was a catapult technician, chief of six enlisted men, commanded by a Lt. J.G. on the USS Guadalcanal (CVE-60). The Guadalcanal was a Casablanca Class escort carrier. The carrier was converted from a Maritime Commission hull, built by the Kaiser Company, Inc. of Vancour, Washington." The carrier was first named Astrolabe Bay (AVG-60), later reclassified as ACV-60 on August 20, 1942. It was launched with the name Guadalcanal on August 2, 1942. Again, it was reclassified on July 15, 1943 as a CVE-60. The carrier was commissioned at Astoria, Oregon on September 25, 1943. After a shakedown training cruise, the carrier performed carrier qualifications near San Diego, California prior to departing on November 15, 1943 to the Panama Canal, onto to Norfolk, Virginia on 3 December. The carrier became the flagship of Task Group 22.3 (TG 22.3).

Gerlach..."During day flight operations launched two to four aircraft every four hours. At night, launched two aircraft every four hours. Pilots flew on compass courses, using a thigh chart to follow course and then return to a designated spot in the ocean to land on the carrier. At night, in the dark, the pilots approaching from the stern only had red lights for landing reference. We continued flight operations 24 hours a day, in all weather conditions. Sailing out of Norfolk, we maintained escort operations for six weeks, refueling at Casablanca and then six weeks back to Norfolk. The carrier had kills:

U-544 on 16 January 1944.

U-515 on 8 April, northwest of Madeira.

U-68 on 10 April, 300 miles south of the Azores.

"We received intelligence on German submarine operating locations because of Enigma intelligence code intercepts."

Enigma was the codename given to the German military cipher code machine developed from a 1918 Dutch design. In 1929, the Enigma machine was adopted by the German military, first for the Army and then the Navy. Use of the code machine expanded to the Luftwaffe, SS, the Abwehr and Reichsbuhn (German State Railways). The code machine resembled a small portable typewriter. Each key depression activated an electric circuit, which transmitted an electric signal impulse to a lamp board illuminating a different letter. Code machine operators were able to insert interchangeable metal rotor wheels at specific periods to make transmitted codes, unbreakable by enemy code breakers. However, a talented group of British code breakers at Bletchley Park cracked the Enigma machine's coding procedures, added by a captured Enigma code machine with intact rotors and settings from a German submarine, along with production information smuggled out of Nazi occupied Europe.

Gerlach..."Captain Galley conducted boarding or salvage operation drills to capture a surfaced German submarine. We were at General Quarters for one week. On 3 June, we had a strong underwater contract, but lost it. The German submarine probably dived below the thermal barrier and we lost the underwater contact. On 4 June, we were off the coast of West Africa, went to General Quarters, launching aircraft with destroyer escorts dropping depth charges. Wildcat fighters located the destroyers who spotted for the aircraft as to where to drop depth charges. The submarine surfaced. Captain Galley ordered all firing to cease. The German crew abandoned the submarine, sinking by the stern. The submarine was circling, due to a jammed rudder with its seacocks open, low battery, hatches dogged down."

The Guadalcanal's logbook and after action intelligence report on the recovery of the U-505. On June 4, 1944, 150 miles west of Cape Blanco, French West Africa, the destroyer Chutelain detected U-505 as it was returning to its base at Breast, France after an 80 day commerce destroying patrol in the Gulf of Guinea. The destroyer dropped a depth charge pattern and guided in for a more accurate drop by circling TBF Avengers, soon made a second. This pattern blasted a hole in the outer hull of the submarine and rolled on its beam ends. Shouts of panic from the conning tower led its captain to believe his boat was doomed, so he blew his tanks and surfaced, 700 yards from Chatelain. The destroyer fired one torpedo, which missed, followed by a combined fire from the escorts, which forced the crew to abandon ship.

Captain Gallery had been waiting and planning for such an opportunity, and having already trained and equipped his boarding parties, ordered Pillsbury's boat to make the German submarine's capture. Under the command of Lt. J.G. Albert David, the party leaped onto the slowly circling submarine and found it abandoned. Lieutenant David and his men captured all important papers and books while closing valves and stopping leaks. As Pillsbury attempted to get a towline on the submarine, the boarding party shut off the engines. A salvage team from the carrier boarded the submarine to rig a towline. After securing the towline and picking up the German crew from the water, the carrier headed for Bermuda. The fleet tug Abnaki rendezvoused with the task group, taking over towing operations, reaching Bermuda on 19 June, after a 2,500 mile tow.

Gerlach..."The group was refueled by a fleet tanker out of Casablanca. After refueling, due to security concerns, the tanker was assigned to the task group, accompanying the carrier to Bermuda. A fleet tug from Casablanca took over the two for the trip to Bermuda at seven knots. While we were so engaged, we did not know of the planned Allied invasion of Normandy on D-Day, June 6, 1944. The capture of U-505 was so well kept secret considering over 1,000 sailors were involved. All but one of the German submariners survived the sinking. The submarine's Captain attended school in Philadelphia and spoke fluent English. The Germans were kept in segregation, in a POW camp so as not to alert German U-boat command that U-505 had been captured intact."

A post World War II report on the capture of U-505, United States Naval War College Library. The capture of the U-505's code books provided crypto-analysts at Bletchy Park, England on June 20, 1944 to have the regular and officer settings for June 1944, current short weather code books, short signal code books and bigram tables for July and August. [50]

---

[50] Charles Gerlach, Rapid City, South Dakota, interview by author at Black Hills Veterans Writing Group, Rapid City, South Dakota, May 8, 2010.

George W. Larson

A Seabee's Story
Tinian and Okinawa, 1944 to 1945

GEORGE W. Larson, during World War II was assigned to the 135th United States Naval Construction Battalion (USNCB), better known by its nickname as the Seabees. On March 17, 1944, Larson entered World War II active duty, giving up his job at an armaments plant in Ankeny, Iowa and war deferment. He departed Des Moines, Iowa on a passenger train for Farragut, Idaho near Lake Pend Oreilla at which time Larson was assigned to Company 351-444, Camp Waldron, U.S. Navy Training Station. Phase I training introduced him to military life. Phase II training consisted of advanced gunnery training. In September 1944, arrived at Oakland Naval Base, issued transit orders and boarded a Liberty ship for the sea voyage to Pearl Harbor, Hawaii.

Once at Pearl Harbor, Larson received the balance of his Navy uniforms, with the rest of his clothes cleaned at Pearl Harbor's laundry. Navy Quartermaster personnel issued him a personalized stencil to mark the sea bag and clothes. Larson kept this all clothes packed, ready for immediate ship boarding once an overseas billet assigned. He had no idea of the final destination or unit. He expected to assignment to a warship because of gunnery training. Meanwhile, the U.S. Navy kept Larson busy working on Pearl Harbor's construction projects and other installations around the island. He had no input to assignment or unit deployment into a forward combat deployment into the western Pacific. One day a Navy Ensign walked down the barrack's center walkway, told Larson to report to the 135th USNCB. The battalion's second echelon, at that time, was in preparation to transport to a forward combat area. Larson climbed into the back of a Navy truck, rode to Pearl Harbor's dock area, climbed out of the truck in front of large transport. The transport was a pre-World War II civilian registry Dutch transport the Motor Ship (MS) Tjisadane. On October 9, 1944, Larson boarded the transport, stowing personnel gear in the forward cargo hold, containing three seemingly endless rows of tripe bunk beds, with little room between the beds. The forward hold was hot, humid and uncomfortable during the 21 day voyage to the battalion's combat duty assignment. Larson decided to spend as much time as possible on deck where at least a cooling sea breeze over the bow, fresh air and open sky made the trip bearable. The 135th had its heavy equipment and supplies loaded in the aft cargo hold.

Every morning and evening, all 135th personnel stood General Quarters, one hour before sunrise and sun set, with every man assigned to a lifeboat station. Each 135th member wore a long-sleeve shirt, cap, life preserver, carrying a full container of water for survival if forced to abandon ship. Destroyers prowled the convoy's perimeter, searching for Japanese submarines, herding strayed transports back into proper position in the slow moving procession. For recreation, battalion personnel listened to shortwave radio broadcasts. One evening, Toyo Rose (a name given to various female English-speaking broadcasters) came on the air, announcing the 135th USNCB was onboard a Landing Ship Tank (LST) somewhere in the Pacific, sunk by an Imperial Japanese Fleet submarine, with all onboard lost (killed). It gave Larson and others listening to the radio goose bumps that somehow Japanese Imperial Navy Intelligence knew the 135th departed Pearl Harbor. Navy escorts and all onboard the transports in the convoy spent the next two days on battle stations, on the lookout for Japanese submarines. There were no sightings, so routine operations resumed. While on the ship, one night Larson was on deck and a seaman came up to him and asked, "would you like me to do a color chalk sketch of you for your family?" Larson agreed and sat for the portrait. Once done, the seaman tore off the finished chalk portrait and gave it to him. Larson never found out who it did his portrait. He rolled it up and placed it into a sea bag and somehow it made it home to Altoona, Iowa with only a small tear in the upper left top. It is one of the author's prized memorabilia of his father's service during World War II as a member of the nation's "Greatest Generation."

The 135th landed on Tinian Island the morning of October 24, 1944. They went over the side of the MS Tjisadane on cargo nets into bobbing Higgins landing craft alongside the transport. Larson was in the second wave, landing on the beach with full combat gear, carrying a carbine. Everything had to be off-loaded from the transport anchored off the beach, first loaded into Landing Craft Tanks (LCTs) for movement onto the beach, loaded into dump trucks for transport inland. It was slow, hot and exhausting work. Seabees worked 18 hours a day unloading heavy equipment and tons of supplies.

The battalion set up its first camp in the middle of a muddy sugar cane field, initially sleeping in two-man pup tents. Larson used his combat helmet to clean off mud and dirt after a hard, 18 hour first day on the island. At first, the weather was ideal, although hot, with gentle trade winds blowing across the island. Later, seasonal rains turned the torn up ground into a mass of sticky mud, which no one could get out of or away from. Meals at the initial campsite were a problem without a permanent mess facility. The first meal consisted of K-rations and hot coffee. Eventually, a large tent was set up to provide hot meals 24 hours a day.

Even after heavy rains hit the island, the men of the 135th lived in pup tents. Shipping crates ripped apart to build wood floors for the tents, later upgraded to pyramid 16 by 16 foot tents erected, electricity provided by a generator, with other items scrounged on the island as needed. Larson got his first break after seven days, hitched a ride on a Navy jeep to ride into the main town at the south end of the island, named by the Japanese as Tinian Town. Concrete constructed buildings were standing shells, most without roofs. Piles of rubble were against exterior building walls, pushed there by bulldozers to clear roads from the beach unloading areas to inland camp areas and construction sites.

Each member of 135th work parties carried carbines, wore combat helmets, as well as maintaining roving armed security patrols around the Seabee camp and work sites. There were constant sightings of stray Japanese soldiers and civilians coming out of hiding at dusk scrounging for food. Eventually, Maries set up a POW camp for surrendering Japanese troops and civilians, along with Korean workers brought to the island as agricultural laborers.

Larson could find no way to get out of the mud, with one either walking or driving through it. Vehicles bogged down, often requiring one or two bulldozers to pull it free. Often, even a bulldozer sank, mired in the sticky mud, needing another bulldozer to pull it free.

As soon as possible, construction started on a permanent 135th camp area, consisting of metal Quonset huts. One of the first completed Quonset buildings was the battalion's permanent mess facility. The battalion's commander relaxed regulations to permit Seabees to wear utility pants cut to short length and go shirtless. The 135th upgraded its camp while working on projects throughout the island.

The 135th worked on building two of the four 8,500 foot long runways at North Field, stressed to accommodate the loaded weight of B-29 Superfortresses. Other Seabee battalions also worked on the runways and facilities. The 135th concentrated on runways one and four. Runway number four was used by the 509th Composite Group's B-29s, dropping the two atomic bombs on Japan (Hiroshima on 6 August and Nagasaki on 9 August 1945), leading to that nation's surrender on 14 August.

On North Field, Seabee battalions operated 80 power shovels, one dozen 12 ton rooters designed to ripe out thick overgrowth, 48 rollers, 90 drills, five well drills, 40 water wagons to keep dust down on coral roads and spread salt water over prepared surfaces to cement together crushed coral. Seabees worked ten hour shifts, with a two hour overlap to repair and service equipment, feed and change out personnel.

Even with the cutting down high spots on runway construction sites, there was not enough material to fill low spots. Huge coral pits dug into hills provided fill and topping material for runways, taxiways and parking aprons. Dump trucks began wearing out from constant loading and unloading of abrasive coral. Seabees welded one-quarter inch steel plates to the floor of each dump truck bed. To increase carrying capacity steel runway mat sections welded to the dump bedsides.

Hundreds of dump trucks shuttled to and from coral pits, load, then dumping coral wherever directed. Dump trucks traveled on designated roads, one way to construction areas, returning by a separate one-way road. Once the coral reached the desired locations, the coral had to spread and leveled by bulldozers and road graders. Larson operated a road grader as part of the runway finishing crew. Coral was additionally impacted by hog teeth rollers, layer after layer, until reaching proper grade. Considerable compaction of the coral surface occurred when heavy dump trucks and construction equipment traveled over the coral surface. The application of salt water on the coral's surface produced a bonding effect, assisted by rolling which created a hard and smooth surface, almost as hard as concrete.

Seabees built a fuel storage and distribution system: a 14,000 barrel fuel storage farm for diesel oil, a 2,000 barrel farm for gasoline and six aviation farms with a capacity of 165,000 barrels. Fuel came ashore through a submerged pipeline, moved inland to aircraft fueling positions.

Seabees built several hundred acres of bomb revetments and ammunition dumps, 1,700 acres of camp facilities, 300 acres of supply dumps, 75 miles of coral surface roads and 50 miles of asphalt topped roads. On December 21, 1944, the first B-29 landed on North Field, while construction work continued. Larson was operating a road grader on the adjacent runway. He stopped the road grader and stared at the landing B-29, a huge four-engine aircraft. Sirens began blowing while jeeps and command cars burst onto the coral runway next to the one Larson was working on, clearing construction equipment and personnel off the runway. This B-29, aircraft number 22-4802, named "Purple Shaft," carried Army Air Forces Brigadier General F.V.H. Kimble (Twentieth Air Force Commander, assigned to coordinated Tinian's North Field operations).

As additional B-29s reached the island, Seabees moved their construction equipment to one side to allow Superfortresses to pass, without slowing their work. To prevent B-29 engines from sucking up coral dust and catching fire, taxiways and then runways coated with heavy asphalt oil, later topped by rolled asphalt.

Larson also directed dump trucks to position for unloading coral. He wore Seabee manufactured goggles to keep coral dust out of his eyes and wore a wet cloth over his nose to keep coral dust out of his mouth. It was hot and dusty work, even when working at night, aided by portable electric floodlights. At the sound of approaching Japanese twin-engine bombers, electric lights shut off, with Seabees heading for the closest slit trench. Larson once had to dive into a slit trench as a Japanese Betty bomber machine-gunned the runway he was working on. Face down in the shallow slit trench, Larson heard bullets smacking into the road grader he abandoned a few seconds earlier.

The biggest irritant was not Japanese air raids but heavy tropical rains, turning everything on the ground into a sea of mud. Seabees' rain ponchos were available, but most never wore them because they were hot and uncomfortable.Japanese snipers occasionally shot at Seabees working on the runways and dump truck drivers hauling coral. Japanese snipers were difficult to locate because they covered their rifle muzzles with bamboo or sugar cane pieces, concealing the flashes. Marines swept the area, killing Japanese flushed into the open. Periodically, Seabee guards killed Japanese soldiers attempting to get into the camp areas scrounging for food.

While operating a road grader, periodically a large piece of uncrushed coral appeared in the runway. Larson stopped the grader, climbed down, taking a pick and shovel to dig out the coral chunk, rolling it off the runway. He shoveled coral into the hole, tamped the loose coral with the shovel, climbed back into the grader, resuming leveling operations to the end of the runway, turning around for another grading pass.

Larson, if not working at night, hiked to a high spot near the active runways to watch B-29s take off. A B-29 barely lifted off the runway, not gaining enough altitude, crashing into the ocean off the end of the runway in fiery flames. Many B-29s crashed while landing after long combat missions to Japan. Larson quietly walked back to his Quonset hut thinking of the crew lost in the flames.

Larson was grading a parking apron when a newly arrived B-29 pulled onto an adjacent parking apron. Larson stopped the grader, climbed down when one of the aircrew motioned for him to come over and climb into the aircraft to look around. It was an impressive aircraft, large, modern, with pressurized crew compartments. Larson later in 1981 had the opportunity to climb into a Boeing B-52 Stratofortress at Andersen Air Force Base, Guam and in 2005, into a B-1B at Ellsworth AFB, South Dakota (arranged by the author who was a Strategic Air Command Strategic intelligence officer on Guam and while at Rapid City, arranged because the 28th Bomb Wing commander was headed to be the 509th BW commander at Whiteman Air Force Base-which Larson had supported under the 509th Composite Group). The 135th adopted a B-29 and its crew, making them honorary battalion members, nicknamed "Wolf Pack," aircraft number 22-4787. A 135th artist drew a wolf riding a falling bomb underneath the copilot's window. The aircraft crashed on a return flight from Japan in the sea, with no survivors.

To keep coral chunks from jamming dump truck rear wheels, Seabees strung a steel cable between the dual axles. The steel cable prevented coral chunks from lodging between the wheels, destroying axles and or truck tires.

It was so hot and humid on Tinian that Larson constantly sprayed medication into his shoes and on heavy work-socks to prevent fungus growth. Every Seabee had to be careful not to severely sun burn and urged to drink large amounts of water to keep hydrated.

While the majority of the 135th worked on North Field, part of the battalion built their permanent camp. As soon as a Quonset hut was completed, 135th personnel tore down tents and moved into assigned permanent living quarters. Each Quonset divided by two rows of bunk beds, holding 30 Seabees under a hard roof and raised structure.

Mail was one of the high spots of life on Tinian. When a dump truck loaded with mail sacks arrived at the battalion's post office, word spread throughout the island. Seabees wrote a lot, giving them contact with family at home.

Later the battalion's Quonset camp became a 1,000 bed Army hospital after the battalion departed Tinian for Okinawa. On June 27, 1945, the 135th loaded men and equipment into five LSTs, sailing north into Saipan harbor for integration into a convoy. Because of limited below deck berthing accommodations, Larson lived on the ship's deck.

He stretched a tarpaulin between two trucks, providing shade from the tropic sun. The 1,200 mile trip was made without incident, arriving at Buchner Bay, Okinawa on 13 July. While entering the harbor, two LSTs grounded on the reef. Rising winds and rough seas placed the ships in harm's way. Every effort to move the LSTs off the reef failed. On 17 July the decision was made to abandon the two LSTs. Larson was on one of the two LSTs, reaching shore without personal gear, later unloaded from the ship, stacked in the battalion's camp area.

Larson and other 135th members were assigned to build an administrative and housing area for U.S. Navy operations base at the southern end of Baten KO. The Japanese surrender on 15 August ended the war in the Pacific. On hearing confirmation of the surrender, a bout of shouting and wild-unauthorized firing of pistols and carbines into the air began as the battalion celebrated the happy day. Two battalion men suffered wounds from falling bullets.

On 16 September, the 135th received warning of an approaching typhoon. All afternoon, Larson and other battalion men worked in a driving rain to secure tents and equipment. The force of the storm blew down 28 tents and most of the buildings under construction. On 9 October a more powerful typhoon struck with winds in excess of 150mph. Larson and other battalion men took shelter inside a large cave near the camp. In the morning, Larson emerged from the cave to witness a scene of total destruction of twisted steel, splintered lumber and smashed debris everywhere.

Many battalion men began heading home, based on points or time in service. Larson eventually received his checkout card, climbed into the back of a dump truck for transportation to a waiting Liberty ship headed for the United States. For Larson, the war ended. On January 31, 1981, Larson returned to Tinian, visiting North Field and his World War II construction sites. He walked the nearly intact runways and visited the battalion's campsite location. The author had a once in a lifetime experience to literally "walk in the World War II footsteps of his father" on Tinian, also accompanied by his son. Larson was part of the massive U.S. World War II effort, which turned Tinian into the world's largest military airport complex, which many Seabee called "A miracle of construction.

Larson suffered from his World War II service from coral dust infestation in his lungs and head injuries when he was blown off a road grader due to an improper detonation of coral to level runway number four. This head injury lead to dementia/Alzheimer's disease in his later years. Larson had kept his Navy Corpsman's records of injuries on

Tinian, which his Chief never asked for. This assisted the author in getting his father great treatment at the Rapid City Veterans Clinic until he died in June 2009 at the age of 94, buried with full military honors in the Black Hills National Cemetery, east of Sturgis, South Dakota, south of Interstate 90. Fortunately, the author talked to his father while he could remember war service to record military service."[51]

---

[51] George W. Larson World War II experiences, Seabees," by Lt. Col. George A. Larson, USAF (Ret.), submitted to American Veterans Center and published as "World War II Experiences: Seabees, Pearl Harbor." George W. Larson, originally of Altoona, Iowa lived the last year of his life as a resident of South Dakota with his son, Lt. Col. George A. Larson, USAF (Ret.), dying of complications from Alzheimer's in May 2009.

Had Taylor

German Prisoner of War
Stalag 17, Krems, Austria

HAD Taylor enlisted in the U.S. Army Air Corps on December 3, 1942, at Cranston, Rhode Island. His initial training was at Miami Beach, Florida, transferred to Laredo, Texas for Aerial Gunnery School. He had additional training at Salt Lake City, Utah; Denver, Colorado (Lowry Field) and Boise, Idaho. He was assigned to a Consolidated B-24 Liberator bomber crew as a tail gunner. The crew was assigned to overseas combat with the Fifteenth Air Force. A mission on April 12, 1944 consisted of 450 B-17s and B-24s assigned to attack German aircraft factories at Fischamend Market and Wiener Neustadt, Bad Voslau assembly plant in Vienna, Austria and surrounding airfields. Fighter escort screen consisted of 200 Lockheed P-38 Lightnings and Republic P-47 Thunderbolts. Enemy AAA and fighters shot down eight bombers with several bombers not returning to base.

Taylor's B-24 was attacked south of Vienna by a group of six German Luftwaffe Bf-110s enroute to Bad Voslau. Two of his crewmembers were unable to parachute out of the aircraft (copilot and a military photographer on the bomber to take photographs). Taylor was in his position as tail gunner able to see the other five B-24s in formation, referred to as tail-end-Charlie grouping of the large bomber force. One Bf-110 approached Taylor's bomber, firing unguided rockets at the aircraft, knocking out number four engine, with shrapnel hitting Taylor's leg. He jumped out of the badly damaged aircraft, getting a good look at the burning aircraft just as one wing fell off the aircraft's fuselage, followed by a violent explosion destroying the aircraft in a ball of flames.

Once on the ground Taylor and the other surviving crewmembers were captured by German troops, transported to a Luftwaffe run POW camp, Stalag 17-B at Krems, Austria on April 12, 1944. He remained in the POW camp until liberated by units of General Patton's 13th Armored Division on May 3, 1945. U.S. troops freed the 4,000 POWs held at the camp. For Taylor, the World War II was over. After the end of World War II, he transferred to the newly created Air Force in March 1948, assigned to Weaver Air Force Base (renamed Ellsworth AFB in 1953). Taylor was a tail gunner on a Boeing B-29 Superfortress, Convair B-36 Peacemaker and later as a gunner in the forward crew compartment on a B-52H Stratofortress. He retired from the Air Force on April 30, 1965 at Ellsworth AFB.[52]

---

[52] Had Taylor, "POW at Stalag 17," Veterans of Foreign Wars, Post 1273, Rapid City, South Dakota, to author, June 2011.

Lt. Commander John C. Waldron

USS Hornet
The Battle of Midway, May 1942

THE state of South Dakota has a long history of honoring its military veterans through memorials and designated historical markers throughout the state. One of the state's World War II famous veterans is U.S. Navy Lt. Commander John. C. Waldron. He was born on August 24, 1900 at Fort Pierre, South Dakota. His father's heritage came from Colonial New Hampshire with his mother from the Oglala Indian tribe of South Dakota. Waldron graduated from the U.S. Naval Academy in 1924, earning his pilot wings in 1927, assigned to the U.S. Navy aircraft USS Hornet (CV-8) in the summer of 1941 as Commander Torpedo Squadron 8 (VT-8), flying the Douglas TBD-1 Devastator. VT-8 was equipped with this arguably obsolete dive-bomber at the time of the Battle of Midway, pending delivery of the new Grumman TBF Avenger torpedo bomber. Six TBFs flown to Midway Island as their initial combat evaluation against Japanese aircraft carrier aircraft. However, their contribution to the air campaign against the four Imperial Japanese Navy aircraft carriers was minimal. The Navy's primary torpedo bomber, the TBD-1 was slow, maximum speed of only 200mph, armed with one torpedo slung below the centerline of the aircraft's fuselage, one forward firing and one rear gunner firing .30 caliber machine guns. The torpedo bomber was an easy target for high-performance Japanese Zero fighters. It suffered the same design flaw as the Japanese Zero, lack of self-sealing fuel tanks, which gave it the tendency to burst into flames when hit by cannon or machine gun shells, knocking it out of the air with the death of the Japanese pilot and the three-man TBD-1 torpedo bomber crew.

In September 1939, the keel of CV-8 was laid down. The carrier's construction was based on a modified aircraft carrier Yorktown design. The Hornet displaced 20,000 tons, 809 ½ feet long, beam 83 ¼ feet, draught 21 2/3 feet, designed to operate 81 to 85 aircraft, with space for a maximum of 100 aircraft, with aircrew and ship's complement of 2,072, carrier able to obtain a maximum speed of 34 knots to launch and recover aircraft.

U.S. Navy Captain Marc A. Mitscher, Commanding Officer, USS

Hornet, "After action report on the battle of Midway."

1. In accordance with CincPAC Operation Plan 29-42, the Hornet got underway from Pearl Harbor at 1130, May 28, 1942, receiving the Air Group at sea at 1530 the same afternoon. One SBD would not start at Ewa Field and the pilot was flown to the carrier in the rear of a TBD. The pilot, Lt. W.J. Widhelm, USN, was later credited with two direct 1,000 pound bomb hits on a battleship or heavy cruiser, on 6 June. An additional SBD, Ensign R.D. Milliman, USNR, pilot, was lost the following morning when it crashed about 15 miles from the ship while on intermediate air patrol, probably due to engine failure. No personnel were recovered. The Air Group consisted of 27 VF (fighters), 35 VSB (dive-bombers) and 15 VTB (torpedo bombers), which the aircraft strength was maintained until contact with the enemy. Except for temporary decommissioning for minor repairs.
2. After passing through Kauai Channel, course 296 degrees True was maintained until the afternoon of 31 May, when course was changed to 290 Degrees True, and maintained until the arrival at "Point Luck" on 1 June. Point Luck was the codename OK'd by Admiral Chester A. Nimitz for the fleet rendezvous point 325 miles northeast of Midway Island to position his carriers to intercept the approaching Japanese carriers, assault and bombardment warships. On the night of 30 May, a CincPAC intelligence report, giving an estimate of the Japanese Midway Task Force organization, was received. During 31 May, two reports were received that Japanese bombers had been sighted northwest of Midway. At 1630, 2 June, Task Force 17 was sighted. The two forces separated, but usually within visual contact. Task Force 16 remained in the vicinity of "Point Luck" until 3 June. Word having been received that the enemy main body had been sighted bearing 261 Degrees True, 700 miles from Midway, course was set to the southwest.
3. It was about the same time that several dispatches were sent to the Task Force Commander in command ciphers. It is strongly recommended the carriers be issued a class five cryptographic allowance; these ships may well become separated during continuous air operations and the carrier commanding officers require all available information. The receipt of this information will obviate the necessity for a large part of the visual traffic so difficult to deliver by semaphore from the Task Force Commander to the carriers.
4. The first indication of the possibility of another enemy force was

received at 0810, 4 June, in CincPAC 041807, which reported the sighting of a seaplane 320 Degrees True, 100 miles from Midway. Two minutes later came a report of many planes in the same vicinity, and 14 minutes later, another of two enemy CV on the same bearing distance 180 miles. This ship was called to General Quarters and remained in that condition until after dark.

5. At 0900 (all times given hereafter are zone plus 10) commenced launching the Air Group for attack; VSB loaded with 500 pound bombs, VTB with torpedoes and VF with MG. ammunition only. The objective, enemy carriers, was calculated to be 155 miles, bearing 239 Degrees True from this Task Force; one division of 10 VF; Squadron Commander (Lieutenant Commander S.G. Mitchell U.S.N.) in charge was sent with 35 VSB and 15 VTB, to afford fighter protection. Deferred departure was used. A combat air patrol had been maintained since one hour before sunrise. An unfortunate aerological feature of the day's action was the fact that the wind was light (about 4 knots) and directly away from the enemy; every time combat patrol was relieved, of forced landing was recovered, our attack planes had a longer run back to the ship, and increased the distance between this force and the enemy. Between 1320 and 2100, launching and recovery operations were being conducted almost continuously on a generally easterly heading and at high speed. The VSB returned from the search in groups, Scouting 8 and Commander Horney Air Group together. One section of Bombing Eight returned alone. These ten planes of Bombing Eight landed at Midway due to lack of gas; two of these ran out of gas and landed in the lagoon at Midway. The remaining eleven were gassed, ordered to attack the enemy, and return to Hornet if possible. They were unable to locate the enemy and landed onboard at 1727.

6. None of Scouting Eight or Bombing Eight made contract on the above flight. After searching the prescribed bearing, the squadrons turned south to search in the direction of the enemy advance. As it turned out, had they turned north, contact would have probably been made. This was due to the fact that when the planes took off, they took course to intercept the enemy, at that time, reported headed on course 140 Degrees True, speed 25 knots. About one hour after the planes had departed the enemy reversed his course and started his retirement. We did not break radio silence to report this to the planes. None of Fighting Eight, which went with the attack group, returned to the ship. They remained with VSB until

forced to head for Midway due to lack of gas. Five pilots have been rescued; without information as to the point of rescue. They are assumed to have landed in the water on a line running 320 degrees True from Midway.

Prior to take-off, Waldron had a vocal disagreement with the Hornet's Commander, Air Group, Stan Hope C. Ring, and Hornet Commanding Officer, Admiral Marc Mitscher over intelligence indicating a contact report that Japanese carriers were southwest of the Hornet. Waldron wanted to fly that course but ordered to fly to the west. After launch, Waldron could not raise the Hornet's strike group on the radio to change course. Waldron's squadron broke away to the contact report's location of the Japanese carriers. He reached the Japanese carriers at a little after 0900, long before (approximately one hour) before the dive bombers and their fighter escort. Waldron did not hesitate, attacked, flying low over the water toward the Japanese carriers to drop their torpedoes. With only one .30 caliber rear facing machine gun the 15 TBDs were quickly shot down by defending Japanese Zero fighters and ship borne anti-aircraft artillery fire. Only one of Torpedo Squadron Eight's crew survived the attack, although his aircraft was shot down, Ensign George H. Gray, Jr., USNR, he was able to crawl out of his TBD when it sank. While floating in the water, he had an eyewitness to following U.S. Navy aviators attack on the four Japanese carriers. He was later rescued by a Midway PBY. During Waldron's squadron attack the four Japanese carriers were unable to complete rearming bombers on the deck from bombs to torpedoes or launch additional aircraft due to evasive maneuvers. The Japanese carrier task force commander did not expect the presence of U.S. carriers at this point in the attack against Midway Island. After the destruction of Hornet's TBDs, Zero fighters intercepted TBDs from the Enterprise (CV-6) and Yorktown (CV-5), shooting down nearly all the attacking American torpedo bombers. Only four TBDs each from the Yorktown and Enterprise were recovered after the Japanese attack on Enterprise's flight deck due to Yorktown's damage. The loss of so many TBDs and their crews was not in vain, as the SBDs arrived over the Japanese carriers, without interception by Japanese Zeros, at low-level, attacking wave-hopping, withdrawing surviving TBDs. The unmolested (intercepted) dive-bombers sank three Japanese carriers: Akagi, Kaga and Akagi, each with flight decks crammed with munitions loaded and fully fueled aircraft.

7. Torpedo Eight, led by Lieutenant Commander John C. Waldron, USN, was lost in its entirety.
8. Very little was seen by this ship of the enemy attacks on the Yorktown. At 1410, enemy torpedo planes were reported to be attacking Task Force 17, which was almost hull down on the horizon to the northwestward. Many anti-aircraft bursts were clearly visible and at least three planes were seen to fall in flames. Heavy columns of dark smoke soon arose from the direction of the Yorktown. Commander Task Force 17's Portland plain language dispatches reporting the air attack were intercepted shortly thereafter. During the attack, VF-8 fighters shot down three enemy Zeros and two Val dive-bombers, with one VF-8 plane shot down. Yorktown fighters were noted approaching this ship to land and one section of VSBs was, for a short while, thought to be enemy VTBs. One Yorktown fighter plane, whose pilot was wounded in the foot, crash-landed aboard. He had not cut his gun switch. Upon crashing, all six of his machine guns commenced firing in the direction of the island and continued firing for about two seconds, with .50 caliber machine gun bullets spraying the after end of the island, killing the after 5-inch control officer, Lieutenant R.R. Ingersol, USN, and four enlisted men and wounding 20 others, the majority of whom were in Battle II behind one-inch especially hardened armor plate. Bullets penetrated not only this armor plate but also penetrated a 1/4-inch steel I-beam.
9. Aircraft operations on easterly course caused this ship to lose sight of the Yorktown. The VSBs were being rearmed. When the 11 planes of VB-8 returned from Midway, they only had to be gassed. Had they located the enemy and made their attack prior to return, they probably would not have been ready to send on the next flight.
10. At 1803 commenced launching the second attack group, consisting of 16 VSBs. The target was then assumed to bear 280 Degrees True, distance 162 miles and was supposed to consist of two or three burning CVs, one or two BBs and DDs. At 1930, the attack was commenced; three hits were made on one BB (two 1,000 pound bombs and one 500 pound bomb); two 500 pound bomb hits were made on a heavy cruiser. The one enemy CV sighted was not attacked, as it was burning throughout its entire length and was assumed to be of no further value as a target. SBDs from the Enterprise, at 1795, attacked and hit the Japanese carrier Hiryu with four 500 pound bombs, setting it ablaze, with the carrier sinking

the next morning at 0820, 5 June.

11. During the night of 4-5 June, the Task Force retired to the eastward until 0200, 5 June, when course was changed to 000 Degrees True and at 0348 to 270 degrees True. At 0110 5 June the casualties resulting from the accidental firing of the VF machine guns, were buried at sea. During the night, information received that an enemy bearing 320 Degrees True, 170 to 200 miles from Midway, on course west to northwest, and that there was a probability that a carrier was still able to operate planes. (The Hiryu was burning, without an operational flight deck, one of many intelligence reports that did not portray exact battle information).

12. At 0930, speed was changed to 25 knots and the force maintained westerly course throughout the day. At 1712, commenced launched the attack group, consisting of 26 VSBs. The enemy force this time was thought to bear 325 Degrees True, distance 240 miles from Midway, and to consist of two BBs, four CAs, one CV (already sunk) and some DDs. At 2004, having failed to locate any major enemy forces after conducting a 315 miles search, the attack group attacked an enemy CL or DD in a position 278 miles, nearing 315 Degrees True from the Hornet's position at time of launching. No direct hits were observed; it is estimated that five 500 pound bombs landed with 100 feet of the target. All planes returned with the exception of one, which landed in the water near the Enterprise due to fuel exhaustion; personnel were recovered in a fine manner in the darkness by the Aylwin. Most of the landings were made after complete darkness had set in. Few of the pilots had previous night carrier landing experience. All planes returned with very little gas; one plane landed out of fuel, in our arresting gear.

13. Course 280 Degrees True, speed 15 knots was maintained during the night, the enemy have been reported to be heading slight south of west, probably to join the southern forces. Shortly before sunrise, Enterprise launched a reconnaissance flight to search the area 180 degrees through west to 360 Degrees for a distance of 200 miles. Contact was made by the pilot in the section 240 degrees True, the enemy bearing 239 degrees True, distance 150 miles from this force. The contact report and due to voice error the expression BB was heard as CV. Accordingly, one CV was reported to Commander task Force 16. The pilot immediately returned to base and reported correctly, one BB, one CA, three DDs, by message drop and verbally. Cruisers were then ordered to gain and maintain con-

tact with their search aircraft, track the enemy and keep the OTC informed.
14. At 0957, commenced launching air group of 26 VSBs and eight VFs. The latter were ordered along in case of previously undetected air opposition. They aided in the attack by effectively strafing destroyers. At 1150, the air group commenced its attack on the enemy force, which consisted of one BB, one CA and three DDs, 142 miles bearing 235 Degrees True from Hornet's 1015 position, resulting in the following: two 1000 pound bombs and one 500 pound bomb hit on the stern of a DD. Four VFs strafed one DD, which probably sustained heavy personnel casualties on the bridge and upper works. One of Hornet's VSB was apparently shot down by AAA fire on this attack. All pilots of this attack insist that the principal target was definitely a BB (probably Kirishima class) and not a CA. All planes, except the one shot down, were recovered at 1245 and rearmed.
15. At 1239, Enterprise launched her first attack of this day; interceptions on the voice frequency indicated a large success.
16. The wind was light but favorable throughout the day, blowing straight from the enemy; launching was conducted occasionally without deviation from Fleet course or speed.
17. Upon the return of the Enterprise Group, 24 VSB were launched at 1530 for what proved to be the final attack of the day action. One deferred landing returned at 1602. At 1645, the attack was begun on the enemy force consisting of one CA (probably Kirugasa Class) or one CL and two DDs. The enemy force was at this time about 110 miles 264 degrees True from the Hornet's position. Results of this attack areas as follows: one 1,000 pound bomb hit on CA, six 1,000 pound bomb hits on CA or CL, one 1,000 pound bomb hit on DD. Very heavy explosions were seen on the CA and it was left completely gutted by fire, personnel abandoning ship. At 1728, the attack group returned, without losses, and was recovered. Retirement was commenced on a northeasterly course. Cruiser seaplanes assumed the inner air patrol.
18. The Commanding Officer desires to commend the entire crew of the Hornet to the Commander-in-Chief as deserving of high praise for their performance during the subject action. All hands conducted themselves in a manner fitting the Navy's best traditions. There were no outstanding individuals, as the activity was purely an air action, and these is no cause for censure.
19. Recapitulation of our losses.

15 TBDs, 4 June (one pilot rescued).

12 F4F-4s, 4 June (six pilots rescued).

5 SBDs, 4-6 June (four pilots and four RMs rescued).

21. In particularly, the Commanding Officer feels that the conduct of Torpedo Squadron Eight, led by an indomitable Squadron Commander, is one of the most outstanding exhibitions of personal bravery and gallantry that has ever come to his attention in the past or present. (Torpedo Eight earned the Presidential Unit Citation with Lieutenant Commander Waldron also receiving the USN Cross, posthumously).

The state of South Dakota honored its World War II, Korean and Vietnam veterans, deceased and living, with a moving memorial along Capital Lake, next to the state's capital of Pierre. A plaque honoring Lieutenant Commander John C. Waldron and the Missouri River bridge, connecting Fort Pierre and Pierre together was placed as a tribute to the veteran who performed beyond the call of duty, creating victories in the Pacific, winning praise as one of "America's Greatest Generation."[53]

---

[53] Lt. Col. George A. Larson, USAF (Ret.), "Lieutenant Commander John C. Waldron and the Battle of Midway," article submission to Military, October 2010. Information from South Dakota Historical Society in Pierre, South Dakota.

Thomas K. Oliver

B-24 down over Yugoslavia, May 1944

DURING World War II, USAAF First Lieutenant Thomas K. Oliver was assigned to 15th Air Force, 459th Bombardment Group, 756th Bombardment Squadron, flying a Consolidated B-24 Liberator out of Giulia Airfield, Italy. First Lt. Oliver remembered mission number 24, especially its following consequences. On this mission, he was breaking in a new copilot, 2nd Lt. Camillas Rechtin. The rest of the crew: navigator, 2nd Lt. John Thibodeau; bombardier, 2nd Lt. Charles Gragz; engineer, Jodie Oliver; radio operator, Donald Sullivan; ball turret gunner, Franklin Bartels; tail turret gunner, Edgar Smith; nose turret gunner, Griffin Goad and waist gunner, William Keepers.

The B-24H Lt. Oliver usually flew was named "Fighting Mudcat," so named because the catfish is a survivor. On 6 May, his regular aircraft was in maintenance, so Lt. Oliver and crew flew a replacement. Oliver..."I had a little superstition. At the briefing before the mission, I always made it a point to enter the estimated time of arrival back at our home base on the briefing sheet or pilot's flimsy and carries the sheet in my pocket during the mission. If for some reason, I missed getting the official pilot's flimsy, I wrote the time of arrival on a scrap of paper and carried that. It seemed good to have an estimated time back at home base written down somewhere on my person. As we taxied out for take-off, the paper blew out the open cockpit window. I remember the flight engineer saying, 'We didn't need that, did we?' I bravely said 'No' and we went. It was 96 days before we saw our base again. It was enough to make one wonder.

"The mission was to the Campina Marshalling Yards near the Ploesti Oil Fields. Our group led the 15th Air Force over the target and caught a full benefit of flak and German fighters before the flak gunners and German fighter pilots got tired. The fighters came right through their own flak to make a nose on attack on our aircraft. One Fw-190 had our airplane singled out. After he passed just beneath us the gunners on my crew said he went down trailing smoke. We will never know for sure whether we hit him fatally or not. We will also never know whether the damage to our plane was done by fighters or flak. Shortly after bombs away, number three engine was losing oil pressure. I tried to feather it, but no success. A look at the engine showed why. The prop governor had been hit, hanging by one bolt. The drag and vibration forced us to slow down and lag behind the formation. Two P-38s came up to us and flew alongside until we were beyond German fighter danger. I would have liked to hug those two pilots, whose names I probably will never know.

"The next excitement came when number three engine seized from running without oil. The vibration was horrendous. The right wing shook in a sine wave pattern, as though one took one of a rope and tied it to a tree and then gave a good shake at the other end. Finally, something snapped. I was later told that the reduction gear must have failed. The propeller now spun freely on its bearing and things went smoothly for a while.

"The next engine on that side of the aircraft lost oil pressure. Not wanting to repeat the experience with engine number three, we got it feathered in a hurry. With two engines dead on the same side we threw out our guns, flak suits, etc., and anything to reduce weight. We managed to maintain about 8,000 feet, just enough to clear the Dalmatian Alps near the Adriatic Sea. I was figuring that I might first to bring a B-24 back from Ploesti with two engines dead on the same side. That should be good for a Distinguished Flying Cross and a little respect back at home base. But, all that was not to be.

"John Thibodeau, our navigator, was trying to keep us on a course that would not take is over any flak batteries. Just after we crossed the Danube River near Turnul Severin and the Iron Gates, we encountered flak at the Yugoslavian town of Boo. It had not been noted on our charts. We lost a third engine, which was set on fire and the crew said that the bomb bay doors looked like the top of a saltshaker. With only one good engine, and no way to put out the fire, the only course of action was to bailout. I gave the order to bailout on the intercom and hit the bailout button. Then I took one more look at the burning engine. It did not look any better. I turned and looked back to see how the crew was coming along at bailing out. All were gone except Jim Thibodeau, who was standing in the bomb bay motioning me to come on. I moved to him to get out. I did not want anyone in my way when I let go of the wheel. He jumped and I jumped.

"As I tumbled through the air, I remember saying to myself that even if the parachute did not open, I was no worse off than when I was in the plane. My attention was drawn to a noise like the loudest siren I ever heard. The free propeller was winding up as the plane dove toward the ground. The plane hit the ground and there was a huge fireball. Cecil B. DeMile never put on a better show. After the fireball cleared, all I could see was a large black spot. At first, I seemed to be descending very slowly. I feared the Germans would have time to have a patrol waiting for me when I reached the ground. As the ground came close, I realized that it was approaching at an alarming speed. I made a good landing, but did have a sore shin for a week or so. I almost landed on top of a group of Yugoslav peasants who were having a picnic lunch. Their table was set near a farmhouse. On the table was a sheep's head, eyeballs and all the rest. As the honored, if uninvited guest, I was offered the eyeballs. Somehow, I lost my appetite. They offered me a glass a wine and it seemed like a marvelous idea. Probably, within ten minutes or less, a couple of men approached wearing military caps with rifles slung over their shoulders and leading a horse. They mentioned Draza Mihailovich and indicated that I was to mount the horse. It had not taken the Serbian guerrilla organization too much time to find me.

"After the Chetniks took us into custody, that afternoon we kept moving rather steadily and a few times, I heard shots fired over the hill. Once we stopped for a few minutes to talk with a Yugoslavian medical doctor who had been educated in France. I discovered that it was much easier to communicate in French with a Yugoslavian educated in France than with a Frenchman. He was very helpful at putting words into mouth. In the evening, we stopped at a peasant farmhouse. The lady of the house offered me a cup of hot goat's milk with some kind of scum floating on the top. I took it because I had to eat to live. Furthermore, these people ate it and they survived. After supper, I was put to bed on a pile of straw. At the same time in the early morning hours, they woke me up and it was time to move on again. By this time, there were about six Serbian Chetniks escorting me. They and I rode horses, with three in front, me, then three more bringing up the rear. We proceeded single file, winding through the hills by moonlight. The Chetniks wore classic style fur hats and tight jackets. Each had a rifle slung over his shoulder. The only sound was horse's harnesses jingling. I pinched myself and silently asked...What am I doing in the middle of this grad B, black and white movie?

"The next day, our pace was more relaxed. We seemed to go from one outdoor café to the next, with a round of drinks at each. I was carrying two hunting knives, one on my belt and one strapped to my leg. The Chetniks would as, via gestures, 'Why two knives?' Then one of them answered. He pointed to one knife and said 'Hitler,' with a throat cutting gesture and an appropriate noise like a death rattle. The he pointed to the other and said 'Mussolini,' with the same gesture and noises. I later used this same line among other groups and it always went over well. That evening there was a religious ceremony. They took me to what obviously were the graves of two American airmen who had been shot or killed. A Serbian Orthodox Priest conducted the service. It was evidently a sort of requiem mass for the dead. This took place at the gravesite. A cup of wine was passed around. Each person took a sip and spilled a small amount on the grave. That night I was put in a house in a little village. In the early hours of the morning, I was raised again. There was an alarm that the Germans were coming, 'Heidi, Heidi,' they cried to me, which by that time I had learned meant, 'hurry, hurry!' In my underwear, I was taken out and hidden in the woods until the danger was over. The stark terror convoyed by their voices is something I will never forget.

"The next day I was reunited with the rest of my crew. There were in fact, parts of three crews, about twenty-four of us, all billeted in one place, a pleasant farmhouse. We had an interpreter, an old man who earlier in his life spent several years in the United States. He had worked in Wisconsin in the logging business, obviously surrounded by Swedes. It was unusual to find a Yugoslavian who spoke English with a heavy Swedish accent. The local Chetnik commander was a man called Kent. He was young, handsome and dynamic, a Chetnik's Chetnik. We were in the region of the Timok Corps.

"Nothing great occurred for about one month. We were still fairly close to the Danube River, near the eastern border of Yugoslavia. The local Chetnik commander was hoping to get us evacuated from there and hoping to get some sort of aid or supplies from the Allies in return. Finally, he was persuaded to send us to the center of Old Serbia, the region where General Mihailovich's headquarters was located. Captain Ivan Milac was assigned the job of leading us over about 150 kilometers to the middle of Old Serbia. He was a Chetnik who had been an officer in the Yugoslav Regular Army. He had learned English on his own, largely by listening to radio broadcasts in English. A finer gentleman has never lived.

"We were issued rifles to carry on the march west. It began on a section of mountain railroad, which evidently was considered safe. We traveled for some distance and got off just before the tracks went into a town of some size. That was the only easy part of the march. The rest is all mixed up, with our sleeping in haystacks or on hard wood schoolhouse floors. John Thibodeau reminded me of one incident. About lunchtime, three of us were led to a place where there were three city girls. The casual peasant girls in the Babushkas were not all that attractive. But these girls were beautiful and they invited us to lunch and indicated that we could spend the night. I was talking to them in whatever French I could remember from school. It seemed like heaven. As we sat down to lunch, the Chetniks indicated that we were to leave immediately the Germans were coming. That was the last time we saw of these three girls.

"We arrived in the area of General Mihailovich's headquarters and were divided up into small groups and billeted in various peasant farmhouses. We had lots of time to kill and would whittle out corncob pipes and smoke whatever local blend of tobacco we could lay our hands on. It was explained to us that cigarettes were in short supply because we, Allied bomber crews, had hit the cigarette factory at Nis. I remember watching a peasant woman baking bread. It was in a little square house, built of square wood timbers. The roof sloped up steeply on all four sides, with a whole in the top of the roof. The floor was clay, hard as concrete, with a fire burning on the center of the room. Most of the smoke rose and went out the hole at the top of the roof. The peasant woman sweep coals from a spot on the hearth on the floor. The bread dough, on a plate, was set on the clay hearth. She then placed a large earthen bowl upside down over the plate with the bread dough. Finally, hot coals were shoveled over the inverted bowl. The bread got baked that way.

"In Yugoslavia, we saw real gypsies. I never saw anyone who needed a bath more than they did. They would come in a village area, carrying an accordion and a couple of violins. Then, that evening the whole village had a party. Food was brought out and everyone had dinner. Then the Gypsies played and there was dancing in the public square. The next day, the Gypsies moved to another town.

"It was an impressive event, each time the 15th Air Force aircraft flew overhead on the way to targets in the Ploesti area. We would hear a faint buzzing sound, like bees. The sound would get louder and louder until it became a roar and the sky was filled with airplanes. We knew we could on other two or three crews, joining us on the ground. Once we saw a B-24 overhead, flying in large circles. All four engines were running. It kept flying in large circles until it eventually went out of sight. Clearly, the plane had been abandoned. I would have loved to have a long rope ladder to climb up to that airplane and fly it home.

"Meanwhile, no great progress was being made at getting us back to Italy. One reason was that the British, who controlled the Mediterranean Theater of Operations, had recalled their mission at and severed relationships with General Mihailovich. Some of the Yugoslavian officers who spoke English would tell us that they had notified their government in Cairo, Egypt about our presence in Yugoslavia. They in turn would notify the British and that was all they could do. We gradually got the idea that we ought to try, somehow, to get a message to 15th Air Force as to how many of us were in Yugoslavia and they would be more likely to act than the British in Cairo. Those in Cairo were probably following Prime Minister Winston Churchill's fear that General Mihailovich was a Communist, under the control of Soviet Union military and political advisors. By now, late July 1940, there was close to 150 Allied airmen in our group, including the crew of one RAF Wellington bomber.

"So far as I knew, as a First Lieutenant, I was the highest-ranking officer in our group. So, I started saying as the American Commander, I wanted to see the Chetnik commander, General Mihailovich. Finding the general of a guerrilla outfit is not easy and it was not unusual for one single person to not know where his commander was located. The route was to ask the Captain, who knows where the Major is, etc., and on up the chain of Chetnik command to reach the General. Finally, I got to see General Mihailovich himself. We spoke through an interpreter. He assured me that he had notified his government. However, he was willing to help us send a message directly to Italy. Now it turned out that among the down Allied airmen the idea of sending an open radio message to Italy was very controversial. Some said 'Don't send any message, the Germans will intercept it and home in on it and capture us!'

"My right hand in the whole process of getting to see General Mihailovich, composing and sending a message was a fighter pilot named Jack Barrett. If we accomplished anything worthwhile, he desires a full measure of credit. Partially, as a concession to the cautious group we decided to formulate a message in American slang, which would accomplish our purpose and at the same time, puzzling as possible if the Germans intercepted the messages. The resulting message went something like this with the explanation in parentheses.

"Mud cat driver to CO APO 520. (My airplane was named the Fighting Mudcat. APO 520 was the 15th Air Force.) 250 Yanks are in Yugoslavia, some sick. Shoot us workhorse. (The workhorse of the U.S. Army Air Forces was the C-47.) Our challenge, first letter of the bombardier's last name, color of Banana Nose's scarf. You authentication, last letter of Chief Lug's name, color of fist on the wall. (The challenge and authenticator were to be done with signal lights and could be transmitted ground to air or air to ground so that each party would know they were dealing with the right people. Banana Nose was Sam Benigno, a pilot in our squadron who wore a white scarf. The Commander, 459th BG, Colonel Munn, once wrote on the wall of the Officers Club at our base, Each lug in the 459th, sign here, and he signed it M.M. Munn, Chief Lug. The fist on the wall was a red fist on the Officers Club wall, part of the 15th Air Force emblem.) Must refer to Shark Squadron, 459th BG for decoding. (Our squadron had shark teeth painted on the noses of our B-24s.) Signed KO, Flat 12 at 4 in Lug order. (Mt tent mates and I back home called our tent Poker Flat. When I signed on the wall below Colonel Munn's signature, I had signed T.K. Oliver, Flat Rat. 4.)

"The message was sent by a Yugoslav radio operator, picked up by a British radio operator in Italy. Eventually, it reached Walt Cannon, Commander, 756th BS. He deciphered it, recognizing it as genuine. This led to a reply, which we received from 15th Air Force Headquarters. Someone in the Escape and Evasion Office, 15th Air Force Headquarters had a great idea. They asked us to transmit our longitude and latitude, coded by adding the numbers to my radio operator's serial number. This we did of course. This task leads to a digression in my story. I had to get longitude and latitude off captured German maps, provided by Yugoslav guerrillas. The Germans did not use Greenwich as reference, but Berlin. I had to convert. About the time we were sending longitude and latitude to Italy, I ran across my West Point roommate, Leo C. Brooks. He had been flying with William Kilpatrick, known as K.P. They were shot down in a B-17 Flying Fortress. Small world.

"Using the serial number code, 15th Air Force sent us a message indicating what day and hour an OSS team would be dropped in to join us. It was about midnight and I remember the beautiful silhouette of a C-47 against the sky. George Muslim, an American of Serbian parentage and who spoke the language well, led the team. He had an assistant who also spoke the language and was a radio operator. They were equipped with a radio, codebooks and everything else needed to arrange the evacuation. The Chetniks prepared a short sod-covered runway along the edge of a hill. I paced it off, taking short steps to be as optimistic as possible about its length. I got 600 yards. The Chetniks filled holes with dirt and stones, tamped it all down by hand.

"The evacuation started about midnight on August 10, 1944. C-47s landed, one at a time. The first took off before the second landed. We sent out the sick and wounded first. After that, those who had been in

Yugoslavia the longest had priority. I was scheduled for the third plane. The first got off nicely. The second went off the end of the strip, disappeared in the valley below. Fortunately, it climbed back up and out again. As we got into our airplane, most of us tossed our shoes out as parting gifts to the Serbians who had risked their lives for us. We had to admire those people. They had something hard to explain. For lack of words, I call it character and integrity. I was told the evacuation continued into the daylight hours the next morning, with additional C-47s coming in. P-51s flew cover the daylight. I know there were Bf-109s stationed at the German airfield at Kralejevo, not far from the evacuation airstrip. I saw them there one time. Evidently, they wisely chose to stay on the ground. As it turned out, about 225 of us were evacuated and flown back to Italy. Back at 15th Air Force Headquarters in Bart, Italy, we were deloused and our clothes burned. We were issued new Khakis and given orders for our return to the United States via the next convoy. [54]

---

[54] Lt. Col. George A. Larson, USAF (Ret.), "Escape from Yugoslavia," Logbook, 1st Quarter 2004, Volume 5, Number 1.

"Operation FRANTIC"

Eighth Air Force Shuttle Bombing Missions Against Germany from England to Russia and Back

AFTER the Japanese attack on Pearl Harbor on December 7, 1941, and subsequent declarations of war by the Axis powers on the United States, and vice-versa, U.S. President Franklin D. Roosevelt decided to conduct a "Europe first" policy, assisting Britain in the defeat of German and Italy, before turning full force on Japan, long-range bombers like the B-17 and B-24 were the key to U.S. strategy. With designated targets scattered throughout Germany and across Nazi occupied Europe, some were too far away for Allied airpower to reach them and return. A solution was devised that required an unusual level of cooperation from Russia. American bombers began recovering to and launching from bases at Russian airfields, close to and behind the front lines with German forces. With the addition of airfields in North Africa, this widened the areas which could be bombed.

USAAF slowly built up a substantial force of B-17s in England, beginning on July 6, 1942. The first Eighth Air Force B-17 raid against German occupied Europe (Rouen, France) was conducted on August 17, 1942, flown by a small force of 12 bombers. The first B-17 raid into Germany was conducted on January 27, 1943, when of 64 B-17s, attacking U-boat production yard at Vegesack. However, complete cloud cover over the U-boat production yard forced the bombers to abort and attack their secondary target, Wilhelmshaven.

Eighth Air Force planners believed that to maximize bomber operations against Germany, shuttle-bombing missions flown from widely scattered USAAF bases would place the greatest possible strain on Luftwaffe fighter resources. The bombers would take off from bases in England, bomb strategic targets in Germany, land at bases in North Africa, return to England after attacking targets in Germany on the return flight. The first such mission was conducted on August 17, 1943, when 317 B-17s bombed Regensburg and Schweinfurt, Germany's primary ball bearing production plants. However, 51 B-17s were shot down, with the surviving aircraft recovering at airfields in North Africa. After Italy was invaded on 9 September, followed by the Italian government (south of Rome) switching to the Allied side in the war against Germany. Fifteenth Air Force prepared airfields in Italy, available for Eighth Air Force bombers performing shuttle-bombing missions. USAAF photoreconnaissance flights identified German war plants east of Berlin and in surrounding occupied countries. These were out of range of Eighth Air Force B-17s and Fifteenth Air Force B-24s. It was reasoned that if shuttle bases could be built in Russia, B-17s could effectively range across German strategic war plants.

1. Shuttle bombing of Germany would force the Luftwaffe to transfer fighters from the Western Front to the Eastern Front to counter/intercept Russian based USAAF bombers on their return to England, weakening German air defenses in the west, which otherwise could oppose the upcoming/planned invasion of the continent.
2. Shuttle bombing would demonstrate to the hard-pressed Russians, fighting Germans on the Eastern Front, the extent to which the USAAF was waging a strategic bombing campaign against German war industries and population centers.
3. Shuttle bombing success against strategic German war industries and targets might help convince Soviet military and political leadership, especially Joseph Stalin, to grant permission for B-29s to be stationed/operate into and out of Siberian airfields. This would allow Twentieth Air Force bombers to take off from Marianas airfields, bomb targets in Japan, recover in Russia, refuel and rearm, take off and bomb targets in Japan on the return flight to the Marianas.

The Allies gave the Russian shuttle bombing program the code name "Operation FRANTIC." In October 1943, General Henry Arnold convinced the U.S. Combined Chiefs of Staff to send a delegation to Moscow to ask and receive permission from the Soviet leadership (Joseph Stalin) for B-17 and long-range fighter recovery and reconstitution airfields to be prepared near front lines on the Eastern Front. The airfields were needed for refueling, rearming and repairing aircraft for return bombing missions over German occupied territory. In November, the American Military Mission to Russia departed Washington DC to talk to the Russians on the viability of shuttle bombing. The mission to Moscow was led by Major General John R. Deane. At the meeting, the concept was accepted but no formal approval until after the "Big Three" met at Teheran (November to December 1943). At

Tehran, Stalin ordered his Army generals to prepare six airfields for shuttle bombing missions.

In February 1944, the Russian Army provided three airfields, not the six as agreed by Stalin. The B-17 airfields were located at Poltava and Mirgorod, with the fighter base at Piryatin. The three airfields were near Kiev, north of the Black Sea. Their proximity to Black Sea ports provided operations support, however, the airfields were father behind Russian front lines than desired by the Eighth Air Force, increasing mission flying distances. More importantly, the airfields needed extensive repair and construction to meet Eighth Air Force operational needs. This meant additional supplies, equipment and personnel had to be brought through the Black Sea ports to upgrade the airfields. The added resources shipped to Russian Black Sea ports and through the Iran supply line allowed Russian construction workers, most women, to lengthen and strengthen the B-17 runways, with improvements completed to all three. The work involved laying down steel Marston mating on muddy taxiways and parking aprons/areas, construction of maintenance hangars and control towers, setting up open-air supply depots for fuel drums, bombs, ammunition, food and aircraft spare parts. U.S. guards had to be posted to protect these depots from theft by Russians to sell stolen items on the black market. Anything not guarded on the three airfields turned up missing, with Russian military officers taking no action to stop theft.

Construction and repair work progressed slowly because Russian Army officers were reluctant to allow U.S. personnel to move openly behind Russian lines, without prior clearance and accompanying Russian Army troops to keep them inside the airfield areas. The Russians were afraid of American personnel collecting intelligence on the Eastern front and conditions behind the front lines. These tight restrictions delayed the movement of U.S. personnel, equipment and supplies from Russian ports. Supplies and equipment disappeared from unloading to delivery at the three airfields. Russian officers restricted the number of U.S. personnel which could enter their country. In response, U.S. officers openly argued with these Russian officers to stop being suspicious of Eighth Air Force shuttle bombing airfield operations, the end result was to defeat the Germans. It was worse when U.S. personnel started setting up communications stations to direct flights of U.S. C-47s bringing in high priority cargo, to replace losses at Russian ports and during transit to the airfields. Russian officers were afraid to trust anyone with a radio because their lives depended on maintaining tight security over all activities in their areas, under constant surveillance by

KGB and political officers.

Soviet officers did not want U.S. aircraft over flying their territory, other than the agreed to B-17s and escorting fighters. Stalin established fear in his officer corps, so that they were fearful of Allied intentions, even though the Soviet Army was responsible for aiding bombing attacks directed by Allied Supreme Commander, General Dwight Eisenhower in support of upcoming "Operation OVERLOAD." General Eisenhower had been given temporary control of U.S. medium and heavy bombers in order to disrupt movement of German troops, equipment, armor and artillery, ammunition and supplies towards the Normandy invasion beaches. It fell to the Fifteenth Air Force in Italy to conduct initial "Operation FRANTIC" missions.

Soviet officers also interfered with shuttle mission planning by demanding target selection approval. General Carl Spaatz selected shuttle-bombing targets, informing Russian officers and political leadership of his decision without prior warning for concurrence.

On May 3, 1944, General Spaatz issued an operational strike preparation order to Commanding General, Fifteenth Air Force for 150 heavy bombers and one fighter group to move to Russian airfields in June. The operational order stated…"Thirty-two Boeing B-17 Flying Fortresses will be provided from each Bombardment Wing (2nd, 97th, 99th and 483rd). The Bomb Groups' first shuttle bombing targets are the marshalling yards and rail workouts at Debrecen, Hungary to be struck on June 2, 1944. The 306th Fighter Wing (70 P-51 Mustangs) will provide target penetration, target coverage and withdrawal escort for the bombers. The 325th Fighter Group will relieve the first escorts, cover the bombers withdrawal and escort the bombers to Russian bases."

Preparation for the first shuttle mission to Russia included instructions relating to precise aircrew standards of conduct and operations, especially if a bailout or crash landing in Russian territory was necessary. "All crewmembers should refrain from any actions which may seem suspicious to Russian troops, such as not trying to conceal themselves nor bear arms, etc. If a Russian Army representative approaches the aircraft or crewmembers, the crewmembers shall raise their arms. It is desirable that each has at all times in his possession an identification certificate printed in Russian with the statement, United States Army Air Forces and the crewman's first and last name."

The precaution was sensible as it could prevent Russian Army troops from shooting at what they otherwise might believe were Luftwaffe crews(who they were ordered to kill, not capture), not

USAAF airmen.

In another order aimed at avoiding friction and maintaining proper coordination between B-17 and B-24 personnel in Italy, B-17 crews were warned not to speak disparagingly about the Consolidated B-24 Liberator. When questions were raised about the type, personnel were instructed to speak highly of the bomber in order to preserve morale. At that time, it was common for Fortress aircrews to refer to the Liberator "as the shipping crate in which the B-17 was delivered!"

At 6:55 a.m., on the designated date, 128 B-17s took off from three bases in Italy, led by General Ira Eaker, with 306th Fighter Wing launching 70 P-51s as cover for the run into the target area. Colonel Chet Sluder, Commander, 325th Fighter Wing, led 64 P-51s to relieve the first fighter escort group. Colonel Sluder joined up with the bombers near the coast of Yugoslavia and onto the Russian airfields. Bomb coverage on the marshalling yards and railroad repair shops were reported to be good. Flak was light although one-97th BG B-17 exploded in the air prior to bomb release. The bombers continued onto the Russian airfields. On landing, B-17 aircrews and P-51 pilots were welcomed by U.S. ground crews as well as high-ranking Russian Army Officers. Russian suspicions of U.S. intentions continued with each U.S. mechanic or ground crewman assisted by two Russian Army troops, under open instructions to assist in aircraft turnaround and to report on activities of U.S. personnel. A tent city on each airfield, complete with sanitary facilities and an open-air mess was ready for aircrews. Many Russian Army troops crowded the mess facilities because the food was plentiful and delicious, nothing comparable in Russian mess facilities for common troops. Bomber crews uploaded their aircraft in a drenching rainstorm, while USAAF and Soviet cameramen scurried from one aircraft to another, taking motion picture and still photography. An official news announcement on the completion of the first portion of the USAAF bombing mission was released by Soviet press officials in Moscow. This was unfortunate because deteriorating weather conditions forced bombers and fighters to remain on the ground at the three Russian bases for three days. The grounding made the aircraft and aircrews tempting targets for the Luftwaffe, once these forward Eighth Air Force airfields were located by aerial reconnaissance.

To honor and celebrate the completion of one half of the first shuttle-bombing mission from U.S. bases into Russia, the Red Army band arrived from an undisclosed front line position to perform a concert. In attendance were high-ranking Russian Army officers, USAAF Lt. General Eaker (airborne combat leader), USAAF Major General

Walsh (USAAF commander of Mirgorod airfield) and USAAF Brigadier General Lawrence (USAAF commander of Fifth Wing). Also at the concert were nearly all combat aircrews and ground support personnel.

Russian Army troops, temporarily transferred from front line units, serviced the American bombers and fighters, requiring constant supervision and on the job training from USAAF ground support personnel. There were many mistakes. For example, one Russian Army mechanic assisting with fragmentation bomb loading improperly secured the canister in a 99th BG B-17 bomb bay. The canister fell out of the bomb bay, striking a glancing head blow to the B-17's radio operator instructing the Russian mechanic. The radio operator dropped to the ground, temporarily knocked out. The Russian was convinced the American was dead and momentarily would be executed by KGB guards roaming the airfield. It took considerable effort to convince the Russian that the radio operator did not die. Both eventually recovered, sat to one side of the bomber as the dropped fragmentation canister was lifted and secured inside the bomb bay. The rest of the bombs were loaded and secured by Russian troops.

Four days later, the B-17s and escorts took off from the three Russian airfields to bomb the German airfield at Galati, Rumania. One hundred four B-17s attacked the airfield, successfully returning to the Russian airfields. Post mission debriefings indicated the airfield thoroughly covered, many German aircraft destroyed, damaged (reported as burning). German flak light and inaccurate. P-51s provided escort to and from the target, losing two Mustangs to German fighters. B-17 aircrews reported seeing no enemy fighters, intercepted by the escorts, unable to break through to the bomber stream.

For the next five days, U.S. Eighth Air Force personnel were given tours of surrounding Russian military bases, something previously denied so that the true conditions behind Russian front lines could be kept secret from the Americans. P-51s were not the only American aircraft at Piryatin airfield. The Russian Air Force operated American Lend Lease delivered Bell P-39 Airacobras, Curtiss P-40 Warhawks, Douglas A-20 Havoc and North American B-25 Mitchells. One of the 99th BG's flight engineers spoke sufficient Russian to carry on conversations and talked with Russian pilots. The Russian pilots indicated their aircraft were Russian built copies of American aircraft, not Lend Lease. Russian political leadership (Stalin) and military officers did not want to admit to their troops and pilots that they were using anything but Russian equipment and supplies.

After nine days in Russia, USAAF and Russian mechanics loaded B-17s with incendiary clusters for another bombing raid on German targets, followed by recovery at Italian airfields. The return bombing target was the German airfields at Focsani, 130 miles northeast of Budapest, Romania. The strike force consisted of 127 B-17s and 60 P-51 escorts. The bomber stream brushed aside light flak and through unfavorable weather over the target, with the lead bombardier releasing his bombs onto the airfield, followed by the remaining bombardiers releasing their bombs on the lead's drop. Many German aircraft were destroyed on the airfield. Escorting P-51s intercepted German fighters, although one Bf-109 shot down one B-17G from the 97th (two parachutes were noted from crew bailout). No bombers were lost to AAA.

The next shuttle-bombing mission took off from England with P-51 escorts. Three German fighters were shot down by P-51s and five by B-17 gunners, with 15 probables near Stendal, along the German coast. The P-51s turned back to England, relieved by another group of 70 P-51s. The B-17 strike force split into two groups: 123 bombers heading for a synthetic oil production plant south of Berlin and 21 B-17s bombing targets of opportunity around Elsterwerda. One B-17 suffered a bomb release malfunction, not repaired until over Riesadue, at which time the bombs were dropped. The B-17 was fortunate, able to rejoin the bomber stream 50 miles southeast of Poznan. The P-51 escorts were relieved by 51 P-51s from England to complete the escort to the Russian airfields.

The Luftwaffe was better prepared to intercept the bombers headed into Russia, after the surprise of the route from the first shuttle-bombing mission. As the bomber stream passed 50 miles southeast of Brest Litovsk, 30 German fighters attacked the bombers, losing six fighters to P-51 escorts, shooting down one B-17 and one P-51. The small raid was a diversion because a long-range twin-engine Heinkel He-111H trailed the bombers. Once into Russian territory, 72 B-17s landed at Mirgorod, 72 B-17s landed at Poltava, with P-51s landing at Piryatin. The He-111H identified the B-17s, withdrew, climbed to altitude, radioed the bomber fields' locations to the Luftwaffe's Eastern Headquarters at 7:00 p.m., remaining hidden in the night's sky.

The Luftwaffe attacked Poltava with one high-altitude He-111H circling above the airfields, periodically releasing parachute flares to illuminate the airfield. This enabled 70 He-111Hs (releasing demolition, incendiary and fragmentation bombs) and escorting Bf-109s (also releasing anti-personnel mines) to methodically bomb and strafe the airfield for two hours. The attack destroyed 43 B-17s, damaging 26 B-

17s. A separate strike force of He-111Hs attacked Piryatin Airfield, destroying 15 P-51s and numerous Russian Air Force aircraft. The attack destroyed 450,000 U.S. gallons of aviation fuel stored in an outdoor 55 gallon fuel drum depot, killing one USAAF airmen. Russian casualties consisted of 25 mechanics and ground support personnel. Russian air defenses were nearly non-existent, knocking down no German aircraft. No P-51s took off to defend the airfields nor any Russian fighters from nearby airfields.

On the morning of June 22, 1944, as a precaution against possible follow on German air attacks, USAAF Eastern Command officers ordered operational B-17s and P-51s shifted farther behind Russian front lines, out of German bomber range. A Luftwaffe reconnaissance aircraft, a Fw-198A-2 located Mirgorod airfield and He-111Hs attacked the shuttle-bombing airfield. German aircraft destroyed on base stocks of fuel, ammunition and bombs, badly damaging the runway and support facilities. Russian officers did not like these determined and destructive attacks on the airfields, rapidly eroding their long-term commitment to USAAF shuttle bombing missions, even though these missions were destroying German war capabilities.

The Eighth Air Force flew in maintenance officers and personnel to salvage and repair damaged B-17s for return to England. It was an urgent mission because their mission was to repair as many aircraft as possible before further German air attacks turned damaged aircraft into hopelessly wrecked hulks. Working with USAAF and Russian mechanics on the Russian airfields, they were able to return a few of the bombers to flying condition. During this time, Russian shuttle bombing missions were suspended. Soon thereafter, repaired bombers took off from the Russian airfields, landing at Foggia, Italy for more extensive maintenance and repairs for the longer flight back to Eighth Air Force bases in England.

USAAF and Russian Army officers discussed how future shuttle bombing missions should be conducted. Recommendations included increased separation between parked aircraft to make them more difficult to destroy, better dispersal of ammunition, fuel and bomb dumps. Even the Russians relented, agreeing that additional and continuously manned anti-aircraft gun emplacements were needed, along with extensive air raid warning drills and training exercises. USAAF officers wanted to bring in night fighters to protect the three airfields to blunt German night attacks. However, ever-suspicious Russian military officers refused, blocking any deployment and stationing of USAAF night fighters and support personnel inside Russia. The Russian military did not want to relinquish any operational control of their airfields to the Americans and openly admitted they were unable to defend the airfields from attacking German aircraft, even when openly stating they had air superiority on the Eastern Front. This forced USAAF officers to modify shuttle-bombing missions by concentrating on German military targets, using one-night stopovers at the two Russian airfields. B-17s would be rapidly refueled, re-armed and prepared for the return-bombing mission. The short turn around reduced ground vulnerability to German air attacks.

Four days later, B-17s attacked the oil refinery at Drohobycz, with Russian shuttle bombing missions continuing through mid-September. Inclement weather often forced gaps of days or weeks between raids.

On 1 August, the Polish underground in Warsaw radioed Allied Command in England for an emergency airdrop of food, ammunition, weapons and medical supplies. The resistance movement went on the offense against German troops inside Warsaw believing Soviet troops outside the city would come to their assistance. Ever concerned about post war political advantages, Soviet leaders (Stalin) had a different agenda, so he allowed the Germans to kill the Warsaw resistance, creating a vacuum for installation of Soviet backed Communist government in Warsaw and in the rest of Poland. The Russian Army halted its advance short of Warsaw, allowing German troops in the city to crush the rebellion. British Prime Minister Winston Churchill was outraged, demanding from Stalin why Russian troops did not enter the city and assist the rebellion. Russian officers outside Warsaw indicated the halt in offensive actions was necessary to replace killed and wounded troops; restock food, ammunition, fuel and equipment prior to resuming their attack into the city. Stalin delayed, finally approving the Allied airdrop on 11 September. This delay further soured U.S. and Russian relations as the war moved into its closing months.

It also took time to organize and prepare the B-17s to drop supplies instead of bombs and it was not until 18 September that 107 B-17s were loaded with specially prepared bundles, fitted with parachutes. The bombers were escorted from their bases in England by 150 P-51s. Shortly after take-off, three B-17s aborted, returning to base. Two were shot down by Luftwaffe fighters prior to reaching Warsaw, at which time the B-17s started circling the city. Four two hours B-17s dropped 1,284 supply containers. Unfortunately, only 130 to 300 bundles reached resistance fighters inside Warsaw. German troops retrieved the bulk of parachuted supplies.

After the supply airdrop. 64 P-51s flew back to England, 86 P-51s continued on with the B-17s to Russia. The following day, the Allied force took off from the Russian airfields to bomb the Szolnok Marshalling Yard. The strike force recovered in Italy, after crew rest and servicing of aircraft, on 22 September the B-17s and P-51s flew back to England.

The time period of Russian shuttle bombing missions ended. By October 1944, only 200 USAAF personnel remained at the three Russian airfields. Russian troops restricted them to the airfield, segregated from Russian Army troops, remaining in virtual isolation until Germany accepted the Allied terms of unconditional surrender.[55]

---

[55] During World War II, B-17 aircrews trained at Rapid City Army Air Base, Rapid City, South Dakota were assigned to Eighth Air Force, flying against targets in Nazi held Europe and Germany. An experiment was conducted to conduct continuous strategic bombing of German targets from England, recovering at airfields in Russia, refueled and rearmed, flying back over German controlled areas, bombing selected targets, recovering at their home airfields in England. One of these airmen was Al Marcello, trained as a B-17 gunner and flight engineer at Rapid City Army Base, assigned to 100th Bomb Group, which took part in the Russian shuttle bombing missions. Following information in this section by Lt. Col. George A. Larson, USAF (Ret.), "The Shuttle Bombing, B-17s and B-24s in Russia," Combat Aircraft, 2001. Additional information provided by Paul Marcello, 28th Bomb Wing Historian, whose grandfather Al Marcello was assigned to the 100th Bomb Group.

Peter Dahlberg

U.S. Army World War II

The Bridge at Remagen

PETER Dahlberg..."December 7, 1941, changed our world forever. Until that day, my life had been comparatively peaceful and quiet. We lived in the Red River Valley, just 50 miles from Canada, where I had the privilege of being raised on a farm, just across the road from the small town of Drayton, North Dakota, population 500. I'll never forget that Sunday afternoon, coming home from church and seeing bold headlines, 'Japan attacks Pearl Harbor!' Although my oldest brother was already in the military service it still seemed far removed. Little did I dream that in just a few years I would be deeply involved in a conflict that affected so much of the world.

"Except for gas rationing, shortages of sugar, rubber and a few other commodities, we managed to survive fairly well. I had just turned 16 years of age and in my junior year of high school. For a time, I considered joining the Navy Air Corps. It sounded exciting. For some reason, I delayed until graduating from high school in the spring of 1943. That fall, I enrolled in Bible College in Minneapolis, Minnesota, knowing full well that a military draft call up might prove inevitable. Almost everyone I knew had been called into service and I wanted to join them and see action.

"Following one semester of college, my draft board issued the call. On January 26, 1944, I was sworn into the U.S. Army at Fort Snelling, Minnesota and given a 21 day furlough. After being home about a week, a rather unusual event took place. My dad wanted to trim a long branch of a cottonwood tree. In doing so, the branch struck the ground, rebounded, hit him in his mid-section, knocking him off the ladder to the rock hard frozen ground. Both his heels and one arm were broken, leaving him bedfast and practically helpless. I was given emergency leave for the next four months to help keep the farm going, the delay that may well have saved my life.

"My friend, Bob Cramer, came from the great metropolitan city of Chicago, Illinois, while my roots were in a small town in the Red River Valley, North Dakota, population 500. He was familiar with bustling city life, while I was raised in a quiet rural area. We had some things in common though. We were both 18 years of age and far from home. Somehow, we came together for basic training in the infantry, at Camp Blanding, Florida in June 1944, and ended up in the same company, where we spent 17 weeks of intense training. Under the hot sun of summer, it was quite grueling out on the white hot sands. This was the first time for troop training during summer months at Camp Blanding because of the extreme heat. We felt like we were being prepared for the Pacific. Instead, Bob and I were getting ready to endure the awful cold winter in Europe, the worst weather in a century during the Battle of the Bulge.

"Bob and I soon became friends. I will never forget one clear starlight night when we were assigned the duty of guarding a machine gun range. As we walked our post around midnight, we began an interesting discussion. Our thoughts focused on how the world came into being. Bob...'You now, I'm an atheist.' As we looked up at the bright heavenly display the stars seemed so close you could almost reach out and touch them. 'How could all this come about without a creator? We discussed the subject for a while. When our shift was over, we returned to settle down in our pup tents for the rest of the night. I suggested to Bob...'Before you go to sleep, why don't you ask God to reveal himself to you.' We never had occasion to broach the subject again.

"Basic training came to a close, and somehow Bob and I continued staying together, the only ones from our company to do so. We spent a few days at Fort Meade, Maryland before going overseas. While there, we had the opportunity of visit Washington, DC and New York City, New York. It was a great experience for this small town boy. Then we prepared to embark from Boston Harbor. On December 12, 1944, as we walked up the gangplank. I wondered if I would ever walk back down one again. After seven days and nights on the stormy North Atlantic, we landed in Liverpool, England. We boarded a train to Southampton, where we were housed in a large tent city. Since reinforcements were sorely needed on the front during the Battle of the Bulge, plans were made to fly us across the English Channel on Christmas Day, but fog proved too dense for C-47s to take-off or land. A few days later, we crossed the English Channel on an LST during the night, evading German U-boats, disembarking at LaHavre, France. From there, we boarded 40 by 8 boxcars (referred to as French forty men or eight horses), headed for Raven, France where we were issued M1 carbines and had an opportunity to zero them in. Shortly before leaving for the front lines to join the 78th Infantry Division, we had one last chapel service in a barn loft where we sat on bales of hay. During the service, the chaplain invited anyone who wanted to share his faith to stand and express it. To my amazement, Bob was first on his feet. Somewhere along the way, he had to come to firmly believe in an almighty God and had courage to acknowledge his faith. In days to come, it proved to be a strong point during combat when he was twice wounded. The first time he was disabled for a few weeks and soon back in action. The second wound was more serious and removed him from combat for the remainder of the war.

"While recovering in a hospital in Holland after his injury, Bob wrote a letter home. 'I've been reading my bible a lot lately, and yesterday while I was thinking about going back up to the front, just by chance, I happened to open my testament to the Book of Psalms, and for some reason, I don't know why, Numbers 91 and 18 stuck in my mind, so I read the 91st and 18th Psalm. I wish you would read them and then you should not worry about me. I have changed a lot, from what I was like eight months ago, a lot of it because of Peter Dahlberg, he influenced me to start taking interest in the bible. I never had much faith in prayers before I was in the Army, but, well, I've had several of them answered, so please, don't worry at all about me, and remember, whatever happens is for the best!'

"The exciting moment came when we crossed the Ludendorff Bridge over the Rhine River at the little German village of Remagen. The bridge was under constant bombardment and we dashed across during a lull in the shelling. The following day, we pressed forward to take a certain objective, when we walked into a deadly trap. Fog lay heavily over the landscape and we captured a few German prisoners along the way who warned us of impending danger just ahead. Bob was given responsibility to take them back to a secured area, so he missed the following action, which no doubt saved his life. We were ordered to spread out across the open hill and dig in, when suddenly the fog lifted. All Hell broke loose! Rifle and machine gun fire raked the open area mowing down our men who had no cover. They did not have a chance to respond; it happened for too quickly. My squad leader had motioned for me to join him in a shell hole, where we had a little protection. As I opened fire, a bullet glanced off my steel helmet and careened off into the air. Then, suddenly, the fog settled down. The agonizing cries of wounded and dying men will always live on in my memory. Minutes later, my squad leader was killed by the explosion of a mortar shell that knocked us both to the ground. I was only slightly wounded, as I wandered somewhat dazed back to where one of our tanks stopped and come on the scene and helped direct their fire to the location of the German troops about a hundred yards away. Soon a long column of some 70 or 80 German troops emerged from the woods, wearing long overcoats, with hands raised high above their heads. We won a costly battle with nearly half our platoon killed. I will never forget the scene as the bodies of our men were carried off the battlefield and laid side by side on the cold, wet ground.

"A day or two later, after trying to reorganize, we pressed on to take another objective. We stopped in a wooded area, waiting for our tanks to take the lead so we could follow them. Suddenly, we came under intense artillery shelling, with tree bursts making it impossible to find adequate cover. I watched one of our tanks take a direct hit, resulting in flames leaping from the turret. This was when Bob was hit by shrapnel in one leg. It was a serious wound and was the end of action for him. He was soon carried back to a medic station, transferred to a hospital in Paris, then onto to England for further care. During his recovery, he began taking real interest in the medical field as he observed the care given to those who were suffering. He later wrote...'I began to think of my future. It was there that I first started to think about becoming a doctor. I wanted to make my life count as one that was worthwhile.' This ultimately led to his decision to follow the medical profession. Had he not been wounded, he probably would have died in further action that very day. Since our tanks could not go ahead because of enemy fire, we were ordered to spread out in a skirmish line at the edge of the trees. At a given signal, we made a mad dash across the open field toward a hill we were to capture. Halfway across the open field, a German 88mm artillery shell exploded midway in our line and very man to my right fell to the ground. Our new squad leader in the center of the line took a direct hit and some of the other men near him were killed. Had Bob been with us, he might have been one of them. The Angels watched over him once again and his life was spared.

"Following his discharge from the Army, Bob began his training to enter the field of medicine. He became an excellent doctor, married a beautiful young woman from the area where he established his medical practice and subsequently raised a lovely family of five children. A few years ago (2007), he was honored at a celebration for having completed 50 years of medical practice in the same community. My path led me in a different direction as I began training for the ministry, which has continued for almost 60 years. Part of this time, I served as a Chaplain at a V.A. Center and S.D. Veterans Home for a period of 30 years. I was privileged to be able to identify with veterans from various wars. By the way, Bob is still practicing medicine (2009) and I am still involved in the ministry, although we both have slowed down just a bit. In the summer of 2010, my wife and I had the opportunity to visit Bob and his wife in their home. It was a delightful experience to see each other again after more than 50 years. Our lives were changed and given direction during those months on the front lines in Germany.

"Not long ago, Bob sent me an interesting book, *Remagen 1945, End Game against the Third Reich*. He concluded on a note...'I always knew that you would make it through the war. I knew that God would protect you. From Blanding on throughout the war I admired your ability to live your religion. You never tried to force your beliefs on anyone but you lived what you believed. Your actions were more telling than words could ever have been. You had quite an effect on me.' All I can say is, thanks Bob, you could not have given me a greater tribute; your words mean more than any medals I have ever received. And thanks, too, for being a life-long friend. It is so good to see what God has done in each of our lives, that we have given the privilege of living out our life's dreams and fulfilling his purpose for having spared us again and again on the battlefield.

"Bob expressed it so well when he wrote...'The war was an experience that none of us would ever go through again, not for all the money in the world, yet on the other hand, we would not trade that experience for anything.' These experiences during World War II certainly played a huge part in preparation for life and for service. I will never forget the lessons I learned, most importantly, I learned to pray and trust in God with all my heart. For his loving protection and care, I will be forever grateful and will give thanks, too, for the privilege of developing friendships that have continued through the years. Bob...'My youth was snatched away from me...I went into combat and was forced to grow up overnight. Combat was terrible and I lost many friends in battle, and yet, I think that ours was one of the most fortunate of all generations. We were privileged to grow up in a time when honor, truth, loyalty, duty and patriotism were real and meant something.' I totally agree, and it is still good to be alive!" [56]

---

[56] Peter Dalhberg, Rapid City, South Dakota to author, June 2009.

Dean Shaffhausen

Amphibious Group Nine, Leyte Gulf

DEAN Shaffhausen..."I was a senior in high school on December 7, 1941, the Japanese attack on Pearl Harbor. I was enlisted under the D-5 Program of Naval Air. Out of the ten men enlisted with me, I was the only one to pass the physical. I was sworn in at the Elks Building in Yankton, South Dakota by Captain Joe Foss. I was assigned to attend classes at Abelfoss College for Officer Candidate School. I finished the first semester and came to the realization this was not what I wanted to get into the active war. I went to my commanding officer and explained why I wanted to leave school and enter active duty into a combat zone. I waited a week and talked to him again. This time, he granted my request. I completed Navy boot camp at Great Lakes Naval Training Facility near Chicago, Illinois.

"After training, I was sent to Treasure Island, in California, waiting for orders to the Pacific. I boarded the U.S. Navy transport S.S. Sea Snipe and while on the ship, for the first and only time, I got seasick. We sailed alone for 30 days to Hollandia, New Guinea. I often wondered how we made it into a forward combat zone without being attacked by a Japanese submarine or aircraft. We first stopped at an intermediary point before sailing onto Hollandia. I was assigned to Amphibious Group Nine, commanded by Rear Admiral Arthur Dewey Strubble, on the Flag Staff. How I ended up on his staff I do not know. The staff consisted of 49 officers and 155 enlisted. I worked in a section of 10 enlisted, which assembled invasion/amphibious plan information. I worked directly with officers who were responsible for writing and putting together our mission plans. I was 19 years old and on the Admiral's staff.

"Leyte was the big one. Admiral Strubble's flagship was a Fletcher Class destroyer, the Dashiell (DD-659). During the trip to Leyte Gulf, the ocean was rough. I could look to see an LST at the top of a 50 foot wave above and another seemingly below the destroyer. The group took part in twenty assault landings, hitting the beached on every major island in the Philippines. The Admiral shifted his flagship to the USS Nashville, a Brooklyn Class light cruiser (CL-43)."

The Nashville's keel was laid down on January 24, 1935, the New York Shipbuilding Corporation at Camden New Jersey. It was launched on October 2, 1937, commissioned on June 6, 1938. On 27 May, the cruiser was part of naval assault force shelling Biak, Schouten Islands, where on June 4, 1944 it sustained moderate damage from a near miss while repelling a Japanese air attack. After repairs at Espiritu Santo, New Hebrides, Nashville transported General Douglas MacArthur and his staff to the invasion of Morotai, Dutch East Indies in mid-September. The cruiser transported MacArthur on his return to the Philippines, for which it carried the General and his staff from Manus on 16 October. The cruiser provided fire support for the Leyte Island landings on 20 October, guarding the troops on the beachhead and the nearby transports. Returning to Manus Island for brief repairs, Nashville left the Admiralties on 28 November as the flagship for the Commander, Visayan Attack Force, enroute to the invasion of Mindoro. On 13 December, the cruiser was struck by a Kamikaze off Negros Island. The Kamikaze crashed in the cruiser's port 5-inch gun mount, with two bombs on the aircraft exploding 10 feet off the deck. Gasoline fires and exploding ammunition set the cruiser's amidships area into a sheet of flames, with 133 sailors killed and 190 wounded. The cruiser's remaining 5-inch guns maintained defensive AAA fire. The Attack Group Commander shifted his flag to another warship and Nashville steamed via San Pedro Bay in the Philippines onto Pearl Harbor, before continuing on to Puget Sound Naval Shipyard on January 12, 1945.

Shaffhausen..."I just had left that location (amidships area) heading below when the Japanese aircraft hit the cruiser. I went back up and saw dead and wounded all over the deck. Admiral Strubble ordered the Dashiell alongside the cruiser to collect dead and wounded. The cruiser remained on station until sailing to the Puget Sound Naval Shipyard. The staff of the group transferred to the Dashiell. I was with Admiral Strubble when General MacArthur and staff waded ashore from a landing craft (LCI) on 20 October. I got to shake MacArthur's hand because I was standing next to the Admiral. I listened and I guess I was just lucky to witness this history. I was with the Admiral after Corregidor was recaptured on February 26, 1945. I was able to walk inside Malinta Tunnel, looking at the lateral tunnels. Again, this was because I was on the Admiral's staff.

"After the USAAF dropped the two atomic bombs on Japan, due to my points accrued, I was given a 30 day leave. I boarded the transport Henry T. Allen. I wanted to go home. I finally got on a train to Las Vegas, Nevada; to Minneapolis, Minnesota; and then onto to Tilden, South Dakota. After leave, I took a train to Bremerton, Washington. I was assigned to an Admirable Class Minesweeper (AM-161). We were to take the minesweeper to San Diego for decommissioning. I was awarded the Navy Commendation Medal prior to be released from active duty."[57]

---

[57] Dean Shaffhausen, South Dakota, interview (during a monthly meeting of the Black Hills Veterans Writing Group, Rapid City, South Dakota), author, May 8, 2010

Gordon Lease

World War II Coast Guardsman

COAST Guardsman Gordon B. Lease of Rapid City was on LST-381 on the beach at Plestion Le. Greve, Brittany, France in August 1944. Lease..."We were supporting the U.S. Army assaults in Brest and St. Nazaire, France. All we carried was ammunition and gasoline in five gallon cans. About Salerno, Italy. The first 200 German prisoners evacuated from the Anzio beachhead were put aboard USS LST-381 on January 23, 1944, and transported to the Naples, Italy area. The 381 was Coast Guard-manned with a 30 man Navy Assault Boat Team aboard at that time.

"During World War II, the Coast Guard was involved in the sinking of the German Navy pocket battleship Bismarck. When the Germans began their Paukenschlag campaign sink ships off the American east coast, Guard units sank 12 German and two Japanese submarines, while capturing surface vessels, resulting in the very first Germans taken in combat by an American force. Working with the Navy and Marines, Coast Guardsmen saw combat in the 1942 North African invasion (Operation TORCH) and the 1943 invasion of Sicily (Operation HUSKY). In addition, Coast Guard cutters were present off all five landing beaches during the Normandy invasion of June 6, 1944, along with Lease himself, providing combat search and rescue operations under enemy fire. He said the worst Coast Guard disaster was off Guadalcanal (Solomon Islands) when 193 Coast Guardsmen and 56 Army soldiers on board were killed. After retiring from the Coast Guard, Lease enlisted in the Marines for a while, and then became a municipal water tester in California before moving to Rapid City."[58]

---

[58] "Gordon Lease (World War II Coast Guard)," Black Hills Veterans Writing Group, "World War II, U.S. Coast Guard service," Rapid City, South Dakota, author, June 2012.

Harold Jansen

U.S. Navy, World War II

HAROLD Jansen was aboard a small landing craft that sat unguarded, along with the rest of the American invasion fleet, off the coast of Leyte Island in the Philippines on October 25, 1944. The fleet of U.S. warships protecting the transports had been lured away by a Japanese decoy force. The U.S. transport ships were sitting ducks for a large Japanese fleet of battleships and cruisers approaching from the north. The enemy warships almost certainly would have annihilated the U.S. invasion fleet if they had broken through a thin group of small American warships. Jansen, a 20 year old ensign, was the second in command of a 200 foot long landing craft, LCT-958. Jansen and the rest of the crew prepared to scuttle their ship if the battleships broke through.

Jansen..."We were nervously sitting there hoping the Kamikazes wouldn't get through. They would have had a field day with us." Luckily, for the U.S. transports, the small force of outgunned American destroyers, along with planes from several small aircraft carriers, fought ferociously against the bigger Japanese warships, which eventually retreated, their commanders mistakenly thinking they had encountered the main force of large American warships. The invasion fleet was saved, but at a high price. The big Japanese warships sank two U.S. escort carriers, two destroyers, and a destroyer escort and damaged four other American ships. More than 1,000 American sailors and aircrew men were killed. The battle, off Samar Island, was one of four major engagements that, together, were called the Battle of Leyte Gulf. The Japanese navy suffered major losses in the rest of the battles, which effectively ended it as a major force for the remainder of the war.[59]

---

[59] "Harold Jansen, U.S. Navy, World War II," Black Hills Veterans Writing Group, "World War II," Rapid City, South Dakota, to author, June 2012.

World War II Consolidated B-24E Liberator Training Crash

Meadow, South Dakota

ON October 20, 1944, a RB-34E training aircraft, number 42-7249, piloted by Second Lieutenant Robert A. Meyer was involved in a catastrophic aerial accident, killing four crewmembers onboard the aircraft. Lieutenant Meyer was scheduled for a cross-country flight: Casper Army Airfield, Wyoming to Fort Peck to Bismarck, North Dakota and return. Before taking off from Casper, Meyer completed a visual pre-flight of the aircraft, the fluorescent lights were inoperative, and there was a moderate amount of oil on top of number two engine cowling and tail surfaces. After the fluorescent lights were repaired and functioning properly, Lieutenant Meyer took off on the proposed flight. Lieutenant Meyer told members of the USAAF Aircraft Accident Investigation Board that the aircraft had a weight and balance index of 92.5 (tail heavy) and that he refused to take onboard eight boxes of ammunition because of the high weight and balance index. The aircraft's take off index was 72.5 with all crew on the flight deck. Meyer stated that number three engine was run in emergency rich while climbing to keep it cool. Lieutenant Meyer stated that although he was briefed and the Form 23 indicated he was to fly Contact Flight Rules (CFR), most of the flight was on instruments. Over Dickinson, North Dakota, Lieutenant Meyer became aware of excessive vibrations and asked the radio operator (Corporal Bernard W. Day) if the vibration was coming from the upper forward gun turret. The radio operator answered, "No." Lieutenant Meyer indicated that he paid no further attention to the vibrations and that all instruments were normal.

About an hour out of Bismarck, Lieutenant Meyer indicated trouble started on the flight. The B-24E was fitted with a single .50 caliber machine gun in the lower section of the tail, which replaced the Sperry twin .50 caliber machine gun turret on the lower rear fuselage. Because of production problems at Ford Motor Company's Willow Run plant at Ypsilanti, Michigan; Consolidated at Fort Worth, Texas and Douglas at Tulsa, Oklahoma aircraft plants, the majority of the B-24Es or 801s as it was classified because on the single lower rear gun, became training aircraft. Lt. Meyer kept the aircraft cruising in auto lean mixture, propellers set at 2,150 revolutions per minute (RPMs) with a manifold pressure of 31 1/2-inches. He stated one of the engines on the right side of the aircraft cut out, so Lieutenant Meyer initiated the emergency three engine procedure, mixture auto rich, advancing the propellers to high RPM. The mixture remained in auto lean. Lieutenant Meyer thought number one engine went out, so he feathered it. Then realizing that the trouble was in number three engine, because they were only pulling 20-inches manifold pressure, 2,000 rpm and that cylinder head temperature was 280 degrees, Lt. Meyer feathered the engine. After feathering the engine, Lieutenant Meyer and William A. McManus (copilot) told the Accident Investigation Board that number four engine went out. All of the engine instruments were reading normal on this engine and the reason they knew it went out from the added control pressure.

Lieutenant Meyer gave the order to bailout of the strickened aircraft, with the copilot repeating the order. The two pilots were able to keep the aircraft level for thirty seconds to give the crew an opportunity to bailout. Three crewmembers successfully jumped out of the aircraft: Corpora Day (radio operator), Corporal Sheldon B. Kaiser (nose turret gunner) and Corporal Sherwood W. Long (tail turret gunner). Lieutenant McManus cut the number two magneto. Five of the crew ordered to bailout remained in the aircraft. By this time, the aircraft had dropped from 8,600 to 4,300 feet. Lieutenant Meyer again gave the order to bailout. At this time, Lieutenant Milan J. Mikulec (bombardier), Flight Officer Alex K. Kalsmavek (navigator), Corporal William Goczewski (engineer) and Corporal Carson A, Bass (lower turret gunner) bailed out of the aircraft. Lieutenant McManus tried to get out of the aircraft but it was impossible and strapped himself back into the copilot's seat. Lieutenant Meyer turned on the aircraft's landing lights in preparation to attempt a night landing. Lieutenant McManus lowered the flaps to control the aircraft as it neared the ground, with landing gear lowered, although neither the pilot nor copilot indicated to the Accident Investigation Board that the landing gear was lowered.

The bomber touched down on top of a slight ridge, skidded 200 to 225 feet with full brakes on. The aircraft slid off the ridge and dropped 10 feet, blowing the left landing gear's tire. This caused the aircraft to skid sideways, breaking off the nose landing gear, dropping the nose onto the ground, thereby plowing through the soft soil. The aircraft continued to plow through the ground for another 400 feet before coming to a full stop. The pilot and copilot crawled out the right front cockpit window, assisted by a farmer who had been working in the field. The three found Corporal Ralph L. Kizer (upper turret gunner) pinned under the wreckage the upper turret. He did not try to jump out of the aircraft when told to do so, twice. The three men had to chop him out of the wreckage, when an ambulance arrived, Corporal Kizer was transported to the Lemmon Hospital to be treated for his injuries. He remained in the hospital until Saturday, 28 October, at which time a C-47 from Casper Army Air Field landed at Lemmon, transporting him back to base. The navigator, Flight Officer Kalsmavek died. His parachute was found open, 40 feet behind the aircraft wreckage, apparently waiting too long to jump out of the aircraft. Three other crewmembers that jumped out of the aircraft died when they struck the ground apparently before their parachutes opened: Lieutenant Mikulec and Corporal Goczewski. Their bodies were recovered and transported to Lemmon. On Sunday, 29 October, a Casper Army Air Field assigned C-47 flew the four dead airmen back to base.

The crash occurred at approximately 10:15 p.m., in Whitney Township, 26 miles south of Lemmon, South Dakota, five miles east and two miles south at 45 Degrees 28.589 Minutes North and 102 Degrees 04.589 Minutes West. Prior to the arrival of Army Military Police from Casper Army Air Field, Lemmon city police established a 24 hour guard around the crash site until relieved by military personnel. The crash site was the scene was carefully examined by an USAAF Aircraft Accident Investigation Board. When their on-site investigation was completed, the aircraft could not be repaired, with usable equipment removed and trucked to Casper Army Air Field. The wreckage was salvaged and trucked to Rapid City for disposal. An examination of the four engines revealed no indications of operational failure, other than engine number three, which showed signs of fire. It was suggested the fire could have been the result of excessive heat from high rpm and manifold pressure from the engines running in auto lean. Even then, piston rings and valves were intact, showed no indications of deteriorating or excessive detonation. The spark gaps were perfect and not fouled in any way. Sufficient aviation fuel remained in all tanks, and carburetors on each engine were functioning.

Although the actual cause of the accident was never officially determined, the reviewing board indicated probable cause of the crash was cockpit confusion between the pilot and copilot. The board published its conclusions.

1. The pilot or copilot knew did know which engine was giving them trouble, as evidenced by their statements.
2. It is highly improbable that number four engine quit in that, as stated by pilot and copilot, engine instruments remained normal.
3. The explosion of number two engine was probably the igniting of excess gasoline vapors resulting for the misuse of throttles.
4. Complete teardown of the engines failed to show any symptoms of engine failure and only in number three engine was there any signs of fire or excess heat.

Even though the Accident Investigation Board did not believe the pilots' being on instruments at the time of troubles with the aircraft hold any direct bearing on the accident. However, the board felt this does reflect on the ability of the pilot, in that he did change his flight plan from CFR to Instrument Flight Rules (IFR) as required by the Civil Aeronautics Authority (CAA) and USAAF regulations. The board recommended additional instruction to be given on emergency procedures, for, as clearly evidenced by statements by the crew to the investigating personnel that they were not fully cognizant of what was going on with the aircraft.

A group of local military veterans and historians commemorated the crash site of the B-24E south of Lemon and the four crewmembers that died with the placement of a plaque at the location. South Dakota was the location of intense training for combat operations during World War II and there were many fatal crashes throughout the state during the war. Most did not make headlines as fighting in the overseas combat zones. They were still part of the sacrifices of those called the Greatest Generation for their country, which allows us to remain free today. The bronze plaque marking the crash site was provided by the Meadow Historical Society and the Sons of the American Legion.[60]

---

[60] Around Ellsworth Air Force Base (last in a series of names since its creation as a military facility in 1941), there have been numerous military aircraft crashes. David Christman was responsible in setting up a memorial for the aircrew killed during a B-24E crash in a training flight during World War II. On Ellsworth AFB is a memorial walk with plaques on pillars indicating the type of aircraft crashed and those who lost their lives,
continued...

...continued
    including the mentioned B-24E. Interview with David Christman, Rapid City, South Dakota, by author on October 9, 2010.

Japanese Balloon Firebombing Attacks Against the United States

Including South Dakota during World War II

THE strategy of large-scale, modern aerial warfare using arsenals of ICBMs began with the raid by 16 North American B-25 Mitchell twin-engine bombers launched from the U.S. Navy aircraft carrier USS Hornet on April 18, 1942. The historic air raid was led by Army Air Forces Lt. Col. James Doolittle, using the unorthodox procedure of launching Army Air Force bombers from the pitching deck of a U.S. Navy aircraft carrier, part of a task force, which penetrated patrolling (screening) Japanese Naval Defense Warming picket ships to within 668 miles of Tokyo. For this raid, the B-25s were modified with an autopilot navigation system, increased internal fuel capacity for longer range to compensate for low-level flying to penetrate below Japanese early warning radars, ventral machine gun and Norden bombsight removed to reduce weight. The B-25 was the only USAAF bomber able to takeoff from an aircraft carrier with sufficient range to reach targets in and around Tokyo with a respectable bomb load. The Doolittle raid was planned to cause confusion and impede Japanese war production by forcing reallocation of that country's scarce military resources to defend the home islands. B-25 bomb loads were not large enough to produce large-scale damage, but enough to inflict a definite psychological blow to the Japanese military. They might be forced to change their Pacific war strategy, allowing the U.S. Navy to concentrate is limited surface warships (especially its aircraft carriers) on a few threats, rather than across a wide operational front from the Indian Ocean, Australia, Solomon Islands, Midway, Hawaiian Islands, Aleutians and Alaska.

The Doolittle raid attacked targets in the Tokyo, Yokohama, Yokosuka, Kobe and Nagoya areas. With the Hornet flight deck crowded with B-25s, the Enterprise provided the task force with its aerial screen in the case the Japanese discovered the approaching ships. At 3 a.m. on April 18, 1942, the Enterprise's radar detected two small Japanese picket ships twelve miles ahead of the task force. The task force changed course to bypass the picket ships, avoiding detection. At dawn, the Enterprise launched three Douglas SBD Dauntless dive-bombers to search ahead of the task force out to a distance of 200 miles to skirt patrolling Japanese picket ships. One SBD located a picket ship 42 miles ahead of the task force. Upon landing on the Enterprise, the pilot reported his aircraft had probably been identified and the sighting radioed to Tokyo Naval Headquarters.

The task force altered course to avoid the picket ship ahead of its course. Japanese picket ship number 23, the Nitto Maru, radioed Tokyo to the presence of a U.S. Navy task force consisting of three probable aircraft carriers, 700 miles east of Tokyo. The final lifting of secrecy of the position of the two carriers resulted from two picket ships within six miles of the task force. Both were sunk by the task force's screen, but operations plans had to be changed. The B-25s had to launch outside planned takeoff range, increasing flight distance to targets, meaning they would have insufficient fuel to reach the China recovery airfields, behind Japanese lines. The Japanese military did not attack the American task force, believing it outside carrier based aircraft launch range. The accepted range was 400 miles. The Japanese military did not know B-25s, not SBDs would conduct the bombing attack. The B-25 raid caught Japanese air defenses unprepared, although Tokyo completed an air raid drill immediately prior to the arrival of the B-25s.

The Japanese military command in Tokyo reacted to the Doolittle raid's far-reaching tactical and strategic decisions. Admiral Yamamoto convinced the Japanese military command to authorize his "Operation MI," an attack on Midway Island to lure the remaining U.S. Navy's aircraft carriers into battle and destroy them, something his attack on Pearl Harbor failed to accomplish. Companion "Operation AO" was a diversionary attack in the Aleutian Islands. This attack was successful but the Japanese lost four fleet carriers, their skilled pilots and support personnel when surprised by three American carriers positioned North of Midway Island, before the Japanese expected them. Remaining Japanese aircraft carriers could not be risked in attempts to penetrate increasing U.S. Navy defenses to launch aircraft to bomb the continental United States. Consequently, the Japanese military forged ahead with development of a long-range, four-engine heavy bomber. It was not until late October 1944 that the Nakajima Aircraft Company completed the bomber prototype, the Nakajima C8N1 Renzan (Liz) heavy bomber with a design range of 4,600 miles. The Renzan never enter production because of the loss of airfields on the Marianas Islands and shortage of strategic materials, especially high-performance engines.

The loss of the Marianas Islands forced the Imperial Japanese Navy to modify its long-range submarines, fitted with watertight, deck-mounted aircraft hangars to transport single-engine aircraft close enough to launch a bombing raid on the western Panama Canal locks. This would disrupt Allied plans for the invasion of Japan. The submarines, aircraft and pilots were ready to depart Japanese home waters in August 1945, but the war ended before the attack force sailed. The Doolittle raid also pushed the Japanese development of the world's first intercontinental weapon, a high-altitude, hydrogen filled balloon, armed with incendiary and anti-personnel bombs. The Japanese had received plans, carried by a Japanese submarine, which dodged U.S. and British anti-submarine patrols from Germany to Japan, to build jet fighters, copy of V-1 pulse rocket, radar, early atomic technology and processed uranium. However, Japanese industry did not have the strategic materials necessary of produce the German wonder weapons. The balloons were designed to travel across the Pacific Ocean on prevailing high altitude jet stream winds to drop bombs on North America. From 1942 to 1944, the Japanese worked to design the balloon, bombing release mechanism. Japanese scientists worked hard to solve the many technical problems for this intercontinental bombing platform.

The Japanese balloon weapon project was classified as "Operation FU-GO." The military bomb carrying balloon launches should be viewed as a historically significant event and the development of waging intercontinental warfare from one's home country to that of another. On the birthday of former Japanese ruler Emperor Meiji, November 3, 1944, at 5 a.m., Japan began its intercontinental air assault on the United States. The first week in November brought strong winds in the jet stream, which rapidly pushed the launched balloons toward North America. The jet stream is a narrow band of high-velocity winds near the base of the stratosphere where the tropopause makes its greatest change in elevation. During winter months, jet stream winds can reach 450mph, with the average somewhat lower, but still high-velocity. The Japanese military launched the balloons up into the Jet Stream which followed the Great Northern Circle Route along the Aleutian Islands, Alaska and Pacific coast to the U.S. northwest.

The balloon's design was simple, but functional. The balloon bag was 32.81 feet in diameter, with an operational capacity of 19,000 cubic feet of hydrogen. The balloon's fabric consisted of four-ply paper upper and three-ply lower paper material. Japanese engineers and scientists designed the balloon with many special features to allow it to reach the target area and drop its bombs, then self-destruct. Launching the balloon was an ingenious process. The balloon was carefully positioned on the ground so that the suspension curtain, attached to the mid-seam of the balloon, secured to three foot long ground screw anchors. The balloon was inflated with hydrogen gas from large hydrogen gas cylinders until the gasbag was approximately 50 percent inflated. The gasbag would fully inflate as it reached maximum altitude. The amount of hydrogen gas vented into the balloon was determined by its ground inflation height since each balloon was handmade and varied slightly in size.

A wood suspension cradle held the balloon's aluminum equipment ring with its altitude-control device and bombs. As the balloon stretched in its moorings, ground handlers let the balloon rise so that the 40 foot shroud lines were fully extended, pulling the ordnance package off the ground. The balloon was released to climb into the jet stream and onto the United States. The balloon launch sites were located in northern Japan to take advantage of the season's prevailing west to east jet stream winds. A balloon launch site consisted of three balloon pads.

The Japanese could not have started their balloon bombing campaign against the United States at a more favorable time. The November jet stream winds were strong, pushing the balloons toward North America. The American public was becoming informed of German V-2 rocket attacks against England, for which there was no defense. Unknown to the American public, U.S. intelligence believed Germany was developing a long-range, multi-stage rocket capable to attacking U.S. east coast cities. Japanese Kamikaze attacks in the western Pacific were increasing American casualties (dead and wounded) from terrific suicide aircraft strikes against U.S. Navy warships. These attacks revealed the extent to which the Japanese was willing to sacrifice its military personnel to inflict serious damage on the U.S. military. More concerning was intelligence reports the Japanese military was training hundreds of thousands, possibly millions of its civilian population into cadres of suicide ground troops to attack U.S. troops during the anticipated invasion of the Japanese home islands. A successful balloon attack against the United States would possibly boost Japanese civilian population morale, which suffered because of U.S. Navy submarine attacks (sinkings) of merchant ships, tankers, and warships, along with increasing frequency and intensity of U.S. Navy aircraft carrier launched strikes against military installations on the home islands. Destruction was worse from attacking B-29 conventional bombing and incendiary (fire-bomb) raids, as well as shipping loses to shipping around the home islands from B-29 sea mining of inland shipping lanes.

After the balloon was launched, a timer (powered by a one and one-half volt wet cell battery, determined bomb release. The balloon's flight time was programmed for a specific length, determined by estimating jet stream wind speed. The balloon was equipped with aneroids to maintain programmed altitude. An aneroid is a disk-shaped metallic capsule with air inside evacuated, able to register sensitivity to atmospheric pressure changes from expansion and contraction. The aneroids served as altitude meters from maintaining the balloon's programmed altitude within the upper and lower estimated jet stream boundary layers. If the balloon dropped below its programmed altitude, the aneroids senses altitude change triggering a sequence release of one or more sand ballast bags until the balloon returned to proper altitude. If the balloon climbed above programmed altitude, the aneroids detected reduced pressure, opening the gas relief valve at the bottom of the balloon until returning to programmed altitude. The release of expanding hydrogen gas to prevent the balloon from climbing to an altitude where pressure increase inside the paper gasbag would burst, destroying the airborne weapons platform. The balloon was still at the mercy of the jet stream's changing directions, which ultimately determined flight path and destination areas in North America.

The Japanese produced approximately 10,000 balloons, launching 9,300. It was estimated only ten percent of the balloons reached North America. The low number successfully completing the high altitude flight over the northern Pacific probably resulted from malfunctioning ballast control mechanisms. Balloons recovered in the United States and Canada retained a high percentage of the self-destruction flash bomb on the instrument ring, providing U.S. intelligence information on their design and operation. The flash bombs were designed to be ignited by a 94 minute fuse ignited after incendiary and anti-personnel bombs dropped. Flash bomb failure was apparently due to either battery or fuse malfunction. When the flash bomb did not detonate, the balloon slowing settled to the ground at widely scattered locations in North America. Most were retrieved by a special unit of USAAF personnel.

Balloon recoveries in the U.S. and Canada provided indications the balloons could survive ballast mechanism malfunctions and still make it to North America. Examination of recovered balloons indicated some of the ballast sand bags and equipment pulled off by ground or water impact. Balloons on which the sequence of ballast release stopped prior to payload release showed the bombs on the equipment ring not to be armed. The bombs did not arm until release from the equipment ring. The balloons were designed to reach the United States within a preset time, release the bombs to ignited fires in the northwest forests. It was a simple concept, released bombs starting fires in isolated areas, which would grow in size to destroy U.S. cities and industries in the fires paths. After bomb release, a 94 minute fuse ignited the flash bomb on the gasbag, destroying it by fire. A demolition charge on the aluminum equipment ring detonated by a 169 second fuse after bomb release to destroy the altitude control instruments and equipment, ballast and bomb release mechanisms.

On November 3, 1944, the first balloons were launched toward North America (primarily aimed at the U.S. northwest). The first indication of this initial attack came on 4 November when the crew of a U.S. Navy destroyer patrolling 55 miles southwest of San Diego, California recovered an unusual mechanical apparatus, deflated balloon envelope and rigging from the Pacific Ocean at 3:55 p.m. U.S. Navy intelligence examined the recovered equipment, determining it was an unmanned balloon weapons platform designed for indiscriminate bombing attacks against the United States. Warnings were sent to USAAF airfields along the probable northern jet stream approaches to and in the United States to be on alert form additional bomb carrying high altitude balloons.

The difficulty in locating the balloons over the United States was demonstrated on the evening of 4 November, shortly after the warning alert to U.S. airfields and ground observers to watch of highflying balloons. Four USAAF Curtiss P-40 Warhawks from Los Angles AAFB scrambled to intercept a possible sighting of a Japanese balloon over Santa Monica, California. The P-40s were not equipped with radar for night interception operations, could not locate the suspected Japanese balloon. The first confirmed shoot down of a Japanese balloon inside U.S. airspace was on November 23, 1944. A Lockheed P-38 Lightning from Santa Rosa AAFB, California intercepted the balloon over Calistoga, shooting it down. The first confirmed Japanese bomb explosion in the U.S. was on December 6, 1944, 15 miles northwest of Thermopolis, Wyoming. AAF personnel recovered fragments from an exploded 15 kilogram anti-personnel bomb. AAF personnel interviewed eyewitnesses who reported hearing an explosion and seeing a bright red flame in the sky.

AAF special recovery teams continued to retrieve as many grounded Japanese balloons as possible while trying to keep or hide the significance of their activities secret from the locals in the areas of their recovery operations. The fear was if the extent of the Japanese bombing became known to the American public, the shock and fear of the indiscriminate bombing might be worse than any actual damage from the small number of bombs. USAAF intelligence learned a lot after translating Japanese manufacturer's inspection tags found on the balloons. On tag on a downed balloon on March 13, 1945, at Chimacum, Washington indicated it was balloon number 262, manufactured at the Sagami Army Arsenal Factory Number 2, 15 miles northwest of Yokohama, Japan. The balloon was manufactured in February 1945, accepted by the launch site on 1 March. Thirteen days later, the balloon was recovered in Washington State.

Balloon Number 11 was recovered at Hay River, Northwest Territory, Canada on June 12, 1945. The identification tag indicated the balloon had been manufactured on January 23, 1945 at the Takaki Factory, 25 miles northwest of Sendai, Japan. The Canadian Army recovery team could not determine when the balloon came down in the territory. Another balloon recovered near Mahogany, Oregon on June 9, 1945, had a tag identifying it as balloon number 165, launch scheduled on January 31, 1945, by Number 10 Balloon Squadron. The last documented recovery of a Japanese balloon was near Indian Springs, Nevada on July 20, 1945. A USAAF recovery teams collected the balloon's gas envelope, shroud lines and gas relief valve. During the closing months of World War II, Japan's industries were unable to produce balloons in sufficient numbers to continue the aerial bombing campaign against the United States. Japanese intelligence had not heard of any American public outrage over their attacks, report of civilian casualties, forest fires in the northwest areas of the United States, or significant damage.

Even though the balloons gas envelope was fabricated from layered paper, shortages of aluminum affected component production. American submarine sinkings of Japanese merchant ships, B-29 aerial mining of inland Japanese shipping channels and ports, combined with B-29 incendiary and conventional bombing raids, dramatically reduced the importation of strategic materials and food to the Japanese home islands. The coordinated American B-29 raids drove hundreds of thousands of Japanese civilians from the cities, disrupting their labor for military production around their homes.

The Japanese military launched 9,300 balloons, with an estimated 1,000 reaching North America. They were recovered over a large area from Attu Island in the Aleutians, as far east as Michigan, and as far south as northern Mexico. In Canada, Japanese balloons were recovered from Northern Yukon Territory in the west, south into British Columbia and east to Lake Winnipeg. Fortunately, Japanese balloon bombs only killed six Americans. On May 5, 1945, a Japanese balloon bomb exploded on Gearhart Mountain, Oregon, killing Elsie Mitchell (pregnant wife of a local minister) and five children on a picnic. The Japanese also booby trapped each balloon's equipment package with a small demolition charge, designed to destroy the equipment on the balloon after bomb release. Sometimes, these demolition charges blew up when the balloon's equipment package on the ground was disturbed by AAF recovery personnel. Recovery personnel treated each balloon with great care as a live ordnance package.

Military historians tend make small significance of the Japanese use of balloons as part of its last effort to retaliate against the United States in World War II. It was still a significant development of a revolutionary concept, predating today's intercontinental ballistic missiles to be launched from underground, concrete hardened silos or from submerged atomic-powered ballistic submarines (the U.S. and Russia). If the Japanese had armed their balloons with biological (germ warfare) canisters, (Japanese scientists in Manchuria used Allied troops as guinea pigs for their biological weapons development) or poison gas cylinders, the number of deaths in North America might have been a pandemic. Regardless, the Japanese balloon terror weapons failed to achieve the desired strategic results. Seven Japanese balloons were recovered in South Dakota, from the North Dakota border, south of Nebraska, in the central part of the state. No major damage resulted from these balloon weapons in the state with little fear or uncertainty from the state's citizens. Today, most Americans do not know that the Japanese tried to set the North American Pacific coast a blaze in the closing months of World War II in the Pacific.

Interestingly, the U.S. military in the 1950s tried a nonlethal variant of the Japanese high altitude, intercontinental balloon concept for photographic aerial reconnaissance. The U.S. military launched high-altitude, helium stratospheric balloons to overfly the Soviet Union. These balloons carried high-speed aerial camera to collect ground photographs for U.S. intelligence on the military capabilities of the Soviet Union and to provide cartographic information for mapmakers required by SAC for its atomic armed bombers to attack Soviet targets. At this time, the U.S. military did not have reconnaissance aircraft, which could fly high enough, with sufficient range, to fly across the

Soviet Union without being shot down. A manned aircraft confrontation might possibly touch off a war between the U.S. and Soviet Union. The requirement to look past Soviet border military installations was one of the reasons for the design of the Lockheed U-2 spy plane, followed by the supersonic Lockheed SR-71 Blackbird. The shooting down of a U-2 over the central Soviet union on May 1, 1960, fortunately did not set off an atomic exchange between the Soviet Union and the United States. It did embolden Premier Khrushchev to place atomic armed MRBMs and IRBMs on the island of Cuba, setting off the Cuban Missile Crisis and a close step to an atomic war.

These balloon flights provided little valuable military intelligence because of cloud cover, out of focus photographs, but primarily the inability of intelligence personnel to determine where the images were taken on the ground. Intelligence personnel could not compare photograph terrain features with maps, because most the area of the Soviet Union was blank on U.S. large and small-scale maps. The U.S. military photographic balloon flights produced about the same level of results as Japanese fire bomb balloon campaign. It took the development of photoreconnaissance satellites to open up the Soviet Union, locating military, industrial and political targets, while providing details to produce air target charts for SAC bomber crews and missile targeting.[61]

---

[61] Lt. Col. George A. Larson, USAF (Ret.), "The fire-bombing of America," Air Classics, April 1966.

A Personal Look at the Battle of the Bulge

Three South Dakota Veterans Recall the Historic Battle

THE "Battle of the Bulge" or as referred to by the Germans as the "Battle of the Ardennes," is a classic example of intelligence failure of the Allies to recognize that the German military was not beaten, still able to launch a powerful, if limited winter offensive in the west. It has been the story of books, military studies and movies. What follows is a look through the remembrances of Allied soldiers thrown into the battle to stop and drive back the Germans in cold and terrible winter conditions. The German objective was to drive through the American front lines. Sweep to the sea and capture the port of Antwerp, Belgium, severing the Allied supply line from England and dividing U.S. troops to the south from British troops to the north of the port. The Germans carefully and secretly collected a striking force of 200,000 troops along a 60 mile front, to a depth of three miles from the advanced American frontline positions. The initial German striking force consisted of five armored divisions with 500 tanks and 1,900 artillery, support by 13 infantry divisions. U.S. forces spread six divisions along the 60 mile front, not expecting a major German offensive to attack at this point. The terrain was not ideal to conduct offensive operations, especially on the winding roads, which made rapid movement difficult. The Ardennes Mountains extend over rough terrain, with deep ravines, narrow valleys, steep elevations, cut by numerous streams and rivers. Heavy snow hampered the movement of men and supplies for the Allies attempting to hold back the German offensive.

Generaloberst DerWaffen SS Josef Dietrich's Sixth Panzer Army, the north wing of the attack, led the German offensive. The Sixth Panzer was to cross the Meuse River, to either side of Liege. Once the German force crossed the river, it was to turn north, forming a unified advance from Maastricht to Antwerp, Belgium. Supporting German infantry would create a front east of the Meuse River, along the Vesdre River. The German 15th Army positioned to protect the Sixth Panzer's Army's right flank and rear. General der Panzer Truppen Hasso-Ecpcard Von Manteuffell's Fifth Panzer Army, once across the Meuse

River would take up a position south of the Sixth Panzer Army, holding a position referred to as the Antwerp-Brussels-Namur-Dinant. On the German left, General der Panzer Truppen Erich Brandenberger's Seventh Army was to protect the attacking southern German flank along the Semois and Meuse Rivers.

The Germans attacked the American front lines on the night of December 15, 1944, under cover of low clouds, snow and cold temperatures. At the time of the German attack, the main U.S. battle tank was the Sherman M-4, outmatched by the heavier German panzers. George Moe, of Rapid City, South Dakota, during the battle was a First Lieutenant, assigned to General George Patton's Third Army, 4th Armored Division, 35th Tank Battalion, a Sherman Tank Battalion commander. During an interview on January 15, 2004, Moe..."General Eisenhower gave orders to General Patton to change offensive direction, moving north to cover the 150 miles into Bastogne, Belgium. As a 25 year old Lieutenant, I had the daunting responsibility of moving north, leading the 35th Tank Battalion, with my 'A' Company. The hardest part was that we did not have any maps. We'd get into these little villages. I'd knock on people's doors until I got someone to come up from their cellar to ask them directions. One night, I banged on the doors of fearful villagers in France, Luxembourg and Belgium, trying to find directions. I used a smattering of French, English and German. The people were not overly helpful, because they did not whether the roaring tanks and trucks were German or Allied. Eventually, we got maps for the Bastogne area from the French, but they weren't as detailed as the ones we usually used but certainly better than nothing.

"Our tank company moved north of Arlon, Belgium toward Bastogne and got to the hillside village of Martelange. Once in the village, the company had to wait for combat engineers to repair a bridge over the Sure River so we could continue our advance. I had my tanks park on the peak side of a junior-sized mountain with the tank crews still aboard. My assistant company commander and I walked down to see how the engineers were coming with the bridge repairs. As our boots clicked on the cobblestone street, I heard the loudest 'whang' of my life. A rifle bullet had ricocheted off the cobblestones right between the two of us. Immediately, I realized that a sniper in the steeple of the historic church at the top of the peak could have killed us if he had wished. We quickly returned to our tanks, mounted up to get a shot at the sniper from our tanks, but because of the angle of the hill, we couldn't get a clear shot without destroying the historic church. I made the call not to destroy the church just to get one sniper. I have always been glad that I didn't destroy that church.

"Soon, we were on our way toward Bastogne. A short distance down the road we waited at a farmhouse to figure out what to do next. A U.S. Army major informed us he was to take his tank into the town of Warnach from the south while another tank entered the town from north to take the town. I positioned my tank just inside Warnacj and waited to see my partner from the north. I waited and waited, but he didn't show. The number one rule for tankers is never go into a town alone. If you do, you are a great target. Finally, I made a right turn and started looking for the other tank company but there was no sign of them. I was desperate. I had my head out of the tank and could hear 9mm bullets hitting my tank. The Germans were firing from occupied Belgian family houses. I could feel paint chips hit my cheeks. I couldn't see a thing in the ink-black night. Next, an unseen German soldier carrying a PanzerFausst (a German anti-tank weapon similar to a U.S. Army Bazooka) got behind my tank and blew a hole through the one and one-half inch thick steel of the tank's turret. I was knocked out for about 10 to 15 seconds. When I came to, the guys in the tank were hollering, 'Get out, Lieutenant. We've been hit.' I got out by jumping the 10 feet down to the cobblestone road. My head hit the cobblestones without the protection of my helmet. I crawled around searching for my helmet so I could have a little protection from the flying debris, but the sky was so dark, I could see absolutely nothing. Since nobody else had seen our route (the tank's hatches were closed), I crawled along a hedgerow fence motioning my men to follow. At one point, the six of us had to stop dead in our tracks. We were afraid the Germans might hear our hearts beating when a German armored vehicle came directly toward us and cross our path. After what seemed like eternity, we reached our troops at the farmhouse. My brand new blanket overcoat was more of a casualty than I was. The back of it was in tatters and shreds. Almost immediately, I was evacuated to a field hospital at Arlon, twenty miles to the south of Warnach.

"When I was getting into the ambulance, I had to surrender by .45 caliber pistol. Imagine my shock when I found myself sitting with an SS Nazi Officer in his dress uniform as though he was going to a ceremony and not fighting a war. He belonged to Hitler's personal guard and special security forces. I demanded that I get my pistol back, but of course, the corpsman wouldn't give it to me. During the entire drive to Arlon, that German never looked at me once. I think he knew the end was near. When this little village (Warnach) finally fell to our troops the next day (so another officer later told me), my tank was glowing red hot from the burning gasoline and ammunition.

"I spent a week at the hospital in Arlon while a companion tank battalion, led by a future U.S. Army Chief of Staff, Lt. Col. Creighton Abrams, stormed into Bastogne, past German resistance. After a week of being 'knocked out' each day at the field hospital in Arlon, Belgium, I was ordered to take a group of three new tanks up to our battalion, now headquartered in the woods south of Bastogne. The tanks were a new version, with different silhouettes: longer cannon (76mm) supporting a muzzle brake, on other words, pretty much like a German tank. Since we were replacing lost tanks, including mine, we had no crews, just drivers and tank commanders. In the dim light and snow flurries, we were acutely aware than an American soldier might take us for hostile and have at us. That did not happen, but we did have real problems. The up and down roads in the Ardennes were coated with ice and our tank tracks were steel. The snow on the shoulder was fine perhaps for a motorcycle, but unless you could get both tank tracks on it, it only turned you around. The ordnance men welded steel studs on our tracks and they were of some help. With a lot of slipping and sliding, we got the tanks to their new home. I was given a new company of tanks and, of course, a new crew. The packaged field rations we ate on the way had left me with a bad case of hunger and I was glad to hear my new gunner mention that we had a real holiday treat in the way of food in the ration box, leftover turkey with white bread. I lost no time checking this out. The ration box was on the sloping front of the tank, held there by a horizontal board. The promised treat was there all right, frozen solid."

The K-rations of World War II fed millions of troops and civilians overseas. It took a lot of research to develop the K-ration kit for U.S. service personnel, compact, but providing a full meal, able to be carried by a solider into combat, with up to three days' supply of food. The K-ration box of food was intended to supplement field kitchens and feed troops when these were not readily available, giving the soldier 3,000 calories a day. However, this was not sufficient for troops in combat who always craved more food. The U.S. Army Corps of Engineers developed the food ration kit, beginning deliveries in May 1942 to combat troops. It was designed to be easily carried, provide the greatest variety of nutritionally balances food, in the smallest package, allowing three per day (a total of nine) to be carried soldier's backpack.

Moe..."Many people think the battle for Bastogne ended on Christmas Day, December 25, 1944, but it raged for 44 days. In addition to fighting the Germans, U.S. personnel had to battle bitter cold, which claimed thousands of men in shallow foxholes, along the ditches and on the narrow, cobbled streets of Belgian villages. At the 'Battle of the Ardennes,' it was time to pause and replace the prodigious losses in men and equipment. Equipment losses were the easy part. Thanks to the U.S. Army's extraordinary logistics system, new tanks, trucks, jeeps, artillery, etc., were soon on hand. However, with men, it was a different matter. Experienced combat replacements were out of the question. The men we received were either rear-area soldiers or arrived directly from the United States, as I had done. Therefore, I could sympathize with the replacements. They had to learn fast, since we were almost continuously on the move, leading the charge for the Third Army. Some unfortunate incidents happened. We refueled the tanks at night, from five gallon Jerry cans brought up by truck, under blackout conditions so as not to give away our position to German troops. A new man, unaware of the danger of static electricity, sparked a fire that brightly illuminated our sector of the front line positions and cost us a tank. Another, on guard in the turret at night, while the other crewmembers slept, challenged a figure approaching from the direction of the enemy. Not hearing or misunderstanding the password, fired one round from the big .50 caliber machine gun. Result, one dead American returning from a patrol. Another time, an exhausted U.S. Army infantryman curled up in his blanket in the snow under the rear of a tank. When the tank was ordered to move in the darkness, the steel tanks crushed and killed him. Again, one of the new men, when moving into a house in Luxembourg, dropped his loaded machine gun onto the wood floor, hitting the floor muzzle up. This caused the machine gun's heavy bolt to cycle back, then forward, firing a bullet through him. A continuous danger that was not solely confined to new replacements was that around machines, like tanks, half-tracks, machine guns, etc., it was impossible to keep one's gloves from becoming oil-soaked and wet. Without the protection provided by gloves in the brutal cold temperatures, one's fingers could freeze to the metal. This caused massive cases of black, bleeding and chapped skin. A U.S. Army Medic gave me a tip, use Burma Shave. It contained lanolin and was a tremendous help. Our infantry suffered greatly from trench foot, the consequences of wet, cold boots, which we could rarely remove to dry out. Many had to be evacuated with amputations common until General Patton ordered that each man be issued a clean, dry pair of wool socks in each day's rations."[62]

Peter J. Dahlberg..."We departed the United States from the port of Boston. We spent seven days and nights on the stormy North Atlantic. We landed at Liverpool, England. From there, we rode a train to Southampton, where we occupied a 'tent city,' a makeshift type of barracks thrown together with canvas tents. On December 25, 1944, we were scheduled to be flown across the English Channel. The 'Battle of the Bulge' was raging fiercely and reinforcements were needed badly. The fog, however, proved too intense, so two days after later we were taken down to the harbor and loaded into an old Spanish flag-registered vessel. Almost immediately after boarding we were ordered off. As we filed off the ship we were met by men carrying their M1 rifles, boarding the ship in our place. The next day, we heard that the ship had been torpedoed in the English Channel with the loss of nearly 500 men, jumping of the ship into the icy waters with their steel combat helmets fastened on, their necks broken as they hit the water, quickly drowning. The following day, 28 December, we boarded a LST and safely crossed the English Channel under the cover of darkness. We landed at LeHarve, France and we were soon in small boxcars, called '40 et 8,' which meant there was room from 40 men or eight horses. Some of the men lit a bonfire in the middle of our boxcar, and almost asphyxiated us. Finally, we arrived in the heart of France. There, we were issued our rifles, loaded into U.S. Army trucks and hauled to the front lines at the edge of the Belgium border. It was the dead of winter in Europe, the worst weather in a century. Deep snow covered the ground and it was bitterly cold! Living in foxholes was not a pleasant experience, but holding the line was far better than the actual combat going on, just a few miles away."[63]

During the "Battle of the Bulge," Colonel Leonel M. Jensen of South Dakota was assigned to the U.S. Army 75th Infantry Division, Field Director, American Red Cross (ARC). The 75th Infantry Divi-

---

[62] Lt. Col. George A. Larson, USAF (Ret.), "Personal look at the Battle of the Bulge," research for World War II display of war memorabilia and personal recollections for Rapid City Journey Museum, Tribute to Local Veterans, January 2004.

[63] Peter J. Dahlberg of Rapid City, South Dakota. During World War II he was one of the stateside replacements, mentioned by George Moe, who was fed into the "Battle of the Bulge" as a rifle infantryman replacement, assigned to the 78th Infantry Division. Information provided during interview with the author on January 15, 2004.

sion departed Camp Breckinridge, Kentucky on October 15, 1944, traveling by train to Camp Shanks, New York. On 22 October, the division boarded a transport for the crossing of the North Atlantic to England, arriving on 3 November. Division training and equipment issue was completed in England. The division was transported across the English Channel in LSTs on 10 December. The division formed up a cohesive element at LeHarve, France, moving by train to Wiljre, Netherlands. While on the train, the division was diverted to Tongres, Belgium. The 75th Infantry Division traveled the 250 miles by train in French railroad boxcars referred to as "40 by 8," with motorized division elements moved by road. The German attack in the Ardennes changed the division's destinations, setting up headquarters at Ocquier, Belgium. Due to pressing battlefield-deteriorating conditions, the 75th personnel and equipment was fed piecemeal into areas to plug the German offensive, December 24, 1944 to January 14, 1945. The division suffered 407 killed, 1,707 wounded, 334 missing in action, and because of fighting in the harsh winter weather suffered another 2,623 casualties, so severely affected to be classified by Army Medics as non-effective personnel, removed from combat.[64]

It is impossible to cover in detail all the fighting during the "Battle of the Bulge." The following is a post battle summary of the 75th Infantry Division's fighting, pulled from the U.S. Army War College Library. On December 24, 1944, the Division's Combat Teams 209 and 289 were assigned to support the Third Armored Division. The bulk of the division was positioned along the L'Ourthe River, defending the line between Bomal and Grandmenil. Combat Team 209 moved south out of Hotton-Soy to create a defensive position along the line of Grandmenil and Blier. The Second Battalion, 291st Infantry was assigned to support the Second Armored Division at Sommeleuze, Bel-

---

[64] During the "Battle of the Bulge," Colonel Leonel M. Jensen of South Dakota was assigned to the U.S. Army 75th Infantry Division, Field Director, American Red Cross (ARC). He had the unique opportunity to travel throughout Belgium and later into Germany because he had a vehicle and pass to travel in the forward combat areas. He carried a camera and took photographs of the areas he traveled through, documenting the effects of the intense fighting during December 1944. He was a great collector of World War II memorabilia and shipped trunks home containing this material. His son, Paul Jensen of Rapid City allowed the author access to this material and it was used for a World War II display for the Rapid City Journey Museum's tribute to area veterans.

gium, creating a ready combat reserve for the VII U.S. Army Corps.

On 25 December, Combat Team 290 cleared the Hotton-Soy road of German troops. However, as it neared the village of Werpin, the Germans were positioned on high ground, blocking the Hotton-Hampteau Road. Company K of Combat Team 290 had to cross a football size open area to conduct a frontal attack on the German defensive positions, taking losses, but with support on its flank by Companies I and L, succeeded in capturing the high ground. From a historical entry into the "Battle of the Bulge," Germans on this high ground represented their farthest advance toward Liege. One soldier from Company K fired his bazooka, knocking an advancing German tank east of Grandmenil. The 75th infantry Division soldiers supported the 3rd and 7th Armored Divisions in the area. They provided ground support to assist in the capture of Grandmenil on 26 December. They were ordered to dig in to protect the town from an expected German counterattack.

On 27 December, the division's troops were assigned to the XVIII Airborne Corps. However, Combat Teams 289 and 290 remained with the 3rd Armored Division. The Second Battalion of the 291st was released from the Second Armored Division. On 28 December, the Second Battalion shifted combat positions, taking up defensive positions south of St. Gertrude, remaining there until the next day. On the night of 27 December, the First Battalion of the 289th Infantry came under attack by the Volks Grenadier Regiment, repulsing the attack. The First Battalion then moved its front lines to the west to shoulder up with the 2nd Battalion. The spreading of troops over a greater distance allowed the 25th and 26th Panzer Regiments, 12th Panzer Division to penetrate U.S. defenses at this location, reaching Sadzot before being stopped by U.S. troops. On 28 December, the 75th Division's ground troops advanced down the Aisne River, attacking and mopping up remaining pockets of German troop resistance. On 29 December, the 289th Infantry was released, returned to the 75th Division. Combat Team 290 remained on defense, under control of the Third Armored Division. In addition, the 291st Infantry relieve units of the 7th Armored Division operating in the Grandmenil-Manhey sector, moving to relieve the 517th Parachute Infantry Battalion on January 2, 1945.

The 75th Division returned to the VII Corps on 2 January. Company F, 289th Infantry attacked Croix St. Jeanne, south against a German company dug in on the heights west of Veiux-Forneaux. The attacking company withdrew to allow U.S. artillery to shell German positions. The division continued to operate against pockets of German resistance through the remaining time of the "Battle of the Bulge."[65]

---

[65] United States Army War College Library, "Battle of the Bulge," research in August 1983, during the author's assignment with the Joint Chiefs of Staff, Alternate Military Command Center, Fort Ritchie, Maryland, for United States Air Force War College paper on "Strategy and Tactics."

Paul Priest

Crossing the Rhine River at Remagen, Germany

The Last Remaining Bridge Over the Rhine River

AS Allied troops advanced along a broad front line toward Nazi Germany in the winter of 1945, the U.S. Army was eager to capture an intact bridge over the Rhine River to allow its troops and heavy equipment to advance rapid into Germany. The Rhine was the last major natural obstacle to Allied forces on their nine-month offensive, which began on D-Day, June 6, 1944, at Normandy, France. U.S. aerial reconnaissance identified two bridges still standing over the Rhine. One was at Oberkassel near Dusseldorf. The 83rd Division moved forward to capture the bridge. As American troops approached, German engineers blew up the bridge. The second remaining bridge was south of Waddington. Units of the 2nd Armored and 98th Infantry Divisions pushed toward the intact bridge. American troops reached and crossed the bridge, but a German counter attack drove them back, allowing their engineers time to blow up the bridge. This near capture of this Rhine River bridge created great fear in Berlin. Adolf Hitler ordered the remaining Rhine River bridges blown up, even if German Army units were still fighting on the west bank, cut off from escaping across the river.

German troops following Hitler's orders blew up the Rhine River bridges except the Ludendorff Railway Bridge at Remagen, a Roman constructed town between Bonn and Koblenz. German engineers had built the 1,000 foot long railroad bridge during World War I to move supplies and troops to the Western Front from the Ruhr Valley. After World War I, France occupied the area and took control of the bridge. French engineers filled the demolition chambers with cement, making the bridge stronger and difficult to destroy. Remagen, which had been fought over, occupied at one time or another by troops from France, Spain, Sweden and Russia was considered a resort location. It contained restaurants, cafes and all types of shops in the old section of the city, which surrounded the four-towered Gothic church of St. Apollinaris and remains of the saint, who was martyred in Italy, AD 79. Beyond the town rose a 600 foot cliff known as Erpelor Ley.

The Rhine River current is strong at Remagen, 300 feet wide with a tributary of the Ahr Rhine adding to the turbulence a mile upriver from the town. The Ludendorff Railway Bridge, which residents of Remagen resented for ruining their fine view down the Rhine, passed through the 1,200 foot tunnel on the Erpelor Ley before continuing east into the Ruhr Valley. The Allies mounted repeated air attacks against the bridge after the Battle of the Bulge in an effort to slow the movement of German troops, equipment and supplies to the fighting in Belgium. U.S. air attacks damaged the bridge, but German engineers repaired the damage. The bridge was scheduled to be attacked on the morning of March 7, 1945, but the bombing raid cancelled because of bad weather.

That morning, a reconnaissance unit of the U.S. 9th Armored Division reached Remagen and reported the sight that the Ludendorff Railway Bridge remained intact. Second Lieutenant Karl Timmermann of the 27th Armored Infantry Regiment, commanded the forward U.S. unit. He was half-German ancestry, the son of an American doughboy who fought in World War I and a German mother. He had been born one hundred miles from Remagen at Frankfurt am Main, immigrated to the United States with his parents as an infant. Leading the scouting party in a Jeep Lt. Timmerman rounded a hillside north of Remagen and looked down to the river. The two white stone supports were intact. German troops laid wooden planks across the bridge's railroad tracks to allow tanks and trucks to cross the river. Thousands of troops and civilians jammed the bridge, making it a tempting target for Allied warplanes. Timmermann radioed his battalion commander, Lt. Col. Leonard Engerman that the bridge was intact.

At noon, Brigadier General William M. Hoge, Commander, Combat Group B, 9th Armored Division, III Corps, First Army received verification from Engerman that the Ludendorff Railway Bridge was intact. Against standing orders not to deviate from the planned objective of Ahrweiler, he ordered Engerman to seize the bridge..."Get those men moving into the town." Engerman radioed back..."Already in their way." Timmermann moved to take a platoon of Pershing tanks assigned to the 14th Tank Battalion, each armed with a 90mm main gun, moving down the hill toward the town. Engerman ordered his troops to..."Go down into the town. Get through it as quickly as possible and reach the bridge. The infantry will follow on foot. Their half-tracks will bring up the rear. Let's make it snappy."

The Pershing tanks clattered down the winding road into Remagen followed by the infantry. The Americans moved and advanced rapidly against spotty German resistance. German soldiers captured from houses on the outskirts of Remagen were asked about the defenses in the town and on the bridge. One German soldier told the Americans that the Ludendorff Railway Bridge was to be blown up at 4 p.m. Similar intelligence had been obtained earlier by troops assigned to the 52nd Armored Infantry Battalion, several miles from Remagen. These reports were relayed to General Hoge who radioed Engerman at 3:15 p.m..."You've got 45 minutes to take the bridge." Engerman radioed the lead Pershing tank commander, Lt. John Grimball..."Get to the bridge as quickly as possible." Grimball radioed back..."Sir, I am already there." The Pershings began firing at a long string of freight cars on the east bank, destroying the entire train.

German defenders at Remagen were commanded by Captain Willi Bratge, a former schoolteacher who had been given the unenviable task of guarding the bridge with a handful of wounded, elderly and conscripted soldiers, some of whom were Russian volunteers captured on the Eastern Front. Bratge ordered the construction an elaborate system of foxholes and bunkers, but only defended by 36 troops. The bridge had been wired with an electric detonation fusing system connected to a control switch inside the entrance to the Erpeler Ley Tunnel. Sixty boxes of high explosives were placed along the bridge's length, ready to be set off at the last minute by combat engineers.

On the morning of 7 March, German Major Hans Scheller was sent to take over the defense of Remagen and destruction of the bridge. Scheller was unfamiliar with the town, the troops and the bridge itself. He had scarcely arrived when news German units on the hill above the town had been attacked by American tanks and accompanying infantry. A German artillery officer approached Scheller indicating his battalion was approaching to seize the bridge. He pleaded with the officers not to blow up the bridge before his troops crossed it. Scheller agreed. Scheller and Bratge established their headquarters inside the mouth of the tunnel on the far side of the bridge and waited for the American to reach the bridge. Much time was lost. The Americans appeared on the far bank and started firing.

Even though German defenders of the bridge waited until the last moment before blowing it up, there was no assurance the American troops could make it across the bridge before the demolition charges were set off. Engerman reasoned the Germans would wait until the tanks roared onto the bridge before setting off the demolition charges. Infantry led by Timmermann advanced through Remagen and toward the bridge. Meanwhile, the Pershings took up firing positions at the west end of the bridge. As troops of the 27th Armored Infantry Regiment, Company A, reached the west end of the bridge at 3:50 p.m., the Germans set off the demolition charges creating a large crater at the west end. The crater prevented Pershings from crossing the bridge. A second demolition charge detonation was set off when Company A reached the two-thirds distance across the bridge. The explosion knocked out the steel diagonal bridge supports on the upstream side, destroying a section of wood planking and flooring, causing the bridge to sag six-inches. The charges failed to drop the bridge into the river below, allowing American troops to continue to move across the bridge.

One of the first infantrymen to cross the bridge was Paul Priest of Flint, Michigan, now living in Box Elder, South Dakota. He recalled many years later in an interview in Rapid City in the author's home..."I almost did not make it to the Rhine River, being involuntarily assigned as a replacement crewman in a Sherman tank. I did not like it and after one day asked the Captain of the tank unit to let me out, which he did. I was assigned to the Division's Headquarters Company, performing reconnaissance patrols. On March 5, 1945, two days before we reached the Rhine River, I was detached from the lead division's reconnaissance group, dropped off at a road checkpoint to guide the division's vehicles as to which one of the three roads to take. I took up my guard post at 3:30 p.m. I was told the division should reach my position by 4 to 4:30 p.m. The vehicles did not reach me by that time. It kept getting later and later. I went out and picked up all the guns I could locate, creating a large pile near the gas station I decided to use as cover for the evening. These weapons were all over the ground. I recovered them from dead German soldiers in the area, fearing that someone may pick one up and turn it on me.

"I was in the building until 9:30 p.m. At that time, I heard the sound of tank tracks coming toward my location. It was the lead column of the 9th Armored Division. I showed the lead tank which road to follow. I climbed onto the lead tank, rejoining my reconnaissance unit in time to make the historic dash across the Ludendorff Railway Bridge over the Rhine River. On the morning of 7 March, I was in the group heading toward the bridge. I was not with the lead group of soldiers, but further back in the reconnaissance column. Our tanks quickly knocked out the train on the eastern bank. There were many secondary explosions. The first tank knocked out the train's engine, bringing the train to a stop in a large cloud of steam released from the destroyed engine.

"I was in the lead group of infantry attacking across the bridge when the tanks had to stop because of the large crater at the west end of the bridge. The demolition charge was set off in front of me. We were taking machine gun fire from the two bridge towers at the east end of the bridge. I was not thinking about anything other than making it safely to the other side of the Rhine River."

Pershing tanks provided covering fire for the advancing Company A, which was quickly followed by the 2nd and 3rd platoons. At about the same time, three 9th Armored Division engineers were on the bridge cutting wires to four-pound demolition charges that had not been set off. The engineers were led by Lt. Hugh Mott and supported by SSgt. John Reynolds and Sgt. Eugene Dorland. They located remaining unexploded demolition charge cables, discovering the cable was too thick to cut with pliers. Lt. Mott used his carbine, firing three shots, cutting the cable. Sgt. Joseph DeLisio knocked out the enemy machine gun in one of the east bridge towers and TSgt. Mike Chinchar knocked out the remaining machine gun. American troops ran across the bridge. The first U.S. infantryman to make it across to the east bank of the Rhine River was Sgt. Alexander Drabik of Toledo, Ohio; he was joined a few seconds later by Timmermann, the first officer of an invading army to set foot on German soil since Napoleon's Grand Army in the early 19th Century.

Priest..."One of our Pershing tanks, fitted with a bulldozer blade, filled in the crater at the west end of the bridge to allow tanks to move across the bridge. Engineers were also on the bridge to repair the hole in the flooring about two-thirds across the bridge. Once the east tower machine guns were silenced, we cleaned out the tunnel of scattered German troops, mostly young kids and older men. I helped paint a sign on a piece of wood planking, nailing it up on the east bank of the bridge: 'cross the Rhine with dry feet/courtesy of the 9th Armd Div.' We moved through the railway tunnel, into the cliffs beyond, attacking the remaining German 88mm and four 20mm flak guns. Our Pershing tanks destroyed some of the 88mm guns and others were abandoned by German troops, which we destroyed with grenades. We did not encounter any real organized German resistance, for one day, until the Germans brought in more troops."

With American troops moving across the bridge, German defenders remained inside the dark railway tunnel. Scheller tried to rally his troops for a counter attack, but they refused to attack. No one wanted to be the last man to die contesting American entry into Germany. Scheller took a bicycle and pedaled to the rear for new orders. On his way back to LXVII Corps headquarters at Aktwied, he was arrested, court-martialed for deserting his post, executed along with two engineers and the anti-aircraft commander, who had failed to blow up the bridge. Back at the bridge Bratge and the remaining troops attempted to exit the opening from Remagen, only to find it blocked by American troops. Bratge noticed another group of soldiers and civilians leaving through the front entrance beneath a white flag. It gave him the necessary cover to save his honor.

The full exploitation of the bridgehead almost did not happen because of a command failure at the highest level of the American Army. Overall, operational planning for offensive operations east of the Rhine was under control of Supreme Allied Headquarters Allied Expeditionary Forces. Major General Harold Bull, in charge of G-3 Intelligence, did not want the broad front plan of advancement to be discontinued. General Omar Bradley, Commander Twelfth Army Group, telephoned General Dwight Eisenhower, Commander Allied Forces, with the news that the 9th Armored Division had captured the Ludendorff Railway Bridge intact across the Rhine River and had established a bridgehead on the east bank. Within 24 hours after the German failure to destroy the bridge 8,000 U.S. troops, large numbers of tanks, self-propelled artillery and trucks crossed the Rhine River into Germany. Not everything went smoothly. Tanks assigned to Company A, 14th Tank Battalion, crossed the Rhine River, but one tank destroyer assigned to the 656th Tank Destroyer Battalion broke through the wood planking on the bridge, blocking following vehicles. U.S. troops in following half-tracks climbed out of their vehicles and walked across the bridge. It took some time to clear the stuck tank destroyer and continue the movement of heavy equipment across the bridge. After the first 24 hours, the German 9th and 11th Panzer Divisions were repositioned around the American bridgehead across the Rhine River, effectively isolating the U.S. 9th Armored Division.

On 9 March, ten German Air Force aircraft, eight of which were Stuka dive-bombers, attacked the bridge, scoring two hits on the bridge. On 15 March, a larger force of 20 turbojet aircraft, a mixture of twin-turbojet engine Me-262 fighters and twin-engine Arado AR-234 B-1 bombers attacked the bridge. These jet aircraft scored no hits on the bridge. Priest..."This was the first time I saw turbojet aircraft. At first, I thought the aircraft had been hit by our on anti-aircraft fire, but the smoke was coming from their twin turbojet engines. They dove from altitude, attacking at a high rate of speed. They were very fast, dropping bombs on the bridge. None of these bombs hit the bridge splashing all around the bridge. The Germans were desperately trying to knock out the bridge."

After General Eisenhower ordered the bridgehead to be exploited, American police on the west bank of the Rhine Rover dealt with a large traffic jam of military vehicles and thousands of infantry. All roads leading to the bridge were packed slowing movement across the river. To protect the bridge from attack by German aircraft, flak vehicles were lined side by side on the west bank of the river, supported by artillery firing across the river at German troops attempting to isolate the one and one-half mile deep and one and one-half mile wide American bridgehead. Beginning on 9 March, German artillery shelled the bridge and engineers from the 51st and 291st Engineering Battalions working to repair the bridge's damage. In addition, engineers from these two battalions constructed pontoon and Treadway bridges across the Rhine River on either side of the Ludendorff Railway Bridge to increase vehicle traffic and tonnage into Germany. They were also a backup against the possibility that the Germans would be able to destroy the railway bridge.

Engineers continued to work during heavy German field artillery shelling. Meanwhile, German civilians were removed from Remagen to eliminate the possibility of German troops receiving clandestine reports on what was happening on the west bank and the accuracy of their artillery shelling. American engineers worked 24 hours a day to keep the Ludendorff Railway Bridge operational. The Germans made continued efforts to destroy the bridge. They floated a barge, containing explosives, downstream in an attempt to destroy the bridge. This was attempted at night but not a hidden effort. U.S. troops intercepted the barge, preventing it from getting close enough to the bridge piers to destroy the structure. Mines were also floated downstream in efforts to blow up the bridge, but U.S. sharp shooters fired at the mines, blowing them up before they could reach the bridge. Volunteer German troops, wearing rubber suits, entered the cold Rhine River waters upstream, towing explosives behind them in efforts to blow up the bridge. They were detected by American troops along the river's east bank, killing or capturing before they could place explosives on the bridge's piers.

The Germans tried to make do with troops and weapons they had along the east bank of the Rhine River. The capture of the bridge isolated 300,000 German troops and their equipment west of the Rhine River. The German secret weapon, the V-2 rocket was even used against the bridge. Prior to the rocket attack, German troops pulled back from the American bridgehead a distance of nine miles, out of the possible rocket warhead impact. The unit assigned to fire the V-2s was located at Hellendorn, Netherlands, 130 miles north of Remagen. They moved into the area on 8 March. Because of repeated Allied air attacks on its supply lines, the V-2 unit suffered fuel and supply shortages. Hitler ordered 50 to 100 V-2s to be fired at the bridge, destroying it over a two-day period, but the rocket unit only was able to fire eleven at the bridge on 17 March. One V-2 impacted and detonated near the Apollinaris church in Remagen, one mile from the bridge. The warhead destroyed several buildings around the church with blast extending out to a distance of 3,000 feet. The resulting ground and air shock wave was felt throughout the town. A second V-2 splashed into the Rhine, one mile from the bridge. A third V-2 landed in Remagen, destroying a building in which 12 U.S. troops were billeted, killing three. A fourth V-2 struck the command and control post of U.S. Army Engineer Combat Group, killing three and injuring thirty-one.

Even though no V-2s hit the bridge, ground shock waves, along with the effects of the demolition charges, constant and heavy U.S. military vehicle traffic eventually weakened the bridge causing it to collapse. At 3 p.m. on 17 March, the bridge feel into the Rhine River, killing 28 U.S. Army engineers. Priest..."I was not in the area when the bridge collapsed from the volley of V-2 rockers. We had moved up into the hills, up through a gulley. This was where I was shot be a German soldier using a wooden bullet in his rifle. The impact took my helmet off. I was kept in the line, the wound considered only a flesh wound. Fortunately, by the time the bridge collapsed, pontoon bridges took up the burden of moving men and equipment across the Rhine River. The bridge was a mass of twisted metal, visible near both the west and east banks of the Rhine River. When I left the United States, I brought with me a small fold out camera, and I was able to take photographs as we moved place to place. I also took photographs from German troops we encountered and disarmed during their personal searches. As we moved away from the Rhine River, many German troops surrendered to us. They threw their weapons onto the ground, raising their arms into the air, surrendering. I did not take part in any large actions after crossing the Rhine River. German troops gave up, surrendering to U.S. or British troops rather than to advancing Soviet Army troops to the east. It was at this time I found out my parents had received a telegram reporting my death in Germany. It was another Paul Priest. However, things like that happen in war. It was a great relief to my parents when they heard I was still alive when they got a letter from me."[66]

---

[66] Lt. Col. George A. Larson, USAF (Ret.), "Bridging the Rhine at Remagen," *Military Heritage,* August 2007.

Gale Holbrook

96th United States Naval Construction Battalion

Philippines and China

THE Japanese attack on Pearl Harbor, dramatically revealed the urgent military requirement for rapidly mobilized construction and repair units. On January 5, 1942, authority was given to the U.S. Bureau of Navigation to recruit men from America's civil construction trades to man Naval Construction regiments, composed to three Naval Construction Battalions. The men in these units were referred to as Seabees. Age range for enlisted men was 18 to 50, averaged 37. Interestingly, after December 1942, President Franklin Roosevelt ordered further USNCB enlistments to come from those registered in the Selective Service System (draft). A Seabee construction battalion consisted of 31 officers and 1,073 enlisted in four companies. A headquarters company was attached, consisting of medical and dental doctors and technicians, administrative personnel, storekeepers, cooks and other specialists.

Gale Holbrook..."I was born in Lemon, South Dakota, in the northwest corner of the state near the North Dakota border. I graduated from high school in Lemon in 1942, after the United States entered World War II on December 8, 1941, the day after the Japanese attack on Pearl Harbor. On December 7, 1941, my father was the Standard Oil agent in Lemon. A warehouse went along with the station's operations. We were at the station on Sunday afternoon of 7 December and one of our customers came along and wanted to get some oil and grease. He said... 'Did you hear about Pearl Harbor?' We answered...'No, we had not.' He told us the facts that the Japanese had attacked Pearl Harbor. I went out to Seattle, Washington and started working in the Boeing B-17 Flying Fortress plant. My brother and his wife lived in Seattle and I stayed with them." At this time in the war, Seattle Boeing was producing the B-17F, with over 2,300 built before production shifted to the B-17G with the forward firing chin turret to discourage head on fighter attacks on the bomber formations. Holbrook..."We returned to Lemon and I stayed for four to five months. I knew damn well I was going to be drafted, because on February 24, 1943, I received my notice of classification to 1-A, order number 10466. I decided just to get on with it. I went to Fort Snelling in Minneapolis, Minnesota to enlist.

"While at Fort Snelling, I had to take a physical examination. Everything was going along fine until we got to the point where they had to check to determine if you were colorblind. I guess it was because the old Navy needed that because they used colored signal flags to send messages between close in ships. You had to know what the correct color was of these flags. In line, this was next for me. I got up to the guy with the color exam and he wanted to know what the number was on the colored chart and I told him...'I don't know.' He told me...'Get to the back of the line and when you get back to me, tell me it is 18.' I said...'O.k., I can do that.' Therefore, that went along fine and I was sent to Farragut, Idaho for Boot Camp training.

"I took my training there. While I was there, one day on the rife range, training on the proper use of the M-1 carbine. They told us to lay day and shoot at the target down range. In my laying down, my rifle went off. The instructor said...'Who in the Hell shot that round?' I was not going to stand up and said I did. I went to Camp Perry, supposedly for more training. However, we did not do too much. I worked as a guard in the military brig. We were shipped/assigned to the 96th USNCB in August 1944."

The 96th USNCB, after activation on June 12, 1943, transferred from Davisville, Rhode Island to Gulf Port, Mississippi, then back to Davisville. On 31 December, the battalion sailed to Terceira, Azores, arriving on January 9, 1944. The battalion built the Santa Rita Camp, worked in the Pria Docks and Logens Airfield at Terceira. The battalion returned to the United States on August 3, 1944 to Bayonne, New Jersey for reorganization for its second overseas deployment, this time to the Pacific Theater of Operations.

Holbrook..."They shipped us to Treasure Island, California in San Francisco, California. I was a replacement for the 96th USNCB. We were shipped to Quoddy Village, Maine by train along the northern route. Once on the train, some of my passenger car mates acted up. The World War II passenger cars were not built for comfort with wood seats/benches. For some stupid reason, some of the guys got to talking...'You know it would be fun for some of us to stand up on one side of the passenger car and some on the other side, then one side jumps up and lands and the other side repeats the jumping.' They did this over and over again, getting the passenger car rocking side to side until stopped by the conductor. I did not want to play that game.

Quoddy Village, Maine was a little community that President Roosevelt helped set up through the Federal government to build a dam across the estuary to harness the high tides to produce electric power, but did not pan out. We were there for six to eight months. Went back to Treasure Island, California. We shipped out on January 27, 1945 for a 45 day sea transport voyage to the Philippines Islands. We were then sent on to Manicani Island."[67]

The 96th USNCB was sent to Manicani Island in the Samara area of the Philippine Islands, beginning construction work there on March 13, 1945. The principal naval development was at the southeastern tip of Samara. The naval base was located on a peninsula, three miles wide and 11 miles long, and on Calicoan Island, which is more than a mile wide and seven miles long, and is separated from Samar by 800 feet of shallow water. Guiuan, site of the headquarters for this area, was in the middle of the Peninsula on the eastern area, was in the middle of the peninsula on the eastern shore of Leyte Gulf.

A major destroyer repair base and a ship repair unit were built on Manicani Island, eight miles west of Guiuan. This project included wharves, berths for several large floating dry docks, administration buildings, shops, water and steam lines, power system, and fire protection system. Construction of a pier to accommodate vessels of 45 foot draft required 100 feet of coral fill and a timber approach 40 feet wide. A 1,500 by 80 foot pier was built, using one floating and two skid rigs to drive 3,400 pilings, up to 100 feet long. Many of the pilings were spliced to reach the required length. Despite a delay of six weeks waiting for long pilings, the project was completed in four and a half months. A pontoon pier and a jetty for LSTs were constructed in the northwest cove.

Ship repair facilities were housed in 80 Quonset huts and 150,000 square feet of large timber trussed structures. When completed, the repair unit had facilities for the repair and maintenance of any ship from the Pacific Fleet, from a battleship to an LCM. Coincident with this work, 25,000 feet of lines were installed for a saltwater fire protection system, sanitation, fresh water and steam systems. Numerous power stations, each consisting of two dozen 75 kilowatt diesel generators and all necessary distribution systems (power lines and transformers) were provided for the entire area. At least six floating dry docks, including the giant sectional ABSD's, were brought to Manicani Island.

---

[67] Gale Holbrook, Rapid City, South Dakota, interview, Lt. Col. George A. Larson, USAF (Ret.), January 6, 2012.

Water for this activity was obtained from local water shed one half mile wide and three-fourths a mile long. The water was pumped from the collection point to a water treatment plant with a capacity of 840,000 gallons per day. Personnel housing and messing facilities for 10,000 men were constructed with tents and frame huts. Approximately 150 acres of swampland were converted to hard ground to accommodate the construction, 150,000 cubic yards of coral being excavated from the bay. Harbor improvements at this activity included the moving of approximately 5,000,000 yards of material by blasting and dredging. [68]

Holbrook..."One of my friends was working on one of the concrete docks, I think with a jackhammer or some sort of power equipment. At that time, the news came the war was over and that friend of mine just picked up the equipment and threw it off the dock into the water. I was a Coxin by this time in the war. We were on Manicani Island and our supply base was on Guiuan. To move supplies from there we had to have boat crews and barges. I don't remember how many barges we operated. The reason I got the Coxin rating advancement was interesting. When I would come back from getting supplies, with my barge fully loaded, I was very cautious coming into the dock. I certainly did not want to hit the docks, damaging the wharf area or my barge. The guys had worked hard to complete the dock and make necessary improvements. So, I came in slow and cautiously. One of our officers noticed and recorded my piloting the loaded barge. I had to learn this on the job and it was something I had not been trained to do in the States. During one time I was pulling into the dock at Guiuan, I saw this Navy guy come off a barge tied alongside the supply pier and he had a case of beer. He moved toward a wood, dugout canoe. He loaded the case of beer into the canoe, placing it by others inside the dugout. Hell, I thought we would just pull alongside that barge a get a couple cases of beer for ourselves. We were about just about ready to cast off from that barge when a guy said...'What in the Hell are you guys doing?' It was pretty clear to figure out what we were doing, loading beer from the barrage into ours. I was taken off my barge, marched to the brig, where I spent the night, accused of attempting to steal beer. Well, the next day I made it back to Manicani, and my commander already had received the report of the incident on Guiuan. I was assigned a Jewish JAG officer, former private attorney

---

[68] *Building the Navy's Bases in World War II: History of the Bureau of Yards and Docks and the Civil Engineer Corps, 1940-1946.*

in the States, who commented to me...'What in the Hell is the guy at Guiuan thinking of. You cannot be charged with or accused of attempting to steal beer. You do it, or you don't do it.' So that is how the lawyer got me out of that mess. We went through the chow line in the evening and the next morning, if my brother had been on duty at that time, I would have seen him in the chow line. I did not know he was on the island. I had not known about his assignment to Manicani Island. So, we had an opportunity to be together for a short time. I was good to see Ellis and realize the war was over with Japan. We were shipped to China." [69]

After the surrender of Japan, the Third Marine Amphibious Corps was detailed to assist the Chinese government on the repatriation of Japanese troops home to Japan. To assist the Marines, four construction battalions and two special battalions were sent to China as the Marine unit set up headquarters at Tientsin, China. In November 1945, part of the 33rd Seabee Regiment, consisting of the 83rd, 96th and 122nd Battalions and the 32nd Special Battalion landed at Tsing Tao and Tang Ku. Part of the 42nd Battalion landed at Shanghai with Naval Advance Base Unit Number 13.

The 96th Seabees, after building quarters for themselves and repairing ten miles of road from the city of Tsing Tao to a former Japanese built airfields, were assigned in early January 1946 the task of rebuilding and expanding the airfield for use by U.S. Marines, Navy and Chinese Air Force. The two 3,800 foot strips were repaired and extended to 5,000 feet and 6,000 feet, respectively, with 900 foot approach strips. The project included the construction of a complete drainage system for the field extension of the runways required the removal of rock hills and the resulting excavation of 350,000 cubic yards of weathered granite. Section B of the 122nd Battalion assisted the 96th in trucking operations at Tsing Tao. Section B of the 32nd Special Battalion handled the stevedore activities. Section A of the 122nd was assigned to Peiping, and Section A of the 32nd to Tang Ku, where the 83rd Seabees had been sent to construct harbor facilities. [70]

Holbrook..."We were at Cheng Tau. What we did there was not too much for my section, except get a flavor of the Chinese culture. No construction. Of course, we were not there very long. The one thing I remember seeing was the Chinese with their small wood dug-

---

[69] Holbrook.
[70] Navy Bases in WWII.

out canoes going along the sides of our barge, picking off the barnacles growing there. These Chinese were hungry and looking for everything possible to eat, almost all the time.

"We did our cooking on the barge. One morning, our cook must have got carried away with the breakfast ingredient proportions and prepared a whole bunch of pancakes, more than we could eat. The excess food was just going to be thrown away so I decided to take the extra pancakes up the gangplank and onto the dock. Some of the Chinese who I had seen picking off barnacles from the barge were on the dock. They saw the food I carried. I was just going to hand out the food, but an intense fight broke out among the Chinese. I dropped the food and immediately retreated. I could have gotten killed. They were hungry and they wanted the food. It was a mess, a real fight for survival. They would have killed for that food. I was very lucky not to have been injured. Another incident I remember was when a Chinese troop ship came in and docked not too far from our barge. I walked over to look at the ship and see what was happening. The first thing the Chinese did was unload a huge iron kettle onto the concrete/stone dock. They filled it with water, stacked and ignited wood around the kettle, bringing water to boil, adding rice to cook. This was what they ate.

"We had no idea of why we were in China. No one told us much about it. We were pretty much separated from the main body of the 96th. I just thought they did not know what else to do with us. I did not have enough points to be sent home because I entered the war later than others in the battalion."[71]

By the end of January 1946, all personnel not eligible for release from the service had been transferred to the 96th and Section B of the 32nd Special Battalion, which remained in China. The other units were inactivated. The 32nd (Section B) was inactivated on May 1, 1946, and the 96th was scheduled to be inactivated on July 1, 1946, when a Seabee detachment was to assume maintenance of the Tsing Tao airfield. By May 1946, Seabees had been withdrawn from the South Pacific and Southwest Pacific area, except Manus and Milne Bay. There were still regiments at Okinawa, Samar, Marianas, Hawaiian Islands and a single groups (for the most part detachments) or maintenance units in the Philippines, Iwo Jima, Eniwetok, Kwajalein, Peleliu and Alaska. Maintenance units were still on duty in Iceland, Argentina, Trinidad, Bermuda, St. Thomas, Panama (Atlantic side of the locks) and a single

---

[71] Holbrook.

detachment at Exter. [72]

Holbrook…"I left China on a troop transport for Treasure Island, California. I was there a short time, discharged. They gave me my back pay and travel allowance to get home. I decided to hitch hike home and save my money and relax, taking in the sights on the way home. That went very well. In those days, you didn't stand on the roadway very long before, you were picked up wearing any kind of a military uniform. I made good time. I went to Great Falls, Montana in the northern part of the state. One of my brothers lived in Great Falls. He had been in the CCC before the war, enlisted in the U.S. Army. He served in North Africa, Sicily, Italy and had a lot of military points to be released from active duty when the war was over. I visited him and then hitch hiked to Billings, Montana where my other brother was. I visited him for a little while. I hitch hiked to Baker, where I bought a passenger train ticket on the Milwaukee Railroad for the short hope to Lemon, South Dakota.

"When I got off the passenger car at the Lemon depot, I left my duffle bag inside, because no one was going to bother a serviceman's duffle bag. I thought I would just walk down main street and see what it looked like. I would then go see my mom and dad. I was walking down main street and my present wife was just coming out of the bank where she worked, earning 20 cents per hour. She saw me, waved, came across the street and visited for a while. Pretty soon she said…'I will buy you a cup of coffee.' Well, thank goodness, coffee was only 5 cents a cup at that time. That was half of what she made in an hour working in the bank. So we went down to Shorty's, a bowling alley and cafe. We had a cup of coffee. I don't recall the type of coffee. For me, the war was over." [73]

---

[72] Navy Bases in WWII.
[73] Holbrook.

Carl Anderson

A Personal View of the United States Occupation of Japan After World War II

ON May 25, 1945, the U.S. Chiefs of Staff (JCS) issued an operational directive to begin the overall and detailed planning for the final battles against the Japanese home islands under code name "Operational DOWNFALL." This allowed the two Pacific Theater commanders (U.S. Army General Douglas MacArthur and U.S. Navy Admiral Chester Nimitz) to begin their offensive planning for the invasions of the Japanese home islands. For "Operation OLYMPIC," after a full-scale air bombardment campaign, an amphibious invasion of the southern island of Kyushu was to be conducted on or about November 1, 1945. The next amphibious operation would be "Operation CORNET," to be conducted no earlier than March 1, 1946, to seize and occupy Tokyo. The invasion of Japan would require a combination of U.S. and British troops currently in the Pacific, augmented by forces and equipment transferred from Europe to the Pacific. One of the divisions scheduled to take part in the invasion of the Japanese home islands was the U.S. Army's 98th Division.

The 98th Division was created during World War I, constituted on July 23, 1918, in the National Army as Headquarters 98th Division at Camp McCellan, Alabama. The division's organization was never completed because of the signing of the armistice in Europe, demobilizing in November 1918. During World War II, the 98th Infantry Division was reorganized on January 30, 1942, moved to Camp Breckenridge, Kentucky on September 15, 1942. Manning was a significant problem with the majority of U.S. Army Reservists already assigned as replacements, spread out to other active duty units. This was necessary to bring under-strength divisions up to combat levels before moving out to overseas combat zones. The War Department tried to fill in manpower gaps in the 98th Division by assigning draftees from New York and New England states. The 98th Division consisted of the 389th, 390th and 391st Infantry Battalions; 367th, 368th and 923rd Light Artillery Battalions; 369th Medium Artillery Battalion and 98th Reconnaissance Troop.

The 98th conducted extensive combat training prior to its scheduled overseas movement, completing two months of combat training in the Tennessee U.S. Army maneuver area in 1943. In April 1944, the 98th transferred to Fort Lawton, Washington for its final overseas deployment. The division sailed for Pearl Harbor on April 13, 1944, replacing the 33rd Division in the defense of the Hawaiian Islands. The 389th Infantry Battalion was assigned to the Kauai District, the 390th Infantry Battalion was responsible for the security in the Maui District. As U.S. forces came closer to the Japanese home islands, the 98th Division was relieved of responsibilities for the security of Hawaii Islands on May 31, 1945. The division began combat training and preparations to allow it to participate in "Operation Downfall." On 28 July, the division was assigned to military forces committed to "Operation OLYMPIC," the amphibious operation on Kyushu. The 98th was to land on the Kaimondaike beaches or on one of the existing beachheads as reenforcements for U.S. troops inland.

Events somewhere else changed planning on how the war would end in the Pacific on the morning of 6 August 1945 on Tinian Island when a flood illuminated "Enola Gay" B-29 was ready to fly the world's first atomic bombing mission. On 15 August, Japanese government officials agreed to accept the Allied terms of unconditional surrender, ending World War II, eliminating the need to conduct amphibious operations against the Japanese home islands. The atomic bombs vindicated the USAAF opinion that Japan could be forced to surrender without amphibious operations.

The 98th Division supplied a 200 man detachment to support amphibious landing operations at Leyte, Philippines. The division also sent troops to other Pacific combat units, with the bulk of the division retained in the Hawaiian Islands, in a reserve capacity. One of the Division's soldiers was Carl Anderson (Rapid City, South Dakota). Anderson..."I graduated from high school in June 1944, while the war in the Pacific still raged, drafted into the U.S. Army in 1945. After completing basic training, I was assigned to the U.S. Army 98th Division, shipped to Hawaii as a replacement. At this time, the 98th Division was training, getting ready for the invasion of Japan. We finished training and during loading into Navy transports for the sea voyage to the Japanese home islands, the Japanese government accepted the Allied terms of unconditional surrender on August 14, 1945." The division boarded U.S. Navy transports in Pearl Harbor on 6 September, assigned as a U.S. occupation force of the Japanese home islands: USS Bottineau (APA-235) and USS Logan (APA-196).

Anderson..."I was on the U.S. Navy transport USS Logan, commissioned in 1944 as a Haskell-class transport. The transport made an intermediate stop at Saipan in the Marianas Islands for resupply before sailing onto the Japanese home islands. It took 21 days sailings to reach Japan after leaving Pearl Harbor. It was necessary to stock up with food before sailing into a Japanese harbor because the Japanese home islands suffered a severe food shortage. It was planned we would live on food brought in on the transport until U.S. sea supply could start delivering the tonnage for occupying U.S. forces and the Japanese population. The sea approaches around Japan had to be cleared of wrecked and sunken ships, and destroyed ground transportation systems repaired. The transports in the convoy, because fighting stopped, did not require continuous and roving escort patrols. We only had one destroyer, the USS Livermore (DD 249) assigned to keep track of the transports during the sea voyage from Pearl Harbor. The division was assigned to disembark at Osaka, Japan, arriving on September 27, 1945. Elements of the division landed at Wakayama on Honshu, Japan on 10 October. The division was to serve as part of the U.S. military occupation, designated 'Operation BLACKLIST,' as well as securing the main island of Honshu." The occupation of Japan was primarily a U.S. operation, under the command of General MacArthur of all Allied military forces in Japan. The United States did not have enough troops to create a military government in Japan, requiring cooperation with existing Japanese political and civil administrators.

Anderson..."We reached Honshu, landing at Wakayama. This was a part of the Japanese home islands targeted for amphibious invasion, but as of that time, no American troops had landed. We did not know whether we would meet with resistance. The Japanese had ordered its troops to lay down their arms and give arriving American troops all the assistance possible in a peaceful occupation of their country. Consequently, not sure of what would meet us on shore, we landed on the beach, combat ready, armed with rifles, full ammunition bandoleers and combat rations. It was raining 'cats and dogs' when our transports approached Wakayama Beach on October 1, 1945. We had to go over the side of the Navy transport on rope cargo nets into Landing Craft Personnel (LCP), which circled around the transport as if in a real invasion, waiting their turn, head to the beach and land the troops. A LCP could hold 20 to 30 men and smaller vehicles such as jeeps. However, our LCP got hung up on the sand bar before reaching shore, so we had to jump out of the LCP into the water that was up to me chin (I am not that tall), holding our rifles over our heads and wading onto shore and the beach. Fortunately, we met no Japanese resistance of any kind, and if we had, we would have been in serious trouble.

"While still in Pearl Harbor, Hawaii, getting ready for the scheduled amphibious assault, we welded snorkels onto our jeeps and trucks since we were going onto the beach through heavy surf, one snorkel to the air intake on the engine and a second to the exhaust pipe. When I was wading through the high water, I remember seeing one of the soldier's head above the water, with two pipes sticking up out of the water allowing the jeep to run under water, heading for the beach under its own power.

"Once up onto the beach, we were ordered to pitch our pup tents for the night. We started a big fire to dry our wet clothes on the beach with most of us remaining huddled around fires to stay warm, as it was cold that time of the year. I eventually crawled inside my tent with a fellow division mate to get some sleep. We had guards posted around the temporary beach camp. The first thing I saw the next morning was a Japanese male running away from the beach area carrying a pair of U.S. Army boots, stolen from one of the division's soldiers. We quickly learned to secure anything of value or find it gone, stolen by Japanese who were short in clothing, or able to sell the item for food on the local black market. Following our first night on the beach, some of us were assigned to guard the supplies unloaded from the transports to prevent the wholesale theft of these items by Japanese. During that time, a powerful typhoon hit near Okinawa on 9 October, then moved on to strike Honshu on 10 October.

"Once on Honshu, we moved into a World War II Japanese air base in our area, where we saw many destroyed remains of shot down and shot up Japanese aircraft. There we set up a temporary shop to serve as a motor pool, where I was assigned to work. All our vehicles that landed on shore by driving through the surf suffered saltwater damage and had to be greased and the oil changed. The engines were sealed but not the chassis. I worked on our division's vehicles continually for several weeks, having the seemingly never-ending line of vehicles waiting to be repaired. These lines increased daily with vehicles damaged in road accidents.

"The building we were assigned as a barracks had one end open to the elements. We had to put up mosquito netting around our beds to keep out the rats, which you could hear running on the rafters above our heads. One night, I was stretched out on my bed and zipped into my mummy sleeping bag, a rat jumped up onto my feet. I jerked my feet upwards inside the sleeping bag, violently throwing off the offending rat against the wall, killing it. I made sure to secure the netting promptly after this incident.

"There were concrete bomb shelters built at this Japanese air base to protect personnel against B-29 raids and later, to provide protection during the expected U.S. invasion. Division engineers drilled holes into some of these so we could use them as latrines. Local Japanese residents would come into our area, very friendly and politely saying they were glad to see us, but they wanted to beg from us. We thought it would be food first, but no, they wanted to clean up. Most were very dirty and dressed in worn out clothing, the remaining effects of the bombing of their cities by B-29s. The destruction was everywhere and extensive. They were also very interested in our heavy equipment, kicking the big tires. Our division interpreter told us these men had been told by their government that the United States was out of rubber and that we used wooden wheels on all our vehicles because Japan controlled all the rubber from Malaya and the surrounding area."

Housing for American occupation troops was a critical problem in immediate postwar Japan because the heavy bombing of the cities and industrial centers. Japanese civilians lived in damp and unheated concrete buildings that remained. Many wooden buildings burned to the ground during B-29 fire bombing raids. Allied troops took control of and occupied any remaining intact concrete buildings with operational steam heat. The 98th supervised demobilization of Japanese troops encountered in the area, along with the seizure and disposal of military supplies, equipment, armaments and installations remaining intact after the cessation of hostilities. The division's headquarters was at Kanaoka Barracks, a former Japanese cavalry post at Sakai, Japan.

Anderson..."After a few weeks, we moved to Osaka, where we were quartered in a seven-story office building with elevators. The top floor had been a restaurant, which we took over and converted into a mess hall. Division engineers began cleaning out a bombed out building located nearby for use as our motor pool. Occasionally they would uncover a dead Japanese while cleaning up the area. It was hard for us to clean out the stench of death all around us, left over from the aerial bombing.

"I was next assigned to the Division Supply Office, which for me was the best job in the motor pool. One of my first assignments was to drive the Supply Officer around the area's neighboring provinces to check on food supplies for the local Japanese." No provision had been made in the U.S. occupation plans for the U.S. military to bring in food for the Japanese population between August 1945 and January 1946. The need eventually became so great that U.S. Navy transports were not only bringing in food for occupation forces but also for the Japanese civilian population. It took the direct intervention of former President Herbert Hoover, Chairman, Special President Advisory Committee on Japan to convince President Harry Truman to authorize the shipment of thousands of tons of food to Japan, increasing that tonnage as the needs were identified.

Anderson..."By rationing, we made sure the Japanese in our area had enough food for the winter. We took a Japanese guide and interpreter when driving to locations around the provinces, but he had been used to going to places by bicycle and not in a jeep. Consequently, some of the trails he directed us to were really only wide enough for a bicycle. On one bridge over a canal we crossed, I had to lean out over the left side of the jeep, looking down at the narrow road bed below, while the officer did the same on the right side to make certain we did not roll off the bridge. The tires were already half off the edge and we did not want them to slip off, sending the jeep into the canal below. We did not take that bridge on the return drive.

"On my first day of driving in Osaka, I was to pick up my Supply Officer at a certain location and drive him on his rounds. We had no reliable road maps, and Osaka is about the size of Chicago with all the road signs in Japanese. I got lost and finally arrived at the designated spot to find the Supply Officer had left a message that he had gotten tired of waiting and caught a ride with someone else to his next appointment. I was to catch up with him at that location and drive him to the next appointment. Well, I got lost again, and it went on like that all day long as I chased him across the city. I did not catch up with him until 5 p.m. I was sure he was going to be angry but he just said I probably learned my way around Osaka that day."

The Division Team from the 389th Infantry Regiment was charged with locating and demobilizing Japanese military target installations in the Wakayama Prefecture, parts of the Osaka Prefecture and on the island of Awaji Shima. During these operations, 279 officers and enlisted personnel supervised 1,200 Japanese workers in demilitarization of 90 industrial plants and one military airfield. The Infantry Regiment also carried out the demobilization of three coastal defense fortresses. Anderson..."We were not allowed to carry any weapons after coming ashore. One day, while we were driving up into the mountains, we came upon a Japanese man carrying a rifle. We were nervous, unsure of what he was going to do, but we kept going when we got close to him we read his armband on which 'official hunter' was written in English. He was apparently allowed to hunt for food. When we got back to our base, the Major received permission to carry a Colt 45 caliber automatic pistol, he never had to use it. The Japanese civilian population respected authority and did not oppose the U.S. military occupation."

Fortunately, Japan's agricultural system, once the land was taken away from control of the landlords under direction of General MacArthur, given to the peasants, food production dramatically increased. Japan still could not grow enough food to feed its population. Anderson..."We were told not to take any food from the local population because of its drastic food shortages. Slowly, the food situation improved, but at a significant cost to the United States in the occupation of Japan. I was stationed in Japan for nearly one year and I enjoyed most of it, departing Japan on September 17, 1946. I was only 20 years old when I got back to the United States and after all I had seen and done, I was still not old enough to vote."

The 98th Division completed its occupation of Japan on February 16, 1946, deactivated at Saki, Japan. The U.S. occupation of Japan, from 1945 to 1948, was a period of great reform for that country, followed by the creating of economic stability. Even though Japan was demilitarized, it became home for many U.S. military bases supporting fighting in Korea, 1950 to 1953. Japan entered the 1950s with a growing economy. In September 1951, the Treaty of Peace was signed in San Francisco, California by former Allied nations that fought against the Empire of Japan, except the Soviet Union. In April 1952, U.S. military occupation of Japan officially ended with the country regaining complete independence as a sovereign nation.[74]

---

[74] Lt. Col. George A. Larson, USAF (Ret.), "A personal view of the United States occupation of Japan," *Military*, October 2005.

114th Fighter Wing

South Dakota Air National Guard

Joe Foss Field, Sioux Falls, South Dakota

ON July 10, 1946, U.S. Congressional Medal of Honor recipient and United States Marine Corps World War II aerial ace over Guadalcanal during World War II, Joseph J. "Joe" Foss was appointed to form an Air National Guard unit at Sioux Falls, South Dakota. The mission of the new unit would be to recruit and train aircrews and supporting ground crews and personnel to a level of operational proficiency, which would enable them to intercept and destroy airborne enemy aircraft penetrating U.S. air space. The equipment authorization for the proposed unit included 25 of the World War II North American P-51 Mustang, a first line piston powered fighter of the time. The USAF was just beginning active duty deployment of the Lockheed P-80 turbojet fighter, the first generation of turbojet fighters. Colonel Foss called a meeting for those interested and plans formulated for organizing the squadron. Authority to activate the 175th Squadron (assigned to the 132nd Fighter Group at Des Moines, Iowa) in Sioux Falls was issued, and on September 20, 1946, the squadron received federal recognition.

The 175th was reassigned to the 133rd Fighter Interceptor Wing, along with units from Fargo, North Dakota; Duluth and Minneapolis, Minnesota in November 1950. The unit was called to active duty on March 1, 1951, moving to Ellsworth AFB to provide support for the 28th BW's B-36 bombers. The unit remained nearly intact and at the end of their active duty deployment returned to the state of South Dakota control, reorganized on December 1, 1952.

Two Lockheed T-33 Shooting Star trainers were assigned in July 1954, beginning the transition for the wing's pilots into turbojet aircraft. The arrival of turbojet fighters started with the F-94A/B Starfire fighters and in rapid succession, the pilots were checked out in flying the turbojet aircraft. On April 16, 1956, the 175th Fighter Interceptor Squadron became part of the newly constituted 114th Interceptor Group (FG), headquartered at Sioux Falls. In May, the first Starfire arrived. In 1958, the F-94s were retired for the more powerful and longer-range F-89 Scorpions. After flying the aircraft for two years, the next aircraft to arrive was the F-102 Delta Dagger, supersonic aerial interceptor. In 1960, the F-102s began replacing the F-89s, with operational control under the U.S. Air Defense Command (ADC). The 114th FG was assigned to the 132nd Fighter Wing (FW). As part of assuming a more active role in the defense of the Continental United States, a number of on duty aircrews were placed on five minute alert, with four aircraft armed and fueled, ready for a scramble launch to intercept and destroy airborne enemy aircraft.

A significant change was made in May 1970, when the 114th FG, Aerospace Defense Command (ADC), Tactical Air Command (TAC). The F-102s were in turn replaced by North American F-100D Super Sabres. The group's mission became that of controlling the combat skies from enemy, used and reinforced friendly combat forces on the ground. In March 1976, the F-100Ds were replaced with the A-7D Corsair IIs. The last F-100D took off from Sioux Falls, Joe Foss Field in June 1977. The group in 1979 began a 12-year participation in "Operation CORNET" at Howard AFB, providing aerial defense for the Panama Canal. Both aircrew and support personnel were active in the summer of 1979, flying missions during the Nicaraguan Crisis. The group was awarded the Armed Forces Expeditionary streamer for combat duty as part of "Operation JUST CAUSE," 1989-1990.

The group began receiving F-16C/D Fighting Falcons in August 1991, with conversion completed on January 1, 1992. The group was redesignated as part of Air Combat Command (ACC) on June 1, 1992. It was one of four ANG units tasked to deploy in support of "Operation PROVIDE COMFORT II," flying out of Incirlik AB, Turkey. Combat patrol missions were flown over the north "NO FLY" zone of Iraq from December 1993 to January 1994. The ground was redesignated as the 114th Fighter Wing (WG) in October 1995. The wing supported "Operation NORTHERN WATCH," based out of Turkey in 1995 and 2003, and "Operation SOUTHERN WATCH," based out of Kuwait in 1998 and Saudi Arabia in 2001. The wing also deployed aircraft to Belgium, Singapore, The Netherlands, Antilles and Israel.

A new chapter opened in the history of the ANG after the terrorist attacks on the United States on September 1, 2001. In addition to the wing's on-going tasking as part of the Air Expeditionary Force (AIF), wing members active to provided support to "Operation NOBLE EAGLE" within the United States and "Operation ENDURING FREEDOM" overseas. Over two-thirds of the wing's 1,000 members have supported the U.S. "War on terror," either at home or overseas.

Mobilization orders were received for members of the 114th Security Forces Squadron, Civil Engineering Squadron, Maintenance Squadron (munitions) and Logistics Readiness Squadron (transportation). Wing personnel have deployed to the United Arab Emirates, Qatar, Oman, Kuwait, Saudi Arabia, Jordon, Cyprus, Pakistan, Romania, Bosnia-Herzegovina, Turkey, Spain, France and Germany.[75]

---

[75] United States Air Forces, "History of the South Dakota Air National Guard," *U.S. Air Force Fact Sheet.*

Weaver Air Force Base B-29s Deploy to Europe in Support of the Berlin Airlift

SAC Forward Deploys its Atomic Capable Bombers

THE Berlin Airlift, which took place between June 24, 1948 and September 30, 1949, kicking off the first round of the "Cold War" between the United States and the Soviet Union. Some Cold War historians believe that when the Soviet Army closed railroad, roads and water routes from Allied occupied Germany into Allied occupied West Berlin, the two former World War II allies formally turned against each other. The Cold War was characterized by an atomic arms race, followed by a more deadly thermonuclear arms race, which lasted, into the 1990s.

On June 24, 1948, the Soviet Army closed overland transportation routes from Allied control Germany through occupied Soviet controlled Germany into West Berlin isolating that city except by air transport. Fortunately, a November 1945, Allied Control Council agreement, of which the Soviet Union signed, allowed three 20 mile wide air corridors from Allied controlled Germany into West Berlin. The Soviet Union had a tradition of abiding by its international legal agreements and because of this allowed the three air corridors to remain open to Allied air traffic. The Soviet military did not believe the Allies could supply Berlin by air and felt they could wait for the city to surrender due to lack of food, fuel and living necessities.

U.S. Army Lt. General Lucius D. Clay, Deputy Commander American Occupation Zone Berlin, only had limited air transport available to keep Western Berlin from falling under Soviet control. He ordered the U.S. Air Forces-Europe (USAFE) transport aircraft to begin preparations to fly supplies into Berlin, under code name "Operation VITTLES."

This was a difficult assignment because of the limited number of available transport aircraft. The USAFE transport force consisted of one hundred twin-engine Douglas C-47 Skytrains and two four-engine Douglas C-54 Skymasters. Smaller twin-engine Fairchild C-82 Packets (forerunner of C-119 Flying Boxcar) were also used. The RAF contributed Short Sunderland flying boats, landing them on a lake in Berlin, delivering high-priority cargo.

The first Berlin Airlift flight was flown on 26 June. On May 12, 1949, the Soviet Union lifted the blockade. The Allies continued to fly in supplies until 30 September to continue the buildup of emergency supply stockpiles in Berlin. During the 276,926 transport flights, the U.S. lost 17 aircraft and the British seven. With the final flights, the Allies delivered 17,835,727 tons of cargo into Berlin keeping the city alive and free of Soviet control.

One little known action taken by the U.S. as a response to the Berlin crisis was the deployment of B-29 Superfortresses to bases in Europe. President Truman hoped this implied threat to unleash the Strategic Air Command's (SAC) B-29s, armed with atomic weapons against Soviet targets would deter the Soviets from further aggressive action.

In 1948, the Soviet Union was attempting to develop its own atomic bomb but had not detonated a weapon. President Truman wanted to use America's atomic bomb monopoly to keep the Soviet Union's expansionism in check. This was an early use of the "Containment Policy," which became the basic strategy used by the U.S. against the Soviet Union. The Berlin Crisis that spawned the airlift brought the U.S. and Soviet Union close to World War III.

After World War II, the U.S. rapidly demobilized and had a relatively small occupying force remaining in Europe compared to that of the Soviet Army. It could only threaten the Soviet Union with atomic weapons delivered by B-29s. A Joint Anglo/American Intelligence Group developed an atomic plan code named "CHARIOTEER," to attack selected Soviet cities and industrial centers. The plan targeted 70 Soviet cities and industrial centers (with eight atomic bombs to be dropped on Moscow and seven on Leningrad). The goal of this plan was to destroy Soviet political and administrative control, the majority of the country's oil industry and 30 to 40 percent of the industrial base. In carrying out the atomic bombing, U.S. war planners estimated seven million Soviet citizens would be killed.

The Berlin Crisis forced U.S. political leadership to contemplate its first atomic military option. President Truman did not want to use ground troops to force open land routes into Berlin, primarily because he did not want to put two U.S. Army divisions in Europe (60,000 troops, of which, only 10,000 were classified as combat ready/capable) against superior Soviet Army occupation troops (300,000 to 400,000 combat veterans who fought on the Eastern Front against German troops in World War II) in East Germany and Eastern Europe. The

Soviet military did not demobilize after World War II, maintaining a huge Army and Air Force.

As the Berlin Airlift started, President Truman and his military advisors looked at a change in U.S. strategic policy. During World War II, thousands of American bombers were stationed at air bases in England, flying combat sorties over Nazi occupied Europe and into Germany. By the end of 1946, these bombers were no longer based in England. These B-17s and B-24s were rapidly scrapped or relegated to secondary missions as B-29s took over the role of long-range, heavy, strategic bombing.

During discussion with U.S. Ambassador to England, Lewis W. Douglas, on June 26, 1948, Ernest Beven indicated the Berlin Crisis required the stationing of B-29s on England. He reasoned that this would signal to Soviet political leadership and military commanders that the Western Allies would not back away from keeping West Berlin a free city.

At the same time, Sir Brian Robertson, British Ambassador to western Germany, informed General Lucius Clay, in his role as Commander of the Office of Military Government and Military Governor of Germany that the British government would approve the stationing of SAC B-29s at RAF bases. On 27 June, General Clay submitted a request for B-29s to be deployed to England. General Hoyt Vandenburg supported his request, forwarding it onto President Truman. On 28 June, President Truman signed the request. However, it took until 13 July for the British Cabinet to sign the formal agreement, allowing SAC B-29s to be flown to England, operating from RAF air bases.

President Truman had three objectives for the United States to achieve during the Berlin Crisis.

1. The U.S. and its allies (England and France) would remain in West Berlin.
2. Supply West Berlin by air transport, not resorting to combat with surrounding superior Soviet military Forces in Eastern Europe.
3. Increase USAF strength in Europe, including the deployment of SAC B-29s.

SAC responded to the Soviet military blockade of Berlin. One B-29 bomb squadron (BS) of the 301st Bomb Group (BG) was already on rotation at training at Furstenfeldbruck, Germany. General George C. Kenny, Commander of SAC, ordered the 301st BG's two remaining squadrons to deploy to Goose Bay, Labrador in preparation to fly onto European air bases. Although the B-29 was considered a long-range bomber, it needed airfields close to the target area in the European Theater of Operations. SAC was in the process of integrating the very heavy (VH), long-range Convair B-36 Peacemaker into its combat units but not operationally ready in 1948.

SAC placed the 28th and 307th BGs on alert. The 28th BG (Weaver AFB) could deploy within 12 hours and the 307th BG within three hours. On July 15, 1948, the U.S. National Security Council approved sending SAC B-29s to England. The Soviet Union's political leadership speculated SAC B-29s could carry atomic bombs because the U.S. demonstrated it could drop atomic bombs in August 1945 on two Japanese cities. By deploying B-29s to England, SAC aircrews were within range of targets in the Soviet Union, such as Moscow. This was an implied strategic threat to the Soviet political leadership.

SAC placed other B-29 bomber groups on twenty-four hour deployment notification. By early 1948, the 301st BG's two remaining squadrons were on the ground at Furstenfeldbuck, Germany. Later in the month, the 28th BG deployed from Rapid City to British RAF Scampton, England for a ninety-day show of force mission. SAC deployed B-29s were assigned to RAF Lakenheath, Marham, Scampton and Waddington. In July 1948, B-29s flew to RAF Lakenheath, assigned to the 2nd BG. Nine B-29s assigned to the 304th BS, 97th BG landed at Marham. Between July 1948 and February 1949, RAF Scampton had thirty B-29s assigned to the 28th BG, relieved later by the 301st BG. SAC B-29s were stationed at RAF Waddington.

The 3rd Air Division (3AD) Provisional was created to serve as a temporary 30 to 60 day deployment command. Due to the ongoing Berlin Crisis, the provisional designation was dropped on August 23, 1948, with the 3ADorganization moving to headquarters at Bushey Park Air Station on September 8, 1948.

The British government provided SAC access to their airfields at no additional expense, as long as operational expenses did not exceed normal RAF operating costs. This agreement was formalized on January 4, 1949, after Major General Leon W. Johnson, Commander 3AD, received financial agreement to support SAC B-29s in England from the British Air Ministry. This would not have been possible if airfield facilities in England had not been upgraded to handle B-29 aircraft. This had happened previously when in 1946, Air Chief Marshall Sir Arthur Tedder, British Chief of the Air Staff and General Spaatz, Commanding General USAAF decided that former B-17 and B-24 runways required upgrading. Over the next two years, runways were lengthened and widened to handle combat B-29 weights. Without these modifications, B-29s could not have been operationally deployment to RAF airfields in England.

The USAF and RAF committed transports to fly supplies into Berlin in a show of united resolve. At the same time, SAC wanted to demonstrate the atomic lethality of its deployed B-29s. In reality, SAC aircrew bombing accuracy left a lot to be desired. In May 1948, prior to the Soviet Army's closing ground routes into Berlin, Major General Clements McMullen, Deputy Commander SAC, began to address this deficiency. He started a bombing competition to develop accurate and precise dropping of atomic bombs. In June 1948, three aircrews from each of SAC's bomb groups flew to Castle AFB, California to compete in SAC's first bombing competition. This was not a sophisticated competition. Each crew dropped three practice bombs by visual identification and three by radar from 25,000 feet. The competition cumulative bombing scores resulted in a Circular Error Probability (CEP) of 1,065 feet for visual and 2,955 feet for radar releases. Using atomic bombs, this would allow the destruction of large area (soft) targets but did not deliver the accuracy SAC desired.

The deployment by the 28th BG was typical for SAC B-29 units being prepared to support the Berlin airlift's operations. On July 15, 1948, a detachment of the 717th BS, consisting of 79 officers and 139 enlisted, took off from Weaver AFB (today Ellsworth AFB) along with a provisional headquarters squadron and a detachment from the 77th and 718th BSs for deployment to England for 30 days. Thirty 28th BG B-29s, carrying maintenance and medical personnel, along with standard aircrews, flew via Goose Bay, Labrador and Prestwick, Scotland, landing at RAF stations Scampton and Lincolnshire. Supplies, equipment and additional support personnel were transported by commercial transport aircraft.

Once at Scrampton, the 28th BG came under the jurisdiction of the 3AD, Provisional, USAFE. Upon arrival in England, members of the 28th BG learned that the duration of their TDY had been extended from 30 to 60 days. News of this change, along with over-crowded barracks, poorly prepared food, lack of recreational facilities brought about a sharp decline in morale of the group.

On July 26, 1948, twenty-six 28th BG B-29s were dispatched to fly an aerial review honoring Mr. Henderson, the British Secretary of State for Air. Three days later, a division mission was flown by the 307th BG, flying over the English cities of Lincoln, Cambridge, Brighton, South Hampton, Plymouth, Bristol, Evesham, Liverpool, Leeds and Cottingham. This gave the British citizenry their first glimpse of Superfortresses. Equally important, Soviet embassy personnel witnessed this show of SAC bomber airpower strength and reported to Moscow that the USAF was flying training missions in England, possibly in preparation for combat sorties against the Soviet Union.

The 28th BG's morale improved in August 1948, when commanders began authorizing personnel 48 hour leaves to travel into London to get away from the constant activities involved in keeping B-29s ready to be launched and flown into West German air bases, taking off to strike targets in Eastern Europe and Russia if authorized by the President. August also brought distinguished VIPs to visit the 28th BG at Scampton: Stuart Symington, Secretary of the Air Force; General Hoyt S. Vandenburg, USAF Chief of Staff and Major General Leon W. Johnson, Commanding General Fifteenth Air Force. In September, more VIPs visited Scampton: Major General Johnson returned on 1-2 September; U.S. South Dakota Senator Cham Gurney made an official inspection of the 28th BG on 3 September; Lord Tedder, RAF, visited on 4 September, watching the group's B-29s take-off on a Joint American-British air defense exercise. This impressed Soviet officials stationed in England, primarily Soviet embassy assigned intelligence officers, of the threat implied by a large force of B-29s stationed near the borders of the Soviet Union. Lt. General Norstad, Commanding General USAFE, visited the group on 4 September.

Toward the end of 1948, the 28th BG was alerted for another TDY to England, but did not deploy. In 1949, the bomb group had a more important role, beginning the transition from the B-29 to the B-36, thereby improving SAC's long-range, thermonuclear delivery capabilities against the Soviet Union.

The 307th BG deployed from MacDill AFB, Florida to RAF stations Marham and Waddington. General Kenny viewed the Berlin Crisis as an opportunity to demonstrate America's willingness and military capabilities to use air power against the Soviet Union. Soviet political and military leaders were surprised by the rapid American military response to the closing of ground routes into Berlin. Soviet leadership did not know how many of SAC's deployed B-29s carried atomic bombs.

On October 19, 1948, General Curtis E. LeMay took command of SAC and immediately started upgrading the force's aircraft, aircrew and support personnel capabilities thereby enhancing its ability to deliver nuclear weapons against the Soviet Union. Even though the Soviet Union had been an Ally during World War II, the U.S. planned to use its monopoly of atomic weapons against the Soviet Union if required. On July 19, 1945, President Truman approved a memorandum prepared by Secretary of War Henry Lewis in which the United States should use its atomic weapons monopoly to force the Soviet Union to adopt a political system that would suit America. The U.S. atomic bomb monopoly could possibly be used to gain political advantage over the Soviet Union in the post-World War II era. After the end of World War II, the U.S. JSC recommended that the United States must be ready to strike a first blow with atomic weapons if needed. The resulting war plan targeted twenty Soviet cities. Included on this list were Moscow and Leningrad. This initial atomic bombing plan was called "TRINITY."

As forward looking as the atomic war plans appeared on paper, the problem of implementation depended on the number and availability of atomic bombs. The first three atomic bombs produced by the United States cost two billion dollars. The first atomic bomb was tower detonated prior to the transfer of two other atomic bombs to Tinian island for the bombing of Japan (Hiroshima on 6 August and Nagasaki on August 9, 1945). The bomb dropped on Nagasaki was referred to as "Fat Man" and became the basis for the U.S. post war Mark III plutonium atomic bomb. In 1948, the U.S. inventory of Mark IIIs was one hundred. By 1949, the number of Mark IIIs reached two hundred. The Mark III had a yield of 18 to 49 Kilotons. A B-29 could carry one Mark III. SAC only had 38 B-29s in 1948 modified of carry the Mark III. By the end of 1949, this increased to 95 aircraft. At the start of the Berlin Crisis in 1948, SAC only possessed a limited number of B-29s to conduct its mission of atomic deterrence. The majority of these were assigned to the 509th BG.

Another problem was the training of the aircrews tasked to deliver atomic bombs against targets in the Soviet Union. This was the time before intense training initiated by General LeMay and the transition of SAC into a credible nuclear deterrence force. For the B-29s deployed to Germany, the forward based squadron commander did not know how to prepare for what type of combat operations against the Soviet Union. He questioned SAC Headquarters as to whether he was to prepare to employ conventional or atomic bombs. He did not have an operational or contingency plan of possible operations against the Soviet Union. Initially, when there was a shortage of transport aircraft to fly into Berlin, it was wrongly believed that the B-29s would be turned into transports, possibly hauling sacks of coal.

The biggest obstacle to atomic arming SAC's B-29s was the assembly of the atomic bombs at the designated forward or deployed operational bases. In 1948, with one hundred Mark IIIs, SAC munitions personnel could only assemble two atomic bombs per day. This did not allow enough atomic bombs to be assembled, loaded into the B-29s for a simultaneous mass launch to destroy the desired targets in the Soviet Union as specified under "CHARIOTEER." Even though SAC deployed B-29s to England and Germany in 1948, President Truman did not authorize the movement of atomic bombs from the United States to England or Germany. The B-29s deployed could only realistically be armed with conventional bombs.

Soviet intelligence probably correctly concluded that SAC's deployed B-29s were not armed with atomic bombs because of the absence of special munitions facilities at the B-29 bases with the required guards and secured storage areas. B-29s on the forward bases were not heavily guarded at the same level as atomic loaded bombers on alert status. SAC's primary atomic bombing group, the 509th, was not deployed from the United States. However, the deployment of large numbers of B-29s to Europe was still a concern to Soviet political and military authorities.

Soviet intelligence personnel reported the arrival of each SAC bomb group and there was no indication by U.S. intelligence that the Soviet leadership believed SAC's B-29s were not armed with atomic bombs. Soviet intelligence officers collected information on SAC B-29 activities in Europe during the Berlin Crisis. Due to the emergency landing in World War II of three damaged B-29s in Siberia, Soviet aviation engineers knew the operational capabilities of the Superfortress. Based on these interned U.S. B-29s, Soviet aviation engineers developed their own copy, the Tupolov Tu-4 Bull. These were later armed with the Soviet atomic bomb, developed because of deep Soviet intelligence espionage of the U.S. top secret World War II Manhattan Project's plutonium atomic bomb.

The sending of SAC B-29s to Europe was one of "saber rattling," giving the Soviet political leadership pause to think about the military ramifications of their blockade of Berlin. General Kenny complained about the inactivity of SAC B-29s..."The Russians may of course be worried about our 90 B-29s now in Europe, but they do not seem to be seeing them as a club. Perhaps in time, the Russians will signal that as long as we do not mention them around the green table that they are no good anyhow." However, it appeared that Soviet Premier Joseph Stalin viewed these B-29s as possible atomic deterrence since he never tried to take the rest of Berlin from the Allies by military force. U.S. intelligence agencies reported combat training and levels of Soviet military forces in Eastern Germany were not preparing for any type of offensive action. There was small scale Soviet military unit tactical training but no large-scale operational training or combat deployments. The movement of two Soviet Army divisions toward the border of Allied occupied West Germany in September 1948 lacked logistical support for initiating offensive operations. On June 30, 1948, U.S. intelligence collected information that the Soviet Politburo discussed preparations and adequacy of Soviet anti-aircraft defenses. This reflected the Soviet political leadership concerns over the U.S. monopoly of atomic weapons and the presence of SAC B-29s in Europe.

Regardless of the lack of atomic weapons for the deployed B-29s, there appeared to be an elaborate effort to convince the Soviet political leadership that President Truman had the will and prepared to use atomic weapons in the defense of Berlin. The deployment of SAC's B-29s to England was publicized as the movement of atomic bombers from the United States to England. The British government allowed SAC B-29s on RAF stations. Comments issued by the British government indicated the issue of who controlled the release of atomic weapons stationed in England was uncertain and under discussion. In reality, SAC only responded to release orders from the President. For Soviet Premier Joseph Stalin, the Berlin Crisis turned into a political setback. In the months after the Berlin Crisis several developments occurred, many with long-lasting effects.

1. President Truman did not and would not recognize Soviet predominance in Germany.
2. The U.S. rapidly turned the Berlin Blockade to its advantage, pushing anti-Soviet propaganda.
3. The rapid creation and maintenance of an air transport capability to move supplies to West Berlin was something the Soviet political leadership did not believe could be sustained.
4. Premier Stalin did not plan to start World War III over Berlin, which U.S. intelligence accurately determined. The deployment of B-29s from the U.S. by SAC certainly played a significant role in the peaceful outcome of the Berlin Crisis.
5. By 1949, Premier Stalin had to recognize a permanent western political right in West Berlin.
6. Countries of Western Europe turned to the United States for protection against a possible Soviet military threat, eventually

leading to the creation of the North Atlantic Treaty Organization (NATO) in 1949.

In April 1949, the United States joined NATO, a European military alliance, an outgrowth of the Brussels Treaty. A key provision of the treaty was that an armed attack against one or more of NATO's members shall be construed as an attack against them all. In this was an implied threat that the United States would use its atomic weapons to retaliate against a massive Soviet ground and air attack against NATO.

President Truman in 1948 was informed by intelligence officers that the Soviet Union would not have an atomic bomb no earlier than 1953. However, on September 3, 1949, a USAF WB-29 collected a high-altitude airborne radiation sample, evaluated, with U.S. nuclear scientists concluding the Soviet Union exploded its first atomic bomb. It was an engineering/production replica/copy of the U.S. World War II "Fat Man" plutonium atomic bomb of World War II dropped on Nagasaki, Japan. The relatively quick development of the Soviet's atomic bomb was aided by dedicated espionage from the spy Claus Fuchs and others working in the U.S. World War II top secret "Manhattan Project."

To give SAC credibility to the Soviets as an atomic deterrent force, General LeMay ordered SAC's second bombing completion, October 3-7, 1949, thereafter an annual competition. The same formant as the first bombing competition was followed. Results improved but additional training was still needed. Another development from the deployment of B-29s to England came after the end of the Berlin Airlift. On March 22, 1950, the first group of B-29s was flown from the U.S. to England, transferred to the RAF under the Mutual Defense Assistance Program. The RAF took possession of 70 B-29s, followed by a second transfer of eighteen. A larger transfer was scheduled but the USAF cancelled it when pulled B-29s from storage at Davis-Monthan AFB were transferred to the FEAF for Korean War air combat operations. The RAF designated its B-29s as the Washington B.1.

In April 1949, Lewis Douglas, U.S. Ambassador to England and Aidan Crawley, British Secretary for Air, came to the agreement that RAF airfields located in East Anglia were vulnerable to a possible Soviet air attack. It was decided to relocate SAC B-29s to RAF station Upper Heyford.

Even though there were not enough atomic bombs or modified B-29s available to carry out a massive atomic bombing against the Soviet Union, the deployment of B-29s to Europe constituted a highly visible signal that the U.S. political leadership would defend access rights of the western powers to Berlin. This political and military response to the Soviet blockade gained approval from the U.S. Congress and led to the establishment of numerous U.S. military bases overseas. Air bases were needed by SAC to ring the Soviet Union's borders with atomic armed bombers. Even though "CHARIOTEER" atomic bomb plan created by the JSC Joint Intelligence Group looked good on paper, realistically at this time it could not be implemented. The dropping of 133 atomic bombs on 70 Soviet targets was beyond SAC's capabilities in 1948 to 1949, but led to the creation of a credible deterrent force in the following years.[76]

---

[76] Lt. Col. George A. Larson, USAF (Ret.), "The B-29 atomic option during the Berlin Airlift," *Friends Journal,* Volume 29, Number 4, Winter, 2006/2007.

South Dakota National Guard

1950 to 1953, Korean War

IN July 1950, South Dakota National Guard units were mobilized with the 196th Regimental Combat Team going to Alaska. The 196th consisted of 147th Field Artillery Battalion, 200th Engineering Company and a medical detachment. The 109th with units in Rapid City, Sturgis and Hot Springs was mobilized on September 3, 1950 and trained at their mobilization station of Fort Bragg, North Carolina for eight months prior to being sent to West Germany. During their one year tour in Germany, they controlled bridging operations over the Rhine. They also had a TDY to France for two months building roads for the French military. All South Dakota soldiers return home in July 1952, never sent to the Korean battlefield. [77]

---

[77] Lt. Col George A. Larson, USAF (Ret.), "South Dakota National Guard, 1950-1953, Korean War." Visit to Camp Rapid, The South Dakota National Guard's open house to celebrate the National Guard's 150 years of service," display set up in the Headquarters Lobby, "2012: Countdown to Withdrawal," June 9, 2012.

Colonel Dale Friend, USA (Ret.)

Korea, Vietnam, Germany

Disputing Myths About the U.S. Military in the Vietnam War

COLONEL Dale Friend..."I was a 15 year old, somewhat of a juvenile delinquent, when a judge gave me a choice between incarceration in a juvenile facility or enlisting in the military. Since I was 15 years old I had to have my father sign that I was 17 years old. I had 12 weeks of Army basic training. I was then sent to Korea for one year, 1950 to 1951. When I was discharged from the Army, I entered the Civil Service in the Army National Guard. I returned to the Regular Army, with an assignment in France at a chemical depot. I applied for Officer Candidate School (OCS) at Fort Benning, Georgia. First, to be qualified, I needed to complete the NCO Academy. I graduated in the top 10 percent. After seven years as enlisted, I went to OCS. I went to Ranger School, four weeks in the mountains of Georgia and four weeks in the swamps of Florida. I was assigned to the 504th Infantry in Germany as a Rifle Company Commander. The Army sent me back to the United States to finish my last year of college at the University of Omaha, in Omaha, Nebraska. I was then assigned to Fort Campbell, Kentucky.

"I was sent to Vietnam in 1966 to 1967, a Captain assigned to the 173rd Airborne Brigade, stationed at a base camp in Bien Hoa. You'd go out for about a month and then go back to base camp for three or four days and get your act together. While with the 173rd, I participated in a parachute jump with 724 other guys and one female French journalist. On February 22, 1967, the 173rd conducted "Operation JUNCTION CITY," the only combat jump of the Vietnam war. The operation saw three brigades controlling eight battalions dropped out of C-130s at an altitude of 1,500 feet into War Zone C, in Tay Ninh Province. During the battle, the brigade operated out of the northeastern part of the war zone along with the 196th Infantry Brigade, as four other brigades from the 1st and 25th Infantry Divisions attempted to surround and destroy the 9th Viet Cong Division in the war zone."

He came home to a country torn apart by the war. Friend..."When we got off the airplane coming home it was not unusual to be called baby killer." While he was earning his Masters' Degree at Michigan State University he saw protests against Marine recruiters. That was a common thing. Friend..."I went to Army Command Staff College at Fort Leavenworth, Kansas, where I was later assigned as an instructor.

In 1974, I was assigned to Germany as a battalion commander. Then to the Army War College at Carlisle Barracks, Pennsylvania. In 1980, I was assigned as Deputy Post Commander. In 1982, I was notified of pending orders to Washington, DC. I did not want to go to the area with its high cost and political atmosphere. I declined the orders, retiring after seven years as enlisted and 23 years as an officer."

Colonel Friend is still fighting the Vietnam War to change lies about the war and the soldiers who served during it. He has collected some interesting facts about the Vietnam War.

1. 9,087,000 military personnel served on active duty during the official Vietnamese era from August 5, 1964 to May 7, 1975.
2. 2,709,918 Americans served in uniform in Vietnam or 9.7 percent of their generation.
3. 240 men were awarded the Medal of Honor during the Vietnam War.
4. 58,148 were killed in Vietnam.
    A. Of those killed, 61 percent were younger than 21.
    B. 11,465 of those killed were younger than 20 years old.
    C. Average age of men killed was 23.1 years.
    D. Five men killed in Vietnam were only 16 years old.
    E. The oldest man killed was 62 years old.
    F. Of these killed, 17,539 were married.
5. 75,000 were severely disabled.
    A. 23,214 were 100 percent disabled.
    B. 5,283 lost limbs.
6. As of January 15, 2004, there were 1,875 Americans still unaccounted for from the Vietnam War.
7. 87 percent of Americans hold Vietnam Veterans in high esteem.
1. According to Colonel Friend, Vietnam Veterans live under a cloud that should be removed. He blames the media, a uniformed public disinterested in the facts and a government that has not corrected the "fiction" that has spread about the war.

Isolated atrocities committed by American soldiers produced outrage from anti-war critics and news media, while Communist atrocities were so common they hardly received any media attention. The U.S. minimized and prevented attacks while North Vietnam made attacks on civilians a centerpiece of its strategy. Americans who deliberately killed civilians received prison sentences, while Communists who did so received commendations. This was backed up by the declassified President Richard Nixon Presidential papers which indicated from 1957 to 1973, the National Liberation Front assassinated 36,725 Vietnamese abducted another 58,499. Death squads focused on leaders at village level and anyone who improved the lives of the peasants such as medical personnel, social workers and schoolteachers.

Colonel Friend indicated most Vietnam Veterans served well and honorably. They came home, married, raised families and held down jobs. He is angry about the "myth" of the messed up, strung-out Vietnam Veteran who cannot forget the war. Unlike some reports, two thirds of Vietnam veterans were volunteers. There was no disparity in the numbers of Blacks who served and died, nor were most soldiers from poor and uneducated backgrounds.

There were many myths about the Vietnam war.

Myth: Common belief is that most Vietnam Veterans were drafted.

Fact: Two-thirds of the men who served in Vietnam were volunteers. Two thirds of the men who served in World War II were drafted. Approximately 70 percent of those killed in Vietnam were volunteers.

Myth: The media have reported that suicides among Vietnam veterans range from 50,000 to 100,000, or 5 to 11 times the non-Vietnamese veteran population.

Fact: Mortality studies show that 9,000 is a better estimate.

Myth: Common belief is a disproportionate number of Blacks were killed in Vietnam.

Fact: Eighty-six percent of the men who died in Vietnam were Caucasians, 12.5 percent were Black and 1.2 percent of all other races.

Myth: Common belief is that the war was fought largely by the poor and uneducated.

Fact: Servicemen who went to Vietnam from well to do areas had a slightly elevated risk of dying because they were more likely to be pilots or infantry officers.

Myth: Kim Phuc, the nine-year old Vietnamese girl running naked from a napalm strike near Trang Bang on June 8, 1972, shown a million times on U.S. television, was burned by Americans bombing

Trang Bang.

Fact: No American had involvement in this incident near Trang Bang. The planes bombing the village were Vietnamese Air Force, flown by Vietnamese pilots in support of Army of Republic of Vietnam (ARVN) troops on the ground. The Vietnamese pilot who dropped the napalm in error is currently living in the United States, escaping the country after the fall of Saigon to Communist North Vietnamese troops. Even Associated Press photographer, Nick Ut, who took the picture, was Vietnamese. The incident took place on the second day of a three day battle between the North Vietnamese Army (NVA) who occupied the village of Trang Bang and ARVN, who were trying to force the NVA out of the village. Reports of the news media that an American commander ordered the air strike that burned Kim Phuc are incorrect. There were no Americans involved in any capacity according to Lieutenant General James F. Hollingsworth, USA (Ret.), the Commanding General of TRAC at that time.

Colonel Friend commented on the Domino Theory, which stated that America had to fight in Vietnam to prevent countries from falling like dominos. The Philippines, Indonesia, Malaysia, Singapore and Thailand remained free of Communist rule because of American intervention in Vietnam. If you ask people who live in these countries who won the war in Vietnam, they have a different opinion than the American news media. The TET Offensive, in which North Vietnamese troops staged an attack in early 1968, has long been portrayed as a major victory for the North Vietnamese. Most historians now agree (including the author of this book), that it was in fact a huge loss for the North Vietnamese in terms of the amount of soldiers killed and the loss of Viet Cong combatants in South Vietnam. It was reported as an overwhelming success for the Communist forces and a decided defeat for the U.S. forces. Nothing could be further from the truth. The TET holiday offensive succeeded on only one front and that was the news front and the political arena.

Myth: The common belief is that the domino theory was proved false.

Fact: The domino theory was accurate. The Association of Southeast Asia Nations countries of Philippines, Indonesia, Malaysia, Singapore and Thailand stayed free of Communism because of the U.S. commitment to Vietnam. Without the commitment, Communism would have swept all the way to Malacca Straits that is south of Singapore and of great strategic importance to the free world. If you ask people who live in these countries who won the war in Vietnam, they have a different opinion from the American news media. The Vietnam War was the turning point for Communism.

Myth: The common belief is that the fighting in Vietnam was not as intense as in World War II.

Fact: The average infantryman in the South Pacific during World War II saw about 40 days of combat in four years. In Vietnam, the average infantryman saw about 240 days of combat in one year, because of the mobility of the helicopter.

Although the percent that died is similar to other wars, amputations or crippling wounds were 300 percent higher than in World War II with 75,000 Vietnam veterans severely disabled.

MEDEVAC helicopters flew nearly 500,000 missions. Over 900,000 patients were airlifted nearly one half were American.

The average time lapse between wounding to hospitalization was less than one hour. As a result, less than one percent of all Americans wounded, who survived the 24 hours, died.

The helicopter provided unprecedented mobility. Without the helicopter it would have taken three times as many troops to secure the 800 mile border with Cambodia and Laos. Politicians thought the Geneva Conventions of 1954 and Geneva Accords of 1962 would secure the border.

Colonel Friend is strongly opposed to the belief that America lost the Vietnam War. The last American soldier left Vietnam on March 29, 1973, but Saigon did not fall until April 30, 1975. The South Vietnamese lost the war to the North Vietnamese. Colonel Friend after retiring from the U.S. Army, was recruited by the Homestake Mining Company as Chief of Security and Fire Prevention from 1981 to 1984.[78]

---

[78] Colonel Dale Friend, U.S. Army (Ret.). He was a U.S. Army battalion commander during the Vietnam War, led troops into jungle combat as part of the 173rd Airborne Brigade Combat Team. Black Hills Veteran Writing Group, Western Dakota Technical Institute, Rapid City, South Dakota, author, May 12, 2012.

Gerald (Jerry) Teachout

Focus on Korea, 1951

GERALD (Jerry) Teachout..."Eventually we all ended up at Tachikawa Air Base. After all, it was the base from which we went to Korea. There were still 'frag order' missions to fly and the ground forces still needed supplies of all kinds. So the flying didn't stop just because we had been driven out of Kimpo. In other words, we were down but far from out. We were two aircraft and one crew short, but that's all, and there was still plenty of "git up and go" left in the unit. he Reserve Wing from Chicago had been recalled as a unit and was on their way over to Brady Field, located on a peninsula just a little south and west of Ashiya. The C-119s were stationed at that Air Base and most air cargo was first brought in to Ashiya and redistributed in Korea from there. Our First Provisional Group was divided up and added to the Chicago Wing.

"We were broken up into three existing squadrons to completely fill out their TOE (Table of Organization and Equipment) because most reserve wings had plenty of openings that were never filled. There was some friction between the two groups as most of their crews had never been near a combat situation but that was soon dispelled. The men that had left families somewhere in the Far East, Kadena Air Force Base on Okinawa or Clark Field in the Philippines, stayed with the squadron at Tachi Base on Okinawa or Clark Field in the Philippines, stayed with the squadron at Tachi because the family living conditions there were a whole lot better than elsewhere. Some families with a short rotation date were sent back to the ZI (Zone of Interior, or the U.S.) while others were in family housing at Tachi. Two more squadrons were at Brady Field, which had been a Japanese field during World War II, therefore no buildings for the troops were involved. We lived in tents that been erected over a two by four frame and floored with rough-cut lumber at least high enough to keep the critters out and heated with the familiar oil-burning heater.

"The runway was long enough but was the old familiar PSP surface. The narrow part of the peninsula that Brady was on was made of sand and further out on the wider part of the peninsula, the 25th Infantry Division made its home at Camp Hakata. I might add that the 25th had borne the brunt of the initial attack on Korea, had taken many casualties, so a lot of the dependents had headed stateside. According to most military historians, the 25th was only there for housekeeping purposes and undermanned and none of its personnel were trained or equipped as a division should be.

"In my estimation, the roller coaster up-down thing had reared its ugly head in the wrong place at the wrong time and the Korean conflict was far from the planners minds. It shouldn't have happened but it did!

"Many missions were flown to Ashiya, then to Korea and back, mostly hauling ammo, spare parts and clothing to the ground troops. The Chinese didn't get as far south as the North Koreans did the first time and were driven back beyond the 38th Parallel, eventually.

"That opened up more airfields for our use and it shortened the flying time to the 'bomb line' considerably. Then there was the mission from Ashiya supposedly to Tachi hauling a bunch of passengers and, of course, at night. I was filling in for a sick copilot as the right seat felt as good to me as the left. We had climbed to our assigned altitude and were cruising along the airway towards Tachi when a passenger came forward to the pilot's compartment and told us that the right engine was streaming fire from the exhaust stacks quite badly and that he didn't think it should be doing that. A quick check of the engine showed nothing amiss so I got out of the seat and headed back to see for myself. Sure enough, the passenger was right. I hurriedly got back into the copilot's seat and we shut down that engine pronto. There was no sense in ruining a fixable engine and if we needed it, we could restart it. That left one good engine to get us to Komaki Air Base, another thirty minutes or so ahead of us.

"The weather was good and a textbook approach and landing was made without 'further ado.' We spent an unscheduled night along with all the passengers at Komaki as though it was done every day. That was the only engine failure that I experienced in well over 2,000 hours of flying in that type of aircraft.

"We did get to drop paratroops on our own island of Kyushu in Japan. It is said that the commanders of the airplanes and the paratroopers made a bet that the airplane CO would not jump with the rest. He did, but broke his leg upon landing and that put him out of commission for a while.

"My faithful copilot (the one that wanted to fly single-engine airplanes) had applied for and gotten in a new squadron that was being formed in Korea. It was equipped with AT-6s and their job was to be the spotters for ground support strike aircraft that were coming in from the south. The AT-6 was the same airplane I had flown at the first part of Advanced Flying Training and after it had been fitted with smoke rockets was a good pick for the job. At least, he was flying single-engine aircraft. I would see him again some fifteen years later at CCK (Ching Chang Kwan airbase) on the island of Formosa, quite by accident, the Air Force had begun to be a great big fraternity because goodbyes became hellos at some later date. There was hardly an Air Force base in the world that didn't have on its roster someone that you had known in yesteryears as illustrated by the friendship mentioned above.

"Fifth Air Force Headquarters had set up a C-119 school at Komaki Air Base near Osaka, Japan. I don't know how their selection process was set up but another pilot and myself came out of their magic ball to attend this school. The C-119 was a newer version of the C-82, which Troop Carrier units had depended on. In the first place, it had been designed by people who would be using the aircraft, both Air Force and Army, and their requirements were well met. There were two R-4360 Pratt & Whitney engines turning a four blade, fourteen foot propeller that was fully reversible for use in short field landings, tricycle landing gear with a steerable nose wheel, twin booms, like a C-82, removable 'clam shell' doors for heavy equipment drops, a cargo compartment center-line monorail used at the same time troops were dropped with accompanying 'bomb bay doors' and a bunch of other amenities that would suit any troop carrier pilot.

"It is now known that it picked up the name 'Flying Boxcar' before it ever got out the factory door. It would haul just about anything you could get inside and drop most of it if so desired. It handled a lot differently than the C-46 and it should, it was a much newer aircraft and had proven its worth right here in this war. I never expected to fly another type of aircraft in any school that close to a war zone but the C-119 had proven itself so successfully in all respects that the head shed people were taking notice. The school only lasted two weeks and was more of a familiarization school than anything else but we did some 25 hours in the left seat. Little did I know of the future of that airplane and how it would affect me.

"In the first part of April, two pilots were picked from all squadrons that were to do things with the C-46 that had never been done before. The job was to fly the big airplane as a spray aircraft to control the mosquito population in and around all Allied installations in South Korea. I happened to be selected as one of them and the other was from the Chicago Wing. We were to have the pick of aircraft and crew including the crew chief because the flying was to be close to the ground and in tight places. The crew chief had to be on the ball for obvious reasons and the airplane had to be one of the most dependable in all respects. I chose an olive-green painted aircraft and her accompanying crew chief, the number of the airplane was 43-7522. That meant that the airplane was made in 1943, and the rest of the number signified the place it took in that particular block of numbers assigned to the manufacturer. Out call sign became COMMANDO FIVE DOUBLE DEUCE and remained as such for the whole summer.

"The crew consisted of me as the aircraft commander, the copilot and the crew chief and that was all. It became our job to take the airplane to the Tachikawa Air Base where FEAMCOM workers were to install two 750 gallon tanks that were usually used as long-range fuel tanks in the cargo compartment of a C-54. These tanks were connected together and held the DDT and the diesel-fuel mix that we were to spray. An electric pump was installed between the tanks and controlled by an ON/OFF switch located on the co-pilots windowsill. Two one-inch metal pipes carried the mix from the pump out of the aircraft to the underside of the aircraft to the underside of the horizontal stabilizers and ended sticking straight down, but cut off at a forty-five degree angle and were located so that the vortex of the propellers would break up the stream into droplets.

"For the benefit of the engineering type, the tanks were located near the aircraft's center of gravity and the tanks already were baffled inside to keep the mix from sloshing around too much on takeoff and landings. The weight of the mix was near seven pounds per gallon and a little arithmetic shows that a full load with all the rest of the equipment has us a load of about eleven thousand pounds. The only thing left was learning to fly the bird in all maneuvers required of a spray airplane. Every bit of it was close to the ground. For some reason, there was always a thin flat deck of clouds over the Tsushima Straits, the body of water between Japan and Korea. That became our training ground, and it afforded flying low on top of the clouds, sharpening our depth perception to aircraft speeds without tearing something up. Our altitude above the cloud deck was about twenty feet.

"We also learned how to turn the aircraft on a dime and get back a nickel change, ready for the next pass. For the pilots reading this: The crew had to be alert at all times ready to expect anything. It took a lot of coordination and cooperation not normally required of any crew, especially flying transports. The C-46 was powered by two R-2800 engines swinging Hamilton Standard three-bladed props, or Curtis Electric three-bladed props, variable speed, and DOUBLE DEUCE was equipped with the latter. We learned that power settings were never changed. The turnaround was all done by maneuvering the aircraft and depending on changeable flap settings and trim tabs. As a matter of further explanation, let us describe a 180 degree turn to the left.

"The heading from the previous run was noted and the ship was started into a right climbing turn to about 45 degrees from the original heading, with airspeed dropping off rapidly and quarter flaps were called for immediately. The aircraft was hung on the props and flaps through the turn back to the left, the airspeed was monitored closely through the turn which determined the position of the nose of the aircraft at least through the ninety degree to the ORIGINAL heading, flaps were retracted to the full-up position, the aircraft continued to turn to the one hundred eighty degree heading with the nose coming down to pick up spray airspeed. Right there was the scary part and everything had to work just right or 7552 and crew would be history. It was no place for the faint of heart with the aircraft nose pointed towards the ground which wasn't too far away, a low but increasing airspeed, and a little airmanship didn't hurt a bit. The angle of bank in any of the turns rarely exceeded thirty degrees.

"The flaps on a C-46 retracted a little slow but when they were full up and airspeed regained as the turn maneuver was completed, spray altitude and position were on the money. Slight variances of these procedures were changed as aircraft weight changed but that basically was how it was done time and time again. It sure made for a close-knit crew and it didn't take long to see the 'makings of the man!' That copilot's switch got a workout and had to be turned on and off at exactly the right time and that had to be determined by me, just another thing to think about.

The equipment had to be in A-1 shape, fixed so that it was, nothing was overlooked that I knew of. You could lay money on the fact that all crewmembers relied on their equipment. We were working with an Air Force entomologist while we found out all these little secrets about spraying. After we had gotten used to flying low over a cloud deck it was time for the real thing. A strip of beach barely out of the water became our next training ground. Approach to the beach was made from the water at spray altitude and a slight pull-up was required to remain at that altitude.

"The entomologist would put four-inch square plates of glass at various places and count the drops of water of the glass we sprayed to make sure the coverage was what it was supposed to be. If there were not enough drops, we probably were not low enough. All of our self-searching was done with full spray tanks of water and that meant a slightly heavier airplane than one loaded with mix. As a matter of note, our 'checker' would fly with us from A to B never on an actual practice mission. The mosquito season was approaching rapidly and we headed for K-37 at Taegu, Korea for the real thing. This was to be our base of operations for the rest of the summer of 1951.

"One fuel truck had been designated for our refill requirements, which were no longer under Air Force supervision but the Fifth Army Surgeon General. Since they were responsible for all forces south of the 38th Parallel, they were now our boss. They knew less about aerial spraying than we did as the whole thing turned out to be a successful experiment. Their requirements consisted of spraying all U.S. and ROK (Republic of Korea) installations south of the parallel. Our first actual spraying mission was the airfield we were on which turned out to be a snap. We notified the airfield control tower who in turn notified all interested parties of the time window when spraying actually took place. Mess halls and hospitals were of special interest because that is where the mosquitoes congregated. A one half mile area surrounding each installation was to be treated to make sure the bugs were killed.

"As the season progressed, earlier and later spray flights were required and seventy degrees F. seemed to be the limit. Anything above that temperature our lethal mix simply floated away and became non-effective. Malaria was rampant amongst the indigenous population because their rice paddies came right up to the edge of most fields. The Fifth Army Surgeon, a full colonel (Medical Corps) visited us one day to show why we were spraying. The crew piled into his jeep and headed for the city of Taegu where he stopped near one of their open-air meat markets. Refrigeration was not part of their culture and what meat they had hung in the open and was covered with black flies and other insects.

"A concrete lined riverbank was nearby and the usual pile of garbage ran over the edge of the concrete. He flipped the top layer off the garbage pile with his swagger stick and the pile was alive with maggots eating their way to adulthood. It was enough for us to see the meat market and its flies but the maggots really brought the reasoning for our mission home to stay. Later on, that same colonel wanted to fly a spray mission with us, to which we readily agreed. Everything was fine until it was necessary to head back for spray altitude after a turn around. The colonel was sitting in the seat normally reserved for the crew chief and could see everything we did to make the mission successful. The color green adorned the cockpit for the rest of the mission and he never wanted to go on another. The four-inch square glass plates were still in use, however.

"Most of the spray missions were of necessity flown very early in the morning and if it cooled off enough, in the evening. Those airfields close to the seas that surrounded Korea were kept cooler from an onshore breeze that was almost always present, but it was some of these fields that gave us the real headaches. As an example, K-10, located on the southern coast of Korea, was an older Japanese seaplane base with one end of the runway sloped into the water to accommodate amphibious aircraft that wanted to get out of same.

"There were a lot of other problems, such as a hangar with an open end that sat so close to approach end of the runway that we used space for a run-up area, the hangar being topless and unused, a very close mountain range that paralleled the runway, the water and some small island being on the other side, a more or less permanent crosswind (there is that onshore breeze again) and an immediate turn was required after takeoff to miss the mountains. The living/operations areas were spread out on what flat land they could muster between the runway and the mountains.

"Approach and landing were always made from the open sea towards the mountains located near the other end of the runway. The South Africans were operating P-51s from that field regularly but it had to be sprayed like any other Allied field. (Some of the South Africans were so tall that they could not fit into the cockpit of a P-51 so they flew them without benefit of a parachute). The colonel from the Fifth Army would have turned a different color than green if he had been along on any spray mission to that field.

"There was one other area occupied by the ROK ground troops that had to be sprayed located south of Taegu and within spitting' distance of K-37, our 'mother' airfield. The quick, small radius turn around came in quite handy because the area was located in a box canyon and on either side of a stream draining the valley. Their buildings were more like our tent areas, low and flat, without many electric wires and poles sticking up for us to miss. The valley narrowed and went uphill like all good valleys do and our turnaround had to be made there. Our mission was made easier as the ROK encampment ended soon enough for us not to leave any wingtips for them to play with.

"I don't know how many missions we flew against the invasive mosquitoes and other strange bugs that airplane taught us to fly in no uncertain terms, to 'FLY IT,' and not the other way around. I cannot thank the crew enough to stay as a cohesive unit and each do their part when the chips were sometimes down.

"We got back to Brady Field in Japan once in a while for needed aircraft inspections and things of that nature. We got a day off but the 'frag' orders still had to be delivered and the air cargo missions from Ashiya to Korea hadn't stopped. We pilots still had a bed in the officers tent area because our duty in Korea was always on TDY (Temporary Duty open-end) orders, sometimes lasting over a week.

"Itazuke Air Base was just a little ways from Brady and the F-84 'bent wings' flew overhead in loose formation on their way to the bomb line in Korea. The wing undersides of that airplane were always loaded with everything from napalm to bombs of various sizes. On one of the trips back 'home' I watched an F-84 climb out with the rest, get just past our base and lose his engine. I am told, since I never flew that airplane, that the electrical system also quit and there was no way to jettison the load.

"I next observed the craft on the final approach to our base, high, hot and long, and as a result, wound up as a ball of aluminum scrap on the runway. The pilot was decapitated and his wedding ring was found in one of the groves in the PSP. On another occasion at K-9 I watched a B-29 on its way north to bomb line that tried to land with his load because the salvo mechanism wouldn't work. The number three engine and prop were feathered and it looked like he was set up for a good three-engine landing. His gear was down and locked, but he was also high, hot and long, and he wound up running off the runway and burying the right gear in the sand besides the PSP. The crew survived that unfortunate incident and so did the airplane.

"Yet another similar day at K-9, I watched a B-26 make a beautiful touchdown and landing, only the nose wheel collapsed when it eased on to the PSP. I have a notion that they are still finding pieces of the nose section of that craft as it was made of glass. The bombardier usually occupies that space at least on a bomb run, but I noticed that it was empty as the aircraft went by. Our parking area was close to the runway, which afforded my crew a ringside seat to many of these 'accidents' which we hoped were not part of the daily menu.

"There were some days that were unsuitable for spraying because of the heat. Nevertheless, we watched predicted weather like a hawk as a summer shower could undo a mission very quickly. There were plenty of missions to fly in the little time we had at 'home' and we got our share. Let it be said that the aircraft from our wing never sat idle if they were in flyable condition. Sometime during the summer the higher-ups had laid out a plan of rotation for the men they had sent over on the spur of the moment and like many others turned out to be one year. The summer was waning into the fall and the rotation date of early October got closer.

"My new station was to be Donaldson Air Force Base at Greenville, South Carolina. There is not a lot to tell about the trip home other than it was all by the same Flying Tiger Airline and the same airplane that had taken us over. The route of return and time enroute were about the same but the attitude was a lot different. Instead of the excitement of what lay ahead, most 'heads' just slept. All of us had screwy schedules and there was no better way to pass the time than sleep. Many of we returnees had stayed together for the whole year and we were going to the same place after our leaves were finished. All of us had a 30 day leave coming and it sure was welcomed.

"A year away from a young family is a long time and many things had taken place in that year. The kids were at home where they should be when my wife met me at the Omaha Airport. It is a different feeling to be in a country like ours and not having to look behind every rock to make sure of your safety and one does not get over that in a day. It was a sobering thought to see the family well taken care of after what we had experienced in Korea. The night was spent in an Omaha hotel and it was a joy to see the little boy and girl the next day. Thirty days of 'vacation' time sounds like forever, but it went by fast and furious. I did think that I had done my part as best I could, and it was time for someone else to shoulder the burden. There was still a lot of flying to be done right here at home and Donaldson was fourteen-hundred miles away to the southeast."[79]

---

[79] Gerald Teachout, "Focus on Korea, 1951," Black Hills Veterans Writing Group, "Korean War," Rapid City, South Dakota, to author, June 2012.

R.A. Jacobsen

Prisoner of War (POW) Riots by North Korean and Communist Chinese Troops During the Korean War

THE Korean War had been referred to as the "forgotten war" and reporting of United States Navy operations during that conflict is even more low-keyed, except for coverage of U.S. Navy and Marine Corps, along with U.S. Air Force exchange pilots, pilots flying off aircraft carriers operating in the Sea of Japan or Yellow Sea. The role that smaller support ships played in the Korean War was just as important and one of the smaller warships, a Landing Ship Medium (LSM) participated in a historic event of the war.

After the RAF narrowly defeated the large air assault from the German Luftwaffe in the "Battle of Britain," some means of carrying large numbers of troops, equipment and supplies across the English Channel to conquer Nazi-occupied Europe needed to be rapidly developed. U.S. naval architects designed the Landing Ship Tank (LST), Landing Craft Tank (LCT) and LSM. However, the LSM design was not finalized until early in 1944 because of other heavy war industrial commitments. The LSM was designed to land troops directly onto enemy held beaches in shallow waters without the need to build docks and breakwaters, speeding the movement of troops over the beach inland to take the fight to the enemy.

LSM-546 was not completed until after World War II. Her keel was laid down at the Brown Ship Building Company at Houston, Texas on July 14, 1945. It was launched on 25 August, commissioned on January 16, 1946, decommissioned on 27 May at Green Cove Springs, Florida, placed into storage at the U.S. Atlantic Reserve Fleet. On September 22, 1950, LSM-546 was re-commissioned to support U.S., United Nations and South Korean forces fighting in Korea.

The subject of Communist POWs is not often discussed when discussing the Korean War, except when the armistice agreement was signed and POWs were swapped, allowing Communist troops to go north and United Nation Command (UNC) troops to cross the 38th Parallel, south. LSM-546 was involved in the support for the large Communist POW camp on Koje-do Island and aftermath of POW riots inside that camp. The riots were a response to attempts by the UNC to regain control of activities inside the POW compounds. After the U.S. amphibious landing at Inchon and advance out of the Pusan Perimeter by the U.S. Eighth Army and UNC troops, the North Korean Army turned and retreated north towards the 38th Parallel.

R.A. Jacobson of Rapid City, South Dakota told his story to the author about service on LSM-546 during the Korean War in the ship's engine room, rating of EN2. His story provides a firsthand account of the Koje-do Island POW riots. Jacobson..."One unusual operation for LSM-546 was out of Pusan, while the North Koreans were desperately trying to break through the perimeter. We took on three Air Force personnel, one officer and two enlisted. I believe the two enlisted were sergeants. They drove two jeeps into the LSM, each equipped with a radio transmitter. We set out to sea and then at night, slowly and carefully edged onto the beach near Pohang, on the north edge of the Pusan Perimeter. The ramp was lowered and the two jeeps drove up onto the beach and disappeared into the dark. There were many North Korean troops operating in the area and it was the job of these forward air controllers to call in air strikes to eliminate these troops. We later learned the air strikes killed over 500 North Korean troops. Unfortunately, the three Air Force personnel did not make it back out."

Large numbers of North Korean troops were captured by U.S. troops after the amphibious landing at Inchon and the crossing of the 38th Parallel into North Korea. By August 1950, approximately 1,000 North Korean troops had been captured. As Communist Chinese troops (referred to by the PLA as volunteers) entered the fighting in North Korea, the UNC had approximately 130,000 troops fighting in Korea by November. During the heat of combat not too much attention had been given on how to secure, clothe, feed or shelter Communist POWs. At first, there were not enough troops immediately available to guard Communist POWs and by January 1951, the number of incarcerated POWs topped 137,000. The UNC decided to move the POWs to Koje-do Island, providing a more secure location, separated from the Korean peninsula.

Neither North of South Korea had any established procedures on how to handle POWs. At first, many South Korean Army troops shot captured North Korean troops, later holding them in open areas until U.S. Army troops took control them. North Korean and Communist Chinese troops were a mix of professional soldiers and civilians (conscripted to replace combat losses). When the UNC started discussions on an armistice, select North Korean and Chinese troops were ordered to be captured, transported to UNC administered POW camps, establishing a formal Communist political control inside the camps, blocking every effort to allow POWs to follow UNC rules and control.

Jacobson..."LSMs were used to transport Communist POWs from the mainland to Koje-do Island. The open cargo deck was separated from the rest of the ship and the sides of the cargo area above the floor, allowing guards to be positioned completely separated from the POWs, thereby providing great security. The voyage from Pusan to Koje-do Island was a four hour trip, usually through rough waters that affected flat bottom LSMs, and those inside the ship. Four LSMs were used to move Communist POWs (LSM-316, 422, 546 and 547), escorted by a patrol craft. We would start early in the morning, departing from the port of Pusan to Koje-do Island. We also carried supplies to support the POW camp."

In January 1951, the UNC undertook a construction program to build a large POW camp to house an estimated 50,000 Communist POWs at War Camp Number One. This camp consisted to four enclosures, each subdivided into eight separate compounds designed to hold and secure 700 to 1,200 POWs, which grew to capacity of 5,000 each. Each compound was separated by barbed wire and secured to what can be referred to as an "untrained guard force." Communists inside the compounds quickly asserted control of the camp. By December 1951, the number of guards on Koje-do Island POW camp reached 9,000 (U.S. and South Korean Army troops), which was still 6,000 under the number deemed necessary to completely secure the large POW camp complex. It should be pointed out that as long as battles raged on the Korean peninsula, constantly changing front line positions, with neither the Communist or UNC forces gaining the upper hand, Communist POWs inside Koje-do Island camp remained relatively quiet. However, as more POWs were transported to the camp, UNC started having problems. Initially, POWs were allowed to control their own affairs inside the camp, which proved not to be a good idea.

In September 1951, 15 POWs were executed after a trial held inside the comp by a POW Communist court. UNC troops entered Compound Number One on 19 September and removed 200 POWs who desired reclassification, resulting in three POWs killed. By November and December, an estimated 37,000 POWs wanted to change their status to that of "Civilian Internees." Communist POWS were screened, except those inside Compound Number 62, which housed 5,600 POWs. With the unsecured nature of the POW camp, Korean War activities of the International Red Cross (IRC) was limited to inspecting the POW camps and providing basic needs to the North Korean and Chinese POWs. The Communists did not accept the IRC and charged this organization was not neutral, pressured POWs inside the camp not to return home, remaining in South Korea to be considered as a unified block, only returning to North Korea together. Eventually, UNC prohibited the IRC from entering Koje-do Island POW camp. Most importantly, Communist POWs were the primary "stumbling block" in the armistice negotiations. The large numbers of Communist North Korean and Chinese POWs were an embarrassing statistic for Communist China and North Korea. These two Communist nations repeated praised the superiority of their social and economic systems over the corrupt western nations.

The Communist leader in control of Compound Number 62 stated everyone in the compound wanted to return to North Korea, requiring no UNC screening. On February 18, 1952, UNC troops entered the compound in full combat gear, resulting in the death of 77 POWs and wounding 140, at the cost of one U.S. Army soldier killed and 38 wounded. UNC truce teams tried to persuade Communist POWs not to return home, with their main effort beginning in April 1952. It should be pointed out that in December 1951, UNC indicated 132,000 POWs and 37,000 others reclassified to civilian internees in custody. Out of these numbers, 16,000 wanted to remain in South Korea rather than cross the 38th Parallel and home to North Korea or onto the Peoples' Republic of China. UNC offered to exchange 70,000 Communist POWs for 12,000 UN POWs held by the Communists in North Korea. By May 1952, the Communists rejected the UNC offer. No further POW screening was attempted. Unrest reached a high level on May 7, 1952 in Compound Number 76 when Communist POWs captured U.S. Army Brigadier General Francis T. Dodd, Camp Commander. On 11 May, Communist POW leaders inside the compound made demands.

1. Immediate ceasing of the barbarous behavior, insults, torture, forcible protest with blood writing, threatening, confinement, mass murdering, gun and machine gun shooting, using poison gas, germ weapons, experiment of A-bomb by your command. You should guarantee POWs human rights and individual life with the base on international law.
2. Immediately stop the so-called illegal volunteer repatriation of NKPA and CVPA PWs.
3. Immediately cease the forcible investigation which thousands

of PWs of NKPA and CVPA be rearmed and failed in slavery, permanently and illegally.

4. Immediate recognition of the PW representative group consisted of NKPA and CVPA PWs and close cooperation to it by your command. This representative group will turn in Brigadier General Dodd, USA, on your hand after we receive the satisfactory declaration to resolve the above items by your command.

Five Republic of South Korea small patrol craft were ordered to a position off Koje-do Island to prevent any possible escape of Communist POWs by water from the camp. Elements of the 187th Airborne Regiment were hastily flown from Japan to Pusan and lifted out by LST, while the rest of the regiment with its heavy gear was brought across by sea. U.S. Navy Task Force 90 ceased all combat operations and maintenance, repositioned near Koje-do Island to provide support for those troops around the POW camp. During July 1952, U.S. Navy ships, including those by LSMs, transported 37,000 POWs to newly constructed and decentralized POW camps.

Brigadier General Charles F. Colson took charge of the command situation outside the POW compound, trying to get General Dodd out of the hands of the Communists. General Colson responded to the Communist demands.

1. With reference to your item 1 of that message, I do admit that there has been instances of bloodshed where many PW have been killed and wounded by UN forces. I can assure in the future that PW can expect humane treatment in this camp according to the principles of international law. I will do all within my power to eliminate further violence and bloodshed. If such incidents happen in the future, I will be responsible.
2. Reference your item 2 regarding repatriation of Korean People's Army and Chinese People's Volunteer Army PW, that is a matter which is being discussed at Panmunjom. I have no control or influence over the decisions at the Peace Conference.
3. Regarding your item 4 pertaining to forcible investigation, I can inform you that after General Dodd's release, there will be no more forcible screening or any rearming of any PW in this camp, nor will any attempt be made at nominal screening.
4. Reference to your item 4, we approve the organization of a

PW representative group or commission consisting of North Korean People's Army and Chinese People's Volunteer Army PW, according to the details agreed to by General Dodd and approved by me.

On May 20, 1952 U.S. Army infantry teams entered Compound Number 3 and advanced against Communist POW resistance. Communist POWs armed with rocks, flails, sharpened tent poles, steel pipes and knives, the defiant POWs screamed insults and challenges against UNC troops. UNC troops maintained excellent discipline, using tear gas and concussion grenades to break up the POWs opposition. One Communists POW was killed and another 29 wounded with one U.S. Army soldier wounded.

On 4 June, UNC troops moved against Communist revolts inside Compounds Number 60, 85 and 96. U.S. Army tanks knocked down Communist flags being flown inside the three compounds, tearing down signs, burning the banners with Communist slogans on each and, in the process, rescuing 10 Communist POWs who were about to face a trial for their actions which supported the enemy. UNC troops forced their way into compound Number 76, bringing out 76 POWs who were also to be tried for similar support to the UNC. In Compound Number 60, UNC troops repeated the military take back process within the Communist POW compound. On 10 June, UNC troops entered Compound Number 76 to gain control of the area, but the fighting resulted in 31 Communist POWs killed, with many killed actually executed by the Communist POWs themselves, 139 wounded with one U.S. Army soldier killed and 14 injured.

Brigadier Generals Dodd and Colson were relieved of command, demoted to full colonel, ordered to retire from active duty, returned to the United States. The new camp commander was U.S. Army General Hydon L. Boatner.

UNC now determined to implement voluntary repatriation regardless and this had the end result of delaying Armistice negotiations with the Communists. On June 8, 1953, Republic of South Korea President Rhee unilaterally ordered the release of thousands of POWs being held, allowing them to disappear into the South Korean countryside. After prolonged and hard negotiations with the Communists, the Armistice was finally signed on July 27, 1953, stopping fighting in Korea, but not officially ending the war. LSMs moved Communist POWs from Koje-do Island to Pusan, from there transported to Panmunjom for transfer back to Communist control. During this initial exchange, referred to as "Operation BIG SWITCH," 75,821 UNC held POWs were released to Communist control in exchange for 12,773 UNC POWs, of which 3,591 were Americans. On 23 September, another 14,704 Communist Chinese and 7,900 North Korean UNC held POWs were released. The balance of UNC held Communist POWs were repatriated on January 21, 1954.

Jacobson..."LSM-546's crew earned the Korean Service Medal for participation in United Nations summer to fall offensive, to November 27, 1951; second Korean winter, 28 November to December 4, 1951 and 19 February to March 15, 1952; and Korean defense, summer to fall, 7 May to July 17, 1952. I left Korea after the end of the war for Japan and then shipping home, but LSM-546 remained in Korea. It was transferred from the U.S. Navy to the Republic of South Korea on February 16, 1953. LSM-546 remained in service until removed from active service in 1959 and scrapped."[80]

---

[80] Lt. Col. George A. Larson, USAF (Ret.), "POW riots on Koje-do Island and the role of LSM-546 during the Korean War," *Military*, April 2004.

Raleigh H. Watson, Jr.

Convair B-36, 77th Bomb Squadron, 28th Bomb Wing, Ellsworth Air Force Base

Electronic Countermeasures Mechanic

RALEIGH H. Watson, Jr., B-36 ECM operator, 77th BS, 28th BW, Ellsworth AFB, South Dakota..."I enlisted in June 1951, at 17 years old, right out of high school. Basic training at Lackland AFB in San Antonio, Texas in June. I went to Airborne Radar Maintenance School at Keesler AFB, Louisiana from August 1951 to April 1952. I arrived at Ellsworth AFB in Rapid City in April 1952, assigned to 4011th A&E Maintenance Squadron as an ECM mechanic. In August 1952, I volunteered to return to Keesler AFB for a two month course to become a fully qualified ECM operator. I returned to Rapid City, assigned to the 77th Bomb Squadron.

"I was assigned to Captain Grissom's crew for training. I flew with them once or twice until checked out. I was asked to fill in for Major Anthony Loving on the Azores trip, as he could not go. I made this trip on Lt. Cummings crew. It was on this exercise that General Ellsworth was killed. I recall that he came down to see us off when we departed Lames Field. I understood from our engineer, then Major Dale Poeot that General Ellsworth was to return with us, but his plans changed so he could sit in for a sick pilot on the RB-36H, which crashed during the return flight to Ellsworth AFB.

"Upon returning to Ellsworth AFB, I requested to be assigned to Colonel Cumming's crew as Airmen/ECM operators were going to be assigned to it. He agreed to have me and I remained in his crew (S-03) until my discharge two years later. I was an Airman Third Class, on a crew, and I received two spot promotions. I made Airman First Class the following month, so I ended my Air Force career as an Airman First Class.

"The flights with that crew were relatively unremarkable. The crew was very cohesive and we never had any serious in flight emergencies. Our ground crew had a superb crew chief, SSgt. Byanes, keeping our B-36 (number 734) in top shape. We had our share of feathered engines, but never had to remain over night while I was with them.

"The most exciting things I recall were not that exciting. One was on return from the Azores, as we were just about to take off, a scanner reported flames from one engine. I was almost asleep in my seat but that woke me up. Later, we determined the flames came from an engine backfire.

"Another interesting flight was a GCA approach under minimum conditions. We returned from a routine 15 to 20 hour flight. The weather was lousy at Ellsworth and I was in the upper blister listening to the radar operator. I heard the Aircraft Commander talking to the base 77th OPS officer on the ground. Major Kuncz told the Aircraft Commander to make one landing approach under GCA control, and then go to Denver and RON if he could not in as our fuel was becoming marginal. I sat in the blister and listened to the GCA ground controller coming in over the radio all the way down. It was a beautiful sight when we broke out and landed on the runway. Speaking of beautiful sights, at daybreak one morning I was standing in the left forward blister, watching a gorgeous sunrise when all of a sudden, a T-33 pulled up right off our left wing tip and flew alongside for a few moments. It was beautiful, but he could stay back with us, so he dropped his landing gear to slow down. One of our pilots said on the interphone 'that is adding insult to injury.' Then the T-33 pilot pulled up his landing gear, peeled off and was gone.

"My crew was away from Ellsworth for six months. They were at bomb tests at Eniwetok Island in the Pacific, leaving the ECM team and gunners on base. During that time, we ran the squadron coffee bar for the 77th BS and maintained our minimum ECM requirements by flying test hops with other Ellsworth crews. I had one short flight, which was probably my most exciting. About four hours after takeoff, we got into a storm with violent turbulence, possible lightning strikes and then something broke off from an antenna stab, which banged against the airplane. Many sick crewmen were on board and I was trying to shoot a Form 'E' on the Ellsworth AFB ground radar site. It was miserable, on landing, the aircraft's hydraulics was out and we had to use the emergency pump to get pressure for the hydraulic operations."[81]

---

[81] Raleigh H. Watson, Jr., interview, B-36 Reunion, Castle Air Museum, October 14, 1995, author.

How Ellsworth Air Force Base Got its Name

THE United States Air Force installation, which presently bears the name Ellsworth AFB has undergone several designations since its creation in October 1941, established on January 2, 1942. Beginning with its earliest planning stages in December 1941, the federal government referred to the military base as the Rapid City Army Air Base, unofficially Rapid City Army Air Field. The U.S. Army renamed it Rapid City Air Field on November 28, 1947, then Weaver Air Force Base after USAF Brigadier General Walter B. Weaver. He was one of the pioneers in the development of the Air Force in January 1948. Public appeals convinced the Air Force to rename it Rapid City Air Force Base on June 24, 1948.

Just after midnight on the morning of Wednesday, March 18, 1953, a Convair RB-36 Peacemaker (tail number 51-13721) assigned to the 718th BS, 28th SRW, took off from Lajes Field, Azores. It had flown sorties with a task force of eleven other RB-36s during five days of intercontinental combat training and crew H15 was ready to go home to Ellsworth. After checking that their aircraft was operational ready for the return trip, the flight crew (Aircraft Commander-Brigadier General Richard E. Ellsworth, pilot-Major Frank C. Wright and Chief of Wing Operational Planning, Aircraft and Crew H15 Commander-Captain Jacob H. Pruett, Jr., and pilot-Captain Orien F. Clark) coaxed their colossal silver bird into the sky and onto its westward course of the United States and Rapid City Air Force Base. Although Captain Jacob H. Pruett was the Aircraft Commander, Wing Commander Brigadier General Richard E. Ellsworth was senior officer on the aircraft. The 3.5 million dollar airplane carried the General and twenty-two fellow crewmembers.

Crew H15's flight westward across the Atlantic would take them several hours, most of which would be over the vast, trackless ocean. Turbulent spring weather conditions were not ideal during the best of days, much less, for low-level, over the water training conducted at 1,000 feet above the whitecaps. The navigator, Captain Harold G. Smith, had factored in head and tail winds, confident that his calculations would alert the pilot to climb to 2,000 feet above the craggy North American coast well before landfall. His computations had to be particularly precise, as forward-looking radar not developed for the B-36.

The weather steadily worsened. Both General Ellsworth and Major Frank C. Wright flew the over water portions of the flight. As they came to within several hundred miles of the Canadian coast, however, Captain Pruitt tackled the difficult chore of piloting number 721 on instruments alone, through steady sleet, freezing drizzle and fog.

The crew reported their position every hour at planned points across the ocean. What they did not know was that five hours into their flight the weather sabotaged one of their position reports. Not only were they unable to gauge their true ground speed, which increased from 160 knots, but they also believed the aircraft was more than 205 nautical miles out to sea and wouldn't need to climb for at least another 30 minutes. In reality, they were 67 nautical miles from the coast and rapidly gaining on land as their ground speed reached 202 knots. They had only 20 minutes before reaching Newfoundland's rugged eastern shore.

With a ceiling of 50 to 100 feet and visibility from zero to one-eighth of a mile, General Ellsworth and the crew H15 were flying blind. Then, to make conditions worse, icing choked two of the plane's four turbojet engines, its six reciprocating pusher engines were still functioning. Radio operators in St. John's, Newfoundland intercepted an emergency declaration that two engines had failed. Residents of the tiny fishing of Burgoyne, Newfoundland watched helplessly as the giant plane rumbled low overhead, crashing just below a hilltop in the nearly trackless forest. The crew probably did not know what they hit. The crash site is in the wilderness area of Random Island, near Burgoyne Cove, 60 miles east of Gander, Newfoundland.

Alerted by the explosion, local woodsmen were first to arrive at the site of the burning wreckage, followed by arrival of authorities who braved horrible flying conditions that had already grounded other aircraft throughout the Province. Fort Pepperell Air Base dispatched an emergency medical team to go by ground transportation and boats, with the Royal Canadian Air Force provided rescue experts who parachuted into the crash site's remote location. Unfortunately, three valiant rescue attempts and efforts were in vain. There were no survivors.

President Dwight D. Eisenhower flew to Rapid City Air Force Base on June 13, 1953, officiating the ceremony renaming the Air Force installation to Ellsworth Air Force Base in honor of Brigadier

General Richard E. Ellsworth, the name, which it carries today.[82]

---

[82] "How Ellsworth Air Force Base got its name," Ellsworth Air Force Base. 28th Bomb Wing Historian.

Ralph Whitaker

B-36 Crewman, Ellsworth Air Force Base

RALPH Whitaker..."During my three years at Ellsworth Air Force Base, I had three events that I call outstanding. First, the sad event involving the August 27, 1954 crash of Cotterill's RB-36 when I lost a close friend named Harry Hertnekly, who was an electrical gunner on the ill-fated crew. His wife asked me to escort his body by train to his home in Colorado Springs, Colorado, where I presented his widow the U.S. flag and gave a short speech of condolences from the Air Force at the burial services. I am not positive that I said anything that I said anything that even resembled the speech I was told to give and that I had practiced.

"The second event involved a 'rum-run' to Ramey AFB in November 1954 and I've gotten the name of the very capable aircraft commander. However, we took off loaded for Ramey AFB and the left inboard flap stopped at about the 15 degree down position and looked loose and dangerous so we pointed out the flap and gear indicators to the aircraft commander. The aircraft commander sent the crew chief to the bomb bay to check the problem out; there was no change so the aircraft commander gave any of the crew the option of bailing out. But, with 15mph ground winds or coming in with the plane still loaded with fuel and he was confident he could stop the heavy bird without inboard flaps down to the maximum, plus we lad two miles of runway available. We all chose to ride it out and proceeded to secure the area and buckled up tight in crash positions. The hotshot pilot touched the main gears down on the very end of the runway and normally we had slowed enough to turn off at the operations turn off, one-half or one mile of the runway. However, today, we went by operations with engines in reverse and operations were just a blur in the blister. We were slowing down but we were in the aft section and could not see the end of the runway rapidly coming at us. However, we sensed somebody had better throw out an anchor. Fortunately, at the end of the two-mile runway, the pilot looped the plane around with the brakes squeaking when it stopped. Our ground crew fixed a broken linkage and we proceeded to Ramey AFB with no further problems.

"The third event was an air show flight to the RB-36 to Billings,

Montana where a new airport celebration was in progress. The airport was built on a high bluff above the town and had an adequate one mile runway for commercial aircraft and our RB-36. However, after setting overnight in the parking area we found our main landing gear sunk into the asphalt about eight-inches. Fortunately, we had enough engine horsepower to pull out and proceed forward to the end of the runway where we had to back up by reversing the six pusher propeller engines into starting position at the end of the runway. We took off with all ten engines (six pusher propellers and four turbojet engines) roaring in only 2,500 feet of runway. The pilots pointed the aircraft's nose in a steep climb to about 10,000 feet, then banked in a chandel type maneuver, coming down, aimed at the center of the runway, pulling out at 200 feet, climbing back up at the end of the runway, leveling off, heading back to Ellsworth AFB."[83]

---

[83] Ralph Whitaker, interview, B-36 reunion, Castle Air Museum, October 14, 1995, author.

Matador Cruise Missile

South Dakota Missileers, America's First Nuclear Ground-to-Ground Guided Missile

DURING World War II, Nazi Germany initiated the modern missile era with the development and operational use of the tactical surface-to-surface missile or SSM. Along the English Kent coastline on June 13, 1944, at 4 a.m., the first German Vergeltungswaffe I (V-1), a tactical missile entered English air space and headed toward London where it delivered a 1,870 pound conventional warhead. It flew at a speed of 400mph and at 4,000 feet. The V-1 (commonly referred to as Vengence-1 weapon) was a surprise to many Allied leaders who believed that after D-Day (June 6, 1944), Germany could no longer threaten English cities with aerial bombs. Later, with the tactical operational introduction of the V-2 rocket, these missiles shaped post-World War II U.S. and Soviet missile development and deployment options.

Post Victory-in-Europe Day or VE-Day inspection of captured German tactical missile depots, factories and launch positions spurred research and development in the United States, as in the Soviet Union. Some say this was the delivery weapons portion of the arms race between the United States and the Soviet Union for the unmanned delivery of atomic then nuclear weapons. Earlier, in October 1944, the United States recovered an intact, although damaged V-1, which landed in England without detonating, shipping, it back to a military research and development center. The resulting knock-off copy had the designation JB-2. Republic Aviation Corporation, powered by an engine produced by Ford (under designation PJ-31-F-1), built the weapon's airframe. World War II ended before the U.S. could deploy the missile to the Pacific Theater of Operations for use against the Empire of Japan, to attack defensive positions prior to amphibious landings. It was a relatively crude weapon, with a cruise speed of 400mph, range 150 miles, able to deliver a 2,100 pound warhead. The JB-2 provided technical data for design improvements to build an advanced cruise missile designs.

With the end of the war in the Pacific, the USAAF in August 1945 published a design production specifications for an advanced winged cruise missile with a range 175 to 500 miles and speed of 600mph. The proposal designation was XB-61 Matador Pilotless Bomber. The Glen L. Martin Company won a one-year design contract in 1946, almost cancelled, but extended because of the Korean War. The design upgraded to carry an atomic weapon, TM-61A or Tactical Missile 61A. It looked like a conventional turbojet fighter without a pilot's compartment, fitted with a 57,000 pound thrust rocket assisted takeoff (RATO) bottle hanging below the rear of the fuselage. This rocket provided a zero-launch capability, boosting speed in three to twelve seconds from 0 to 200mph, at which time the 4,600 pound thrust JSS-A-37 (Allison J-33) turbojet engine fired up, increasing speed to 600mph, driving it down range to 600 to 690 miles. It carried a 3,000 pound conventional or atomic warhead. Initial range was limited to 250 miles because guidance had to be line of sight. In 1954, the guidance system upgrade allowed increased range, although still functioned as line of sight, vulnerable to ECM. The design deficiency remained until deployment of the MACE cruise missile.

Another shortcoming of the Matador was overall launch to target reliability, one never completely corrected. By the end of test launches, the Matador obtained 71 percent launch reliability. Given today's zero-zero or pinpoint accuracy of cruise missiles, Matador CEP of 1,600 to 2,700 feet with an atomic warhead made up for the lack of conventional accuracy.

Harvey Holzwarth..."I joined the Air Force after graduating from high school in 1948, trained as a heavy-equipment operator (crane operator) and assigned to the first Matador unit, 1st Pilotless Bomber Squadron at Patrick Air Force Base at Coca Beach, Florida. Patrick AFB was near Cape Canaveral. The Matador was the first U.S. missile test flown at Cape Canaveral. Testing was a new part of the Air Force and to warn civilians around the test launch area, Air Force transports fitted with loudspeakers flew low over the waters around Cape Canaveral, using mounted loudspeakers underneath the wings to warm fishing boats a test launch was about to take place."

When one pictures the name "Cape Canaveral," the mental image of the huge Saturn V moon launch rocket and shuttle launches comes into view. In the early 1950s, it was an empty area, desolate landscape, referred to by locals as the "Cape." The Cape had its first missile launch on July 24, 1950, a German V-2 rocket, shipped to the U.S. after capture of V-2 weapons in Germany. It was fitted with an American second stage (WAC Corporal Rocket), under launch designation "Bumper 8." By June 2000, the Cape passed 3,200 missile launches.

There were 280 Matador launches between 1951 to 1954. Testing was under direction and control of the 6555th Guided Missile Squadron. The squadron was responsible for OJT for Martin Company employees (follow on to Glen L. Martin Company), Missile Assembly Shop training, contractor and military personnel missile training, and simulated launch training. The first live Matador launch by a military crew was on December 7, 1951.

Holzwarth..."During test launches, two USAF F-86 Sabre turbojets followed the airborne Matador, both increasing power (screaming) to catch up to the missile, which had accelerated to 300mph. You just cannot believe the sounds from the missile and the F-86s. The launches were nothing less than spectacular."

The 6555th s Matador Training Program consisted of three phases.

1. Phase I: Personnel assigned to propulsion and missile assembly received 13 days of individual training, and those assigned to missile guidance, 43 days of instruction.
2. Phase II: Individual technicians were gathered into three teams (assembly, checkout or launch) to start working on the Matador missile.
3. Phase III: Normally required six weeks, but the continued lack of training missiles and ground equipment extended this time. This phase of training was when guidance, propulsion and assembly teams were mated as crew. Note: crew training was projected to last 43 days, but its actual length and completion depended on the availability of training missiles.
4. An additional training phase, not considered part of the programmed training phase, was conducted separately by the missile squadrons (independently), turning crews into operational squadrons, each with its own staff officers and commander.

The 1st and 69th Pilotless Bomber Squadrons, after training, were assigned to the USAF Tactical Air Command (TAC) for deployment to West Germany. Even with nagging reliable problems, in March 1954, the Matador was shipped to West Germany, and in 1955 operational at Bitburg AB. Eventually six missile Matador squadrons were deployed to Bitburg, Hahn and Sembach Air Bases, with 200 missiles. All missiles were deployed to pre-surveyed, fixed launch sites in clearings around each base, within 150 miles of Soviet controlled East Germany. It required twenty vehicles for each missile site. This was a large convoy: transport vehicle trailer, launchers, 20 ton Garwood mobile crane, a "bread van" used as the guidance and control vehicle, warhead transport vehicle, and mobile 10 kilovolt generator. Permanent site buildings consisted of Quonset crew huts and concrete bunker, which served as the launch block house. Not all missiles deployed to the launch sites. A squadron deployed two missiles to the field, with two missiles at the primary base maintained in a standby status if the primary missiles became non-operational.

The launcher was parked and set to correct orientation. The transporter was pulled alongside the launcher. The crane was positioned between the two vehicles to swing the missile from the transporter onto the launcher, then the wings were attached. Holzwarth..."After the missile was assembled, I assisted in moving the auxiliary boost unit (RATO) and positioned it on the lower, rear of the missile's fuselage. This provided a 57,000 pound solid rocket motor to zero-launch the missile, dropping off with three to 12 seconds, boosting speed to 200mph, which permitted the missile's turbojet engine to kick in and continue to propel the missile to its designated cruise speed to target." The vehicles pulled away and power added by the 10 kilovolt generator. All the wires had to be connected and run from the missile to control/guidance ban and to the concrete blockhouse. The warhead section attached the warhead to the missile. The crew was not told if the warhead was conventional or atomic. Once the missile was checked, the blockhouse assumed launch control. The time for arrival to alert or launch ready was 45 minutes. If time permitted after the initial launch, a reload and second launch could be completed in 15 to 16 minutes.

Beginning in 1959, the Matador was replaced by the Martin CGM-13 Mace. It was similar in appearance to the Matador, but required fewer support vehicles, once launched it operated under an automatic terrain recognition and navigation system, which guided the missile to its target, with a longer range of 1,200 miles. Today, one would look at the pilotless cruise missile as an updated version of the World War II German V-1, but it provided the United States with a nuclear missile able to strike targets inside the Soviet Union during the early years of the Cold War.[84]

---

[84] Lt. Col. George A. Larson, USAF (Ret.), "Matador: America's First Cruise Missile," *Friends Journal*, Volume 25, Number 1, spring 2002. On October 6, 2000, during an interview with Harvey Holzwarth (Pierre, South Dakota) and sixty former "Cold War" members of the 38th Tactical Missile Wing (B-61 Matador ground-to-ground nuclear armed cruise missile) at the Rapid City Ramkota, details of the United States Air Force's first nuclear attack

continued...

...*continued*

missile was discussed. South Dakotans don't' realize those from their state also manned missile sites other than the Titan I and Minuteman I and II ICBMs.

Titan I Intercontinental Ballistic Missiles at Ellsworth Air Force Base

THE Intercontinental Ballistic Missile (ICBM) Scientific Advisory Committee planted the seeds of the Titan I ICBM program in July 1954, when it recommended that the Air Force Western Development Division (WDD) explore alternative missile configurations before deploying the Atlas ICBM as America's first strategic missile. In August 1954, the WDD directed its system engineering and technical direction contractor, Ramo-Woodridge Corporation hired Lockheed Aircraft Corporation and Glen L. Martin Aircraft Company for assistance. WDD and Ramo-Woodridge Corporation determined it was not a sound strategic defense decision rely on the Atlas ICBM for America's long-leg strike nuclear deterrence against the Soviet Union. This was a concern because Convair's Atlas ICBM design relied on an unconventional approach. Although many engineering tests had been made on the Atlas ICBM, it had not been test fired. This would not happen for three years. Based on an October 1954 study, WDD recommended Convair go ahead with the Atlas ICBM. At the same time, WDD suggested the Air Force broaden its ICBM program to include an ICBM with a rigid aircraft type fuselage and alternate engine configuration. The WDD stressed the development of a second ICBM, which would allow the Air Force to follow a more ambitious design and create a healthy competition with the Atlas program.

In January 1955, the ICBM Scientific Advisory Committee reviewed the WDD's findings and recommended the Air Force pursue an alternate ICBM configuration. This approach would most probably be a two-stage propulsion missile. Based on the committee's recommendation, in April 1955, the Secretary of the Air Force, Harold Talbott, authorized the WDD to begin work on a second ICBM. The only stipulation was that the winning contractor agree to build its missile production facility somewhere in the central United States. The Air Force requested bids for this ICBM in May 1955, and in October, a contract was awarded to the Glen L. Martin Company of Baltimore, Maryland. Its production facility was to be near Denver, Colorado.

The Air Force's goal in starting the Titan I ICBM development program was to serve as a backup ICBM in case the Atlas ICBM program failed. Other goals were to develop a large, two-stage ICBM with a longer range and heavier payload delivery capability, and develop a rocket that could also be used as a heavy payload launch vehicle for scientific space research flights. At the beginning of the development of the Titan I ICBM, referred to as Weapon System 107A-2 Program, it was given the designation SM-65/LGM-25. The program would take advantage of new developments in missile technologies not used on the Atlas SM-65/HGN-19. The Atlas ICBM was developed to provide nuclear deterrence against the Soviet Union. The Atlas ICBM was one large fuel tank, with guidance equipment and warhead on the nose, and engines at the bottom. The fuel tank served as the main component of the missile's structure. It was classified as a single stage ICBM.

Development problems slowed the Titan I's development, with the first test flight not launched until February 6, 1959. Three companies submitted bids to the USAF to develop and produce the Titan I: Martin, Douglas and Lockheed. On October 27, 1955, the Glen L. Martin Company won the bidding competition and selected to build the Titan I airframe. Subcontractors were brought into the program to support missile production. It was not until April 20, 1962 that the first Titan I ICBM was lowered into an operational silo, later elevated to alert. It was assigned to the 703rd SMW at Lowry AFB, Colorado.

To support SAC's ICBM operations, on June 3, 1959, bids were opened from contractors for remodeling Building D on Offutt AFB. During World War II, the building was used as a production facility to build the Martin B-26 Marauder and later, Boeing B-29 Superfortress. SAC modified Building D into a guided missile assembly facility. It had a short life span and on December 15, 1965, the 549th SMS was inactivated with missile assembly no longer performed in the huge building.

The U.S. Army Corps of Engineers Ballistic Missile Construction Office directed the construction of the Titan I complexes. They were configured as a cluster of three silos together because the missile required ground-based radar and guidance computers during the launch phase. The Titan I did not have an inertial guidance system that came with the Titan II and following Minuteman and Peacekeeper ICBMs. To protect the missiles from a near missile from a Soviet ICBM attack, the Titan I complex was underground, connected by underground tunnels.

The Titan I complex layout was distinctive. At one edge of the complex, three silos were located, each 160 feet deep and 44 feet in diameter. The silos were constructed of re-enforced concrete, ranging two to three feet thick. Within the silo, a steel framework housed the missile and an elevator to raise it to the surface prior to ignition and launch. The only sections of the silo above ground level were two horizontal blast doors, each weighing 125 tons. Located next to each silo was the propellant and equipment terminal building buried 17 to 24 feet underground. Seven hundred feet from the silos were the control room (100 feet in diameter) and powerhouse (27 feet in diameter), each built of re-enforced concrete, 10 to 17 feet underground. Controlling access to these two buildings was a portal, buried 72 feet underground, 38 feet in diameter.

At the base of the Titan I ICBM complex were two radar antennas for the ground-based missile guidance system. The antennas were protected by their placement inside two silos, each 67 foot deep and 38 feet in diameter. The launch crew raised the two antennas prior to the missiles, each on an elevator. The two antennas were 1,300 feet from the farthest missile silo. The complex used 2,500feet of corrugated steel tunnels, nine feet in diameter, 46 feet underground. The tunnels connected all the buildings and silos in the complex. Once alerted, the first of three missiles could be fueled and launched in 15 minutes. After receiving a verified launch order, the missile crew filled the ICBM's tanks with 200,000 pounds of liquid oxygen and RP-1 kerosene. After the missile was fueled inside the silo, it was raised to the surface for ignition and launch. The first stage burned for 134 seconds, propelling it at an altitude of 35 miles.

As the first stage fell off, the second stage ignited, burning for 156 seconds, pushing the missile to an altitude of 150 miles, at a maximum speed of 22,554 feet per second. After the second stage rocket engine burned out, two small vernier rocket engines ignited, burning for 50 seconds. The two small engines provided final powered course correction. After the vernier rocket engines burned out, the re-entry vehicle with its warhead followed a ballistic trajectory, reaching a maximum altitude of 541 miles, then beginning its high-speed descent to a designated target in the Soviet Union. At this time, because of the time for the Titan I RV to begin its non-powered ballistic flight, the ground-based radar at the launch site remained active for seven and one-half minutes, at which time the second missile could be launched, followed the by the third missile after another seven and one-half minutes.

Titan Is were deployed at Lowry AFB, Colorado; Ellsworth AFB, South Dakota, Beale AFB, California; Larson AFB, Washington and Mountain Home AFB, Idaho. In August 1957, the Air Force selected Lowry AFB as the first Titan I ICBM operational facility. Construction of launch facilities began on May 1, 1959. By August 4, 1961, construction all on planned Titan I silos at Lowry AFB was complete. On April 18, 1962, the 724th SMS was declared operational; turned over to SAC for operational control. The 725th SMS was turned over to SAC on May 4, 1962 and declared operational on 10 May. Both missile squadrons remained on operational alert for three years. These Titan I ICBMs started coming off alert on February 17, 1965. The last Titan I was removed from its silo on March 26, 1965. Both missile squadrons were inactivated on June 25, 1965.

On December 1, 1960, the 850th SMS was activated under control of the 28th BW, Ellsworth AFB, South Dakota. On June 22,1961, the 28th BW received its first Titan I ICBM. The squadron became operational on 28 September. On January 1, 1962, control of the squadron came under the 44th SMW. On December 1, 1962, the 44th SMW was reassigned to the 28th Air Refueling Squadron (AR EFS), making the wing, along with two others, the 456th Strategic Air Wing, at Beale AFB, California and 462nd at Larson AFB, Washington, the only SAC wings to operate B-52s and Titan Is. On February 1, 1965, Ellsworth's last Titan I was removed from alert, with the 850th SMS inactivated on March 25, 1965. The 851st SMS was activated at Beale AFB on April 20, 1962.

During 1962, a tremendous explosion blasted a Titan I ICBM silo, destroying the missile and heavily damaging its silo during contractors' checkout at Complex 4C. An Air Force accident investigation report indicated the two liquid tanks exploded because of blocked oxygen vents and valves. On June 6, 1962, a flash fire at the Chico complex killed a worker.

On September 8, 1962, the 851st SMS was declared operational, turned over to SAC. The squadron remained operational for the next two and one-half years. On January 4, 1965, the first Titan I was removed from alert. The decommissioning process was complete by 22 January. On March 25, 1965, the squadron was inactivated.

The 568th SMS at Larson AFB, Washington was activated on April 1, 1961, assigned to 4170th SW. On September 26, 1962, the 568th became operational, turned over to SAC. On March 18, 1963, the squadron suffered an accident with a Titan I in its silo. During maintenance, Air Force missile maintenance personnel inadvertently disconnected the cable between the missile and the silo, resulting in the inter-stage separation rockets firing, blasting off the second stage from the first stage. The accident heavily damaged the silo and the missile inside, but fortunately, it did not injure any maintenance personnel. The missile was not fitted with a nuclear warhead at the time of the accident. The squadron's missiles started coming off alert on January 4, 1965, completed by February 2, 1965, inactivated on 25 March.

The 569th SMS was activated on June 1, 1961 at Mountain Home AFB, Idaho. On August 16, 1962, it was declared operational, turned over to SAC. The first missile was removed on February 17, 1965, with the final missile pulled from its silo on April 1, 1965. The squadron was inactivated on June 25, 1965.

The 6,300 miles range of the Titan I was a major factor in determining site locations. The Air Force placed sites between Colorado and Washington state. Titan II ICBMs, with a longer range of 9,000 miles, could be based further south in the United States. Launch silos for the Titan II were located in Arizona, Kansas and Arkansas, allowing a wider silo separation. With storable liquid fuel and an all inertial guidance package, the missile could be fired from inside the silo as soon as launch door slid away. Other factors affecting the site location of each Titan I and II launch complexes were the surrounding civilian population densities, the missile's projected flight path to Soviet targets and distance to supporting Air Force bases. The operationally deployed Titan I force life span was from 1962 to 1965.

On May 16, 1964, Secretary of Defense Robert McNamara directed an accelerated phase out of the Atlas and Titan I ICBMs. The Titan Is were removed from their silos and transported to Mira Lomas Air Force Station in the spring of 1965. The missiles were stored in the open for nine months. Because there was no national requirement for these missile as space launch vehicles (mission performed by the Atlas missile air frames) or anti-missile targets, in the spring of 1966 the Aerospace Corporation advised to not to continue their storage. Most of the missiles were scrapped. Select museums acquired a Titan I ICBM for display, including the South Dakota Air and Space Museum. It has not be refurbished and is not on display (as of 2015).[85]

---

[85] Lt. Col. George A. Larson, USAF (Ret,), "Titan I, America's first heavy two-stage intercontinental ballistic missile," *Friends Journal*, Volume 29, Number 2, Summer 2006.

MSgt. Robert O'Daniel

U.S. Navy and U.S. Air Force

54th Fighter-Interceptor Squadron Air Defense Command at Clear, Alaska

"Operation NEW LIFE," Wake Island

ROBERT O'Daniel was born in 1933 in Redfield, South Dakota. He graduated from Rapid City High School on May 1, 1952. He joined the U.S. Navy on November 7, 1952, with the rank of Yeoman, Third Class. Upon his discharge from the Navy on September 17, 1956, he joined the U.S. Air Force, trained as a Flight Records/Administrative Clerk, assigned to the 54th Fighter-Interceptor Squadron, Ellsworth Air Force Base, South Dakota. In 1959, as Chief Clerk of Wing Administration Section he maintained publication files, prepares correspondence, reports and messages, maintains suspense files, assigns tasks to personnel under him, commensurate with their capabilities.

In December 1959, he was assigned to 731st Radar Squadron at Sundance Air Force Station, Wyoming, SSgt., NCOIC of the Administrative Section. He was later assigned to Detachment 2, Headquarters 71 Surveillance Wing with Air Defense Command at Clear BMEWS, Alaska on June 13, 1962. He was assigned to Headquarters, Pacific Air Forces, Hickam Air Force Base, Hawaii. He had temporary duty assignment to Wake Island, earning a Letter of Commendation for his assistance in handling South Vietnamese refugees as part of "Operation NEW LIFE," assigned to the 15th Operations Squadron. He retired from the Air Force on April 1, 1977.

The following expands on important aspects of MSgt. O'Daniel's assignments on the defense of the United States, starting with the 54th Fighter-Interceptor Squadron's history, before and during operations at Ellsworth Air Force Base. Information from typed history of 54th Fighter-Interceptor Squadron, Ellsworth Air Force Base as provided by records retrieved and documented by MSgt. O'Daniel.

1941

The 54th was activated at Hamilton Field on 15 January.

1942

22 January–The Squadron moves to Paine field, Washington. Flying conducted in P-40s and P-36s.

13 February–First P-38 arrives.

9 March–Designation of Squadron changes from 54th Pursuit Squadron (INT) AFCC to 54th Pursuit Squadron (INT) AAF.

2 April–1st accident, Lt. Morse injured when his P-38 crashes into mess hall, killing two airmen.

5 April–Lt. Pinson crashes into Puget Sound-killed.

9 April–Reconnaissance mission to Elmendorf, returned on 22 April, first step toward combat.

12 April–Designation changed from Pursuit to 54th Fighter Squadron AAF.

23 May–1st Air Echelon (pilots and mechanics) leave for Elmendorf, arrives 2 June then to Cold Bay and Umnak.

24 May–2nd Echelon to Elmendorf, arriving 2 June.

25 May–Departure rest of Squadron to Kodiak via sea transport by 29 May.

31 May–Arrival at Elmendorf.

3 June–Initial tactical operation of 54th air alert, two-hour patrol, no bandits.

4 June–First planned mission (escort), no contact with enemy.

5 June–first part of air echelon leaves for Cold Bay, 2nd flight to Fort Glen, Umnak.

6 June–Search mission for enemy carriers, no success from Cold Bay. First active strike from Fort Glenn, Umnak. Strafe Russian freighter flying Japanese colors.

14-15 June–A&B Flights leave Elmendorf for Fort Randall, Cold Bay, Alaska.

18 June–Captain Jackson (CO) makes major.

21 June–Lt. Millton killed in crash, weather the cause.

5 July–C-53 crashes killing four officers.

21 July–Lt. Stoland, one of flight of four, killed in crash into mountain in bad weather, he was number four in flight.

21-23 July–second part of air echelon departs Fort Glen, Umnak, arrives Adak Island on 31 August.

3 September–Squadron begins attacking enemy on Kiska. Lieutenants Walter and Laven strafe and bomb.

11 September–Squadron switched to 342nd Fighter Group from 55th Fighter Group.

11-19 September–third part of air echelon arrives at Adak-PCS.

13 September–Lieutenants McCoy and Hsenfus contact Zero's, later badly shot up. McCoy damages one Zero.

14 September–Lieutenants Mills, Gardner and Laven get one Zero a piece. Major Jackson (CO) killed in air collision with Lt. Crowe (also killed). 1st Lt. Victor E. Walton, CO for six days.

20 September–Major Ashkin from 11th Fighter Squadron assumes command.

23 September–1st Tactical operation against Amchitka Island, bomb radio shack and sink submarine.

3 October–Lieutenants Walton and McDonald get two more Zeros.

7 October–Lieutenants Long and Ambrose, air medaled, first decoration.

14 October–2nd Lieutenant Luther B. Stockard shot down, died in water bailout.

18 October–1st Lieutenants Walton and Laven receive DCS.

27-31 October–Captain Francis Pope new CO.

9 November–first attack on Attu, eight kills in strafing .

28 November–1st Lt. Kenneth Ambrose killed in crash returning P-38 to United States.

17 December–1st Lt. Richard B. Gardner, 1st Purple Heart.

26 December–Captain Matthews killed in combat.

30 December–Lieutenants Kaiper and Leighton lost.

1943

9 January–Captain Morgan A. Griffin new CO.

13 February–Mitsubishi Type 97 downed by Captain Griffin and Lt. Moore. Captain Laven and Lt. Evans each get a Zero.

March–Replacement 1st Lieutenants Long and Hasenfus first to go home.

12 March–Four C-47s and 10 P-38s leave Adak for Amchita strip.

2 April–Captain Harley Taulkes succeeds Major Griffin as CO.

30 April–Remained of squadron arrives at Amchitka from Adak.

May 4-5-6–Pre-invasion bombing and strafing of Attu (54th played a large role in each). Early attempt at ground support by fighters.

26 May–More victories. Lt. Col. Wattl-one Betty, later lost on mis-

sion. Lt. Moore, three Bettys. Lt. Higgins, one Betty.
4 June–Concluded operations against Attu Island.
11 June–Attacks against Kiska Island. Lt. G.B. Martin killed in weather.
18 July–Captain William T. Samways assumes command of 54th.
July–Ten missions over Kiska, no aerial combat.
14 August–Last tactical mission flown against Kiska.
15 August–Invasion by Canadian and American troops of Kiska.
30 September–Second part of air echelon TDY to 344th Fighter Squadron to participate in practice flights with bombers.
18 October–Squadron ordered to Shemya-PCS. At this time, detachment from the squadron were both at Shemya and Attu.
October–Bad living, bad living conditions, only training, low morale.
November–Official change of station of entire 54th to Alexai Point, Attu Island.
November-December–Digging in and setting up on Attu.
25 December–Christmas turkey and trimmings on Attu

Awards Received by 54th (15 January 1941 to 31 December 1943)

Distinguish Service Cross: 2
Silver Star: 2
Distinguished Flying Cross: 33
OLC to DFC: 4
Air Medal: 38
OLC to Air Medal: 11
Purple Heart: 3

Losses of 54th (15 January 1941 to 31 December 1943)

Tactical: 9 officers killed, 6 wounded
Non-tactical: 10 officers killed, 7 enlisted killed

Accomplishments

59 enemy aircraft destroyed and damaged
10 vessels damaged

1944

15 January–Third anniversary party of the squadron.
27 January–Lt. Banks killed in weather during routine search mission.
4 February–Lieutenants Garver and Dailey killed in mid-air collision.
May–Opening of Pilots Rehabilitation Center, training flights continued.
June–Completion of Day Room, "Pride of the Aleutians."
6 June–D-Day in Europe.
July–Routine training-first rotation.
August–Two of original Sgts. Stevens and Price killed in auto crash due to bad weather, routine training.
September–Routine training. "Rags" the mascot killed by a truck.
October–Squadron acquires live cow from Navy, named Saide, only cow on the Aleutians, routine training.
November–Twenty-one pilots arrive, eleven of the old ones leave.
24 November–Rehabilitation Center burns down.
December–Rotation of 37 enlisted men, 36 new ones arrive. Fifteen new pilots relieve nine old ones.
3 December–Three pilots killed, two in mid-air collision, one with engine fore, bailed out, died in water, rash of accidents. Six majors, destroying four planes. Two minors, attributed to low pilot flying time.
25 December–Christmas Party.

1945

15 January–Fourth anniversary. Squadron wins pool table.
14 February–Six new P-38Ls arrive.
13 April–First sighting of Jap balloons. Six shot down.
May–V-E Day.
11 May–Lt. Wilson killed, engine failure on take-off. Al Jenkins and troop (USO) arrive, big party, with girls.
25 July–Lt. Col. Samways CO, TDY to C&GS School, not expected to return. CO from 18 July 1943 to 25 July 1945. Major Andis assumes command.
14 August–V-J Day.
August–Many inspections by generals. 54th does quite well. Considered as an example to other squadrons in area.

9 October–Major Harrison assumes command.
26 October–Squadron leaves Alexai Point for Anchorage.
1 December–Lt. Bickett relieves Major Harrision as CO.

1946

January–Lt. Preble relieves Lt. Bickett as CO.
15 January–Fifth anniversary party.
21 March–54th Fighter Squadron deactivated.

Squadron inactive until 1 December 1952. When reactivated, the squadron was built mainly about a nucleus of personnel from the 175th Air National Guard Squadron of South Dakota. The following is the summary from September 1946 to 1 December 1952 for the 54th Fighter-Interceptor Squadron.

1946

September–175th ANG Squadron formed at Sioux Falls, South Dakota. Squadron previously carried on records as 387th Fighter Squadron. Lt. Col. Joe Foss first 175th CO.

1948

Summer camp held in Sioux Falls.

1949

Summer camp at Casper, Wyoming. During the year, the 175th received Spaatz Trophy for best squadron in ANG. F-51 acrobatic team made up of Lt. Col. Foss, Lt. (now Captain) W.J. Downy, Lt. J. Beyer and Lt. R. Reid.

1950

Summer camp at Camp Williams, Sparta, Wisconsin. Major D.L. Corning promoted to Lt. Col and made CO.

1951

18 January–Squadron alerted for activation in March.
1 March–Squadron went on full time active duty without ceremo-

nies.

17 May–Squadron went on alert status.

14 June–Lt. P.J. Kirkby killed in crash in F-51, lost control in pattern.

27 June–Major General R.R. Acheson of CG of CADF informed squadron of move to Rapid City Air Force Base, in near future.

19 July–Lt. Helder, with Captain W. Swenson in the back seat, ground looped the squadron's T-6 ($1,400 in damages).

16 August–Squadron completed move to Rapid City, equipped with F-51s.

September–Alert hangar completed and F-51s moved in.

15 November–Lt. K.D. Frank killed after complete engine failure during a gunnery mission.

1952

21 January–Fire destroyed Squadron Supply building, $4,000 in damages.

January–175th won $100 base ground safety award, also leadership trophy. Winds up to 100mph and temperatures below zero held down flying.

March–Twenty-one Squadron pilots participated in gunnery exercises at Yuma, Arizona. Twenty pilots rated expert.

May–Flying virtually halted because of nation-wide gasoline strike.

August–Permanent alert hangar completed and F-51s moved in, much more comfortable for pilots and crew chiefs.

15 September–Lt. J.D. Brown bellied in from GCA pattern, dry fuselage tank.

27 November–Lt. V.G. Howe landed gear up at Sioux Falls, pilot error.

1 December–54th Fighter-Interceptor Squadron reactivated, takes over from the 175th. New CO, Lt. Col. Paul J. Imig.

18 December–Squadron received word that turbojet were forthcoming to the 54th, morale boost.

28 December–Lt. Norris brought in first flight of three F-84Gs. Aircraft used on alert until replaced by the F-86D, all-weather interceptor took its place in January 1954.

1953

- 16 February–Squadron transferred from 31st AD to 29th AD. During the month, heavy snow held flying to a minimum.
- 16 March–First gunnery mission in F-84.
- 23 March–First night flying in F-84.
- 31 March–F-84s assumed alert duties.
- 24 May–Fifteen aircraft and 22 pilots departed for gunnery at Yuma, Arizona.
- 5 June–Lt. Harre bailed out after explosion and fire returning from gunnery mission, first squadron ejection.
- 10 June–Lt. E.M. Koski killed in crash, inclement weather.
- 24 June–Captain Cobb killed in crash of F-84, cause unknown.
- 18 September–Lt. Col. W.P. Benedict relieved Lt. Col. Imig as CO.
- November–Squadron began making preparations for change over to F-86D in near future. Many pilots TDY to "Dog School." Technical representatives for several companies are conducting F-86D maintenance courses.

1954

- 22 January–Col. Benedict brings in first F-86D.
- January–Two dozen more F-86Ds arrive shortly thereafter. F-84s continue on alert until about half of the pilots are checked out in the "Dog." All personnel on seven-day work week to speed checkout in "D."
- March–Pilots get first taste of all-weather flying the "Dog." Six Aircraft scrambled (practice) and recovered with 200 feet and ½ mile visible. Same thing next day only with four birds, 100 feet and ½ mile.
- 20 March–Lt. Cook bailed out at night after fuel starvation flameout.
- 25 March–Major William H. Fairbrother relieves Col. Benedict as CO.
- 27 March–F-86Ds take over alert, last of F-84s ready to leave.
- April–AIO advises that F-86D simulator will be installed in near future.
- 10 May–All pilots completed at least one air-to-ground rocketry mission in the F-86D for familiarization with the Pod Drop System of firing.
- 12 June–Lt. A.N. Weber bailed out from 35,000 feet after fire in engine, no injuries.

6 July–Flying curtailed in preparation for "Operation CHECKPOINT" this month.

July–Squadron flew more than 97 sorties during "Operation CHECKPOINT," came out of exercise with two more aircraft in commission than beginning. Lt. Newell made dead stick landing at Dickenson, North Dakota after throwing several buckets.

10 August–Phase II mission being run in preparation for Yuma rocketry, two T-Birds were targets.

September–Open house held for families and friends. Lt. C.E. Proudfit made a dead stick landing after turbine failure shortly after becoming airborne.

8 October–Twenty pilots and F-86Ds depart for Yuma.

5 November–Squadron returned to Ellsworth Air Force Base, 19 hits.

December–Squadron had two nights to work out on B-47 aircraft interception, 112 interceptions in two nights.

16 December–Four F-86Ds to Great Falls to back up 29th Fighter Interceptor Squadron, TDY only.

1955

5 January–Six F-86Ds to Scott AFB for "Operation SPOTLIGHT," night interception of B-47s.

February–About half of squadrons F-86D-40s replaced by "Operation ROLLOUT," modified F-86D-36s with drogue chutes and other improvements. All F-86D-40s to be replaced in near future.

17 February–Captain D.C. Baker killed in bailout attempt at low-altitude after engine fire and explosion.

March–All pilots fire rockets, air to ground, at night for familiarization.

12 April–Jo-Jo installed in neon operations building.

May–All F-86s back from "Operation PULLOUT," improvements include new flight control system, improved radar and drogue chute.

10 June–Improvements underway on alert hangar.

24 June–Jo-Jo the lion, 54th mascot returned to Hill City Zoo.

10 July–Lt. Col. Benedict leaves 29th for Air Command and Staff School.

22 July–29th FIS downs 54th in rocketry competition.

27 October–Lt. McMillan lands gear up, minor aircraft damage.

16 November–Lt. Sims airlifts rare blood to ten year old Huron girl.

1956

5 February–54th returns from Yuma after 30-days of air-to-air rocketry.

15 February–Lt. Col. O. Schultz relieves Major Fairbrother as CO.

6 May–Major Fairbrother leaves for England.

21 May–54th will carry 29th Division colors to CADF shoot off at Yuma.

July–Computer fuses plague 54th, finishes CADF meet in sixth slot.

August–Col. Marshall's CADF tactical evaluation team compliments 54th. Major Lane flies cobra serum to cobra bitter in New Orleans youth.

4 October–Lt. Kowal makes successful low level ejection after compressor failure.

1957

January–Major Alma R. Flake relieves Lt. Col. Schulze as CO.

1 March–Major Flake leads 12 ship deployment to Great Falls, Casper, Sioux City, Lincoln and return, no aborts.

April–Eighteen pilots qualify as 54th fires air to air on Badlands range.

5 May–54th ends 39 day alert at Malmstrom, as 29th FIS transitions into F-89J.

12 June–Inclement weather forces postponement of CADF tactical evaluation.

22 June–54th scores 109 hits in two weeks rocketry at Wendover Air Force Base, Utah.

10 July–Five F-86Ds sent to Iran as the first step in F-86D phase out.

16 August–Tactical evaluation proves 54th to be one of CADF's top units, primarily as a result of outstanding rocketry and subsequent evaluations.

August–Col. Marshall submits Captain Norris and Captain Levy for "expert" rating.

September–54th once again to Great Falls to pull alert for the 29th.

October–54th misses first place in CADF rocket meet due to bad wing film. Captain Norris takes individual honors in CADF rocket meet.

28 October–First day of F-89J MTD for 54th pilots.

10 November–First F-89J arrives to replace F-86D.

December–Squadron transitioning from F-86D to F-89J.

19 December–Newly assigned Air Police men arrive to take charge of guarding Special Weapons Section.

1958

January–F-89J transition proceeding successfully.
February–Conversion F-89J complete, takes over alert.
26-29 May–Inspector General of Central Air Defense Force conducts inspection of squadron, rated excellent.
24 June–CWO Hudson takes over new completed ADC Special Weapons Area.
26 June–First "Dining-In" held. Guest speaker was Major General Alfred E. Kolberer.
11 July–Deployed to Vincent Air Force Base, Arizona for weapons training.
16 July–returned to Ellsworth without completing training due to international situation and increased alert commitment.
21 August–Squadron participated in exercise against 28th Bombardment Wing's B-52s.
11 September–Participated in exercise against 28th Bombardment Wing's B-52s, which were using extensive ECM.
16 September–Visit to squadron by Major General Stevenson, Commander of the 29th Air Division and Brigadier General Neely, Commander of the 29th Air Division.
19-20 September–"Exercise TOP HAND."
25 September–Central Air Defense Force tactical evaluation.
22 October–13 November–Squadron participates in six training exercises in preparation for ADC Operational Readiness Inspection.
3-7 November–ADC Inspector General conducts weapons inspection.
6-7 November–CDAF tactical evaluation of Squadron.
17-21 November–ADC Operational Readiness Inspection and tactical evaluation.
28 November–19 December–Squadron deployed to Vincent Air Force Base, Arizona for weapons training. Squadron breaks thirty-one world records during this period.

1959

February–Major James C. Brown arrives as new Executive Officer.
10 March–Major Robert W. Gibson replaces Captain William Norris

as Operations Officer.

7-22 March–Two Air Force Academy students, Gordon S. Savage, Jr. and Kerry D. Miller spend a training tour with the squadron.

15 May–Lt. Col. Flake departs for new assignment. Major Brown assumes command until arrival of Lt. Col. Ernest B. Nuckols, Jr.

May–54th FIS lost shoot-off for representation at William Tell meet to 29th FIS due to malfunction of an RME.

2 June–Five aircrews gave flyover to first graduating class at Air Force Academy.

2-4 June–CADF Tactical Evaluation. This was the largest exercise attempted by CADF. 54th FIS rated outstanding.

21 July–Lt. Col. Ernest B. Nuckols, Jr., assumes command.

28 July–Practice mass loading of aircraft.

August–Engine shops established a world performance record by maintaining a J35-H-35 engine from an F-89J for 1104.30 hours without a major overhaul.

19 August–Lt. James B. Gormely, pilot and Lt. John P. Trulove, R/O, catch on fire while taxiing an F-89J to take-off position. Lt. Trulove is severely burned, Lt. Gormely, uninjured.

20 August–Squadron awarded Hughes Achievement Award. This award is presented annually to the outstanding fighter-interceptor squadron.

September 1-5–Col. Nuckols and a representative group of the squadron attend the annual Air Force Association at Miami, where General Lawrence S. Kuter presented to the squadron, the Hughes Award.

14 September–Alert crews move to Operations Area to enable workers to modify and redecorate the Alert Hangar.

September-October–54th FIS suffering from an R/O shortage. Four R/Os from Davis Monthan AFB, Arizona arrival for thirty days TDY to alleviate the situation.

8-10 November–Squadron is given tactical evaluation by CADF.

3 December–A luncheon was held at the Sheraton Johnson Hotel for General Lessig to enable him to meet Rapid City businessmen.

7 December–Inspection team for USAF Headquarters here. Headed by General Stewart, they were primarily interested in our Special Weapons area.

16 December–General Atkinson, Commander, ADC, arrives at

Ellsworth to present 54th FIS the USAF Safety Award. [86]

---

[86] MSgt. O'Daniel, Rapid City, South Dakota served at Ellsworth Air Force Base with the 54th Fighter-Interceptor Squadron as an administrative Clerk. He provided original records on the 54th Fighter-Interceptor Squadron, long assumed lost, especially by the South Dakota Air and Space Museum located outside the main gate of Ellsworth Air Force Base. He served in an important role as part of the nation's Ballistic Missile Early Warning System (BMEWS) and later TDY from Hickam Air Force Base, Hawaii to Wake Island to assist in "Operation NEW LIFE." The author was on Andersen Air Force Base, Guam and sent thousands of Vietnamese refugees to Wake for temporary housing prior to their processing to go onto new homes in the United States. Information provided to the author.

First Lieutenant Charlie Piper, USAF (Ret.)

F-86D Pilot, 54th Fighter Interceptor Squadron Ellsworth Air Force Base

FIRST Lieutenant Charlies Piper..."The 54th Fighter-Interceptor Squadron was a tenant unit at Ellsworth Air Force Base, which was part of the Strategic Air Command (SAC). The 54th FIS was a unit of the Air Defense Command, which later became the North American Air Defense (NORAD) Command. We flew F-86D's, which was a single seat, all-weather plane with radar fire control and armed with rockets. I was a fighter pilot in the 54th, with a rank of 1st Lt. We had very little contact with base operations as we had our own Operations Section. I think that things were much stricter than they are now on base. (However, with the attacks by terrorists on military bases and recruiting stations, military bases are back on 100 percent identification checks with increased on base security.) We could not wear flight clothes off the flight line. You had to show ID coming onto base and going off. I don't know how things are now, but we had a separate pass to get on the flight line. he role of the 54th FIS was air defense. We were part of the 29th Air Division, which was at Great Falls, Montana, and it was composed of two fighter squadrons and numerous GCI (radar) sites. We were on 24 hour alert and if one of the GCI sites picked up an unknown plane, we were to scramble to intercept it and see who it was. Most of the intercepts were over North and South Dakota, and sometimes Wyoming and Montana. In those days, there were many cities, which had fighter–interceptor squadrons. The 54th FIS alert hangar became part of the South Dakota Air and Space Museum by the main gate, with the alert hangars moved from the flight line to its current location. My first year in the 54th FIS, I was one of the alert pilots and were on alert 24 hours and off 24 hours. Later, we switched to a day or night alert schedule, and a normal day, which involved flying training and ground training."⁸⁷

---

[87] First Lieutenant Charlie Piper, USAF (Ret.), F-86D pilot, 54th Fighter-Interceptor Squadron, Ellsworth Air Force Base, interview, 28th Bomb Wing Public Affairs to author.

Minuteman I and II Intercontinental Ballistic Missiles at Ellsworth Air Force

THE ICBM race between the former Soviet Union and the United States began after the end of combat in Europe during World War II, referred to as Victory in Europe or VE Day, on May 8, 1945. The Soviet Army and U.S. Army units competed against each other to capture German rocket scientists and the Vergeltungs Waffe 2 V-2, technically referred to by the U.S. Army engineers as the A-4. The U.S. Army scored a major coup when many of the top German rocket scientists, including Werner Von Braun, surrendered to them. U.S. Army units captured large stocks of V-2s, spare parts, support and launch vehicles, and missile related technology. Soviet Army units also captured German rocket experts and missiles. These German rocket scientists, at the end of the fighting in Europe, were working on a longer-range rocket, with possible intercontinental range, but the project never got beyond the initial design stage because of deteriorating conditions in Germany from U.S. and British strategic bombing.

It was the Soviet Union's successful launch of the world's first man-made or artificial satellite into low-earth orbit on October 4, 1957, named Sputnik, which pushed the U.S. into a space race. A modified ICBM, SS-6 surface-to-surface ballistic missile, fueled by kerosene and liquid oxygen, launched the 184 pound satellite into orbit. To obtain added power to launch a satellite, the rocket had four strap-on boosters, each with four rocket engines. The SS-6 would allow the Soviet Union to launch thermonuclear weapons over the North Pole to hit relatively soft strategic targets in the U.S., primarily SAC bomber bases.

In 1946, Convair, later a division of General Dynamics, awarded a contract to design and build an ICBM, referred to as the Atlas or SM-65/HGM-19, an upgraded version of the German V-2. The Atlas exterior skin was paper-thin, stainless steel, requiring inert nitrogen for use when empty, to maintain interior pressure to keep it from collapsing. The thin skin reduced the missile's weight, giving it the necessary intercontinental range carrying a single nuclear re-entry vehicle or RV. The Atlas force grew to 148 missiles by 1964, removed from the Air

Force and SAC inventory in 1965.

The second liquid-fueled U.S. ICBM became known as the Titan I. The design was started by the Martin-Mariette Company in 1955, under the military designation SM-68/LGM-25A. The Titan I was a two-stage ICBM, with its framework constructed of an aluminum copper alloy, supported by fuel and oxidizer tanks, 10 foot diameter booster stage with two engines providing a combined thrust of 200,000 pounds. The second stage sustainer engine was eight feet in diameter, providing 50,000 pounds of thrust. The Titan I had a range of 6,300 miles. The 98 foot long Titan I was stored in a 115 foot deep and 40 foot wide concrete silo, deployed in a grouping of three missiles per complex. The missile was also a liquid-fueled ICBM, raised on an elevator for an above ground launch, taking approximately 15 minutes for the fueling to be completed. The Titan I used a radar-initial guidance system, which followed a radio beam powered flight, susceptible to jamming or other electronic counter-measures.

In October 1960, Ellsworth AFB entered the "space age," with the activation of the 850th Strategic Missile Squadron, initially assigned to the 28th BW. For more than a year, this squadron prepared for the emplacement of the Titan I ICBM, which occurred on 1962, shortly after the activation of the 44th Strategic Missile Wing (SMW) in January. At that time, Headquarters SAC named the 44th SMW as host wing at Ellsworth AFB. The Titan Is' life span was short in western South Dakota. In July 1962, SAC rendered the missile obsolete by activating the 66th SMW, the first of three such units selected to operate 150 Minuteman I (MMI) ICBMs, under the 44th SMW.

The Titan II replaced the Titan I, 50 percent heavier than the first missile, equipped with an inertial targeting and navigation guidance system, a nine megaton warhead, operationally deployed in a 146 foot deep and 55 foot wide concrete silo, covered by a concrete door mounted on railroad rails weighing 758 tons. The Titan II was launched from inside the silo. The missile system was deactivated on May 5, 1987, replaced by the solid-fuel MMI.

SAC wanted a solid-fuel ICBM, which could be produced and deployed in large numbers to counter expanding numbers of deployed Soviet ICBMs. The solid-fueled ICBM could be launched under warning of an incoming Soviet ICBM attack within five minutes. In March 1958, the USAF reviewed seven different missile aerospace and aircraft company designs and production proposals for a three-stage, solid fuel, 68 foot long and silo launched ICBM In October 1958, the Boeing Aircraft Company's design was selected. Boeing engineers put together a sub-contractor team of six companies to build the MMI, then MMII and MMIII. The MMI's first flight was on February 1, 1961, launched from Cape Canaveral, Florida with a dummy warhead hitting its designated target 25 minutes later at a down range of 4,600 miles into the Atlantic Missile Test Range. The MMI, approximately one half the size of the Titan II, could destroy a pinpoint or hardened target inside the Soviet Union.

Minuteman silo, Launch Control Facility (LCF) and Launch Control Center (LCC) construction was standardized to reduce construction and maintenance costs, along with construction time to maximize the number of ICBMS to be fielded in the shortest time. The MMI was designed to meet the Soviet ICBM threat, providing a credible and survivable nuclear deterrence. Silo construction began with earth scrappers digging a twelve foot deep trench, deepened to 32 feet by backhoe excavation. A crane equipped clamshell bucket dug the silo to the final depth of 84 feet. A heavy crane lowered steel cylinder 12 feet in diameter into the excavation. Re-enforced concrete was poured around the steel cylinder, allowed to harden, back-filled with dirt, covered by additional hardened concrete, fitted with a ballistically activated door mounted on three railroad guide rails.

Each silo is connected to its LCF by an underground trench, several miles long, containing shielded cables. Communications backup was provided by hardened UHF radio receivers, an aboveground mast antenna receiver, and alternate buried cables from other LCFs providing redundant command and control. Each LCF was an above ground building with the LCC 31 feet below. A large excavation was dug by earth scrappers for the external shell, 29 feet in diameter, 54 feet long, built of re-enforced concrete, four feet thick, poured around the hardened steel shell was added. Suspended inside the plate steel shell is a box like acoustical enclosure containing two LCC consoles, communications, missile monitoring equipment and crew accommodations. Its entrance is protected by an eight ton, blast proof, steel and concrete door.

The LCC has two consoles, each with a swiveling, high-backed, aircraft type seat, fitted with a seat belt and shoulder harness. The Deputy LCO Commander's chair slides along a double rail mounted on the LCC's floor to permit his monitoring of the equipment. The LCO Commander's console is positioned at the far end of the LCC, opposite the entrance, with instruments to monitor the operational and security status of the flight's ten missiles as well as those from other flights to provide redundant launch and control capabilities. The

Deputy LCO Commander's console area contained the radio, telephone, decoding and other communications equipment.

Each of the two consoles has a spring-loaded, key-operated, missile launch switch. The two keys are secured inside a red, double-padlock steel box (one lock for the LCO Commander and one for the Deputy LCO Commander), positioned above the Deputy LCO Commander's console. Audio-alarm alerts the two LCOs to an incoming, coded missile launch warning message. After verifying the coded launch message, with both officers must agree on the message has formatted content, unlock the padlocks on the red box, removing the missile launch keys. Each officer takes a key to his console, inserts it into the launch switch, and then continues the proper launch sequence. Both officers strap themselves into their chairs and complete the final missile launch countdown sequence. At the proper time, both turn their key simultaneously, launching their ten missiles. Because the two LCO consoles containing the launch switch are 12 feet apart, no one officer can independently launch the missiles. Before the flight's missiles can be launched, the proper Nuclear Weapons Release Authorization message must be authenticated and verified by another LCC or airborne command post. This adds another layer of positive nuclear control to prevent an unauthorized missile launch. Once launched, a MM ICBM in approximately 30 minutes could deliver the warhead(s) to strike its target(s). With constant guidance system improvements, the RV's accuracy nears pinpoint strike capability.

Even though the LCC receives its day to day electrical and air conditioning from the LCF above, it can be completely sealed off, operating independently on emergency power, air conditioning and oxygen equipment. This isolation was only done if an incoming Soviet missile attack was detected, requiring operation in a nuclear environment.

The above ground LCF is secured by a chain link fence, monitored by video cameras, with entry through a remote-controlled, chain link, vehicle size sliding gate. The support building provides lodging and cooking facilities, security patrol/control, environmental and electrical equipment for the LCC. It is manned by two Security Controllers, (two) two-person armed response (Security Police) teams, a cook and facility manager. The two missile launch officers in the LCC remain on duty for 24 hours before being relieved by another two missile launch officers. Support personnel worked a three day shift. The LCF support area contains a vehicle storage building, containing two security vehicles and a frontend loader for snow removal at the LCC and missile solos, two hardened high frequency (HF) antennas, one ultra-high frequency (UHF) antenna and one underground, survivable low frequency (LF) communications system antenna to provide continuous communications with surviving National Command Authorities during a nuclear attack. A helicopter-landing pad is located outside the security fence for emergency support.

The USAF began building its first MMI ICBM field on March 16, 1961 at Malmstrom AFB, Great Falls, Montana. The first ten silos and corresponding LCF and below ground LCC became operational on October 27, 1962, at the height of the Cuban Missile Crisis when both the Soviet Union and the United States were at the brink of a nuclear missile exchange. By 1967, SAC controlled 1,000 Minuteman ICBMs, reduced from the planned 1,500. MMI ICBM fields were constructed at Malmstrom AFB, Montana; Ellsworth AFB, South Dakota; Minot and Grand Forks AFB, North Dakota; Whiteman AFB, Missouri and Frances (F.E.) Warren AFB, Wyoming.

The only launch of a MM I ICBM from an operational silo, N-02, located north of Newell, SD, took place on 1 March 1965. The launch of an unmanned ICBM, with a dummy warhead, proved the launch capability of SAC's ICBM force. The test missile only had fuel for seven seconds of powered flight in the first stage, with the rest of the missile's propellant inert. The further two test operational silo test launches were cancelled. MMIs remained on alert until each flight of ten missiles was replaced by the MMII. MMII remained the backbone of America's silo-based nuclear deterrence until replaced by the MMIII at those silos remaining active. By July 1975, SAC's ICBM force consisted of 550 MMIIIs, 450 MMIIs (F.E. Warren, Minot and Malmstrom AFB) and 57 Titan IIs.

By January 1980, SAC completed a major silo upgrade program to increase MMII and MMIII survivability, to offset increasing numbers of deployed Soviet ICBMs fitted with MIRVs. The upgrade program increased the Minuteman's protection against the effects of nuclear blasts overpressure and ground vibration or shock waves caused by nearby nuclear detonations, along with the effects of Electro Magnetic Pulse (EMP). A high-altitude detonation of a nuclear warhead produces Gamma Rays, which interacts with the upper atmosphere, creating a layer of intense EMP radiation spreading out from the explosion, assisted by high-altitude jet stream winds, to cover thousands of square miles. EMP bursts impact all types of electric components, especially communications equipment. A series of EMP, high-altitude bursts could knockout or block U.S. command and control, post-attack communications as well as nuclear command orders to silo based ICBMs. The silo and LCC upgrades were designed to detect a possible EMP burst, automatically shutting-off and isolating susceptible electronics equipment for a microsecond to protect electronic circuits prior to resuming normal operations.

The U.S. developed the LGM-118A (MX) Peacekeeper to replace the MMIIIs, which had become vulnerable to the new Soviet SS-18 ICBMs. The SS-18 was classified by U.S. intelligence agencies as a first strike weapon designed to saturate U.S. ICBM fields, with each SS-18 carrying eight MIRVs. The SS-18 could deliver large numbers of warheads on MMII and MMIII silos, LCFs and LCCs, destroying SAC's primary ICBM retaliatory capabilities to ride out a Soviet first nuclear strike and then respond accordingly. This was at the height of U.S.-Soviet nuclear warhead proliferation time period. With the signing of START, both nuclear powers shifted from adding more delivery system and multiple warheads to an actual reduction of deployed warheads. The Peacekeeper was a four stage, solid-fuel ICBM with enhanced accuracy. The Peacekeeper was viewed by the Soviet political leadership as a first strike U.S. ICBM, deployed in response to their SS-18. The peacekeeper was armed with ten AVCO Mark 21, MIRVs, each tipped with a W87 (300 to 475 kilotons) warhead. The Peacekeeper was cold-launched by a powerful gas generator to push the missile out of its silo, at which time, the first stage's rocket motor ignited. The cold launch was used to allow the Peacekeeper to be deployed in a mobile configuration, complicating Soviet SS-18 ICBM targeting, eliminating that missile's first strike threat.

The Peacekeeper was to be operationally deployed in horizontal, underground shelters, with one missile randomly rotated between ten shelters, carried on mobile transporter/erector/launchers. Each group of ten missile shelters would have to be targeted by one or more Soviet SS-18s in an effort to hit the mobile ICBM possibly hiding inside. U.S. missileers referred to this concept as the hidden shell game. When it was determined the ground area required to hide 200 Peacekeepers in 2,000 underground shelters took up too much land, another deployment option was proposed. The Peacekeeper's deployment was shifted to an option using a train shuttling along the U.S. railroad network. The proposed train consisted of a diesel engine; two Peacekeeper missiles, one each in a railroad car 89 feet long, 9feet 6-inches wide and 15 feet 9-inches high; one missile launch control car; two maintenance cares and one crew support car. The Peacekeeper trains were scheduled to be garrisoned at F.E. Warren AFB, Wyoming; Little Rock, AK;

Barksdale AFB, Louisiana: Wurtsmith, AFB, Michigan; Grand Forks, AFB, North Dakota; Fairchild AFB, Washington and Dyess AFB, Texas. Peacekeeper missile trains, while in garrison would be parked inside protective igloos, only moved onto U.S. railroad system during a period of increased nuclear alert, referred to as DEFCON I (Defense Condition 1), the highest alert.

SAC planned to deploy a force of 200 Peacekeepers, but this number was reduced to 50, deciding not to deploy the ICBM in expensive underground shelters or on mobile trains. The option selected was to pull 50 MMIIIs from their silos at F.E. Warren AFB, modified to hold and cold launch the heavier missile. On September 27, 1991, President George H. Bush, ordered MMII ICBMs removed from nuclear alert with their silos and LCCs below LCFs destroyed. The deactivation and destruction process used at the MMII force at Ellsworth AFB was followed at other MMII fields.

The destruction process at Ellsworth AFB started on December 3, 1991, when the first MMII ICBM was pulled out if its silo, G-02, located north of Red Owl, SD. The remaining 149 ICBMs followed as each warhead and missile was removed from the silo, along with equipment which could be salvaged. Each silo was destroyed by a demolition charge, blowing it up down to a depth of 20 feet 6-inches. The last Ellsworth AFB MMII silo was blown up on September 13, 1996. After each blast, the 30 foot diameter silo headworks were mechanically demolished using large excavators. The concrete rubble was dumped into the silo and recovered steel set to one side for scrap recovery. Approximately 140 tons of structural steel and rebar was salvaged from each silo. During demolition, an observation cone 20 feet deep and 70 feet wide was dug over the remaining portion of the silo. This allowed a 90 day observation period specified under START to allow Russian verification of the destroyed silos and LCCs by on-site inspection and/or aerial/satellite reconnaissance, with all verifications completed by January 1997.

The final phase of destruction consisted of the site's back fill, compacted and rough graded. Next, gravel was dumped in the silo area, enclosed the by the existing security fence. The underground LCC facility was destroyed by back filling and sealed with a concrete floor poured over the elevator shaft. Above ground LCFs remained intact, offered for sale to current surrounding land owner(s). The sewage lagoon was back filled and graded. One silo, D-09 and LCF/LCC, D-01, remained intact under START rules, allowance for conversation into a Cold War museum.

On December 2, 1991, President William Clinton signed a bill, establishing the Minuteman Missile National Historic Site, located east of Wall, SD, along Interstate 90 (I-90) to commemorate the role of the Minuteman Defense System missiles and personnel played in the Cold War with the Soviet Union, maintaining America's nuclear deterrence. Two facilities, Delta-one (D-01), along with LCC/LCF Delta-Nine (D-09), now make up part of the U.S. National Park System (NPS).

Air Force personnel assigned to F.E. Warren inserted a boilerplate or dummy training MMII ICBM into the Delta-Nine silo. Air Force personnel covered the silo with a concrete frame and glass plates to allow visitors to look down into the silo to see how a missile was set for nuclear alert. On June 19, 2001, this first activity took place at the Cold War missile silo since April 7, 1994. Under START, Russian inspection would occur within 30 days verifying the missile in the silo as inert, non-operational as a museum display under the 1991 treaty clauses.

On September 16, 2002, the USAF transferred D-09 and D-01 to the NPS, Department of Interior to become the first NPS system site dedicated to telling one of the major events of the Cold War. At 10:00 a.m. a 28th BW B-1B flew low over the crowd of 500 people at the missile silo. Badlands National Park Superintendent William Supernaugh opened the formal dedication, introducing Fran P. Mainella, NPS Director who commented..."These two new Park Service sites will help teach children about the Cold War era. They need to know the terms such as the Berlin Wall, fallout shelter and Natural Assured Destruction or MAD. This is a tribute to American morals while others, bullies, are hiding their weapons; America is turning hers into a national park. This shows who believes in peace."

Lt. General Robert Hinson, Vice Commander, Air Force Space Command..."The missiles were so effective that they eventually put themselves out of business. We celebrate that victory here today. I remembered when stationed at Ellsworth AFB, seven years ago, that two of the missile sites should be presented to help tell the Cold War story. Young people have a hard time understanding the fear and tension of a time when many thought nuclear war would breakout."

Arnold L. Orr, Deputy Assistant Secretary of the Air Force for Installations, Environment and Logistics..."The Minuteman II ICBMs succeeded in their mission of deterrence because they were reliable and could not be destroyed." Craig Manson, Assistant Secretary for Fish and Wildlife and Parks, Department of the Interior..."This is a particularly personal day because I was an Air Force Missile Launch Office in the mid-1970s, assigned to Delta Flight, LCC Delta-Nine. If you had told me 26 years ago, I would have considered it pure science fiction. In those middle years of the Cold War, we believed this was a permanent condition, something that would have made this transfer impossible." Colonel James Kowalski, Commander 28th BW..."The missiles' effectiveness helped win the Cold War. This was a war we had to win without any direct combat. It was the war we could not afford to lose."

Because the 44th SMW had previously been inactivated, the tradition in the Air Force of passing the unit's flag from one commander to another could not be performed. Instead, Colonel Kowalski passed a set of ceremonial keys to D-01 and D-09 to Badlands National Part Superintendent Supernaugh, along with General Hinson and Ronald Orr. This concluded the formal dedication ceremony at the missile silo. Then, selected distinguished guests went to the LCF and associated LCC (including the author and his wife).[88]

---

[88] Lt. Col. George A. Larson, USAF (Ret.), "New Life for a Cold War warrior, The Minuteman Missile National Historic Site, September 2001." Request by the South Dakota Department of Tourism, Pierre, South Dakota.

South Dakota National Guard

The Berlin Blockade and Resulting International Crisis

THE mounting East-West military and political tensions over the situation in Berlin, Germany during August and September 1961 prompted increased U.S. military preparedness. The South Dakota National Guard was called into active Federal duty in October 1961. The 740th and 741st Transportation Companies from Milbank and Clear Lake reported to Fort Carson, Colorado. The 211th Engineer Company from Lemmon reported to Fort Lewis, Washington. The 1st Battalion, 147th Field Artillery (Headquarter and Headquarter Battery); Battery A, B, C and Service from Sioux Falls, Madison, Flandreau and Canton reported to Fort Sill, Oklahoma. The 115th Signal Company Wire Platoon from Yankton and Vermillion reported to Fort Riley, Kansas. The 214th Engineer Company from Mobridge reported to Fort Polk, Louisiana and the 730th Medical Company to Fort Riley, Kansas. All units were released from active duty between August 6-12, 1962.[89]

---

[89] Lt. Col George A. Larson, USAF (Ret.), "South Dakota National Guard, The Berlin Blockade and resulting international crisis." Visit to Camp Rapid, The South Dakota National Guard's open house to celebrate the National Guard's 150 years of service," display set up in the Headquarters Lobby, "2012: Countdown to Withdrawal," June 9, 2012.

MSgt. Robert O'Daniel

Ballistic Missile Early Warning System (BMEWS) Clear, Alaska

EARLY in 1958, the United States Air Force announced the selection of the Radio Corporation of America (RCA) as Weapons System Manager for the Ballistic Missile Early Warning System (BMEWS) Project. The over-all management responsibilities for the creation of this powerful space radar net was delegated to RCA. The RCA Service Company had assumed the tremendous responsibilities to install, checkout, integrate, operate and maintain this BMEWS. The project is a momentous endeavor to establish a giant electronic system to probe thousands of miles over the polar waters, to detect and track an invading missile, and to predict its point of impact. The success of such an endeavor depends greatly upon the cooperation and teamwork of the organization working within the project. In addition to RCA, there are many other subcontractors doing their parts for this vital project such as General Electric, Sylvania, IBM, Goodyear Aircraft, Continental Electric and Western Electric.

Brute force radar transmitters illuminating small cross-section targets at extreme range; ultrasensitive radar receivers, reading microvolt echoes through intensive electro-magnetic disturbances, and generating precise position information; data converters, translating data to digital information, complex solid state computing systems, making microsecond decisions. These are the basic components of BMEWS. BMEWS is an epoch-making endeavor that was inspired through common purpose and need. The problems of environment, capacity, and performance inherent in the development, design, and installation of the Ballistic Missile Early Warning System make it unique in the history of military electronics. The swift advance warning provided by BMEWS is the most effective known deterrent of surprise missile attack, and this plays a major role in maintaining the security and well-being of the free world.

The history of Clear, Alaska-Site II continues that of the frontiers of Alaska. Alaska derives its name from an English corruption of the native word "Al-ay-ek-sa," probably meaning "the great land" or "mainland." The region now known as Alaska was discovered by a

Danish Captain by the Russian Navy, Vitrus Bering, on 16 July 1741. Russian traders and trappers soon entered the country, under the initial leadership of Grigor Shelekof and through their activities other nations became interested in this region. Spanish expeditions in 1774 and 1775 visited the south-eastern shore and in 1778 the English explorer, Captain James Cook, made extensive surveys of the coast for the British government. The first settlement was made by the Russians under Shelekof at Three Saints, on Kodiak Island, on August 3, 1784, and in 1804 the Russian-American Company founded Sitka, making it the seat of government in 1805. The leader of the eastern most extension of the new Russia was Alexander Andreevich Baranof, a Russian merchant employed by Shelekof. In 1799, the trade and regulation of the Russian possessions in America were given over to the Russian-American Company, for a term of 20 years, a continent, which was twice renewed for similar periods. In 1821, Russia attempted to exclude foreign navigators from the Bering Sea and the Pacific coast of her possessions. This created tremendous controversy with the United States and Great Britain. The question was settled by a treaty with the United States in 1824 and one with Great Britain un 1825, by which an attempt was made to fix permanently the boundaries of the Russian possession in America.

In March 1867, Alaska was purchased by the United States for 7,200,000 dollars in gold. American history of the Territory of Alaska dates from March 30, 1867, when the Treaty of Purchase was signed at Washington by Secretary of State William Seward for the United States, and Baron de Stoeckl for Russia. By this treaty, ratified by the Senate and proclaimed by President Andrew Johnson on June 20, 1867, the United States acquired an area of approximately 590,000 square miles. The formal transfer of sovereignty took place at Sitka, the Russian capital, on October 28, 1867. Under the terms of the treaty, all natives of Alaska acquired full rights of American citizenship. Secretary Seward, who had negotiated this treaty, was severely criticized for the purchase of what was referred to as "Seward's Folly," and "Seward's Ice Bar." For many years the federal government took little interest in the development of the territory. Finally in 1884, a civil government was established for Alaska through a bill approved by President Arthur. The discovery of gold in the Klondike in 1896 brought an influx of settlers, and thereby created need for additional laws. Congress in 1899 and 1900 provided for a code of civil and criminal law, and in 1903 passed a Homestead Act. The Act of May 7, 1906, empowered Alaska to elect a delegate to Congress. The Territory of

Alaska, with Juneau as the capital, was finally created in 1912, with a legislature of two houses elected every two years by popular vote, and a Governor appointed by the President and confirmed by the Senate for a term of four years. In 1959, Alaska became the forty-ninth state.

Site II Milestones

January 1958–Award of contract and start of equipment design.
April 1959–Start procurement.
May 1959–Start construction.
July 1959–Start production.
July 1960–Start emplacement and installation.
September 1960–Complete equipment design, start checkout and test.
December 1960–Complete procurement, start integration, powerhouse initially operated.
January 1961–Initial radiation.
May 1961–Complete rearward communications first link.
June 1961–Complete emplacement and installation.
July 1961–Complete checkout and test, initial operating capability.
September 1961–Complete construction, production and integration.
October 1961–Operating capability.

MSgt. O'Daniel's assignment to Detachment 2 in the Administration Section at Clear, Alaska. Clear Alaska Missile Early Warning Station (Site II BMEWS) is located in the interior of Alaska, eighty-four miles south of Fairbanks in the Broad Nenana River Valley, which lies just north of the Alaskan Mountain Range. The reservation encompasses some 35,000 acres of land and was selected as the ideal BMEWS location for several reasons. The first and most important reason being a clear and unobstructed radar view over the North Pole region from where the most likely ICBM threat would be launched. Other reasons being that the land was already owned by the Air Force, it has a good solid gravel base that adequately supports the massive antennas and heavy equipment for this type of operation, there is an unlimited supply of palatable water that flows at a constant 35 degrees temperature, both in winter and summer. The station is under the direct control of a select number of Air Force and enlisted personnel. The actual operation and maintenance of the facility is being accomplished by the RCA Service Company, under an Air Force contract, which is renegotiated on an annual basis.

MSgt. O'Daniel had access to a full range of onsite facilities due to the isolated location of Site II. A complete medical dispensary is available with one civilian doctor and civilian nurses in attendance. This medical service is available to all personnel permanently employed on the site. For military personnel requiring more extensive medical care, medical and dental facilities are available at Eielson AFB near Fairbanks and Elmendorf AFB near Anchorage. A branch of the First National Bank of Fairbanks is located on site to provide services to all shift schedules. The site dining facility is a field ration mess, operated by a professional civilian employees. Meals are available on a twenty-three hour a day basis, with breakfast being available along with any regular meal being served. Dormitory type housing is provided to all personnel, approximately 1,300 people, with 560 in the permanent dormitories. Television is available in each lounge of the dormitories with all programs approximately 30 days behind (at that time) the same program in the Continental United States. Permanent dormitory rooms are immediately accessible without the need to go outside in the cold and northern weather, to the Main Exchange, gymnasium, movie theater, bank, mess facilities, Air Force offices, dayroom, mail room, post office, and barber shop.

An airfield with a 4,000 foot gravel runway is maintained on Site II; able to handle (at that time) aircraft as large as C-54s. Consequently, Clear is in reality, a city within itself, providing all the necessities of any small community. It provides housing and all the amenities. A power plant, which is operated by the Alaskan Air Command, provides electrical power for the technical site and steam heat and electrical power for housekeeping. There are nine miles of roads, serviced by an on-site bus service. [90]

---

[90] MSgt. Robert O'Daniel, Rapid City, South Dakota. Information provided to author, May 15, 2012. MSgt. O'Daniel was assigned to Detachment 2, Headquarters 71 Surveillance Wing, Air Defense Command on June 13, 1962 after the 54th Fighter-Interceptor Squadron was discontinued at Ellsworth Air Force Base, South Dakota. The following information comes from "Welcome to Site II, Clear, Alaska, BMEWS, 71st Surveillance Wing and RCA.

Gerald Teachout, USAF

Air Force Pilot in Vietnam, 1964

GERALD (Jerry) Teachout..."Things were beginning to happen in the Southwest Pacific area almost like the 'no you don't' of Korean War times. Communist forces had walked all over the French troops in the country of Vietnam. Most people, as with Korea, hardly knew where it could be found on a globe. The U.S. had advisory troops in that area if no more than to keep our intelligence at a decent level so officials would know what was going on. The hammer finally fell in the summer of 1964 when other KC-135 squadrons were alerted to send crews and airplanes to the Philippines to fly out of Clark Field over the Tonkin Gulf just east of Vietnam itself. We were to refuel anything that belonged to us that needed a drink. My crew was picked to go in the letter part of October of that year but there are two things that make a difference in the rest of this autobiography.

"Number one was the fact that Air Force retirement entered the picture in about 1965 and both my wife and myself were looking out for ourselves in the planning. It all goes back to the alert business and the ninety-six hours per week that SAC had put on our backs. Some crewmembers got off alert and spent their time at the lake fishing and enjoying their boats and beer, others had to have something else to do and I was one of the latter. I had a flight scheduled after my mandatory off time so I reported for it, ready to go. For some reason, a myopia of dire proportions hit me and they got another aircraft commander to take the flight. I ended up in the hospital, knocked out for two days while this myopia subsided. Myopia is a severe muscle cramp and it hit me in the shoulder.

"The squadron took its turn and headed for the Viet Nam area in 1966 for six months where aerial refueling duties were needed. Part of the squadron had to stay home to man the EC-135s used to maintain the radio links with SAC Headquarters and its Air Forces. I stayed home and watched the war escalate to a full-blown conflagration and knew I'd have all I wanted of this, the third major conflict for me. The Old Man upstairs was looking after me for sure, never putting me in direct contact with an enemy but close enough to make my services necessary. Korea was simply a leftover from World War II, as was the Cold War time spent in Europe during what destiny had for me and what I loved best, flying airplanes. Hardly a day goes by that I don't review some of the good things that have come my way and also the bad choices considered as part of the life that has nothing to do with aircraft.

"A year to a child is forever, but to an adult that same period of time goes by like a racecar. Time didn't mean a lot to me, only what I could do with time I had so a year went by and the squadron was alerted that it was their turn again to spend another six months near where the actual fighting was occurring. In the meantime, the alert schedule never dropped a day and the mission to take fighters across the Pacific kept up its pace. Crossing the Pacific was like taking a daily stroll with the exercise instructor. One such mission was to mother hen some F-4s out of George Air Force Base, California and we were to meet them near the Farrilon Islands off the coast of San Francisco at a given time the next day. My crew was to stage out of March AFB, California, so we had to get a briefing as to times, altitudes, air speeds, offloads, etc. We took off from Ellsworth as planned, climbing to our assigned altitude when I felt a pain like I had never experienced before. My right side almost doubled me up and point of trouble didn't go away. Just got a little better as the flight continued. I told the copilot that a flight surgeon would have to look me over when we got on ground at March or they had better plan on another aircraft commander if the pain didn't subside.

"By the time we arrived over 'high station' at March, the pain had gone away enough to allow me to make the letdown and landing, but it still persisted. The flight surgeon was never called and alerted to my condition. The crew, bless their hearts, unloaded what baggage we had onto the crew bus and we headed for the assigned quarters. Upon arrival there, I had to urinate 'pronto' like yesterday of there was such a thing. It felt like someone had stuck and ice pick into my right side and drug it around to the front when simultaneously the pain ceased and I heard a 'clunk' as the only kidney stone I had ever had hit the porcelain of the stool. Several months later I told another flight surgeon about it and got royally reamed about it for not reporting the incident. The mission continued and the fighters were delivered to do their jobs. So ended my first encounter with kidney stones.

"I took another trip to the Far East as scheduled when the wing took its turn. We had airplanes all over to cover the necessary missions. Some of us ended up a Kadena AFB, Okinawa, also at CCK near Taichung (Formosa), Utapao (Thailand) and Andersen AFB, Guam, all for 179 days and if that isn't six months I'll eat your hat. I have to tell you about this six months because I got promoted during this time and that meant a lot of changes in future life. I landed at Kadena and parked the airplane. I was met immediately, before I had filled out the necessary paperwork so the mechanics would know what was wrong before the next flight. Before I had loosened the seat belt shoulder harness. A friend of mine came aboard that had been at Ellsworth some months before. He was called the 'Alert Force Commander,' which meant that he took care of the billeting and other regards for incoming crews. Unlike the flight crews, he could accompany him to see the 'Old Man' and I wondered 'what did I do now to rate this?' He assured me all was okay and that I was to meet an old friend of mine, that's all. The staff car pulled up in front of a decrepit Quonset Hut where the Controlling Wing had been formed. I was ushered into the Wing Operations Officer's room and sure'nuff, there sat my friend as Director of Operations. He had been the Squadron Operations Officer during my KC-135 training days at Roswell AFB, New Mexico, was the Operations Officer that I had hauled to the Philippines some three years before from Glasgow, AFB, Montana. He was by this time a Bird Colonel, I was just a major, but rank didn't seem to enter the picture at all. We recalled old times and people like Air Force people are supposed to do when the subject of 'WHY' I was in his office came up. I had never been to Kadena before, my bags were taken care of by an a airmen unknown, and assignment to quarters had all been arranged simply because my friend from Ellsworth, the Alert Force Commander, knew that I was a bit handy with woodworking and carpenter tools.

"The 'Old Man' and my friend stashed me in a staff car and away we went to a new building on the other side of the runway that was to house the wing when it was ready. I had not been to the assigned quarters yet and knew nothing about the base. Our first stop in the building was a very large and new briefing room and the 'Old Man' asked me if I could frame the painted insignia of every bomb wing and squadron that had participated in the wing activities, forty-four of them, simply for wall decor. Each panel was some 24 by 30-inches, an easy job with the right molding and proper tools. I made the excuse that all my tools were still back in the States and if I had known. He assured me that the base carpenter shop and base supply would furnish anything needed to complete the job and further drove me to each facility to make sure they knew who they were serving.

"Majors in flying suits are not their regular customers and I had little to say other than 'yes sir' to everything he asked. After all it was a new building and decorations came few and far between. The second and third day found me looking at the rest of the building, some 144,000 square feet of it, and not a piece of wood adorned any of it. I had said yes to the frames and thought that would be the end of it and I was dead wrong. The frames were finished in a couple of days with the help of some excellent base carpentry shop saws, the next thing asked for was a frame around a huge area of responsibility wall map behind the desk of the operations officer. I quickly found that visiting Washington heads frequently visited this office and first impression were paramount. The knowing and curious will want to know how permission was granted so quickly for me to use the base equipment, such as the 'dangerous' saws. Machinery like this were my meat and had been for years. Ability was the answer and had to be demonstrated to the shop chief's satisfaction. Shop safety practices showed up repeatedly and the permission to use any machine in the shop was granted.

"The building had been built to Air Force specs by Okinawan contractors without a speck of cabinetry involved. Why the Air Force 'bought' the building without such amenities will never be known. When I was introduced to the American GI that actually ran the carpenter shop, the Okinawan workmen looked at me in utter bewilderment as though an officer couldn't do anything but order another person around. Their personal respect showed up at Christmas time in the form of a complete teakwood sewing cabinet for my wife, which she still has. It also showed up in the form of a turkey invite from the NCOIC of the shop and spending that time with a family with a lot better than anything the officer's club had to offer. At a later date, a teakwood table showed up as another present for my wife, from these same Okinawan workmen. I was a bit overwhelmed.

"I was assigned an Air Force pickup for my twenty-four hour a day transportation, old but very serviceable. I found that my friend had put me in a swanky corner downstairs room, more like a suite than a room, and that it had been previously designated as a VIP room. By this time, I figured that more was expected of me than just flying airplanes and further duty was unjustified as far as the Air Force was concerned. My primary job was to fly that KC-135 to the best of my ability. I cannot take all the credit because my crew kept the action oiled like a proper machine, the extra activity is and was unheralded.

"All this extracurricular activity took the better part of a week. I flew twice during this first week to get acquainted with the route and procedures, which were not much different than back home, except they were mostly over water. Again, this was where a good navigator as part of the crew was a necessity. The flying duties were passed around, that is, thirty days at Kadena, thirty days at CCK on Formosa, both refueling B-52s, thirty days at Utapao, Thailand, refueling all kinds of fighters, nine days at Andersen AFB, Guam, again standing by for B-52s needing fuel as they returned from 'in country' and then the routine started all over again until the 178th day when the leapfrogging trek to Ellsworth would begin. I found that the 'old man' had ordered my torus cut to fifteen days at each place and that I was not to repeat any of it. That meant I was stuck pretty much to Kadena. The crew loved it because Kadena was considered a 'plush' assignment of the lot.

"To set the record straight, my crew flew just one mission short of the highest number flown by any crew from our base. I was lucky in that none of the crew were bar hangers or carousers but they didn't help any with the chores, which I seemed to be saddled. My spare time was taken up with a hobby that had followed me all the days of my life and I was grateful. I flew missions that had to be flown anyway even though I was more of less restricted but I had a 'thing' to look forward to when the mission was finished. And there was one more thing in my favor, that of being a senior major and an experienced lead crew commander, therefore the lead position in a flight of three or more always fell to my lot."[91]

---

[91] Gerald (Jerry) Teachout, USAF. "Air Force pilot in Vietnam, 1964." Black Hills Veterans Writing Group, "Vietnam War," Rapid City, South Dakota, author, June 2012.

USS Proteus

Cold War Nuclear Submarine
Ballistic Missile Tender
Apra Harbor, Guam

THE keel of the submarine tender USS Proteus (AS-19) was laid on September 15, 1941, at the Moore Shipbuilding and Dry Dock Company, Oakland, California. With World War II approaching, the United States Navy (USN) increased construction of its surface warship fleet in preparation to fight a two-ocean war. The Proteus was one of a new class of USN submarine tenders, named after the first one commissioned, the USS Fulton (AS-11).

This class was built at a slow rate. The construction program had to be altered after the Japanese raided the USN base at Pearl Harbor, Hawaii on the morning of December 7, 1941. The Fulton was on its shakedown cruise when Japan attacked. The second of the class, the Sperry (AS-12), was still on the building ways, rushed to completion to clear the construction yard. As soon as it was launched, the Sperry was assigned to the Pacific Fleet at Pearl Harbor to support fleet submarine operations. The remaining five Fulton class submarine tenders (Bushnell AS-15, Howard W. Gilmore AS-16, Nereus AS-17, Orion AS-18, and Proteus AS-19) had their construction priority reduced, allowing for personnel and construction materials to be switched to other vessels.

As fighting in the Pacific increased, the USN authorized the completion of the five Fulton class submarine tenders and others. The Proteus was launched on November 12, 1943. However, because of demands of a two-ocean war, was not commissioned until January 31, 1944.

After its shakedown cruise off San Diego, California, the Proteus sailed up the California coast to the Oakland Navy Yard prior to deployment to the Pacific. It departed San Francisco Bay on March 19, 1944, for Midway Island to serve as a submarine tender for Submarine Squadron 20's operations against Japan. It arrived at Midway on May 3, 1944, operating out of Midway Island until December 1, 1944. While anchored at Midway Island, the Proteus completed 51 voyage repairs and 14 refits. The forward deployed Proteus allowed U.S. submarines to be serviced for return to combat faster than returning to Pearl Harbor.

The Proteus returned to Pearl Harbor on December 4, 1944, for refit. On February 5, 1945, the Proteus deployed to Apra Harbor, Guam in the Northern Marianas Islands. When the Northern Marianas were captured from the Japanese (Saipan, invaded on 15 June and declared secure on August 6, 1944; Guam, invaded on 21 July and declared secure on August 10, 1944; and Tinian, invaded on 24 July and declared secure on August 1, 1944), the USN had excellent forward support bases. While at Apra Harbor, the Proteus completed four voyage repairs and 24 refits. The submarine tender was operating from Apra Harbor on August 15, 1945, when Japan accepted the Allied powers unconditional surrender terms, ending World War II.

The unconditional surrender demand on the Japanese was declared in the final document of the Conference of Berlin (better known as the Potsdam Conference) on July 31, 1945 that: "The agreed summary of conclusions reached at the Terminal (Potsdam) Conference...is that the over-all objective...in conjunction with other Allies to bring about at the earliest possible date the unconditional surrender of Japan." Japan was warned by the United States, England, and China (the Soviet Union did not declare war on Japan until August 9, 1945): "We call upon the government of Japan to proclaim now the unconditional surrender of all the Japanese armed forces, and to provide proper and adequate assurances of their good faith in such action. The alternative for Japan is prompt and utter destruction."

The Proteus lifted anchor and sailed out of Apra Harbor, joining the Third Fleet, proceeding to Sagami Bay, then entering Tokyo Bay for the formal surrender ceremony on the battleship USS Missouri. During the signing of the formal surrender documents, the Proteus served as the flagship for Vice Admiral Lockwood. After the surrender ceremony, the submarine tender was temporary berthing home for the Japanese submarine I-400, which at that time, was the largest submarine in the world.

The Japanese built three of these submarines, but because of a lack of forward bases by November 1944, they did not employ them against the United States. They decided to attempt a suicide air raid against the Panama Canal locks, blocking movement of freighters and warships from the Atlantic to the Pacific. Each submarine had a waterproof (enclosed) aircraft hangar, holding one disassembled and three complete floatplanes. They could be launched off the submarine's bow-mounted catapult and normally landed alongside the surfaced submarine, hoisted back onto the deck by a crane. With a displacement of 3,530 tons, there were the largest submarines built prior to the construction of nuclear powered submarines. While USN experts examined the I-400, the Proteus served as the flagship for 26 USN ships off the Honshu coast until August 26, 1945.

On August 28, 1945, the Proteus anchored at Sanami Wan to support Submarine Squadron 20 as it demilitarized Japanese submarines, human suicide torpedoes, torpedo carrying suicide boats, as well as the suicide boats at Yokosuka Naval Base and at other locations in the Sagami Wan-Tokyo Bay areas. Starting in September 1945, and continuing to the end of the month, the Proteus supported the supply and repatriation of Allied Prisoners of War (POWs), and the continued demilitarization of the Japanese World War II naval units.

The Proteus departed Tokyo Bay on November 1, 1945, returning to Pearl Harbor for repairs prior to sailing to the United States. On December 6, 1945, the Proteus transited the Panama Canal on its way to the New London Navy Base. Later, the submarine tender deployed to Argentina, supporting SubRon 8's operations in South America during November 1946. After operating at New London for almost one year, the submarine tender was decommissioned on September 26, 1947. Even after decommissioning, the Proteus was not placed into ready storage, but instead, served as station ship until January 1959.

The USN, after World War II, declared most of its diesel-electric submarine fleet obsolete, reducing their numbers and supporting tenders. The USN began research and development on nuclear propulsion. With the commissioning of the USS Nautilus in 1954, the USN's submarines no longer had to surface to recharge batteries, their underwater range only limited by the endurance of its crew. At the same time, ballistic missile technology was introduced.

The USN created a new class of submarine, the ship submersible ballistic nuclear (SSBN), armed with 16 long-range fleet ballistic missiles (FBMs), on December 31, 1957. To shorten deployment time (due to worsening relations with the Soviet Union), two attack submarines (already on the building ways) were converted to carry the solid-fuel Polaris FBM (Polaris A1).

The Polaris A1 (UGM-27A) weighed 28,800 pounds, 28 feet six-inches long, 54-inches in diameter, with a range of 1,000 miles. The A1's first stage weighed 18,400 pounds, with a steel motor case, powered by 15,200 pounds of polyurethane propellant with ammonium perchlorate oxidizer and aluminum additives. The second stage weighed 9,400 pounds, also with a steel motor case, powered by 7,300 pounds of solid fuel propellant.

With compromises in building schedules, the USN in January 1958, slipped the launch dates for two hunter-killer Skipjack class submarines (Scorpion, SSN-589 and Sculpin, SSN-590), pulling funding from other warship construction, to modify the two attack submarines and build three additional SSBNs. The first two SSBNs were essentially hunter-killer nuclear submarines with a missile compartment inserted between the control navigation areas and nuclear reactor compartment. The keels of the first two SSBNs were already laid at the Electric Boat Division at Groton, Connecticut.

The Scorpion (George Washington) was cut into two sections, to insert and weld in a 130 foot long missile section, referred to as "Sherwood Forest" (nicknamed by submarine personnel who walked through the area with eight missile launch tubes on either side of the submarine, describing its appearance as a man-made, steel forest inside the submarine's hull).

While these SSBNs were under construction, preparations began to have a submarine tender ready to support the George Washington SSBN-598. The George Washington sailed on its first nuclear alert patrol on November 15, 1960. The submarine tender, USS Hunley (AS-31) was under construction and would not be operational in time. Consequently, the USN decided to modify the Proteus into an SSBN tender. It was moved to a large dry dock and was cut into two sections.

To the casual observer, it appeared the ship was being cut apart for scrap. A new section, designed for "special weapons handling" (to accommodate the Polaris A1 FBMs) and nuclear servicing of the submarine's nuclear power plant (S5W pressurized water-cooled nuclear reactor) was welded to the separated hull sections. This added 500 tons in weight and 44 ½ feet in length to the submarine tender. The Proteus was re-commissioned on July 8, 1960.

The Proteus crew increased to 1,329 to handle the workload associated with servicing the SSBNs. On its shakedown cruise, the Proteus went to the Charleston Navy Yard to pick up the Navy's first operational FBMs and transport them back to New London. Once back at New London, the Proteus dropped anchor, ready to service its first SSBN. On January 20, 1961, the George Washington berthed alongside and the Proteus and was loaded with 16 Polaris A1 FBMs. Eleven days later, the George Washington departed on the USN's first SSBN nuclear alert patrol.

The USN decided to forward deploy the Proteus to Holy Lock, Scotland, reducing transit time to and from nuclear alert patrol zones.

The Proteus dropped anchor in Holy Lock harbor on March 3, 1961, establishing the USN's first advanced Polaris deployment anchorage. The first SSBN to berth alongside the Proteus at Holy Lock was the Patrick Henry (SSBN 599). The Proteus completed the first overseas FBM exchange with the Patrick Henry.

To accomplish this, the Proteus used its outward extending gantry crane, holding a tube-like structure, which was fitted and locked onto one of the Patrick Henry's 16 missile launch tubes. This holding tube was necessary so the motion of the SSBN and submarine tender did not affect the alignment of the Polaris A1. The missile handler tube was fitted with an internal hoist, which raised or lowered the missile in or out of the missile launches tube. The missile handler tube had to re-positioned over each missile launch tube.

Over the next two years, the Proteus completed 38 refits. The submarine tender was relieved by the Hunley, allowing it to return to Charleston Navy Yard for refit and over haul in 1963, including dry-docking for a fresh coat of paint. Once out of Charleston Navy Yard, the Proteus relieved the Hunley at Holy Lock on January, 1964, so the Hunley could undergo refit and overhaul. After the Hunley returned to Holy Lock, the Proteus established the USN's second advanced Polaris deployment anchorage at Rota, Spain. The submarine tender remained at Rota Harbor until returning to Holy Lock on April 12, 1964, when it relieved the Hunley.

On 29 June, the Hunley resumed station at Holy Lock, so the Proteus could return to Charleston Navy Yard, where it received orders to set up the USN's third advanced Polaris deployment anchorage at Apra Harbor, Guam in the Northern Marianas Islands. On November 29, 1964, the Proteus arrived back at a familiar anchorage, Apra Harbor.

The Daniel Boone (SSBN 629) was the first SSBN to berth alongside the Proteus at Apra Harbor. The Proteus resumed submarine tender operations in Apra Harbor after an absence of 19 years, becoming an almost permanent fixture in the western Pacific. It remained in Apra Harbor for the next seven years, only relieved by the Hunley for five months in 1968, while completing a self-overhaul (remaining in Apra Harbor).

In order to increase the patrol range of the Polaris SSBN, the range of the Polaris FBM had to be increased, bringing more Soviet targets within striking distance. The next upgrade was the Polaris A2, with a range of 1,500 miles (a modest range increase), weighing 32,500 pounds, and 31 feet long. It was the same diameter as the A1, allowing it to fit inside the SSBN's missile launch tubes without expensive and time-consuming dry dock modifications. The Polaris A2 became operational on June 26, 1962, when the Ethan Allen (SSBN 608), the first SSBN designed from the keel up, loaded 16 A2s into its missile launch tubes.

In order to achieve its 1,500 mile range, the weight of the second stage was reduced, thereby increasing the thrust potential and range. A reduction in the second stage's weight returned an eight-fold increase in range increment than a similar weight reduction in the first stage.

The next FBM upgrade was the Polaris A3, with a range of 2,500 miles (a significant range increase over the A2). It was 31 feet long and weighed 35,700 pounds. Its design was restricted by the volume available in the Polaris SSBN's launch tubes. The A3's first stage weighed 24,600 pounds, with a fiberglass motor case, powered by 12,800 pounds of nitro plasticized polyurethane propellant. The second stage weighed 10,800 pounds, also with a fiberglass motor case, powered by 9,000 pounds of double base propellant. The missile was fitted with three re-entry vehicles (RVs) which tilted outward and ejected by a small rocket motor.

The A3 became operational on the USS Daniel Webster (SSBN 626) on September 28, 1964. The A3's 2,500 mile range extended the Polaris SSBN's operational area to counter the growing lethality of the Soviet Navy's surface and long-range aircraft anti-submarine operations in the western Pacific and North Atlantic.

However, the USN wanted to strike more than three targets per missile and development the Poseidon C3 FBM. It was 74-inches in diameter (compared to 54-inches for the A3), 34 feet long (compared to 31 feet for the A3), and weighed 65,700 pounds (30,000 pounds more than the A3). The Polaris SSBN's maximum growth potential was stretched to the limit, to fit the C3 inside its missile launch tubes. An advanced, multiple individual targeted re-entry vehicles (MIRVs) fire control system was installed for the SSBN's missile launch officer.

The C3 was a two-stage, solid-fuel FBM, with a range of 2,500 miles (the same as the A3), fitted with up to 14 Mark 3 RVs (compared to three RVs on the A3). This revolutionary multiple target capability per C3 changed USN nuclear targeting policy, strategic force structure, employment doctrines, and operational planning. On March 31, 1971, the USS James Madison (SSBN-627) took 16 C3 FBMs to sea on nuclear alert patrol for the first time.

In 1971, the Proteus arrived at the Mare Island Navy Yard for extensive overhaul and propulsion system upgrade, which increased the ship's weight to 20,295 tons, reduced the crew to 1,258, increased maximum speed to 18 knots, and increased draft by two feet (25 feet six-inches). The Proteus made its retrofit shakedown cruise to Pearl Harbor, with a port call at Sydney, Australia prior to returning to Apra Harbor in January 1973, establishing a pattern of regular swap outs with the Hunley.

The Proteus took part in "Operation NEW LIFE," beginning on April 23, 1975, when Guam military authorities were ordered to prepare reception camps for an estimated 50,000 South Vietnamese refugees fleeing the North Vietnamese. Guam based military personnel renovated World War II facilities and built huge tent camps to receive, process, and house the South Vietnamese refugees. Approximately 5,000 South Vietnamese arrived each day at Anderson Air Force Base, at the north end of Guam. By June 1976, Guam military personnel had handled 130,000 refugees to and out of Guam. The author was involved in "Operation NEW LIFE" and frequently visited the tender, providing updates on the numbers of refugees and schedules. He was part of the staff effort, especially when the Commander of COMNAVMARIANAS learned his father had been a Seabee during World War II, assigned to nearby Tinian Island and Okinawa, temporarily assigned to the Admiral's staff to assist in processing arriving South Vietnamese refugees.

In 1978, the Proteus (previously scheduled to be retired) was ordered to the Long Beach Navy Shipyard for overhaul and refit. It returned to Apra Harbor in May 1980, resuming refit responsibilities for SSBNs in the western Pacific. The Poseidon modification changed the makeup of the SSBN fleet. In July 1981, the Polaris Robert E. Lee, sailed from Apra Harbor, ending the Polaris SSBN presence in the western Pacific, replaced by Poseidon SSBNs. At this time, the Proteus was converted from a SSBN tender to a general fleet support ship.

One of the reasons the Proteus was pulled from SSBN support was the introduction of the Trident SSBN. Starting in 1979, the USS Francis Scott Key (SSBN 657), referred to as an Ohio class SSBN, sailed on its first nuclear alert patrol, armed with Trident I (C4 FBMs). The Ohio class SSBNs are specifically designed for extended deterrent patrols, each armed with 24 C4s, with a range of 4,000 miles, fitted with MIRVs.

A total of 18 Trident SSBNs were to deployed (at that time in the cold war), based at the Naval Submarine Base at Kings Bay, Georgia and Naval Submarine Base at Bangor, Washington. Tridents replaced the Poseidon SSBNs, and armed with the C3 FBM provide near pinpoint accuracy over intercontinental range.

The Proteus was assigned to the U.S. Seventh Fleet operating from Diego Garcia in the Indian Ocean, supporting USN warships and submarines in the Indian Ocean and Persian Gulf. The submarine tender returned to Apra Harbor in April 1982, departing in October 1982, for a three-month deployment to Subic Bay to support USN fleet operations in the Far East.

Again, in 1983, the Proteus deployed for three months to Subic Bay for fleet support and upkeep of USN vessels operating in the Far East or on their way to the Indian Ocean and Persian Gulf. The Proteus returned to Apra Harbor in late June 1983. The author provided intelligence support to the tender during his second tour on Guam, 1978 to 1983. The submarine tender deployed again to Subic Bay in September to conduct fleet support operations and perform ship maintenance, returning to Apra Harbor in December.

On January 31, 1984, the crew of the Proteus celebrated the submarine tender's 40th birthday on active duty with the USN, marked by an island-wide celebration, presided over by the Catholic Archbishop of Guam. On May 14, 1984, the Proteus deployed from Apra Harbor, stopping at Singapore before sailing to Diego Garcia, returning to Apra Harbor on October 12, 1984.

From January to July 1985, the Proteus completed the first phase of an incremental overhaul, three months of which was spent in a floating dry dock, at the Naval Ship Repair Facility, Apra Harbor. Even while undergoing repairs and in dry dock, the Proteus continued to service submarines, as well as Tiger Team support to submarines operating in the western Pacific. On 3 July, the submarine tender deployed to Subic Bay to support USN fleet operations, returning to Apra Harbor on August 31, 1985.

The Proteus deployed to Subic Bay on February 12, 1986, for one month. After a rest and relaxation port call at Hong Kong, the submarine tender sailed to Chinhae, South Korea for three weeks. The Proteus provided logistic and repair support for USN fleet operations, and repaired six South Korean Navy submarines. Following return to Apra Harbor on April 3, 1986, the Proteus became the first USN submarine tender in the western Pacific to berth a Trident SSBN alongside (USS Georgia, SSBN 729 from 30 April to May 10, 1986). Throughout the summer and fall of 1986, the Proteus provided repair and logistic support to submarines entering Apra Harbor. In addition, from July to October, the submarine tender's crew completed the second phase of a self-incremental overhaul, continuing to service visiting submarines.

1987 and 1988 was a period of numerous deployments for the Proteus to support submarines operating in the western Pacific: Chinhae, South Korea; Subic Bay, Philippines; Hong Kong; Sasebo and Yokosuka, Japan. In January 1989, the crew of the Proteus celebrated the submarine tender's 45 years of active service. In March, the Proteus deployed to Chinhae, providing logistic support for the U.S. Seventh Fleet, with port calls at Sasebo, Japan; Pattaya Beach, Thailand; and Subic Bay. In September and October 1989, the Proteus made port calls to the Marshall Islands, New Guinea, and Cebu, Philippines.

From March to June 1990, and again in 1991, the Proteus completed cruises to Hong Kong, Philippines, and Japan. An emergency deployment was made to Subic Bay to provide assistance after the eruption of Mount Pinatubo. "Operation FIERY VIGIL," mission was to dig out U.S. military facilities at Subic Bay Naval Base and the nearby Philippine town of Olongapo. The Proteus returned to Apra Harbor on August 15, 1991. The Proteus made its final operational deployment, April to May 1992, painted in its 1945 World War II camouflage scheme, to commemorate the 50th anniversary of the U.S.-Japanese carrier air battle, referred to as the Battle of the Coral Sea (April 29 to May 4, 1942).

By winning this battle, where neither surface fleet engaged each other, U.S. naval aviators stopped the Japanese invasion fleet from reaching Port Moresby, New Guinea. The Proteus made port calls at Sydney and Brisbane, Australia to participate in the Coral Sea festival. After returning to Apra Harbor, the submarine tender was inactivated on July 11, 1992. It sailed to Bremerton, Washington for decommissioning in September 1992, going into fleet reserve storage. However, the submarine tender did not remain in storage very long.

In 1994, the Proteus was re-instated to the USN's active ship roll, designated as IX 518, as a USN berthing auxiliary. The Proteus is currently supporting overhaul crews at the Bremerton Navy Yard. Since its commissioning on January 31, 1994, the Proteus had served for over 50 years.[92]

---

[92] The author, while an intelligence officer on Andersen AFB, Guam provided intelligence briefings to the U.S. Navy Fleet ballistic nuclear submarine crews in Apra Harbor during crew change outs (one crew coming off the submarine at the conclusion of its patrol and the relieving crew which will take the submarine back out on patrol). This was a vital part of America's sea based portion of the TRIAD of nuclear weapons, secure at sea, ready to strike back at the Soviet Union if the United States was attacked by ICBMS, SLBMS, and/or long-range bombers.

Alan B. Walker

May 28, 1968, Foxtrot Ridge, South Vietnam

ALAN B. Walker..."I have been in the bush for more than six months. I am no longer the 'Boot,' and except for a few close firefights, it's been a good experience. Six months ago, I was a lowly mortar jumper; now I am a squad leader in Foxtrot Company...the nightmare has started. We get our mortar ready to fire; all of us get into the mortar pit. We are very fortunate that we have a claymore mine in front of us. It isn't long, and we can hear voices and movements in front of us. We can hear them dragging up equipment. We can hear their canteens clanking on their belts. We can hear them lock and load their weapons. More of the elephant grass is pushed down. It seems like it's right in front of us. My squad tells me to hit the claymore. I tell them very softly that we need to wait a little more. I am so scared. If someone were to say...'Let's get the Hell out of here,' we would; but no one has told us to leave. More movement in the grass, soon they will be right in our faces. I don't want my squad to know that I am scared. I think everyone is. In fact, Holes, my 'A' gunner, lies down in the mortar pit and starts to cry. I hit the plunger on the claymore and nothing happens. I do it again and still nothing. I start to pull in the wire and I find it has been cut. My heart falls out of my chest. I know that we will all die tonight. Death is just a few feet from our mortar pit. I pray to God to let us live until morning. That's when help will be here. I pray again and again.

"A flare is sent into the sky and the whole hill rises up in front of us. Hordes of enemy soldiers charge at us. NVA soldiers are shooting farther up the hill. They think we are farther up. Instead, we are shooting them in their bellies. They don't even know that they are being shot at. They fall into our mortar pit and outside of it, and soon we have more than ten bodies lying around us. I put my empty pistol magazine in my pocket so I can reload them later. Now I am out of bullets. I am loading my magazines as fast as I can. I can hear people dragging up behind us. I push the last bullet into the magazine and quickly push the magazine into the .45 caliber pistol. I pull the slide back and turn around and I am looking into the muzzle of an AK-47. Before the NVA soldier can squeeze the trigger, I put a .45 slug into his forehead and I hit his buddy in the face with the next bullet.

"My autobiography traces my Omaha-Winnebago roots, which is the history of the Ho-Chunks from the Treaty of 1832 to my fighting as a Marine in South Vietnam during the Vietnam War. The Treaty of 1832, part of the Indian Removal Act of 1830, under President Andrew Jackson, removing Indian tribes west of the Mississippi River. My grandfather (who at this time I will call William Cloud because I do not really know his last name). So in 1832, William was moved to Black River Fall, Wisconsin. The Ho-Chunks wanted canvas for their teepees to replace the heavy hide coverings. Even more desirable was cast iron cooking utensils. We moved to northeast Iowa where the Federal government considered the area to be neutral ground near Fort Atkinson. After signing another treaty with the Federal government, some of the Ho-Chunks moved to Minnesota, others to South Dakota. The Winnebago Indians purchased land from the Omaha tribe in the northern part of the reservation around Fort Thompson. At this time, one of my ancestors, Chief Little Priest, joined the U.S. Army as a scout with 74 others out of a total tribe population of 1,200 to 1,500. Interestingly, the U.S. Army's Indian opponents, the Sioux, Cheyenne and Arapahos started raiding the Winnebago's homes. The 75 Winnebago's were valuable in combat. William Cloud proved himself in battle, earning a song, which is the title of my book, 'Every Warrior has his own song.' In 1865, William changed his last name to Hatchett.

"The federal government wanted the Winnebago Indians to be farmers. William Hatchett's son, Louis, was sent to a missionary school for three years. My grandfather, Ed Hatch, was taken from his parents at night, forcibly transported to an Indian school. Taken at night so they could not escape and find their way home. The Indian school was at Genoa, Nebraska, 30 miles north-northwest of Lincoln, Nebraska. The children had to speak English. Government run Indian schools were set up and run like a U.S. Army Post. Indian children were told they were orphans. Ed Hatch was at the school for 11 years, eventually returning home to his grandparents.

"Interestingly, the merchants on the reservations were mostly white people. Winnebago's, when they received their government rations, traded excess items in town with the white merchants. It was at this time, Ed met a daughter of one of the white merchants, Mable Wilcox. When she became 21, she married Ed. They moved to the west end of the reservation. It was hard for them, being in an interracial marriage. But, the banks loaned Ed money because he was a good farmer. Then like hundreds of thousands of farmers throughout the United States, the October 1929 stock market crash and resulting

Great Depression, they lost their farm. They moved back in with Ed's grandparents, U.S. Grant. Ed went to work on President Franklin Roosevelt's created Works Projects Administration (WPA) in 1940. He needed work to provide for his wife and five children. During a heavy rain, Omaha Creek flowed over its banks, flooding their home. They moved to the southeast edge of the Winnebago Reservation until 1955. My grandparents passed away in 1969 in a nursing home in Nebraska.

"I graduated from high school on May 22, 1966, with my United States Marines Corps (USMC) entrance into active duty moved up to 25 May. I was sent to San Diego, California for Marine Corps Boot Camp. I went to 81mm mortar school and then onto to Okinawa in 1967. I was in Okinawa for three weeks as the 3rd Marines were rebuilt after losses in combat in South Vietnam. I was assigned to Foxtrot Company, 2nd Battalion. We were sent to Vietnam, stationed as a 'float' troops inserted by helicopters into hot spots throughout the country. My Foxtrot Company named me 'Chief.' When operating in the 'Bush,' I found it exciting. In December 1967, I was assigned mess duty. When operating in the Bush, we survived (ate) on C-rations. Our Company worked an area south of DaNang. I walked point for the company. On one operation we were to move through a town with lepers. We were warned not to allow anyone in the village to touch us. On point, when I entered the village it was empty. I realized something was wrong. The company was far behind me. The NVA must have ran these people in the village away.

"On January (TET) 30, 1968, the all-out NVA offensive began. We saw the Viet Cong (VC) set up 122mm rockets, aimed or targeted against DaNang. They placed the Rockets on a wood, tree yoke, lighting off the rockets toward DaNang. We could see the flame of the rockets when ignited, whooshing overhead, lighting up the clouds, then flaming out, exploding on the ground in and around DaNang. We could see NVA running around, lighting the rockets to fire them off to DaNang. It was amazing they could be so accurate and hit DaNang.

"I manned a machine gun bunker on the ridge while this was going on. We shot off some flares. I thought I saw something so I fired my M-60 machine gun. Well, nothing happened. We moved north and I again walked point. I broke my glasses, my second pair, so I was flown to a hospital ship for two new pair. I was on the hospital ship when our company commander was wounded.

"We moved into and through Hue, northwest of DaNang along the coast of the South China Sea. Wow, the city was full of street lights, paved roads, sidewalks and shops. We moved north to Khe Sanh on 1 April. There were lights everywhere. We found the lights were from B-52 bombs hitting the ground. The ground troops referred to this as Operation Pegasus. This allowed Route 9 to be opened and Marines in Khe Sanh relieved from its intense siege by NVA forces. Most of the NVA moved out of the B-52 strike areas. We moved again, our company bolstered by replacements, into Landing Zone (LZ) Hawk, simply a wide spot in the road. There were 106mm recoilless rifles nearby. They were needed somewhere else, but did not want to move them out and let the NVA see they were no longer supporting our positions. Engineers took empty 106mm shell canisters welding them together, mounted on a wheel dolly, creating a dummy 106mm recoilless rifle battery. We moved into a position on the last bridge before Khe Sanh. I wanted to wash up in a water filled B-52 bomb crater. The North Vietnamese had artillery in caves dug back into the hillsides, rolling them out, firing three shells and rolling the guns back into the caves before we could locate and destroy them, either by artillery or aircraft attacks. The North Vietnamese started to shell us. We moved on.

"While we operated in company levels, the NVA operated in Battalion level (1,000 to 1,200 troops) versus our 88 to 100 men. We captured some NVA maps, to the same scale as ours. When we overlaid them on ours, we were sometimes only 1,000 yards away from superior NVA forces. On May 28, 1968, we took position on top of a high ridge along Route 9, a landing zone near Khe Sanh. There were 88 of us in the company and on the third night, we were attacked by 1,100 NVA. We saw movement and started getting hit by NVA. Most of the company pulled back, but we in the mortar crater (pit) did not get the order. We could hear the NVA coming. The Gunnery Sgt. popped a flare. There were 1,100 NVA attacking. Then Khe Sanh started shelling. The something unfortunate happened. We saw a figure coming toward us. We thought he was an NAV and we killed him. He was a Marine who had been manning the listening post and was trying to get away from the NVA into our lines. By the third wave of the NVA attack, we were running out of ammunition. We never received orders to fire the 81mm mortar. I dropped a grenade into the mortar tube to blow it up so the NVA could not use the 81mm shells against us. Foxtrot Ridge was hit by rocket propelled grenades (RPGs), artillery and mortar shells. The back side of the ridge was pretty steep and as the NVA over ran us, we played dead and the NVA ran past us.

"We had a combat engineer in our foxhole. He was crying out loud and shaking badly. He would not crawl out of the foxhole. We found him dead the next morning. I was with a group of Marines when a short round fell among us, wounding me in the left eye and ear. The artillery at Khe Sanh had reached their minimum ammunition level and ceased fire on the NVA. Our commander called them...'You start firing again on the NVA or I will fire on you.' They resumed firing. At daylight, we attacked the NVA with a C-47 gunship called 'Puff the Magic Dragoon' and F-4s dropping napalm on the hill. Our dead were burned in the attack. Forty-four out of our 88 in the company walked out of Foxtrot Ridge. I was sent to Da Nang because I had been wounded. In December 1968, I was home in the United States.

" On May 5, 2012, I received my own song, like my grandfather. Every Warrior has his own song." [93]

---

[93] Alan B. Walker, "Foxtrot Ridge, South Vietnam, 28 May 1968," Rapid City, South Dakota: Western Dakota Technical Institute, Black Hills Veterans Writing Group, Rapid City, South Dakota, author, June 9, 2012.

Mark St. Pierre

December 1968
"Operation FAYETTE CANYON"

"MARK St. Pierre..."In the mountainous rain forests of northern South Vietnam, not far from Da Nang, Frank Jealous Of Him stood alone looking across the helicopter-landing zone called Landing Zone (LZ) Baldy. The LZ, about a hundred meters in diameter and built mostly of sandbagged bunkers and empty shell boxes, sat on a hilltop cleared from the jungle and overlooked a long range of coastal mountains. The terrain below the firebase ranged from flooded rice paddies interspersed with thick hedgerows on the valley floor to thick brush that covered the lower hillsides. Higher up the mountains the cover changed to thick triple-canopied jungle. LZ Baldy sat high above it all, and to Frank seemed perched like a lonely eagle's nest on a craggy mountaintop.

"A misty ceiling at five hundred feet shrouded the distant forest floor where two lakes were fed by the numerous streams that cascaded down the steep mountains. Trails, which aided movement for both sides of the conflict, converged amid the thick bush on the valley floor.

"Winter monsoons had brought rain every few days, keeping the sky a gloomy overcast, and sent him into dark thoughts of home and whether he would or, better, should go home again. Showers would commence late at night and leave the jungle floor a cool, slippery red mush in the morning that would turn steaming hot by noon.

"Fog clung to the lower reaches of the area most days, creating an eerie isolation for the men of the landing zone. At 1100, in the command bunker at the center of the LZ, Captain Larry Stanford addressed the assembled platoon leaders. As usual, Frank was invited to the meeting by his lieutenant but felt out of place and squatted just outside the circle listening. 'Intelligence from Chieu Hois and our own reconnaissance patrols indicate the NVA and Vietcong are again utilizing Base Area 116 as a hospital and training site.' He indicated a set of circles in the northeast quadrant of the map. 'We have good information that a trail north of Alligator Lake is being used to purchase rice and resupply enemy units.' Again, the young officer's hand went to the map. 'We know they are getting rice from Dien Ban, Duy

Xuyen, and Khe Sanh districts. This route gives the enemy access to Goi Noi Island in the northern part of the lake. Sniffer missions and aerial observations have us convinced that the 36th NVA Infantry has reestablished their headquarters here at location 9656, while the 38th Quang Da Provincial Headquarters are here at Victor Bravo-Tango 0254. Our mission for the next two months is to discourage these people from thinking they've got control of this area.' He studied the faces of the men in the half-light of the bunker's interior. 'Company C is to attack and secure position one, here. Company A is to seize and hold objective two over here, while Company D will seize objective three. B Company will secure LZ Baldy, including the immediate vicinity.'

Pierre..."With that, Frank slumped against the sandbagged wall, part of him relieved that for now at least life would be easy, but also a little annoyed that his company would see little action for this mountaintop stronghold.

"Under the cover of a makeshift roof constructed of empty wooden mortar cases, he looked out through the rain, down at the misty world below him. He drew some writing paper from his pack and began a letter home.

Dear Dad:

"We've been moved again, this time further north to a place called LZ Baldy. Lieutenant Chellis who I've been working under is a short timer and will be leaving soon. He says that I am one of the main reasons he will be going home. These guys tell me I'm pretty important part of the platoon because I'm so good on point. Point means that I'm like a scout out in front of the squad and the rest of the platoon looking for sniper trip wires and booby traps.

"When our platoon goes on a company sized operation, I'm what they call point of point. That means I'm point man of our squad, point man or point platoon, out in front of the rest of the company. These guys tell me that the lives of point men usually only last a few days, sometimes only a few minutes or hours before they get blown away.

"They think that because I'm an Indian, I'm good at this. How do you tell these guys how crazy that is? 'Hey, I'm from the prairie where we can see for miles.' It's kind of weird bit I have gotten good at it. It's kind of up to me to see that we don't get lost, that we end up at night where we're supposed to be. Lots of times, I don't even look at maps. I try to feel where I'm going. Sometimes I look for animal trails through the jungle and just like hunting at home, here they kinda go towards water but I don't know really how I do it. The lieutenant says it's something he calls instinct.

"The Vietnamese people over here are all the same. By that I mean, the enemy and the civilians are the same people, so we don't know who is who. Remember I told you about the Chu Hois, they're former Viet Cong who now live with and work with us. They know I look more like them than the guys in the outfit. I feel like these people stare at me. They wonder why I'm even here with these Americans because I don't look like other soldiers. Sometimes I feel like they hate me for fighting here at all.

"But maybe that's how I survive. I try to think like them. Like Crazy Horse fighting the cavalry soldiers with his mind instead of having the best weapons. That's how these Viet Cong are always having to outsmart the U.S. Army.

"They guys in my outfit still call be 'Chief' even though I tell them that I'm not a chief. I guess it's because I'm an Indian.

"It's pretty rainy up here so when we're out on patrol our fatigues usually don't last long. I took to just wearing an olive drab towel, split down the middle, like a poncho over my head, instead of a shirt. Now all the other guys are doing that too. It's kind of become our uniform in the Bush.

"I think a lot of these guys are really scared, and they think that I'm going to get them home alive. I guess that's why I take point so much. Nobody orders me to, in fact we're supposed to rotate on point, but some of these guys are so bad at it that I figure they'll get killed or get the rest of us killed. Lt.'s calling me.

"So much for now.

"Tell Congo that it's a good thing he's not old enough to be here. Say hi to Bernice and give the girls a big hug. I miss you all a lot and think of you all the time. I sure look forward to the letters I get from the Hollow Horns to,

See you in the funny papers!

"LZ Spec 4 Frank W. Jealous of him.

"The next seven days were light duty except for occasional patrols in the vicinity of the landing zone. B Company enjoyed the meager comfort in the firebase, including warm showers and a steady supply of C-rations.

"On 22 December, Lieutenant Chellis called together the platoons of B Company. 'We're ordered on a reconnaissance in force patrols at the base of Baldy tomorrow at sunup. Sniffer patrols say activity has stepped up. So get some rest, we might be out for a while.'

"Because the platoon lieutenant was a 'short timer,' the pace of the patrol the next day was cautious. The first night the lieutenant sat reading map. He called for Frank to join him in the command post. What he did not need right now was to run into the enemy: 'Frank, tomorrow I want you back on point. If you see or hear anything unusual, I want to hear about it first. Right now I'm one superstitious and nervous bastard and I'm putting my faith in you to get my tired ass on the Freedom Bird.'

"I said, 'You got it, sir,' was all Frank had to say, and the lieutenant relaxed a bit.

"The next morning, after coffee and beef chips, under a gray sky, Frank moved slowly ahead, down through the triple canopy, studying the ground. He didn't have a map, but as usual sensed where the location of that night's camp should be. With total concentration he took it all in: the matted jungle floor, the low-lying branches, and the trees had become his textbook, and was an A student. The deer in these woods were tiny; the noise of the war in their mountains had made them rare and elusive, but they left tiny trails and in his heart Frank thanked them as he crept forward.

"At noon he sat near a buddy named Carl Schofer. Both were reading letters from home. Frank's letter from Clynda carried news about school and volleyball. It spoke of Christmas and his dad's church and Bernice being pregnant again. All of it made him smile. He read parts of it to Carl, who had come in country not long after Frank. The two shared almost everything.

"By 1300 he was out on point again. A sixth sense made him edgy, told him to stay on his toes. At 1400 he stopped, crouched, then raised his hand for the squad to halt. Chellis and his men froze. Lying on the dim jungle floor only a few feet ahead was an intact American C-ration can, looking for all the world like a discard. Only somehow Frank knew it wasn't. He had found the source of his intuitive nervousness.

"His eyes studied the jungle ahead and to the sides and then went back to the mysterious tin. After a pause that unraveled the nerves of the men behind him, he turned slowly around and grinned at the lieutenant and pointed at the can. Sure enough, a fine wire was stretched tightly between the can and the trunk of a sapling. He signaled Chellis to come forward. The lieutenant moved up quietly and crouched nervously behind his point man. Frank said in a whisper, 'Sir, I think I got something here you might want to see.' He pointed to the can.

"The officer stepped up beside him and returned a nervous whisper. 'What is it, Frank?' 'It's a can of chipped beef and gravy, sir! The

Vietcong must have good intelligence,' he said chuckling. 'Because they wanted one of us to pick it up! If it was ham and cheese, the booby trap wouldn't work.' Frank laughed. The he signaled the lieutenant and his men back. Stepping back quickly himself, closer to the squad, he pulled a pin from a grenade and tossed it toward the deceptive tin. A muffled blast and a spray of earth were followed by a loud explosion from the right side of the trail, toppling a small tree. Chellis signaled the squad to move quickly away from the noise, knowing every Vietcong in the area now knew exact where they were.

"Later, two klicks away, the RTO radioed in a situation report to base camp. Frank walked over the lieutenant, 'Wouldn't want you to miss that plane ride sir!' He said slapping the officer on the back. The other man shook his head and forced a nervous smile."[94]

---

[94] Mark St. Pierre of Rapid City, South Dakota provided an excerpt from his book Of Uncommon Birth: Dakota Sons in Vietnam, to the Black Hills Veterans Writing Group, Rapid City, South Dakota. He graciously allowed this to be included in the stories told here.

Dean Muehlberg, U.S. Army

REMF War Stories
17th CAG-Nha Trang, Vietnam (1969)

DEAN Muehlberg..."I was stationed in Fort (Ft.) Ord, California when I received the news that I was going to Vietnam. I was not quite 21 years old, just an un-traveled and green farm boy from North Dakota lonesome for home. So far (I had been in the service for 10 months), I had missed all of the levies for overseas and was beginning to feel quite confident I would get to miss out on the Southeast Asian tour. Maybe Uncle SAM and the great administrative jungle of the army had forgotten about me. I would have been content to miss Vietnam and even the tour to Germany that I wanted. I just wanted to serve my time and get out of the Army as soon as possible. It did not happen that way.

"I was a clerk-typist in a personnel company and was busy typing away when our NCOIC (Non Commissioned Officer in Charge) popped in and asked a couple of us into his office. Mystery? There were a couple of fellows from my section and few from other sections in the office. 'What's up?' I kept asking myself. Promotion? Demotion? Detail? I knew there was no special honor the Army would want to bestow on me or these others.

"The NCOIC called off a list of names and everyone was present. Then he spoke. 'By Christmas all of you men will be in Vietnam. You will be put in for thirty days of leave before you go. We will have orders for you in a few days.'

"Bang! I felt like I had been hit by a brick. My lungs contained no air. Most of us tried to manage a half-hearted smile or lousy joke, then ambled out of the room to look for a chair or some solitude to grapple with this new thing. A few were actually happy and that confused me too. 'Vietnam, Vietnam, Vietnam,' I kept saying to myself as if it would bring a more meaningful shape or color to the word. Up until this time that is all it was – a word that brought newsreel footage to mind or reminded you of someone that had been there. Now the word grew bigger like a fence or wall behind which you could not see because it was so high. 'Vietnam, Vietnam, Vietnam, I am going to Vietnam!' For the first few hours that is all my mind accomplished.

"I should have been ready for it, especially since I was in the Army! Maybe when I first went in I thought about it more, for like most civilians I linked the thought of the Army with war. People are prone to settling into a routine, however, and forgetting about events outside their sphere of action. This was my fault, putting the war and its possibilities out of my mind and then letting it surprise me. It made me realize how many others were doing this same thing, allowing the war to be just another news report, just another highway fatality or armed robbery.

"On the night of the news I called home to tell my family. I had to tell someone close, someone that would be shocked and afraid, someone that I might comfort so I could assume a different role, one in which I could become the strong figure. It is a natural defense, but does not always work. My family is relative stoic and laconic. My mother only managed an 'Is that right?' and though I knew she probably was surprised and somewhat afraid, I could not comfort someone who did not react according to her appointed part. Maybe she had been prepared as a mother with a son in the Army would have been at that time. I did not realize that until later, however, and at the time and after the conversation felt more alone and cut adrift with my future.

"I tried the same with my girlfriend with much the same reaction, though maybe not for the same reason. We were close but that closeness was jeopardized and the alienation of over two years in the army. She was off enjoying college life and could not be blamed.

"So I was still very much alone. Events beyond the date of my departure (22 December) were still a blank, but I had to put my remaining time in this country into perspective. I still had a couple of month's duty at Ft. Ord and a month of leave at home before I went. The bulk of my time was taken up within the romanticizing about my upcoming days at home, but within the confines of my E4 pay I tried to get off the post when I could to see the sights and to drink and party. My best friends on post had also been levied for overseas duty and would be leaving at about the same time. One had a Volkswagen and the three of us putted around California to see what we could before we left.

"On one balmy, westcoast evening we decided to 'celebrate' our new assignments. My friends were really celebrating as they had been picked for Germany. I was the butt of a good many of their 'bad luck' jokes and we did laugh about it a lot, they enjoyed it more than I. The evening was to be a long one.

"After a couple of beers we decided on a whim to drive to Santa

Cruz. We picked up some booze on the base to take with us. I do not know what was in Santa Cruz except a college and maybe we had the ridiculous notion we might meet some girls. That was a real joke as all soldiers were felt to be illiterate hicks by young, pretty college girls at that time, and to tell the truth we probably were. We were also warmongers in their eyes. Being a 'G.I.' during this era was much different than being one during the previous wars. We were scum and during those longhair days there was no disguise for us, we could not blend into the crowd.

"Predictably, nothing of note happened in Santa Cruz but we were well on the way to inebriation by the time we headed back. Mike, the driver and owner of the car we were in, was weaving back and forth on the interstate and was not dimming his lights (or so the highway patrol's report read). We were stopped and caught with open containers in the car. Mike was of legal drinking age but not Chuck or myself. We gave the patrolman a 'story' that we had all just been ordered to Vietnam (one-third the truth, I though ironically). This must have helped some. He could have hung us all, as well as reporting us to the military authorities, but he did not. What he really got us for I do not know but it cost me $70 and Mike $120 with no loss of license. Chuck was asleep in the back and got off unscathed. I could almost hear him holding his breath as he feigned sleep and the subsequent chuckle and relief at his good fortune.

"We continued on our way and went to Carmel Beach to ponder over the evening and our future and finish a couple of last beers. I was ready for the sack but the others weren't ready to give up the evening. On the way we chided Chuck for his 'cowardice,' his lack of interest in meeting the patrolman and his unbelievable luck.

"The beach was a light streak that divided the dark of the pulsing ocean from the dark of the trees and town. The moon was out enough to reflect on the millions of grains of sand and provide contrast for any objects that moved over their surface. There were no others but us and a few misshapen pieces of driftwood. It was peaceful, beautiful at this late, late hour with only the event, small crashes of minor waves reminding us that there was a gut-beat of life waiting for the morning light to legitimize.

"There wasn't much talk; the shock of the tickets and the onset of fatigue and too many beers turning all thoughts inwards. There was an occasional 'Yep' and a 'Well, what can ya say?' We sat leaning against an old driftwood log and I sifted sand through my fingers and stared off into the west not really seeing or focusing on anything. I wondered about that piece of land a couple of thousand miles beyond my eyes and was sad and alone.

"My probing fingers ran onto an obstruction a few inches under the surface of the sand. It relieved the lack of direction and enthusiasm of the moment. With growing interest I focused my attention on freeing the object, digging down and around it. For each handful, I pulled away a half a handful ran back into the depression. What did I have here? A watch maybe? A movie star's bracelet? A Wallet? Finally I got a grasp on an end and could extract it knowing already it was none of these. It was a small figurine of some sort. I lit a match to see what I had and immediately wished I had never felt it, found it. In my hand lay a toy soldier and in the flickering light provided by the match I could see clearly that it had no head. The green plastic torso stood gallantly on its little pedestal but the missing part explained how successful that posture had been.

"The match went out and I held the broken toy a few moments in my hand while my companions tried to laugh. Even they were struck by the unbelievable timing and chances of the find. I mumbled to myself and shook my head in the darkness while I reburied the fallen fighter. I had come down considerably on meeting the patrolman, but this really took me all the way. Omens and superstition were things of myths and legend, kid's stuff, weren't they? 'I don't mean nothing!' I told myself. But it did. I imagined he worst in my wait to get my year in Vietnam started and this did not help at all. The memory of that discovery would hang with me the whole year I was there. If it never came true for me it did forecast an outcome for a nation; but I wouldn't know that for years to come.

"We toured the land and the sea, taken in by the beauty and wonder of vast landscapes and the life and color in them. A friend had duty in the great Hunter-Liggett Military Reservation, several thousand acres of uninhabited mountains and tress. We visited him and he took us out along the trails and high in the hills to see the ocean huge and lingering blue and magnificent in the west. We skinny-dipped in the mountain pools. We spent a weekend camping on the beaches of the Pacific, fenced in between the awesome cliffs at that extremity of our continent and the pounding of the surf of the ocean. We felt the land and its greatness. It made me proud to be a part of it and sad that I was leaving it. This was too grand a land though to think it or the people that sprung from it could be doing something wrong. I had an obligation and I would fulfill it so that I might return.

"I tried to forget about Vietnam but the college of imagined circumstances kept creeping back into my resolve to put it out of my mind. I tried to look at it as an adventure and a challenge but the possibility of not returning always took the excitement out of it. I was too young to die and worse, to die a million miles from nowhere. There was that horrid fear of dying where no one would see you die, not necessarily that fear of dying for nothing. If you died there it was like it confirmed your unimportance, like it placed you irretrievably among the masses with never a chance to rise up as this country willed you, formed you to do. This was the greatest fear, where even your family could not see you, feel you die to give credence to your very existence. You had to go on though, put one foot in front of the next, and you succeeded. I told my girl we'd forget that I was going until just before I actually had to leave.

"An important prelude to going to Vietnam was RVN (Republic of Vietnam) training. This was three or four days of orientation on the Vietnamese people, their language and culture, ambush defense tactics, and proficiency with the M16 rifle, a small, light-weight, low-caliber, high velocity weapon developed for jungle fighting. The best thing about the training was that it got us out of the office for a few days into regular fatigue dress (like trading a suit for levis). For the most part we played war games, being designated to different mock units and trudging through rough terrain until being attacked by the enemy (other soldiers dressed up in Vietnamese clothing). In one exercise I was designated squad leader because I outranked many of the other guys. I led a reconnaissance squad along one ridge while a second squad infiltrated another ridge across a small valley. The second squad was ambushed by a few 'Viet Cong' in a machine gun nest (It all sounded pretty realistic as our weapons were filled with blank ammunition). I proceeded to lead my squad across the valley in a full-scale attack on the enemy position to assist the other squad. It was the wrong move. I got chewed out because of it. Apparently I was told to hold my position and protect that flank. My entire squad was massacred. So much for John Wayne. I was thankful it was only training. It was something I wouldn't forget. If their evaluation of my performance was correct, it made you see how lives could be lost quickly and unnecessarily through the incompetence and inexperience of one man. I had only followed my prior day's training. The previous day we had been loaded aboard trucks and driven through rough terrain when also ambushed by the enemy. In this instance we were told to dismount the trucks and attack directly into the fire of the enemy positions. The instructors explained that though we would lose a great many this way we had a better chance of at least surviving. In the end the two days of war games seemed awful short education for the business as important as life or death. Then again we were not front line troops and if they spent more time on preparing those poor guys I did not mind.

"We also spent a half-day firing the M16. This weapon looked more like a prop from Star Wars than a real rifle. It was black and short with a triangular grip that tapered off from the chamber up to the end of the barrel. The sight on the weapon also served as a handle, hand-sized and rose up like a grip on a suitcase. The trigger handgrip extended down from the plane of the rifle like a pistol. This weapon fired either semi-automatic (squeezing one round after another) or full automatic (like a machine gun). The rifle had very little 'kick' to it but it was amazingly difficult to hold it on target when on full automatic. The barrel would rise up and out of the target area. At the end of the day we were all judged proficient in the handling the M16.

"Perhaps the best thing happening during RVN training was winning a hundred dollars on a World Series pool. That year the Detroit Tigers won it in seven games. They had lost, I think, the first three games of the Series. I had a dollar in a pool that picked Detroit to win 4-1 in the seventh game. Needless to say, I had forgotten all about my chances of winning. Then while sitting in some bleachers listening to a black sergeant I could not understand trying to explain how to survive an ambush. I got the news. The trooper next to me pulled a transistor plug covered with waxy buildup from his ear and simply stated, 'Detroit just won 4-1!' I spent half of the winnings sending roses to my mother and girl – neither of whom had ever before gotten flowers. Both later related they cried and I was duly compensated.

"My last month at Fort Ord went quickly. I got my orders and flew home to frigid Sioux Falls, South Dakota where my girl was to meet me. My mind jumped with the excitement of anticipated romantic encounter as the plane bounced down on the frosty runway. My girl went to school in Brookings, 75 miles to the north, and had driven down to pick me up. We embraced and hurried to her car, she letting me drive while sitting next to me. I couldn't wait to get where we were going so that I could plant a big kiss on her face. The car was equipped with power steering and power brakes, features I was not familiar with, frivolous luxuries to my frugal upbringing. Talking excitedly on leaving the airport parking lot and not paying much attention to traffic, I saw a car out of the corner of my eye coming down the street where there hadn't been done before. I reacted accordingly, hitting the brakes hard. The power brakes took hold immediately. My head and shoulders shot forward, the motion stopping as my mouth slammed into the steering wheel. The blood began to flow evenly and my mouth swelled to clown-like proportions. We continued on, I holding a handkerchief to my face and issuing black oaths through my puffed face, my girl not completely succeeding in containing her amusement. So much for the brave, dashing figure returning home. It was funny, but for me only years later. It took nearly the entire leave to get my passion provoking lips back in shape.

It was one of the stormiest and snow-laden winters on record with snow nearly inundating our small farmstead. This and my puffed-out mouth are all I remember of that leave, except that I did not have much Christmas spirit knowing I would be many thousands of miles away on foreign soil, in foreign circumstances, and in the middle of a country at war. My family had Christmas early and they gave me a fancy cigarette lighter with my name on it. I thought it was sharp. Sometimes you get some little thing like that and it is the greatest gift in the world, a thousand dollars or a new car would have been good. I suppose it was kind of a link to this country I was leaving and an even more special link to those people from whom I had sprung. I cherished it and holding on to it was like holding onto a life or flow of life.

"It is difficult to say how I felt about the war at the time. I can relate how I think I felt but there was nothing sure or absolute. I do not care how much one felt that he had to go, that it was right, that it was the tradition of our fathers that it was to those poor subdued people; no matter what there was a cog in the works that kept you from feeling there was no question about it.

"It was a difficult time. There were peace demonstrations, draft dodgers, and conscientious objectors. There were thousands of people being killed on both sides or lines were not that easily discerned. And the mood of the country was not of full consent. Somehow that uniform was not what it used to be. Our fathers had not questioned authority but were brought up in an analytical age and we did question. While many citizens did not praise the uniform neither did many of the soldiers wearing it.

"Perhaps the worst thing was the sin of youthful optimism, of hope, the growing belief or feeling that maybe this was indeed the 'Age of Aquarius.' Maybe man really was coming to his senses, maybe man could really live in peace, maybe killing was not a part of man's nature. All of the wonderful youth of that age had a dream, a good dream, and it hurt, really hurt to go off to Vietnam, which meant an immediate rejection of that dream. It meant killing a bud that could quite possibly (it seemed at the time) blossom into something so beautiful. We needed that dream. It was a time for needing something like that. God was dead and so was everyday fulfillment and meaning. Putting a foot in Vietnam was killing it because you immediately put yourself into a position to kill it. If some son-of-a-bitch shoot at you enough times most people are damn well going to shoot back no matter what they believe. It was a rejection of your youth, your hope, and your times. It was a damming of yourself by yourself and by a lot of people back home who you needed to have believe in you. Even the ones who patted you on the back were beginning to pat a little lighter.

"So, Vacuum! A vacuum where what you believed meant nothing and where life meant nothing. And insult to injury added to injury with the seeming incompetence and ridiculous management of the military. To place oneself in this position seemed all but too much.

"The soldier went to Vietnam fighting shadows. Even the grunt who killed actual bodies was shooting at that shadow trying to corner it. When the smoke cleared he found the shadow had escaped only to harass him again later and all he really had was blood on his hands and a little more of his dream and of himself chipped off to join forces with the shadow.

"This was the situation or what it seemed at the time. I gave much thought to it and decided I had to go because I still believed in the American Dream. If that was not the reason, I decided I had to play the game. I was not quite idealistic enough or sure enough for that seemingly not so heroic end run north of the border. I did not want to preclude seeing my family and friends again. And I was not sure that those going north were going because of the ideals they should have been going for or because of what they were saying they were going for.

"As far as practical preparation goes, I was ready for Vietnam. I had all my specially developed tropical underclothes right down to the green army boxer shorts. I could never figure out that detail. I did not plan on seeking out the enemy in my shorts. I packed them faithfully in my duffel bag for the chance that should I have to attack than damned machine gun nest and all my clothes were blown off save my shorts they would not see me coming and I might survive!

"I took my malaria pills according to the guidelines two weeks in advance to insure that I would be protected by the time I reached Vietnam. It seemed kind of strange taking malaria pills in North Dakota when it was twenty degrees below zero and the snow was ten feet deep.

"I left North Dakota on the afternoon of December 20, 1968. My family accompanied by my girlfriend drove me to Fargo to await the plane. I had made most of my farewells when they announced that the plane would be two hours late. Ouch! Now I had to do it all over again and it was hell waiting two more hours on that nice secure ground that I probably would not see again. I hated standing there holding my poor girl's clammy hand. If she would have cried it would have helped some but she did not. It would have made it harder to leave but still have made me feel more missed.

"The plane finally came down and I made all the big hugs again and it was hard holding back the tears, but I did. I turned and walked to the ramp but stopped at the top to wave one more time and take one of those scanning, noble looks at the countryside. That was a guaranteed heartbreaker even if all I saw was airport and windblown snow banks.

"I found my place next to a window and looked out at those funny, unreal people that were my loved ones standing there so somber, now turning and walking back to their everyday lives in Dakota while I headed for the unknown. It was then I grabbed my lighter, held it tight, real tight. A single tear ran down my face until I tasted the salt and decided it was time to get ready for Vietnam. I wiped the tear away and smiled a hello to the lady seated next to me, then sat back to wonder what it was all about, what I was all about, and what it would have been like if it were 1943. There would have at least been a lot less doubt and a lot more certainty as to our goal.

"I had a long wait in the Minneapolis Airport where I had to wait to hook up for a flight to the west coast. I sent my girlfriend a card from there in which I said, 'When a person is leaving home, I don't think there is anything more lonely or desolate than a large airport. It is a cold, unfeeling place to spend hours waiting for a plane after being warm and happy for the days of my leave.'

"I got to Fort Lewis, Washington late that night, checked in and was sent to a barracks for the night. Transient barracks are usually the next thing to slum living. The building was cold and we had no sheets or blankets. There were only five to ten bunks set up on the floor. The rest were disassembled or broken, the mattresses being salvaged with GIs lying here and there shivering and trying to get as much warmth as possible from their rumpled dress greens.

"We were all up at 5:30 a.m. the next morning to eat and get issued Vietnam fatigues and boots. The fatigues were baggy affairs with all kinds of pockets, four on the shirt and two huge ones on the sides of the trousers. They proved great for carrying beer cans and other bulky items but were so numerous you could lose things in them for months at a time. The boots had thick rubber grips with the biggest part of the tops made out of canvas rather than leather for coolness. After the issue we went back to the barracks and prayed we would not get caught for a detail or KP. There is nothing like slopping greasy dishes after a sleepless night and being headed for Vietnam at the same time. It does not do anything for your morale.

"We formed up the next morning for our flight, a dark green huddle over over-sized, ill-fitting uniforms looking like an unmade bed. Faces filled with fatigue, worry, and doubt topped the shuffling mass. I wondered how many were infantry and had a lot more to worry about than myself and how many would not come back or would come back much different than they were now.

"We boarded a huge plane especially chartered for hauling G.I's to the romantic Orient. It was the same plane used on commercial flights and even carried attractive young stewardesses. As luck would have it I ended sitting up in the very front of the plane, directly across from that little fold down seat where the stewardesses sit when the plane takes off or lands or when they are not busy at their appointed tasks. This was good luck or bad luck depending on how you thought about it. I am a sucker for beautiful legs and a beautiful girl showing them off up to her derriere. At the time though, it just reminded me of what I was leaving behind. There is so much creativity, serenity, and comfort in a beautiful thigh as well as mystery and excitement. I did not feel I could afford that luxury right then. I looked at the ceiling and tried to sleep, faltering in my fortitude and wisdom once or twice.

"We neared the coast of Vietnam early on the morning of the 23rd of December. Just prior to landing, the pilot came on the air to let us know where we were and to give the weather and ground conditions. The guy had a real sense of humor, again depending on how you looked at it. The ground conditions consisted of "light to scattered automatic weapons fire" and a few other things I don't remember but designed to scare the crap out of you. So there we were preparing ourselves right off for the worst, probably everyone hoping like myself that he would not be a complete coward.

"It was a funny feeling descending the ramp to Vietnamese soil. The ground conditions reported were completely false but there were plenty of wary, wide-eyed soldiers that left the plane, moving out only because they followed the soldier in front of them. I remember saying to myself, 'Well, here is another silly thing you have gotten yourself into. Here is to a year, or however long I last.'

"It was still dark in Cam Ranh Bay and from the first appearances it looked like we had just made another stop at some airport completely unassociated with war and blood and death. After a few moments some flares popped off in the far out perimeter areas completely illuminating a hillside and wiggling down to their death like a flickering candle carried by a ghost hunter descending into a spooky and foreboding cellar. Then I knew it was no ordinary airport and I stared apprehensively into the dark outside of the secured areas.

"Tired, uneasy, and awestruck, we were loaded into buses and transported to sorting areas where we would be broken down into small groups heading for the same area.

"In transit military travel is like being suspended in time and space, watching a being with a form such as you imagine your own to resemble, proceeding forward in time and leaving you behind until such time as a destination is reached and orderly living pattern is again resumed. At least it was that way for me. Ordinary daily functions did not work when I traveled. I did not eat, sleep or go to the bathroom right.

"Standing around dazed and bleary-eyed, we waited for our assignments but were sent to transit barracks for a couple hours of sleep. We were roused from fitful, damp sleep and shown to the mess hall for breakfast, then sent back to our barracks to lounge around. During this time, we were told we go to the USO for "something special." See as how it was 23 December, we knew it had something to do with Christmas and were curious enough to investigate. The USO provided some cookies and a bag for everyone who ventured forth. The bag contained playing cards, a washrag and sundry other items that actually were quite dear to me that day.

"On the trip to the USO and back we saw assorted Vietnamese men and women wandering around the camp working at their seemingly slow but steady and effective pace either washing clothes, digging ditches, or some other chore they had managed to pressure from the rich U.S. soldiers and their government. It made me uneasy at first, much as it would make a country boy like myself uneasy to get stuck downtown in some big city bus terminal with all its assorted derelicts and weirdoes and unfamiliar patterns. I was not acclimated to all this and I felt new and was obviously green with my store-fresh Southeast Asia fatigues and boots. So even as I started and stared at the sing-song patterns and strange attire they wore, they returned the stares seemingly in never ending curiosity over the fresh boys that kept coming. I became inwardly dramatic thinking that these people right here might be VC sympathizers. As I threw out 'Chow' (hello, about all I could remember from orientation) and a smile with one I watched their apparent cunning with my other.

"All this time and for a month to come I still was standing in the wings watching myself function, reaching out now and then to grab a few impressions or make a few suggestions but mostly just letting the form carry on. I imagine this is the way it was for most, knowingly or unknowingly, only for the apprehension made the dreamlike state a little worse. None of us at the transit camp knew yet where we were going so the anxiety level was still quite high for all no matter what the MOS, for even clerks were known to go to besieged outposts.

"We gathered nervously for the assignments. Names were called and attached to obscure, unpronounceable names of no-doubt hideous places. 'Muehlberg, Nha Trang!' I had never heard of it! It scared the hell out of me! It was probably another Khe Sanh only never heard of any worse, some little hilltop fifty miles from any really support with only a strand of barbed wire between you and the murky jungle and the death that that lay there waiting for you.

"Death scared me. I did not want to die, yet I felt that getting stationed at the wrong place in the wrong circumstances meant certain death for me. In situation of violence or danger I have never reacted well, never reacted quickly. No killer instinct. I was not smart enough to back off in critical situations though. Pride and self-respect made me jump into things even with little chance of outlasting an opponent or topping the situation. And because of that infinitesimal instant of hesitation that was a part of me, I always jumped in at the worst moment. It was either too late to get the jump or too early to provide a defense with plans of re-attack. Or so I have always pictured myself. In Vietnam where the statistical chances of encountering danger multiplies, I did not think I had a chance.

"I remembered there were a few others that had been associated with the same place, and tried to find one of them with no luck. Finally, instructions were given for people going to different areas and I met up with a few others going to Nha Trang. None of them knew anything about Nha Trang either so we just speculated amongst ourselves what it could be. We did learn it was north of Cam Rahn Bay and along the coast and that made me feel some better, a chance for escape by the sea! The next morning we were trucked to an airfield and an awaiting C-130. There were several of them parked in three-sided metal reinforced revetments of rocket shelters without roofs. The C-130 was one of those fat fuselage planes used to carry cargo. In the butt of the plane was a tailgate that lowered to the ground like the lower jaw of a great whale and that allowed cargo to be brought aboard. The plane was big enough for jeeps and other equipment to be driven into it. It could land and take off in short runway situations and I believe had the unique feature of reversible props, allowing the plane to quickly decelerate on landing.

"Today the cargo was us men only. There were about twenty of us with our duffel bags. Every few feet on the floor of the plane was a cargo strap that could be adjusted and tightened down to secure the cargo. They instructed us to place our duffel bags under this strap and to sit on them after the straps were tightened. If we needed to hang onto something during the flight we could grab the straps.

"So we left for Nha Trang, four or five rows of frightened troops in store fresh fatigues, holding onto cargo straps as much to just hold onto something as to keep from falling off our perches. As the plane made its turn away from the airfield to Nha Trang a mile or two out over the jungles, I felt as if I were crawling into a dark cave with no idea if there was a way out of the other end. The plane creaked, groaned, and rattled all the way to Nha Trang. I will never forget that I thought we were being fired upon the entire way as the rattling sound so much like automatic weapons fire. I pictured the rounds streaking up from the dense growth on the ground below and contemplated the vulnerability of my butt. I surely did not want to get shot in the ass. I also looked ahead to the possibility of being shot down and crash in the jungle, estimating where the safest place in the plane would be to survive it. We did not have weapons on us and that did not comfort me at all. The only weapon I saw was a pistol hanging in its holster ahead of the rear of the pilot's compartment.

"All of the worrying was misplaced, we had not been fired on and we flew over relatively secure ground. The plane circled, landed and taxied to the Nha Trang terminal. I did not know it at the time but we had dropped into what could be a picturesque, tropical paradise outside of war and which was an actual resort area for wealthy Vietnamese and French colonials in better times.

"It was early afternoon and the two or three of us with orders for the 17th CAG (Combat Aviation Group) were picked up by someone with a 3/4 ton truck. We drove away from the terminal and through a U.S. Air Force base that looked like it could have been transplanted lock, stock, and swimming pool right from the good old USA, except that the perimeters were close enough so that what was outside them told you the truth. The route we took carried us towards a bay and out of the air base. We were on a road that paralleled the shore of the bay, a road we later knew well as just 'Beach Road.' It took us north. On the right a couple hundred yards of beach filled the space between the road and the Pacific. It was a beautiful view, one that made it difficult to believe that a few miles in the opposite direction was blood and death and suffering. On the left side of the road was an endless string of villas, half in disrepair and half holding their own, but all telling of past beauty, wealth and prestige. On the road we followed, we met or passed other military vehicles of every size and description and several military personnel on foot. Following into, around, over, under and through the hubbub of military activity were the omnipresent Vietnamese. These included the basket laden pineapple vendor ladies from the beach, the husband, wife and two kids on a Honda 50 weaving through traffic, prostitutes and the flypaper kids in packs of twenty surrounding walking soldiers and relieving the unwary of anything that wasn't nailed down. After a half mile of this we made a left turn that took us into the crowded, close traffic of the city of Nha Trang. The street was the main road from what was later to be my permanent residence to the beach. It was somewhat wider than most of Nha Tang's streets, yet compared to what I was used to, it was close. The gaps between objects caught in the street were filled with the smells and the immediacy of a sweaty, fishy, garlicky, too intimate life.

"The street ran for only about a quarter of a mile when it came to guard posts manned by both American and Vietnamese military police. The truck drove through the checkpoint without acknowledgement by either set of guard and proceeded to the compound that was to be my home for a year. I did not know this at the time. We bounced and bumped to a stop in front of an unpainted two story barracks about the size of a barn. We were told to dismount the truck with our things and, after our names were crossed checked with forwarded orders, to grab a bunk in the lower level open bay of the barracks.

"I went through a set of circumstances then that took my spirits up and down. At the approach to the barracks I saw in big letters 17th Combat Aviation Group on a sign on its front. I thought 'Well, this is it. It is not great but it does not look too bad.' I thought I had finally reached the end of my immediate traveling. As we got down from the truck I noticed the smaller letters on sign, Replacement Billets, and I got that sick feeling that there was another leg or two of the trip to go. I was later to learn that the 17th had several battalions and units located in the "boonies" which I very might have been sent to.

"As it was I grabbed a bunk and lay down to contemplate the

whole situation. In the back of it all was the fact that it was the afternoon of Christmas Eve. People have gone through much worse and I have nothing to complain about, but I was overwhelmed by it all. I was a farm boy from North Dakota. I had not been away from home much if you discounted my earlier army days in the states, and I am the type that travel tires out. Here was a totally new situation, the changes in climate from the frigid North Dakota plains of my month's leave to the hot, humid weather of Vietnam, the holiday season, the days of travel and sleepless nights of not knowing where you were going or when if you would come back, the mosaic of completely different sights, sounds and smells of a foreign culture. A person's body and mind work overtime in these situations putting out sentries in the senses to protect one against the unknown. Rest comes hard. It was not battle fatigue but it was fatigue of a type that must have been timeless, fatigue associated with anticipation and with, if not a great event, an even bigger than the person. It was a pre-pre battle exhaustion that millions of others in ages past must have experienced, above and away from the warmth of the schedule and the known.

"I lay on the bunk for an hour or two trying to put everything into perspective, feeling depressed with the thought of moving on yet again to more new situations. It was then that Bill came bouncing down the long aisle of the barracks, grabbed my bags and told me to follow him. I asked where I was going and he said only 'You want a home for Christmas Eve, don't you?' I did not have time to ask more or was too tired to care. I felt I might as well get the rest of the trip over and followed directly behind him. I gave the two or three other 'intransists' lying on their bunks a shrug and left.

"Bill Skyes was tall, dark and good looking. His skin was darker than an ordinary Anglo and with his high cheekbones he could have been a handsome Indian but his mustache belied a different heritage. The heritage was Spanish. Later, I would learn that he came from the very south of Arizona close to the Mexican border. His appearance was that of the aristocracy and his vocabulary and personality fit this idea. He was a charmer with the ladies I guessed. I always pictured Bill in other, earlier times as a Spanish cavalier or diplomat surrounded by the accouterments of class and wealth or as the don of a great ranch and magnificent adobe hacienda. Yet Bill was such a charmer I was never sure if what he told of himself was real or invented. In the end, and after getting to know him more, it did not seem to matter. I liked him and liked him more in the setting of my mind had created for his past.

I followed Bill and my bags out of the transient barracks and over the dusty, dry earth of the compound adjacent barracks. These barracks were two-stories, with an access to the upper levels gained by an open wooden stairway at either end of the structure. These stairways ran across the face of the building from the lower left corner of the bottom level up to a platform that was at the upper floor level. The platform was only as wide as the door and carried a railing. We ascended this stairway and entered the top level, taking a right at the first doorway. Bill threw my bags in a sagging bare bunk and told me we would go to the 'office' where I would work and then get me some things I would be needing.

"'The office where you will work!' He said it so quickly and I had been so much in a trance that I nearly missed it. Relief swelled up in me. No more travel. I could begin getting settled and into a new schedule. I wanted to ask if they had to fight much here in Nha Trang but did not for fear of sounding like an anxious fool. I wanted to ask a million other questions but did not for the same reason.

"I followed him like an obedient pup to a large Quonset a hundred feet from my barracks. Inside the Quonset were ten to fifteen desks arranged in little groups of one to four, each section heralded by its function, 'Personnel Records, Orders, Awards and Decorations, NCOIC, etc.' Bill guided me to a huddle of three desks to the right. The sign above it said Awards and Decorations. He showed me a desk, told me it would be mine and introduced me to Pete, the other fellow in A & D. Pete was a big fellow who talked like the fighters in the old movies or like Rocky in the new one. He gave me a hearty welcome and told me I would like it here and that I was lucky I was here. That sounded awfully good to me. Bill, Pete and I exchanged a few other generalities and then Bill and I moved on again. He told me he would introduce me to other fellows in the office later, but that there were not many others around this afternoon as everyone but one man per section was off since noon for Christmas. This sounded halfway civilized and my apprehensions began to subside a bit. The warmth of two new friends and protectors also helped a great deal. I had roots.

"We went to supply and procured bedding and a mosquito net and then to the arms' room for my weapon, surprisingly an M14. I had thought the heavier, bulkier M14 was obsolete. I found out that they were in use in the relatively safer support areas such as I was in. That was okay with me as I had more training with and was more familiar with the M14 anyway.

"We trudged back to the barracks with my new gear, locked my

M14 in the gun rack and dropped my bedding and net off in my room. Bill said we could get the bedding on and the net up later as a Christmas party was just beginning and he did not want to miss any of it.

"We proceeded to a square, white plaster building a block away that appeared to be part of a larger pattern of the same kind of buildings, maybe a main compound. On entering the main room we encountered a party in an early level of progress. There were eight to 10 people and munching on a fairly impressive tray of snacks. Bill introduced me to several whose names I immediately forgot. We stayed at the party for an hour or so exchanging more general information. The people I talked to felt Nha Trang was a pretty secure area and it did not seem they were just trying to make the new gut feel good. It was easy to feel good too, having found a new home and already partying in fairly decent surroundings. I had prepared myself for the worst, a malaria ridden, rat infested filthy corner of the damp jungle, but now I was sipping eggnog and eating cheese in a training room much as back in the states. It was almost too good to believe.

"The party never really got beyond the first stage so Bill suggested with we hook up with a couple of others from personnel and go to the bars. We walked across the compound and across a dirt road to a line of wood and metal shacks that extended for approximately a half a block. There were several openings along the front, shaded part of this row with attractive little Vietnamese women or girls standing half in and half out or just outside these entrances. As we approached the first opening two or three girls suddenly attacked my paying little attention or no attention to the other fellows. 'Hey G.I., U come in. Ha drink. Okay? You numah one G.I.!' Before I knew it I was sitting down on a small sofa next to the door with a pretty girl sitting on my lap and almost imperceptibly sliding back and forth. I was overwhelmed with all the attention and felt warm and good from drinks I had just had. My reactions were mixed however. As I sat there nearly overpowered by the vitality of that little creature, I could see the other guys smiling and nodding to each other. At another time I would probably have felt conspired against but was enjoying myself too much to care. My ego was doing just fine. As the center of attention a person rapidly goes through some chemical process that makes oneself bigger in one's own eyes. I loved it. At the same time I felt a slight discomfort with this rapidly progressing familiarity with an oriental. I was still a North Dakota farm boy, and though are not too many prejudicial veins in my body, these people were still totally new, totally alien. Without the few drinks I had had, this feeling would probably have been stronger.

"My reverie was cut short by Bill or some other pulling the vexed girl from my lap while she was alternately demanding, then begging coyly that I but her a drink. I felt mildly annoyed myself, feeling I was developing quite a nice relationship in such a short time. I had not realized that my only contribution was a fresh, unfaded set of fatigues that carried a reputation of easy money, naiveté,' and gullibility. As the girls shrieked and carried on their singsong repartee, obviously scolding Bill and the others, we moved on to the next entrance, went inside and sat up to a bar. There were several girls on or next to the few G.I.s in this bar but none approached us. From the ordering going on from our small group I could tell my friends were regulars. A cute little dark haired beauty of 16 or 17 peered at us from behind the bar. She could barely reach the top with her elbows and the winning smile she gave was almost all you noticed above the bar. She gave me a glance and then Bill a knowing look saying, "New G.I., huh?" It began to dawn on me then. I stuck out like a sunflower in a potato patch.

"We had several drinks there, my new friends paying for them all with Piastres, the Vietnamese currency. All my money was in MPC (Military Provisional Currency), the funny money the American soldier was paid in to prevent loss of greenback. I was told this was the personnel bar and for the most part the bar girls left the personnel people alone unless their company was sought after. The little girl behind the bar was straight and a good friend along with two others that ran the bar.

"I learned a little more about my new unit, the 17th CAG. The company I was in was a Headquarters Company, which meant we were on the very top of a very large military organization. The 17th CAG had seven or eight helicopters and air battalions under it. These units carried troops into combat zones and out and provided support for ground actions. Our company supported the commanding officer of this group, a full colonel, coordinated troop replacements and movements for the group, and provided other administrative services such as write-ups for medals and decorations.

"I learned that I was fortunate to get picked off for duty in Nha Trang and how that had happened. My personnel file had been scanned by NCOIC. The Awards Section needed a clerk-typist and my military aptitude score was higher than average. This was a major factor in my favor. The personnel department was close to an elite sector with new personnel being picked either by educational background or aptitude score. My score was good enough to get me into a group of well read, intelligent, and very interesting people from all over the states.

"Talk turned to the Christmas Eve bonanza at the NCO Club. A 'round-eye' (Caucasian) stripper was going to appear there in a couple of hours. It was rumored that she went all the way. I was not thrilled by the fact that she was Caucasian but I was knocked over by the fact that she might go 'all the way.' I had never seen anything like that and it was all I could think about from there on out. The other guys seemed just as excited about the fact that she was a Caucasian. I did not learn until months later what a treat this was. Gazing on the features of a pretty 'round-eye' was a rarity in Vietnam and caused as much commotion as a rocket attack. The only difference was that the alert siren was not blown.

"I drank a lot that afternoon and ate only a small egg sandwich and some kind of chop suey that they sold at the bar. When we left to catch the stripper I found it hard to walk. We had been sitting in the dark, relatively cool bar for three or more hours. When I hit the hot, bright receding sun around 7 p.m. my head reeled and I had to fight throwing up. I fought hard. I did not want to miss seeing everything on a real live girl.

"We staggered to the club and pushed our way into an overcrowded, smoke-filled hall, into a stiflingly hot mass of bodies. We never got further in than a few feet from the front door, a good 25 feet from center stage. It was announced that the show would not start for another half hour. We managed to procure drinks and stood drunkenly sipping it for another quarter of an hour. Suddenly I could stand no longer. I made it through the band's first number, 'My Girl,' a song that has been indelibly dated in my mind from that time. I begged leave, embarrassed and disappointed that I had to go. My new friends voiced concern at my condition and my ability to find the barracks. I assured them I could make it and staggered out, away from the closeness, the heat and the noise of the club back to the barracks that was now my home.

"The bunk wasn't made. I remember trying to get up that spark of resolve needed to make the bed and set up mosquito net apparatus. I managed only to set up a folded up folding chair on one end of the stained mattress and to lean it against a wall at the end of the bunk. Over this I draped the net, tucking the other end under the mattress. I crawled into this little enclosed world and lay down still fighting the nausea and feeling strange and so alone again without my new friends. I pined for the missed stripper now, felt a million miles from nowhere, then fell into a drunken stupor, not seeing the abundance of inch round holes in my mosquito net that would not have kept the sparrows out.

"I woke up the next morning with a head splitting, throbbing hangover and felt dirtier and sweat grungier than I ever had before in my life. In addition I was covered with hundreds of mosquito bites. My skin was puffed and hardened and itched all over. There were more mosquitoes inside my net than in all of the rest of Nha Trang. It took me minutes to realize where I was." [95]

---

[95] Dean Muehlberg provided an exert of his book, REMF "War Stories": 17th CAG-Nha Trang, Vietnam-1968, to the Black Hills Veterans Writing Group in Rapid City, South Dakota. He helped found this organization so that Veterans would have a place to tell their stories and information on how to do so. As a friend and fellow author, Dean graciously allowed his story of life in South Vietnam, a different look than the images on daily evening news of the death and destruction during the Vietnam War to be included here. Dean now lives in Median, Idaho after moving from Rapid City.

William L. Walker, U.S. Army

Sketch of My Daily Life in Vietnam

WILLIAM L. Walker, U.S. Army Sergeant Major, Ret., Belle Fourche, South Dakota..."My Battalion Headquarters was in Da Nang, Republic of South Vietnam, on the perimeter of the Air Force base. The actual base, hangars, runways, etc., had its own fence. Surrounding it was a cluster of smaller compounds, including mine. There was a fence around that too, plus each compound had its own fence. One side of ours was the outer perimeter. The guard towers were manned by two guards with M-60 machine guns. The inner fence towers were manned by single guards with M-16s. The actual city was a few miles away and off limits, unless you were on official business.

"We had a steam and cream, but it was usually closed because the girls couldn't pass the health inspection. Besides, it was so far away we couldn't get there easily. After I became a Section Chief, I had a jeep and occasionally had to go to other places, so I got to cheat. The USO was also too far away, but using my jeep, I made it there twice, making a side trip while on official business. I got a hamburger both times. It was like a special treat.

"There were places we could go to get girls, but it didn't seem worth the effort. They had diseases there where the germs were bigger than I was. At night, our compound was closed and you needed a pass to get off base. Twice a week, the Air Force had movies at their theater, about a mile from our compound, but still within the base perimeter. We were allowed to go there. I made it there, three or four times. It was a real treat. They had a popcorn machine, a soda fountain that dispenses orange soda and soft serve ice cream machine. Best of all, it was air-conditioned. For a couple of hours, you could feel like a human. Other than that, we had our own Enlisted Mess Club, and the 'skeeter flick,' an outdoor movie theater. I slept with my rifle next to me and didn't leave home without it.

"We had two company parties at China Beach during the year that I was there. I managed to check out a surfboard once, so I can honestly say that I surfed the South China Sea. I went to Cam Rahn Bay a couple of times. We mutually supported a unit there. I got to goof off at the Air Force beach club while thee. Other than that, it was buck up, and go to work.

"I thought I had it very easy compared to many of my friends. As for being a Rear Echelon (MF), I always thought I was one. Our unit statement of purpose was to avoid contact. Most of the time we did. I was in DaNang about half of the time, the rest I was somewhere in I Corps. Got home without a scratch. Went to sick call twice, both for ear infections. Once I wound up in the hospital for a few days. Some kind of stomach bug. I lived through my share of rocket attacks and have been shot at many times, shot back too, but I am certainly no hero and never pretended to be. I came home with a Good Conduct Medal and other medals for showing up in Vietnam.

"Busted a guy once for being under the influence of Marijuana. He was on guard duty and I was Sergeant of the Guard. Found him passed out in a bunker. I saw very little drug use. Did do some serious drinking at our EM club but never touched dope. Looking back, I wonder how smart it was to get plastered in a combat zone. I had been so drunk; I doubt I could have reacted in an emergency. Only got drunk like that a couple times and always in DaNang at our compound. Fortunately, nothing ever came of it.

"One of my best memories was Sunday mornings. I often rode shotgun with the mail clerk. Regulations required an armed E-5 to leave the compound with a vehicle. Sundays, he needed to go off base. The mail clerk was an E-4. We almost always stopped for breakfast at Air America's compound. They had a snack bar where you could get breakfast sandwiches. I still like salami and fried eggs on toast." [96]

---

[96] William L. Walker, U.S. Army Sergeant Major, Ret., Belle Fourche, South Dakota. He served in Vietnam from April 1969 to March 1972. His story first told in the Black Hills Veterans Writing Group, Rapid City, South Dakota. He graciously allowed this to be included in the stories told here. As an author himself, he has a novel, To Ride a Hurricane, as well as numerous short stories, some dealing with the war in Vietnam.

Donald R. Smith

World War II, Korean War and Vietnam War

Airman's Career Covers 32 Years

DONALD R. Smith, Lt. Col., USAF (Ret.), Black Hawk, South Dakota..."I was born in Milwaukee, Wisconsin in 1922, growing up in rural Wisconsin Dells. I joined (enlisted) in the U.S. Army Air Corps Aviation Cadet Program on September 10, 1942. I began flying training at Chishay Army Air Field, flying the Fairchild PT-19, a two-seat, open cockpit, low-wing monoplane trainer. I then went to Enid, Oklahoma, flying the Boeing/Stearman PT-13 Model 75. This was a two-seat, open cockpit, biplane trainer. I went to Altus, Oklahoma for advanced training in the UC-78. At Sioux City Army Air Field I flew the Boeing B-17 Flying Fortress. I was sent to Salt Lake City Army Air Base to be assigned to a B-17 crew. We went to Sioux City Army Air Field for additional B-17 crew training. I was commissioned a Second Lieutenant on January 7, 1944. I was now officially a B-17 co-pilot.

"We took off for England, but due to bad weather, after we landed in Iceland on June 7, 1944, we were grounded for three days. We reached England on 10 June. We were a replacement crew, assigned to Eight Air Force, 303rd Bombardment Group, 427th Bombardment Squadron. Our crew was not kept together used a replacements where needed. We had arrived after the June 6, 1944 D-Day landing and all the bombing operations prior to the invasion operations. I want to speed up at this point.

"One of the Group's B-17s, aircraft number 41-24577, named 'Hells Angels' was the first heavy bomber (not crew) to complete 25 missions. The Memphis Belle's crew was the first intact crew to complete 25 missions, returning home to the United States. In 1948, two members of the group, taking the name of the aircraft and group formed the Hells Angels motorcycle club/gang.

"We were assigned to Molesworth, England Royal Air Force Base. It had wood barracks, with the control tower along the edge of the runway. It took me eight months for me to record 34 missions as a B-17 co-pilot, on combat missions bombing targets in Germany and

Czechoslovakia. I guess I was fortunate, I arrived at the time of long-range fighter escorts (especially the North American P-51 Mustang), lower numbers of German fighters and less qualified German Air Force fighter pilots. Because of this, the 303rd Bomb Group flew the most bombing missions of any bomb group in the European Theater of Operations (364 missions).

"On one flight in November 1944, there were nine ships in tight formation. We were on the right of the leader. I had a close friend, a navigator in the nose of the lead B-17 inside the plexiglass nose took a direct AAA blast, tearing away the nose section. My friend and two others were blown out of the nose of the aircraft just before it fell out of formation, spiraling to the ground. The remaining eight B-17s in the formation were trying to get out of the way of each other. I grabbed the controls and yelled at the pilot, I am going to get us out of the way.

"On another mission, our flight engineer and top forward turret gunner were wounded. The forward gunner's oxygen hose was shot away and he passed out. The pilot told me to get him down. I got the spare or walk-around oxygen bottle, hooked this on his mask. The radio operator helped me get him down. Then I gave him a shot or morphine to ease his pain. As we approached Molesworth, one of the crew fired a flare to indicate a wounded man needed medical attention upon landing.

"Our aircraft sustained damage on about 70 percent of the missions. I certainly didn't enjoy being shot at. That's one of the things that really scared me. But they didn't send you somewhere for a joy ride, there was a plan. I was never wounded, fortunate. I did have my rudder pedal shot off by a piece of 88mm flak shrapnel. Another piece of 88mm flak shrapnel hit the bottom of my armor plate underneath my seat. In heavy flak bursts the pilot and myself pulled our legs up on to the seat, creating a ball to protect ourselves. We were just trying to survive, scared to death. We wore flak helmets and vests to protect us. One occasion a piece of 88mm flak shrapnel hit my co-pilot's window, partially penetrating the plexiglass, later vibrating loose, falling to the ground somewhere.

"It was remarkable the mechanics could patch the damaged B-17s back together for the next mission, sometime the next day. Later, I would be in Air Force Maintenance. I remember only one Bf-109 fighter attack. It dove from high-altitude, speeding through the bomber formation and the squadron, directly at us, but as he fired we were no hit. AAA fire was always rough. When I came home from Europe, I wanted to wipe all that out of my mind. As a co-pilot, flying the B-17 required attention all the time. The aircraft was very reliable. However, we received less battle damage than those who flew with the Eight Air Force prior to the June 6, 1944 D-Day invasion. The Eighth Air Force flew during daylight to draw up German fighters, shoot them down, thereby securing the air space over the Normandy invasion allow the amphibious forces and airborne units to land in France. It still was not a cake walk. It is scary when you lose two engines, having to worry about airborne prowling German fighters, hiding in the clouds, waiting to attack stragglers. We did lose two engines, one on each side, but since we had dropped our bomb load, carrying a reduced fuel load, able to land at Molesworth.

"Since I was not assigned to a specific or permanent crew, I flew in many different B-17s and with many crews. Between missions I rarely left Molesworth. I didn't drink or smoke. I did go to the officer's club to eat, drink a Coke, play cards, eat Red Cross donuts and talk with the Red Cross ladies, and write letters home. After completing 34 missions, I returned to the United States, temporarily assigned to Atlantic City, Florida. I was in the States when the war in Europe ended. After combat in Europe, I transferred to transport aircraft. First, I was assigned to fly factory fresh Consolidated B-24 Liberators from the giant Ford Willow Run factory to the Arizona desert for storage. They were no longer needed in Europe or the Pacific.

"I was assigned to Presque Isle to fly four-engine C-54s. I flew as a co-pilot from Maine to Africa. With the surrender of Japan, our crew flew to Kadena Air Base, Okinawa to move supplies and personnel to Japan to support the U.S. Occupation Forces. After this mission ended, flew supplies and materials from eastern India into China. After returning to the United States, assigned to Fairfield Suisan AFB, later renamed Travis AFB, California. Due to reduction of wartime U.S. military force levels in 1946, released from active service, receiving a reserve commission as a Captain with the Wisconsin Air Force Reserve.

"In 1952, assigned to Moses Lake AFB, Washington to fly four-engine C-124 Globemasters. After the base closed, moved to Donaldson AFB, South Carolina as an Instructor Pilot and flight test aircraft pilot. I had additional duty as squadron maintenance officer. I flew 6,600 hours in the C-124, participating in the Cuba, Suez and Congo Crises, as well as 'Operation GYROSCOPE' and 'Operation DEEP FREEZE,' many landings north of the Arctic Circle during the building on the Distance Early Warning (DEW) Line. In 1957, I applied for a received a regular commission as an Air Force Captain. I had three months Temporary Duty to Rheine-Main AB, Germany as squadron maintenance officer, also flying regular missions throughout Europe and the Middle East. I was then assigned to the 53rd Weather Reconnaissance Squadron, known as the 'Hurricane Hunters.' I also became the Staff Maintenance Officer, flying missions into hurricanes so that weather scientists and forecasters could gather information in order to better predict when and where a hurricane might reach the United States coast line areas. In 1968, at the end of a three year tour, I was assigned Director of Aircraft Maintenance, Engineering Headquarters, Scott AFB, Illinois.

"In 1970, assigned to the 14th Field Maintenance Wing, Special Operations, Phan Rang Air Base, South Vietnam, with additional duties as Wing Chief of Maintenance. In 1971, returned to Dover AFB, Delaware, 436th Military Aircraft Wing, Military Airlift Command as Control Staff Officer until 1974. At this time, retired from active military service with 9,000 hours as a Command Pilot, 32 years of professional service with the Air Force, rank Lieutenant Colonel." [97]

---

[97] Donald R. Smith, Lt. Col., USAF (Ret.), Black Hawk, South Dakota. Pilot during World War II, Korea War and Vietnam War. Interview, author, July 22, 2012. According to the United States Census Bureau, there were 23.2 million veterans living in the United States in 2008. Out of that number, 92,000 consecutively served in World War II, Korea and Vietnam.

South Dakota National Guard

Rapid City Flood of June 1972

ON June 9-10, 1972, extremely heavy rains over the eastern Black Hills of South Dakota produced record flooding on Rapid Creek and other streams in the area. Nearly 15-inches rain fell in approximately six hours near Nemo, and more then 10-inches of rain fell over a watershed area of 60 square miles. According to the Red Cross in Rapid City, the resulting flooding left 238 people dead and 3,057 injured. In addition to the human suffering, total damage exceeded 160 million dollars, which included 1,335 home and 5,000 automobiles destroyed. The South Dakota National Guard was pressed into service to save those stranded by the water and debris, provided shelter, medical care and heavy equipment to clear debris. The devastation was compared to the Allied bombing of Berlin during World War II. [98]

---

[98] Lt. Col. George A. Larson, USAF (Ret.), "South Dakota National Guard, Rapid City Flood-June 1972." Visit to Camp Rapid, The South Dakota National Guard's open house to celebrate the National Guard's 150 years of service," display set up in the Headquarters Lobby, "2012: Countdown to Withdrawal," June 9, 2012.

Linebacker II

The End of the Vietnam War and America's 10,000 Day Involvement in Southeast Asia

ELLSWORTH Air Force Base B-52 Stratofortress bomber crews and support personnel were heavily involved in the Vietnam War. These personnel served and fought in the air war over South and North Vietnam. They helped end the 10,000 day war in Southeast Asia, assisting in forcing North Vietnam to release long held U.S. POWs held in brutal captivity in North Vietnamese prisons. With the passage of decades, the events of Linebacker II have not lost their importance. The eleven day air operation proved the capabilities of the B-52 Stratofortress fleet to project conventional bombing power over long distances, in all types of weather, against a highly sophisticated enemy air defense system. The losses in aircrews and aircraft were sobering and SAC personnel exhibited exceptional fortitude in completing their combat missions against the world's heaviest concentration of Soviet supplied air defense equipment (fighters, surface-to-air missiles and anti-aircraft artillery).

SAC B-52s flew their first conventional bombing mission in Southeast Asia (SEA) in support of U.S. Army ground operations on June 18, 1965. With its first bombing mission in SEA, SAC B-52s began the transition from a total nuclear to conventional bomber. SAC B-52s were able to complete this and subsequent mission changes in stride, adapting to new strategic bombing missions, which went far beyond those imagined by Boeing Aircraft Company engineers and designers in the 1950s. The B-52F carried either an internal bomb load of (27) MK-82 500 pound or (27) MK-117 750 pound bombs. Later, it was modified to carry an additional six MK-117s on each under wing weapons pylon. By the spring of 1966, B-52Ds replaced B-52Fs, supplemented by B-52Gs. Due to political considerations from the White House, SAC was denied permission to bomb targets inside the Hanoi/Haiphong area.

By October 1972, the Vietnam Peace Talks in Paris, France, resumed but little was accomplished. Negotiations were terminated on December 13, 1972. Henry Kissinger, National Security Advisor to President Richard Nixon, had been unable to convince North Vietnam's negotiator Le Duc Tho to agree to cessation of hostilities and release American POWs held in North Vietnam. President Nixon was frustrated with North Vietnam's blocking negotiations and ordered unrestricted conventional strategic bombing of restricted military targets around Hanoi and Haiphong to force that country back to Paris, sign a peace treaty, ending the Vietnam War and bring U.S. POWs home, ending the unpopular war to the American electorate. The bombing operation was code named "Linebacker II."

USAF and USN planners created a comprehensive list of 59 targets: railroad yards, radio communications facilities, power generating facilities, SA-2 sites, SAM support storage facilities, airfields and high-priority strategic military targets. The U.S. assembled a force of a large variety of aircraft for the eleven-day air war of Linebacker II. Andersen AFB, Guam was packed with (53) B-52Ds and (99) B-52Gs. The B-52D had gone through the "Big Belly" configuration which modified its bomb bay to hold (84) MK-82 500 pound or (42) MK-117 750 pound bombs, as well as bombs on the two external wing pylons, (12) MK-117s on each pylon. This gave each B-52D the capacity to drop 60,000 pounds of bombs on a single combat sortie. The B-52D also underwent an extensive electronic countermeasures (ECM) equipment upgrade to counter increasing North Vietnamese AAA and SA-2 threats as the Soviet Union continued to ship large quantities of military equipment.

The B-52G had a shorter tail with the tail gunner's position moved inside the main crew compartment. B-52Gs had begun to be upgraded to carry ECM equipment as on the B-52D, but only 50 percent of the fleet had been upgraded by the start of Linebacker II operations against targets in North Vietnam. A short-term, temporary fix or upgrade was made to unmodified B-52Gs at Andersen to give them enhanced ECM capabilities against North Vietnamese air defenses. This modification involved the installation of either one AN/ALE-25 forward-firing chaff dispenser rocket pod or one AN/ALQ-119 countermeasures pod mounted under a pylon between the engine pods.

Another (54) B-52Ds were based at U-Tapao Royal Air Force Base, Thailand. In April 1967, diplomatic and military negotiations with the Royal Thai government succeeded. Permission/authorization granted to the USAF to base and operate B-52s at U-Tapao Air Base. U-Tapao Air Base was only two to five hours round trip flying time from North Vietnamese targets, rather than the 12 hour round trip from Andersen AFB. The use of U-Tapao Air Base permitted a larger total strike force since Andersen only had a limited number of aircraft parking spaces, for up to 152 Stratofortresses and support aircraft. U-Tapao Air Base permitted the spreading out of bomber parking spaces, facilities, maintenance which increased sortie rates. It also provided an emergency landing runway if a battle damaged B-52 could not make it back to Andersen AFB.

The USAF and USN would be fully committed to providing a wide variety of support aircraft to support B-52Ds and B-52Gs in penetrating and exiting North Vietnamese air space. Air Force General Dynamics F-111As was tasked to attack North Vietnamese airfields and SAM suppression. Ten F-111As were assigned to support each B-52 attack wave to assist to the bombers in getting through enemy defenses. Ten McDonnell-Douglas F-4 Phantom fighters protected each B-52 cell. Air cover coordination was extensive. B-52Ds and B-52Gs flew at altitudes of 31,000 to 40,000 feet, with F-4s flying lower at 25,000 feet, five miles in trail and to one side of the bombers, positioned to keep any North Vietnamese Air Force fighters able to get airborne from attacking from the rear of the bomber stream. Escorting F-4s flew racetrack formations over each B-52 cell. Another ten F-4s flew as MiG cap suppression cover, roaming near the bombers and to one side to counter any North Vietnamese Air Force fighters approaching the bomber stream from the North. The USAF and USN committed 260 F-4s to protect the bombers.

A combination of Republic F-105Gs and F-4C Wild Weasels, eight per bomber wave, were assigned to take out active North Vietnamese radars supporting SA-2 and AAA sites. Wild Weasel crews fired antiradiation missiles at active radars, which homed on the radiation signals, tracking back to the source of emissions, destroying the radar site. If the radar was supporting an SA-2 site, destruction of the radar site would cut the ground guidance link to the launched SA-2. If weather conditions did not permit a sold missile lock onto the radar emission, cluster bombs were used on the radars and associated SA-2 and protecting AAA sites. Because the USAF's fleet of 23 F-105Gs was limited, the aircraft was supported by six F-4Cs. These Wild Weasels were assigned to protect bomber waves one and two.

The USN committed eight Grumman A-6A Intruders from aircraft carriers to protect bomber wave number three. The A-6A was primarily a carrier-based, ground-attack fighter, able to attack enemy radars, SAM and AAA sites, bridges, power plants and hardened facilities with pinpoint accuracy. A Lockheed C-130 Hercules was modified into an airborne command, control and communications (C3) aircraft, providing strike directions to the bomber support aircraft. The C-130 carried airborne controllers, directing multiple aircraft over a wide area. It was assisted by more the more distant orbiting Lockheed EC-121 Warning Star airborne radar aircraft, which provided detection and warning of approaching NVAF MiGs. It was fitted with a top and bottom mounted fuselage radar, providing lookdown surveillance capabilities covering the bomber stream while it was inside North Vietnamese airspace. Due to its vulnerability of size and slow speed because of its piston engines, the EC-121 had to operate far outside North Vietnamese airspace. C-130s were an important link in providing airborne assistance to downed U.S. airmen by directing USAF HH-53 Jolly Green helicopters to pick up these downed crewmembers, usually inside enemy controlled areas. Airborne rescue operations were shielded by USAF Douglas A-1 Skyraiders and other available aircraft controlled/directed from the orbiting C-130. Additional support aircraft were committed to assist or defend the bombers. One hundred ninety four Boeing KC-135 Stratotankers provided aerial refueling. The tankers were essential in refueling B-52s from Andersen. Badly damaged aircraft made calls for emergency refueling to safely exit North Vietnamese airspace to make it the nearest U.S. air base.

Russia supplied air defense equipment and systems delivered to North Vietnam included SA-2 missiles, launchers and radars, AAA and fighters. The substantial North Vietnamese air defense network posed a significant threat to the bombers, requiring countermeasures. Eight F-4s carried chaff dispensers to drop aluminum strip bundles to create false radar signals, masking the location of U.S. aircraft, a dense corridor through which the bombers penetrated to their assigned targets. By the end of Linebacker II, over 25 tons of chaff was dropped, enhancing onboard B-52 ECM capabilities.

Douglas EB-66s were used as electronic jammers. The aircraft was designed to transmit an electronic signal on the same frequencies as the SA-2 radars; thereby degrading the downlinks so SA-2 ground radars had difficulty locking onto airborne targets and guide missiles to the bombers. Active jamming took place approximately eight to ten minutes prior to B-52s time-over-target. With only 17 EB-66s, they were tasked to support bomber waves one and two. USN EA-3s supported bomber wave number three. The assumption was that SA-2s could be defeated by jamming, which proved to be inadequate alone since SAM radars were able to burn through ECM jamming to counter B-52 penetration tactics.

Vought A-7 Corsair IIs and F-4 fighter-bombers attacked designated targets in support of Linebacker II during daylight with first generation laser guided munitions to destroy bridges. Seventy-two A-7s dropped bridge spans, blocking rail and road transport of supplies out of threatened supply and warehouse depots under attack.

The critical task of bomb damage assessment was conducted by 18 RF-4Cs, providing low-level and detailed photographs to determine if a target had been destroyed sufficiently to move onto other targets on the Linebacker II strategic targets list. These RF-4C missions started on day two, continuing through day nine. RF-4C aircrews flew 81 photographic sorties by the end of Linebacker II.

This complement of support aircraft was required to counter Soviet supplied military equipment in North Vietnam. North Vietnam had 145 MiGs (including the supersonic delta-wing MiG-21 Fishbed), 26 SA-2 sites (21 which protected Hanoi and Haiphong), large numbers of light, medium and heavy AAA with supporting radar sites, overlapping early warning radar sites, repetitive C3 facilities and ground observers.

The mission plan for U-Tapao based B-52Ds launched after Andersen B-52Ds and B-52Gs. During the eleven-day air war, 729 B-52 combat sorties were flown. Linebacker II operations and subsequent American newspaper headlines concentrated on the B-52s and not the huge fleet of support aircraft. B-52 strike missions could not have been flown without direct support during daylight: 126 tactical air strikes to suppress SA-2 sites, 273 fighter combat sorties, 89 fighter chaff dispenser missions, and 46 various ground attack strikes. Night support missions consisted of 170 SA-2 suppression strikes, 390 fighter combat sorties and 209 chaff dispenser missions to protect the bombers. The USN contributed 505 aircraft from five aircraft carriers for a variety of missions: aerial mining, attacking SA-2 and AAA sites, bombing shipyards and docks in Haiphong, bombing railroad and truck stations. For the first time during the war in Southeast Asia, North Vietnam suffered the full force of American air power during the unrestricted air campaign against Hanoi and Haiphong.

Day one of Linebacker II started on December 18, 1972. Eighty-seven B-52Ds from Andersen and forty-two from U-Tapao launched and positioned into three attack waves. U-Tapao B-52Ds were each armed with 108 MK-117 bombs. Andersen B-52Ds were armed with 66 MK-117s with the B-52Gs each carrying 27 MK-117s. Their targets consisted of Hoa Lac Airfield, Kep Airfield, Phuc Yen Airfield, Kinh No Vehicle Repair Facility, Yen Vien Railroad Yard, Hanoi Repair Facility and Hanoi Radio Station. One hundred twenty-seven B-52s released bombs on target with B-52Gs of Agua 02 Cell and Red 03 Cell unable to release their bombs. Wave one consisted of 48 B-52s, arriving over their targets at 7:45 p.m. At bomb release time, one B-52D tail gunner in Brown 03 Cell shot down a NVAF MiG-21, which approached close to the rear of the bomber stream. At 9:03 p.m., a B-52D from Andersen, flying at 38,000 feet near Kinh No Vehicle Repair Facility came under attack by an SA-2 from SAM Site VN 133. The B-52D was hit, but able to exit North Vietnamese air space, making an emergency landing at U-Tapao Air Base. At 9:14 p.m., an Andersen B-52G at 34,000 feet near Yen Vien Railroad Yard was hit by two SA-2s fired from SAM Site VN 119. The B-52G crashed, with only three of the crew successfully ejecting from the badly damaged bomber. They were captured once on the ground by North Vietnamese troops.

Wave two consisted of 30 B-52s, assigned to attack the Yen Vien Railroad Yard and Kinh No Vehicle Repair facility. An Andersen B-52G was hit by an SA-2 in the left wing. It remained airborne, able to exit North Vietnamese air space. The aircraft was badly damaged with the crew bailing out, picked up and flown by helicopter to U-Tapao Air Base, then flown back to Andersen. Wave three consisted of 41 B-52s, assigned to attack the Hanoi Radio Tower. One B-52D was hit by an SA-2 fired from SAM Site VN 549. The bomber crashed, with four of the crew ejecting, captured by North Vietnamese troops. B-52D, aircraft number 56-583, at 34,000 feet was hit by an SA-2 over the Hanoi Railroad Repair Yard, exiting North Vietnamese air space, making an emergency landing at U-Tapao Air Base. The North Vietnamese fired approximately 200 SA-2 at B-52s during day one. The losses to the bombers and their aircrews was sobering to SAC's Stratofortress aircrews, ground and support personnel. The author was a SAC Headquarters, briefing on bomb damage assessment, loss of aircraft and crews. It was a very tense scene in the briefing room.

Day two, December 19, 1972, Linebacker II primary targets were the Kinh No Vehicle Repair Site, Yen Vien Railroad Yard and Thai Nguyen thermal power plant. The attack force consisted of 93 B-52s. Andersen launched 27 B-52Ds and 36 B-52Gs, with U-Tapao adding 30 B-52Ds. The night sky was filled with the exhaust flames from 180 SA-2s, fired at the Stratofortresses. One Andersen B-52D was hit, exited North Vietnamese air space, making an emergency landing at U-Tapao Air Base. One Andersen B-52G was hit, but its damaged was not severe, allowing it to land back at Andersen, the only B-52G to survive an SA-2 hit. The Stratofortresses released bombs on all assigned targets, evaded the launched SA-2s, which, unfortunately, would not be repeated during following night raids over North Vietnam.

Day three, December 20, 1972, raids consisted of 99 B-52s. Andersen launched 66 B-52s, with U-Tapao 33. The night's primary targets were Yen Vien railroad yard, Ai No storage area, Thai Nguyen thermal power plant, Bac Giang shipment area, Kinh No vehicle repair site, Gia Lam railroad repair facility and Hanoi fuel storage sites. North Vietnamese SA-2 sites fired 220 missiles at the bombers with disastrous results. Six B-52s were shot down (two B-52Ds and four B-52Gs). These losses caused Andersen based SAC officers to recall two airborne B-52G cells from wave two which did not have upgraded ECM equipment rather than risk losses to SA-2s. No B-52Gs were pulled from wave number three. None of the B-52s hit by SA-2s carried upgraded ECM equipment. Headquarters SAC revised strike tactics. Interestingly, no specific and repeated attacks were made on SA-2 sites until December 23, 1972. Revised tactics directed the three B-52 cell configurations would be continued to maintain ECM protection, but B-52 cell separation distance was reduced. Time-over-target was reduced to 90 and 120 seconds. Altitude separation between B-52 cells was increased. Post target withdrawal routes were altered to provide exit over the Gulf of Tonkin with the bombers retrofitted with ALT-28 ECM transmitters to block/jam SA-2 downlinks. B-52s flew in stepped altitudes from 34,500 feet to 35,000 feet to take advantage of densely laid airborne chaff corridors and evasive action was finally authorized during inbound and outbound target routes. To give B-52G crews the opportunity to recover from losses to SA-2s, they stood down for two days. The air war was picked up by B-52Ds assigned to U-Tapao Air Base.

Day four, December 21, 1972, 30 U-Tapao B-52Ds launched. This allowed the majority of KC-135s to stand down, only requiring the use of ground alert and emergency airborne tankers for required refueling. B-52Ds went into North Vietnamese air space accompanied by 75 USAF and USN aircraft. The reduction in strike activity allowed crew and support personnel rest, providing maintenance personnel an opportunity to work on damaged aircraft. The bombers primary targets were the Bac Mai storage depot, Van Dien storage depot and Quang Te airfield. However, the success of North Vietnamese site sites continued, bringing down two B-52Ds, using mass launches to burn through combined B-52D ECM.

Day five, December 22, 1972, 30 U-Tapao B-52Ds launched, assigned to attack railroad yards, petroleum storage and distribution sites. SAC again revised bomber tactics:
1. Bomber approach flight paths into the target were changed, bypassing AAA concentrations, radar sites and Sa-2 sites

around Haiphong and its harbor, as well as storage and distribution facilities.
2. It was decided to increase the severity and number of tactical air strikes on defending SAM sites.
3. Increased intensity of jamming SA-2 radar and SA-2 sites to prevent salvo launches to defeat B-52 ECM.

Day six, December 23, 1972, consisted of a split force of 30 B-52Ds (18 from Andersen and 12 from U-Tapao). A further alteration of tactics prior to bomber take-offs came from SAC, designed to eliminate SAM sites.

1. Each North Vietnamese SAM site would be attacked separately by two B-52Ds.
2. The SAM sites were to be over flown, which eliminated Stratofortresses ECM support, reducing vulnerability.
3. Single B-52D strikes would make it more difficult for SA-2 sites to lock onto following bombers.
4. Allow for destruction of SAM sites before SA-2s could be fired at following aircraft.

These tactics worked, with no B-52 losses.

Day Seven, December 24, 1972, 30 Y-Tapao B-52Ds attacked the Kep and Thai Nguyen railroad yards, 40 miles from Hanoi. Headquarters SAC ordered additional changes in tactics.

1. Change in the approach to target from U-Tapao by flying overland from Thailand through Laos, entering the target area from the north, as opposed to the previous (expected) routes over the Gulf of Tonkin.
2. Bomber routes were selected in order to bypass SAM concentrations until the run from IP to Target.

Once again, no bombers were lost to North Vietnamese air defenses, possibly due to the changes in operational tactics. This ended what was referred to as Phase 1 of Linebacker II attacks against North Vietnam. The switch in tactics on day five and six seemed to be effective since even though 70 SA-2s were fired at the B-52Ds, no hits were scored. This strengthened the belief that the Stratofortresses could bring the North Vietnamese back to Paris in an attempt to end the fighting.

On December 25, 1972, President Nixon ordered the B-52s to stand down. He wrote in his memories about the Christmas Day stand down..."At 6 p.m., Saigon time, on 24 December, a twenty-four Christmas truce I had approved began in Vietnam. No planes flew. No bombs were dropped. For a day, we were at peace." However, the Christmas Day stand down was viewed by the North Vietnamese leadership as a sign of American weakness and not as an opportunity for them to surrender and end the bombing of their country. President Nixon ordered the bombing to be renewed on December 26, 1972.

Day eight, 26 December, became the largest B-52 concentrated strike against North Vietnam. The bombers were assigned to attack ten targets in the Hanoi and Haiphong areas, with all bombers releasing their bombs on the targets within ten minutes. One hundred twenty bombers took off from Andersen and U-Tapao. It was decided to alter tactics further, committing B-52Ds, equipped with upgraded ECM package to penetrate and attack heavily defended targets in the Hanoi area. The targets to be attacked were the Thai Nguyen railroad yard, Hanoi railroad yard, Hanoi petroleum storage, Giap Nhi railroad yard, SAM Site VN 549, Van Dien vehicle storage facility, Haiphong railroad yard and Haiphong transformer complex. SAM Site VN 549 had inflicted considerable damage to the attacking Stratofortresses. U.S. intelligence believed the SAM site was operated by Russian missile officers and enlisted personnel, training North Vietnamese who then were assigned to SAM sites throughout North Vietnam.

The night's bomber support package consisted of 113 aircraft. An aircraft accident at Kadena Air Base, Okinawa nearly wrecked the carefully planned support for the day's bomber strike. A Military Airlift Command Lockheed C-141A Starlifter declared an in-flight emergency, landing at Kadena, coming to rest on the runway. The C-141A accident held up the scheduled take-offs for the KC-135s. The 15-minute take-off delay required a quick airborne change in the operational flight plan for mission refueling. Nine B-52Ds attacked the Hanoi Duc No railroad yard, approaching the target from the northwest. Eighteen B-52s attacked the Giap Nhi railroad yards from the southwest. To lessen dangers to B-52Gs flying over North Vietnam, three B-52Ds attacked SAM Site VN 549, flying over the missile site, approaching from the southeast. Fifteen B-52Ds attacked the Van Dien vehicle repair depot in Hanoi, approaching the target from the southeast. Fifteen B-52Gs and three B-52Ds (equipped with upgraded ECM equipment) bombed the Thai Nguyen railroad yards north of Hanoi, approaching the target from the northwest. Fifteen B-52Gs attacked the Haiphong transformer station, approaching from the northeast. A second group of 15 B-52Gs attacked the Haiphong railroad yards, approaching the target from the southeast. It was believed multiple IPs to target approaches would complicate North Vietnamese SAM defenses. Sixty-eight SA-2s were fired at the Stratofortresses. In Ebony Cell, two U-Tapao B-52Ds at 36,500 feet, approached the Giap Nhi railroad yards in the southeast part of Hanoi. Ebony 01 indicated TWS and uplink signals approximately four minutes prior to the Bomb Release Point, going to maximum jamming of the TWS sources, using two transmitters on the down link frequency. Ebony 02, aircraft number 56-0674, was hit by one SA-2 at 11:42 p.m. during its post target turn away from the target, near SAM Site VN 271, exploding in an immense fireball. Ebony Cell was in the midst of approximately 27 to 30 SA-2s, which had been salvo launched within six-minutes.

At 11.45 p.m., Ash Cell from U-Tapao, consisting of B-52Ds was at 36,500 feet. Two B-52Ds from the cell were nearing Kinh No vehicle complex north of Hanoi. NVAF MiG-21s attacked the cell, forcing it 8 to 11 miles off course. Ash 02 suffered a partial ECM jammer malfunction and only able to operate two jammers against defending SA-2 down links identified. Ash 01, aircraft number 56-0584, was hit by one SA-2, remained flying. The crew struggled to keep the bomber airborne, able to exit North Vietnamese air space, making an emergency landing at U-Tapao Air Base. Unfortunately, the badly damaged B-52D landed too fast, over shooting the runway, running off the runway, tearing itself apart at a distance of one mile beyond the overrun, bursting into flames. Only the co-pilot and gunner managed to escape the flames and survive. Two B-52Ds from Cream Cell were damaged by SA-2s during their attack on the Hanoi railroad yard. The resulting damage was minor and not noticed until landing. Even though 99 support aircraft were airborne over North Vietnam to screen and protect the bombers, North Vietnamese SA-2s got through to the bombers. A post Linebacker II review of Day eight's Stratofortress losses indicated it was dangerous to allow one bomber to fly alone to strike its target. If any aircraft dropped out of its cell, it was to join up the closest bomber cell to achieve maximum/mutual ECM protection from tracking SAM sites.

President Nixon, after the 26 December raid wrote in his personal diary…"That afternoon the North Vietnamese sent the first signal that they had had enough. We received a message from them condemning what they called extermination bombing, but they did not required the bombing stop as a precondition to their agreeing to another meeting, which they proposed for 8 January in Paris." The word from the North Vietnamese did not go far enough and the decision was made to continue the bombing raids. This resulted in three Stratofortress attacks against North Vietnam, the final one on Day 11, which finally convinced the North Vietnamese political leadership they had had enough.

Day nine, 27 December, consisted of 30 U-Tapao B-52Ds and 30 Andersen B-52s attacking SAM Sites VN 234, VN 243, VN 549 and four other targets. North Vietnamese SAM sites continued their lethality. One U-Tapao B-52D was hit by an SA-2 launched from SAN Site VN 243, remaining airborne long enough to exit North Vietnamese air space, at which time the crew bailed out over Thailand. They were recovered by USAF rescue personnel. Earlier in the evening, an Andersen B-52D was shot down by a SA-2 while attacking the Trung Quan railroad yard.

Day ten, 28 December, consisted of 30 U-Tapao B-52Ds with Andersen adding 15 B-52Ds and 15 B-52Gs, attacking the Long Dang railroad yard, SAM support facility 58, Duc Noi, SAM Site VN 158 and 266. The five targets were successfully attacked with losing any Stratofortresses. On this raid, there were fewer SA-2s fired and those that managed to be launched appeared to act erratically, probably because of inadequate down link guidance. Defensive AAA fire was ineffective.

The final bombing raid of Linebacker II was conducted on day 11, 29 December. The raid consisted of 30 U-Tapao B-52Ds and Andersen launching 12 B-52Gs and 18 B-52Ds. The Stratofortresses attacked Phuc Yen Sam support facility, Lang Dang railroad yard and Trai Ca surface to air missile storage facility. All targets were effectively bombed with no B-52s lost. The North Vietnamese could only launch 23 SA-2s at the Stratofortresses. The last Linebacker II to land was an Andersen B-52G, at 12:01 p.m., 30 December.

President Nixon wrote in his diary..."At 7 p.m., Washington time on December 29, 1972, bombing above the 20th Parallel was suspended. The next morning we announced that the Paris negotiations would be resumed and that Kissinger would meet with Le Duc Tho on January 8, 1973,...finally, on January 23, I made a brief statement announcing that a settlement had been reached in Paris and that a Vietnam cease fire would begin on January 27, 1973." Henry Kissinger wrote in his diary..."The Paris Accords with all their ambiguities reflected the balance of forces in Vietnam in the wake of climatic battles of 1972. As with any peace settlement, it depended on the maintenance of the balance of forces. We had no illusions about Hanoi's long-range goal of subjugation of all Indochina."

The cease-fire agreement released 591 American POWs held by the North Vietnamese. Whatever the successes of Linebacker II, a high price was paid. During the eleven-day air campaign, 729 Stratofortresses sorties were flown, losing 15 bombers and 92 aircrew members. Thirty-three Stratofortress crew members, captured during the eleven-day war were released after the cease-fire, another twenty-six were rescued by USAF Search and Rescue personnel, with 33 Missing in Action (MIA) or killed. Other losses consisted of two F-111As, three F-4s, two A-7s, two A-6s, one EB-66, one HH-53 and one RA-5C.

The use of Stratofortresses during Linebacker II was impressive and historical; nothing like this air war had occurred with a modern turbojet bomber force. Even though historic, one must remember that this was only one part of SAC's (including Ellsworth 28th BW) effort during the Vietnam War between June 1965 and August 1973, scheduled a total of 126,663 B-52 scheduled combat sorties, with 126,615 (50 percent against targets in South Vietnam, 27 percent in Laos, 12 percent in Cambodia and 11 percent in North Vietnam) efforts in Southeast Asia. SAC lost 18 B-52s shot down and 13 lost from other causes. Even with the end of Linebacker II operations, this did not mean that SAC's participation in Southeast Asia ended. It was not until January 15, 1973 that SAC Stratofortress bombing missions below the 20th Parallel ended. The final B-52 mission was flown on January 27, 1973 in South Vietnam, in Laos on 17 April and Cambodia on 15 August.[99]

The author was an intelligence officer at SAC Headquarters and briefed the SAC staff on Linebacker II operations, including the B-52 losses, destruction of targets and all corresponding events for the bombing strikes. It was not a fun time to be briefing general officers when the reports of the Stratofortress shoot downs started coming in. Later, photographs of the targets allowed following strikes to be planned and conducted. It was a sobering experience and one which does not fade from memory.

---

[99] Lt. Col. George A. Larson, USAF (Ret.), "Strategic Air Command's Linebacker II," *Friends Journal*, volume 28, Spring 2005.

South Dakota National Guard

Service During the Vietnam War

THE South Dakota National Guard did not mobilize or deploy units to the Republic of South Vietnam. However, many returning Vietnam Veterans over the following years joined various National Guard units to share their experiences and skills. We salute those veterans for their service as well by establishing a Vietnam War display thanking them for their services and remembering those who were killed in action (KIA).

Fall of Saigon. Schlesinger announced early in the morning of April 29, 1975 the evacuation from Saigon by helicopter of the last U.S. diplomats, military and civilian personnel. "Operation FREQUENT WIND" was arguably the largest helicopter evacuation in history. It began on 29 April, as hysterical crowds of Vietnamese vied for limited space. In the United States, South Vietnam was perceived as doomed. President Gerald Ford gave a televised speech on 23 April, declaring an end to the Vietnam War. "Operation FREQUENT WIND" continued around the clock, as North Vietnamese Army tanks breached Army of the Republic of Vietnam last-ditch defenses on the outskirts of Saigon. In the early morning of 30 April, the last U.S. Marines evacuated the embassy by helicopter, as civilians swamped the perimeter and poured into the embassy grounds and buildings. Many of these had been employed by the American government and left to their fate in the occupied city. On 30 April, North Vietnamese Regular Army troops quickly overcame and put down all resistance, capturing key government buildings and military installations. A North Vietnamese tank crashed through the gates of the Imperial Palace, and at 11:30 hours, local time, the NFL flag was raised above it. President Duong Van Minh, who had succeeded Huong two days earlier, surrendered. His surrender marked the end of 116 years of Vietnamese involvement in conflict either alongside or against various countries, primarily China, France, Japan and the United States.[100]

---

[100] Lt. Col George A. Larson, USAF (Ret.), "South Dakota National Guard, Service during the Vietnam War." Visit to Camp Rapid, The South Dakota National Guard's open house to celebrate the National Guard's 150 years

continued...

...*continued*
of service," display set up in the Headquarters Lobby, "2012: Countdown to Withdrawal," June 9, 2012.

The Capture of South Vietnam by North Vietnamese Forces

The End of America's 10,000 Day War in Southeast Asia

AFTER the signing of the Paris Peace Agreement on January 27, 1973, the United States military withdrew from South Vietnam. North Vietnam then set 1975, as the year to bring down the South's military and political leadership. Its troops would attack and destroy at least one third of the Army of the Republic of Vietnam (ARVN), occupy 50 percent of the South's countryside, interdict all major highways and transportation systems to isolate Saigon. These planned actions would demoralize the South's population and cripple the country's agricultural based economy. The North's ultimate goal was to bring down the government of President Nguyen Van Thieu, unifying the two Vietnams by military force.

Le Duan, North Vietnam's Communist Party First Secretary stated about this planned effort: "Victory will take two years. In 1975, the fight will be in the countryside. The North Vietnamese Army (NVA) will establish staging and supply bases close to the South's major cities, from where attacks will create conditions for a general offensive in 1976. By then, ARVN troops will be so weak and demoralized that the North can easily win the war."

North Vietnam's military and political leaders selected the South Vietnamese city of Ban Me Thout to begin their conquest and unite the two Vietnams. Ban Me Thout is located 155 miles northeast of Saigon and 31 miles east of the Cambodian border in the Central Highlands. NVA units attacked with a force of 30,000 troops, overwhelming the South's defenses. The NVA attack began at the start of the Vietnamese Lunar New Year, March 10, 1975, continuing up until the beginning of the rainy season, in late May or early June.

With only 4,000 ARVN troops in or around Ban Me Thout, it only took NVA troops 48 hours to isolate and cut off the South's Central Highlands. Fighting was fierce, and the NVA lost many of its attacking tanks, but its sheer weight of numbers of men and equipment staggered ARVN I Corps troops. This corps was cut off from support from ARVN II Corps with its two divisions to the South because of heavy fighting around Plieku. With the capture of Ban Me Thout, the South's Central Highlands and Northern provinces were behind NVA lines, isolated and cutoff from Saigon. Many ARVN troops were now operating behind NVA positions, effectively removed from the fighting.

South Vietnamese President Thieu, on 15 March, decided not to attempt to retake the Central Highlands or the Northern provinces, making them an unrecognized part of North Vietnam. ARVN forces had no other option, but to pull troops and equipment from the area to a strong line of defense to be created east of Qui Nhon and south to Nha Trang.

The northern provinces of Quang Tri and Thua Thien, located adjacent to the Demilitarized Zone (DMZ), the geopolitical dividing line between the two Vietnams, became an access for military supplies from North Vietnam as ARVN troops fled south. NVA support troops used trucks to move supplies directly to the south without traveling down the winding and Ho Chi Minh Trail, in its attempt to support the fluid and changing military situation in the South. At the same time, the South's provinces of Kontum, Quang Due, Phulong, Pleiku, Darloc, and Binh Long were under heavy NVA attack.

NVA General Vo Nguyen Giap made a statement to the press in Hanoi that..."The NVA's victory at Ban Me Thout and the subsequent route of ARVN units in the Central Highlands, as well as in the Pleiku-Kontum corridor, the ARVN army is on the run."

The South temporarily controlled the coastal lowlands between Da Nang to Saigon. However, the rice-producing delta was threatened by an increased tempo in Communist attacks (NVA and Viet Cong troops). Four ARVN divisions were spread throughout the delta region, constantly harassed and attacked by the NVA 5th and 6th Regiments, and Viet Cong D3 Regiment. These Communist forces were later augmented by the NVA 8th Division.

President Thieu believed an ARVN defensive line east of Qui Nhon and south to Nha Trang would be able to protect Saigon and give ARVN units in the delta time to secure it from Communist troops. His defensive plan pulled ARVN forces from much of South Vietnam: from Ban Me Thout north, through the western part of the country. This would concentrate remaining ARVN forces around the South's major population centers and important lines of transportation.

President Thieu had no other military option, given the reality of the military situation in the Central Highlands and northern provinces. After January 23, 1973, the date of Paris Peace Treaty ending United States active participation in the Vietnam War, ARVN combat losses averaged approximately 1,000 per month. More significantly, after 1974, United States economic and military air was reduced to the point that the south could not replace its destroyed or captured weapons, or restock its rapidly diminishing stocks on munitions.

By early 1975, the South was unable to replace its helicopter and field artillery losses, which previously had been transferred from in-country U.S. Army supply depots. Probably the most crucial deficiency was the absence of a sustained air umbrella, previously provided by the United States Air Force (USAF), Navy, Marine Corps, and Army gunships.

As ARVN units pulled out of the Central Highlands, NVA troops increased the tempo of their attacks, inflicting heavy casualties, turning a planned strategic withdrawal into a panic route. In what is referred to as the "Convoy of Tears," of the approximately 50,000 ARVN troops and civilians attempting to reach the coast along Highway Number 7, only 12,500 survived the North's attacks.

ARVN withdrawal from the Central Highlands resulted in the abandonment of Hue, scene of fierce house to house fighting and tank battles during the North's January 21, 1968, TET offensive. ARVN units, which had been able to reach Tan My, began to move down a strip of land between Hue and the ocean toward Da Nang. Unfortunately, for ARVN units in the corridor, NVA forces cut Highway Number 1, the main route to Da Nang, blocking the ARVN evacuation route.

Inside Da Nang, between 750,000 to 1,000,000 refugees, ARVN troops and deserters milled around, looking for an escape route south, away from NVA troops. NVA troops fired heavy rockets into the city and airfield, beginning on 26 March, increasing panic in the city, creating an atmosphere of desperation to escape by any method. World Airways managed to airlift thousands from the city but stopped these flights when a Boeing 727 was commandeered by ARVN troops, demanding exit from the city. It was the last aircraft to depart Da Nang's airport.

ARVN Lieutenant General Nho Quang Troung radioed Saigon's military headquarters that further defense of Da Nang was impossible and withdrawal the only military option. However, with increased intensity of NVA shelling of the city and rioting by ARVN troops prevented orderly troop movement to the south, out of the city.

By 28 March, after the NVA lobbed 300 to 500 rockets into Da

Nang's airport, it had to be closed, cutting off the city to the outside world. The South Vietnamese Air Force was able to fly out a few of its military aircraft prior to the rocket attack, but many operational aircraft were abandoned to the North. No attempt was made to destroy these aircraft, because Air Force personnel left in a panic to escape the approaching NVA forces. Many could not be flown because of a lack of fuel and spare parts to make them operational.

When NVA troops entered Da Nang, they also captured large amounts of abandoned military equipment, supplies, and munitions, which provided them desperately needed supplies for their troops. The NVA drive south moved faster than originally planned, out distancing most of their advancing logistic columns. NVA troops used captured ARVN trucks to move supplies and munitions to resupply advancing troops, often replacing inferior weapons with captured U.S. rifles, machine guns, mortars, artillery, and boxed rations.

With the NVA's rapid advance south, it lacked sufficient troops to occupy surrendered or captured areas, requiring a departure from their normal procedures of terror and assignation. NVA political officers directed that local South Vietnamese could take care of injured ARVN troops without fear of being shot. This tactic was a calculated risk, but it permitted NVA troops to maintain constant pressure on retreating or withdrawing ARVN troops, not giving them time to pull back and prepare a strong line of resistance.

The North's offensive initially brought 15 of South Vietnam's 23 provinces under its control; captured 100,000 ARVN troops, and killed or wounded another 20,000 in Da Nang; with an additional estimated 50,000 ARVN troops killed, wounded, captured, or ineffective due to the loss of weapons, equipment, or desertion.

As NVA troops advanced toward Cam Ranh Bay, ARVN troops commandeered cars, trucks, and jeeps to get out of town; fired on helicopters and chartered civilian aircraft landing at the airfield to force their way onto these flights. The city was captured along with its airfield, harbor, and expansive military storage facilities intact containing thousands of tons of U.S. military equipment, food, munitions, and assorted supplies.

These supplies had been pre-positioned to support ARVN operations in the northern provinces. However, once they were captured by the North Vietnamese, retreating ARVN units had no sources of replacement military stockpiles, except those in Saigon. However, roads north of Saigon were blocked by masses of refugees fleeing south, making it impossible to move supplies or troops. The South Vietnamese military did not have enough operational helicopters to move the amount of supplies north to resupply ARVN troops to give them a better chance to halt NVA troops.

To complicate the resupply situation, NVA forces cut the highways into Tay Ninh City, 45 miles north of Saigon, blocking supply to ARVN units attempting to hold back the advancing Communist forces. ARVN troops managed to temporarily force Communist troops back, opening the highway, but only to complete a strategic withdrawal to defensive positions closer to Saigon.

South of Saigon, the situation was not any better. Communist troops in the delta attacked Can Tho and My Tho, keeping three ARVN divisions fighting, unable to assist fighting north of Saigon. When Route Number 4 from the delta to Saigon was blocked by NVA troops, these three ARVN divisions were sealed off from the final battle for Saigon.

As Communist, troops (NVA and Viet Cong) circled Saigon; most well to do South Vietnamese began fleeing the country by any means possible, taking with them U.S. dollars, gold, silver and precious gems to live outside the country. The mass flight of these Vietnamese triggered a general population exodus out of the country. This panic forced President Thieu to accept the resignation of Prime Minister Tran Thien Khiem and his cabinet on 4 April, in a last ditch attempt to stabilize the government's deteriorating political situation. However, the North was no longer interested in a political settlement with the South, because of what appeared to be an almost certain military victory nearby.

The North's military successes changed its strategy for the conquest of the South. Xuan Thue, North Vietnamese Communist Party Central Committee Secretary, at a press conference in Hanoi, stated..."The offensive in South Vietnam's northern provinces had only been a punitive blow against the Saigon government. Our ultimate objective is President Thieu's resignation, the withdrawal of all remaining U.S. personnel from the South, and reunification of Vietnam."

NVA's propaganda units were assigned to forward units, to broadcast surrender appeals over loud speakers and on field radio stations to ARVN units. These broadcasts contained surrender procedures and how to safely approach NVA ground troops or land on their controlled airfields. South Vietnamese military personnel were instructed to bring with them their weapons, trucks, jeeps, tanks, aircraft, and ships when they surrendered. They were told, "Surrendering prior to the North's ultimate and certain victory would earn them rehabilitation merits."

Approximately 50,000 ARVN military personnel took advantage of the North's surrender terms and withdrew from the fight for Saigon. They were later joined in re-education camps set up by the North Vietnamese, by 200,000 former ARVN troops, South Vietnamese bureaucrats, police officials, and former United States employees.

The situation in the air around Saigon became as dangerous for those flying combat air strike missions as for those fighting fierce ground battles near the capital. The North Vietnamese moved hundreds of anti-aircraft-artillery (AAA) guns south, shooting down many of the South's aircraft. As aircraft loses grew from the intense AAA fire around Saigon, South Vietnamese Air Force pilots refused to fly what they viewed as one way, suicide ground-attack missions against NVA and Viet Cong troops. The closer NVA troops advanced toward Saigon, the more intense became the ground fighting with ARVN units.

By 18 April, the North had moved approximately 100,000 troops (NVA and Viet Cong) within a two day's march to Saigon. Effective ARVN countering strength consisted if only 30,000 troops, without reserves or re-enforcements, adequate supplies, close air support, and field artillery ground fire.

The North Vietnamese then virtually grounded the South Vietnamese Air Force after moving SA-2 Guideline surface to air missiles (SAMs) from North Vietnam to hastily prepared sites around Saigon. These SAMs eliminated the South's remaining possible air threat to their offensive. Prior to the positioning of these SAMs around Saigon, the United States managed to airlift approximately 60,000 South Vietnamese to Anderson Air Force Base on Guam in the Marianas Islands. Guam eventually processed approximately 130,000 South Vietnamese who fled from the country. By the time the North took control of all of South Vietnam, it is estimated that over 300,000 South Vietnamese fled by a variety of means. Most settled in the United States, with others going to England, France, Canada, and a scattering of other nations.

On 21 April, Saigon's Bien Hoa airfield was heavily shelled by Communist artillery, rockets, and heavy mortars. It had been the largest administrative and logistic support airfield for air strikes against advancing Communist forces until the rocket attack closed the airfield. When the North Vietnamese captured Vung Tau, Saigon's ocean port, shipping to and from the outside was sealed off, isolating Saigon.

On 24 April, President Thieu realized the war was lost and resigned. He remained in Saigon until Ben Hoa's runway was cleared and repaired for limited operations. On 26 April, Thieu left the country, accepting exile in England.

After President Thieu's resignation, Doung Van Minh became temporary president. He agreed to the North's terms of surrender on the evening of 24 April, prior to Thieu's departure two days later. The United States completed a hasty evacuation of its remaining personnel from its Saigon embassy grounds, along with U.S. citizens and dependents, South Vietnamese employees (not all were evacuated), journalists, and those able to force their way into the embassy's grounds. The last helicopter lifted off from the embassy's roof on 28 April. On 30 April, North's military forces entered Saigon and took control of the government.

The North's capture of Saigon closed the door on the 10,000 day United States involvement in South Vietnam's struggle against the Communist North. It has taken years for the hostility between Vietnam and the United States to slowly mend and move toward normalization of relations. [101]

---

[101] The author was stationed at the 43rd Strategic Wing, Andersen Air Force Base, Guam when the North Vietnamese began their military campaign against the South Vietnamese military, ending in the U.S. evacuation of Saigon. He prepared daily intelligence briefings to the Commander, Third Air Division on the status of fighting in South Vietnam. He read the daily State Department updates sent from their Saigon Embassy, unclassified cables that were also used by U.S. news networks to report on the final Communist victory in South Vietnam. The material was included in an article submission to Vietnam Magazine, although only the section on "Operation NEW LIFE" was published. He had a front row seat on the final Communist offensive, which ended the U.S. 10,000 day war in Southeast Asia and then led to "Operation NEW LIFE," the movement of over 130,000 South Vietnamese from their country through Guam, escaping the Communist authorities. The author took part in this and it will be covered following this account.

Review of "Operation NEW LIFE" on Wake Island

Report Prepared for
Commander Naval Forces Guam

Captain George A. Larson, USAF
Chief, Combat Intelligence Branch,
Eighth Air Force, Andersen Air Force Base, Guam

WAKE Island is a coral atoll having a coastline of 12 miles in the North Pacific Ocean, located approximately two-thirds of the way between Honolulu, 2,300 statute miles to the west and Guam, 1,510 statute miles to the east. It is an unorganized, unincorporated territory of the United States, administered by the Office of Insular Affairs, U.S. Department of the Interior. Access to the island is restricted, and all activities on the island are managed by the United States Air Force. There is also a missile facility operated by the United States Army. The largest island, Wake Island, is the center of activity on the atoll, and has an airport and runway of 9,800 feet. On January 6, 2009, President George W. Bush included the atoll as part of the Pacific Remote Islands Marine National Monument.

There is no evidence to suggest there was ever a permanent settlement by the Marshallese who traveled to the island. On October 20, 1568, Alvaro de Mendanade Neyra, a Spanish explorer, with two ships, discovered the island. In 1796, British schooner Captain William Wake landed on the island. On December 20, 1840, U.S. Navy Commodore Charles Wilkes landed on the island. The United States annexed the island on January 17, 1899, setting up a telegraph station. In 1935, Pan American Airways constructed a small village, "PAAville," to serve flights on its U.S.-China Clipper passenger route. In January 1941, the U.S. Navy constructed a military base on the atoll. On 19 August, the first permanent military garrison, elements of the 1st Marine Defense Battalion (449 officers and enlisted), along with 68 U.S. Navy and 1,221 civilian workers. On December 8, 1941, the Japanese bombed the island. On 23 December, the Japanese captured the island. On September 4, 1945, the Japanese garrison on Wake Island surrendered to a detachment of U.S. Marines. As indicated previously, from late April to the middle of August 1975, Wake Island served as a refugee center for more than 15,000 Vietnamese refugees who fled their homeland after North Vietnamese military forces captured Saigon. [102]

---

[102] Report prepared for Commander Naval Forces Guam, Captain George A. Larson, USAF, Chief, Combat Intelligence Branch, Eighth Air Force, Andersen Air Force Base, Guam. The author, on Guam during "Operation NEW LIFE," and his intelligence section personnel, processed many refugees to fly onto Wake Island for temporary housing and processing for entrance into the United States.

Airmen Bring New Life to South Vietnamese Refugees on Wake Island

THE *Wake Special Edition, The Hawaiian Falcon*, Hickam Air Force Base, Hawaii, Public Affairs and Information Office, June 27, 1975...In the past two months, a metamorphosis has taken place for "Operation NEW LIFE" at Wake Island. Two months ago, 25 April, "Operation NEW LIFE" was launched. Tired, hungry refugees poured onto Wake Island from USAF C-141s and civilian aircraft, 8,000 of them in the first wave. The camp was in an emergency state. The basics of survival were at stake: children, clothing, a full stomach. During the early days of the operation, it was not unusual to see children stuffing their mouths with food as they left the dining room. Today, 60 days later a transformation has come about from those bleak, early days. The morning brings with the songs of children: songs in French, Vietnamese and English. Patient, volunteer teachers, recite the English A-B-Cs and numbering system. Over 1,000 children are now enrolled in area schools taught by Vietnamese volunteers and Americans during their off-duty times. Under trees, Kindergarten children play "ring-around-the-roses," tumble down slides and giggle with glee as they swing. No longer are there long lines of people at the dining halls. There is plenty of food. Volunteers worked through the day and night in at most every phase of the Task force operation as translators and typists and helpers at the 657th Tactical Hospital, information, security police, personnel processing, dining halls, billeting and laundry. [103]

---

[103] As part of "Operation NEW LIFE," MSgt. Robert O'Daniel, while assigned to Headquarters, 15th Air Base Wing, Pacific Air Forces, Hickam Air Force Base, Hawaii was sent TDY to Wake Island to support the administrative processing id South Vietnamese refugees, on 2 May 1975. As previous noted the author was heavily involved on Guam with the processing of over 130,000 South Vietnamese refugees who passed through the island of Guam and Andersen Air Force Base. The actions of these two South Dakotans crossed in support for those fleeing the Communists in South Vietnam on Wake Island, marking the end of the Vietnam War. The information for this section comes from the *Wake Special Edition, The Ha-*
continued...

...continued
waiian Falcon, Hickam Air Force Base, Hawaii, Public Affairs and Information Office, June 27, 1975.

Pacific Backwater Comes to Life Again

Wake Island, "Operation NEW LIFE"

THE arrival of thousands of Vietnamese refugees on Wake Island brings that tiny, sleepy atoll back into an unaccustomed spotlight in the world news. The Wake Island story come at a time when all three of the islands closest to Hawaiian chain; Wake, Midway and Johnson Islands are drifting along as forgotten backwaters. All three have lost population in the last five years. All retain military ties of lessening importance. Until the refugees reopened bungalows on Wake, life of the atoll had been very slow. The only time Wake caught the world's attention was when it surrendered to a Japanese invasion force in 1941, and when President Harry Truman and U.S. Army General Douglas MacArthur there in 1950 to discuss the Korean War and whether Communist Chinese troops would enter the war on the side of the retreating North Korean forces as they neared the Yalu River. Today (May 1975), Wake has only about 225 civilians and five Air Force personnel, whom keep the place going for one reason: to supply passing fliers with food, fuel and beds. Kenton Hawaii supplies the work force to operate a postal service, fuel the planes, run the airstrip, control tower and fire trucks. The coming of jet aircraft did much to make Wake an unnecessary rest stop for military planes crossing the Pacific. In 1970, Wake supported 1,647 people. Earlier, in 1960, the population was 1,097. At the height of the Vietnam War, Wake's three square miles of land supported more than 600 Federal Aviation Administration workers and their families, 450 housekeepers of the Facilities Management Corporation, more than a dozen Air Force, Navy and Coast Guard personnel. Most housekeepers are Filipino nationals. In 1965, Wake handled 800 aircraft per month, served 27,000 meals, processed and housed 8,000 transient servicemen. At that time, the Army employed 30 Page Communications personnel to man a Troposcatter system and Standard Oil had 25 men to pump aviation fuel.

Midway's population, mostly Navy personnel, has dropped from 2,200 to 1,168 as of February 1975. Midway made international headlines in 1970, when U.S. President Richard Nixon and South Vietnamese President Nguyen Van Thieu met on the island to discuss the changing U.S. involvement in South Vietnam. Currently (1975), Midway's personnel service transiting aircraft, while providing search and rescue service in that area, support ships at the port on the island to support missile projects and classified operations. [104]

---

[104] "Pacific 'backwater' comes to life again," *Honolulu Star Bulletin*, Honolulu, Hawaii, May 5, 1975.

Refugee Business Rewards with Memories

Wake Island, "Operation NEW LIFE"

ON Wake, there were nearly 8,000 homeless Vietnamese seeking refuge and respite from a lifetime of strife. Wake Island got into the refugee business quite quickly and unexpectedly. Colonel W. E. Y. Paxton, Commander, 15th Air Base Wing, flew there with a team in 24 April to plan for such a contingency, but before they could complete their preparations, the refugees began arriving. Wake had been closed for two years; its houses emptied of all furnishings and boarded up against the elements. Paxton's airmen began getting the houses ready, fixing the plumbing, installing cots, turning on electrical power. The two and three bedroom houses each became home for 30, 40 or more refugees. The aircrew that flew Paxton's team was pressed into service setting up cots. The three man Royal Air Force Detachment joined the effort, loading cots and escorting refugees to their new homes. Efforts were made to keep families together, donated clothing was passed out, showers with privacy walls were built in the streets alongside the houses to help with hygiene, four dining halls were opened, a fully staffed tactical hospital was flown in from Clark Air Base, Republic of the Philippines. [105]

---

[105] "Refugee business rewards with memories," *The Hawaiian Falcon*, Hickam Air Force Base, Hawaii, Public Affairs and Information Office, June 27, 1975.

Lucky Rains, Hard Work, Mark Early Success

Wake Island, "Operation NEW LIFE"

AFTER arriving, the first task of the initial survey team was to determine how many people could be accommodated in the old, closed housing facilities on Wake. After the first survey, it was decided that up to 8,000 refugees could be accommodated, using a criteria of 30 to 35 square feet per individual. To get started, it was decided Wake could accept 1,000 refugees within three days. The immediate concern was to plan to receive the people, a reception center (where MSgt. O'Daniel was sent TDY from Hickam AFB to man the reception and administration/processing center on Wake Island), medical facility, a dining hall, food and quarters. Each building selected for use had to be cleaned up and have electricity, and in many cases, water turned on. A building on the flight line was selected for administration, another for a reception center, and two old barracks nearby were converted into a dispensary with living space for the medical types, plus an isolation ward. Many of the buildings that belonged to Pan American Airlines, when they used to serve Wake, were pressed into service. The processing center was the old Pan American Airlines Reception Center. The original work of connecting the facilities was done by the aircraft crew and the initial survey team. They were augmented by a Civil Engineering Prime Beef team from Hickam AFB. The on island Kenton employees and five USAF members, along with Coast Guard, National Weather Service, and Royal Air Force.

During the first week, the Air Force team of 36 people averaged 16 to 18 hours a day. They often found themselves doing jobs that were a far cry from their normal duties. For example, processing center interviews were conducted by two Prime Beef site developers and two Kenton employees. Water was a main concern in the beginning, but with the help of three water producing stills and a couple of lucky early rains, an adequate water supply was established. This was in spite of the fact that soon, with an average population of 5,000, the daily consumption of water was over 100,000 gallons per day. Supply was another early problem. There was very little at Wake, which could be used to support the great influx of people. However, with excellent support from Hickam, the problem was very quickly controlled. Everything was timely, adequately and most helpful. The Military Airlift Command (MAC) dedicated one C-141 Starlifter just for support on Wake. It began flying round robin shuttle missions carrying supplies and food. One typical mission carried 42,000 pounds of rice from Hickam to Wake Island.

Three housing area were opened. Typical was a three bedroom complex with an enclosed lanai. Twenty-five people were put into each side of this type of house. At first, the Air Force was trying to get a bed or a cot for each individual, but after talking with the first group of refugees, it was discovered that many of the Vietnamese preferred to sleep on the floor. They ended up with about a 50 percent ratio of cots to people. The very young and the very old slept on the cots; the others preferred a pallet on the floor. Three dining halls were set up, using existing facilities, including an old Pan American dining room and an old American Legion Hall. Two field kitchens, one flown in from Hickam and one from Clark Air Base, Philippines, provided the refrigeration and equipment for the three facilities. After the first refugees arrived, the ranks of workers were increased with Vietnamese volunteers. The jungle had been rapidly reclaiming many of the unused areas, but when a supply of rakes, hoses and shovels arrived, the Vietnamese went to work cutting it back. They kept two trucks busy, 12 hours a day, just cleaning up and clearing the areas. [106]

---

[106] "Lucky rains, hard work, mark early successes," *The Hawaiian Falcon*, Hickam Air Force Base, Hawaii, Public Affairs and Information Office, June 27, 1975.

Wake Island Reviewed

"Operation NEW LIFE"

NOW that the dust has settled from supporting "Operation BABY LIFT" and "Operation NEW LIFE," some impressive information is surfacing on the extent of support given by Air Force Hawaiian personnel. The massive support ended earlier this month (2 August) a 3 a.m., when 22 refugees stepped off a C-141 aircraft from Wake Island. On board with the refugees were some 30 military TDY (including MSgt. O'Daniel) and civilian contractors. The primary responsibility for "Operation NEW LIFE" at Wake as an overseas receiving center and for "Operation BABY LIFT" here fell on the 15th Air Base Wing, with Colonel W. E. Y. Paxton, Wing Commander, at the helm. Colonel Paxton..."The immense task undertaken during the past four months by Air Force Hawaiian people in support of "Operation BABY LIFT" and "Operation NEW LIFE" was overwhelming. However, whether military, civilian employee and contractor, or dependent volunteer...each of you did an outstanding job, and I'm proud of you and your achievement."

Some of the impressive stats chalked up here and at Wake are:

1. Nearly 15,000 refugees were housed and fed, clothed and given medical attention as they passed through Wake from 25 April to 2 August.
2. Over 1,700 tons of cargo was airlifted into Wake onboard MAC C-5 and C-141 aircraft. By mid-July, this represented over 85 cargo and passenger flights. At the peak of activity, nine were on the Wake ramp unloading passengers and cargo.

Meanwhile, back at Hickam, over 92,000 refugees, evacuees and babies passed through the MAC terminal and Honolulu International airport (The author's intelligence section personnel processed those departing Andersen Air Force Base, Guam for the long flight to Hawaii) or HIA, from Wake Island, Andersen AFB, Guam and Clark AB, Philippines, involving over 500 aircraft. Both these flying operations were locally controlled by the 61st Military Airlift Support Wing personnel.

The Supply Squadron, during a three day period in late April, pumped over two million gallons of JP-4 fuel for aircraft in support of "Operation NEW LIFE."

Not outdone, the Transportation Squadron processed and shipped over two-million pounds of supplies and equipment to Wake. In addition, over 4,000 requests were handled, carrying some 30,000 people for a total distance of over 100,000 ground miles.

The Services squadron made and delivered thousands of box lunches for aircrews and passengers alike, as well as reopen the dining hall of short notice to feed the hungry refugees.

Throughout both operations, the majority of the flights at Hickam and HIA were met by medical, security police, services, personnel and chaplain representatives as well as hundreds of military, civilian and dependent volunteers.

At Wake, over 8,000 tubes of toothpaste, 370,000 pounds of rice and 3,875 gallons of soy sauce were distributed to the refugees by supply and food service personnel. Over 13,000 meals were prepared daily in the four refugee dining halls.

In the early days of "Operation NEW LIFE" on Wake, Civil Engineering Squadron's Prime Beef Team initially kicked-off the action, with C-118 crewmembers and Wake permanent party personnel, by opening housing areas long since boarded up. The project included turning on the electricity and fixing the plumbing. Furniture was removed so that the houses could accommodate some 30 refugees each. Mattresses, blankets, cots and sheets were moved in. After seven days, at 18 hours per day, there were 7,000 sleeping accommodations set up.[107]

---

[107] "Wake Island Reviewed," *The Hawaiian Falcon*, Hickam Air Force Base, Hawaii, Public Affairs and Information Office, August 22, 1975.

Second Honor Roll Listed

"Operation NEW LIFE" for 15th Air Force Personnel

"OPERATION NEW LIFE" activities on Wake Island AFB ended earlier this month. The nearly four month long operation hit Air Force Hawaii in mid-stream during support of "Operation BABY LIFT," the evacuation of orphans from Vietnam during late March and April (1975). In addition to some 300 personnel sent TDY to Wake Island in direct support of the Task Force set up there, many other military, civilian and dependents throughout Air Force Hawaii and the Pacific helped. Expressing appreciation for the Command, CINCPAC Logistics Directorate..."On 2 August, Wake reduced its 'Operation NEW LIFE' population to zero. Since its inception, Wake received, housed, processed and educated 14,597 refugees. The professional competence and effectiveness of the 15th Air Base Wing and medical hospital personnel and those of Kentron of Hawaii, Ltd., reflected the highest in military/contractor cooperation and assistance. Leadership and humanitarian contribution by all involved was the hallmark of Wake's operation." General Louis L. Wilson, Jr., CINCPACAF..."The willing response and dedicated professionalism exhibited in support of this historic humanitarian undertaking is indeed gratifying. Please pass my personal appreciation to all those involved." [108]

---

[108] "Second honor roll listed," *The Hawaiian Falcon*, Hickam Air Force Base, Hawaii, Public Affairs and Information Office, August 22, 1975.

B-52Ds in the Defense of the Republic of South Korea

Major George A. Larson, USAF
43rd Strategic Wing, Strategic Air Command, Andersen Air Force Base, Guam

IN 1976, North Korean troops entered the Demilitarized Zone (DMZ) and killed two United Nation's Command officers (U.S. Army officers) who were directing the cutting down of a large tree blocking the view into North Korea. The tree was south of the "Bridge of No Return," on one of the roads leading into North Korea. Today, the location of the "Tree Chopping" incident is marked with a bronze plaque mounted on a short concrete pedestal.

The only available long-range conventional bomber force to project a military show of force over the Korean peninsula was stationed at Anderson Air Force Base, Guam (Northern Marianas Islands). The 43rd Strategic Wing (SW) had 14 Boeing B-52D Stratofortresses. They had undergone the "Big Belly" configuration during the Vietnam War allowing it to carry an internal bomb load of 42,000 pounds and 18,000 pounds on two under wing pylon positions.

Four B-52Ds at Anderson were always cocked on nuclear alert, each armed with four gravity hydrogen weapons in the forward bomb bay. None of Anderson's B-52Ds were loaded with conventional bombs, sitting on conventional ground alert, available for a quick response to changing events in Korea. The wing went back to Vietnam era conventional 500 pound bomb clip loading procedures to prepare for a Korean War contingency. The wing was tasked to put four B-52Ds over South Korea within six to eight hours of hostilities initiated by North Korea into the South. These B-52s were to be quickly loaded with 500 pound bomb clips in the bomb bay. Following B-52Ds would also be loaded with 18,000 pounds of bombs on external pylons to make a 60,000 pound bomb load.

The wing's intelligence staff, in coordination and cooperation with bomb navigation staff personnel, photographic interpreters and B-52D bombardiers selected offset aiming points (OAPS) in South Korea. The majority of these were located near and along the top one third of

South Korea.

Electronic beacons were placed at the OAP locations by South Korean troops and USAF (SAC) personnel. The B-52Ds were equipped to receive the location signals from the beacons while airborne. They were numbered and plotted on charts given to the crews as part of their Korean Contingency War packages. Intelligence personnel built 14 contingency bags, one for each B-52D at Anderson, all identical, and complete except for the addition of the current codes prior to aircraft launch.

The wing created a Strategic Advanced (ADVON) Team, which was tasked to move from Guam to South Korea within four hours of activation. They took with them a pre-assembled ADVON kit, which contained all the necessary charts, manuals, equipment and items needed to support B-52D operations in Korea. A Boeing KC-135 Stratotanker transported the ADVON team to Osan AFB, South Korea. On arrival, the team setup operations in the command center, ready to coordinate battlefield air support requests. The 16 person team was to fight the SAC portion of the air war in Korea for the first 72 hours until augmented by additional personnel and command staff from Headquarters SAC, Offutt AFB, Nebraska.

The first four conventional loaded B-52Ds took off as soon as the ADVON team was operational at Osan. They entered South Korean air space from the south and received a coded message as to what OAPs were to be loaded into the computer for target selection. In this manner, the bombing capability of the B-52D was enhanced to act more like a tactical than strategic bomber. Later, the iron bomb load was changed to cluster munitions (anti-personnel and armor) which increased ground area lethality.

In this process, a single B-52D could be vectored to a specific target while airborne without the time-consuming, pre-mission briefings, and labor-intensive construction of Combat Missions Folders (CMFs). The basic CMF was already built, with up-to-date information, only requiring weather and security codes to be complete. During an Operational Readiness Inspection (ORI), SAC inspectors spent as much time reviewing contingency CMFs as the Single Integrated Operational Plan (SIOP) CMFs.

The ADVCON Team concept was tested during Team Spirit 1980, when it deployed to Osan. The system worked and added to the defense of South Korea. This concept with the B-52Ds remained in operation until 1983, when the last B-52D was retired. SAC's conventional precision munitions have been added to that of iron bombs carried on the B-52H and B-1B, and B-2. [109]

---

[109] The author was assigned to the 43rd Strategic Wing, 1974 to 1976 and again 1978 to 1981. The second assignment was as Chief of Target Intelligence Division and responsible for SAC's weaponeering mission with the wing, to include the defense of South Korea. This was a "Cold War" mission to protect the integrity of the Republic of South Korea against another massive invasion by the Democratic People's Republic of North Korea.

B-52 Stratofortress Reconnaissance Missions During the Iran-Iraq War

"Operation BUSY OBSERVER"

ON September 22, 1980, Saddam Hussein, ordered Iraqi military forces to invade Iran. However, Iraq suffered the same fate as German military forces during their invasion of Russia: they had to attack across long distances, while fighting a larger army. The fighting soon turned into a war of trenches and earthworks, with terrible losses on both sides. The war threatened the world's access to the Persian Gulf oil fields.

Israel's attack on Iraq's nuclear reactor made the situation even tenser and threatened to spread the conflict throughout the Middle East. On June 7, 1981, Israeli F-15s and F-16s bombed the Osibak nuclear reactor near Bagdad, eliminating a possible future nuclear threat from Iraq. Fortunately, Iraq was so heavily involved in the war with Iran that it could not respond. The Iran-Iraq war did not end until July 18, 1985, with the implementation of a United Nations ceasefire.

United States presence in the Persian Gulf increased during the war to protect the vital Persian Gulf oil route. During the war, the United States supported Iran against Iraq, because it did not want Iraq to win the war and become even more of a threat, positioned at the end and along one side of the Persian Gulf.

The 43rd Strategic Wing (SW), Strategic Air Command (SAC), on Andersen Air Force Base (AFB), Guam and its B-52Ds became an important intelligence collection source during the war. The 43rd SW commander received daily intelligence briefings on the situation in the Persian Gulf, briefed to the aircrews. The author briefed most of the events on the war to the Strategic Wing commander and staff.

The 43rd SW's area of responsibility included the Indian Ocean and the Persian Gulf. SAC directed the 43rd SW to conduct Special Indian Ocean Missions to track ship movements in the area. These missions, at the time, were classified as sensitive reconnaissance flights, designed to track Soviet and Communist bloc countries, as well as other nation's shipping in the Persian Gulf.

In October 1980, 43rd SW intelligence personnel began training B-52D crews on Soviet warship and merchant vessel recognition, and general ship identification techniques and classification procedures. Crews also learned how to use hand held, 35mm cameras fitted with telephoto lens, to photograph moving ships from a moving aircraft. The author, because of his training while enrolled in the U.S. Navy War College Correspondence Program and self-education with the Navy at Apra Harbor, and previous advanced photoreconnaissance training at Headquarters SAC became the primary trainer on Soviet ship recognition for the aircrews on Andersen. His office also handled the construction of all the mission bags for the aircrews.

Mission planning was complicated. Each Indian Ocean Busy Observer mission required the launch of three B-52Ds. Each aircraft carried two additional pilots to provide relief on the 33 hour flight to and from the Persian Gulf.

The B-52Ds first refueling point was north of the Philippine Islands. Two tankers refueled the primary bombers, with the mission spare returning to Guam. A ground alert spare KC-135A tanker was at Kadena Air Force Base, Okinawa.

The second aerial refueling point was northwest of Australia, after the B-52Ds cleared Singapore and Indonesia air space, by KC-135A tankers based at the Royal Australian Air Force Base at Darwin.

The third aerial refueling location was north of Diego Garcia, which allowed the B-52Ds to patrol the entrance to the Persian Gulf to identify ships in the crowded shipping lanes. The U.S. Navy provided F-18 Tomcats to shield the bombers. F-18s also used the B-52Ds to simulate approaching Soviet Bear long-range turboprop naval reconnaissance aircraft, which staged out of Vietnam from the air base at the former U.S. Cam Ranh Bay military complex. The Bears flew reconnaissance missions to the Indian Ocean and Persian Gulf approaches, collecting information on U.S. ship movements.

On the return to Guam, the B-52Ds were air refueled three times. After landing, intelligence personnel collected the exposed film, processed it, and brought the photographs to post-mission intelligence debriefing. Crew identification of ships photographed was verified by intelligence personnel prior to the mission's report were transmitted to higher headquarters. The author oversaw the entire process and received letters of commendation from SAC as well as Pacific Air Force (PACAF) at Hickam AFB, Hawaii, along with his intelligence staff on Andersen.

The reconnaissance report was transmitted to Pacific Air Force

Headquarters in Hawaii; SAC Headquarters at Omaha, Nebraska; and the Joint Persian Gulf Intelligence Command Center on Diego Garcia.

Later in the Iran-Iraq war, B-52Hs flew these missions from Guam, since their longer range required less air to air refueling resources. To reduce flight time to the Persian Gulf, on May 5, 1981, a B-52H from the 410th Bomb Wing at K.I. Sawyer, Michigan landed at Darwin. It was the first B-52 to land in Australia. The aircraft went on public display before its first mission. On June 22, 1981, the first Indian Ocean reconnaissance mission was flown from Darwin as a test of flying from a forward base in Australia.

Until the end of the Iran-Iraq war, SAC's B-52s supported U.S. naval forces operating in the Indian Ocean and Persian Gulf. This showed the ability of the manned bomber to adapt to changing international threats, which it continues to do today. [110]

---

[110] The author was an intelligence officer assigned to the 43rd Strategic Intelligence Wing, Andersen Air Force Base, Guam when the Strategic Air Command tasked his office to prepare B-52 aircrews to fly from Andersen AFB to the Persian Gulf and back, non-stop, taking photographs and collecting information on Soviet and Eastern Bloc nations shipping delivery military equipment and supplies to Iran. At this time, the United States back Iraq in the war against Iran, evening though Iran had been a one-time ally with support for the Shan of Iran. This was a precursor to the later Coalition attack on Iraq during the "First Gulf War."

South Dakota National Guard

"Operation DESERT STORM"

IN 1990, the South Dakota National Guard mobilized six units for duty in Saudi Arabia and Iraq. These units were 109th Engineer Group, 730th Medical Company, 1742nd Transportation Company, 740th Transportation Company, 747th Highway Regulating Company and the 57th Movement Control Team. [111]

---

[111] Lt. Col. George A. Larson, USAF (Ret.), "South Dakota National Guard, Operation DESERT STORM." Visit to Camp Rapid, The South Dakota National Guard's open house to celebrate the National Guard's 150 years of service," display set up in the Headquarters Lobby, "2012: Countdown to Withdrawal," June 9, 2012.

A View of the Cold War Between the United States and the Soviet Union

After Tearing Down the Berlin Wall and Fall of the "Evil Empire"

THE end of the "Cold War" between the United States and the former Soviet Union reset thinking on what transpired between the two nuclear superpowers after World War II to the 1990s. The author was one of the U.S. intelligence officers whose responsibility it was to analyze report on and probe the Soviet Union for military indicators. These evaluations followed the changing status and thinking of the Soviet Politburo and military leaders, followed by Eastern European Bloc countries on military capabilities against NATO in western Europe. After the Berlin Wall came down without any military reaction from the Soviet Army, this took a great deal of getting use to and interpretations of future implications. The opportunity to meet four former Soviet intelligence officers, of the author's counterparts across the intelligence table was exciting. The initial exchange was set up between the Russian Association of National Security Alumni and the Association of Retired Intelligence Officers. The idea of such an exchange started after contacts developed between U.S. intelligence officers who served in Vietnam. The author was a photo-intelligence officer assigned to the 544th ARTW (Aerial Reconnaissance Technical Wing, Headquarters SAC, Offutt AFB, Bellevue, Nebraska), with part of his duties reporting on Southeast Asia as well as the Soviet Union. He was a briefer during Linebacker II to SAC commanders, reporting on bomb damage, aircraft and crew losses and availability of crews and aircraft for the next day's strikes. Opposite U.S. intelligence officers were those Soviet intelligence officers who served in Afghanistan, often referred to as the Soviet Union's Vietnam. Just as the United States pulled out of Vietnam, the Soviet Union extracted its military forces from Afghanistan. Interesting, President Obama and the Secretary of Defense Leon Panetta (at that time) are trying to do the same thing after U.S. forces have been in Afghanistan for the past ten years. Both nation's former intelligence officers looked ahead to define intelligence commitments while attempting to remove some of the suspicion between each side. As a comment, suspicion continues between the United States and Russia.

In January 1992, former U.S. intelligence officers were invited to travel to Moscow to meet their professional counterparts (the author was unable to attend), in what former U.S. President Ronald Reagan coined as "Evil Empire." During a meeting in the Protocol Room of former KGB Headquarters, U.S. intelligence officers invited members of the Russian National Security Association to come to the United States to discuss issues between the United States and former Soviet Union.

The United States lecture tour was set up to focus on the continuing need for expensive intelligence collecting organizations in the post-Cold War era between the two superpowers. The threat posed by the Russian military's growing nuclear strategic capabilities, revitalized in 2000 and after because of inflow of large amounts of petro dollars to modernize its weapon systems, grows as Russia demonstrates a renewed belligerency against U.S. efforts in former Eastern Bloc nations to build an anti-missile shield against a possible Iranian missile threat (missiles armed with chemical or nuclear warheads). The lecturers also looked at U.S. intelligence capabilities, which appeared to be under examination, and re-evaluation, shifting toward threats from Middle East and Southwest Asia based terrorist organizations. Discussion never approached the threat, which eventually rose, to disaster on September 1, 2001 from external terrorist groups. In 1993, the U.S. intelligence unconfirmed budget (did not include top secret or "Black" intelligence programs) was 25 billion dollars. Eighty percent of this U.S. intelligence budget was earmarked or dedicated to pry out secrets and intentions of Soviet military capabilities and operations. U.S. military and civilian intelligence agencies used sophisticated intelligence collection platforms. The tours of the four Soviet intelligence officers was an attempt to start and open up a public debate on the need of existing methods to extract and collect intelligence information. These Soviet intelligence officers presented a different and personal perspective on intelligence collection not previously available to the American public. Activities on Ellsworth AFB were of great concern to Soviet military because of B-52H, KC-135 and Minuteman II ICBMs operating from and controlled by the base, along with the top secret nuclear weapons storage facility at the north end of the base.

The four retired former Soviet intelligence officers filled a wide variety of intelligence positions. Colonel Vladmir B. Barovsky, PHD, a

1939 graduate of Moscow Technological Institute spent World War II with Soviet Intelligence in London, England. After the war, he was posted to New York City. He retired in 1984, from the Deputy Chief of the KGB's Science and Technology Directorate. Colonel Yuri I. Modin joined Soviet intelligence in 1934. He graduated from the Moscow Institute of Foreign Languages in 1946, and assigned to London, England for ten years. Later, he served in New Delhi (today called Mumbai), India. He retired in 1988, as Deputy Director of the Research Institute on Intelligence Problems. Colonel Vsevelod I. Capon holds a law degree from Kiev University, beginning his career in the Ukrainian Foreign Service in 1954. He was posted with the Ukrainian mission to the United Nations in New York City from 1958 to 1960. He joined the Soviet Intelligence Service in 1962. From 1964 to 1967, he was with the Soviet Mission to the United Nations. From 1981 to 1987, he was in Prague as a ranking member of the Soviet Union's delegation to the Conventional Arms Limitation negotiations. He retired as Deputy Chief of Division in 1991. Colonel H. Totrov graduated from Moscow State Institute of Foreign Relations in 1957, specializing in Far East Studies. Originally, with the Ministry of Foreign Affairs, he joined the KGB in 1960. He spent over ten years in Japan in various assignments and retired in 1992, as a Section Head in Counter Intelligence, monitoring Central Intelligence Agency operations around the world and against the Soviet Union.

A large percentage of the U.S. intelligence community efforts support U.S. Armed Forces, which with the end of the "Super Power" conflict between the United States and the Soviet Union, are geared to prepare for projected foreign contingencies. Not only is intelligence support provided to the U.S. military, but also to United Nations peace keeping forces, of which, the U.S. Armed Forces contributes personnel and equipment. Even in the era of military downsizing (1993), prior to September 1, 2001 terrorist attacks on the United States, the U.S. intelligence community (civilian and military) continued to provide thousands of defense planners and contractors, concentrating on foreign capabilities, which are needed for "assessing U.S. military needs."

For over twenty years, the author worked to bring down the Soviet Union and when its collapse occurred, all of a sudden the author and other intelligence professionals were no longer needed. The author and other intelligence officers helped win the Cold War and were considered expendable. The author blames the disaster of September 1, 2001 on the lack of shared and reported intelligence warnings on the approaching disaster, with intelligence assets spread out across military and civilian intelligence agencies, lacking dedicated inter-agency communications and sharing of intelligence information, review of all inputs in one central location to determine possible resulting actions or consequences, and training of dedicated intelligence officers to be aware of terrorist threats.

Intelligence activities across once hostile borders of the United States and Soviet Union is easier under terms of the Open Skies Treaty signed by twenty-seven countries on March 22, 1992. The author worked on intelligence information for this treaty while assigned to the 544th ARTW (second tour 1989 to 1992). The treaty allowed signatory states to fly over each other's territory and collect intelligence, which was shared with all treaty members. South Dakota was part of this when Ellsworth AFB's 150 Minuteman II ICBM silos were destroyed in compliance with the U.S.-Soviet Strategic Arms Reduction Treaty (START). The silo headworks were blown up, left undisturbed for verification by Soviet intelligence, on-site visit and overhead aerial reconnaissance, then cleaned up.

The 55th SRW at Offutt AFB made the U.S. intelligence flights. Interestingly, the "Open Skies" policy was first proposed by U.S. President Eisenhower at the June 1960 Geneva Conference. The timing was bad. After the shoot down of a CIA U-2 reconnaissance aircraft near the Ural Mountains in Central Soviet Union, Premier Nikita Khrushchev turned down the request due to the violation of Soviet air space by a CIA spy plane. The Soviets captured the pilot, Francis Powers and put him on trial, found guilty of espionage against the Soviet Union, sentenced to a long prison term. He was eventually traded for a Soviet intelligence Agency (captured) spy. The spy game continued between the United States and the Soviet Union.

The four retired Soviet intelligence officers toured the United States for five weeks, participating in forums held at universities and civic meetings, discussing the post-Cold War role of national intelligence organizations. The author was invited by the Greater Des Moines, Iowa Chamber of Commerce Federation to attend a breakfast with the four Soviet intelligence officers on November 18, 1993, at the Metropolitan Club in Capital Square. He also attended larger meetings at Drake University in Des Moines, Iowa and at Iowa State University (the author graduated from ISU with a degree in history in 1969). These four Soviet intelligence officers openly discussed spy techniques, the changing Soviet intelligence collection, domestic Soviet politics and opportunities for cooperation. However, the author's intelligence training and instincts of "do not trust without verification" kicked in.

Colonel Vsevelod Gapon..."There is room for intelligence operations in the new era of cooperation, but only if each group is governed by laws. I want to separate my opinions from what I note or refer as counter-intelligence as in suppression of Russian dissidents by the KGB or stealing atomic bomb secrets from the U.S. Manhattan Project, the cornerstone of old-style Soviet spy operations. To avoid abuse, all intelligence gathering activity should be conducted according to laws about intelligence. Our country has already passed laws about the boundaries which intelligence should conduct its activities. This is the best way to avoid the abused of the past." Colonel Vladimir B. Barkovsky..."On the one topic asked, I will not explain the Russian story of how the Soviet union acquired the atomic bomb from scientists at Los Alamos, New Mexico, the birthplace of the U.S. nuclear weapons program. My visit to the United States would have been unthinkable a couple of years ago." Colonel Yuri H. Totrov..."Russian intelligence has closed about 30 spy stations around the world since the collapse of Communism in 1991. Even though my country has fallen apart, American counterintelligence efforts have actually increased. I am referring about your FBI and CIA recruitment of Russians in Washington, DC. There have been many efforts to enlist Russian nationals to provide information to the United States. It's getting bolder, when the Cold War is supposedly over. I, myself, rejected an overture by CIA operatives when assigned to Osaka, Japan, only two weeks after the failed coup in Moscow in 1991. During the Vietnam War, however, I did the same thing while stationed in Japan. I was involved in intelligence efforts to persuade U.S. soldiers on rest and relaxation (R & R) in Japan to desert from their unpopular military service and fighting in South Vietnam." Colonel Yuri I. Modin..."I want to respond to the United States as an enemy. No difficulty at all, but it took some time. In the dark days of the Cold War, about the only cooperation between each country's spies was not to kill each other. Intelligence services existed and they will continue to exist. All nations intelligence services look at each other's activities with suspicion. But the time has come when we can quite realistically hope for an end to covert actions." This appears to be the case with discovered Russian intelligence collection operations in the United States over a period of three years (2009 to 2012), including the Cold War Soviet spy techniques of using outdoor information drops, later going back for recruited agents to pick up money. Vigilance goes on to protect America's secrets, more threatened now by Communist Chinese cyber-hacking and old-fashioned KGB spying techniques. The current threat to the United States continues (In July of 2015 the Communist Chinese were found to have completed a cyber-attack into the Department of Defense's data system containing sensitive information on military, federal and family information for those who had security clearances). The following comment made in 1993 by Colonel Modin is very revealing in 2012. Modin..."I do not think American corporations need to worry excessively about industrial espionage because of their own defensive security measures. But as companies pursue joint ventures in Russia, you maybe can share your secrets with your friends in Moscow." Spying activities continues and security is even more critical given the spiraling growth and use of computers. We use passwords, lockouts, security programs, and on-line security companies to protect our computers. We shred all documents but it only takes one's corporation a momentary lapse to compromise thousands of people's personal security. The same for federal and military security. One person's secrets are any other person's target to be collected. No one seems to take responsibility and lapses in security go unpunished. [112]

---

[112] The author was a career strategic intelligence officer with the United States Air Force from 1970 to 1992, serving with the former Strategic Air Command, Defense Intelligence Agency, Pacific Air Forces and other intelligence organizations. In 1993, the author attended lectures by four retired former Soviet intelligence officers touring the United States for five weeks.

South Dakota National Guard

Spencer Tornado of May 30, 1998

ON May 30, 1998, the most destructive and the second deadly in the history of South Dakota, struck Spencer, South Dakota. The 1998 Spencer tornado required the guard to provide search and rescue, and many other support activities. [113]

---

[113] Lt. Col. George A. Larson, USAF (Ret.), "South Dakota National Guard, Spencer Tornado of May 30, 1998." Visit to Camp Rapid, The South Dakota National Guard's open house to celebrate the National Guard's 150 years of service," display set up in the Headquarters Lobby, "2012: Countdown to Withdrawal," June 9, 2012.

South Dakota National Guard

Oglala Tornado of 1999

A twister tore through the Pine Indian reservation overnight in June 1999. Governor Bill Janklow and the South Dakota National Guard personnel deployed to Oglala to assess the damage and assist in clean-up operations. Guard members brought in a clean water drinking tanker truck for Pine Ridge residents to pick up water. Guard troops also assisted in search and rescue operations throughout the reservation. [114]

---

[114] Lt. Col. George A. Larson, USAF (Ret.), "South Dakota National Guard, Oglala Tornado of 1999." Visit to Camp Rapid, The South Dakota National Guard's open house to celebrate the National Guard's 150 years of service," display set up in the Headquarters Lobby, "2012: Countdown to Withdrawal," June 9, 2012.

South Dakota Veterans War Memorial

Pierre, South Dakota

IN March 2000, South Dakota Governor William J. Janklow announced that the State of South Dakota would build a World War II memorial to honor past and present South Dakota residents who contributed to winning the war. The memorial was dedicated on Saturday September 15, 2001. The memorial consists of six bronze, full-size figures representing the branches of the U.S. Armed Forces. They are portrayed as warriors in battle, not on parade, appearing as everyday combat troops. Each figure is lighted at night, creating a dramatic effect. The figures are set on a man-made peninsula jutting out into Capital lake. They face the Korean and Vietnam War memorials on the north shore, separated by steps and a fountain. The bronze figures range in height from six feet to six feet 7-inches, each weighing approximately 2,000 pounds. A South Dakota quarried granite slab is positioned in front of the figures with a simple inscription..."South Dakota World War II warriors: why they fought for flag for country for all of us." These bronze figures represent the branches of the U.S. military service as well as those who volunteered to assist combat troops from South Dakota who participated in fighting during the Second World War.

"U.S. Marines Corps...A tall Marine in a tattered uniform from the jungles of the South Pacific, carrying a slung Browning automatic rifle.

"Woman volunteer...Portrayed as a nurse with medical kit and stethoscope ready to assist the wounded. She represents the Women's Army Corps (WACs), women accepted for volunteer service in the Navy (WAVs) and SPARs (acronym derived from the USMC "Semper Paratas," always ready) for women volunteers in the U.S. Coast Guard.

"Sailor...In his working uniform with bandaged hands from fighting an onboard fire. He also represents those who received the Purple Heart.

"Air pilot...Dressed in flight gear and wearing a parachute, short stub of a cigar lit upon landing. He is armed with a .45 caliber automatic pistol.

"Coast Guard and Merchant Marine...Dressed in foul weather gear on duty in the North Atlantic while on watch for prowling and/or attacking German submarines (U-boats) and on ships transporting war equipment and troops.

"U.S. Army G.I...Depicted as a Native American fighting in the European Theater of Operations, specifically performing duties as a "Code Talker," equipped with open ammunition pouches and a Garand M-1 rifle, held by a sling.

"These sculptures and those of the Korean and Vietnam Memorials were created by Sherri Treeby (art professor at Presentation College and Aberdeen Ventral High School at Aberdeen, South Dakota along with Lee Leuning (Conservation Officer with the South Dakota Department of Game, Fish and Parks on the Missouri River produced sculptures in Pierre, South Dakota.

"The Korean War Memorial features a seven foot tall bronze statue of a Korean War soldier dressed in winter battle clothing. It was dedicated on Saturday September 18, 2004. The memorial portrays a determined U.S. soldier, facing attacking hordes of Communist Chinese troops and extreme cold weather during the battle of the Chosin Reservoir. One hundred twenty five thousand Communist Chinese troops attacked 25,000 U.S. troops and their South Korean supporting troops, inflicting 6,000 casualties. An equal number succumbed to the harsh, bitter cold weather, resulting in severe cases of frostbite. The bronze figure depicts a soldier still fighting, protecting his fallen comrades with their names engraved before him on a marble wall slab. The soldier is low on ammunition, suffering from frostbite, tired and unshaken, but with a look of determination as he completes his mission. Unlike World War II veterans, those who fought and suffered in the Korean War returned home without parades, fanfare or recognition for a job well done. They were not embraced, as those of World War II referred to as "America's Greatest Generation." Korean War veterans fought in what has become known as the "Forgotten War."

The latest addition to South Dakota's tribute to its veterans is the Vietnam War Memorial dedicated on September 15, 2006. The bronze statue of a Vietnam serving soldier balances out its Korean War companion. He also faces a marble slab wall with the names engraved of South Dakotans killed during the Vietnam War. His jungle pack is slung low on his back, wearing a helmet, ammunition belt strung over his neck, knife at the ready, M-16 rifle in his hand, open shirt and sweat towel around his neck. At this time in the Vietnam War, he is not wearing a flak vest later issued as standard combat equipment to protect soldiers from fatal chest and upper torso wounds. The memorial honors those who fought in an unpopular war, fought in the front of world and American television crews, with nightly national newscasts showing the horrors of the ear, death and destruction, generally uncut and unedited for sensationalism. The bronze figure is dramatic, recreating a moment frozen in time on a Southeast Asia battlefield.

During the dedication of the Vietnam War memorial, a bronze statute was unveiled, that of an American eagle. It is dedicated to South Dakota's Native American Indian population as a memorial to their important contributions to the U.S. military and American freedom. The eagle connects the Korean War memorial's wall with the names of those killed from 1950 to 1953, to that of the Vietnam War memorial's wall with the names of those killed in the 10,000 day war in Southeast Asia (1961 to 1975).

The memorials at South Dakota's capital grounds in Pierre are just part state's tribute to its war dead, as well as a lasting remembrance to those who gave the ultimate sacrifice in the defense of America, as well as honoring those who served, fought and lived the statement..."Freedom is not free!" [115]

---

[115] Lt. Col. George A. Larson, USAF (Ret.), "South Dakota Veterans Memorial," article submitted to *Military*, April 2011.

South Dakota National Guard

Jasper, Flagpole and Maitland Fires (2000)

SOUTH Dakota National Guard members were activated to help maintain the Maitland Fire near Spearfish, South Dakota. On the 7,000 acre Flagpole Fire, west of Angostura Reservoir in August, Governor Bill Janklow ordered 17 South Dakota National Guard bulldozers to respond to the fire. The Jasper Fire later burned more than 84,000 acres in the southern Black Hills west of Custer, making it the biggest ever in the Black Hills. The National Guard also played a significant role in providing helicopter and heavy equipment support by 250 soldiers and airmen to fight these fires as if deployed into a combat zone. The enemy was the raging fires threatening homes and property in the Black Hills. [116]

---

[116] Lt. Col. George A. Larson, USAF (Ret.), "South Dakota National Guard, Jasper, Flagpole and Maitland Fires (2000)." Visit to Camp Rapid, The South Dakota National Guard's open house to celebrate the National Guard's 150 years of service," display set up in the Headquarters Lobby, "2012: Countdown to Withdrawal," June 9, 2012.

South Dakota National Guard

"Operation ENDURING FREEDOM" Afghanistan

FOLLOWING the attack on the United States by terrorism on September 11, 2001, America began to prepare, and implement operations against world terrorism. President George W. Bush set in motion the largest call up of military forces since World War II. The South Dakota National Guard mobilized and deployed more than 3,500 citizen soldiers to support this great nation. These deployments became known and referred to as "Operation NOBLE EAGLE," "Operation IRAQI FREEDOM," and "Operation ENDURING FREEDOM." Nearly 1,000 soldiers and airmen deployed from South Dakota in support of "Operation ENDURING FREEDOM." SDNG units served in a variety of roles. Units like the 211th Engineers (support) performing route clearance operations to higher headquarter units like the 196th Maneuver Enhancement Brigade acting as installation manager. On May 1, 2011, President Barrack Obama announced the death of Osama Bin Laden, leader of Al Qaeda. President Obama said bringing him to justice was a huge step toward closure for Americans remember the 911 attack on the United States homeland and deaths of thousands of Americans. President Obama also made it clear this was not the goal. The Taliban regime fell after Bin Laden's death. The Afghan military force continues to grow stronger and more independent moving American troops closer to returning stateside. President Obama plans to gradually withdraw forces through 2014 as the Afghan military forces take on more responsibilities to protect their own country and combat Al Qaeda attacks. [117]

---

[117] Lt. Col George A. Larson, USAF (Ret.), "South Dakota National Guard, Operation ENDURING FREEDOM Afghanistan." Visit to Camp Rapid, The South Dakota National Guard's open house to celebrate the National Guard's 150 years of service," display set up in the Headquarters Lobby, "2012: Countdown to Withdrawal," June 9, 2012.

South Dakota National Guard

"Operation IRAQI FREEDOM"

THE beginning phases of the "War on Terrorism," thirteen South Dakota National Guard units mobilized and deployed to various locations. Their time on active duty varied from six months to eighteen months. Some of the units were involved in the initial push from Kuwait into Iraq and Bagdad. Their missions, including transporting supplies, ammunition, equipment, building bridges, airport and base camp construction, and security. Units who deployed to Kuwait and Iraq were the 722nd, 744th and 1742nd Transport Companies, 109th Engineer Battalion, Company B 109th Medical Battalion, 204th and 842nd Engineer Companies, and the 114th Civil Engineering Squadron of the South Dakota Air National Guard. The units not deployed overseas provided security and training of troops at Stateside locations were the 235th Military Police Company at Fort Carson, Colorado; Mobile Public Affairs Detachment at Fort Riley, Kansas; 1st Battalion/147th Field Artillery at Fort Sill, Oklahoma; Battery C, 2nd/147th Battalion Field Artillery at Fort Campbell, Kentucky; 196th Regimental/Training Institute at Fort Sill, Oklahoma and Fort Bragg, North Carolina. Detachment 3, Company E; 238th Aviation Detachment 3; Company A 249th Aviation were mobilized to Iraq for air support missions transporting personnel and supplies. 1st Battalion, 147th Field Artillery was mobilized to support security operations.[118]

---

[118] Lt. Col George A. Larson, USAF (Ret.), "South Dakota National Guard, Operation ENDURING FREEDOM Afghanistan." Visit to Camp Rapid, The South Dakota National Guard's open house to celebrate the National Guard's 150 years of service," display set up in the Headquarters Lobby, "2012: Countdown to Withdrawal," June 9, 2012.

South Dakota National Guard

"Operation NOBLE EAGLE"

OPERATION NOBLE EAGLE" is the name given to military operations related to "homeland security" and support to federal, state and local agencies. The ongoing operation began September 14, 2001, in response to the September 11, 2001 terrorist attacks on the United States. "Operation NOBLE EAGLE" began with the mobilization of the arsenals of the national guard and reserve personnel to perform security missions or protect military installations, civil airports and potential soft targets such as bridges, power plants and critical unloading facilities at major ports. These reservists were called to active duty under a mobilization authority known as "partial mobilization." The 665th Maintenance Company mobilized in South Dakota to support security operations at Ellsworth Air Force Base at Rapid City and Joe Foss Field at Sioux Falls (home of the South Dakota Air National Guard). Detachment 3 was primary responsible for security operations while the rest of the company conducted similar operations at the National Guard Training Camp. [119]

---

[119] Lt. Col George A. Larson, USAF (Ret.), "South Dakota National Guard, Operation NOBLE EAGLE." Visit to Camp Rapid, The South Dakota National Guard's open house to celebrate the National Guard's 150 years of service," display set up in the Headquarters Lobby, "2012: Countdown to Withdrawal," June 9, 2012.

South Dakota National Guard

"Operation ENDURING FREEDOM" Afghanistan

The War in Southwest Asia

ONE month after the traumatic attacks on September 11, 2001, President George W. Bush declared war on the Taliban and Al Qaeda forces in Afghanistan. President Bush outlined his vision for how the United States would counter-attack terrorism..." We have suffered great loss, in our grief and anger, we have found our mission and our moment. Americans' should not expect one battle but a lengthy campaign unlike any other we have seen (This continues on in 2015 and the war against ISIS can possible go on for 10-15 years." South Dakota National Guard members felt the first large scale effect of the war in 2004, and the first SDNG unit deployed overseas in support of "Operation Enduring Freedom Afghanistan." More than 75 soldiers of the 109th Engineer Group served as a nine-month tour. Since that time, nearly 1,000 soldiers and airmen have deployed from South Dakota. State Command Sgt. Major Larry Zimmerman, SDNG..."These deployments have given us the edge for unit readiness. We learn to shoot, move and communicate at optimum levels. Our citizen soldiers bring personal experiences to the flight. City business managers, lawyers, farmers, construction workers, all of those trades bring additional skills to the typical warrior tasks." SDNG units deployed to Afghanistan have served a variety of rolls from units like the 211th Engineers (sapper) performing routine clearance operations to higher headquarters units like the 196th Maneuver Enhancement Brigade (MEB) acting as installation management and logistical support. The impact South Dakota service members have made throughout the conflict weaver through the entire U.S. operation in Afghanistan. The National Guard is no longer a strategic reserve to the active component as the war clearly proves. National Guard troops form an operational force directly integrated into active duty deployments and missions. SSgt. Rebecca Linder, 196th MEB..."My recruiter told me there was a definite possibility of deployment when I enlisted in 2005. That didn't stop me. I was more than willing to serve my country and go overseas."

On May 1, 2011, President Barrack Obama announced to the world that an operation carried out by American forces lead to the death of Osama bin Laden, leader of Al Qaeda…"Over the last ten years, thanks to the tireless and heroic work of our military and our counter terrorism professionals we've made great strides in that effort. Bringing Bin Laden to justice was a huge step for justice for the September 11th attacks. Bin Laden's death did not end the U.S. mission. There is no doubt at Al Qaeda will continue to pursue attacks on us. We must, and we will, remain vigilant at home and abroad."

The effort of American troops helped the Afghan people break free from the grip of the terrorists controlling their country. As the influence of Al Qaeda faded from Afghanistan and the Taliban Regime fell, the mission for U.S. forces changed direction. Now the Force Military Protection members have priorities to help train and educate the Afghanistan forces and citizens. SSgt. Adam Hermann, deployed with the South Dakota Embedded Training Team in 2008…"It was rewarding to work side by side with the Afghans. In order for our mission to be successful we need to have them the soldiering skills to one day operate on their own." [120]

---

[120] Lt. Col George A. Larson, USAF (Ret.), "South Dakota National Guard, Operation ENDURING FREEDOM Afghanistan" to War in Southwest Asia. Visit to Camp Rapid, The South Dakota National Guard's open house to celebrate the National Guard's 150 years of service," display set up in the Headquarters Lobby, "2012: Countdown to Withdrawal," June 9, 2012.

South Dakota National Guard Goes to War to Protect America

March 19, 2003

ON March 19, 2003, President George W. Bush addressed the nation with the words that would impact the lives of many soldiers and airmen in the South Dakota National Guard..."My fellow citizens, at this hour, American and Coalition forces are in the early stages of military operations to disarm Iraq, to free its people and to defend the world from grave danger." Since President Bush addressed the Nation, 30 communities and more than 3,360 citizen soldiers and airmen throughout South Dakota have experienced a unit mobilization in support of "Operation IRAQI FREEDOM and "Operation NEW DAWN." The U.S. military and Coalition forces have now withdrawn from Iraq. The last two units to support the war in Iraq were Company C, 1st Battalion, 189th Aviation Regiment of Rapid City and the 139th Brigade Support Battalion of Brookings. These units deployed to Iraq in 2011, then moved to Kuwait. They were part of the historic withdrawal process from Iraq and finished their deployments conducting follow on missions of retrograde operations, including the transfer of personnel and equipment from the Iraq Theater of Operations back to the United States.

"It's a good feeling for us to be finally out of Iraq," said Major General Tim Reisch, Adjutant General of the SDNG. "This war has gone on a long time." The Iraq war is the second longest in American history. It is also said to have changed the National Guard from a strategic reserve to an operational force. We went from "on the bench" component during the Vietnam and Cold War eras, to one that has served in combat zones continually for the past decade. There are few, of instances during our 150 year history that the South Dakota National Guard has been relied to the extent that it has been during that period since 911. Reisch..."Virtually every unit deployed from the SDNG has received the Meritorious Unit Commendation Award." The award is given to units for exceptionally meritorious conduct in performance of outstanding service for at least six continuous months during the period of military operations against an armed enemy. Reisch..."Our soldiers and airmen are of truly the highest caliber. The tremendous legacy of the South Dakota National Guard has been elevated even higher during this period of time."

While more than 3,360 soldiers and airmen and their family members made significant sacrifices to the Iraq War, seven SDNG soldiers made the ultimate sacrifice and lost their lives while serving in Iraq. "We have had enormous sacrifices from our South Dakota National Guard soldiers," said Lt. Colonel Lynn Wilson, full time Support Chaplain for the SDNG. "I have gone to homes as a Casualty Notification Officer and have gone to families to bring the news that loved one, their son, their soldier is now dead, and that news is absolutely devastating. So is the cost of war, it is always severe, it is always great." Lt. Col. Wilson deployed to Iraq in 2004, with the 2nd Battalion, 147th Field Artillery, as a Chaplain where he not only experienced the devastation and cost of war but also witnessed the positive effects. Wilson..."I think the accomplishments as well as the loss, and the losses are terrible and severe. I don't think you ever get over it. It is still a scar and it is deep, but then there are the accomplishments that we gave to a country. Wilson..."I went to Babylon, to one of Saddam's places. They would take teenage girls, and rape them, murder them and toss their bodies down the Euphrates River. We stopped that...that didn't go on after we were there." During Lt. Col. Wilson's time overseas, he also witnessed a defying moment in Iraq's history. For the first time, they had more than one option on their election ballot. [121]

---

[121] Lt. Col George A. Larson, USAF (Ret.), "South Dakota National Guard Goes to War to Protect America, March 19, 2003." Visit to Camp Rapid, The South Dakota National Guard's open house to celebrate the National Guard's 150 years of service," display wet up in the Headquarters Lobby, "2003: South Dakota National Guard goes to War," June 9, 2012.

Major Bob Liebman

B-1B Weapons Officer

Combat in Southwest Asia, 28th Bomb Wing Ellsworth Air Force Base

MAJOR Bob Liebman... "In Southwest Asia, B-1Bs were stationed at undisclosed locations so the host countries would have plausible deniability the bombers were stationed on their home soil. B-1B crews flew 10 to 16 hour combat missions. Evening during the Iraq War, B-1Bs flew missions over Afghanistan. This was a coordinated effort between aircrews, maintenance and munitions personnel to keep the bombers mission ready and airborne. There could be up to eight to 10 B-1Bs airborne. For instance, for operations into Iraq and Afghanistan (one grouping for each country of operation).

"One B-1B prepared to take-off for its in-country mission.

"One B-1B entered the country to transit to its assigned patrol area.

"One B-1B orbited over its assigned patrol area.

"One B-1B exited the country on its return flight back to its home base.

"There has been a great political debate over the existence of "Weapons of Mass Destruction" (WMD), primarily chemical weapons. Troops on the ground found FROG-7 (Free Rocket Over Ground) ground to ground tactical missiles, which appeared to be equipped with chemical warheads (as documented in an *Aviation Week and Space Technology* photograph). No warheads but before and after the Coalition attack, large convoys of trucks moved north, out of Iraq into Syria, possibly Iran. They were possibly carrying out WMDs from Iraq. This was of great concern to President George W. Bush and one of the reasons given for the invasion of Iraq, as well as removing terrorist training facilities in that country. B-1B attacks destroyed the Salman Pak terrorist training camp outside Bagdad. Overhead photography showed a derelict Russian passenger jet in the camp, with its wings blown off. I suspect the wings were cut off to enable easier to transport the airframe to the middle of their training facility. It's in the middle of a field, a Tupolev airliner. The camp was also a probable source of equipment and funds for terrorists. In my opinion, Saddam was probably more of a regional terrorist enabler and facilitator, rather than an operational leader.

"B-1Bs in Southwest Asia had a multitude of roles. This includes non-technical intelligence surveillance and SCUD hunting. MTISR stands for Non-Traditional IRR; non-traditional for bombers I suppose, but bombers did do some of this stuff in the Pacific in World War II and Korea; interdiction and strategic strikes; time sensitive targets (TST/dynamic targets); close air support (CAS). B-1Bs and other Coalition aircraft were striking Bagdad even as the ground offensive started. It took the Coalition forces about two weeks to get to Bagdad. B-1Bs traveled at high-speed, working on TST as directed. A B-1B from Ellsworth took out Saddam Hussein's staff early on in the war on April 7, 2003. This was described in an article in *Time Magazine* as 'The Hit.' We believed we might have taken out Saddam, until he reappeared later. The Saddam strike took only 12 minutes. We were referred to the strike area by ground commanders. I believe the CENTCOM Air Commander/CENTAF, Lt. General Michael Mosley said this 'His headquarters was the CAOC.'

"When hunting SCUDs, B-1Bs patrolled specific areas of Iraq. The aircraft's Doppler radar assisted the crew in locating ground targets. Before a crew released a weapon, it required positive identification so as not to hit friendly forces. Even when receiving targeting information from forward ground controllers, the crew carefully plotted and determined where the bombs would fall, sometimes preventing accidental friendly fire casualties. B-1Bs conducted interdiction and strategic strikes to block or reduce the flow of supplies from rear depot areas to front line troops. Strikes were conducted against Iraqi command and control centers, attacked concentrations of ground forces and support infrastructure. After the first day of air strikes, B-1Bs only had one pre-programmed target. Normal airborne operating procedures were to strike targets on the ground by information passed in flight. While airborne, retargeting was through communications with the ground control network. The real time, in flight re-planning was mostly accomplished by the aircrews in the jet, an important point in a world where some would trust everything to remotely controlled vehicles. We had airborne WACs for de-confliction as well as direction by the Combined Air Operations Center. CAS information also came from ground controllers to the Command and Control Center/AWACS. IF nothing happened, if TST or CAS were not tasked, then there was a specific default target set for the B-1B to strike. Again, real time targets took priority.

"B-1B crews in Southwest Asia followed a dynamic targeting procedure, using satellite radio communications, Combat Track II along a well-practiced command structure. B-1Bs also completed Collateral Damage Evaluation, CDE-as defined by Rules of Engagement, which was also part of Battle Damage Assessment (BDA). During CAS operations, challenges to minimize collateral damage because of geo-political impact and significance. This is the fundamental reason we have ROEs, in addition to protecting the good guys. During the air war, everyone at one time or another wanted to improve authority over selection of targets and release of weapons. 'Everyone' may be too general, but the spirit of this comment is probably close to the mark, as an aircrew perception, anyway. This impact was reduced or eliminated, somewhat mitigated, by a series of weapons and tactics conferences with all parties involved ons striking targets to prevent delays in effective employment of advanced weapons. Interestingly, this process has again slipped back to the restrictions on targets, referred to as ROE. It was heavily tilted toward geo-political implications and significance, especially as developed in Afghanistan as of the summer of 2010. The term ROE has been in use to define these constraints and procedures from the beginning of "Operation IRAQI FREEDOM" and "Operation ENDURING FREEDOM." CENTCOM drafts, promulgates, evaluates and updates the theater ROEs continuously. I suspect that the level of external interference on their execution goes through seasons defined by the current political environment, directives and sensitivities."

Major Liebman, from June to December 2007, served a combat duty tour on the ground with the U.S. Army in Afghanistan..."Before that, I had three OIF and OEF flying deployments between 2003 to 2004, to include 40 combat missions in the B-1B, plus a brief stint-supporting mission planning and ATO production at the CAOC. As an Electronics Warfare Officer (EWO), assigned to Afghanistan to assist the U.S. Army in country with Improvised Explosive Devices (IEDs). These Air Force deployments in support of the U.S. Army were called ILO by the Pentagon, deployed in lieu of Army resources. These are particularly nasty weapons, designed to kill U.S. troops and independent Afghanistan truck drivers who supply goods and services to isolated villages throughout the country. After the end of the Cold War, the U.S. Army reduced (cut) its combat electronic warfare capabilities. The Army was not equipped or manned to do the job on the new explosive dangers found in Afghanistan. We assisted and eventually (at the time of this material) the U.S. Army will rebuild its EW capabilities. I was at a Forward Operating Base (FOB) at Sharana, Afghanistan. Sharana was a base, originally built and occupied by Russian Army troops during their occupation of Afghanistan. It was upgraded and enlarged by U.S. Forces. I was to assist in countering the IED threat, part of Joint Task Force Paladin. I worked with the U.S. Army 36th Engineer Brigade on the base. One of their many missions in Afghanistan included the Route Clearance Package (RCP) Team who hunted for, located and removed or destroyed IEDs. Air Force Explosive Ordnance Disposal (EOD) personnel assisted Army personnel in the dangerous IED removal operations. There was a fleet of specially designed and constructed vehicles to complete the dangerous mission such as the Joint EOD Rapid Response Vehicle. The terrain is rugged in country with high mountains down to narrow low-valley terrain. Many tribal villages in some of these isolated and remote areas date back to the time of Alexander the Great.

"The Taliban's region of terror is less of a local issue, but more of one from refugees, previously living in Afghanistan and escaped to Pakistan during the Russian occupation and brutal attacks by the Russian Army. They operate somewhere out of the rugged mountains of the Pakistan/Afghanistan border area. This is a fertile area for Taliban recruitment, assisted by Moslem clerical schools which spread the Jihadist philosophy for those who transit into and fight in Afghanistan. The Pakistani government is the key U.S. ally in the area and faces the turmoil of the Taliban in their country, which also impacts political and military outplay with India. The situation is even more intense because both countries are equipped with nuclear warheads and missiles to deliver them. Much of the equipment and weapons used by the Taliban appear to be provided by external sources, to include that provided from the People's Liberation Army (PLA). Al Qaeda is part of this too, but I'm not sure how." [122]

---

[122] Major Bob Liebman, to author, USAF (Ret.), December 16, 2010.

Senior Airman James Pyeatt

28th Munitions Squadron
B-1Bs in Southwest Asia
Ellsworth Air Force Base

SENIOR Airman James Pyeatt..."Our days in Southwest Asia to support B-1Bs are very important. We first load the munitions trailer, check the munitions to be certain they are secured for transport, slowly pulled to the flight line. The munitions are delivered to a specific aircraft depending on the mission load requirements. The bomb load is determined by that day's combat sorties. We do not know that information until we get to the flight line. This changes from one sortie to the next. This is usually a mix of conventional precision guided munitions. We will also load counter-measures for the specific mission to be flown. Weapons are now at the aircraft. The loader takes over to correctly configure the munitions in the bombs bays. The loader signs for the munitions. The expediter at the aircraft handles all the required paperwork to direct which munitions goes to what aircraft. I also collect any unused munitions from aircraft, which completed a mission if not retained on the aircraft. Once the loaders place the munitions, the expediter makes sure the bombs are properly positioned and ready for operational release. The cycle is repeated throughout the day as required. During a 24 hour cycle, our munitions personnel normally handle four to six sorties per day. I worked the 12 midnight to 12 noon, from January to July 2007. During this time period, our squadron never had or encountered any problems with the sophisticated, precision guided munitions. But, it was the aircraft's crew chief who make sure the bomber was ready to launch for that day's mission." [123]

---

[123] Senior Airmen James Pyeatt, 28th Bomb Wing, 28th Munitions Squadron, interview, Ellsworth Air Force Base, author, July 15, 2008.

SSgt. Ryan Walker

34th Maintenance Squadron, 28th Bomb Wing
B-1Bs in Southwest Asia
Ellsworth Air Force Base

SSGT. Ryan Walker..."From wakeup to recovery, my day is full. I like to get up early, go to the gym, eat, head for the bus stop to go to work. Others I worked with just barely got out of bed and headed straight for the bus. Once to the work area, I checked out my normal tool set, wait for that day's aircraft work schedule. On my aircraft, I may have to take with me additional tools, which I sign for at the tool desk. A bread truck (a large van) drives us to my aircraft on the flight line, drops us off at the aircraft. I do a pre-flight and depending on the situation, complete either a generic flight check or possibly heavy maintenance as required. This varies on the aircraft from day to day. Every day is different, so then you've gotten all that accomplished and your jet (B-1B) is ready for the crew (ERED), so you wait there, get your jet pinned and wait for the crew to show up. They get there and you brief them on any current maintenance that has occurred on that jet so if it happens to reoccur, they will be ready for it. You do your walk around with the crew and then they tell you are good to go. You hand over the jet and you operate the headsets to the crew inside the aircraft until they clear you off and they taxi put to the main runway.

"There is a whole slew of things that can go wrong on a launch with no indicated 'Red Balls' (write-ups) or many, it just depends and the crew will try and help you work through them and get the jet fixed so it will be ready to be launched. An average launch could take an hour or four. So you launch the jet and they take their sorties, usually 12 hours and if it didn't catch the jet you launched, the other shift would do it in that time. You would do other maintenance that needed to be done as a crew chief. You seldom had any dead time while at work. You always strived for a 100 percent FMC rate. That way, if anything were to pop off, we were always ready and that is a day deployed at work in Southwest Asia.

"There are always difficulties, which require attention to be fixed each day. Everything that breaks on the aircraft over there you don't expect to break and we don't have it in the kit or all the jets have gone through that same item and depleted the kit. It always seemed that what we needed, for some reason, we just didn't have. The work is conducted in unforgiving heat. Sometimes the workload can get to the people or the fact that you're away from your family or the constant 12 hour shifts. Those things can wear on a person making their willingness to work less and that makes it hard on that person and everyone else because you have someone not pulling their weight and this is a commitment from a person who has been to the island of Diego Garcia. Living a life like that has many restrictions during a six-month combat tour. I've been to Iraq and I've seen how everyone had to dress off work. But, I think that if you can run around in swim shorts and whatever shirt you want within taste kind of helps you feel that you're away from work and gives you peace of mind. Just the small things over there makes life better.

"I did not see or feel there were too many personal hardships when deployed to Southwest Asia. Personally, if I am pushed then I can push right back. I will make sure my work is good. Some people may work faster and miss things to keep up with the pace. The potential is there for that to happen. There is a constant pressure on everyone there to get the work done fast because the ground pounders rely on us, just as badly as our jets need us.

"My family takes it differently every time I go overseas. I go to Iraq in the heat of battle no matter how many times I tell them I'm not. Always think I am so obvious they worry. My wife knows the situation and takes it well, but still hates it. When we talk, we seldom have much to say. She will talk about her day and life that is going just as it was when I left, minus me! I will say, well I launched a jet, worked on a jet, went to the gym, went to sleep, just like I did last week when she called and the week before. For me, that's the worse because I never have much to say so she takes that the hardest when I don't chat with her." [124]

---

[124] SSgt. Ryan Walker, 28th Bomb Wing, 34th Maintenance Squadron, interview, Ellsworth Air Force Base, author, July 15, 2008.

Major Brian (Sea Bass) Witkowsky

34th Bomb Squadron, 28th Bomb Wing
B-1Bs in Southwest Asia
Ellsworth Air Force Base

MAJOR Brian Witkowsky..."A typical mission during a stateside training week is as follows. We will have a formal briefing for the entire squadron where we will get a chance to get caught up on current or pressing matters that can be accomplished at a Group level. At that point, we will go to our vault area to execute our mission. We usually mission plan one day and fly the next. During mission planning, we do initial coordination where we determine the scenario; take inputs from intelligence (real or training scenario), objects for the day or mission. The rest of the day is pretty well set for the mission. In case of close air support mission, you are trying to contact Joint Tactical Air Controller (JTAC) or get intelligence on the area of operations or imagery, maps or charts and all those types of things at some point complete an attack meeting on which you are trying to do. Weaponeer specific targets, what kind of fusing to mate to the weapon. The end of the day concludes with a formal mission briefing, the mission lead will conduct the briefing, review all the objects, scenarios and how the mission is to be tactically executed.

"The next day you show up for the mission at the step desk. That is where the squadron supervisor provides weather briefing guidance for the mission, information on what aircraft you will be flying. You get to the aircraft about one hour prior to take off and execute a mission. For missions around South Dakota, about an hour in a military operating area, 50 percent at low-level and 50 percent at high-altitude. For a close air support sorties (CASS), we do such things as a show of force at low-altitude, non-kinetic engagements against a potential enemy or hostile force. We also try to get air refueling in and then come home to do some practice approaches at Ellsworth AFB's runway. Once landed, you begin a mission debrief.

"In Southwest Asia, take off was similar to mission planning as back at Ellsworth. A mission-planning cell does most of that planning for us. We step to the jet where we have pre-flight crews. Enroute depends on what theater we are going to and at what point we prepare the aircraft, get the radio set up, make sure our computers are all set up the way we like it to be, make sure the aircraft systems are top notch. Once we are in country, we have to check in with the command and control element there. They will either provide us with a new tasking or continue with the current mission. In theater, we are there to provide 'over-watch' for those ground forces and again a typical tasking may not require the release of weapons. The JTAC will be contacted to give them an update on our status. Then we get an update on the ground situation. Once we do that if there are no troops in contact, no hostile action or situation, they will usually give us information on a specific area in the country to familiarize us with that area. If there is a troop contact situation the command and control element can move us to any area of operations there and we go support from there. We check in with JTAC. This will be a little more expeditious. JTAC will give us a close air support brief, tell us what the target is, location, elevation, and nearest friendly troop elements. At that point, our weapons system officer uses his radar to get a picture of that area based on the coordinates of that area and with the JTAC talking to the Weapons System Officer and then we will reconfirm that target. The Defense System Officer works his laptop computer and imagery. We try to minimize kill time over the target. Once the target us located, confirmed by the crew and personnel on the ground, at that point, the JTAC will give us clearance and the aircraft will turn into the target and we will release our weapons. If at that point the desired result is not met, there is an option for a re-attack. Also, we fly non-kinetic to include show of force. Those would be used in situations, maybe where the enemy's location is not precise where we can let them know there is a B-1B on station. When we go low and fast, we get their attention.

"Any mission where you can provide that support to those guys who needs it. We are like on call airborne artillery. Especially in a lot of those areas you cannot get in artillery due to the elevation. We can help those guys and you can hear the relief in their voices even if you do not release weapons. This always means a lot. JTAC personnel will often come up to us when we area at our base and tell us how much they appreciate our mission. There have been specific missions when you could hear gunfire in the background over the radio and when you provide that support and you achieve the effects that gut is looking for. When you hear the gunfire stop you can hear the relief in their voices.

"A lot of guys, including me, did a tour on the ground as an air liaison officer. There have been eight-to-ten officers from the squadron who served as an air liaison officer and that experience working with the ground commander helps us understand what is going on and share with other members of the squadron, opened their eyes to what is going on, especially on the ground. Up in the sky you sort of get a displacement as to what is going on. There was one time when we were flying around we were the only asset available to the ground commander. It was a support for the troops. Working as a team, this is important.

"Even if the guy on the ground is not actually hostile combatants, just to hear their voice and relationship is unique. Everyone has everyone else's back. Away from combat, our life has gotten a whole lot better with access to the internet, phone calls home, sending photographs, and with squadron support my family is well cared for, even from our sister squadron, the 37th BS. We take care of our deployed members' families." [125]

---

[125] Major Brian Witkowsky, 28th Bomb Wing, 34th Bomb Squadron, interview, Ellsworth Air Force Base, author, July 15, 2008.

Lieutenant Colonel Lucien Case

Chief of Plans, 28th Bomb Wing, Operations Group Ellsworth Air Force Base

LT. Col. Lucien Case..."The sniper pod for the B-1B is another sensor we can use to improve our accuracy and improve the timeliness of a strike we are performing in support of our ground forces (July 2008.). Ellsworth AFB crewmembers are being trained from the 337th Test and Evaluation Squadron. Other Air Force units are already equipped with the sniper pod, with Ellsworth B-1B equipped by July 2008. The bringing of this technology to B-1Bs has gone more quickly than expected because B-1B program officers were able to configure it with laptop computers on board aircraft rather than having to reprogram it into the bomber's avionics system. They took a three plus year integration program, and reduced it to 15 months. One difference between the Sniper Pod and current B-1B (July 2008) technology is that it can pick up targets that does not show up on the regular B-1B radar. Using the Sniper Pod and its infrared sensors, aircrews can move more easily track targets identified by teams on the ground. That will reduce the chance of friendly collateral damage and increase our chances of finding the target he actually wants us to strike in an accurate manner." [126]

---

[126] Lt. Col. Lucien Case, Chief of Plans, 28th Bomb Wing, Operations Group, interview, author, July 15, 2008.

Major Eric Upton

37th Expeditionary Controller Squadron, 28th Bomb Wing Ellsworth Air Force Base

MAY 2008) Major Eric Upton..."I am about to culminate my one-year tour in Southwest Asia. It was an outstanding year. I want to share with you what I believe to be one of the most significant aspects of our service as airmen. The significance of my tour is not marked by a piece of cloth on my chest or even the work I did while I was here, but by the relationships I forged with fellow airmen in a time of war and the indelible mark their relationships left on my heart. You see, it is relationships that enrich an individual; achievement, bring a team victory and give life meaning. A hallmark of our relationships as airmen is that we take care of one another. From fellow commanders leaning forward offering their support to each other and airmen cooperating in their daily efforts, to friends and family back home sending care packages or words of encouragement and love. I've seen what generates air power, wingmen! Let me give you an excellent example of this relationship making. We bring more than 3,500 active duty, guard and reserve airmen together and swap out an entire wing over a 30 day period. We do this all the while executing the air tasking order, keeping food on our plates, running chapel services, constructing and occupying new facilities, moving cargo north, guarding the perimeter, trans-shipping blood units. Delivering communications theater wide, contracting and paying for every single requirement. We do a remarkable job taking care of each other and never give those feats a second though. How is this possible? All of the above accomplishments and more are made through teamwork, enthusiasm, selfness and trust. An when you test an airmen you get an 'A' for air power every time. We can bring sword or shield at a moment's notice. It's truly impressive and it's marked by our individual nature coupled with the organized and disciplined manner with which we carry out our daily missions.

"We can is the attitude of the day around here. Airmen are self-reliant, expected to figure it out. Here, airmen participate in morale teams and community service and have a sense of urgency in getting materials and services delivered to form the nucleus of sortie generation. They do it, knowing other airmen are counting on them. Wingmen at each echelon, non-commissioned officers, senior NCOs, officers and civilians all mentor through action, encouragement and good, old-fashioned hard work. We have a big job to do and we know no one else can do it. Our friends and family back home are counting on us. The support we receive through their gifts, prayers and words remind us that we have to keep them flying, get the bombs on target and endure a grueling sustained effort to achieve victory.

"My experience here over the past year taught me a lot, but I will reflect most often on the mark. Airmen here and those back home make every day special. See airmen lending hands to make work manageable, excluding positive attitudes, putting others first and relying on each other to get the job done right makes my heart happy. We are friends, family and fellow fighters. Wingmen make me so proud, I sing our Air Force song as loudly and proudly as I can each chance I get! I am absolutely convinced as long as there are wingmen, there will be airmen, and as long as there are airmen, there will be the United States of America." [127]

---

[127] Major Eric Upton, "A is for airpower," Ellsworth Air Force Base, 28th Bomb Wing Public Affairs, May 2008.

South Dakota Army National Guard in Afghanistan

Lt. Col. John P. Weber, Commander
South Dakota Embedded Training Team
January 2008

LIEUTENANT Colonel John Weber was born on September 13, 1968, in Honolulu, Hawaii. He is a graduate of Ethan High School in Ethan, South Dakota. He earned a Bachelor of Science in Geography and Education in 1991 from South Dakota State University. Lt. Col. Weber enlisted in the South Dakota National Guard in 1986, as a member of Alpha Battery, 1st Battalion, 147th Field Artillery as a 13B Cannon Crewmen in Mitchell, South Dakota. Lt. Col. Weber served in Alpha Battery until at which time he attended officer Candidate School and was commissioned as a Second Lieutenant in 1990. Lt. Col. Weber later attended the Field Artillery Basic Course at Fort Sill, Oklahoma in 1991. Lt. Col. Weber has served 1st Battalion in many staff positions such as Targeting Officer, Battalion Fire Direction Officer and S-4. He also held the Battery positions of Fire Direction Officer, Executive Officer and from 1997 to 2000, as Commander of Charlie Battery in Yankton, South Dakota where he led the unit through the M270 MLRS transition and certification. Lt. Col. Weber has also served as the Battery Commander of HHB 147th FA Brigade. Later he served as Brigade Liaison Officer and the Brigade S4. Lt. Col. Weber first came to the South Dakota National Guard to work full-time as ADSW in 1999. Then he worked as the Drug Demand Reduction Administrator for the South Dakota National Guard in Rapid City, South Dakota. At that time, Lt. Col. Weber was instrumental in the development of the in-school substance abuse prevention program for Counter-Drug.

In 2003, Lt. Col. Weber moved over to the Recruiting and Retention Command after being hired on AGR as the Executive Officer/Operations and Training Officer for Recruiting. Among his many duties, he was responsible for the development of the State of South Dakota's first ever Recruit Sustainment Program. There he served as the Operations and Training Officer until July 2005, when he was selected as the Battalion Commander for the Recruiting and Retention Battalion. Lt. Col. Weber served as the Battalion Commander until January 2008. As the recruiting and Retention Battalion Commander, the South Dakota Army National Guard posted the highest recruiting numbers in 15 years with over 1,100 accessions, which is one third of the current strength of the Army National Guard. South Dakota also consistently ranked number one nationally in recruiting measures during his tenure.

In January 2008, Lt. Col. Weber deployed to Afghanistan as the Commander of the South Dakota Embedded Training Team. Upon his arrival he was subsequently assigned as the Commander of Forward Operating Base Konduz in Afghanistan. During this deployment, Lt. Col. Weber commanded Four Mentor teams and FOB Konduz, which housed U.S. and Coalition Forces. Lt. Col. Weber's teams had the responsibility to train and mentor Afghan Army and Police Forces in both Konduz and Baghlan Provinces. Upon return from Afghanistan, Lt. Col. Weber was assigned as the Commander of 1st Battalion, 196th RTI, which is the Officer Candidate School (OCS) Battalion for the Western Region of the United States. Under his command, Lt. Col. Weber had the responsibility for training Officer Candidates from all over the United States to become Army Officer. Lt. Col. Weber also had training oversight for 13 states and one territory. During his Command, the South Dakota OCS Battalion received its accreditation evaluation from the Active Duty Proponent School out of Fort Benning, Georgia. As a result of that evaluation, the South Dakota OCS Battalion was rated a "Learning Institute of Excellence" which is the highest rating that can be received. This is also the first time ever that any battalion from across the country had achieved that level of rating.

(2012) Lt. Col. Weber worked as the full-time Deputy Directorate of Plans (J5) for the South Dakota National Guard. In his job, he has responsibility for the State Partnership Program, the National Guard State Strategic Plan, Army Communities of Excellence, Continuous Process Improvement and Continuity of Operations Plan. Lt. Col. Weber is a graduate of the Field Artillery Officer Basic and Advance Courses, the Combined Arms Staff Services School, Command and General Staff College, the Recruiting and Retention Commanders course, Pre-Command Course, the Human Resources Management

Course and the Military Transition Team Course. [128]

---

[128] Lieutenant Colonel Weber, Rapid City South Dakota to author, July 13, 2012.

South Dakota Air and Space Museum

Berlin Airlift Memorial Dedicated October 3, 2008

RETIRED USAF Lt. Col. Charles Childs, Rapid City, and other surviving members of the Berlin Airlift Association and their families visited the South Dakota Air and Space Museum on October 3, 2008 for a memorial dedication ceremony to celebrate the Berlin Airlift's 60th anniversary. Childs was a Captain during the Berlin Airlift, flying a four-piston engine Douglas C-54 Skymaster military transport..."I flew through the open air corridors over western Berlin, delivering food, coal, blankets, medical supplies and other items necessary to support those in need. The air corridors were so crowded there that simply there was not any room for error or attempt to make a second landing. If you missed your approach, you had to take your load back. I never missed. We had to face problems with Russian military forces, which had control of airfields on either side of the air corridors. Russian military forces would direct and shine powerful spotlights into my C-54's cockpit in an attempt to blind us. They also tried their hand at electronic warfare, interfering with aircrew communications. These actions had the potential to bring the world closer to war than some may have recognized at that time. If any of our planes had been shot down, we would have been in World War III (which possibly would have turned from conventional to nuclear)."

During the Berlin Airlift Lt. Col. Childs and Colonel Hail Halvorson flew many missions into Berlin. During the reunion, these two former Berlin Airlift fliers climbed into a stationary, mechanical lift, raised high over the Douglas High School football field, east of Ellsworth Air Force Base and the South Dakota Air and Space Museum. Once 50 feet off the ground, the two dropped Hersey chocolate bars, suspended by small white cloth parachutes to waiting Douglas School District students in a reenactment of their candy drops to German children during the Berlin Airlift. Over 15 months, 1948 to 1949, Allied airmen delivered over two million 300,000 tons of food and supplies to the blockaded residents of western Berlin, isolated from ground transport routes by Soviet Army troops. As part of this massive air delivery, Allied airmen delivered 23 tons of chocolate and candy. Supplementing the regular cargo, Allied airmen dropped chocolate and candy, suspended underneath miniature, homemade parachutes to hungry German children on the ground. The first to do so was Halvorson, earning him the nickname as "the candy bomber." Other airmen quickly adopted this procedure, calling it "Operation LITTLE VITTLES." By the end of the Berlin Airlift, these airmen dropped an estimated 15 tons of chocolate and candy to German children.

Dr. Paul Reinke, Dentist from Rapid City…"My father was an Air Force Chaplain. I attended Munich High School during the Berlin Airlift. I remember my father conducting memorial services for two U.S. airmen who died during the Berlin Airlift." Dr. Reinke led efforts to acquire and ship two sections of the pre-fabricated concrete sections of the Berlin Wall, located between the Brandenburg Gate and Checkpoint Charlie between 1961 to 1989. These two sections are the central display of a Berlin Wall memorial on display at Memorial Park, south of the Civic Center. Dr. Reinke told 60 Berlin Airlift veterans, 70 family members and a large crowd in attendance…"It was an important victory at the beginning of the Cold War. What you did ultimately resulted in the defeat of Soviet tyranny. You revealed America's total commitment to the freedom of western Europe." [129]

---

[129] Lt. Col. George A. Larson, USAF (Ret.). "Activities surrounding the South Dakota Air and Space Museum's dedication of the Berlin Airlift Memorial on October 3, 2008."

Battleship USS Arizona Memorial, Preservation Project

A South Dakota School of Mines Engineering Contribution

DANA J. Medlin..."I became involved in the USS Arizona preservation project by accident of location and education. I was an undergraduate student in metallurgy at the University of Nebraska at Lincoln, Nebraska. One of my professors, Doctor Don Johnson, who in 1998, was visiting Pearl Harbor, Hawaii on the battleship USS Arizona memorial, asked a National Park Service (NPS) employee, who turned out to the memorial's superintend, about the corrosion rates of the battleship's underwater steel structures and if a long-term evaluation program was on-going. This is how the project started to answer many questions on the viability and stability of the battleship's structure."

Construction of the USS Arizona (BB-39), second of the Pennsylvania class 14-inch main gun battleships, started on March 16, 1914, with the laying down of its keel. It launched on June 15, 1915, commissioned on October 16, 1917. It left New York on its shakedown cruise on November 16, 1917, down the east coast of the United States to Guantanamo Bay, Cuba and back to New York Naval Ship Yard for identified repairs and modifications. It was ready for combat too late during World War I, serving as a gunnery training ship, primarily because of a lack of adequate stocks of fuel oil in the European Theater of Operations. Most of the battleships, or dreadnaughts as classified by Great Britain, Germany and other European naval powers, fueled their large warships with coal.

Arizona completed its post shakedown cruise and overhaul at New York Naval Shipyard on April 3, 1917. During World War I, the Arizona served as a gunnery training ship because of a lack of fuel oil supplies in the European Theater of Operations. In September 1921, the battleship transferred from the Atlantic to the Pacific, based at San Pedro, California. It went back to the Atlantic and Norfolk, Virginia on May 4, 1922. On April 2, 1941, the USS Arizona transferred to Pearl Harbor, Hawaii. It underwent a final overhaul at Puget Sound Naval Shipyard, Washington. Work completed on January 23, 1941.

On the morning of December 7, 1941, the USS Arizona was moored inboard to the U.S. Navy repair ship Vestal. During the Japanese air attack, a Japanese high-altitude horizontal bomber dropped one 1,760 pound armor-piercing bomb with a 500 pound warhead, penetrating into the ship's interior spaces near turret number two igniting the nearby munitions' magazine. The battleship burned for three days. After salvage operations and retrieval of the accessible dead, the USS Arizona was stricken from the active duty list on December 1, 1942.

The USS Arizona's hull still entombs 1,102 Navy personnel out of the 1,177 killed during the attack. The Navy considered those remaining inside as personnel buried at sea. The Pacific War memorial was created in 1949 to build a permanent national war memorial. The memorial was designed by Honolulu architect Alfred Preis.

The USS Arizona Memorial is in the form-stylized bridge, which appears to be floating about the sunken battleship. It is 184 feet long, with a sag in the middle, rising to a higher point at each end. This is a symbolic representation by the architect to depict the low point in the middle of the American public's morale after the Japanese attack on Pearl Harbor on December 7, 1941. It rises at both ends to depict the American victory in the Pacific and the signing by the Japanese Imperial government in Tokyo Bay aboard the USS battleship Missouri on September 2, 1945. The memorial was dedicated on May 30, 1962. It was added to the National Register of Historic Places on October 15, 1966. The USS Arizona was declared as a National Landmark in 1989.

The National Park Service (NPS) has an action plan to develop cultural resources management program for the USS Arizona and memorial structure. The following objectives are part of the overall resources management program.

1. Lab analysis of metal samples from the Arizona's hull. Analysis should determine amount of corrosion, contributing factors, rate and corrosive nature of present condition.
2. Develop computer model of rate of corrosion. Project life if nothing is done. Identify point of no return after which there would be no way to slow or stop the deterioration process.
3. Develop long-term plan for the continuous monitoring of data collection stations. Schedule dives for continuous data collection of USS Arizona photo stations.
4. Obtain and test equipment such as ultrasound, sonar and hologram with outside organization support. Determine hull

thickness, internal structural integrity extent and location of internal oil/fuel reserves and projected life of hull.
5. Finish survey for the Japanese mini-sub sunk by the USS Ward. Document location and condition of submerged cultural resources as well as areas surveyed and found to be void of such resources.
6. Continue to monitor the memorial and docks, including mooring chains, pilings and memorial structure. Identify potential long and short-term effects/impact on memorial and/or the USS Arizona.
7. Develop a computer map of the USS Arizona using data collected from dive surveys. Develop a mapping technique that can identify types of growth on the ship, and changes detected over time, where corrosion rates are highest and other relevant factors. Note deterioration and dates recorded. Photo document the fabric/structural changes.
8. Analyze preservation alternatives for original quays, temporary mooring quays added to the ship in 1942, chains running from the ship to the dock and the flagstaff. Decide on appropriate actions and develop plans to implement.
9. Develop position statement on the long-term disposition of the USS Arizona salvaged materials located at Waipo Point. Work with U.S. Navy to implement and enforce the position.

The NPS's Arizona Preservation Project has specialized goals.

1. Fully characterize the cultural process.
2. Determine rate of structure deterioration.
3. Develop long-term management plan for site preservation.
4. Develop research strategy for environmental impact risk assessment and abatement.
1. Conduct operations with respect due an American War Grave and Memorial and with minimum impact of the site.

Even though more than 1.6 million people visit the Arizona Memorial each year it is still and an active U.S. military cemetery. Those who survived the Japanese attack while aboard the USS Arizona can have their ashes entombed inside the battleship by a U.S. Navy diver. For those who served on the Arizona after its commissioning can have their ashes scattered in the water above the sunken battleship. As a symbol of respect, U.S. Navy, Coast Guard and merchant ships as they enter Pearl Harbor, "man the rails," as a salute of honor and continuing reverence for those who died serving onboard the USS Arizona. They have been joined by crews of foreign ships entering the harbor.

One of the biggest questions is whether to conduct preservation or do nothing. The ship is a tomb for those who died on the battleship during the Japanese air attack or buried onside the USS Arizona. The question of an environmental disaster from the fuel oil still within the ship's bunkers is not if but when. There are plans in place to contain an oil spill, but more questions arise on what to do with the USS Arizona.

1. What to do about the rusting remains of the USS Arizona's superstructure that had been removed during the salvage operations and dumped on nearby Waipo Point in Pearl Harbor?
2. What to do about the mooring quays that were attached to the partially submerged USS Arizona during salvage operations in Pearl Harbor?
3. What to do about the non-historic flagstaff attached to the ship's mast?
4. What to do about the mooring chains between the hull and the memorial deck?
5. What to do about the USS Arizona's original mooring quays?

Interestingly, under Cultural Resource Management guidelines, possibly there exists the interpretation that the USS Arizona cannot be regarded as a historic structure and therefore preservation treatment may be inappropriate. The USS Arizona Memorial, however, does fit the definition of a cultural resource under NPS-28 Glossary Appendix A, page five, and should be regarded as more than just a structure. The memorial's reason to be is the USS Arizona, and it is inextricably tied to the battleship. The relationship between the memorial and the battleship becomes clear when one considers the chain securing the memorial boat dock to the shipwreck and the flagstaff. The flagstaff appears to be part of the memorial. It is actually attached to the ship's structure.

Medlin... "Conduct modeling to predict what is going on inside the battleship, with more data to be collected and entered. This has been created fir interior spaces of the battleship and with data collected, to be collected, this may give stability issues some conclusion. Monitoring systems in and around the Arizona indicates the battleship's metal structure acts like a giant battery, only working in reverse. This allows current density to measured levels, possibly what is going on inside the ship's interior spaces. We carefully drilled into the concretion on the ship's external hull before penetration the steel hull. When the drill plug was removed, due to differences in water pressure, clear water squirted out for a distance into the harbor's water to a distance of 12-inches. At this time the water stream turns to a red color, indicating an iron oxidation process is ongoing. This will help to establish levels of iron content. Ultra sounding investigation determines the remaining steel plates' thickness. Some areas of the hull have or exhibit a fairly high corrosion rate, similar to that recorded on underground steel pipelines transiting through wet areas in the United States."

The effect of corrosion on the USS Arizona indicates that biofouling has created a uniform layer of stable hard fouling that covers most of the hull and superstructure remnants of the USS Arizona. That layer maintains toxic conditions near the exterior steel surfaces and encourages formation of stable black and grey iron oxides. Corrosion products on hull showed a moderate trend toward decreasing thickness as water depth increased.

Medlin..."On the first five to ten feet of depth, more corrosion due to wave effect, oxygen in the water from tide inflow and outflow, changes in salinity, with temperature fairly constant due to the depth limitations of 35 feet."

Most rapid corrosion has occurred on superstructure surfaces located six feet above and below the sea level. In this high oxygen and high-water motion zone, corrosion has extensive deterioration and exfoliation of steel surfaces.

Medlin... "At frame number 75, center of the battleship, the Preservation Project team was allowed to drill eight core samples at different levels down to the mud line. The battleship has settled deeply into the mud and steel plates not accessible."

Application of protective coatings, such as epoxy paints, to surfaces in the high corrosion zone would probably not be practical because of their advanced state of deterioration. Proper preplanning preparation of such surfaces would entail removal of oxide products to a degree that would likely cause further structural weakening.

Medlin..."Testing and analysis provides information that at the five foot level, corrosion is two mils per year and little to no corrosion at lower depth. The test cores drilled indicated that up to 50 percent of steel plate has been compromised with the one half inch thick steel plate at lower level of 34 feet nearly intact. The problem is that some corrosion occurred for ten years before the layer of concretions formed on the outside of the steel plates. Interestingly, the percent of iron in the concretion versus water depth closely matches that of the corrosion figures. There seems to be less corrosion inside the ship's interior spaces primarily due to the sealing off the compartments from the effects of the outside environment."

Corrosion damage did not appear significant in the few interior spaces examined. Water quality environment and presence of hydrocarbons should maintain reduced rates or levels of corrosion in interior volumes of the ship as long as water flushing in those spaces remains low. The potential exists for a decline in the abundance of live biofouling on the ship due to a projected long-term decline of nutrients in the water available for filter feeders. It has been recommended that biofouling be monitored at the permanent photo stations on an annual basis so that such an event can be detected.

The underwater examination by the ROV will assist in determining oxygen levels inside the hull. To continue this study, the South Dakota School of Mines & Technology Metallurgy Department received 250 pounds of steel plates from the USS Arizona. The steel was not extracted from the sunken memorial, but taken from multiple sources. This included the pile at Waipo Point, removed during salvage operations in 1942, as well as the tearing down to below the waterline of the sunken battleship. There are many variations in steel, with different microstructures of the same density because of the different manufacturing companies involved in providing steel for the USS Arizona, which creates different corrosion rates.

The few areas on the submerged USS Arizona superstructure and hull that are presently devoid of fouling organisms should be mapped on at least an annual basis. How such areas form and how biofouling recolonizes such surfaces is not known at this time. There are more questions than answers as the research on the sunken battleship continues. Deck areas receive substantial protection from corrosion and wood-burrowing mollusks by a layer of sediment that varies considerably based on the thickness and composition. That layer would be expected to be less stable on the long-term in shallow water, where higher water notion from the effects of waves can move sediments. Colonial Feather-Duster worms and sponges provide cohesiveness and stability to a large percentage of shallow water sediments.

Sediment thickness on deck surfaces should be monitored on an annual basis to determine if those layers are increasing or eroding. The status if organisms binding sediments in shallow water should be examined periodically. Fish-egg nest depressions should be monitored to determine their year-round abundance and effect on Teak decomposition. If nesting activity is found to be a chronic problem, it may be possible to discourage Maomao fish from schooling and nesting in specific areas by closing off access to hatches by plastic mesh glued in place with epoxy. Openings in one selected area could be closed first as a pilot experiment. It has been generally determined that survey of areas where fouling growth had been removed during the course of sampling procedures should be covered to prevent rapid corrosion of those areas. Initially, areas where biomass scrapings were made also used as areas where PVC flange studs were to be attached. However, it was found that the epoxy did not bind to clean steel underwater and the use of those areas as attachment surfaces was abandoned. The conclusions of the study recommended that those scrapped areas be covered with thin sheets if rigid plastic bonded to deal fouling surrounding the areas.

Medlin..."During evaluation at the South Dakota School of Mines on the metal segments received from Pearl Harbor identified a concern note previously considered on the stability of the steel hull. There appears to be a higher corrosion rate on the steel rivets than on the surrounding steel plates. This could result in the collapse of steel structure sections more serious or imminent than previously considered or estimated. Steel used for the rivets came from different manufacturers, as did the steel plates. This galvanic corrosion on the steel rivet heads appears to be at a higher corrosion rate than that of the surrounding steel plates."

Information on the amount of steel thickness remaining at nearly all accessible locations on the ship would be very useful in determining more precisely the deterioration state of the USS Arizona. High priority should be given to efforts to locate and test by nondestructive means to determine the battleship's remaining steel interior and exterior steel plate thickness. This research and evaluation was conducted by the use of ultrasound penetrations of the hull. These initially soundings at Frame Number 75, on the port and starboard sides of the battleship indicated corrosion rates of approximately three mils at the surface, two mils at a depth of five feet and one mil at the mud line. The USS Arizona has settled deeply into the mud and provides positioning stability at the current time for the sunken ship.

Medlin..."The ship is rigged with a Global Positioning System (GPS) monitors. This indicates that the USS Arizona is either sinking deeper into the mud or moving horizontally. Some cracks appear to be increasing or opening to a width of two to three-inches, possibly showing that some part of the warship is being slowly pulled away from a more securely positioned section since full examination of interior spaces cannot be made, damage to those spaces cannot be determined. This is critical when determining a future course of action on deciding either to attempt to remove or leave the fuel oil in the bunkers. There has been no definite determination if there is any damage to interior fuel bunker compartments on the rear section of the USS Arizona."

The Japanese attack on Pearl Harbor resulted in the United States first declaring war on the Japanese empire and then against Germany and Italy when those nations declared war on the United States. There is a historical artifact and war memorial in Pearl Harbor and more on site research is planned for the 2010. This is an interesting project on an underwater wreck for which research results can be applied to other World War II sunken wrecks throughout the Pacific. Many of these wrecks are accessible to divers and contain unstable munitions. The U.S. Navy is very interested in the spinoff from the USS Arizona Preservation Project for this reason. The USS Arizona is a steel structured vessel in a saltwater environment that has had little, or no maritime annual maintenance to inhibit the natural corrosion reactions of salt water. The structural integrity of the submerged warship has been questioned and this research project is continuing to determine the rate of corrosion since December 7, 1941 and the eventual integrity of the USS Arizona. The research will also assist the NPS and U.S. Navy to determine a long-term remedial action plan. The eventual existence of the USS Arizona Memorial will depend on the research. [130]

---

[130] Dana J. Medlin, PhD, P.E., Associate Professor, Materials and Metallurgical Engineering, South Dakota School of Mines in Rapid City, South Dakota discussed the ongoing battleship USS Arizona preservation project during a presentation at the School of Mines on October 22, 2009. Recorded and expanded by author.

South Dakota National Guard

January 2010 Blizzard Relief

A major winter storm swept across South Dakota in late January 2010, taking down 6,300 utility poles across the State, leaving 11,500 residents without power. Ice from the storm weighed down utility lines causing the poles to snap in half. A utility cooperative made up of Guard members and utility company personnel, made quick progress in dropping the total number of rural South Dakotans without power to 3,000 within a few days. The Guard put more than 70 personnel on State active duty, supported by nine bulldozers to work power restoration, along with eight Heavy Expanded Mobility Tactical Trucks (HEMTTs). [131]

---

[131] Lt. Col. George A. Larson, USAF (Ret.), "South Dakota National Guard, January 2010 Blizzard Relief." Visit to Camp Rapid, The South Dakota National Guard's open house to celebrate the National Guard's 150 years of service," display set up in the Headquarters Lobby, "2012: Countdown to Withdrawal," June 9, 2012.

South Dakota National Guard

James River Flood Support

THE South Dakota National Guard mobilized soldiers and equipment to the Aberdeen area to assist Brown County Emergency Management sand bagging operations in response to spring flooding in late March 2010. More than 63 Guard Palletized Load Systems (PLS) and Heavy Expanded Mobility Tactical Trucks (HEMTTs) were used in the sandbagging operations. According to the U.S. Geological Survey, the James River hit a record level peaking at 20.08 feet, compared to the previous year's record of 19.98 feet. [132]

---

[132] Lt. Col. George A. Larson, USAF (Ret.), " Visit to Camp Rapid, The South Dakota National Guard's open house to celebrate the National Guard's 150 years of service," display set up in the Headquarters Lobby, "2012: Countdown to Withdrawal," June 9, 2012.

"Operation ODYSSEY DAWN"

28th Bomb Wing B-1Bs over Libya
Ellsworth Air Force Base

EVEN though President Obama did not commit U.S. ground forces to support anti-Gaddafi rebels operating out of Benghazi, Libya, the decision was made to support NATO coalition air strikes in the country with Air Combat Command (ACC) ordering two 28th Bomb Wing B-1Bs to attack military targets in in Libya. Colonel Jeffrey Taliaferro, 28th Bomb Wing Commander..."In just two days of our initial notification (March 25, 2011), we were able to generate several (two B-1Bs) aircraft, hundreds of weapons and launch those aircraft to get them all the way around to the other side of the world to strike targets." Inside the former Rushmore Air Force Station munitions assembly building, 28th Munitions Squadron worked inside the heated building, brushing snow off the two thousand pound conventional bombs on 26 March. Squadron munitions personnel added GPS guidance packages, fins and fusing to the bomb casings to create a 2,000 pound Mk-84 or BLU-109 penetrating warhead mated with a Joint Direct Attack Munitions (JDAM) kit. The JDAM kit consists of a Global Positioning System (GPS) receiver, guidance computer that takes inputs from the GPS and Inertial Navigation System (INS), with adjustable airfoil fins to change the bomb's trajectory after release to target. A CEP of less than 10 feet is normal.

Two 28th B-1Bs took off on Sunday, 27 March, under less than ideal weather conditions to participate in NATO authorized air strikes against military forces under control of Colonel Moammar Gaddafi to assist anti-Gaddafi rebel forces advancing on Tripoli in fierce fighting, under the protection of a NATO enforced no-fly zone, imposed on 19 March. Taliaferro..."We were striking military targets, dropping 100 weapons (2,000 pound JDAMs) on 100 targets." No specific information was released on specific targets attacked, but those would be military related targets to limit Colonel Gaddafi's armed forces from effectively resisting approaching rebel fighters: supply depots, air defense systems, command and control systems, all without inflicting damage and casualties to surrounding civilians. The two 34th BS B-1Bs were part of NATO air strikes to protect the Libyan population from attacks by Gaddafi's military and to assist the advance of rebel forces, made difficult due to almost non-existent ground-to-air communications from the rebel ground troops to airborne NATO aircraft. This was the first time B-1Bs were deployed to attack targets directly from a continental U.S. air base to an overseas target and return, without landing at an intermediate air base.

The two B-1Bs landed back on Ellsworth's runway on Wednesday, 30 March, 24 hours after releasing their JDAMs on Libyan targets, at 11 a.m. The author was at Ellsworth AFB when the bombers landed. What a reception the two bomber crews received. As the two B-1Bs turned off the taxiway into the aircraft parking area off the north end of the taxiway, the bombers taxied under an arch of water jets from two Ellsworth Fire Department trucks, past lines of 28th BW personnel and parked B-1Bs.

Taliaferro..."The B-1Bs were launched from Ellsworth, flew halfway around the world, air refueled and without landing, attacked targets in Libya." This is what Ellsworth B-1Bs do repeatedly, answering the call to protect America's interests around the world. The author was among gathered representatives of local press members as one of the B-1B Weapons Systems Officers, Captain Matt Tull, 34th BS commented on the completed mission..."We met a tight operational deadline, but this is what we train for at Ellsworth. We are very flexible. We pride ourselves on that ability and really, it was just an amazing effort of teamwork. I think we were all a little too focused on the task to think too much, about how we really feel. We were proud to do what we did. It was a bit exhilarating and we are just happy that everything turned out well." This showed the flexibility of air power when tasked by the National Command Authority. Again, our freedom is not free. Libya is no longer ruled by a military dictator who attacks his own people to remain in power. [133]

---

[133] Lt. Col. George A. Larson, USAF (Ret.), excerpt, *Thunder over Dakota, The History of Ellsworth Air Force Base, 1941-2011*, Schiffer Publishing, Ltd., 2013.

South Dakota National Guard

Missouri River Flood, May 2011

GOVERNOR Dennis Dauguard called up approximately 1,300 South Dakota Army and Air National Guard members as the State experienced record water flows on the Missouri River. The high water volume rates was the result of record snow melt runoff in Montana and heavy spring rain runoff in eastern Wyoming, Montana and western North and South Dakota. All this water flowed into the streams and rivers of South Dakota. The U.S. Army Corps of Engineers had no option but to begin releasing record amounts to water at all dams on the Missouri River to make room for the water flowing into the upper Missouri River Reservoir Basin. On May 27, 2011 the initial Guard response was directed to the state capital of Pierre and nearby Fort Pierre where soldiers worked 24 hour operations filing sandbags, building levees and directing traffic. As high water levels moved downstream Guard members moved operations into Dakota Dunes and areas of southeast South Dakota. By mid-June, levee construction and sandbagging operations in and around Pierre, Fort Pierre and Dakota Dunes communities had come to a close.Guard members placed an estimated three million sandbags in the Pierre and Fort Pierre area, with another 500,000 in Dakota Dunes. Guard troops remained on active duty as water levels remained high and security levee patrols and quick response repair forces were still needed. In July, National Guard members were still supporting the massive flood relief efforts in maintaining levee security and around the clock maintenance. Guard members remained on site until August. At the height of flood prevention operations, more than 1,300 South Dakota National Guard members served on recall orders from the governor to protect homes, business and infrastructure in the flood threatened areas along the Missouri River.[134]

---

[134] Lt. Col. George A. Larson, USAF (Ret.), "South Dakota National Guard, Missouri River Flood, May 2011." Visit to Camp Rapid, The South Dakota National Guard's open house to celebrate the National Guard's 150 years of service," display set up in the Headquarters Lobby, "2012: Countdown to Withdrawal," June 9, 2012.

South Dakota National Guard

The End of the War in Iraq

SINCE taking office, President Barrack Obama has fulfilled his promise to the American people by withdrawing all U.S. troops from Iraq (However, in 2015 the President has been forced to send troops and aircraft back to Iraq to fight ISIS) by the end of 2011. In his first speech about the Iraq War, President Obama spoke of the sacrifices and dedicated service members have made in Iraq over the last decade..."By any measure, this has already been a long war. For the men and women of America's armed forces, and for your families. This war has been one of the most extraordinary chapters of service in the history of our nation. You have endured tour, after tour, after tour of duty. You have known the dangers of combat and the lonely distance of loved ones. You have fought against tyranny and disorder. You have bled four your best friends and for unknown Iraqis. And you have borne the enormous burden for you fellow citizens, while extending a previous opportunity to the people of Iraq. Under the circumstances, the men and women of the United States military have served with honor and succeeded beyond any expectations." [135]

---

[135] Lt. Col George A. Larson, USAF (Ret.), "South Dakota National Guard, The End of the War in Iraq." Visit to Camp Rapid, The South Dakota National Guard's open house to celebrate the National Guard's 150 years of service," display set up in the Headquarters Lobby, "2012: Countdown to Withdrawal," June 9, 2012.

175 Years of Serving the United States

Celebration of the U.S. Army National Guard

Birthday Celebration of the South Dakota National Guard (1862-2012)

THE journey of the Dakota militiamen began during the Civil War with Companies A and B of the Dakota Cavalry. On March 2, 1861, President James Buchanan signed the act establishing the Dakota Territory. By that time, Vermillion, Bon Homme and Elk Point were growing communities. The territory tended to be people who were genuine settlers, mostly immigrants from Germany, Norway and Sweden. Earlier in the 1850s, the U.S. Army had established garrisons at Fort Pierre and Fort Randall on the Missouri River. Their mission was to protect the 5,000 settlers from the threat of Native American attacks. However, when the Civil War started, the Army withdrew three companies from Fort Randall, leaving it in an exposed position. This led to the December 7, 1861 proclamation, by the Territorial Governor William Jayne, to raise two companies of volunteer militia. Recruiting centers were then established in Yankton, Vermillion and Bon Homme. The citizens were very patriotic with a lot of local pride, and in just over one month, enough men had enlisted to assemble the first company of citizen-soldiers. On January 27, 1862, Captain Nelson Miner, Company Commander, formed the unit in Yankton, Company A, Dakota Cavalry. This unit was the first unit of the Dakota Militia. This was the birth of the South Dakota National Guard (SDNG). Since that historic date in 1862, the SDNG has since seen combat during the Spanish-American War, World War I and World War II, "Operation JUST CAUSE" and "Operation DESERT STORM." The National Guard was also called up during the Mexican Border Conflict, Korean War, Berlin Crisis and peacekeeping missions in Bosnia and Kosovo.

Following the September 11, 2001 attacks on the United States, each of South Dakota's 28 National Guard communities has experienced a unit mobilization in support of "Operation NOBLE EAGLE,"

"Operation ENDURING FREEDOM," "Operation IRAQI FREEDOM" and "Operation NEW DAWN." More than 4,600 soldiers and 1,500 airmen have deployed in support of these operations and continue to deploy today. The National Guard is the only military component that holds a dual-mission, consisting of both federal and state roles. The Federal mission is to maintain trained and equipped units available for prompt mobilization for war or a national emergency At the state level, the Governor reserves the ability under the Constitution, to call up members of the National Guard in times of domestic emergencies. Throughout the years, natural disasters have called forth the Guard's spirit of teamwork and sacrifice to battle floods, fires, blizzards and tornado destruction. From the Rapid City flood of 1972 to the 1997 Spencer tornado to Hurricanes Katrina and Rita, and the 2011 Missouri River flood, the SDNG has helped its fellow South Dakotans and Americans in times of need.

Today's SDNG remains strong with nearly 4,400 soldiers and airmen available to execute its dual-mission on the state and federal level. The National Guard is not in 28 communities throughout South Dakota and is comprised of 64 separate Army Guard units and detachments, and 16 Air Guard units. These units perform a variety of missions; everything from command and control, administration, engineering, field artillery, transportation, logistics, communications, maintenance, aviation, public affairs, military police, fire fighting and medical. The National Guard is no longer a strategic reserve to the active component, but an operational force directly integrated into active-duty deployments and missions. The force structure of the SDNG is designed to meet the needs of the future force; giving the Guard an enhanced capability to respond in times of emergencies and natural disasters and to support overseas contingency operations.

The SDNG has a significant impact on the State's economy with more than 181 million dollars in expenditures and wages in 2011. The SDNG is also one of the largest employers in the State with more than 960 full-time employees along with nearly 3,400 traditional Guard members who train on a part-time basis while pursuing a career or civilian education. These full-time employees, along with state employees and civilian contractors, work to assist the traditional Guardsmen by providing administrative training and logistical support. This support collectively goes into helping units meet mobilization and readiness requirements. The SDNG remains strong with nearly 3,400 soldiers, available for state and federal missions. The nerve center for the SDANG resides at the state headquarters at Camp Rapid, Rapid City;

an 84 acre training site first developed in 1924. The SDANG is located on the southeast corner of Joe Foss Field in Sioux Falls and was federally recognized in 1946. It has nearly 1,100 airmen assigned to its headquarters and the 114th Fighter Wing. The mission of the SDANG is to provide combat capability to the war fight, security for the homeland and to provide combat-ready units in the three roles: federal, state and community.

The proud heirs of the militia tradition can be found in the men and women of today's SDNG (2012). They stand ready to leave the comforts of home and family to help their friends and neighbors, defend the nation's interests and bring peace and hope to people throughout the world. [136]

---

[136] "Birthday celebration South Dakota National Guard, 1862-2012." Camp Rapid: Joint Force Headquarters Readiness Center, Rapid City, South Dakota, June 8, 2012

Visit to Camp Rapid to Celebrate 150 Years of National Guard History

THE author listened to South Dakota's Governor, Dennis Daugaard address the large crowd of guard soldiers, their families, local citizens and honored guests in the New Camp Rapid headquarters..."During times of war, disaster and incredible need, you've proven we can count on you. It was the Guard's help during the flooding of the Missouri River, defending Pierre, the capital and Fort Pierre, which saved lived and property. We are a better state and a better people because of the South Dakota National Guard. When one looks back, in the early days of the National Guard, Guardsmen were exempt from jury duty and poll tax, and they could not be arrested while on duty. Also, Guard members had the right of way on all roads while they were on duty. That's history now." Major General Timothy Reisch, Adjutant General, South Dakota National Guard..."Yes, much has changed in 150 years. But, a century and one half later, our men and women of the South Dakota National Guard are still responding to emergencies in South Dakota and abroad. Our National Guard members have been deployed continuously since September 11, 2001. We've had someone on duty continuously for over ten years. I think this is noteworthy. Camp Rapid started as a training facility and turned into the state headquarters. The National Guard's involvement in disasters like the 1972 flood in Rapid City, 1997 blizzard and 2000 Jasper, Flagpole and Maitland fires cemented good relationships with the people of South Dakota. There is a bond between the South Dakota National Guard and the Rapid City community that will never be broken." [137]

---

[137] Lt. Col George A. Larson, USAF (Ret.), "Visit to Camp Rapid, The South Dakota National Guard's open house to celebrate the National Guard's 150 years of service," June 9, 2012.

South Dakota National Guard

2012: Countdown to Withdrawal from Afghanistan

AS the Afghanistan military forces grow stronger and more independent, the U.S. troops get closer to returning Stateside. The South Dakota National Guard has more than 160 troops (June 2012) in three units continuing to support the mission in Afghanistan. President Obama said that he still plans to gradually withdraw forces through 2014 as Afghan forces take on more responsibility, cautioning that no one should expect..."Any sudden, additional changes," in the pace of withdrawal. "There needs to be mutual trust between the Afghan and U.S. forces," said Security Assistant Force Command Sgt. major Michael T. Hall..."We will be here as long as we need to be to be able to support them." The SDANG has six units scheduled to be deployed between now and July 2013: 935th Support Battalion, 927th Survey and Design Team, 1987th Contingency Contracting Team, 129th Mobile Public Affairs Detachment, 235th Military Police Company and HHC 152nd Combat Sustainment Support Battalion. As of June 2012, the United States currently has approximately 90,000 troops in Afghanistan. President Obama plans to drop that number to 68,000 by late September, but has offered no specific withdrawal plan after that. [138]

---

[138] Lt. Col. George A. Larson, USAF (Ret.), "South Dakota National Guard, 2012: Countdown to Withdrawal from Afghanistan." Visit to Camp Rapid, The South Dakota National Guard's open house to celebrate the National Guard's 150 years of service," display set up in the Headquarters Lobby, "2012: Countdown to Withdrawal," June 9, 2012.

SSN 790 South Dakota

The Third U.S. Navy Warship Named for South Dakota

THE third U.S. Navy warship to be named for the state of South Dakota is a Virginia Class attack submarine, SSN 790. The U.S, Secretary of the Navy, Ray Mabus, on June 23, 2012 at the USS South Dakota battleship memorial in Sioux Falls, South Dakota named the new submarine in a naming ceremony. [139] Construction began on the New South Dakota in 2013, with operational deployment sometime in 2017 (depending on Department of Defense funds to the Navy's warship construction program). Marbus..."This ship is named the South Dakota to honor the citizens who have so strongly supported our military in so many ways including many South Dakota veterans. The ship will remain in service for more than three decades." The next generation attack submarine will provide the Navy with the capabilities required to maintain the nation's undersea supremacy with enhanced stealthy sophisticated surveillance capabilities and special warfare enhancements that will enable the Virginia Class SSNs to meet the Navy's multi-mission requirements. The new South Dakota will have the capability to attack targets with highly accurate Tomahawk cruise missiles and conduct long-term surveillance of land areas, littoral waters or other sea based forces. It is also designed for special forces delivery and support. [140]

---

[139] "Navy Secretary to host USS South Dakota naming ceremony," Washington, D.C., Department of Defense, Secretary of Defense, Navy Social Media, June 1, 2012.

[140] "Virginia Class SSN," Washington, D.C., Department of Defense, Secretary of the Navy.

The Author

LT. Col. George A. Larson, USAF (Ret.), standing on right side of a North American F-86H Sabre, at the South Dakota Air and Space Museum, outside Ellsworth Air Force Base, South Dakota. The F-86H is displayed in front of the former four-bay 54th Fighter-Interceptor Squadron alert hangar, moved from its operational location on Ellsworth Air Force Base.

The author graduated from Iowa State University at Ames, Iowa with a Bachelor of Science degree in History and a commission as a Second Lieutenant United States Air Force in May 1969. He earned a Master of Arts degree in History from the University of Stanislaus at Turlock, California in June 1978. During the Cold War with the Soviet Union he served as a strategic intelligence officer with the Strategic Air Command and the Joint Strategic Target Planning Staff, Defense Intelligence Agency, Pacific Air Forces with an assignment with Republic of South Korea Air Force, Alternate National Military Command Center, and Joint Chiefs of Staff at the Pentagon. He had a career broadening assignment as Commandant of Cadets with Air Training Command's Air Force Reserve Officer Training Corps at the University of Iowa in Iowa City, Iowa. While in the Air Force, the author completed Air Force Squadron Officers School, Air Command and Staff College, Air War College, Industrial College of the Armed Forces, Naval War College, Foreign Service Institute program on the Middle East, Soviet Union and Eastern Europe, and specialized military courses required for his Air Force duties as an intelligence officer.

Merriam Press has published the author's *A Seabee's Story, Tinian and Okinawa, The B-29 Air War Against Japan*. Larson has published over 300 magazine articles on military history, aviation, naval and general history. The author is a member of the Rapid City Military Veterans Writing Group, which assists the researching, writing and publishing stories on veterans to carry on their military accomplishments and history. He lives in Rapid City with his wife Victoria.

www.ingramcontent.com/pod-product-compliance
Lightning Source LLC
Chambersburg PA
CBHW071933220426
43662CB00009B/893